D0619525

The
SMITH AND KRAUS
Monologue
Index

2nd Edition

Smith and Kraus *Books For Actors*

THE MONOLOGUE SERIES

The Best Men's / Women's Stage Monologues of 1998
The Best Men's / Women's Stage Monologues of 1997
The Best Men's / Women's Stage Monologues of 1996
The Best Men's / Women's Stage Monologues of 1995
The Best Men's / Women's Stage Monologues of 1994
The Best Men's / Women's Stage Monologues of 1993
The Best Men's / Women's Stage Monologues of 1992
The Best Men's / Women's Stage Monologues of 1991
The Best Men's / Women's Stage Monologues of 1990
100 Men's / Women's Stage Monologues from the 1980's
2 Minutes and Under: Character Monologues for Actors
Street Talk: Character Monologues for Actors
Uptown: Character Monologues for Actors
Monologues from Contemporary Literature: Volume I
Monologues from Classic Plays
100 Great Monologues from the Renaissance Theatre
100 Great Monologues from the Neo-Classical Theatre
100 Great Monologues from the 19th C. Romantic and Realistic Theatres
Ice Babies In Oz: Original Character Monologues
Kiss and Tell: Restoration Scenes, Monologues, & Historical Context
A Brave and Violent Theatre: 20th Century Irish Monologues, Scenes and Historical Context
The Ultimate Audition Book: 222 Monologues, 2 Minutes & Under

FESTIVAL MONOLOGUE SERIES

The Great Monologues from the Humana Festival
The Great Monologues from the EST Marathon
The Great Monologues from the Women's Project
The Great Monologues from the Mark Taper Forum

YOUNG ACTORS SERIES

Monologues and Scenes for Middle School Actors
Great Scenes and Monologues for Children
Great Monologues for Young Actors Volume I
Great Monologues for Young Actors Volume II
Multicultural Monologues for Young Actors
Multicultural Scenes for Young Actors
Great Scenes for Young Actors Volume I
Great Scenes for Young Actors Volume II

SCENE STUDY SERIES

The Ultimate Scene Study Book, Part I: 102 Short Scenes for Two Actors
Scenes From Classic Plays 468 B.C. to 1960 A.D.
The Best Stage Scenes of 1998
The Best Stage Scenes of 1997
The Best Stage Scenes of 1996
The Best Stage Scenes of 1995
The Best Stage Scenes of 1994
The Best Stage Scenes of 1993
The Best Stage Scenes of 1992
The Best Stage Scenes for Men / Women from the 1980's

If you require pre-publication information about upcoming Smith and Kraus books, you may receive our semi-annual catalogue, free of charge, by sending your name and address to *Smith and Kraus Catalogue,4 Lower Mill Road, North Stratford, NH 03590. Or call us at (800) 895-4331, fax (603) 922-3348. WWW.SmithKraus.com.*

The
SMITH AND KRAUS
Monologue
Index

2nd Edition

Edited by Karen Morris

Career Development Series

SK
A SMITH AND KRAUS BOOK

Published by Smith and Kraus, Inc.
PO Box 127, Lyme, NH 03768

Copyright © 1995 by Smith and Kraus, Inc.
All rights reserved
Manufactured in the United States of America
Cover and Text Design by Julia Hill Gignoux

Second Edition: June 1999
10 9 8 7 6 5 4 3 2

Library of Congress Cataloging-in-Publication

The Smith and Kraus monologue index, second edition / edited by Karen Morris.
p. cm. --(Career development series)
ISBN 1-880399-75-X
1. Monologues--Indexes. 2. Acting--Indexes.
I. Morris, Karen (Karen K.), 1951– . II. Series.
PN2080.S6 1994
016.80882'45--dc20 94-48262
CIP

CONTENTS

How to Use This Guide

You are now at the gateway to a universe of monologues wherein any conceivable audition or class monologue requirement can be found. A specific search need only take minutes, but hours may be spent wandering about, seeking ideas and inspirations.

The process of a specific search is simple:

1. While looking at the Table of Contents on page v, define one or more elements of the character you are seeking.

2. Refer to the Index page (1–50) indicated for that element and locate the monologue number(s). Obviously multiple parameters will help to zero in on the desired monologue.

3. Locate the Monologue Synopses (pages 55–285) and determine which appear suitable.

4. Access the monologue *itself* in the appropriate book in the Smith and Kraus monologue library as indicated by the code under the synopsis. (Key to Book Titles is on page 53.)

Sample Monologue Synopsis

monologue number — **125**

character name, age — **Wylie, 50s**   **Wylie's home, Present** — setting, time

Wylie returns home after being mugged and is greeted by
Kingfish, his large Doberman. Here, Wylie tells his story to } synopsis

book code,   Kingfish, who barks constantly. Dramatic.

running time — **BMSM91, 4 minutes**

title of play, author — *Kingfish by Marlane Meyer*

Part One

INDEX

FEMALE CONTEMPORARY - DRAMATIC

Age 15 and Under

177, 178, 181, 281, 418, 424, 462, 463, 472, 587, 663, 692-700, 705, 706, 707, 945, 1116, 1192, 1234, 1838, 1839, 1844, 1851, 1856, 1857, 1858, 2076, 2494, 2520, 2527, 2531, 2532, 2533, 2536, 2537, 2540, 2544, 2550, 2554-56, 2561, 2564, 2565

Age 16-25

58, 59, 64, 70, 72, 85, 87, 88, 91, 94, 159, 191, 192, 198, 211, 265, 266, 269, 284, 285, 295, 297, 298, 304, 305, 306, 317, 372, 374, 379, 380, 392, 399, 401, 402, 409, 412, 413, 415, 421, 422, 457-461, 464-471, 473-481, 508-513, 544, 548, 552, 555, 556, 562, 566-569, 575, 578, 586, 591, 595, 602, 622, 629, 630, 638, 639, 640, 646, 660, 661, 666, 667, 668, 669, 674, 882, 885, 886, 887, 894, 907, 920, 923, 931, 932, 935, 946, 947, 1056, 1062, 1088, 1097, 1098, 1108, 1111, 1114, 1116, 1129, 1133, 1148, 1177, 1181, 1191, 1192, 1194, 1198, 1200, 1203, 1205, 1211, 1213, 1225, 1227, 1234, 1241, 1246, 1290, 1302, 1304, 1310, 1311, 1367, 1572, 1578, 1587, 1588, 1598, 1615, 1722, 1723, 1729, 1751, 1755, 1770, 1786, 1789, 1798, 1800, 1803, 1807, 1808, 1809, 1811, 1813, 1815, 1817, 1820, 1826, 1827, 1833, 1834, 1835, 1840, 1841, 1842, 1843, 1845, 1847, 1848, 1849, 1851, 1852, 1853, 1854, 1855, 1857, 1955, 1959, 1964, 1966, 1967, 1972, 1981, 1992, 1994, 1997, 2003, 2004, 2075, 2087, 2092, 2095, 2102, 2103, 2104, 2106, 2108, 2117, 2118, 2128, 2129, 2289, 2290, 2297, 2298, 2427, 2438, 2439, 2441, 2476, 2477, 2482, 2483, 2486, 2489, 2493, 2503, 2508, 2524, 2525, 2527, 2528, 2529, 2531, 2533, 2534, 2537, 2538, 2539, 2540, 2541, 2542, 2543, 2544, 2545, 2546, 2550, 2552, 2553, 2557, 2559, 2560, 2561, 2562, 2563, 2564, 2565, 2566, 2568

Age 26-40

65, 73, 74, 79, 83, 84, 85, 89, 92, 97, 98, 100, 169, 170, 173, 193, 200, 209, 267, 269, 270, 271, 272, 273, 274, 275, 276, 279, 280, 285, 286, 291, 293, 295, 298, 300, 302, 305, 306, 307, 308, 310, 314, 315, 318, 319, 372, 376, 385, 392, 400, 401, 403, 409, 412, 417, 422, 425, 426, 428, 547, 548, 551, 552, 554, 558, 559, 561, 563-567, 568, 571, 572, 574, 575,

578, 580, 586, 589, 592, 598, 601, 622, 624, 629, 631, 632, 633, 634, 636, 640, 645, 647, 651, 652, 655, 657, 658, 659, 671, 672, 879, 880, 881, 882, 883, 885-888, 890, 892, 894, 907, 913-916, 919, 929, 923, 926, 944, 946, 947, 1055, 1056, 1066, 1071, 1078, 1088, 1090, 1092, 1094, 1097, 1098, 1102, 1107, 1111, 1114, 1129, 1132, 1135, 1142, 1148, 1176, 1177, 1181, 1185, 1191, 1192, 1194, 1198, 1200, 1203, 1205, 1206, 1212, 1214, 1215, 1225, 1227, 1230, 1231, 1239, 1241, 1242, 1243, 1246, 1286, 1289, 1290, 1300, 1302, 1304, 1310, 1311, 1314, 1345, 1347, 1348, 1350, 1353, 1354, 1356, 1358, 1359, 1360, 1361, 1367, 1574, 1585, 1589, 1590, 1748, 1752, 1754, 1758, 1761, 1764, 1768, 1771, 1773, 1774, 1775, 1776, 1777, 1779, 1781, 1784, 1785, 1787, 1789, 1792, 1794, 1795, 1798, 1801, 1805, 1810, 1812, 1813, 1814, 1817, 1818, 1820, 1823, 1824, 1825, 1826, 1829, 1830, 1831, 1832, 1946, 1952, 1958, 1959, 1962, 1964, 1966, 1967, 1972, 1974, 1977, 1978, 1981, 1982, 1984, 1987, 1988, 1989, 1991, 1992, 1993, 1994, 2000, 2002, 2073, 2075, 2080, 2081, 2088, 2092, 2093, 2095, 2097, 2104, 2105, 2106, 2107, 2108, 2110, 2114, 2121, 2123, 2126, 2128, 2129, 2130, 2284, 2288, 2289, 2290, 2292, 2427, 2429, 2430, 2432, 2436, 2442, 2445, 2476, 2477, 2479, 2481, 2482, 2483, 2486, 2489, 2493, 2494, 2503, 2505, 2508, 2517

Age 41-50

57, 59, 66, 69, 70, 88, 89, 97, 101, 102, 162, 200, 264, 267, 268, 288, 298, 303, 381, 384, 387, 551, 557, 558, 560, 566, 567, 582, 610, 627, 637, 640, 641, 645, 648, 649, 650, 656, 658, 659, 662, 665, 670, 673, 879, 914, 915, 916, 1051, 1089, 1105, 1106, 1115, 1128, 1137, 1145, 1176, 1185, 1192, 1194, 1198, 1212, 1214, 1215, 1221, 1227, 1230, 1231, 1239, 1246, 1249, 1286, 1288, 1292, 1300, 1301, 1302, 1311, 1314, 1345-1350, 1353, 1354, 1356, 1358, 1359, 1360, 1361, 1366, 1603, 1604, 1616, 1725, 1726, 1746, 1747, 1750, 1756, 1759, 1762, 1763, 1769, 1783, 1790, 1821, 1822, 1951, 1960, 1987, 1988, 1990, 1996, 2001, 2072, 2082, 2109, 2111, 2113, 2124, 2127, 2132, 2291, 2293, 2427, 2428, 2430, 2431, 2435, 2436, 2442, 2445, 2479, 2482, 2484, 2486, 2493, 2505, 2508, 2517

Age 51-60

52, 103, 172, 203, 268, 292, 311, 316, 545, 549, 550, 553,

560, 566, 567, 570, 573, 593, 594, 606, 607, 608, 613, 625, 637, 640, 641, 644, 648, 662, 664, 897, 909, 910, 912, 918, 1052, 1053, 1075, 1095, 1137, 1185, 1192, 1198, 1239, 1246, 1288, 1300, 1311, 1346, 1349, 1356, 1361, 1366, 1742, 1757, 1772, 1783, 1790, 1821, 1822, 1951, 1960, 1987, 1988, 1990, 1996, 2001, 2072, 2082, 2109, 2111, 2113, 2124, 2127, 2132, 2291, 2293, 2427, 2428, 2430, 2431, 2435, 2436, 2442, 2445, 2479, 2482, 2484, 2486, 2493, 2505, 2508, 2517

Age Over 60

165, 194, 287, 289, 290, 301, 309, 313, 390, 553, 566, 567, 609, 664, 884, 1104, 1124, 1185, 1192, 1246, 1349, 1351, 1361, 1362, 1740, 1741, 1745, 1806, 1954, 2286, 2427, 2428, 2446, 2482, 2486, 2493, 2497, 2505, 2508

FEMALE CONTEMPORARY - SERIOCOMIC

Age 15 and Under

163, 164, 207, 386, 398, 696, 1054, 1734, 1836, 1837, 1973, 2069, 2526

Age 16-25

53, 54, 55, 60, 62, 78, 80, 86, 87, 93, 95, 104, 159, 161, 167, 184, 195, 201, 202, 204, 205, 206, 298, 378, 388, 389, 394, 396, 397, 404, 408, 414, 427, 1054, 1065, 1079, 1082, 1084, 1085, 1110, 1121, 1123, 1127, 1131, 1134, 1138, 1144, 1182, 1186, 1187, 1188, 1190, 1294, 1305, 1307, 1309, 1319, 1599, 1609, 1619, 1724, 1734, 1743, 1760, 1767, 1778, 1780, 1799, 1836, 1846, 1956, 1975, 1976, 1980, 1985, 1986, 1999, 2006, 2068, 2070, 2084, 2090, 2091, 2098, 2101, 2106, 2112, 2119, 2125, 2131, 2296, 2301, 2424, 2433, 2434, 2437, 2443, 2444, 2474, 2478, 2484, 2490, 2492, 2507, 2509, 2511, 2514, 2526, 2530, 2547, 2558, 2567, 2569

Age 26-40

53, 55, 61, 63, 65, 66, 71, 76, 81, 82, 90, 105, 159, 160, 161, 167, 171, 174, 175, 176, 179, 180, 182, 183, 184, 185, 187, 188, 189, 190, 195, 199, 201, 202, 206, 210, 283, 294, 307, 312, 373, 375, 377, 382, 383, 388, 389, 394, 396, 397, 404, 405, 406, 407, 408, 414, 420, 423, 427, 429, 1049, 1054, 1057, 1058, 1065, 1070, 1073, 1074, 1079, 1080, 1082, 1085, 1086, 1089, 1091, 1093, 1096, 1099, 1100, 1109, 1118, 1119,

1120, 1123, 1125, 1126, 1129,
1130, 1131, 1134, 1136, 1139,
1141, 1143, 1144, 1149, 1174,
1179, 1180, 1182, 1184, 1186,
1187, 1188, 1189, 1190, 1193,
1196, 1291, 1293, 1294, 1295,
1298, 1305, 1307, 1309, 1319,
1344, 1726, 1727, 1734, 1735,
1736, 1737, 1738, 1739, 1744,
1753, 1765, 1766, 1782, 1788,
1791, 1799, 1804, 1949, 1953,
1956, 1963, 1968, 1969, 1980,
1983, 1985, 1986, 1999, 2005,
2006, 2068, 2070, 2071, 2077,
2083, 2084, 2085, 2090, 2091,
2094, 2096, 2099, 2100, 2101,
2106, 2112, 2115, 2116, 2119,
2125, 2131, 2283, 2285, 2299,
2301, 2424, 2437, 2443, 2444,
2474, 2478, 2484, 2490, 2492,
2507, 2509, 2514

Age 41-50

51, 56, 60, 68, 77, 78, 96, 106,
107, 180, 186, 208, 278, 294,
394, 395, 416, 420, 1050,
1054, 1060, 1061, 1064, 1076,
1081, 1087, 1101, 1103, 1113,
1140, 1146, 1173, 1174, 1179,
1180, 1182, 1184, 1187, 1189,
1190, 1193, 1194, 1291, 1293,
1295, 1298, 1299, 1305, 1319,
1344, 1577, 1728, 1734, 1828,
1948, 1961, 1965, 1979, 1985,
1986, 1995, 2074, 2078, 2086,
2120, 2285, 2287, 2301, 2423,
2424, 2474, 2478, 2484, 2490,
2492, 2507, 2514, 2522

Age 51-60

51, 73, 74, 106, 107, 212, 263,
277, 278, 391, 394, 420, 1054,
1059, 1067, 1076, 1083, 1112,
1122, 1173, 1182, 1184, 1299,
1306, 1730, 1734, 1965, 1995,
1998, 2086, 2120, 2294, 2300,
2301, 2423, 2474, 2484, 2492,
2507, 2514, 2521, 2522

Age Over 60

106, 107, 166, 296, 393, 394,
410, 411, 419,1299, 1306,
1734, 1796, 1957, 2122, 2478,
2484, 2507

FEMALE CONTEMPORARY - COMIC

Age 15 and Under

1068, 1734

Age 16-25

99, 1178, 1183, 1195, 1296, 1303,
1308, 1312, 1357, 1734, 1948

Age 26-40

75, 282, 1063, 1069, 1072,
1120, 1172, 1175, 1178, 1183,
1195, 1285, 1287, 1297, 1303,
1308, 1312, 1315, 1316, 1357,
1363, 1364, 1365, 1734, 1948

Age 41-50

168, 197, 1172, 1175, 1178,
1183, 1195, 1284, 1287, 1297,

1303, 1312, 1313, 1315, 1316,
1363, 1364, 1365, 1734

Age 51-60

67, 1077, 1195, 1297, 1303,
1312, 1313, 1315, 1316, 1317,
1318, 1364, 1734

Age Over 60

1195, 1313, 1316, 1317, 1318,
1734

FEMALE CLASSIC - DRAMATIC

Age 15 and Under

690, 691, 701, 702, 703, 704,
2203

Age 16-25

11, 84, 490-494, 497, 498, 511,
512, 513, 830-835, 838, 839,
840-846, 848, 849, 853, 857,
859, 860-866, 868, 869, 873,
876, 882, 1370, 1373, 1376,
1378, 1379, 1380, 1381, 1383,
1385, 1392, 1399, 1402, 1405,
1409, 1413, 1416, 1417, 1470,
1471, 1472, 1473, 1479, 1480,
1481, 1482, 1483, 1485, 1486,
1492, 1496, 1497, 1501, 1503,
1506, 1509, 1510, 1511, 1512,
1513, 1514, 1519, 1571, 1575,
1576, 1580, 1582, 1583, 1584,
1602, 1610, 1611, 1731, 2200,
2201, 2203, 2204, 2209, 2211,

2212, 2213, 2214, 2215, 2217,
2219, 2220, 2221, 2227, 2229,
2234, 2236, 2239, 2243, 2245,
2250, 2252, 2255, 2258, 2260,
2262, 2263, 2264, 2265, 2267,
2272, 2280, 2281, 2549

Age 26-40

12, 13, 14, 18, 832, 833, 834,
835, 837, 838, 839, 840, 842,
843, 844, 845, 846, 848, 849,
854, 857, 859, 860, 861, 862,
864, 867, 868, 869, 870, 876,
879, 880, 881, 882, 883, 1369,
1370, 1371, 1374, 1382, 1383,
1384, 1385, 1387, 1392, 1400,
1401, 1402, 1409, 1410, 1411,
1414, 1415, 1472, 1473, 1492,
1496, 1497, 1500, 1501, 1503,
1511, 1512, 1513, 1514, 1517,
1518, 1519, 1520, 1586, 1595,
1600, 1601, 1605, 1606, 1612,
1613, 1614, 1617, 1618, 1733,
2204, 2206, 2207, 2209, 2212,
2213, 2214, 2215, 2218, 2219,
2220, 2221, 2227, 2228, 2229,
2233, 2234, 2237, 2239, 2245,
2248, 2250, 2255, 2256, 2260,
2265, 2267, 2270, 2272, 2274,
2275, 2276, 2278

Age 41-50

97, 98, 871, 879, 1386, 1404,
1477, 1478, 1487, 1491, 1492,
1494, 1504, 1507, 1520, 1579,
1597, 1598, 2222, 2223, 2246,
2247, 2253, 2254, 2259

Age 51-60
874, 1492, 1515, 1516, 1520,
1581, 2222, 2223, 2230

Age Over 60
874, 875, 1492, 1515, 1516,
1520, 1740, 1741, 2261, 2277

FEMALE CLASSIC - SERIOCOMIC

Age 15 and Under
1474, 2202

Age 16-25
836, 855, 856, 1375,1377,
1389, 1391, 1395, 1396, 1397,
1398, 1403, 1406, 1407, 1474,
1484, 1489, 1490, 1493, 1495,
1502, 1508, 1918, 1419, 2202,
2210, 2225, 2226, 2232, 2235,
2238, 2241, 2249, 2269, 2271,
2273, 2279, 2548

Age 26-40
836, 850, 851, 855, 856, 858,
877, 878, 1372, 1388, 1389,
1390, 1393, 1395, 1396, 1397,
1406, 1407, 1408, 1418, 1419,
1469, 1490, 1493, 1495, 1498,
1499, 1505, 2205, 2208, 2210,
2225, 2226, 2231, 2235, 2238,
2240, 2268, 2269, 2282

Age 41-50
852, 856, 858, 878, 1372,

1390, 1394, 1407, 1488, 1498,
1505, 2216, 2224, 2257

Age 51-60
878, 1372, 1390, 1407, 1412,
1475, 1476, 1498, 1505, 2216,
2266

Age Over 60
1372, 1390, 1407, 1498

FEMALE CLASSIC - COMIC

Age 15 and Under
737

Age 16-25
92, 94, 96, 495, 496, 725-729,
733, 735, 738, 741, 744, 745,
746, 749, 750, 751, 752, 754,
755, 756, 757, 758, 759, 760,
1591, 1592, 1593, 1594, 1596,
2244

Age 26-40
725-729, 733, 735, 738, 741,
744, 745, 746, 749, 750, 751,
752, 753, 754, 755, 756, 757,
758, 759, 760, 761, 1732, 2244

Age 41-50
725, 726, 727, 728, 729, 735,
749, 750, 751, 752, 755, 758

Age 51-60
725, 726, 727, 728, 729, 749,
750, 751, 758

Age Over 60

725, 726, 727, 728, 729, 749, 750, 751, 758

ETHNIC/ NATIONALITY/ RELIGIOUS AFFILIATION

Asian and Asian-American

191, 192, 413, 466, 467, 646, 698, 699, 700, 935, 1104, 1144, 1776, 1833, 1847, 2092, 2528, 2529

Black (includes African-American and non-American)

88, 89, 101, 102, 103, 106, 107, 163, 164, 192, 194, 200, 266, 303, 305, 475, 551, 557, 558, 561, 637, 638, 639, 654, 656, 660, 664, 665, 1051, 1097, 1109, 1134, 1735, 1736, 1740, 1741, 1773, 1789, 1790, 1817, 1832, 1836, 1848, 1849, 1851, 1853, 1854, 1855, 1991, 2005, 2079, 2080, 2128, 2133, 2267, 2288, 2517

Canadian

198, 269, 288, 314, 415, 1787

European and British

10, 73, 74, 75, 76, 81, 86, 87, 88, 96, 97, 98, 162, 189, 190, 197, 267, 270, 271, 275, 281, 284, 286, 289, 300, 302, 306, 313, 316, 318, 319, 381, 410,

462, 463, 479, 493, 587, 622, 624, 645, 661, 662, 674, 836, 838, 840, 842, 843, 844, 845, 846, 850-859, 860, 861, 862, 863, 864, 867, 868, 870, 871, 873, 874, 892, 897, 907, 918, 1050, 1055, 1064, 1065, 1069, 1075, 1082, 1085, 1095, 1112, 1117, 1118, 1123, 1130, 1131, 1133, 1136, 1137, 1142, 1145, 1349, 1371, 1374, 1375, 1377, 1383- 387, 1388, 1389, 1390, 1391, 1392, 1393, 1394, 1395, 1396, 1397, 1398, 1402, 1403, 1406, 1409, 1412, 1414, 1415, 1417, 1418, 1419, 1469, 1470, 1471, 1474, 1476, 1478, 1484, 1487, 1488, 1489, 1490, 1491, 1494, 1495, 1499, 1500, 1501-1504, 1506, 1508, 1512-1518, 1572, 1574, 1575, 1576, 1581, 1586, 1587, 1588, 1591-1594, 1597, 1598, 1600, 1602, 1605, 1609, 1610, 1617, 1618, 1755, 1756, 1767, 1768, 1769, 1809, 1810, 1823, 1824, 1825, 1844, 1948, 2005, 2106, 2119, 2121, 2129, 2200, 2201, 2202, 2203, 2205, 2208, 2209, 2210, 2211, 2212, 2216, 2217, 2220, 2221, 2222, 2223, 2224, 2225, 2226, 2228, 2229, 2231, 2232, 2233, 2234, 2235, 2236, 2236, 2239, 2240, 2241, 2242, 2243, 2244, 2245, 2246, 2247, 2248, 2249, 2250, 2253, 2254, 2255, 2256, 2257, 2258, 2259, 2260, 2261, 2264, 2265, 2266, 2273, 2279,

2280, 2290, 2423-2446, 2526,
2527, 2548, 2549, 2554, 2555,
2556

Hispanic
84, 85, 90, 210, 376, 894, 909,
910, 1051, 1103, 1115, 1116,
1778, 1798, 1845, 2536, 2557

Irish
275, 1145, 1809, 1810, 1982,
2246, 2247, 2423, 2424, 2425,
2426, 2427, 2428, 2429, 2430,
2431, 2432, 2433, 2434, 2435,
2436, 2437, 2438, 2439, 2440,
2441, 2442, 2443, 2444, 2445,
2446

Jewish
380, 462, 463, 666, 667, 668,
669, 1057, 1136, 1364, 1835,
1840, 1850, 1946, 2090, 2521

Mennonite
1834

Middle Eastern
835, 841, 865, 866, 1369, 1835

Mormon
2524, 2525

Native American
1098, 1198, 1213, 1749, 1786,
1837, 1838, 1839, 1856, 2252

Russian
918, 1844, 2119, 2244

TIME PERIODS

Ancient
267, 490, 492, 830, 832, 833,
834, 839, 848, 849, 1065,
1088, 1369, 1370, 1373, 1376,
1380, 1381, 1399, 1400, 1402,
1404, 1410, 1411, 1473, 1487,
1496, 1497, 1507, 1509, 1510,
1511, 1519, 1520, 1571, 1579,
1595, 1596, 1606, 1607, 1608,
1611, 1732, 1733, 1754, 2204,
2206, 2207, 2213, 2218, 2219,
2262, 2263, 2430, 2544, 2566

Medieval
162, 493, 674, 835, 836, 873,
1055, 1123, 1133, 1382, 1414,
1415, 1416, 1419, 1491, 1501,
1502, 1575, 1576, 1591-1594,
1601, 2202, 2203, 2228, 2239,
2279, 2280

1500s
838, 840, 841, 1470, 1471,
1472, 1474, 1475, 1476, 1484,
1490, 1492, 1493, 1499, 1503,
1504, 1505, 1508, 1521, 1522,
1524, 1525, 1526, 1529, 1530,
1537, 1538, 1540, 1541, 1583,
1584, 1597, 1662, 1663, 1664,
1668, 1732, 1733, 1948, 2200,
2201, 2202, 2548, 2549

1600s
491, 496, 497, 498, 725-731,
733, 735, 737, 738, 741, 744-
746, 749-761, 844, 845, 846,

850, 851, 1085, 1136, 1137, 1371, 1390, 1391, 1392, 1395, 1396, 1397, 1398, 1402, 1406, 1407, 1408, 1409, 1413, 1417, 1469, 1477, 1478, 1494, 1495, 1500, 1506, 1512, 1513, 1514, 1516, 1518, 1602, 2106, 2205, 2208, 2209, 2210, 2211, 2212, 2214, 2215, 2216, 2217, 2220, 2221, 2222, 2223, 2252, 2554, 2555, 2256

1700s

91, 92, 266, 300, 495, 701, 702, 852-857, 1097, 1117, 1118, 1213, 1371, 1372, 1374, 1375, 1377, 1378, 1379, 1383, 1384, 1385, 1386, 1387, 1388, 1389, 1393, 1394, 1403, 1412, 1418, 1582, 1586, 1749, 1809, 1810, 1823, 1824, 2224, 2225, 2226, 2227, 2229, 2231, 2232, 2233, 2234, 2235, 2236, 2237, 2240, 2241, 2251, 2569

1800s

159, 200, 427, 474, 476, 624, 637, 858, 859, 860, 861, 862, 863, 864, 867, 868, 920, 926, 1082, 1098, 1112, 1120, 1121, 1198, 1242, 1572, 1573, 1574, 1577, 1578, 1580, 1581, 1586, 1599, 1600, 1601, 1602, 1603, 1604, 1605, 1610, 1612-14, 1615, 1616, 1617, 1618, 1619, 1731, 1740, 1741, 1825, 2127, 2242, 2243, 2244, 2246, 2247, 2248, 2249, 2250, 2253, 2254,

2255, 2256, 2257, 2258, 2259, 2260, 2261, 2264, 2265, 2266, 2267, 2526, 2568, 2569

1900-1930

107, 181, 182, 194, 211, 318, 319, 379, 380, 427, 481, 587, 595, 653, 655, 870, 871, 872, 874, 875, 876, 909, 910, 1050, 1102, 1214, 1215, 1585, 1587, 1588, 1589, 1590, 1609, 1966, 1967, 2268, 2269, 2270, 2271, 2272, 2273, 2273, 2274, 2275, 2276, 2277, 2278, 2281, 2428, 2439, 2441, 2442, 2528, 2529, 2550, 2562, 2563, 2564, 2565

1930s

58, 59, 275, 647, 897, 918, 1830, 1974, 2542, 2543, 2545, 2546, 2567

1940s

73, 74, 293, 434, 463, 464, 478, 479, 608, 698, 699, 700, 877, 878, 918, 1095, 1134, 1725, 1790, 1850, 2296

1950s

75, 76, 106, 107, 163, 164, 197, 219, 288, 316, 473, 622, 653, 654, 663, 665, 880, 881, 882, 883, 1119, 1784, 1785, 1848, 1974, 1976, 2540

1960-1980

175, 176, 177, 178, 204, 205, 272, 297, 298, 574, 589, 660,

892, 935, 1059, 1075, 1077,
1078, 1138, 1142, 1145, 1232,
1234, 1241, 1776, 1784, 1785,
1797, 1814, 2003, 2004, 2087,
2088, 2098, 2112, 2297, 2298,
2433, 2434, 2530, 2561

1980s

187, 188, 269, 270, 273, 274,
276, 279, 281, 285, 286, 287,
291, 302, 303, 304, 305, 306,
307, 308, 309, 311, 312, 314,
315, 1062, 1107, 1776, 1777,
1778, 2299, 2557

1990s

1793, 1827, 2103, 2104, 2443,
2444, 2479, 2531, 2532, 2533,
2534

GEOGRAPHICAL AREA

Africa

66, 263, 276, 264, 276, 671,
884, 1062

Ancient World

830, 833, 834, 835, 839, 848,
849, 865, 866, 1369, 1370,
1376, 1399, 1400, 1401, 1410,
1411, 1472, 1473, 1496, 1497,
1519, 2204, 2206, 2207, 2213,
2218, 2219, 2262, 2263, 2430,
2544, 2566

Appalachia

181, 182

Asia and the Pacific

75, 76, 935, 1762, 1763, 1776,
1833, 1847, 2528, 2529

Australia and New Zealand

1790, 1813, 1812

Canada

198, 269, 288, 314, 415, 1837,
1838, 1839, 2102

Europe and Great Britain

73, 74, 77, 78, 91, 92, 96, 161,
189, 190, 191, 192, 197, 267,
270, 271, 281, 284, 286, 289,
300, 302, 306, 313, 316, 318,
319, 381, 410, 462, 463, 479,
622, 662, 674, 836, 838, 840,
842, 843, 845, 846, 850-859,
860, 861, 862, 863, 864, 867,
868, 870, 871, 873, 874, 882,
892, 897, 907, 918, 944, 1049,
1050, 1051, 1055, 1056, 1064,
1065, 1066, 1069, 1075, 1082,
1085, 1095, 1117, 1118, 1123,
1130, 1131, 1133, 1136, 1137,
1142, 1143, 1145, 1384, 1385,
1386, 1387, 1388, 1389, 1390,
1391, 1392, 1393, 1394, 1395,
1396, 1397, 1398, 1403, 1406,
1409, 1414, 1415, 1417, 1418,
1419, 1425, 1469, 1470, 1471,
1474, 1475, 1476, 1477, 1478,
1484, 1487, 1488, 1489, 1490,
1491, 1494, 1495, 1499, 1500,
1502, 1503, 1504, 1506, 1508,
1512-1518, 1572, 1575, 1576,
1577, 1578, 1581, 1582, 1583,

1584, 1586, 1587, 1588, 1591-
1594, 1597, 1598, 1600, 1601,
1602, 1603, 1604, 1605, 1606,
1609, 1610, 1612-1614, 1615,
1616, 1617, 1618, 1619, 1729,
1742, 1743, 1754, 1755, 1756,
1758, 1767, 1768, 1769, 1778,
1809, 1810, 1823, 1824, 1825,
1844, 1948, 1950, 1951, 1966,
1967, 1982, 2005, 2106, 2121,
2129, 2200, 2201, 2202, 2203,
2205, 2208, 2209, 2210, 2211,
2212, 2216, 2217, 2220, 2221,
2222, 2223, 2224, 2225, 2226,
2228, 2229, 2230, 2231, 2232,
2233, 2234, 2235, 2236, 2238,
2239, 2240, 2241, 2242, 2243,
2244, 2245, 2246, 2247, 2248,
2249, 2250, 2253, 2254, 2255,
2256, 2257, 2258, 2259, 2260,
2261, 2264, 2265, 2266, 2273,
2279, 2280, 2290, 2423-2429,
2431, 2433-2446, 2526, 2527,
2548, 2549, 2554, 2555, 2556

Ireland

275, 1145, 1809, 1810, 1982,
2246, 2247, 2423, 2424, 2425,
2426, 2427, 2428, 2429, 2431,
2433, 2434, 2435, 2436, 2437,
2438, 2439, 2440, 2441, 2442,
2443, 2444, 2445, 2446

Latin America and the Caribbean

90, 909, 910, 1097, 1115,
1116, 1803, 1845, 1954, 1955,
2432, 2536

Middle East

835, 841, 865, 866, 1413,
1416, 1464, 1465, 1472, 1473,
1519, 2237

Midwest (USA)

52, 86, 87, 97, 163, 164, 175,
176, 272, 273, 274, 287, 310,
311, 343, 422, 476, 655, 660,
913, 1215, 1740, 1741, 1749,
1848, 1954, 2075, 2083, 2087,
2098, 2128, 2133, 2535

New England/Northeast (USA)

53, 54, 79, 80, 81, 210, 212,
305, 307, 308, 561, 1783,
1793, 1794, 1797, 1806, 1819,
1827, 1830, 1947, 1955, 2127,
2278, 2287, 2293

New York City Area

51, 57, 63, 64, 65, 84, 88, 89,
94, 95, 106, 107, 167, 168,
177, 178, 186, 203, 268, 291,
297, 298, 303, 304, 309, 312,
315, 375, 376, 379, 380, 396,
397, 666, 667, 668, 669, 1057,
1073, 1074, 1093, 1139, 1144,
1175, 1181, 1299, 1302, 1307,
1317, 1318, 1581, 1589, 1590,
1765, 1777, 1590, 1765, 1777,
1780, 1791, 1792, 1795, 1815,
1850, 1964, 1995, 1997, 1998,
1999, 2077, 2078, 2095, 2114,
2116, 2117, 2118, 2119, 2123,
2124, 2126, 2274, 2281, 2282,
2283, 2295, 2508, 2530

OCCUPATIONS

Clown
1981

Dancer
397, 477, 1173, 1745

Door to Door Saleswoman
2514

Dressmaker
312

Entertainer
81, 382, 389, 397, 413, 427,
477, 675, 1122, 1173, 1183,
1191, 1728, 2119, 2131

Farmer
75, 76, 101, 102, 103, 422,
589, 606, 870, 1974

Flower Shop Clerk
2271

Fortune Teller
878

Gardener
1751

Heiress
1578

Hollywood Agent
2283

Household Helper
2293

Housewife
858, 872, 1349, 1355, 1358,
1361, 1577, 1591, 1593, 1594,
1612-1614, 1615, 1752, 1772

Journalist
640, 641, 645, 661, 1102

Kings/Queens/Royalty
82, 837, 838, 841, 848, 863,
865, 866, 1369, 1399, 1404,
1410, 1411, 1413, 1487, 1491,
1493, 1501, 1507, 1512, 1513,
1519, 1507, 1512, 1513, 1823,
1824, 2207, 2252, 2262, 2263,
2450, 2544, 2566

Landlady/Proprietress
1616, 1734, 2266

Lawyer/Judge
173, 407, 1239, 2505

Magician
2218

Medical Clinic Director
2286

Medical Doctor
387, 635, 918, 1241, 1768

Midwife
2109

Miner
1599, 1790

Missionary
1293

Motel Owner
582

Musician
413, 867

Nightclub Owner
2132, 2517

Night Watchperson
1767

Nobility
2216, 2228, 2238, 2240, 2257,
2268

Nun
172, 197, 1123, 2203

Nurse
557, 1350

Pilot
1779

Plantation Owner
1731

Playwright
641, 1876, 1995, 2049, 2364,
2369, 2407

Poet
1821, 1822, 2558

Police
1354, 1758, 1804, 2002

Political Lobbyist
1946, 2484

Politician/Government Figure
662

Postal Worker
394

Prostitute
383, 660, 1096, 1126, 1141,
1177, 1190, 1494, 1495, 1586,
1603, 1604, 1732, 1825, 1842,
1998, 2092, 2259, 2281, 2285,
2424

Red Cross Volunteer
276

Secretary
307, 308, 592, 607, 655

Self Defense Instructor
1829

Servant
513, 587, 877, 944, 1115, 1418,
1475, 1476, 1733, 1852, 2243,
2276, 2438, 2537, 2554-56

Shepherdess
1502

Social Services Evaluator
2295

CHARACTER TYPES/ SITUATIONS

Affectation/Pretentions
2216, 2282, 2300

Agoraphobia
649, 2524, 2525

Aging Issues
68, 289, 290, 301, 411, 1488,
1589, 1616, 1745, 1759, 1796,
1957, 2078, 2086, 2114, 2294,
2445, 2446

AIDS and AIDS Victims
57, 392, 412, 1083, 1317,
1318, 1726, 1766, 1786, 1807,
1808, 1955, 1968, 1969, 1984,
1992

Air Raid Drill
1975

Alcohol/Drug Abuse
171, 285, 391, 638, 639, 890,
1126, 1128, 1184, 1725, 1798,
1851, 1961, 1962, 1971, 2071,
2095, 2112, 2123, 2522, 2524,
2525

Alienation/Loneliness
1948, 1951, 1995, 2071, 2094,
2095, 2099, 2103, 2106, 2131,
2265, 2272, 2275, 2286, 2426,
2432, 2445, 2527, 2531, 2538,
2539

Alzheimer's Disease
1772

Ambition
1789, 2205

Animal Abuse
2288, 2296, 2301

Armed Conflict/War
276, 918, 2219, 2228, 2277,
2428, 2435, 2441, 2442, 2544,
2566

Art/Theater Patron
1146

Art/Theater, Reflections On
1372, 2286, 2528

Artistic Creation
2270, 2528

Betrayal
2239, 2240, 2242, 2244, 2256,
2258, 2276

Betrothal
2217, 2548

Blackmail
1809

Body Image Issues
102, 199, 310, 427, 562, 696,
1063, 1117, 1243, 1380, 1493,
1589, 1782, 1816, 1826, 1828,
1832, 1956, 1965, 2085, 2086,
2101, 2111, 2114, 2282

Bureaucratic
2492

Environmentalists
1734, 1774

Euthanasia
1955, 2288

Exiled Persons
892, 1501

Family Dynamics
2292, 2299, 2497, 2532, 2536,
2538, 2539, 2545, 2546, 2551,
2552, 2559, 2560, 2563, 2564,
2565

Father/Child Relationship
73, 181, 381, 400, 403, 426,
867, 935, 1054, 1061, 1075,
1379, 1772,1812, 1842, 1969,
1982, 2004, 2073, 2107, 2109,
2130, 2132, 2217, 2252, 2299,
2440

Flashback - Vietnam Veteran
2301

Friendship
1092, 1730, 1955, 2282, 2297,
2298, 2530, 2551

Fundamentalists
69, 399

Fun-Loving/Joyful
2006, 2122, 2443, 2444, 2511,
2541, 2550

Gambling
2238

Gossiping
2266, 2569

Grieving
57, 74, 181, 209, 211, 212,
315, 390, 392, 418, 555, 831,
835, 843, 863, 866, 874, 1054,
1059, 1089, 1092, 1128, 1148,
1351, 1360, 1370, 1373, 1376,
1382, 1383, 1472, 1473, 1477,
1487, 1503, 1504, 1585, 1611,
1722, 1723, 1726, 1730, 1739,
1741, 1742, 1744, 1748, 1759,
1762, 1763, 1769, 1802, 1812,
1813, 1819, 1830, 1852, 1948,
1954, 1958, 1960, 1962, 1974,
1995, 2001, 2002, 2072, 2074,
2075, 2081, 2088, 2104, 2109,
2113, 2123, 2130, 2132, 2204,
2229, 2230, 2234, 2245, 2250,
2255, 2277, 2426, 2439, 2546,
2554, 2555, 2256

Hallucinations
70

Heroism
2219, 2544

Hillbilly
2277

Hippies
2102

Historical and Well-Known Persons

82, 83, 318, 319, 462, 463,
493, 574, 640, 641, 644, 645,
651, 652, 653, 654, 661, 662,
665, 674, 1050, 1056, 1065,
1084, 1102, 1112, 1133, 1232,
1369, 1370, 1579, 1597, 1598,
1601, 1602, 1606, 1607, 1608,
1611, 1732, 1733, 1754, 1779,
1823, 1825, 1965, 1985, 1986,
2088, 2100, 2108, 2127, 2204,
2206, 2207, 2251, 2252, 2262,
2263, 2544, 2566, 2568, 2569

Hollywood Scene

2283, 2299

Homelessness

376, 656, 657, 1367, 2120,
2126, 2264, 2508, 2536

Hostage

401

Incest

560, 849, 1132, 1506, 1519

Infanticide

2508

Infidelity

575, 862, 1572, 1573, 1819,
1958, 1966, 1967, 2105, 2116,
2200, 2214, 2215, 2226, 2229,
2242, 2244, 2255, 2257, 2258,
2278, 2280, 2443, 2444

Introspection

374, 2286, 2559, 2560

Jealousy

1972, 2213, 2225, 2242, 2278

Kidnapping and Kidnappers

1993, 1994

Literature, Reflections On

2526

Lost Loves

92, 169, 182, 194, 279, 395,
568, 833, 834, 839, 843, 854,
857, 860, 862, 863, 868, 871,
883, 1085, 1369, 1370, 1382,
1383, 1385, 1392, 1400, 1401,
1402, 1410, 1470, 1473, 1477,
1479, 1482, 1490, 1576, 1583,
1586, 1587, 1588, 1592, 1593,
1594, 1599, 1605, 1609, 1617,
1737, 1756, 1963, 1997, 2209,
2212, 2229, 2234, 2250, 2256,
2261, 2540

Love

373, 2202, 2204, 2207, 2220,
2227, 2234, 2235, 2241, 2249,
2550

Make-Out Artists/ On The Make

414, 1364, 1393

Male/Female Relationship

64, 96, 416, 546, 575, 863, 1080,
1760, 1800, 1814, 1819, 1857,

1858, 1951, 1953, 1963, 1983,
1984, 1997, 2070, 2078, 2087,
2089, 2091, 2098, 2101, 2108,
2129, 2202, 2207, 2209, 2211,
2212, 2214, 2215, 2221, 2232,
2234, 2235, 2236, 2239, 2241,
2242, 2244, 2249, 2256, 2257,
2260, 2261, 2263, 2269, 2284,
2297, 2298, 2301, 2427, 2433,
2434, 2437, 2438, 2443, 2444,
2445, 2490, 2503, 2530, 2533,
2542, 2543, 2548, 2549, 2551

Man Hater
2233

Marital Relationship (see also Divorce, Love, Infidelity, Jealousy, etc.)
96, 105, 165, 166, 170, 185,
189, 190, 206, 270, 271, 279,
377, 422, 428, 547, 563, 564,
565, 572, 591, 631, 632, 634,
656, 670, 671, 672, 735, 744,
746, 752, 753, 755, 756, 757,
836, 838, 844, 845, 846, 849,
851, 852, 855, 861, 864, 870,
871, 872, 876, 880, 881, 888,
1055, 1057, 1078, 1107, 1112,
1122, 1130, 1147, 1124, 1355,
1358, 1361, 1362, 1371, 1374,
1375, 1374, 1387, 1388, 1389,
1402, 1404, 1406, 1409, 1410,
1411, 1417, 1418, 1470, 1471,
1490, 1495, 1517, 1519, 1571,
1572, 1575, 1576, 1590, 1591,
1592, 1593, 1594, 1600, 1601,
1612-1614, 1615, 1619, 1731,

1733, 1738, 1740, 1741, 1754,
1755, 1756, 1763, 1772, 1773,
1774, 1793, 1797, 1814, 1818,
1819, 1820, 1822, 1948, 1954,
1958, 1966, 1967, 1970, 1971,
1972, 1983, 1986, 2000, 2003,
2074, 2084, 2087, 2088, 2089,
2090, 2105, 2107, 2121, 2200,
2201, 2205, 2206, 2208, 2213,
2217, 2220, 2224, 2225, 2230,
2246, 2248, 2253, 2255, 2257,
2258, 2273, 2276, 2278, 2279,
2280, 2280, 2290, 2423, 2425,
2426, 2431, 2436, 2441, 2474,
2524, 2548

Marriage Proposals
2211, 2542, 2543

Melancholy
2228, 2245, 2254

Mental Illness
180, 186, 187, 188, 284, 293,
423, 545, 555, 562, 563, 570,
573, 610, 649, 650, 1058, 1073,
1074, 1099, 1100, 1105, 1355,
1574, 1580, 1614, 1729, 1734,
1821, 1822, 1830, 2075, 2081,
2120, 2288, 2489, 2507, 2562,
2563, 2566

Mother/Child Relationship
51, 59, 61, 84, 86, 94, 162,
164, 192, 212, 264, 268, 292,
296, 373, 384, 385, 391, 392,
399, 403, 409, 421, 513, 553,
560, 573, 578, 637, 643, 647,

648, 679, 680, 681, 760, 849,
859, 874, 875, 883, 932, 1051,
1052, 1061, 1089, 1095, 1097,
1109, 1142, 1213, 1249, 1366,
1472, 1478, 1491, 1494, 1572,
1573, 1579, 1581, 1726, 1797,
1798, 1603, 1604, 1731, 1740,
1741, 1745, 1746, 1747, 1749,
1752, 1753, 1754, 1759, 1762,
1763, 1769, 1794, 1800, 1801,
1802, 1806, 1811, 1812, 1813,
1826, 1852, 1958, 1959, 1960,
1962, 1968, 1974, 1980, 1986,
1987, 1988, 1990, 1994, 1996,
2001, 2004, 2005, 2072, 2073,
2081, 2089, 2093, 2104, 2110,
2113, 2121, 2124, 2128, 2205,
2224, 2230, 2237, 2246, 2247,
2253, 2264, 2274, 2277, 2289,
2291, 2294, 2428, 2429, 2435,
2477, 2509, 2545, 2546

Murder, Reflections On
2527

Murderers and Murder
79, 201, 202, 209, 578, 834,
854, 947, 1471, 1497, 1611,
1754, 1779, 1781, 1825, 1987,
2111, 2201, 2251, 2277, 2280,
2330, 2425, 2426

Mystics
1817, 1840, 1849, 1853, 1854,
1855, 1856, 2429, 2439, 2525,
2526

Nazism, Reflections On
381, 2527

Nightmares
2107, 2127, 2494

Orphans
58, 1809, 2536

**Otherworldly Figures
(angels, animals, devils,
ghosts, nymphs, etc.)**
383, 830, 869, 1380, 1479,
1483, 1484, 1492, 1498, 1505,
1607, 1608, 1735, 1736, 1764,
1766, 1780, 1794, 1798, 1849,
1857, 1964, 1985, 1986, 1989,
2076, 2103, 2117, 2118, 2493

Panic Attacks
2096

Philosophizing
2068, 2077, 2082, 2123, 2129,
2131, 2271, 2444, 2524, 2525,
2527

Pioneers/Explorers
75, 76, 159, 624, 1120, 1175,
1176, 1779

Plague
2554, 2555, 2256

Political Activists/ Militants
96, 266, 303, 306, 637, 679,
832, 897, 1618, 1767, 1768,
1769, 1845, 2251

Poverty
88, 1356, 1414, 1415, 2106,
2230, 2264, 2265, 2536

Pregnancy
94, 177, 192, 204, 295, 377,
378, 385, 386, 396, 421, 513,
655, 883, 892, 1055, 1095,
1097, 1131, 1213, 1294, 1514,
1749, 1770, 1775, 1776, 1800,
1830, 1836, 1952, 2098, 2110,
2289, 2290, 2433, 2434, 2534

Prisoners/Interned Persons
201, 202, 401, 422, 468, 479,
578, 698, 699, 674, 700, 873,
1399, 1580, 1786, 1787, 1823,
1824, 2227, 2237, 2251, 2252,
2289, 2554, 2555, 2556

Promiscuity
2078

Prostitution
383, 1126, 1141, 1177, 1190,
1494, 1495, 1586, 1603, 1604,
1732, 1825, 1842, 1998, 2092,
2259, 2281, 2285, 2424, 2259,
2281

Racism and Racial Issues
66, 191, 192, 194, 200, 276,
536, 665, 884, 1062, 1731,
1773, 1788, 1789, 1790, 1832,
2080, 2133, 2267, 2298, 2486

Rape
192, 266, 401, 1088, 2001,
2002, 2080, 2087, 2221, 2297,
2533

Rebels
266, 831, 2252, 2542, 2543,
2559, 2567, 2568

Religious Faith
208, 297, 302, 548, 674, 861,
869, 873, 879, 1135, 1136,
1137, 1416, 1795, 1840, 1946,
1959, 1996, 2097, 2109, 2128,
2203, 2204, 2426, 2531, 2553

Religious Intolerance
2442

Sadists
1732

Self Sacrifice
2544

Sexuality/Sexual Orientation
96, 197, 204, 212, 383, 601,
1080, 1738, 1787, 1805, 1818,
1830, 1947, 1968, 1969, 1979,
1980, 1992, 2094, 2095, 2116,
2211, 2218, 2297, 2437, 2438,
2490

Sexual Discrimination
1947

2257, 2259, 2268, 2269, 2273,
2275, 2276, 2279, 2287, 2282,
2431, 2481, 2521, 2526, 2542,
2543, 2547, 2548, 2552, 2557,
2568

Widow

571, 1473, 2074, 2088, 2210,
2228, 2244, 2295

Working Class Persons

90, 96, 175, 176, 210, 376,
379, 380, 419, 480, 508, 558,
587, 858, 872, 882, 894, 944,
1051, 1225, 1408, 1600, 1610,
1735, 1736, 1784, 1795, 1974,
1991, 1996, 2084, 2108, 2247,
2271, 2293, 2446, 2530, 2537,
2557

Worldly Sophisticated Types

1609, 2210, 2231, 2257, 2283,
2522, 2526

MALE CONTEMPORARY - DRAMATIC

Age Under 15

618, 709, 710, 711, 713, 714, 720, 721, 722, 723, 724, 902, 925, 927, 1710, 1859, 1866, 1867, 1869, 1872, 1883, 1884, 1885, 1891, 1916, 2494, 2515, 2520, 2575, 2576, 2577, 2579, 2583, 2590, 2591, 2601, 2602, 2604

Age 16-25

1, 4, 5, 8, 9, 10, 34, 112, 121, 132, 139, 142, 158, 214, 218, 220, 245, 251, 327, 329, 334, 342, 346, 358, 431-456, 499, 500, 501, 502, 503, 504, 506, 507, 514, 515, 522, 525, 526, 527, 535, 536, 537, 544, 581, 612, 620, 628, 680, 682, 825, 828, 889, 903, 904, 921, 930, 968, 971, 972, 977, 983, 1000, 1018, 1149, 1156, 1161, 1207, 1216, 1245, 1247, 1248, 1259, 1274, 1325, 1343, 1671, 1672, 1683, 1686, 1694, 1718, 1720, 1859, 1862, 1863, 1864, 1865, 1866, 1867, 1870, 1871, 1873, 1874, 1875, 1876, 1877, 1878, 1879, 1880, 1881, 1882, 1885, 1886, 1887, 1888, 1889, 1890, 1892, 1893, 1894, 1896, 1902, 1903, 1905, 1907, 1909, 1916, 1929, 2022, 2024, 2027, 2044,

2053, 2057, 2065, 2066, 2149, 2150, 2157, 2158, 2159, 2163, 2164, 2167, 2169, 2194, 2401, 2412, 2413, 2418, 2420, 2453, 2455, 2457, 2461, 2465, 2469, 2470, 2473, 2482, 2486, 2493, 2494, 2501, 2508, 2510, 2512, 2515, 2570, 2573, 2574, 2575, 2577, 2578, 2579, 2580, 2581, 2582, 2588, 2589, 2590, 2591, 2592, 2593, 2594, 2595, 2596, 2597, 2598, 2603, 2604, 2607

Age 26-40

3, 5, 8, 9, 16, 19, 22, 25, 26, 30, 31, 32, 33, 37, 38, 39, 40, 45, 47, 49, 50, 109, 115, 116, 120, 121, 123, 124, 126, 132, 137, 142, 147, 149, 216, 219, 220, 228, 232, 234, 239, 241, 256, 257, 322, 329, 335, 341, 345, 346, 348, 358, 360, 363, 366, 371, 514, 516, 518-522, 524, 527-533, 536, 537, 539, 540, 541, 542, 544, 579, 581, 584, 585, 590, 600, 603, 604, 605, 611, 612, 615, 616, 617, 619, 628, 677, 678, 686, 687, 688, 689, 825, 826, 828, 889, 896, 905, 906, 908, 911, 917, 921, 924, 928, 937, 940, 941, 952, 960, 968, 970, 975, 977, 983, 985, 991, 995, 997, 1000, 1018, 1019, 1027, 1039, 1042, 1149, 1156, 1161, 1197, 1199, 1201, 1202, 1207, 1210, 1216, 1217, 1220, 1223, 1224, 1226, 1228, 1229, 1235-1238, 1244,

1245, 1247, 1248, 1253, 1255, 1257, 1259, 1265, 1274, 1282,1323-1325, 1343, 1671, 1672, 1677, 1679, 1683, 1686, 1687, 1692, 1694, 1696, 1703, 1718, 1719, 1897, 1899, 1900, 1901, 1902, 1903, 1905, 1907, 1909, 1911, 1917, 1919, 1922, 1926, 1929, 1941, 1942, 1943, 1944, 1945, 2008, 2018, 2022, 2027, 2032, 2033, 2034, 2041, 2046, 2047, 2053, 2055, 2056, 2057, 2064, 2067, 2138, 2139, 2141, 2142, 2150, 2154, 2157, 2158, 2159, 2161, 2163, 2164, 2167, 2169, 2175, 2177, 2181, 2182, 2191, 2194, 2404, 2405, 2422, 2450, 2452, 2457, 2458, 2461, 2462, 2465, 2466, 2469, 2470, 2479, 2480, 2482, 2486, 2488, 2491, 2493, 2494, 2505, 2506, 2508, 2510, 2512

Age 41-50

17, 18, 22, 23, 27, 32, 37, 40, 49, 50, 113, 126, 144, 147, 217, 222, 226, 227, 231, 233, 234, 235, 239, 240, 246, 249, 252, 256, 257, 258, 259, 261, 322, 330, 333, 339, 340, 356, 359, 364, 366, 369, 517, 519, 520, 521, 523, 538, 542, 543, 588, 603, 614, 616, 617, 621, 626, 677, 678, 679, 681, 686, 906, 934, 936, 938, 951, 953, 955, 960, 961, 966, 967, 982, 984, 1017, 1022, 1032, 1034, 1154, 1156, 1161, 1197, 1199,

1204, 1208, 1209, 1210, 1216, 1217, 1220, 1222, 1226, 1228, 1229, 1235, 1236, 1237, 1238, 1240, 1244, 1245, 1247, 1253, 1255, 1257, 1259, 1264, 1323, 1324, 1325, 1338, 1712, 1713, 1897, 1914, 1915, 1924, 1934, 1936, 1937, 1939, 1943, 2010, 2011, 2019, 2029, 2043, 2145, 2153, 2402, 2406, 2410, 2450, 2456, 2458, 2459, 2463, 2466, 2468, 2472, 2479, 2480, 2482, 2486, 2488, 2491, 2493, 2499, 2505, 2506, 2508, 2512, 2518, 2519, 2523

Age 51-60

15, 23, 37, 41, 42, 44, 147, 213, 215, 217, 225, 229, 230, 234, 236, 239, 242, 244, 249, 370, 534, 596, 597, 623, 679, 685, 686, 823, 827, 829, 898, 899, 900, 906, 922, 942, 957, 961, 999, 1047, 1154, 1199, 1204, 1208, 1209, 1217, 1226, 1228, 1229, 1235, 1236, 1237, 1238, 1244, 1259, 1283, 1689, 1711, 1715, 1717, 1925, 1930, 1931, 1935, 1937, 2039, 2045, 2062, 2136, 2137, 2140, 2183, 2184, 2199, 2456, 2458, 2459, 2463, 2468, 2472, 2480, 2482, 2486, 2488, 2493, 2497, 2499, 2505, 2506, 2508, 2518, 2523, 2400, 2419

Age Over 60

13, 36, 150, 223, 224, 229, 234,

244, 247, 260, 352, 367, 534, 576,
577, 583, 599, 686, 891, 893, 895,
901, 906, 933, 939, 943, 981, 1010,
1031, 1048, 1204, 1208, 1209,
1218, 1219, 1226, 1235, 1244,
1259, 1283, 1329, 1338, 1675,
1682, 1688, 1697, 1709, 1714,
1721, 1895, 1932, 2009, 2016,
2028, 2051, 2052, 2148, 2160,
2165, 2192, 2193, 2198, 2415,
2416, 2417, 2463, 2482, 2486,
2493, 2497, 2499, 2505, 2508

MALE CONTEMPORARY - SERIOCOMIC

Age 15 and Under
720, 721, 1860, 1861, 1868,
2023, 2162, 2189, 2587, 2590,
2608, 2609, 2610

Age 16-25
6, 33, 38, 46, 48, 117, 129,
141, 146, 151, 237, 248, 255,
331, 332, 347, 350, 351, 357,
954, 958, 973, 978, 988, 989,
996, 1007, 1009, 1023, 1024,
1030, 1040, 1041, 1045, 1152,
1157, 1158, 1160, 1250, 1252,
1261, 1281, 1333, 1335, 1680,
1912, 1913, 1923, 1928, 1938,
1940, 2007, 2020, 2025, 2026,
2036, 2037, 2048, 2059, 2061,
2134, 2135, 2147, 2155, 2156,
2168, 2170, 2171, 2178, 2179,
2185, 2186, 2189, 2190, 2408,

2411, 2421, 2454, 2471, 2478,
2487, 2492, 2498, 2571, 2572,
2586, 2587, 2590, 2599, 2600,
2608, 2609, 2610

Age 26-40
2, 6, 16, 17, 26, 29, 31, 33, 38,
46, 47, 108, 110, 111, 117,
118, 119, 122, 127, 128, 130,
131, 133, 134, 136, 140, 141,
145, 148, 154, 155, 156, 157,
238, 248, 253, 254, 255, 324,
325, 331, 332, 336, 338, 347,
349, 350, 351, 353, 354, 355,
357, 361, 365, 368, 948, 954,
959, 964, 965, 969, 978, 980,
986, 989, 992, 993, 994, 996,
998, 1001, 1005, 1007, 1008,
1009, 1011, 1015, 1020, 1021,
1023, 1025, 1026, 1030, 1033,
1035, 1036, 1037, 1038, 1041,
1043, 1044, 1045, 1046, 1151,
1152, 1153, 1155, 1157, 1158,
1160, 1162, 1164, 1165, 1167,
1170, 1171, 1250, 1251, 1252,
1254, 1256, 1260, 1261, 1266,
1267, 1268, 1269, 1277, 1278,
1281, 1284, 1321, 1326, 1327,
1330, 1331, 1333, 1334, 1337,
1341, 1342, 1673, 1676, 1680,
1690, 1691, 1693, 1701, 1702,
1705, 1706, 1716, 1898, 1912,
1918, 1920, 1921, 1923, 1927,
1928, 1933, 1940, 2007, 2012,
2015, 2017, 2020, 2021, 2025,
2026, 2030, 2031, 2036, 2037,
2038, 2040, 2048, 2059, 2061,
2063, 2134, 2135, 2143, 2144,

2146, 2148, 2152, 2155, 2156, 2166, 2170, 2171, 2173, 2174, 2176, 2180, 2185, 2186, 2187, 2188, 2190, 2196, 2197, 2407, 2408, 2411, 2421, 2448, 2449, 2451, 2464, 2471, 2475, 2478, 2484, 2487, 2492, 2495, 2498, 2500, 2502, 2504, 2513, 2516

Age 41-50

7, 16, 17, 20, 21, 24, 31, 43, 46, 47, 135, 136, 138, 145, 152, 153, 221, 243, 250, 325, 326, 337, 343, 344, 362, 949, 950, 962, 963, 979, 980, 986, 987, 1002, 1006, 1016, 1028, 1041, 1151, 1153, 1155, 1157, 1160, 1162, 1163, 1164, 1165, 1167, 1170, 1171, 1250, 1251, 1254, 1256, 1260, 1268, 1321, 1326, 1327, 1330, 1331, 1334, 1337, 1341, 1342, 1676, 1678, 1681, 1684, 1685, 1695, 1699, 1700, 1898, 1906, 1908, 1920, 1940, 2013, 2014, 2037, 2042, 2048, 2049, 2050, 2151, 2170, 2172, 2399, 2409, 2414, 2421, 2448, 2449, 2451, 2471, 2475, 2478, 2484, 2485, 2492, 2495, 2498, 2500, 2502, 2504, 2513, 2516

Age 51-60

14, 15, 20, 28, 35, 46, 47, 125, 143, 145, 262, 320, 321, 323, 956, 963, 976, 990, 1003, 1012, 1013, 1014, 1151, 1153,

1157, 1158, 1164, 1165, 1170, 1171, 1251, 1256, 1270, 1271, 1272, 1321, 1322, 1326, 1327, 1330, 1341, 1342, 1694, 1704, 1898, 1920, 1940, 2013, 2014, 2035, 2048, 2049, 2151, 2170, 2403, 2421, 2460, 2471, 2475, 2478, 2484, 2485, 2492, 2495, 2498, 2500, 2504, 2516

Age Over 60

12, 28, 35, 46, 114, 143, 328, 1157, 1165, 1256, 1322, 1324, 1332, 1674, 1898, 1940, 2013, 2014, 2020, 2048, 2049, 2060, 2170, 2421, 2460, 2471, 2478, 2484, 2485

MALE CONTEMPORARY - COMIC

Age 16-25

430, 1166, 1168, 1169, 1273, 1279, 1328

Age 26-40

11, 49, 50, 1104, 1150, 1159, 1166, 1168, 1169, 1258, 1320, 1336, 1339, 1340

Age 41-50

21, 24, 49, 50, 1150, 1159, 1258, 1262, 1263, 1265, 1273, 1275, 1276, 1279, 1280, 1320, 1336, 1339, 1340

Age 51-60
1159, 1262, 1276, 1320, 1339, 2447

Age Over 60
974

MALE CLASSIC - DRAMATIC

Age 15 and Under
703, 704, 708, 712, 715, 716, 717, 718, 719, 2606

Age 16-25
482, 483, 484, 485, 486, 487, 489, 505, 506, 712, 770, 775, 787, 788, 790, 792, 794, 802, 808, 815, 825, 828, 1430, 1432, 1433, 1437, 1450, 1452, 1455, 1462, 1522, 1537, 1552, 1553, 1560, 1563, 1564, 1565, 1566, 1621, 1631, 1632, 1636, 1640, 1650, 1651, 1652, 2319, 2322, 2323, 2332, 2333, 2341, 2342, 2344, 2346, 2352, 2354, 2356, 2357, 2359, 2360, 2367, 2368, 2373, 2388, 2390, 2392, 2393, 2584, 2585, 2597, 2606

Age 26-40
770, 774, 775, 776, 778, 779, 780, 781, 782, 787, 788, 790, 792, 794, 796, 797, 800, 801, 802, 803, 804, 812, 815, 822, 825, 826, 828, 829, 1422,

1423, 1431, 1433, 1437, 1438, 1441, 1450, 1459, 1462, 1464, 1465, 1522, 1524, 1529, 1534, 1536, 1539, 1547, 1552, 1553, 1556, 1559, 1560, 1561, 1562, 1563, 1564, 1565, 1566, 1567, 1570, 1620, 1623, 1625, 1628, 1630, 1632, 1633, 1636, 1637, 1639, 1641, 1646, 1647, 1650, 1651, 1652, 1653, 1656, 1657, 1661, 1668, 1669, 2303, 2309, 2319, 2322, 2323,, 2324, 2339, 2341, 2342, 2344, 2346, 2347, 2349, 2352, 2354, 2355, 2356, 2357, 2358, 2359, 2360, 2364, 2367, 2368, 2373, 2377, 2378, 2381, 2385, 2388, 2392, 2393, 2396

Age 41-50
772, 776, 779, 780, 786, 793, 804, 806, 813, 814, 815, 816, 818, 819, 820, 822, 824, 1368, 1420, 1421, 1426, 1441, 1533, 1535, 1550, 1554, 1559, 1629, 1632, 1636, 1641, 1642, 1643, 1644, 1650, 1651, 1652, 1663, 1664, 1665, 1670, 2312, 2313, 2324, 2334, 2335, 2340, 2362, 2363, 2372, 2373, 2376, 2391, 2394, 2397

Age 51-60
771, 772, 773, 776, 795, 805, 809, 813, 815, 817, 819, 820, 822, 823, 827, 1436, 1441, 1451, 1461, 1532, 1557, 1558, 1626, 1627, 1632, 1636, 1638,

1650, 1651, 1652, 1667, 2306,
2307, 2312, 2324, 2325, 2337,
2343, 2361, 2362, 2366, 2372,
2373, 2376, 2398

Age Over 60

776, 1441, 1632, 1636, 1650,
1651, 1652, 2373

MALE CLASSIC - SERIOCOMIC

Age 16-25

784, 785, 789, 1424, 1445,
1448, 1456, 1458, 1521, 1523,
1526, 1527, 1537, 1543, 1546,
1548, 1549, 1551, 1569, 2304,
2305, 2308, 2315, 2316, 2317,
2318, 2348, 2365, 2382, 2384,
2605

Age 26-40

783, 785, 789, 791, 798, 799,
807, 811, 1425, 1427, 1428,
1429, 1435, 1440, 1444, 1445,
1448, 1456, 1457, 1463, 1467,
1468, 1521, 1523, 1526, 1530,
1531, 1537, 1538, 1540, 1543,
1545, 1546, 1548, 1549, 1551,
1568, 1569, 2302, 2304, 2305,
2308, 2310, 2314, 2315, 2316,
2317, 2318, 2320, 2328, 2338,
2348, 2350, 2351, 2365, 2369,
2370, 2371, 2374, 2382, 2384,
2395

Age 41-50

798, 799, 1429, 1434, 1439,
1442, 1447, 1449, 1453, 1454,
1456, 1457, 1463, 1467, 1468,
1541, 1545, 2302, 2311, 2375,
2386, 2389

Age 51-60

1456, 1525, 1542, 1544, 2326,
2327, 2345, 2380, 2387

Age Over 60

2383

MALE CLASSIC - COMIC

Age 15 and Under

737

Age 16-25

488, 725, 726, 727, 728, 729,
731, 732, 734, 736, 739, 748,
749, 750, 751, 762, 763, 764,
765, 766, 769, 810, 1645,
1648, 1662

Age 26-40

725, 726, 727, 728, 729, 731,
732, 734, 736, 739, 740, 742,
743, 747, 748, 749, 750, 751,
762, 763, 764, 765, 766, 767,
768, 769, 810, 1622, 1625,
1634, 1635, 1654, 1655, 1658,
1659, 1660, 2379

Age 41-50

725, 726, 727, 728, 729, 731,

736, 742, 748, 749, 750, 751, 762, 765, 766, 767, 768, 2353, 2379

Age 51-60
725, 726, 727, 728, 729, 731, 748, 749, 750, 751, 766, 767, 768, 1649, 1666, 2379

Age Over 60
725, 726, 727, 728, 729, 731, 749, 750, 751, 766

ETHNIC/ NATIONALITY/ RELIGIOUS AFFILIATION

Asian and Asian-American
435, 436, 1027, 1674, 1675, 1688, 1718, 1890

Australian
1909, 1910

Black (African-American and non-American)
48, 141, 142, 144, 216, 226, 227, 242, 248, 249, 252, 320, 321, 329, 335, 443, 444, 515, 529, 530, 531, 714, 742, 786, 889, 902, 951, 965, 966, 967, 988, 1000, 1009, 1011, 1032, 1325, 1676, 1677, 1683, 1709, 1710, 1862, 1867, 1870, 1871, 1875, 1876, 1877, 1882, 1891, 1892, 1893, 1907, 1909, 1910,

1923, 1925, 1941, 1942, 2054, 2063, 2064, 2187, 2199, 2332, 2333, 2418, 2488, 2499

Canadian
240, 342, 1716, 1717, 1860, 1861

European and British
41, 42, 126, 136, 138, 215, 219, 225, 229, 230, 232, 236, 250, 251, 253, 255, 257, 326, 328, 344, 345, 362, 410, 588, 623, 685, 891, 933, 939, 748, 779, 780, 783, 785, 787, 788, 790-799, 800, 802, 803, 804, 805, 807, 808, 810, 811, 812, 814, 816, 817, 828, 829, 927, 933, 939, 940, 941, 942, 943, 944, 950, 955, 961, 963, 979, 982, 989, 990, 993, 999, 1010, 1015, 1024, 1025, 1028, 1029, 1045, 1046, 1424, 1425, 1427, 1428, 1429, 1431, 1432, 1433, 1434, 1435, 1436, 1437, 1438, 1439, 1440, 1442, 1443, 1444, 1445, 1446, 1447, 1450, 1451, 1453, 1456, 1457, 1458, 1459, 1460, 1461, 1462, 1463, 1466, 1467, 1468, 1521, 1522, 1523, 1524, 1525, 1526, 1527, 1528, 1529, 1530, 1534, 1536, 1537, 1538, 1539, 1540, 1541, 1542, 1543, 1544, 1545, 1546, 1547, 1548, 1549, 1550, 1551, 1552, 1553, 1554, 1555, 1558, 1560, 1561, 1562, 1569, 1668, 1673, 1696, 1714, 1715, 1868, 1869,

1879, 1880, 1886, 1887, 1892, 1893, 1894, 1927, 1930, 1931, 1933, 1944, 2008, 2028, 2038, 2042, 2049, 2063, 2064, 2153, 2175, 2182, 2191, 2193, 2302, 2303, 2307, 2308, 2309, 2310, 2311, 2314, 2315, 2316, 2317, 2318, 2319, 2320, 2322, 2323, 2324, 2326, 2327, 2328, 2329, 2330, 2331, 2338, 2339, 2340, 2341, 2342, 2343, 2344, 2345, 2346, 2347, 2348, 2349, 2350, 2351, 2352, 2353, 2356-2364, 2365, 2366, 2367, 2368, 2369, 2370, 2371, 2372, 2373, 2374, 2375, 2376, 2377, 2378, 2379, 2380, 2382, 2384, 2386, 2387, 2389, 2390, 2391, 2394, 2395, 2403, 2406, 2407, 2412, 2413, 2419, 2420, 2447-2473, 2572, 2578, 2584, 2585, 2597

German-American
2586

Hispanic
5, 6, 29, 30, 43, 121, 447, 500, 911, 951, 958, 1006, 1007, 1207, 1208, 1209, 1335, 1686, 1859, 1863, 1864, 1865, 1873, 1874, 1878, 1883, 1884, 1885, 1888, 1889, 2501

Irish
27, 225, 230, 1046, 1880, 2042, 2447, 2448, 2449, 2450,

2451, 2452, 2453, 2454, 2455, 2456, 2457, 2458, 2459, 2460, 2461, 2462, 2463, 2464, 2465, 2466, 2467, 2468, 2469, 2470, 2471, 2472, 2473

Italian-American
2409

Jewish
12, 13, 37, 143, 260, 261, 331, 332, 367, 801, 901, 917, 955, 960, 992, 1010, 1672, 1713, 2044, 2050, 2060, 2061, 2153, 2162, 2416, 2417, 2583

Middle Eastern
781, 782, 809, 1237, 1464, 1465, 1535, 1556, 1642, 1643, 1644, 1881

Mormon
2524, 2525

Native American
22, 1860, 1861, 2598

Russian
68, 1607, 1617, 1618, 1755, 1756, 1767, 1768, 1769, 1868, 1869, 1894, 2353, 2370, 2371, 2372, 2373, 2379, 2390, 2391, 2394

South African
226, 227, 529, 530, 2415, 2581

TIME PERIODS

Ancient
482, 770, 771, 772, 773, 774, 775, 776, 801, 809, 865, 866, 968, 1420, 1421, 1422, 1423, 1426, 1430, 1452, 1455, 1464, 1465, 1532, 1533, 1535, 1559, 1563-1566, 1567, 1570, 1636, 1642, 1643, 1644, 1661, 1667, 2306, 2312, 2313, 2321, 2325, 2334, 2335, 2381, 2397, 2456

Medieval
35, 236, 244, 777, 778, 779, 780, 781, 782, 783, 785, 786, 789, 790, 804, 957, 1431, 1432, 1450, 1459, 1467, 1468, 1539, 1556, 1561, 1562, 1657, 2304, 2305, 2322, 2323, 2347

1500s
244, 483, 484, 485, 487, 792, 793, 794, 795, 982, 1451, 1527, 1528, 1531, 1536, 1542, 1544, 1545, 1551, 1553, 1554, 1597, 1598, 1627, 1637, 1638, 1639, 1665, 1944, 2153, 2302, 2303, 2304 + 2305, 2307, 2322, 2323, 2347, 2362, 2584, 2585, 2597

1600s
126, 488, 489, 725-729, 731, 732, 734, 736, 739, 740, 742, 743, 747-751, 762-69, 787, 788, 791, 811, 1428, 1429, 1437, 1441, 1442, 1444, 1445, 1446, 1447, 1456, 1457, 1461, 1466, 1521, 1522, 1524, 1525, 1526, 1529, 1530, 1537, 1538, 1540, 1541, 1543, 1546, 1547-1550, 1552, 1555, 1557, 1558, 1568, 1569, 1653, 1662, 1663, 1664, 1668, 2182, 2308, 2309, 2310, 2311, 2314, 2315, 2316, 2317, 2318, 2319, 2320, 2324, 2326, 2327, 2605, 2606

1700s
44, 45, 486, 719, 798, 799, 963, 999, 1000, 1024, 1025, 1424, 1425, 1427, 1429, 1433, 1434, 1435, 1438, 1439, 1440, 1443, 1448, 1453, 1454, 1458, 1460, 1462, 1463, 1620, 1621, 1626, 1628, 1629, 1696, 2328, 2329, 2330, 2331, 2332, 2333, 2336, 2337, 2338, 2339, 2340, 2341, 2342, 2343, 2344, 2345, 2346, 2349, 2350, 2351, 2360, 2361

1800s
145, 147, 216, 242, 258, 259, 320, 321, 340, 435, 679, 807, 808, 810, 812, 814, 821, 822, 921, 922, 927, 928, 929, 1028, 1029, 1199, 1216, 1217, 1247, 1424, 1620, 1622, 1623, 1624, 1625, 1630, 1631, 1633, 1634, 1635, 1640, 1641, 1645, 1646-1652, 1654-1660, 1666, 1669, 1670, 1683, 1716, 2007, 2134, 2135, 2175, 2352, 2353, 2354, 2355, 2356, 2357, 2358, 2359, 2363, 2364, 2365, 2366, 2367,

2368, 2369, 2370, 2371, 2372, 2373, 2374, 2375, 2376, 2377, 2378, 2379, 2380, 2382, 2386, 2387, 2452, 2455, 2457, 2473, 2572, 2588

1900-1930

49, 50, 141, 142, 146, 154, 219, 221, 222, 329, 438, 451, 816, 818, 898, 911, 939, 940, 941, 942, 949,1632, 1633, 1654, 1666, 1896, 1897, 2038, 2388, 2389, 2390, 2391, 2392, 2393, 2394, 2395, 2396, 2398, 2460, 2462, 2465, 2586

1930s

8, 9, 225, 328, 331, 332, 954, 965, 966, 1008, 1009, 1023, 1035, 1197, 2578, 2607

1940s

112, 432, 448, 449, 504, 521, 612, 623, 823, 955, 956, 989, 990, 1010, 1030, 1048, 1676, 1909, 1910, 2148, 2193

1950s

1, 37, 158, 240, 925, 441, 442, 825, 1026, 1027, 1906, 2601, 2602

1960-1980

5, 6, 18, 124, 151, 214, 215, 228, 248, 249, 255, 342, 430, 535, 603, 687, 891, 933, 934, 943, 960, 971, 972, 973, 975, 1046, 1233, 1240, 1692, 1714,

1717, 1718, 1906, 1925, 2136, 2137, 2149, 2159, 2162, 2168, 2185, 2186, 2402, 2415, 2418, 2491, 2573, 2574, 2589

1980s

222, 213, 226, 227, 443, 444, 948, 967, 978, 1045, 1920, 1937, 2044, 2192, 2581

1990s

2178, 2179, 2190, 2466, 2479, 2571, 2575, 2576, 2577, 2592, 2593

GEOGRAPHICAL AREA

Africa

18, 41, 42, 158, 226, 227, 441, 442, 443, 444, 529, 530, 531, 925, 967, 1000, 1023, 1032, 2169, 2415, 2481

Alaska

10, 2598

Ancient World

770, 771, 772, 773, 801, 809, 1642, 1643, 1644, 1929, 2170, 2306, 2312, 2313, 2321, 2325, 2334, 2335, 2382, 2397

Asia and the Pacific

687, 688, 934, 971, 972, 973, 997, 1017, 1027, 1708, 1718, 1890, 2149

Australia and New Zealand

1909, 1910, 1936

Canada

240, 342, 1716, 1717, 1860, 1861, 2147

Europe and Great Britain

2, 21, 35, 37, 44, 45, 49, 50, 112, 126, 135, 136, 138, 139, 215, 219, 225, 229, 230, 232, 236, 250, 251, 253, 255, 257, 328, 344, 345, 410, 483, 504, 587, 623, 685, 777, 778, 779, 780, 783, 785, 786, 787, 788, 789, 790-799, 800, 802, 803, 804, 805, 807, 808, 810, 812, 814, 816, 819, 820, 828, 829, 891, 908, 933, 939, 940, 941, 942, 943, 949, 950, 955, 956, 957, 961, 982, 989, 990, 1015, 1024, 1025, 1028, 1029, 1045, 1046, 1048, 1424, 1427, 1428, 1429, 1431, 1432, 1433, 1434, 1435, 1436, 1437, 1438, 1439, 1440, 1442-1447, 1450, 1453, 1454, 1456-1463, 1466, 1467, 1468, 1521-1527, 1529, 1528, 1530, 1534, 1536, 1537, 1538, 1539, 1540-1550, 1551, 1552, 1553, 1554, 1555, 1558, 1560, 1561, 1562, 1568, 1569, 1622, 1623, 1626, 1627, 1628, 1629, 1630, 1631, 1632, 1634, 1635, 1637, 1638, 1639, 1645, 1646, 1647, 1649, 1650, 1651, 1652, 1653, 1654, 1655, 1657, 1658, 1659, 1660, 1662, 1663, 1664, 1665, 1669, 1670, 1673, 1714, 1868, 1869, 1879, 1880, 1886, 1887, 1892, 1893, 1894, 1925, 1930, 1931, 1944, 2008, 2018, 2028, 2038, 2042, 2044, 2063, 2064, 2153, 2175, 2182, 2191, 2193, 2302, 2303, 2304, 2307, 2308, 2309, 2310, 2311, 2314, 2315, 2316, 2317, 2318, 2319, 2320, 2322, 2323, 2326, 2327, 2328, 2329, 2330, 2331, 2332, 2333, 2338, 2339, 2340, 2341, 2342, 2343, 2344, 2345, 2346, 2347, 2348, 2349, 2350, 2351, 2352, 2353, 2356-2364, 2365, 2366, 2367, 2368, 2369, 2370, 2371, 2372, 2373, 2375, 2376, 2377, 2378, 2379, 2380, 2382, 2385, 2387, 2389, 2390, 2391, 2394, 2395, 2403, 2407, 2412, 2413, 2419, 2420, 2448-2450, 2452-2470, 2472-2473, 2572, 2578, 2584, 2585, 2592, 2593, 2597

Ireland

27, 225, 230, 1046, 1880, 2042, 2448 , 2449, 2450, 2452, 2453, 2454, 2455, 2456, 2457, 2458, 2459, 2460, 2461, 2462, 2463, 2464, 2465, 2466, 2467, 2468, 2469, 2470, 2472, 2473

Latin America and the Caribbean

43, 911, 958, 992, 993, 1207, 1208, 1209, 1451, 1640, 1641, 1686, 1865, 1908, 1936, 2581

Middle East
158, 361, 362, 781, 782, 801, 809, 1450, 1531, 1535, 1556, 1881

Midwest (USA)
248, 249, 432, 521, 692, 1882, 1896, 1897, 2013, 2014, 2045, 2062, 2150, 2159, 2168, 2192, 2194, 2196, 2197, 2506, 2589, 2590, 2591, 2594

New England/Northeast (USA)
26, 239, 821, 822, 969, 1620, 1621, 1633, 1668, 1882, 1896, 1897, 2013, 2014, 2045, 2062, 2150, 2159, 2168, 2192, 2194, 2196, 2197, 2506, 2589, 2590, 2591, 2594

New York City Area
1, 3, 4, 11, 12, 13, 14, 15, 16, 17, 24, 25, 29, 30, 33, 47, 48, 109,110, 118, 149, 150, 155, 252, 325, 326, 327, 329, 331, 332, 500, 683, 825, 905, 978, 985, 988, 1010, 1049, 1152, 1153, 1160, 1163, 1164, 1167, 1210, 1266, 1267, 1268, 1270, 1271, 1272, 1277, 1278, 1878, 1898, 1899, 1921, 1922, 1939, 2010, 2011, 2019, 2027, 2032, 2033, 2043, 2046, 2060, 2160, 2167, 2177, 2188, 2189, 2190, 2508, 2402, 2416, 2417, 2571, 2573, 2574, 2579, 2580, 2583, 2586

Russia
1868, 1869, 1894, 2353, 2370, 2371, 2372, 2373, 2379, 2390, 2391, 2394

South (USA)
8, 9, 19, 20, 114, 141, 142, 145, 146, 147, 154, 214, 216, 223, 249, 346, 806, 898, 899, 900, 965, 1011, 1043, 1044, 1218, 1219, 1656, 1683, 1693, 1870, 1871, 1920, 2009, 2031, 2098, 2385, 2408, 2588, 2607

South Africa
226, 227, 529, 530, 967, 2415, 2581

Southwest (USA)
2026, 2162

Suburbia (USA)
1904

Washington DC
1905, 1923

West (USA)
121, 436, 440, 603, 902, 903, 904, 1006, 1007, 1008, 1009, 1034, 1036, 1037, 1237, 1247, 1633, 1943, 2164, 2135, 2138, 2139, 2140, 2199, 2406, 2418, 2575, 2576

OCCUPATIONS

Actor/Theater Figures
3, 126, 155, 238, 258, 259, 320, 321, 344, 516, 737, 789, 991, 992, 997, 1015, 1032, 1033, 1036, 1037, 1048, 1150, 1155, 1424, 1546, 1923, 1927, 2035, 2050, 2180, 2181, 2383

Advertising
523, 2043

Alchemist
2310

Artist
119, 120, 214, 254, 323, 324, 371, 937, 949, 1645, 1687, 1944, 2197, 2369, 2386

Astrologer
1429

Athlete/Sports Figures
148, 224, 501, 1672, 1704

Atomic Bomb Aircrew
2148

Atomic Bomb Inventor
23

Bartender
1342

Beauticians
1043

Beggar
1545

Bridge Painter
2570

Book Publisher
2416, 2417

Border Guard
121

Boxer
1909, 1910

Bus Driver
614

Businessmen
233, 245, 246, 523, 626, 1255, 1263, 1281, 1326, 1339, 1697, 1895, 1907, 1912, 1921, 2157, 2167, 2376, 2398

Caterer
2600

CIA Official
28

Clerk
2156

Clown
2605

Comedian
155

Construction Worker
542

Defense Contracter
2138, 2139, 2140

Disaster Instructor
1943

Drug Dealer
47, 1867, 1885, 2573, 2574

Entertainer
155, 221, 222, 238, 242, 243,
250, 1328, 1333, 1681, 1693,
2459, 2500

Farmer
345, 604, 605, 773, 821, 1216,
1217, 1645, 1670, 1934

Film Maker
2013, 2014, 2031

Gambler
340, 2389

Gangsters/Mobsters
48, 132, 139, 370, 584, 585,
618, 893, 902, 903, 904, 905,
980, 1011, 1018, 1019, 1692,
2025, 2026, 2046, 2047

Geologist
2018

Grave Digger
583

Grocer
2452

Hitman
1922, 1924, 2025, 2026, 2161,
2510

Hustler
340, 522, 1248, 1548, 1549

Journalist
41, 42, 113, 431, 439, 1197,
1936, 2147

Junkman/Junk Dealer
2176

Kings/Queens/Royalty
771, 809, 819, 957, 1423,
1445, 1455, 1464, 1465, 1535,
1539, 1547, 1555, 1557, 1558,
1561, 1562, 1567, 1570, 2305,
2306, 2585

Knight
1525, 1540, 1563, 1565, 1566

Land Surveyor
2022

Landlord
2387

Lawyer/Judge
522, 603, 623, 813, 893, 948,
1042, 1647, 2337, 2395, 2505

Loan Shark
232

Magician/Necromancer
1536, 1544, 1557, 2303, 2367, 2368

Mathematician
1673

Mayor
2495

Mechanic
2485, 250

Medical Doctor
231, 533, 677, 779, 780, 966, 986, 1035, 1244, 1536, 1713, 2314, 2358, 2406

Medical Researcher
2375, 2377, 2378

Mercenary
1924

Militia Leader
2062, 2199, 2462

Miner
1633

Minister/Priest/Religious Leader
19, 27, 35, 225, 352, 359, 616, 617, 936, 938, 950, 980, 1000, 1235, 1240, 1689, 2153, 2183,
2184, 2312, 2362, 2363, 2381, 2415, 2463, 2469, 2470, 2516, 2595, 2596

Missionary
225

Mortician
2468

Movie Director
2592, 2593

Musician
141, 215, 221, 222, 242, 341, 346, 684, 719, 1009, 1028, 1029, 1038, 1224, 1321, 1669, 1677, 1681, 2044, 2136, 2137, 2175, 2458, 2459, 2488

Nobility
2304, 2309, 2311, 2316, 2326, 2327, 2329, 2330, 2340, 2349

Nurse
962

Opera Singer
221, 222

Orator
1449, 1466

Performing Animals Agent
2586

Philosopher
2037, 2048, 2049

Pilot/Astronaut
112, 220, 975, 2148

Pimp
437, 1167

Plantation Owner
1656

Playwright
328, 1876, 2049, 2364, 2369, 2407

Poet
1866, 1932, 1933, 2057, 2491, 2351

Police
2, 90, 325, 1034, 1163, 1210, 1712, 1721, 1930, 1931, 1935, 2010, 2011, 2177

Politician/Government Leader
28, 685, 742, 763, 957, 981, 987, 1233, 1235, 1420, 1422, 1426, 1454, 1531, 1532, 1533, 1628, 1629, 1642, 1643, 1644, 1647, 1657, 1663, 1664, 1667, 1714, 1715, 1716, 2199, 2307, 2325, 2334, 2335

Postal Worker
544

Prison Guard
453, 2066

Prostitute
1537, 1538, 1549, 1913

Rabbi
2153

Rest Home Owner
2035

Retired Dry Cleaner
2060

Sailor/Seafarer
145, 147, 244, 817, 921, 922, 1208, 1624, 1625, 1665, 1694, 2319, 2355, 2397, 2460, 2472

Salespersons and Merchants
248, 626, 814, 823, 1047

Scientist
23, 930, 979, 2154, 2182, 2375, 2377, 2378

Screenwriter
2009

Servant
739, 790, 808, 1446, 1448, 1453, 1456, 1527, 1622, 2155, 2341

Shepherd
2322, 2323

Slaughter House Worker
2053, 2054

Slave Owner
2385

Slave Trader
999

Social Worker
322, 2063

Soldier/Military Figure (see also War Veteran/Vietnam Vet in Character Section)
112, 137, 142, 448, 449, 506, 781, 782, 792, 801, 803, 928, 929, 940, 941, 942, 949, 953, 958, 963, 968, 971, 972, 973, 989, 994, 1030, 1335, 1420, 1450, 1451, 1522, 1525, 1553, 1556, 1606, 1620, 1621, 1642, 1643, 1644, 1671, 1888, 1889, 1904, 2149, 2168, 2169, 2193, 2313, 2352, 2359, 2410, 2455, 2456, 2462, 2584

Sports Instructor
2064

Spy
28, 933, 934, 979, 1621

Stockbroker
2061

Stoker (Ship)
2392, 2393

Students and College Students
151, 515, 925, 1938, 2044, 2418

Talent Agent
2504

Taxi Driver
220

Teacher
4, 31, 32, 967, 1160, 1235, 1678, 1695, 1699, 1719, 2380, 2572

Thief
2394, 2451

Torturer
43, 383, 958

Toxic Dump Owner
2046

Tramp
2373

Trucker
1920

Waiter
262

Writer
113, 143, 152, 153, 219, 231, 235, 255, 328, 516, 534, 824, 956, 996, 1157, 1265, 1342, 1368, 1634, 1635, 1679, 1684, 1716, 1925, 1930

CHARACTER TYPES/ SITUATIONS

Artistic Creation
949, 1944, 2009, 2136, 2137, 2351, 2364, 2380, 2386

Atomic Bomb, Dropping Of
2148

Body Image Issues
685, 796, 811, 114, 1040, 1327, 1719, 2608

Bureaucratic
2492

Childhood Memories
334, 2191, 2506

Childlessness
1897, 1945, 2056, 2192

Class Struggle/Issues
543, 2390, 2391, 2392, 2393, 2586

Competitive Sports
1860, 1861, 1867

Corporate World
1912, 2157, 2599

Con Artists
522, 980, 1248, 1277, 1278, 1283, 1340, 1427, 1429, 1435, 1467, 1468, 1529, 1548, 1676, 2310, 2314, 2326, 2327, 2512, 2513

Crime and Criminals
48, 132, 139, 370, 527, 584, 585, 618, 893, 902, 903, 904, 905, 961, 980, 1011, 1018, 1019, 1425, 1623, 1637, 1639, 1641, 1710, 1719, 1875, 1885, 2025, 2027, 2046, 2161, 2302, 2309, 2328, 2342, 2370, 2394, 2451

Death and Dying
4, 12, 13, 333, 367, 449, 503, 803, 898, 899, 948, 962, 1228, 1229, 1230, 1343, 1420, 1621, 1650, 1651, 1652, 1660, 1661, 1671, 1677, 1709, 1939, 2016, 2145, 2167, 2377, 2378, 2495

Debauchery
2309

Delusions
2401

Despair/Desperation
2372, 2375, 2383, 2389, 2402, 2405

Disabled Persons and Disability Issues
15, 628, 939, 994, 995, 1237, 1238, 1268, 1701, 1702, 1872, 1878, 1934, 1945, 2042, 2058, 2177, 2194, 2395, 2458, 2480

Disasters
329, 611, 2396

Discrimination
2061, 2586

Fun-Loving/Joyful
2021, 2134, 2135, 2582

Gambling
2389

Gang Members
902, 903, 904, 1710

Gangsters/Mobsters
48, 132, 139, 370, 584, 585,
618, 893, 902, 903, 904, 905,
980, 1011, 1018, 1019, 1692,
2025, 2026, 2046, 2047

Government Corruption
28

Greed
2311, 2366

Grieving
112, 122, 137, 218, 247, 261,
362, 537, 539, , 541, 611, 712,
787, 898, 982, 983, 1017,
1253, 1259, 1323, 1338, 1421,
1436, 1437, 1534, 1535, 1552,
1554, 1650, 1651, 1652, 1687,
1702, 1703, 1711, 1897, 1915,
1926, 1945, 2018, 2024, 2029,
2032, 2058, 2067, 2141, 2150,
2151, 2158, 2160, 2175, 2177,
22307, 2322, 2323, 2332,
2344, 2355, 2417, 2470, 2519,
2583, 2585, 2604, 2610

Hallucinations
359

Hippies
678, 1164, 1937

Historical and Well-Known Persons
23, 146, 216, 221, 222, 236,
323, 328, 341, 603, 685, 719,
824, 826, 948, 949, 956, 963,
1028, 1029, 1199, 1233, 1240,
1368, 1621, 1628, 1638, 1663,
1664, 1667, 1920, 1923, 1925,
1944, 2050, 2134, 2135, 2148,
2151, 2165, 2175, 2182, 2303,
2306, 2313, 2361, 2381, 2397,
2414, 2584, 2585

Holocaust Experience
37, 2416, 2417

Homecoming
2397

Homelessness
146, 252, 256, 325, 326, 596,
597, 903, 904, 1331, 1334,
2508

Hostages
361, 362

Hostage Taker
994

Hunting
1012, 2065

Hypochondriac
2379

2318, 2319, 2322, 2325, 2327, 2328, 2331, 2339, 2347, 2348, 2350, 2353, 2360, 2363, 2366, 2379, 2382, 2388, 2409, 2411, 2412, 2418, 2420, 2422, 2452, 2456, 2460, 2469, 2475, 2487, 2573, 2582, 2597, 2599

Marital Relationship (see also Divorce, Infidelity, Jealousy, Love etc.)

51, 53, 113, 117, 127, 241, 246, 248, 337, 348, 354, 355, 356, 364, 590, 747, 767, 775, 777, 783, 797, 798, 816, 898, 900, 960, 1016, 1031, 1250, 1329, 1338, 1428, 1442, 1453, 1457, 1458, 1460, 1463, 1521, 1523, 1524, 1527, 1528, 1531, 1534, 1541, 1547, 1569, 1630, 1649, 1666, 1700, 1709, 1717, 1906, 1914, 1921, 1926, 1945, 2008, 2032, 2034, 2042, 2045, 2046, 2056, 2060, 2042, 2145, 2050, 2153, 2159, 2160, 2163, 2180, 2181, 2308, 2320, 2329, 2330, 2338, 2355, 2395, 2402, 2412, 2413, 2475, 2519

Marriage Proposals

2379, 2420

Mental Illness

111, 514, 521, 819, 820, 827, 828, 939, 1337, 1154, 1256, 1268, 1685, 1698, 1899, 1932, 2165, 2400, 2401, 2491, 2498, 2502, 2594

Men's Issues/Identity

2411, 2592, 2593, 2596

Midlife Crisis

2039, 2043

Misanthrope

1444, 1559, 1937

Miser

1447

Misogynist

2353, 2412

Mistaken Identity

2156, 2365

Mother/Child Relationship

38, 122, 156, 806, 1040, 1522, 1873, 1916, 1929, 2151, 2189, 2190, 2408, 2451, 2470, 2579, 2583, 2604, 2607, 2610

Murder, Reaction To

603, 2581, 2583

Murderers and Murder

43, 139, 233, 327, 516, 518, 603, 778, 793, 816, 818, 905, 958, 1039, 1260, 1431, 1438, 1443, 1534, 1631, 1656, 1694, 1696, 1899, 1900, 1901, 1922, 1924, 1930, 1931, 1936, 2020, 2027, 2147, 2158, 2161, 2302, 2307, 2343, 2344, 2390, 2391, 2463, 2464, 2510, 2515, 2518

Murder Victim
2575

Music, Reaction To
24, 1669, 2597

Mystics
1869, 2312, 2465, 2472, 2591

Nightmares
2494, 2520

Orphans
1640, 1896, 1897, 2590

Otherworldly Figures (angels, animals, devils, ghosts, nymphs, etc.)
46, 236, 776, 784, 790, 792, 793, 822, 1407, 1441, 1532, 1553, 1636, 1671, 1898, 1905, 1920, 2007, 2020, 2033, 2037, 2048, 2049, 2170, 2171, 2178, 2179, 2189, 2367, 2368, 2373, 2414, 2493, 2495, 2575, 2591, 2606

Philosophizing
2194, 2340, 2374, 2394, 2421, 2485, 2570, 2572, 2574, 2577, 2578, 2592, 2593, 2598, 2605

Pioneers/Explorers
345, 1023

Political Activists/Militants
216, 255, 257, 339, 804, 967, 1035, 1325, 1628, 1683, 1714,
1870, 1871, 1872, 1893, 2062, 2336, 2337, 2358, 2361, 2390, 2419, 2420, 2450, 2461, 2462, 2467, 2491

Politics, Reflections On
2589, 2598

Poverty
146, 2372

Poverty, Reflections On
2387, 2398

Power Hungry
1627, 2303, 2376, 2397

Preaching
2381, 2595

Pregnancy and Childbirth, Reactions To
964, 1033, 1710, 2041, 2150, 2197, 2603

Prisoners/Interned Persons
37, 122, 803, 361, 362, 585, 902, 940, 955, 956, 968, 981, 1011, 1032, 1149, 1459, 1539, 1555, 1626, 1661, 1718, 1859, 1873, 1874, 1881, 2066, 2328, 2404, 2405, 2450

Prostitution
1537, 1538, 1549, 1913

Prostitution, Reaction To
2573

Racism and Racial Issues
215, 226, 227, 249, 327, 335,
965, 966, 967, 971, 1034, 1044,
1276, 1697, 1862, 1870, 1871,
1874, 1875, 1876, 1877, 1891,
1893, 1907, 1909, 1925, 1927,
1942, 2054, 2062, 2063, 2187,
2199, 2385, 2414, 2418, 2486

Rape
348, 902, 1710, 2159, 2422

Rebels
216, 713, 720, 721, 803, 804,
1683

Refugees and Immigrants
1859, 1874

Religious Faith
115, 216, 256, 260, 328, 616,
617, 775, 776, 780, 801, 815,
930, 950, 979, 989, 1009,
1450, 1934, 2018, 2162, 2405,
2415, 2451, 2465, 2473, 2495,
2516, 2595, 2596, 2601, 2602

Retirement, Reflections On
2600

Returning Hero
2397

Revolutionaries
1628, 2419, 2420

Rogues
1880, 2316, 2327, 2328

Sadists
43, 806, 1627, 1696

Sexuality and Sexual Orientation
25, 108, 115, 140, 213, 347,
522, 1903, 1904, 1908, 1917,
1918, 1919, 1923, 1928, 1941,
2015, 2030, 2035, 2057, 2064,
2067, 2136, 2137, 2172, 2174,
2188, 2317, 2607

Sexual Problems/ Abuse/Harassment
132, 342, 347, 370, 536, 1719,
1896, 1907

Siblings
538, 2021, 2158, 2177, 2183,
2184, 2189, 2198, 2581, 2587

Slaves and Slavery
216, 320, 321, 1000, 1683,
2332, 2333

Social Standing/Position
1320, 2376

Street People
596, 597, 1273, 1331, 1334,
2499, 2508, 2603

Suicidal/Self-Destructive
39, 221, 367, 772, 981, 1426,
2154, 2164, 2177, 2191, 2370

Survivors
2396, 2416

Tough Types
1631, 1935, 1941, 1942, 2010, 2011, 2392, 2393, 2505

Transformative Experience
2354, 2377

TV Addict
1940

Vengeance/Revenge
2029, 2306, 2321, 2322, 2333, 2339, 2348, 2357, 2362, 2390, 2606

Victims
26, 31, 37, 49, 50, 124, 125, 218, 226, 227, 249, 250, 256, 257, 330, 334, 361, 362, 770, 956, 965, 981, 988, 995, 1027, 1032, 1149, 1161, 1253, 1324, 1527, 1640, 1708, 1718, 1872, 1896, 1897, 2158, 2169, 2341, 2575

Vietnam War, Reactions To
2589

Visionaries
1866, 1882, 1890, 2182, 2358, 2465

War Crimes/Criminals
971, 1936, 2028, 2044

War Veterans/Vietnam Vets (see also Soldier/Military Figure in Occupations Section)
5, 6, 38, 39, 142, 252, 256, 687, 688, 928, 929, 994, 995, 1026, 1030, 1268, 1688, 1888, 1889, 1904, 2022, 2024, 2065, 2066, 2149, 2168, 2169, 2193, 2410, 2480, 2518, 2523

Women's Status/Identity, Reflections On
1442, 1537

Wordly Sophisticated Types
253, 785, 807, 1322, 1716, 2038, 2167, 2311, 2316

Working Class Persons
121, 138, 147, 217, 218, 230, 232, 239, 249, 262, 331, 342, 343, 499, 500, 505, 515, 517, 530, 542, 543, 778, 789, 798, 799, 814, 817, 818, 927, 969, 970, 998, 999, 1003, 1007, 1159, 1166, 1169, 1886, 1887, 1892, 1893, 1920, 2017, 2155, 2392, 2393, 2399, 2409, 2422, 2485, 2570

Part Two

MONOLOGUE SYNOPSES

Key to Book Titles

1

Chris Boyd, 16   **Staten Island, 1955**
Mrs. Boyd is a live-in nurse who has been hired by Mr. DiPardi to care for his dying mother. When Mrs. Boyd and her son, Chris, move into the DiPardi household, it soon becomes evident that nothing is at it seems. It seems that Mr. DiPardi is gay and has a thing for teenage boys. Unknown to Mrs. Boyd, Chris is also gay. Mr. DiPardi feels that there is something familiar about Chris. When Mrs. DiPardi finally dies, the Boyd's prepare to leave. Chris stays behind a moment to tell Mr. DiPardi that they once spent the night together.
BMSM90, 1.5 minutes
Amulets Against the Dragon Forces by Paul Zindel

2

PC Honey, 20s–30s   **London, Present**
During a long day in court, a London bobby tells an overworked Magistrate how he came to arrest a transvestite for disturbing the peace.
BMSM90, 3 minutes
Apples by Ian Dury

3

Tony, 30s   **New York City, Present**
Tony, Max and Billy are AIDS patients who share an apartment on the Upper West Side of Manhattan. As they await the inevitable, they each reveal deep emotions concerning their lives and fates. Tony desired to be an actor, but the picture he paints of his experience with show business is filled with bitterness and regret.
BMSM90, 3 minutes
A Quiet End by Robin Swados

4

Max, 30s   **New York City, Present**
Max is the intellectual of the trio; an ex-teacher who struggles with grim resolve to accept the decisions he has made in life. When Jason, his lover, arrives to bring him back to their apartment, Max reveals his anger and frustration with his illness.
BMSM90, 2 minutes
A Quiet End by Robin Swados

5

Santana, 20s   **Okinawa, 1960s**
Santana is a U.S. Marine preparing to leave his present station on Okinawa. A turn of events has placed him in a hotel room with Kimiyo, a beautiful young woman who is the daughter of his tailor. Santana is a Vietnam vet haunted by past tragedy, but feels comfortable with Kimiyo. Here, he describes what it was like growing up in an orphanage as a Puerto Rican.
BMSM90, 2 minutes
A Silent Thunder by Eduardo Ivan Lopez

6

Santana, 20s   **Okinawa, 1960s**
After awaking from a terrible nightmare, Santana finally reveals that he feels responsible for the death of Keller, his friend and fellow Marine. He describes they're being sent to Vietnam and the grisly events that led to his friend's death.
BMSM90, 7 minutes
A Silent Thunder by Eduardo Ivan Lopez

7

Rod, 40s
A home on the Hudson River, NY, Present
Billy has traveled from Utah to the Hudson River with the ashes of his friend, Joey, who has died of AIDS. Billy searches for Rod, Joey's older brother, at a party at his house on the river but cannot bring himself to tell Rob of Joey's death. Here, the affable Rod tells Billy a story of the first time that he ever went swimming in the river.
BMSM90, 2 minutes
At the Still Point by Jordan Roberts

8

Neal Avery, 20s   **North Carolina, 1937**
Neal Avery is a young man who is being pulled in many different directions at once. His wife resents the time he spends with Porter, his best friend from childhood. His mother resents the fact that he's gotten married. Porter wishes that he and Neal could run away and be adventurers. Here, Neal reveals that no one who loves him really knows him.
BMSM90, 2 minutes
August Snow by Reynolds Price

9

Porter Farwell, 20s   **North Carolina, 1937**
Porter Farwell is a clerk in Avery's clothing store where he expects to work for the rest of his life. He has always lived in this small southern town and has grown to crave the anonymity it affords. Here Porter comments on the danger of revealing too much of your true nature to people who know you well.
BMSM90, 3 minutes
August Snow by Reynolds Price

10

Henry Harry, 20s   **Alaska, Present**
Rosannah is a confused young woman who leaves her fiancé at the altar, jumps into her car and then drives as far as she can before a blizzard forces her to seek refuge in the converted barn occupied by Henry Harry, a young man

who has been devastated by life. The two slowly reveal insights into their inner torments as the storm continues to rage outside. Henry Harry has accidently burned Rosannah's satin wedding slippers in an attempt to dry them. Frustrated by his feelings of inadequacy, he tells her of his young daughter, Annabelle, and how he let her down as well.

BMSM90, 5 minutes
Brilliant Traces by Cindy Lou Johnson

11
Warren Ives, 20s-30s
New York City, Present
Warren and Lesley have moved into a new home that happens to be a converted synagogue. They are very happy until they hear the singing. It seems that their new home is also inhabited by the ghost of the synagogue's cantor. Warren, a non-Jew, angrily confronts the musical spirit and tells him to leave.

BMSM90, 2 minutes
Cantorial by Ira Levin

12
Bernie, 60s-70s   New York, Present
Bernie is an elderly Jew who is dying. He and his wife have returned to New York from Florida in order to be with their family at the end. Bernie's grandson, Neal, is an artist living in the Village. When he confronts Bernie with his own fears of death, Bernie offers his own vision of how life should be ordered.

BMSM90, 2 minutes
Dividends by Gary Richards

13
Bernie, 60s-70s   New York, Present
Bernie was never bar mitzvahed, and now that the end is near, he feels that it's important to have the ceremony. His great inner strength and determination carry him through the proceedings and he uses this very special occasion to express his deep love for his family and the life that they have shared.

BMSM90, 3 minutes
Dividends by Gary Richards

14
Augie, 50s-60s   New York, Present
Augie is the boorish and brutish patriarch of a clan boasting 21 children. He is a man filled with hatred and uncontrollable lusts. Here, he describes a typical day in rather graphic detail.

BMSM90, 1 minute
Each Day Dies with Sleep by Jose Rivera

15
Augie, 50s-60s   New York, Present
Nelly is the only one of Augie's children who cares enough to see that he gets safely into bed every night. Despite her father's efforts to keep her in thrall, she has fallen in love with the handsome Johnny, who returns her love. Paralyzed from the waist down in an accident, Augie despairs when Nelly and Johnny marry and move to California. The helpless Augie rages at being left alone with his wife, who has taken a lover.

BMSM90, 3.5 minutes
Each Day Dies with Sleep by Jose Rivera

16
Phil, 30s-40s   New York City, Present
Elliot and Joanna have fallen in love and Elliot wishes to introduce her to his friends. When they have all gathered, Phil, a close friend of Elliot's who has recently quit drinking, comments on the possibility that the world's greatest innovations were most likely thought of while their inventors were in a state of intoxication.

BMSM90, 4.5 minutes
Elliot Loves by Jules Feiffer

17
Bobby, 30s-40s   New York City, Present
Elliot, Joanna, Phil, Larry and Bobby have all gathered in Bobby's study for an evening of drink and story telling. The conversation drifts to contemporary theater, and Bobby is reminded of a scene in "Fences" that was reminiscent of an event in his childhood.

BMSM90, 2 minutes
Elliot Loves by Jules Feiffer

18
Jonathan Balton, 40s   South Africa, 1970,
The tragedy of South Africa's system of apartheid is reflected in the relationships among the white faculty of the Blenheim School for Boys in Natal Province. Jonathan Balton is a man torn between his hatred for the system and his need to survive within it. Recently promoted to headmaster at Blenheim, Blaton is faced with the unpleasant task of firing Nan, his longtime friend. Before doing so, he tells a story of his childhood in which he was unable to slaughter a cow.

BMSM90, 4 minutes
The Film Society by Jon Robin Baitz

19
Reverend Thompson, 30s-50s
Florida, Present
Grandmother drags the family to her fundamentalist church, where they are subjected to this hellfire and brimstone sermon delivered by the Reverend Thomp- son, who is more showman than a man of the cloth. Today his topic

of obsession is the cosmetics industry and how it makes "Jezebels" out of young women.
BMSM90, 6 minutes
Florida Girls by Nancy Hasty

20
Tommy, 40s-50s
A Small Georgia Town, Present
Gal Baby's husband, Tommy, is on the edge. He's having an affair and the bank is threatening to foreclose on the plantation. He finally snaps under the pressure and explains to Gal Baby why everyone's talking is driving him crazy.
BMSM90, 5 minutes
Gal Baby by Sandra Deer

21
Melon, 40s **England, Present**
Melon, an irresponsible publisher who seems to teeter on the edge of sanity, addresses the ladies of the Cheltenham Women's Institute with various anecdotes of his life. Here he announces his suspicion that many of the ladies present have secretly written romance novels as a means of getting more love in their lives.
BMSM90, 3.5 minutes
The Holy Terror by Simon Gray

22
Indian, 30s-50s
The American desert, Anytime
Set against a desert backdrop, "Infinity's House" tells the story of three different eras in American history while an impassive Southwestern Indian offers occasional allegorical and poetic narratives. Here, he tells a story of man's fruitless quest to become master of the universe.
BMSM90, 2.5 minutes
Infinity's House by Ellen McLaughlin

23
Oppenheimer, 40s-50s
The American desert, Anytime
Here we find Oppenheimer, the creator of the Atomic Bomb, wandering in the desert. He is a man haunted by his relentless need to control and to be near madness.
BMSM90, 3.5 minutes
Infinity's House by Ellen McLaughlin

24
Mendy, 40s **New York City, Present**
Mendy is middle-aged, gay, and a devotee of the opera. He is passionate about Maria Callas, and here talks on the phone to a young man from Portugal who may have seen Callas perform Traviata.
BMSM90, 3.5 minutes
The Lisbon Traviata by Terrence McNally

25
Mike, 20s-30s **New York City, Present**
Mike and Stephen have been lovers for a long time. Mike confronts Stephen with the disintegration of their relationship citing alienation as the root of their now irreconcilable differences.
BMSM90, 2 minutes
The Lisbon Traviata by Terrence McNally

26
Roger, 30s **Marblehead, MA, Present**
Izzy and Annie want to stop their sister, Monica, from marrying a man they know is a crook. Roger is Monica's true love and the man she has left to marry the crooked banker. Roger arrives at her family's home on the evening before the nuptials are to take place and presents Izzy with Monica's diary, which she had evidently left behind when she left him. Roger tells Izzy that he refused to read through the diary and describes the events that led to the end of the relationship.
BMSM90, 1.5 minutes
Maids of Honor by Joan Casademont

27
Priest, 40s **Anyplace, Anytime**
An Irish priest has converted from Catholicism to Protestantism and now considers himself neither. In an allegorical speech, he calls for the "children of Ireland" to turn their backs on their faiths and look at both with new eyes.
BMSM90, 3 minutes
Mary and Lizzie by Frank McGuinness

28
Wylie Slaughter, 50s-60s
Washington, DC., Present
In this satirical look at the Watergate and Iran-Contra scandals, the absurd nature of our bureaucracy is brought to hilarious and sometimes painful light. At the play's climax, Wylie Slaughter, the recently deceased head of the CIA, appears before the House Select Committee via a prerecorded hologram and informs all assembled that he was behind the insidious "Mastergate." He continues to warn that before his death, he set many other similar plans into action.
BMSM90, 4 minutes
Mastergate by Larry Gelbart

29
Nando, 30s **New York City, Present**
Nando and Delfina mourn the death of their young son, Puli. Nando visits Puli's grave and tells his son of the responsibilities of men. As he speaks, the depth of his loss becomes evident.

BMSM90, 3 minutes
Miriam's Flowers by Migdalia Cruz

30
Nando, 30s   **New York City, Present**
The grieving Nando visits Puli's grave and tells a story of a time that he stepped in ice cream while wearing new shoes. This eventually turns into an allegory of his love for Delfina.
BMSM90, 3 minutes
Miriam's Flowers by Migdalia Cruz

31
Ned, 30s-40s
Hopkins Hycroft Academy, east coast prep school, Present
Ned is the worm that turns in this tale of the caste system within a prep school faculty. Ned is a weakling who collapses when his wife walks out, taking everything with her. A darling among the faculty, he isn't at a loss for company as his friends rally to his support. Allan, for one, loans him $50 and is shocked to discover that he used the money to buy a tie. Ned defends his weakness in a self-pitying monologue.
BMSM90, 2.5 minutes
Neddy by Jeffrey Hatcher

32
Ned, 30s-40s
Hopkins Hycroft Academy, east coast prep school, Present
Like the proverbial phoenix, Ned is finally to rise from the ashes of his wasted life and proceeds to metamorphose into a veritable dynamo of a handyman. At first his friends are pleased that Ned has taken control of his life, but when his success uncovers their own weaknesses, they begin to resent him. Ned is finally shunned by all of his former friends including David, a chemistry teacher who has been assigned to take over Ned's history classes. David addresses the class on the subject of charity, and the roots of his resentment of Ned become clear.
BMSM90, 3 minutes
Neddy by Jeffrey Hatcher

33
Jeremy, 20s-30s   **New York City, Present**
Jeremy is a private music teacher who believes that he is being seduced by the wealthy (and sexy) mother of one of his students. Here, he tells Josh, his friend, of a rather sensual fantasy that he had about this woman while watching his wife sleep.
BMSM90, 3.5 minutes
Oh, the Innocents by Ari Roth

34
Ray, late teens-20s
Rural America, Present
As a rural family struggles to cope with the desertion of their father, Ray, the oldest son, discovers a place of calm from which he can objectively contemplate their domestic situation.
BMSM90, 2 minutes
One-Act Play by Yannick Murphy

35
The Bishop of Prague, 50s-60s
City of Prague, 1316 A.D.
The complexities of both political and spiritual intrigue of 14th century Europe are illustrated in this tale of the Bishop of Prague. As he introduces himself to the audience, we are treated to a glimpse of his wry humor.
BMSM90, 2.5 minutes
Players in A Game by Dale Wasserman

36
Old Man, 60s-70s
New York City Area, Present
The soul of a young woman and a dying old man trade places in this unusual love story. As both struggle with their new lives and bodies, they learn that they need desperately to return to their true selves. Rita, the young woman, addresses the audience in the body of the old man.
BMSM90, 2 minutes
Prelude to A Kiss by Craig Lucas

37
Finkelbaum, 30s-50s
Outskirts of Berlin, 1950,
Finkelbaum is a survivor of Birkenau living in Berlin in 1950. His experiences in the concentration camp, including the death of his wife have driven him to the edge of madness. When a friend from the camp finds him, he helps to pull him back to reality. Finkelbaum is finally ready to face the memory of finding his wife in a pile of bones to be burned. As he tells his friend this dreadful memory, healing finally begins.
BMSM90, 2 minutes
The Puppetmaster of Lodz by Gilles Segal

38
Silvio, 20s-30s   **VA Hospital, Present**
Silvio is a street-smart vet struggling to cope with life in a VA Hospital. His good-humored propensity to flash the nursing staff has earned him quite a reputation among the staff and his fellow vets. In a session with the hospital psychiatrist, Silvio reveals, among other things, his love for his mother.
BMSM90, 2.5 minutes
Pvt. Wars by James McLure

39
Natwick, 20s-30s **VA Hospital, Present**
Natwick feels as though he has failed at life. When his friends go out for a night on the town without him, his feelings of uselessness and alienation drive him to the contemplation of suicide.
BMSM90, 2.5 minutes
Pvt. Wars by James McLure

40
Eugene, 30s-40s
New York City, Present
Poverty has often led Eugene to commit petty crimes in order to stay alive. Here, he tells his friends of the time he was almost recruited to play college basketball.
BMSM90, 3 minutes
Queen of the Leaky Roof Circuit by Jimmy Breslin

41
Dove, 50s **Northern Nairobi, Present**
Dove is a British journalist stationed in Nairobi. He has spent his entire life trying to separate himself from the drama of daily events, and the effort has left him bitter. When Neal, a young American journalist, turns up at his door with tales of brutality in Uganda, Dove reacts with frustration. Here, he blames his destruction on Africa.
BMSM90, 2 minutes
Rebel Armies Deep into Chad by Mark Lee

42
Dove, 50s **Northern Nairobi, Present**
When Neal accuses Dove of not caring about anything, he responds with passion about the numbing consequences of being presented with starvation and poverty on a daily basis.
BMSM90, 1 minute
Rebel Armies Deep into Chad by Mark Lee

43
Husband, 42 **Santiago, Present**
In this absurdist look at the perils of daily life in Santiago, the Husband is a vicious torturer, employed by the government to ferret out "confessions" from enemies of the state. He revels in his work, as can be seen in this monologue in which he defends his vocation to his wife by comparing his killing to her choice to abort their children.
BMSM90, 3.5 minutes
Santiago by Manuel Pereiras

44
Sir William, 50s **England, 1755**
Sir William has followed Sara, his beloved daughter, and her lover to an inn. He sends his servant to her with a letter in which he forgives

them both. When the servant returns with the news that Sara still loves him, he rejoices.
BMSM90, 2 minutes
Sara by Gotthold Ephraim Lessing

45
Mellefont, 30s **England, 1755**
Mellefont, a selfish rake, here considers the possibility of marriage with his beloved Sara. This is the first time that he has truly been in love, and yet he cannot bring himself to commit to the idea of marriage.
BMSM90, 2.5 minutes
Sara by Gotthold Ephraim Lessing

46
Crow **Any Age, Anytime, Anyplace**
An outspoken crow explains the symbiotic nature of his relationship with the scarecrow in this absurdist retelling of The Wizard of Oz.
BMSM90, 1.5 minutes
Scarefield by Louis Phillips

47
Ron, 30s-50s **New York City, Present**
Martin is desperate to raise money for a film project and is determined to do anything to get what he wants – including selling drugs. His search for cash takes him to New York City, where he is introduced to Ron, a desperate character who hides his drug dealing behind a guise of selling landscape equipment. Here Ron tells Martin why he loves New York.
BMSM90, 4 minutes
Search and Destroy by Howard Korder

48
X- Blow, 20s **New York City, Present**
A homeboy ex-con considers Ronald Reagan, power and Batman in a rap-style stream of urban consciousness. The young man reveals the fact that he has killed and that it felt good.
BMSM90, 3.5 minutes
Sex, Drugs, Rock & Roll by Eric Bogosian

49
Aleksander Tarasovich Ametistov, 30s-40s
Moscow, 1922
Aleksander Tarasovich Ametistov is a man forced to survive by his wits since the Russian Revolution of 1917. In 1922, he appears, penniless, at his cousin Zoya's Moscow apartment seeking a place to live. He tells Zoya the complex tale of his adventures and misadventures since the Revolution in hopes of being invited to stay.
BMSM90, 4 minutes
Zoya's Apartment by Mikhail Bulgakov

50
Ametistov, 30s-40s   **Moscow, 1922**
Ametistov comes to Boris, the money-man and power broker to further his scheme. When he finds Boris dead and robbed he knows that his luck has run out in Moscow. He regretfully prepares to set out for yet another new beginning.
BMSM90, 2 minutes
Zoya's Apartment by Mikhail Bulgakov

51
Mrs. Boyd, 40s-50s   Staten Island, 1955
Mrs. Boyd has been hired by Mr. DiPardi to care for his dying mother. Mrs. Boyd moves into the DiPardi home with her son, Chris, and soon discovers nothing is as it seems. Mrs. Boyd learns that Mr. DiPardi is a homosexual. Here she tells a story of her ex-husband's infidelity. Dramatic.
BWSM90, 5.5 minutes
Amulets Against the Dragon Forces by Paul Zindel

52
Jennie Woodson, 60s-70s   Ohio, Present
Jennie and Harley Woodson are an elderly couple faced with evacuating their Ohio farm due to an illegal toxic waste dump. Dramatic.
BWSM90, 3 minutes
A Murder of Crows by Ed Graczyk

53
Trudi, 20s-30s   Maine, Present
Trudi becomes involved in an affair with Hank whose marriage is on the rocks following the birth of his first child. Dramatic.
BWSM90, 1 minute
Apocalyptic Butterflies by Wendy MacLeod

54
Muriel, 20s-30s   Maine, Present
Muriel tells Hank's mother of her plan to move to a city and live in a hotel room where everything is clean. Dramatic.
BWSM90, 1 minute
Apocalyptic Butterflies by Wendy MacLeod

55
Delilah, 20s-30s   Present
Delilah speaks bitterly about the influence that men have had in her life. Dramatic.
BWSM90, 2 minutes
Apples by Ian Dury

56
Beth, 40s   Present
When a gate-crasher, Billy, arrives at the party, Beth is delighted to learn that he knows Joey, who was her first big crush, and lapses into a humorous anecdote of their first kiss. Dramatic.
BWSM90, 4.5 minutes
At the Still Point by Jordan Roberts

57
Sarah, 40s   New York, Present
Billy tells Sarah of Joey's death from AIDS. Sarah is shocked and saddened by the news and helps Billy with his grief by revealing some of her own fears for her future. Dramatic.
BWSM90, 2.5 minutes
At the Still Point by Jordan Roberts

58
Taw Avery, 20s   North Carolina, 1937
Taw tells of a dream in which she used those lessons on her first day of teaching school. Dramatic.
BWSM90, 3 minutes
August Snow by Reynolds Price

59
Genevieve Slappy, 20s
North Carolina, 1937
Genevieve shares a memory of her mother and of her mother's strength on the night that she died. Dramatic.
BWSM90, 3 minutes
August Snow by Reynolds Price

60
Peggy, 40   Memphis, Present
Peggy struggles to keep the family together via the phone lines. An obscene phone caller is treated to a taste of her sharp wit. Dramatic.
BWSM90, 3 minutes
Belles by Mark Dunn

61
Aneece, 30s   Philadelphia, Present
Aneece is haunted by events in her past, and here imagines a phone conversation with her mother, with whom she hasn't spoken in years. Dramatic.
BWSM90, 3.5 minutes
Belles by Mark Dunn

62
Rosannah, 20s   Alaska, Present
A blizzard forces Rosannah to seek shelter in a converted barn occupied by Henry Harry, a young man wounded by life. After sharing their inner torments, Rosannah attempts to comfort Henry by revealing her personal demons which manifest as alienation and loneliness. Dramatic.
BWSM90, 2.5 minutes
Brilliant Traces by Cindy Lou Johnson

63
Mary, 30s   **New York, Present**
Mary is currently the mistress of a crime boss.
Mary has spent many nights in motel rooms
and is an expert on the Bible. Here she ex-
presses her admiration of Biblical heroines.
Dramatic.
BWSM90, 2 minutes
Demon Wine by Thomas Babe

64
Nelly, 20s-30s   **New York, Present**
Nelly has fallen in love with Johnny, despite
her father's efforts to keep her in thrall. Johnny
tries to make love to Nelly in her father's house
and she tells him that she can't. Dramatic.
BWSM90, 1.5 minutes
Each Day Dies with Sleep by Jose Rivera

65
Joanna, 30s-40s   **New York, Present**
An evening ends in disaster for Joanna and
Elliot. They argue over the phone and Joanna
is forced to reveal her fear of intimacy.
Dramatic.
BWSM90, 3 minutes
Elliot Loves by Jules Feiffer

66
Nan Sinclair, 40s   **South Africa, 1970**
Nan assumes her husband's classes in a private
school for boys after her husband has been
fired for inviting a black minister to a school
function. Here Nan rebukes the students for
their shallow understanding of their country.
Dramatic.
BWSM90, 4.5 minutes
The Film Society by Jon Robin Baitz

67
Eulene, 50s   **Florida, Present**
Eulene looks after her neighbor's home while
they vacation. Here she wishes them a "bon
voyage" as only a true pessimist can.
Seriocomic.
BWSM90, 3 minutes
Florida Girls by Nancy Hasty

68
Gal Baby, 40s
A small town in Georgia, Present
Gal Baby introduces herself to the audience.
She is an aging southern beauty whose lifestyle
is threatened with collapse. Dramatic.
BWSM90, 5.5 minutes
Gal Baby by Sandra Deer

69
Actor Six, 20s
Various locations in the U. S., 1983 - Present
Actor Six shares her memory of the day J.F.K.
was shot. We can see that protestant funda-
mentalism already played a major role in her
life. Dramatic.
BWSM90
God's Country by Steven Dietz

70
Actor Two, 40s
Various locations in the U. S., 1983 - Present
An hallucinatory monologue in which the buy-
ing of a time capsule is transformed into a cos-
mic event. Dramatic.
BWSM90, 5 minutes
God's Country by Steven Dietz

71
Dana Sue Kaye, 30s   **Nashville, Present**
Dana Sue confronts a newcomer in church and
seeks to learn why the newcomer's husband,
Brad, never appears in public. Dramatic.
BWSM90, 4 minutes
Imagining Brad by Peter Hedges

72
Brad's wife, 20s   **Nashville, Present**
Brad's wife describes how their first meeting
occurred when she was hired to deliver a
singing telegram to him. Dramatic.
BWSM90, 2 minutes
Imagining Brad by Peter Hedges

73
Nora Joyce, 50s   **Zurich, 1941**
Nora, a woman of great spirit, visits Zurich
with James. While there, the two go to see
their daughter, Lucia, who is in a home for the
insane. Here, Nora reads a letter from Lucia to
James, who is quite ill. Dramatic.
BWSM90, 2.5 minutes
Is He Still Dead? by Donald Freed

74
Nora Joyce, 50s   **Zurich, 1941**
Joyce is near death. Nora stays by his side and
fantasizes to him about better times ahead.
Comic.
BWSM90, 4 minutes
Is He Still Dead? by Donald Freed

75
Mary Lou, 30s   **New Guinea, 1950s**
Mary Lou has followed her fiancée, Dr. Arthur
Roman, into the heart of the cannibal-infested
jungles of Paupau New Guinea. Here she in-

structs the native women on the best way to prepare a Thanksgiving dinner. Comic.
BWSM90, 4 minutes
Kuru by Josh C. Manheimer

76
Mary Lou, 30s   **New Guinea, 1950s**
Mary Lou stumbles onto the cure for the disease Kuru. Her husband, Arthur, humiliated that his wife has discovered the cure for a disease he has been researching for years, begs her to return to Iowa. She tells him firmly that she intends to stay in New Guinea. Dramatic.
BWSM90, 2.5 minutes
Kuru by Josh C. Manheimer

77
Lettice Douffet, 40s-50s
England, Present
Lettice, a highly imaginative and romantic woman, embellishes her speeches to the tour groups with her own exciting interpretations of a dull family history. Seriocomic.
BWSM90, 3 minutes
Lettice & Lovage by Peter Shaffer

78
Lettice Douffet, 40s-50s
England, Present
Lettice conducts yet another rousing tour through the musty old manor house. Seriocomic.
BWSM90, 5.5 minutes
Lettice & Lovage by Peter Shaffer

79
Mona Kale, 30s
Massachusetts courtroom, Present
Mona, bitter about her loneliness, addresses the jury and declares her innocence. She explains she is a victim of a nation addicted to sensationalism. Dramatic.
BWSM90, 4 minutes
The Magic Act by Laurence Klavan

80
Izzy, 20s   **Marblehead, MA, Present**
Izzy and Annie try to stop their sister, Monica, from marrying a crook. Here Izzy describes to a fellow journalist an event from her life as a runaway model. Dramatic.
BWSM90, 2 minutes
Maids of Honor by Joan Casademont

81
Monica, 30s   **Marblehead, MA, Present**
Monica defends her bitchiness to Annie by pointing out that she has managed to survive in the very competitive world of TV. Seriocomic.

BWSM90, 2 minutes
Maids of Honor by Joan Casademont

82
Queen Victoria, 30s   **Anyplace, Anytime**
Marrie and Lizzie Burns, travellers, encounter a young Queen Victoria, who offers an insightful rumination on the future of her country. Dramatic.
BWSM90, 2 minutes
Mary and Lizzie by Frank McGuinness

83
Jenny, 30s   **Anyplace, Anytime**
Mary, Lizzie and Engles are entertained by the Marx's. Jenny serves fresh strawberries and then confronts her guests with what displeases her about her husband. Dramatic.
BWSM90, 5.5 minutes
Mary and Lizzie by Frank McGuinness

84
Delfina, 30s   **New York City, Present**
Delfina packs Puli's clothes for the church while her grief-stricken husband, Nando, sleeps. Delfina speaks softly to Nando about the sneakers that Puli had wanted so badly, and of the clothes he had been dressed in for his funeral. Dramatic.
BWSM90, 3 minutes
Miriam's Flowers by Migdalia Cruz

85
Miriam, 16   **New York City, Present**
Miriam's inability to express her very deep grief has helped to start a ritual of self-mutilation. She cuts herself with a razor, and yet still does not feel pain. In church, she confronts a statue of Christ, and questions him about his own wounds. Dramatic.
BWSM90, 2 minutes
Miriam's Flowers by Migdalia Cruz

86
Molly, 16   **Midwest, Present**
Molly has seen her father loose two wives since her mother left them. Here she describes her parents' first meeting and courtship. Dramatic.
BWSM90, 3 minutes
More Fun Than Bowling by Steven Dietz

87
Lois, 20s-30s   **Midwest, Present**
Molly shared Jake's love of life. Here, she describes a night in her youth to her best friend, Loretta, who was to become wife number three. Seriocomic.
BWSM90, 4 minutes
More Fun Than Bowling by Steven Dietz

88
Juliet Queen Booker, 45
New York, Present
Juliet gives a moving account of life in a New York welfare hotel. Dramatic.
BWSM90, 4.5 minutes
Queen of the Leaky Roof Circuit by Jimmy Breslin

89
Beatrice Jackson, 30-50
New York, Present
Beatrice details a frightening story of being raped by her husband. Dramatic.
BWSM90, 5 minutes
Queen of the Leaky Roof Circuit by Jimmy Breslin

90
Pilar, 38   **Santiago, Present**
Pilar describes her disappointment when government takeover ruined the "high society" life she and her husband enjoyed. Dramatic.
BWSM90, 3.5 minutes
Santiago by Manuel Pereiras [Garcia]

91
Sara, 20s   **England, 1755**
Tortured by guilt over her lost chastity, Sara is plagued by nightmares. Here, she tells her lover of a nightmare in which she is stabbed by an imaginary twin. Dramatic.
BWSM90, 3.5 minutes
Sara by Gotthold Ephraim Lessing tr. by Ernest Bell

92
Marwood, 30s   **England, 1755**
Sara schemes to win Mellefont back. Here, she drops her guise of a concerned relative and we see she is filled with self-loathing. Dramatic.
BWSM90, 2 minutes
Sara by Gotthold Ephraim Lessing tr. by Ernest Bell

93
Marie, 20s   **Present**
Marie tells her dinner date, film producer Martin Mirkheim, that she has written a screenplay for a horror film. Here, she entertains him with a bloody synopsis. Dramatic.
BWSM90, 2 minutes
Search and Destroy by Howard Korder

94
Tina, 20s   **Coney Island, Present**
Tina, confronted by her sister Angela, and her lover, Sonny, reveals that she feels responsible for her mother's death and believes she will inflict the same pain on her own baby. Dramatic.
BWSM90, 3 minutes
The Secret Sits in the Middle by Lisa-Marie Radano

95
Angela, 20s-30s
Coney Island, Present
Angela and Mr. Runey discover their mutual love for "It's a Wonderful Life." Angela describes a scene in the film. Dramatic.
BWSM90, 4.5 minutes
The Secret Sits in the Middle by Lisa-Marie Radano

96
Shirley Valentine, 42,   **Greece, Present**
In Greece, Shirley meets Costas. As she describes Costas, it becomes evident that he has reawakened her sexuality. Dramatic.
BWSM90, 2.5 minutes
Shirely Valentine by Willy Russell

97
Dora, 30s-50s   **Nebraska, Present**
A swan crashed through Dora's window. She nurses it back to health and it metamorphoses into a human male with whom she develops a romantic relationship. Here, she tells the swan of a strange man who appeared at her door and then just disappeared. Dramatic.
BWSM90, 2.5 minutes
Swan Play by Elizabeth Egloff

98
Dora, 30s-50s   **Nebraska, Present**
As Dora and the swan play checkers, Dora offers an explanation for the behavior of men. Comic.
BWSM90, 2.5 minutes
Swan Play by Elizabeth Egloff

99
Waitress, 20s-30s,
West Virginia, Present
A spunky young waitress leaves her job as a nude waitress and hitches a ride across the country with a religious fanatic. Dramatic.
BWSM90, 2.5 minutes
Vital Signs by Jane Martin

100
A Lover, Any Age   **Anyplace, Anytime**
A love affair is heading for disaster as evidenced here when one lover can no longer tolerate the sounds her partner makes. Dramatic.
BWSM90, 2 minutes
Vital Signs by Jane Martin

101
Laura, 47
North Carolina, December 22-25, Present
Laura's sister, Lila, has returned to the farm for Christmas. Laura reveales her resentment of a

life spent behind the plow with no thanks from her family. Dramatic.
BWSM90, 2.5 minutes
Woman from the Town by Samm-Art Williams

102
Laura, 47
North Carolina, December 22-25 , Present
Here, Laura mourns the loss of her femininity. Dramatic.
BWSM90, 2 minutes
Woman from the Town by Samm-Art Williams

103
Hazel, 58
North Carolina, December 22-25, Present
Hazel is desperate to keep their farm, for she hopes her sons will return to work the land. Here, Hazel begs Lila not to buy the overdue mortgage. Dramatic.
BWSM90, 2 minutes
Woman from the Town by Samm-Art Williams

104
Margery, 20s-30s   Southwest, Present
Margery has hitched a ride with Mel. Here, she shares a childhood memory with Mel that she hopes will spark a conversation. Dramatic.
BWSM90, 3 minutes
Zara Spook and Other Lures by Joan Ackermann-Blount

105
Ramona, 30s   Southwest, Present
While at a fishing derby, Ramona is bitten by a rattlesnake that she suspects Mel placed in her boat. While waiting for help, she discusses Mel's inability to express emotion. Dramatic.
BWSM90, 2 minutes
Zara Spook and Other Lures by Joan Ackermann-Blount

106
Zora Neale Hurston, 40s-60s
Bus Station, New York, 1950s
Zora, an outspoken black writer, has fallen on bad times, but doesn't seem full of regret as she remembers her childhood and early education. Dramatic.
BWSM90, 5 minutes
Zora Neale Hurston by Laurence Holder

107
Zora Neale Hurston, 40s-60s
New York City, Late 1920s
Zora's genius is seen here in her tale of the origins of the power struggle between men and women. Seriocomic.
BWSM90, 7.5 minutes
Zora Neale Hurston by Laurence Holder

108
Suit, 30s   Upstate New York, Present
Suit finds himself playing host to Spaz, a man whose homosexuality makes Suit uncomfortable. Over a board game, Suit reveals that he was less together in his youth. Dramatic.
BMSM91, 2.5 minutes
Advice from A Caterpillar by Douglas Carter Beane

109
Leo, 28   New York City, Present
Here, Leo tells his friend, Ricky, how Al Pacino helped to save his life. Dramatic.
BMSM91, 3 minutes
Al Pacino by Bryan Goluboff

110
Bill, 30s   New York City, Present
Bill arrives home stoned and responds to his wife's concerns about the safety of their apartment in a flippant manner. Dramatic.
BMSM91, 4 minutes
Babylon Gardens by Timothy Mason

111
Alvin, 30s   A balcony, Chicago, Present
Alvin, an agoraphobic, has managed to live happily in the self-contained world of his apartment until Karen moves in next door. His attraction to Karen helps him to tackle the crippling phobia. Here, Alvin describes the first venture outside the building. Dramatic.
BMSM91
The Balcony Scene by Wil Calhoun

112
Roscoe, 20s   Italy, 1941
Roscoe, a member of the elite United States Air Corps., the Black Eagles, is saddened by the death of a friend in a firefight. Here, he recalls his favorite aunt for whom he also mourns. Dramatic.
BMSM91, 2 minutes
Black Eagles by Leslie Lee

113
Garland Landow, 40-50   NYC, Present
Garland must watch as his life falls apart when his wife files for divorce and his publisher fires him. Here, Garland confronts his soon to be ex-wife. Dramatic.
BMSM91, 3 minutes
Blackwater by J. Dakota Powell

114
Pete, 60s   South, Present
Pete tries to give his nephew, Joe, some good advice when Joe returns home in search of clues about his own life. Dramatic.

BMSM91, 3.5 minutes
Blood Issue by Harry Crews

115
Denny, 30   **New Jersey, Present**
Denny, a homosexual in a failed relationship, returns from Europe and seeks out Sky, his former partner. Sky is reluctant to accept Denny back in his life. Denny tells Sky that he made a pilgrimage to Assai in honor of the book Sky wrote about St. Francis. Dramatic.
BMSM91, 3.5 minutes
Body and Soul by John Glines

116
Denny, 30   **New Jersey, Present**
Later that evening, Denny finally forces Sky to confront their love for one another. Dramatic.
BMSM91, 2 minutes
Body and Soul by John Glines

117
He, 20-30   **Here and Now**
A modern courtship culminates in the following marriage proposal. Dramatic.
BMSM91, 3.5 minutes
Breaking Up by Michael Cristopher

118
Howard, 30-40
New York City, Present
Howard arrives at his new apartment on moving day and recounts his harrowing cab ride from the airport. Seriocomic.
BMSM91, 4 minutes
The Closer by Willy Holtzman

119
Ty, 30s   **An artist's studio, Present**
Ty, a recovering alcoholic, tries to remember Donna, a fellow addict who helped him to change his life. Dramatic.
BMSM91, 4.5 minutes
The Colorado Catechism by Vincent J. Cardinal

120
Ty, 30s   **Rehab clinic in Colorado, Present**
Ty finds himself growing closer and closer to Donna. When she finally asks him to tell her about his former lover, Artie, he complies. Dramatic.
BMSM91, 4 minutes
The Colorado Catechism by Vincent J. Cardinal

121
Teto, 20s   **Texas, Present**
Teto, a Mexican-American border patrol agent, defends his job to his fiancée, Felicia,

who has questioned his arrest of a family trying to cross the border. Dramatic.
BMSM91, 4 minutes
De Dónde? by Mary Gallagher

122
Dizie, 30s   **Las Vegas, Present**
Dixie, a released prisoner, returns home to learn that his mother has died. Dixie struggles to come to terms with his past and with his feelings for his parents. Dramatic.
BMSM91, 2 minutes
The Geography of Luck by Mariane Meyer

123
Pete, 20s   **Terre Haute, IN, 1980s**
Pete has learned that his younger brother, John, is not his father's son. John's fiancée offers some unsolicited advice. Pete snaps back. Dramatic.
BMSM91, 1 minute
Grotesque Lovesongs by Don Nigro

124
Pete, 27   **Terre Haute, IN, Summer, 1980**
Pete returns home alone after leaving to marry a woman. After many months of silence, Pete confesses the truth to his brother's fiancée, the woman he has always loved. Dramatic.
BMSM91, 4.5 minutes
Grotesque Lovesongs by Don Nigro

125
Wylie, 50s   **Wylie's home, Present**
Wylie returns home after being mugged and is greeted by Kingfish, his large Doberman. Here, Wylie tells his story to Kingfish, who barks constantly. Dramatic.
BMSM91, 4 minutes
Kingfish by Marlane Meyer

126
Elomire, 30-50
Languedoc, France, 1654
Prince Conti decides his troupe should be joined by a vulgar troubadour. Elomire is offended and forces the Prince to choose between the troubadour and himself. Elomire is defeated and here, prepares to leave the estate to face life as a wandering player. Dramatic.
BMSM91, 2.5 minutes
La Bete by David Hirson

127
Sam, 36   **A country inn, 1980**
Sam and Molly reunite with friends, Bob and Lily, at a country inn where both couples spent their honeymoons. When Sam notices that Lily

seems depressed, he lectures Bob on the pitfalls of a sad wife. Dramatic.
BMSM91, 3 minutes
The Last Good Moment of Lily Baker by Russell Davis

128
Sam, 36   **A country inn, 1980**
Here, Sam reveals to Bob that he has always desired Lily, Bob's wife. Dramatic.
BMSM91, 4.5 minutes
The Last Good Moment of Lily Baker by Russell Davis

129
Howard, 16   **An apartment, Present**
Howard and his mother, Gale, look into a security system. As a salesman describes the system to Gale, Howard returns home and tells a wild tale of being abducted. Dramatic.
BMSM91, 4 minutes
Life During Wartime by Keith Reddin

130
Man, 30s   **Here and Now**
A woman seeking a sexual encounter approaches a strange man in a bar and is totally unprepared for the tirade with which he responds to her proposal. Dramatic.
BMSM91, 3 minutes
Love Lemmings "What He Wants" by Joe DiPietro

131
Doug, 30s   **Here and Now**
Doug and Jackie go shopping. Jackie falls in love with a clock but Doug hesitates to buy it for her for fear the purchase will lead to further commitment. Dramatic.
BMSM91, 4 minutes
Love Lemmings "First a Clock, Then...." by Joe DiPietro

132
Milton, 20s   **Bronx, Present**
Here, Milton reveals his tendency towards sexual deviation as he relaxes in his tub. Dramatic.
BMSM91, 2 minutes
Lucy Loves Me by Migdalia Cruz

133
Vinnie, 30   **A big city, 1989**
Vinnie meets Patsy and Rica on the street and proceeds to regale them with his unique insight into the complexities of modern relationships. Dramatic.
BMSM91, 3 minutes
Lusting After Pipino's Wife by Sam Henry Kass

134
Vinnie, 30   **A big city, 1989**
Vinnie enjoys carrying on long conversations with Pipino, a dishwasher at Vinnie's bistro. Here, Vinnie reveals his fascination with Pipino's wife. Dramatic.
BMSM91, 3 minutes
Lusting After Pipino's Wife by Sam Henry Kass

135
Tony, 42   **London, Present**
Tony, awaiting a visit from a successful friend, responds to his wife's comment that the pain in his hand is due to his rheumatism. Dramatic.
BMSM91, 4 minutes
Marriage Lines by Donald Churchill

136
Bill, 40s   **London, Present**
Upon arriving at Tony's house for a golf date, Bill realizes that the funny kind of sleep that a house guest is exhibiting is in fact a suicide attempt. Bill calls the hospital. Dramatic.
BMSM91, 3 minutes
Marriage Lines by Donald Churchill

137
Swift, 30s   **SAC base, Omaha, NB, Present**
Swift has limited his understanding of events that occurred outside of daily military routine. Here, he tells the tale of having to kill his dog. Dramatic.
BMSM91
Nebraska by Keith Reddin

138
Ollie, 40-50   **England, Present**
Ollie seems to have won his battle against loneliness. Here, he prepares for an evening of roller-skating. Seriocomic.
BMSM91, 2 minutes
Our Own Kind by Roy MacGregor

139
Steve, 20   **England, Present**
Steve gets very drunk after an argument with his girlfriend and allows his friends to talk him into stabbing a man to death. Here, Steve panics when he realizes what he has done. Dramatic.
BMSM91
Our Own Kind by Roy MacGregor

140
Jake, 30s   **A farm by the sea, Present**
Jake has experienced his first orgasm in years. Here, he recalls his lovemaking with Andrea. Dramatic.
BMSM91, 2 minutes
Out the Window by Neal Ball

141
Johnny Harper, 20-30
Rural Mississippi, 1920
Johnny, a bluesman with a traveling minstrel show, finds himself involved in one scrape after another. During a calm moment, Johnny shares the story of his first encounter with a harmonica. Dramatic.
BMSM91, 3 minutes
The Rabbit Foot by Leslie Lee

142
Reggie, 20s
Rural Mississippi, 1920
Reggie's life has been changed by his experiences in France in World War I. Here, Reggie tells his wife a story about a fellow soldier. Dramatic.
BMSM91, 3 minutes
The Rabbit Foot by Leslie Lee

143
Itsik Manger, 50s   Here and Now
At the end of his life, Itsik remembers the moment of his birth. Dramatic.
BMSM91, 7 minutes
A Rendezvous with God by Miriam Hoffman

144
Marvin, 40-50
Street corner in W. Oakland, Present
Here, an acquaintance of Dr. Huey Newton describes his descent into the horrific world of crack. Dramatic.
BMSM91, 7 minutes
Salaam, Huey Newton, Sallam by Ed Bullins

145
Captain, 30-60
Rural southern United States, 1850
Here, the Captain spins an unbelievable yarn about alligators. Seriocomic.
BMSM91, 3 minutes
Southern Cross by Jon Klein

146
Huey P. Long, 19   Rural South, 1912
Huey, a homeless person, reveals his ambition to a traveling salesman who has found him hungry and cold in a railroad shack. Dramatic.
BMSM91, 1 minute
Southern Cross by Jon Klein

147
Captain, 30-60   Rural South, 1850
Here, the Captain tells a tale about the biggest steamboat he ever saw. Dramatic.
BMSM91, 3.5 minutes
Southern Cross by Jon Klein

148
Hurricane, 30
Prison in the South, Present
On the eve of his electrocution, Hurricane muses over his past. Here, he fantasizes about entering the boxing ring one more time. Dramatic.
BMSM91, 2.5 minutes
Sparky's Last Dance by Richard Lay

149
Martin, 30-40   New York City, 1987
When Martin joins his family to discuss the future of their publishing business, tempers flare. Here, Martin reveals his reasons for not caring what happens. Dramatic.
BMSM91, 4.5 minutes
The Substance of Fire by Jon Robin Baitz

150
Isaac Geldhart, 60s   New York City, 1987
Isaac is blamed by his son, Aaron, for the declining fortunes of the publishing house. Aaron calls for the removal of Isaac as president of the company. Isaac has the controlling shares and here, he speaks to his sister, Sarah. Dramatic.
BMSM91, 2 minutes
The Substance of Fire by Jon Robin Baitz

151
Casey, 17-20   Poolside, suburbia, 1970s
Here, Casey, a college student, shares a joint and some sociological observations with his friend, Art. Dramatic.
BMSM91, 2.5 minutes
The Summer They Stopped Making Ludes or How Taking Peyote Turned Me into a Coyote by Steven Tanenbaum

152
Jeremy, 40s
Riverside Park, New York City, Present
Jeremy, a writer, bumps into Marlene, his ex, and gives her a copy of a play to read. When they meet to discuss his work, Jeremy reveals his fantasy relationship with Anton Chekhov and the effect it has had on his life. Dramatic.
BMSM91, 3.5 minutes
Talking Things Over with Chekhov by John Ford Noonan

153
Jeremy, 40s   New York City, Present
Jeremy's ex reads a play he has written and discovers it is about them. Here, Jeremy explains why he wrote the play. Dramatic.
BMSM91, 2.5 minutes
Talking Things Over with Chekhov by John Ford Noonan

154
Shelby, 28   Manard, North Carolina, 1920s
Shelby is drunk at his wedding and boasts of
his important connections and bright future.
Actually, he is being set up to take the fall for
dishonest politicians. Dramatic.
BMSM91, 2.5 minutes
Unchanging Love by Romulus Linney

155
Jimmy Bonaparte, 28   New Jersey, Present
After ten years of playing amateur nights at a
comedy club, Jimmy's frustration is reaching a
critical point. When his quarrelsome grandmother falls ill, his fear and anxiety of losing
her permeate his act. Dramatic.
BMSM91, 5 minutes
Veins And Thumbstacks by Jonathan Marc Sherman

156
Chess, 30s   Boston, Present
Here, Chess shares the story of his parent's
double suicide and his struggle to cope with
the loss. Dramatic.
BMSM91, 4 minutes
Walking the Dead by Keith Curran

157
Bobby, 30s   Boston, Present
Bobby is angry that his homosexuality is mon-
itored by society. Dramatic.
BMSM91, 4 minutes
Walking the Dead by Keith Curran

158
Christopher, 16-17
Alexandria, Egypt, 1952-1956
Christopher tries to explain what living in
Egypt during a time of brutality and instability
implies about the tides of life. Dramatic.
BMSM91, 2.5 minutes
White Chameleon by Christopher Hampton

159
Macon Hill, 20s   Wyoming Territory, 1860's
Macon sees a young woman sitting on a bench
outside a stagecoach station. She stops to
speak to her.
BWSM91, 2 minutes
Abundance by Beth Henley

160
Jennifer Collins, 30s
New England, Present
At a party, Jennifer tells Nathan about her
brief attempt at a career as an actress in
Hollywood.
BWSM91, 2 minutes
Amateurs by Tom Griffin

161
Karen, 20-30   Chicago, Present
Alvin and Karen have recently met on their adjoining balconies. Alvin is neurotic to the ex-
tent of barely being able to leave his apartment. Karen gives him some commiseration
and advice.
BWSM91, 3 minutes
The Balcony Scene by Wil Calhoun

162
Beatrice, 40
A French village, 14th Century
After spending many years in a dark little cell,
Beatrice is finally released by the Inquisition,
who tried her for witchcraft. She must tell her
story to the villagers in hopes that they will
forgive her the crime of having had an affair
with a priest and allow her to live out the rest
of her life in peace. Years of confinement with
no one to speak to have left their mark on
Beatrice, who tends to ramble. Here, she
speaks of her daughters and of her love for
them.
BWSM91, 6.5 minutes
Beatrice by Ian Brown

163
Betsey, 12   St. Louis, 1959
On her way to school, young Betsey fantasizes
about life and marriage.
BWSM91, 2.5 minutes
*Betsey Brown: A Rhythm and Blues Musical by
Ntozake Shange and Emily Mann*

164
Betsey, 12   St. Louis, 1959
Betsey's mother has left her father and here,
Betsey longs for her return.
BWSM91, 2.5 minutes
*Betsey Brown: A Rhythm and Blues Musical by
Ntozake Shange and Emily Mann*

165
Mabel, 70   Rural Georgia, Present
At an explosive family reunion, Mabel is
forced to confront her past by the persistent
questioning of her younger son, Joe, who has
long suspected that his mother was keeping a
secret from the family. It seems that when it
was proved that Mabel's husband, Frank, was
incapable of fathering a child, Mabel and
Frank turned to their best friend, Lonny, who
became the biological father of their children.
Here, Mabel wanders the house on a sleepless
night, remembering Frank and Lonny, both
now dead, and her love for them.
BWSM91, 5 minutes
Blood Issue by Harry Crews

166
Mabel, 70s   **Rural Georgia, Present**
Mabel is under pressure from her son, Joe, to reveal the dark truth about her relationship with his father, Frank, and his father's best friend, Lonny. Here she begins to talk.
BWSM91, 2.5 minutes
Blood Issue by Harry Crews

167
She, 20-30   **New York City, Present**
She has just met a man she thinks she likes and is talking to a friend about him on the telephone.
BWSM91, 4.5 minutes
Breaking up by Michael Cristofer

168
Mrs. Howard, 40-50
Sak's Fur Department, New York City, Present
Here, a woman who has devoted her life to the fine art of shopping reveals the genesis of her vocation.
BWSM91, 3 minutes
Charge It, Please by Carlos Gorbea

169
Iris, 30-40   **New York City, Present**
Iris is puzzled when Howard, her ex-husband, invites her to dinner. As they discuss their young son and his problems, Iris is struck by Howard's inability to understand how difficult life has become for her since their divorce. Here, she describes a typical week in her new life.
BWSM91, 2.5 minutes
The Closer by Willy Holtzman

170
Iris, 30-40   **New York City, Present**
When Howard reveals that his new apartment is, in fact, the very place to which he used to bring the women he slept with while they were still married, Iris reveals a recent experience in which her own morality was put to the test.
BWSM91, 5.5 minutes
The Closer by Willy Holtzman

171
Donna, 30s
A rehab center in Colorado, Present
Donna is a woman struggling to overcome her alcoholism in order to regain custody of her young son. At the rehab center, she finds herself drawn to Ty, an artist and fellow addict. Here, Donna tells Ty the sad tale of her senior prom.
BWSM91, 2.5 minutes
The Colorado Catechism by Vincent J. Cardinal

172
Lillian, 50s
The American Southwest, Present
Here, Lillian, a nun who has devoted her life to providing shelter for refugees from El Salvador, explains her motivation to a younger sister.
BWSM91, 2 minutes
¿De Dónde? by Mary Gallagher

173
Lynne, 30s-40s
A Texas courtroom, Present
Lynne, the senior partner of a Texas law firm, sums up her defense of a young Salvadoran who has entered the United States illegally, and whom INS is trying to deport.
BWSM91, 2.5 minutes
¿De Dónde? by Mary Gallagher

174
Teddy, 30s   **Las Vegas, Present**
When Dixie, a once-famous singer, is released from prison, he returns to his home in Las Vegas where he meets Teddy, the daughter of his cellmate. Teddy and Dixie are immediately attracted to one another and spend a lot of time in Teddy's shack in the desert. Here, Teddy tells Dixie of a time she almost got married.
BWSM91, 2 minutes
The Geography of Luck by Marlene Meyer

175
Romy, 22
Terre Haute, Indiana, Summer 1980
When Romy's fiancé, John, inherits a fortune, the two sit down to discuss their future and it soon becomes evident that John is still too young to settle down. Romy has already done all the adventuring she wants and is ready for a home and a family. Here, she describes her feelings to John.
BWSM91, 4 minutes
Grotesque Lovesongs by Don Nigro

176
Romy, 22
Terre Haute, Indiana, Summer 1980
Romy has just dropped John for his brother Pere. Confused feelings and some incipient cold feet appear. Pete asks Romy what she wants. Romy responds.
BWSM91, 2 minutes
Grotesque Lovesongs by Don Nigro

177
Lillian, 13-15   **The South Bronx, 1970s**
When Lillian discovers that she is pregnant, she becomes determined to have the baby.

Despite her resolve, Lillian is often apprehensive of the future and here describes an experience on the subway that helped to bolster her confidence.
BWSM91, 2 minutes
The Have-Little by Migdalia Cruz

178
Lillian, 13-15   The South Bronx, 1970s
Lillian's mother dies at the exact moment that she gives birth to her son, leaving young Lillian alone in a demanding world. She is haunted by feelings of grief and begins smoking cigarettes as her mother did in an effort to feel closer to her. Here, Lillian describes a nightmare.
BWSM91, 4.5 minutes
The Have-Little by Migdalia Cruz

179
Woman, 30s   Here and Now
A woman emerging from a disastrous sexual encounter with one of her students here reveals the feelings of loneliness and despair which drove her into his young arms.
BWSM91, 5 minutes
I Stand Before You Naked by Joyce Carol Oates

180
Lady, 30-50   Here and Now
Here, a society matron greets the audience in the middle of her morning routine, which consists of writing checks to charitable organizations. Her isolation seems to have resulted in a poor grasp of reality which becomes increasingly more evident as she speaks.
BWSM91, 5.5 minutes
I Stand Before You Naked by Joyce Carol Oates

181
Ivy Rowe, various ages
Appalachia, 1920s-1930s
Ivy, age 12, displays a remarkable talent for capturing the emotion of a moment on paper as she describes the death of her father to her teacher in a letter.
BWSM91, 2.5 minutes
Ivy Rowe adapted by Mark Hunter and Barbara Smith from Fair and Tender Ladies by Lee Smith

182
Ivy Rowe, various ages
Appalachia, 1920s-1930s
After losing the father of her child in World War I, Ivy settles into married life in the Appalachian hollow of Sugar Fork. The calm of her life is disrupted by a passionate encounter with a bee man as she describes in the following letter.
BWSM91, 6.5 minutes
Ivy Rowe adapted by Mark Hunter and Barbara Smith from Fair and Tender Ladies by Lee Smith

183
Molly Kass, 32   A country inn, 1980
The time is shortly after the fall of the US embassy in Tehran and the world has become a more hostile environment for executives abroad, provoking a deepening paranoia. Molly and her husband are spending the weekend with friends whom they haven't seen for some time. Molly tells about a dream she had the previous night.
BWSM91, 3.5 minutes
The Last Good Moment of Lily Baker by Russell Davis

184
Sandy, 20-30   Suburbia, Present
When Sandy and her brother, Orin, are paid a visit by the mysterious Frieda, they are challenged by the odd young woman to give more love in their lives. When Frieda suggests that Sandy go to the nearest hospital and tell as many strangers as possible there that she loves them, Sandy finds herself responding to the challenge. Here, Sandy returns from the hospital and relates her amazing   experiences.
BWSM91, 2 minutes
Love Diatribe by Harry Kondoleon

185
Martha, 30s   Here and Now
Here, an anxious divorcée assails her date with a load of unsolicited information regarding her failed marriage.
BWSM91, 4.5 minutes
Love Lemmings: The Very First Date of Martha Mitz by Joe DiPietro

186
Cookie, 40s   The Bronx, Present
This one-time beauty queen is slowly going crazy in her apartment as the following monologue reveals.
BWSM91, 7 minutes
Lucy Loves Me by Migdalia Cruz

187
Lorraine, 30   A big city, Present
Lorraine is a troubled woman who has a hard time relating to people, especially men. Here she engages in a rather fruitless session with her therapist.
BWSM91, 3 minutes
Lusting After Pipino's Wife by Sam Henry Kass

188
Lorraine, 30   A big city, Present
Lorraine's increasing instability becomes quite evident in her following account of a rather primal encounter with a hunter in a parking lot.

BWSM91, 3 minutes
Lusting After Pipino's Wife by Sam Henry Kass

189
Ruth, 40 **London, Present**
When Ruth's husband, Tony, returns home after an evening of drunken revelry, she reveals her fear that he will leave her for a younger woman. When Tony turns the tables by asking her why she never once confessed to a misdeed herself, she offers the following explanation.
BWSM91, 2 minutes
Marriage Lines by Donald Churchill

190
Ruth, 40 **London, Present**
Ruth's conscience forces her to confess her only marital infidelity in 19 years to her husband Tony. He takes it very well and asks if she enjoyed it. Ruth responds.
BWSM91, 2 minutes
Marriage Lines by Donald Churchill

191
Naila, 16 **England, Present**
Following the murder of an Asian in a British council estate, the Asian community stages riots and protests. Here, young Naila shares her feelings on race hatred.
BWSM91, 3.5 minutes
Our Own Kind by Roy MacGregor

192
Lorna, 16 **England, Present**
Lorna has been attacked and raped: a brutal reprisal for her father's testimony in a murder trial. Here, the courageous young woman defends her decision to keep the baby that was the result of the racially motivated attack.
BWSM91, 4 minutes
Our Own Kind by Roy MacGregor

193
Pitz, 30 **Connecticut, Christmas, Present**
Joe has suffered a traumatic brain stem injury as a result of a motorcycle accident and is wheelchair-bound. He is able to leave the institution where he has lived since the accident to spend Christmas with his family. On Christmas night, he and his sister, Pitz, spend the night alone in the house they grew up in. Here, Pitz shares her memory of the night of his accident.
BWSM91, 3.5 minutes
Pitz and Joe by Dominique Cieri

194
Viola, 60s **Rural Mississippi, 1920**
When Viola's grandson, Reggie, returns from fighting in World War I, he reveals to his wife,

Belinda, that he has had an affair with a French woman. Here, Viola tries to comfort Belinda by sharing a secret from her own past.
BWSM91, 1.5 minutes
The Rabbit Foot by Leslie Lee

195
Reef, 20-30 **Here and Now**
Reef and Particle's stormy relationship eventually helps to land Reef in group therapy. Here, she describes her first meeting with Sexaholics Anonymous.
BWSM91, 2 minutes
Reef and Particle by Eve Ensler

196
Reef, 20-30 **Here and Now**
When Reef knocks at her door after an absence of two years, Reef is reluctant to accept him back into her life. Passion prevails, however, and here Reef addresses her feelings of love to Particle, who is sleeping.
BWSM91, 1.5 minutes
Reef and Particle by Eve Ensler

197
Mother Superior, 40-50
A convent in Ireland, 1950
The sexual repression of the 50s combines with the rather limited view of the Church in the Mother Superior's following explanation of sexual intercourse.
BWSM91, 2.5 minutes
Same Old Moon by Geraldine Aron

198
Javalene, 17 **Toronto, Present**
Champion swimmer, Javalene and Sandra have been best friends since they were little girls in Toronto. Sandra's idealism brought her to South Africa where she was arrested and placed in prison. Javalene risks her own life to find Sandra, and here reveals her earliest memory of her friend.
BWSM91, 3 minutes
Say Zebra by Sherry Coman

199
Pearl, 38
A posh hotel's powder room, Present
While on a date, Pearl confronts her reflection in the powder-room mirror. Years of loneliness and life as a single parent have taken their toll, as can be seen in the following monologue.
BWSM91, 4.5 minutes
Shades by Sharman Macdonald

200
Hattie, 30s-50s **Rural South, 1850**

Hattie tells of the night she tried to flee across the river in a rowboat to escape slavery.
BWSM91, 2 minutes
Southern Cross by Jon Klein

201
Nancy, 20-30
A prison in the South, Present
A hard-living woman with a thing for ex-cons, here tells of her children and their respective fathers.
BWSM91, 1.5 minutes
Sparky's Last Dance by Richard Lay

202
Lily, 20-30   A prison in the South, Present
On the eve of her execution, Lily, an accomplice in murder and robbery, reveals her romantic notions of death by electrocution.
BWSM91, 1.5 minutes
Sparky's Last Dance by Richard Lay

203
Marge Hackett, 50-60
New York City, Present
Marge Hackett is a social worker and the widow of a dishonest politician who committed suicide. She visits Isaac Geldhart, a shut-in, at his home where she had been to a cocktail party years earlier when Isaac was riding high.
BWSM91, 1.5 minutes
The Substance of Fire by Jon Robin Baitz

204
Eve, 17-20   Poolside, Suburbia, 1970s
When Monique and Eve share memories of their adolescent sexual exploits, Eve reveals that she was pregnant when she was 13.
BWSM91, 2 minutes
The Summer They Stopped Making Ludes or How Taking Peyote Turned Me into a Coyote by Steven Tanenbaum

205
Monique, 15-20
Poolside, Suburbia, 1970s
Monique is romantically pursued by Art, a young man into peyote. When she finally agrees to go out with him, they wind up talking in the moonlight. As Art trips, Monique weaves a tale of her childhood for him.
BWSM91, 4.5 minutes
The Summer They Stopped Making Ludes or How Taking Peyote Turned Me into a Coyote by Steven Tanenbaum

206
Marlene, 20s-30s
New York City, Present
Marlene runs into her ex while jogging in the

park. Some of the old feelings surface, both good and bad. He asks her about the man she now lives with. She replies.
BWSM91, 2 minutes
Talking Things Over with Chekhov by John Ford Noonan

207
Glad Aggy, 12   Here and Now
When Glad Aggy's family gathers for dinner, they are treated to an extra special performance of the 12-year-old's storytelling skills as she spins an outrageous yarn of the Scandal at the Babies' Hospital.
BWSM91, 2 minutes, 9.5 minutes
The Tattler: The Story and Stories of a Pathological Liar by Terri Wagener

208
Glad Aggy, 50   Here and Now
The years haven't served to diminish Glad Aggy's penchant for embellishment as can be seen in her interpretation of the crucifixion and resurrection of Jesus.
BWSM91, 6 minutes
The Tattler: The Story and Stories of a Pathological Liar by Terri Wagener

209
Woman, 30-40   Here and Now
Here, a woman shares the horrific memory of the death of her sister.
BWSM91, 4 minutes
Telling Tales by Migdalia Cruz

210
Woman, 30-40   Here and Now
Having made the move from the South Bronx to suburban Connecticut, a woman finds it difficult to let go of some of the more extreme elements of her past.
BWSM91, 8.5 minutes
Telling Tales by Migdalia Cruz

211
Jody, 15-18
Manard, North Carolina, 1921
Judy is sold by her parents to the well-to-do Benjamin Pitman, who wants her to marry his eldest son and provide him with grandchildren. When Judy's son is murdered by Leena, the jealous wife of Benjamin's younger son, Judy brings his body to Benjamin to say goodbye.
BWSM91, 1.5 minutes
Unchanging Love by Romulus Linney

212
Dottie, 50s   Boston, Present
Conservative Dottie has agreed to attend a

memorial gathering for her daughter, a transsexual, hosted by Maya, her daughter's lover. Here, Dottie reveals her anger and grief.
BWSM91, 2 minutes
Walking the Dead by Keith Curran

213
Jim Conroy, 53   **New York, 1984**
After 30 years of friendship, Jim confesses to conservative Kay that he is gay. Dramatic.
BMSM92, 2.5 minutes
After the Dancing in Jericho by P.J. Barry

214
Carl, 19
A gas station/luncheonette in Mississippi, 1962
A young southerner with a photographic eye recalls his past. Dramatic.
BMSM92, 4 minutes
...And the Rain Came to Mayfield by Jason Milligan

215
Leonard, 51
Recording studio in London, 1985
Leonard, a concert pianist, has recently decided not to perform in his native South Africa. He offers the following explanation to his son. Dramatic.
BMSM92, 4.5 minutes
Another Time by Ronald Harwood

216
Nat Turner, 30   **Virginia, 1831**
The voice of God has instructed Nat to lead a rebellion on the plantation where his people have labored and suffered. On the eve of the insurrection, Nat prays a final time to God. Dramatic.
BMSM92, 2 minutes
Ascension Day by Michael Henry Brown

217
Pop, 45-60
The dusty basement of a home in the Bronx
When his attitudes are confronted by his son, Pop reveals his contempt for his family. Dramatic.
BMSM92, 2.5 minutes
Beggars in the House of Plenty by John Patrick Shanley

218
Johnny, 20s
The dusty basement of a home in the Bronx
Following a childhood devoid of love and acceptance, John confronts his father with his failure. Dramatic.
BMSM92, 2.5 minutes
Beggars in the House of Plenty by John Patrick Shanley

219
Maksudov, 20s-30s
A flat in Moscow, 1924
After receiving several rejection letters for his novel, Maksudov contemplates suicide. Dramatic.
BMSM92, 5 minutes
Black Snow by Keith Dewhurst

220
Freddy, 20-30   **A suburban home, 1950s**
Here, Freddy, a driver for a taxi company, tells a woman he called for by mistake about his experience flying planes in the Pacific during the war. Dramatic.
BMSM92, 3 minutes
Blue Stars by Stuart Spencer

221
Enrico Caruso, 40-50
Caruso's dressing room in the Metropolitan Opera House, Christmas eve, 1920
While awaiting the evening's performance, Caruso entertains reporters in his dressing room. Here, he talks about his family. Dramatic.
BMSM92, 2.5 minutes
Bravo, Caruso! by William Luce

222
Enrico Caruso, 40-50
Caruso's dressing room in the Metropolitan Opera House, Christmas eve, 1920
While awaiting the evening's performance, Caruso entertains reporters in his dressing room. Here, he talks about his beloved mother's death. Dramatic.
BMSM92, 3 minutes
Bravo, Caruso! by William Luce

223
Gordon Pound, 83   **Rural Texas, 1983**
Gordon's wife may have been kidnapped by Shiite terrorists. As he and his daughter await word from the State Department, Gordon bemoans his age and physical deterioration. Dramatic.
BMSM92, 3 minutes
Captive by Jan Buttram

224
Kid, 70
The locker room of a boxing arena in Cementville, Texas, Present
Kid shoots Bigman, an obnoxious manager, during a riot at a wrestling event. As Kid prepares to exit through a secret door, he tells Bigman of his boxing heyday. Dramatic.
BMSM92, 2 minutes
Cementville by Jane Martin

225
Jack, 53
The home of the Mundy family, Ballebeg,
County Donegal, Ireland, 1936
Malaria has forced Jack, a missionary priest, to return to Ireland. As he recovers in the the home of his sisters, he shares some of his missionary experiences. Dramatic.
BMSM92, 5.5 minutes
Dancing at Lughnasa by Brian Friel

226
Simon Kgoathe, 40s
A house in the poorer section of Soweto,
South Africa, 1988
Several Red Cross buses are attacked in Soweto and Simon, a black South African, manages to save Lydia, a white woman. As they hide in Simon's house, he tells Lydia of the murder of his brother. Dramatic.
BMSM92, 7.5 minutes
Dark Sun by Lisette Lecat Ross

227
Simon Kgoathe, 40s
A house in the poorer section of Soweto,
South Africa, 1988
Simon lashes out at the white government and their systematic destruction of his people. Dramatic.
BMSM92, 4 minutes
Dark Sun by Lisette Lecat Ross

228
Joe Clay, 30-40
A meeting of Alcoholics Anonymous, 1960s
Joe is finally able to face his demons. Here, he addresses the members of AA for the first time. Dramatic.
BMSM92, 4 minutes
The Days of Wine And Roses by J.P. Miller

229
J.P., 50s
A home in the Midlands, England, Present
The caustic J.P., who first appeared in "Look Back In Anger," now wears his anger as a protective mantel. Here, he takes on the local minister. Dramatic.
BMSM92, 4 minutes
Dejavu by John Osborne

230
The Father, 57   A flat in Dublin, Present
The Flynn's return home after an evening out and prepare for bed. Somewhat muddled by alcohol, The Father reminisces about singing, his father and his job. Dramatic.
BMSM92, 2 minutes
Down the Flats by Tony Kavanagh

231
Sleen, 40-50   A city street at night
Following a day of treating the poor, whom he despises, this man walks and muses on the consistency of war. Dramatic.
BMSM92, 1.5 minutes
The Early Hours of a Reviled Man by Howard Barker

232
Tex, 20s   Glasgow, Present
Tex confronts the daughter of the man he has been trying to bully money from. Dramatic.
BMSM92, 2.5 minutes
The Evil Doers by Chris Hannan

233
Lloyd, 40-50
A hit man's apartment, Present
When his business is threatened by a corporate raider, Lloyd hires a hit man. The hired killer asks to postpone the murder so he can attend the Ice Capades. Lloyd explodes. Dramatic.
BMSM92, 3.5 minutes
Evil Little Thoughts by Mark D. Kaufman

234
A delirious traveler, male or female,
Any Age, Here And Now
A traveller in a third world country is stricken with a fever, and is confronted by the hostility of the masses towards wealthy people. Dramatic.
BMSM92, 2 minutes
The Fever by Wallace Shawn

235
Gustave Flaubert, the novelist, 40-50
The garden of a country home in western
Connecticut, mid-summer, Present
A seance accidently delivers Gustave to a party in Connecticut. The misplaced novelist takes a moment to share a bit of his philosophy. Dramatic.
BMSM92, 7.5 minutes
Flaubert's Latest

236
Polonius, 50-60
The Castle of Elsinore, Denmark, immediately
following the events of Hamlet
Here, the ghost of Polonius describes his death to the audience. Dramatic.
BMSM92, 2.5 minutes
Fortinbras by Lee Blessing

237
Brian, 20s   A park in Manhattan, Present
Brian has been trying without success to date

Joanne. Here, he tells her of his love affair with the silver screen. Dramatic.
BMSM92, 2.5 minutes
Gorgo's Mother by Laurence Klavan

238
Andrew, 30s
A brownstone apartment in New York, Present
Andrew's acceptance to play the role of Hamlet prompts a visit by the ghost of John Barrymore. Here, Andrew describes his performance to his phantom coach. Dramatic.
BMSM92, 2.5 minutes
I Hate Hamlet by Paul Rudnick

239
Doug, 25-55
A logging operation, Judevine, Vermont, late December, Present
Doug arrives for work and offers some early morning philosophy to a coworker. Seriocomic.
BMSM92, 4.5 minutes
Judevine by David Budbill

240
Jean-Marc, 48
A log cabin home at Duhamel, Quebec, 1950
Jean-Marc purchases the house that served as his family's summer home and finds his thoughts turning to their experiences there. Dramatic.
BMSM92, 3 minutes
La Maison Suspendue by Michael Tremblay

241
Sam, 30-40
A beach house on Fire Island, Present
Sam discovers that his wife has been unfaithful and has difficulty coping with her betrayal. Dramatic.
BMSM92, 3 minutes
Lips Together Teeth Apart by Terrence McNally

242
Tambo, 50-60
A Pullman car in a railroad yard, 1895
Members of a minstrel show share memories as they hunker down in a Pullman car. Here, Tambo remembers a story behind an interesting song. Seriocomic.
BMSM92, 6.5 minutes
The Little Tommy Parker Celebrated Minstrel Show by Carlyle Brown

243
Vic Parks, 40s
The pool area of a Mediterranean villa, Present
Vic, a popular British talk-show host, finds himself being interviewed for a competitor's show and offers the following dissertation on the art of interviewing. Seriocomic.
BMSM92, 5 minutes
Man of the Moment by Alan Ayckbourn

244
Ancient Mariner, 50-80
The flagship of Christopher Colombus, 1492
As the sailors grumble about not sighting land, the eldest of their number ruminates on their special lot in life. Dramatic.
BMSM92, 2 minutes
Mariner by Don Nigro

245
Aaron, 25
The bathroom of a luxury apartment in New York City, Present
Aaron has just closed a $2 million deal for the family firm and here brags to his father of his coup. Dramatic.
BMSM92, 4 minutes
My Side of the Story by Bryan Goluboff

246
Gil, 40-50
The bathroom of a luxury apartment in New York City, Present
Gil has been drinking tequila in his bathroom all afternoon and, when discovered by his son, explains that he fears that his wife is having an affair. Dramatic.
BMSM92, 3 minutes
My Side of the Story by Bryan Goluboff

247
Old Man, 60s   **Here and Now**
Here, an old man shares a sad memory about a family pet. Dramatic.
BMSM92, 2 minutes
One Thing Is Not Another (A Vaudeville) by Kenneth Bernard

248
Al, 23-33
A basement in a tenement on Chicago's South Side, 1973
Following a domestic squabble, Al shares his angst with his buddies. Dramatic.
BMSM92, 3.5 minutes
Phil Hill by Samuel L. Kelley

249
Charlie, 42-52
A basement apartment in a tenement on Chicago's South Side, 1973
Charlie, an African-American steel worker,

tells a horrific tale of racism when he and his family drove from Chicago to Mississippi. Dramatic.
BMSM92, 6.5 minutes
Phil Hill by Samuel L. Kelley

250
Andrew, 50
A country cottage, England, Present
In the middle of a discussion of the nature of truth, Andrew reveals a sordid event from his childhood. Dramatic.
BMSM92, 3.5 minutes
It's Ralph by Hugh Whitmore

251
Dave, 20
A country cottage, England, Present
Andrew discovers his wife is in bed with another man. When he turns to Dave for sympathy, he is treated to the following story from Dave's childhood. Dramatic.
BMSM92, 3 minutes
It's Ralph by Hugh Whitmore

252
Ujamma, 40s
An apartment in New York City, Present
This wandering Vietnam vet is a desolate voice in the wilderness expressing years of frustration and despair. Dramatic.
BMSM92, 2.5 minutes
The Resurrection of Dark Soldiers by William Electric Black

253
Anthony Saxton, 38
A gymkhana, Present
When confronted with his infidelity, Anthony reveals his callous nature. Dramatic.
BMSM92, 2 minutes
The Revenger's Comedies by Alan Aykbourn

254
Jonathan   **London, Present**
Jonathan, an artist, visits London and is interviewed by a German reporter for an art magazine. He offers the following dissertation on the state of art and the media. Dramatic.
BMSM92, 4.5 minutes
Sight Unseen by Donald Margulles

255
Tantra, 20s   **Union, the Soviet Union, 1969**
Here, young Tantra addresses the Writer's Union one last time before his censure. Dramatic.
BMSM92, 7 minutes
A Slip of the Tongue by Dusty Hughes

256
Joe Humboldt, 30-50
God's waiting room, Heaven, Present
Humboldt finds himself in God's waiting room and makes the following introduction which reveals his Job-like tendencies. Dramatic.
BMSM92, 5 minutes
Thou Shalt Wise Up by Kelly Masterson

257
Constantin, 30-50
An artist's studio, Present
This Romanian has been trying to persuade artists to donate their work to this country. When his motives are questioned, he lashes out fiercely against the world that deserted his country. Dramatic.
BMSM92, 3 minutes
Three Birds Alighting a Field by Timberlake Wertenbaker

258
William Charles Macready, 40-50
New York City, 1849
Macready, an English actor, meets his American counterpart, Edwin Forrest. When Forrest asks Macready why he acts, he offers the following explanation. Dramatic.
BMSM92, 2.5 minutes
Two Shakespearean Actors by Richard Nelson

259
William Charles Macready, 40-50
New York City, 1849
When his performance of Macbeth causes a riot, Macready suffers from nightmares which he shares here. Dramatic.
BMSM92, 3 minutes
Two Shakespearean Actors by Richard Nelson

260
Walter, 80   **New York City, Present**
Walter is discussing his grandson Daniel's future with him. When Daniel disavows religion, Walter lectures him. Dramatic.
BMSM92, 1.5 minutes
Unfinished Stories by Sybille Pearson

261
Yves, 45-50
Yves father, Daniel's grandfather, has just died, and Daniel fears he let the old man down at the end. Yves speaks to Daniel. Dramatic.
BMSM92, 2 minutes
Unfinished Stories by Sybille Pearson

262
The Waiter, 50-60
A coffee shop, late at night, Present
Waiter is annoyed with a couple who have

been drinking coffee and philosophizing all day at his counter. He drives them out and then does some philosophizing of his own. Dramatic.
BMSM92, 2.5 minutes
What Is This Everything? by Patricia Scanlon

263
Rose, 51   Cape Town, South Africa, 1950s
Rose's nephew is a gifted pianist and has been told he should study in Vienna or New York. Here, Rose insists that he study in London. Dramatic.
BWSM92, 5.5 minutes
Another Time by Ronald Harwood

264
Belle, 40s   Cape Town, South Africa, 1940s
After her husband's sudden death, Belle vows to make a better future for herself and her son. Dramatic.
BWSM92, 6 minutes
Another Time by Ronald Harwood

265
Louise, 20s   A psychiatric center, Present
Louise speaks to her ex-boyfriend who is confined in a catatonic state. Dramatic.
BWSM92, 2 minutes
Appointment with a High Wire Lady by Russell Davis

266
Cherry, 20s   Virginia, 1831
Cherry tells her husband the bitter story of her rape by the plantation owner. Dramatic.
BWSM92, 1.5 minutes
Ascension Day by Michael Henry Brown

267
Rance, 30-60
Rome, a shrine in a wood, 78 BC
During the bloody riots of 78 BC, a healer enjoys a peaceful moment in a shrine. Dramatic.
BWSM92, 3 minutes
The Baby by Chris Hannan

268
Ma, 45-60
A dusty basement of a home in the Bronx
When her adult son turns to her for love, Ma bitterly rejects his overtures. Dramatic.
BWSM92, 2 minutes
Beggars in the House of Plenty by John Patrick Shanley

269
Spike, 20s   Cape Breton, Canada, Present
Here, a woman of great confidence explains herself to her lover's ex. Dramatic.
BWSM92
Black Fridays? by Audrey Butler

270
Marie, 30s
A flat in Belfast, Northern Ireland, Present
Marie, a young woman who has been widowed as a result of the violence in Northern Ireland, recalls her wedding day. Dramatic.
BWSM92, 4 minutes
Bold Girls by Rona Munro

271
Marie, 30s
A flat in Belfast, Northern Ireland, Present
Marie tidies the kitchen and muses on the unhappy fates of all of the men in her life. Dramatic.
BWSM92, 3.5 minutes
Bold Girls by Rona Munro

272
Zoe Ann, 30-40
A curio shop in Missouri, Present
Zoe Ann pays a visit to her old friend, Julie. They smoke some pot and Zoe Ann recalls a drug-induced experience. Dramatic.
BWSM92, 3.5 minutes
Bubbling by Le Witheim

273
Ata, 30s   Chicago, Present
After Ata's husband leaves her with only the clothes on her back, her condo is broken into. Here, Ata reassures her alerted neighbors that all is well. Dramatic.
BWSM92, 3 minutes
Criminal Hearts by Jane Martin

274
Ata, 30s   Chicago, Present
Here, Ata releases years of stored-up angst as she confronts her insensitive husband. Dramatic.
BWSM92, 5.5 minutes
Criminal Hearts by Jane Martin

275
Maggie, 38
Ballybag, County Donegal, Ireland, 1936
Maggie remembers a happier time in the past. Dramatic.
BWSM92, 3 minutes
Dancing At Lughnasa by Brian Friel

276
Lydia De Jager, 30-40
Soweto, South Africa, 1988
Lydia, a white South African, organizes Red Cross bus tours of Soweto and is the sole survivor of a violent attack on the bus. Lydia here describes the attack. Dramatic.
BWSM92, 3 minutes
Dark Sun by Lisette Lecat Ross

277
Lily, 50-60
A garden in the middle of nowhere
Lily is unimpressed as she and her daughter, George, watch men do battle for George's hand in marriage. Here, Lily recalls a time that was far more idyllic. Dramatic.
BWSM92, 2 minutes
Devotees in the Garden of Love by Suzan-Lori Parks

278
Madame Odelia Pandhar, 40-60
A garden in the middle of nowhere
Madame Odelia reports from the "front" where divided camps of men do battle for the hand of her protégée. Dramatic.
BWSM92, 2.5 minutes
Devotees in the Garden of Love by Suzan-Lori Parks

279
Helen, 30s   **Malibu, Present**
Massey and Helen have separated. Helen wants some answers. Dramatic.
BWSM92, 3.5 minutes
The End of the Day by Jon Robin Baitz

280
Mary Ann
The worn down kitchen of an old house in the city, Present
After her parent's home has been broken into, Mary Ann tells one of the policemen her theory on what she believes will save her dysfunctional family. Dramatic.
BWSM92
Escape from Happiness by George F. Walker

281
Tracky, 15   **Glasgow, Present**
Track shares some of the darkness of her family life with an uncaring friend. Dramatic.
BWSM92, 2 minutes
The Evil Doers by Chris Hannan

282
Gert, 30s   **Here and Now**
A new man in Gert's life asks about her previ-ous lovers. She offers the following description. Dramatic.
BWSM92
Four Play by Gina Barnett

283
Anastasia, 30-40   **The deck of a ship**
A woman claiming to be a missing Russian princess describes how she came to be in possession of Rasputin's penis. Dramatic.
BWSM92, 4 minutes
Free Ride On the Queen Mary by Kate Moira Ryan

284
Ophelia, 18-20   **Elsinore Castle**
In this comic retelling of Hamlet, Ophelia is rescued from the pond and here recounts her experience. Seriocomic.
BWSM92
Gertrude, Queen of Denmark by Pat Kaufman

285
Nicole, 20s-30s
A suburban home, Present
Nicole sinks into alcoholism following the death of her baby. Here, she describes her apathy. Dramatic.
BWSM92, 2.5 minutes
Gulf War by Joyce Carol Oates

286
Jenny, 20-30
A home in England, Present
Jenny, unable to communicate honestly with her husband, speaks the truth into a tape recorder. Dramatic.
BWSM92, 7.5 minutes
Infidelities by Richard Zajdic

287
Madear, 90
Lakeland, Illinois, Present
At her 90th birthday party, Madear hallucinates that her husband, who left her when she was young, is returning. Dramatic.
BWSM92, 1.5 minutes
Jar the Floor by Cheryl L. West

288
Albertine, 41
A log cabin,   Duhamel, Quebec, Present
Albertine confronts her brother about his homosexuality. Dramatic.
BWSM92, 3 minutes
La Maison Suspendue by Michael Tremblay

289
Laura Cunningham, 80s
A shabby, cluttered one-room apartment,

Present
Laura, forced to face the reality that she can no longer care for herself, here reveals her fears and feelings about the future to her nephew. Dramatic.
BWSM92, 7.5 minutes
The Last Act Is A Solo by Robert Anderson

290
Laura Cunningham, 80s
A shabby, cluttered one-room apartment, Present
Laura, forced to face the reality that she can no longer care for herself, here reveals her fears and feelings about the future to her nephew. Dramatic.
BWSM92, 2.5 minutes
The Last Act Is A Solo by Robert Anderson

291
Chloe, 30-40
A beach house on Fire Island, Present
Chloe's husband has been sleeping with her brother's wife. When both couples spend July 4th together, the closeness of her rival causes Chloe to be less than cheerful. Dramatic.
BWSM92, 2 minutes
Lips Together Teeth Apart by Terrence McNally

292
Bernadette, 50s   **Present**
Bernadette responds to her son's belief that his daddy is better than she is. Dramatic.
BWSM92, 4 minutes
Man, Woman, Dinosaur by Regina M. Porter

293
Juana, 20s-30s
The flagship of Christopher Columbus, 1942
King Ferdinand declares Columbus to be insane. The famous sailor asks Juana if she shares her father's opinion. The mad princess offers the following reply. Dramatic.
BWSM92
Mariner by Don Nigro

294
Adele Gaither, 30-50
A luncheon meeting of the Friends of the Primate House Women's Committee
At the close of her term as chairwoman, Adele addresses the membership and lists the accomplishments of her administration. Seriocomic.
BWSM92, 6 minutes
The Monkey Business by David Bottrell

295
Esther   **Here and Now**
A woman who gave up her child recalls her teenage pregnancy. Dramatic.

BWSM92, 4 minutes
Mother's Day by Kate Aspengren

296
Mary, 60s   **Here and Now**
A woman remembers the day she and her husband adopted an infant. Dramatic.
BWSM92, 3 minutes
Mother's Day by Kate Aspengren

297
Megan, 23
A small apartment in New York, 1970 and 1976
While helping a friend to move, Megan tells about her search for God. Seriocomic.
BWSM92, 3 minutes
Moving by Lee Kalcheim

298
Diana, 21
A small apartment in New York, 1970 and 1976
Diana tells her friend of an experience in her prep school that changed her life. Seriocomic.
BWSM92, 2.5 minutes
Moving by Lee Kalcheim

299
Woman, a performer, any age
A theatre, Present
A woman responds to a list of unrelated words offered by the theatre manager by organizing them into a speech. Comic.
BWSM92, 2.5 minutes
Nevertheless (Transition) by Kenneth Bernard

300
Jane Austen, 40, the reclusive novelist
Jane Austen's cottage in Chawton, Hampshire, England, 1817
Jane sickens and dies, leaving a letter behind for her newly found beloved. (she appears on stage to speak the words of the letter). Dramatic.
BWSM92, 2.5 minutes
The Novelist by Howard Fast

301
Old Woman, 60s   **Here and Now**
Here an old woman in a wheelchair shares a memory of her legs and a school friend. Seriocomic.
BWSM92, 2.5 minutes
One Thing Is Not Another (A Vaudeville) by Kenneth Bernard

302
Claire, 40

A country cottage, England, Present
Claire has shared some wine with Ralph, a friend of her husband's, and here, she tells him of her desire to believe in God. Dramatic.
BWSM92, 4.5 minutes
It's Ralph by Hugh Whitmore

303
Makeeba Parks, 40s
An apartment in New York City, Present
When her husband wonders why their son has turned against their struggle for civil rights, Makeeba offers the following explanation. Dramatic.
BWSM92, 2 minutes
The Resurrection of Dark Soldiers by William Electric Black

304
Janet Wilson, 20
An apartment in New York City, Present
Janet recalls her kidnapping at the hands of black radical Batu Parks. Dramatic.
BWSM92, 2 minutes
The Resurrection of Dark Soldiers by William Electric Black

305
Beatrice, 20s
A studio apartment in Back Bay, Boston, Present
Beatrice's life has taken a few bad turns. She calls her one-time lover and asks him to visit. Here, she tells him a bittersweet tale of her father. Dramatic.
BWSM92, 2 minutes
Servy-N-Bernice 4Ever by Seth Zvi Rosenfeld

306
Katya, 20-30
A flat in Eastern Europe, Present
Katya offers the following explanation for her involvement with the new organization of Eastern Europe. Dramatic.
BWSM92, 3.5 minutes
A Slip of the Tongue by Dusty Hughes

307
Georgie, late 20s   Boston, Present
Georgie reveals her frustration over her new secretarial job to her friend, Andrew. Dramatic.
BWSM92, 1 minute
Spike Heels by Theresa Rebeck

308
Georgie, late 20s   Boston, Present
Georgie admits to throwing a pencil at her boss. Andrew suggests she couldn't hold a job

at McDonald's with such behavior. Georgie responds. Dramatic.
BWSM92, 3 minutes
Spike Heels by Theresa Rebeck

309
Edna, 60s   New York City, Present
Murray asks Edna how her sister is when she returns from a hospital visit. Dramatic.
BWSM92, 2 minutes
Spilt Milk by Glenn Alterman

310
Liz, 30s   Remers, Minnesota
Liz tells Leonard about her daughter and about beauty. Dramatic.
BWSM92, 2.5 minutes
Stories from the National Inquirer by Jeanne Murray Walker

311
Rosalee, 50s   Remers, Minnesota
Rosalee, a woman possessed by angels, tells Leonard, a *National Inquirer* reporter, about her angels. Dramatic.
BWSM92, 2.5 minutes
Stories from the National Inquirer by Jeanne Murray Walker

312
Gretchen, 35   Present
Gretchen tells Becca, who she is fitting, a story of infatuation. Dramatic.
BWSM92, 5.5 minutes
Trust by Steven Dietz

313
Aunt Augusta, 60-70   A flat in London
Following her sister's cremation, Augusta shares a gruesome anecdote with her nephew. Seriocomic.
BWSM92, 2.5 minutes
Travels With My Aunt by Graham Greene (adapted for the stage by Giles Havergal)

314
Benita, 30s   Edmonton, Alberta, 1988
A woman of alleged psychic abilities, Benita muses on a folktale. Dramatic.
BWSM92, 1.5 minutes
Unidentified Human Remains And the True Nature of Love by Brad Fraser

315
Carol, 30s
An apartment in New York, Present
Carol leaves her rural area to travel to New York for her father's funeral. She meets her half brother for the first time. Here she describes her life at home. Dramatic.

BWSM92
Unpublished Letters by Jonathan C. Levine

316
Claire, 50s
A small town in Central Europe, 1950s
Claire returns to the town of her youth to punish the man who once disgraced her. Here, she confronts her one-time lover. Dramatic.
BWSM92, 2 minutes
The Visit by Friedrich Duerrenmatt (Adapted by Maurice Valency)

317
Madeline, 25   **Here and Now**
Here, a young woman tells a pleasingly erotic tale about an encounter with a rainstorm. Dramatic.
BWSM92, 2 minutes
Winchelesa Dround And Other Plays by Dan Nigro

318
Katherine Mansfield, 31, a writer of short fiction
A villa in Menton on the French Riviera, 1920
Katherine has come to Menton in search of a cure for her tuberculosis. Here, she confronts her doctor with the fact of his own illness. Dramatic.
BWSM92, 5.5 minutes
The Winter Wife by Claire Tomalin

319
Katherine Mansfield, 31
A villa in Menton on the French Rivera, 1920
Katherine has completed a story and is able to put her illness at bay for a moment and share memories from the past with her companion, Ida. Dramatic.
BWSM92, 2 minutes
The Winter Wife by Claire Tomalin

320
Papa Shakespeare,50-60
New York City, 1821
All the members of Billy Brown's African Theater have been arrested for performing Richard III. Here, the senior member of their troupe reflects upon his character, William Catesby. Seriocomic.
BMSM93, 3 minutes
The African Company Presents Richard the Third by Carlyle Brown

321
Papa Shakespeare, 50-60
New York City, 1821
Here, Papa Shakespeare tells of his life in the Caribbean and of the origin of his distinctive name. Seriocomic.

BMSM93, 4 minutes
The African Company Presents Richard the Third by Carlyle Brown

322
Connors, 30-50   **An office, Present**
Connors works with sexually abused children and here contemplates the workings of the human mind. Dramatic.
BMSM93, 2.5 minutes
All Fall Down by Wendy Lill

323
Andy Warhol, the artist, 50s
New York City and Brooklyn, Present
In the months before his death, the pop icon contemplates the people in his life; including his secret girlfriend, Rosie. Seriocomic.
BMSM93, 4 minutes
Andy Warhol's Secret Girlfriend by Richard Lay

324
Boris, 30s
New York City and Brooklyn, Present
A convoluted course of events has landed Boris, a house painter, in the home of one of the world's wealthiest women. To his amazement, she has offered to pay him $1 million to paint her fabulous Manhattan apartment. Here, Boris muses on his fate, and on the woman who once broke his heart. Seriocomic.
BMSM93, 5 minutes
Andy Warhol's Secret Girlfriend by Richard Lay

325
A policeman, 30-50
Thompson Square Park, NYC, Present
Here, a member of the NYPD explains how to deal with unruly homeless people. Seriocomic.
BMSM93, 6 minutes
Antigone in New York by Janusz Glowacki

326
Flea, 40-50
Thompson Square Park, NYC, Present
Years of living on the streets of New York and alcohol abuse have driven Flea to the edge of madness. Here, he describes his own vision of the American Dream. Seriocomic.
BMSM93, 2.5 minutes
Antigone in New York by Janusz Glowacki

327
Ed, 20s   **Bensonhurst, Brooklyn, Present**
Driven to despair by his participation in the racial murder of a black teenager, Ed here makes the best confession that his denial will permit. Dramatic.
BMSM93, 4 minutes
Aven'u Boys by Frank Pugliese

328
George Bernard Shaw, the playwright, 60s
England, 1930s
Here, the irrepressible Mr. Shaw muses on the existence of God. Seriocomic.
BMSM93, 2 minutes
The Best of Friends by Hugh Whitemore

329
Baby Creole, 20-30
New York City, 1911, the night of the Triangle Shirtwaist Company fire
Baby Creole, a black boxer and bodyguard, volunteered to help the firemen at the horrific fire that claimed so many young lives. Here, he tells his story. Dramatic.
BMSM93, 2 minutes
Big Tim and Fanny by Jack Gilhooley and Daniel Czitrom

330
Rudolph, 40s   **Germany, Present**
Writer Peter Sichrovsky is in the process of researching a book on the children of Nazis. Here, he interviews Rudolph, who details his childhood spent in exile in South America. Dramatic.
BMSM93, 1 minute
Born Guilty by Ari Roth based on the book by Peter Sichrovsky

331
Eddie, 20-30
A tavern on Canal Street, NYC, 1936
Eddie has been made hard by life, and he here tries to impart some tough philosophy to his infant son. Seriocomic.
BMSM93, 6 minutes
Conversations with my Father by Herb Gardner

332
Eddie, 20-30
A tavern on Canal Street, NYC, 1936
When he is accused of turning his back on his Jewish heritage, Eddie offers the following bitter reply. Seriocomic.
BMSM93, 7 minutes
Conversations with my Father by Herb Gardner

333
Ned Weeks, 40s
Washington, DC, Autumn, 1992
After many frustrating years of battling social ignorance, political treachery, and disease, Ned, an AIDS activist, allows himself to become a human guinea pig for the very establishment he despises. Here, he vents his anger and despair. Dramatic.
BMSM93, 1.5 minutes
The Destiny of Me by Larry Kramer

334
Buddy, 25   **A home in Jericho, RI, 1923**
Buddy is a simple man who has taken a room in the home of his employer's mother. He soon falls in love with Maggie, his boss's outspoken sister. Here, he tells her of his painful childhood. Dramatic.
BMSM93, 3 minutes
A Distance from Calcutta by P.J. Barry

335
Foos, 30s
A Maryland construction site, Present
When Foos, an African-American construction worker, is accused of being involved in the race riots that are plaguing the community, he tells a bitter tale of a walk he took on a hot summer night. Dramatic.
BMSM93, 3.5 minutes
Distant Fires by Kevin Heelan

336
Hertel, 30-40
A California pet cemetery, Present
Hertel is far more in tune with his need to survive than are most people. When he senses that his wealthy mother is about to make a deal with a powerful real estate company to sell his land, he is reminded that life feeds on itself. Seriocomic.
BMSM93, 3 minutes
Dog Logic by Thomas Strelich

337
Michael, 40s   **A bedroom, Present**
Michael can no longer tolerate his wife's constant quest for perfection and here tells her of his malcontent. Seriocomic.
BMSM93, 2.5 minutes
Domestic Violence by Frederick Stroppel

338
MJ, late 20s   **Present**
MJ has returned home to suburban Philly after several years of drifting from one job to another. When he encounters his 15-year-old sister, he is shocked to discover that she barely remembers him. Here he tries to jog her memory with a story of a long-forgotten family vacation to the seashore. Seriocomic.
BMSM93, 4 minutes
Down the Shore by Tom Donaghy

339
Uttyersprot, 40-50
A country enduring a military dictatorship, Present
Uttyersprot, a henchmen for a corrupt regime, has led a good and honest man to his doom. As he watches his victim bleed to death, he

tells him of the inner torment that has driven him to his present state of being. Dramatic.
BMSM93, 2 minutes
Dream of the Red Spider by Ronald Ribman

340
Hayes, 40's
A sidewheeler, just before the Civil War
Hayes has traveled the Mississippi as a gambler for many years. Loneliness has taken its toll as he reveals to a fellow traveler. Dramatic.
BMSM93, 2 minutes
The Gamblers by Val Smith

341
The Puritan, 30-40   **Present**
Keyboard player Glenn Gould was a complex genius. Here, the puritanical aspect of his mind discusses performing, art and morality. Dramatic.
BMSM93, 3 minutes
Glenn by David Young

342
Les, 18
A police station in Saskatchewan, 1967
Les, accused of indecent assault, maintains the swimming pool at the local club. During his interrogation at the police station, he tells the sergeant that he feels isolated from the other kids. Dramatic.
BMSM93, 4.5 minutes
I Had A Job I Liked. Once. by Guy Vanderhaeghe

343
Junior, 40s
An ice-fishing house on a lake in northern Minnesota
A man of simple taste, Junior here reveals his dislike for artists. Seriocomic.
BMSM93, 5 minutes
The Ice Fishing Play by Kevin Kling

344
Colin Bradshaw, 40s   **London, 4 years ago**
When a pretty young reporter from the *Washington Post* interviews this well-known Shakespearean actor, he breaks his own rule and speaks of his divorce. Seriocomic.
BMSM93, 6.5 minutes
The Interview by Amy Hersh

345
Frederick, 38
A poor farm in the Ukraine, summer 1909
To avoid military service in the upcoming war, and against the wishes of his pregnant upper-class wife, Frederick, a Russian farmer, has decided to move his family to America. Dramatic.

BMSM93, 3 minutes
Inventing America by Jeanne Murray Walker

346
Ferdinand, 20s
His father is a Ku Klux Klansman and his mother lives in a world of dreams and visions. To escape, Ferdinand travels to the city where he plays his horn on the street. Dramatic.
BMSM93, 4.5 minutes
Isabella Dreams the New World by Lenora Champagne

347
Jeffrey, 20-30   **New York City, Present**
Here, Jeffrey, a gay man, bravely renounces sex. Seriocomic.
BMSM93, 3 minutes
Jeffrey by Paul Rudnick

348
Cole, 30s
A basement in Rhode Island, Present
Cole has brutally raped his ex-wife, Keely, who was subsequently kidnapped by a militant anti-abortion group. It is the group's intention to keep Keely a prisoner until the child she carries is at term. In the meantime, they have sought out Cole and cleaned him up in hopes that Keely will forgive him and want to become a family again. Here, the newly "saved" Cole begs Keely for forgiveness. Dramatic.
BMSM93, 7 minutes
Keely and Du by Jane Martin

349
Lou, 30s
An apartment in Hell's Kitchen, Present
Lou searched for a mate at the New School in Manhattan and believed that he had discovered the perfect woman in Mona, a classmate. They moved to Vermont with the intention of starting a brand new life together. After a short while, Lou returns to New York City with the following tale of woe. Seriocomic.
BMSM93, 7 minutes
Light Sensitive by Jim Geoghan

350
Charlie, 20-30   **A singles bar**
When Charlie is approached by a woman claiming to know him, he feels compelled to deliver the following diatribe. Seriocomic.
BMSM93, 3 minutes
The Line That Picked Up 1000 Babes (And How It Can Work for You) by Eric Berlin

351
Alan   **A singles bar**
When Alan approaches Diane with the inten-

tion of getting to know her, her chilly response brings out the worst in him. Seriocomic.
BMSM93, 4 minutes
The Line That Picked Up 1000 Babes (And How It Can Work for You) by Eric Berlin

352
Father Hayes, 60s
When Father Hayes is visited by a man he thought dead, he confesses that he has always felt responsible for his death. Dramatic.
BMSM93, 5 minutes
Lion in the Streets by Judith Thompson

353
Carl, 30s   **A small map store, Present**
Carl, a frequent visitor to "Jody's Maps," here denounces the bland nature of human intercourse. Seriocomic.
BMSM93, 4 minutes
Lonely Planet by Steven Dietz

354
Robert   **A home in Queens, Present**
Robert has fallen in love with Susan, but is afraid of what marriage may do to their relationship. Here, he reveals his deepest fears. Seriocomic.
BMSM93, 4 minutes
The Marriage Fool by Richard Vetere

355
Walter, 30s
A wedding chapel in Las Vegas
When a couple whose marriage he has witnessed decides to file for divorce, Walter lectures them on the importance of making a commitment. Seriocomic.
BMSM93, 4 minutes
The Midnight Moonlight Wedding Chapel by Eric Berlin

356
Mickey, 40s   **The home of Mickey and Gi**
Years of drinking and a failed career have taken their toll on Mickey, who announces at Thanksgiving dinner that he is leaving his wife. Dramatic.
BMSM93, 6 minutes
Northeast Local by Tom Donaghy

357
Angel, 20-30
A bombed-out museum in a country experiencing a civil war
As Angel and his partner loot a museum that has been destroyed by war, he tells the story of how the conflict began. Seriocomic.
BMSM93, 6 minutes
On the Open Road by Steve Tesich

358
Tony, 20-30   **A city, Present**
Tony has been given the gift of living parts of his life over again, but soon finds himself trapped in a repeating loop. Here, he reencounters a couple in a pub for the second time. Dramatic.
BMSM93, 5 minutes
Play with Repeats by Martin Crimp

359
Preacher, 40s
A small town along the shore of an immense lake in Northern Saskatchewan, Present
Here, Preacher recounts a hallucinatory experience to a friend who has heard this story many times before. Dramatic.
BMSM93, 4 minutes
Serpent in the Night Sky by Dianne Warren

360
Jonathan, 30-40   **A house in LA, Present**
Jonathan has just discovered that his wife slept with his best friend, Michael, just before they were married. Michael, who is gay, has just tested positive for HIV, and Jonathan confronts his friend with his own feelings of fear and loss. Dramatic.
BMSM93, 2 minutes
Snakebit by David Marshall Grant

361
Adam, 30-40   **A cell, Present**
Adam shares a cell in Lebanon with Michael and Edward who both hail from the British Isles. Here, Adam laments his lack of American underwear. Seriocomic.
BMSM93, 1 minute
Someone Who'll Watch Over Me by Frank McGuiness

362
Michael, 40s   **A cell, Present**
Michael and his fellow hostage, Edward, celebrate Christmas in their dismal cell in Lebanon. Here, Michael tells how he lost his wife. Seriocomic.
BMSM93, 1 minute
Someone Who'll Watch Over Me by Frank McGuiness

363
Atkinson, 30s
A river property on the Tennessee-Tombigbee Waterway, Present
In this isolated moment, Atkinson speaks of the necessity of letting go in order to find ecstasy. Dramatic.
BMSM93, 2 minutes
Spinning into Blue by Sally Nemeth

364
Ron, 40
A small service station in upstate Missouri, Present
On the day of his ex-wife's marriage, Ron tells a fellow traveler of his sorrow. Dramatic.
BMSM93, 2 minutes
Stanton's Garage by Joan Ackerman

365
Mutt, 35   **Here and Now**
Here, Mutt enjoys a game of garage poker with his buddies. Seriocomic.
BMSM93, 3 minutes
Strangers on Earth by Mark O'Donnell

366
A Traveling Penitent, 30-50   **A beach**
Here, a traveling penitent tells the tragic tale of a woman who lost both her father and her lover on the same day. Dramatic.
BMSM93, 2 minutes
The Transformation on the Beach—A Sexual Noh Drama by Dick Bonker

367
Walter, 80
An apartment on the Upper West Side, NYC, Present
At the end of his life, Walter wishes to die with dignity at the time of his choosing. Here, he gives his grandson the responsibility of making sure that no heroic measures are taken to save him should his attempt at suicide fail. Dramatic.
BMSM93, 3.5 minutes
Unfinished Stories by Sybille Pearson

368
Arnold, 30s
A home in suburban Kentucky, Present
Maple and Stan have been trying to have a baby for 12 years. They've tried just about everything—including wearing wigs to look like different people in bed. Here, a neighbor muses about their plight as it pertains to his own. Seriocomic.
BMSM93, 2 minutes
The View from Here by Margaret Dulaney

369
Haseltine, 40s   **Here and Now**
After seducing many, many women, Haseltine confesses his desire for something that will remain once his lust has been sated. Dramatic.
BMSM93, 4.5 minutes
What a Man Weighs by Sherry Kramer

370
John, 50-60   **Here and Now**
John abused his daughter when she was a little girl. Now she confronts him as an adult, and he is incapable of anything save denial. Dramatic.
BMSM93, 2 minutes
What We Do with It by Bruce MacDonald

371
Andrew, 30s   **Here and Now**
On the day of his cousin's wedding, Andrew, a young photographer, tells her of his need to capture life's moments on film. Dramatic.
BMSM93, 2 minutes
The Years by Cindy Lou Johnson

372
Pheenie, 20s   **Cocoa Beach, Florida, Present**
Pheenie has left her dry Alabama home in search of the ocean. She is eventually drawn to Cocoa Beach in Florida, where she finally dips her toes into the water. Dramatic.
BWSM93, 3 minutes
Alabama Rain by Heather McCutcheon

373
Ruth, 30s
An apartment in Manhattan, Present
Ruth and Anna wanted a child for a long time. When Nathan is born, Ruth speaks to his biological father of her love for Anna and her desire to be a parent. Seriocomic.
BWSM93, 3 minutes
And Baby Makes Seven by Paula Vogel

374
Alice, 18-20   **Mythical Tudor England**
Alice is driven to thoughts of murdering her husband by her desire for Thomas, a servant in her husband's household. Here, she speaks to Thomas of her lonely life. Dramatic.
BWSM93, 2 minutes
Andy Fafirsin by Don Nigro

375
Rosie, 30s   **NYC and Brooklyn**
Rosie is a simple Brooklyn gal who works in the garment district. One day she encountered Andy Warhol on a bus and lent him five dollars. A strange romance ensued. Here, Rosie contemplates her first love, a house painter named Boris. Seriocomic.
BWSM93, 3.5 minutes
Andy Warhol's Secret Girlfriend by Richard Lay

376
Anita, 30-40
Thompson Square Park, NYC
Here, good-hearted Anita tells the story of how she came to be homeless.

BWSM93, 2.5 minutes
Antigone in New York by Janusz Glowacki

377
Molly, 30s   **NYC, Present**
Just days away from her due date, Molly tells her best friend of the trouble that she has been having with her husband. Seriocomic.
BWSM93, 4.5 minutes
Approximating Mother by Kathleen Tolan

378
Jen, teenager   **Indiana, Present**
Jen tells of her visit to a social worker to discuss her accidental pregnancy. Seriocomic.
BWSM93, 2 minutes
Approximating Mother by Kathleen Tolan

379
Kathleen, 18-20
New York City – the night of the fire at the Triangle Shirtwaist Factory
Here, a young girl with street smarts offers an eyewitness account of the horrific fire at the Triangle Shirtwaist Factory. Dramatic.
BWSM93, 2 minutes
Big Tom and Fanny by Jack Gilhooley and Daniel Czitrom

380
Esther, 18-20
New York City – the night of the fire at the Triangle Shirtwaist Factory
Esther, an employee of the Triangle Shirtwaist Company, was fortunate enough to have escaped the fire. Here, she tells her story. Dramatic.
BWSM93, 2 minutes
Big Tom and Fanny by Jack Gilhooley and Daniel Czitrom

381
Sibylle, 40s   **Germany, Present**
Writer Peter Sichrovsky is in the process of researching a book on the children of Nazis. Here he interviews Sibylle, who describes the brutal fascism with which she was raised. Dramatic.
BWSM93, 3.5 minutes
Born Guilty by Ari Roth. Based on the book by Peter Sichrovsky

382
Carolee, 30s
The bedroom on a country western band's tour bus, Present
Carolee's heart has broken, her voice is all but shot and now she's expected to do a show. Here, she describes her plight. Seriocomic.
BWSM93, 8 minutes
Cruising Close to Crazy by Laura Cunningham

383
Dominatrix, 30-40
An otherworldly S&M classroom
Once condemned for witchcraft, this angry spirit now gives instruction in the art of sexual torture. Seriocomic.
BWSM93, 5.5 minutes
Cute Boys in Their Underpants Go to France by Robert Coles

384
Sally, 40s
An apartment in New York City, Present
Sally has struggled for years to keep David, her handicapped son, out of an institution. Pursued by guilt and a relentless social worker, she has finally come to accept the fact that he would be better off in a program geared to his special needs. Here, Sally tells David of her decision. Dramatic.
BWSM93, 2 minutes
David's Mother by Bob Randall

385
Rena, 30-40
Just outside Washington, D.C., Autumn 1992
Here, Rena tells her son the sad and horrifying tale of her miscarriage. Dramatic.
BWSM93, 3 minutes
The Destiny of Me by Larry Kramer

386
Luke, 15
On the street next to a church outside of Philadelphia, Present
Luke (really Lucy) is pregnant. Here, she tells her story to her long-lost brother, MJ. Seriocomic.
BWSM93, 2.5 minutes
Down the Shore by Tom Donaghy

387
The Doctor, 40s
A head trauma ward; late at night
When a neurosurgeon runs afoul of a bullet, she is placed in the same head trauma ward that she once managed. Now her consciousness wanders from memory to memory. Here, her mind pays a visit to a patient that she had once found to be particularly disturbing. Dramatic.
BWSM93, 3 minutes
Freakmakers by Jocelyn Beard

388
Constance, 20-30
Queens University, Present
For years, Constance has devoted herself to the selfish Professor Night. She is shocked when he announces that he is: (A) marrying a young

student; (B) taking the position that Constance desired for herself at Oxford, and (C) getting her a job at an isolated college on the Canadian prairie. Seriocomic.
BWSM93, 2 minutes
Goodnight Desdemona (Good Morning Juliet) by Ann-Marie MacDonald

389
Torchy, 20s
Rocco's Pussycat Lounge, Las Vegas
Torchy will do anything to promote her career as a singer/songwriter; including working at Rocco's Pussycat Lounge. Seriocomic.
BWSM93, 2.5 minutes
Hi-Rollers by Jack Gilhooley

390
Bonnie, 60s   **A living room, Present**
Bonnie and Glen have gathered their family together to announce that Glen is dying of an incurable disease and intends to take his own life. When he dies, Bonnie goes into shock. Dramatic.
BWSM93, 2.5 minutes
Homeward Bound by Eliot Hayes

391
Countess, 50-60   **An AA meeting**
Countess has waged a long and successful war against alcoholism. Here, she addresses her AA group. Seriocomic.
BWSM93, 2.5 minutes
The Hope Zone by Kevin Heelan

392
Mona, 20-30
A quilting bee for the Names Quilt Project, Present
Mona has become involved with the Names Quilt Project in order to help deal with the death of her son by AIDS. Here, she shares a special memory of her little boy with her fellow quilters. Dramatic.
BWSM93, 3 minutes
in Stitches by Brian Christopher Williams

393
Mrs. Cavendish, 60-70
A quilting bee for the Names Quilt Project, Present
Mrs. Cavendish had donated the use of her basement to a group that makes panels for the Names Quilt Project. An evening of quilting and discussion has led to speculations about the hereafter. Here, Mrs. Cavendish describes her Near Death Experience. Dramatic.
BWSM93, 1.5 minutes
in Stitches by Brian Christopher Williams

394
Helen, Any age
A parking lot outside of a six-plex, Present
Helen, a postal worker, here tells the frightening story of the day one of her co-workers ran amok with a gun. Serio-comic.
BWSM93, 3.5 minutes
The Innocent's Crusade by Keith Reddin

395
Laura, 43   **A beach house, Present**
Laura fears that her lover of 20 years is about to leave her as she here confesses to Daniel, her lover's brother. Seriocomic.
BWSM93, 4 minutes
It Is It Is Not by Manuel Periras García

396
Jane, 20s   **A bedroom, Present**
Here, Jane makes a series of frantic calls in an effort to raise $250. She dials a number, obviously getting an answering machine. Seriocomic.
BWSM93, 8.5 minutes
Jane Amphetamine by Annie G.

397
Laurie, 20s
A train compartment, Penn Station, NYC, Present
It can be extremely difficult to find fame and fortune in NYC, as Laurie, a young dancer, here confesses to a stranger on a train. Seriocomic.
BWSM93, 3.5 minutes
Jay by Anthony Giardina

398
Jenny Glass, 14
A den, New Year's Eve
Jenny has holed up in her parent's den with some junk food and a telephone. Here, she gabs with her best friend as the world waits to welcome a new year. Seriocomic.
BWSM93, 9 minutes
Jenny's New Year by Annie G.

399
Johanna, 17
A farm outside a small town in Ontario, 1939
Johanna is a young woman who longs to escape the dreary life she shares with her father. Here, she confides an unhappy memory of her mother to a farmhand who she is encouraging to stand up to her father. Dramatic.
BWSM93, 2 minutes
Johannesburg by James Harrison

400
Portia, 30s
A nearly-deserted coal mining town, Present
As a child, Portia was sexually abused by her father, an ill-tempered coal miner. Years later, she returns home and finds him dying of black lung disease. Dramatic.
BWSM93, 1.5 minutes
Julius and Portia Jones by Brian Christopher Williams

401
Keely, 20-30
A basement in Rhode Island, Present
Keely has been brutally raped by her ex-husband. While seeking an abortion, she is kidnapped by members of the underground anti-abortion group who intend to force her to carry the child to term. Here, she longs for solitude. Dramatic.
BWSM93, 1 minute
Keely and Du by Jane Martin

402
Julia, 20-30   A prison in a desert
Julia longs for love and beauty, but the world in which she lives is filled with hatred and pain. Here, she tells a story that mirrors her feelings. Dramatic.
BWSM93, 4 minutes
The King of Infinite Space by Andrew C. Ordover

403
Edna, 30s
An apartment in Hell's Kitchen, Present
Edna has fallen in live with Tom, a blind man to whom she has volunteered to read. When Tom's best friend arrives on the scene, Edna fears that he will waste no time in supplying Tom with an unflattering description of her. Here, she begs him to remain silent. Dramatic.
BWSM93, 9 minutes
Light Sensitive by Jim Geoghan

404
Fran, 20-30   A singles bar
When Fran meets an interesting man in a bar, she tells him of her frustration with "guys." Seriocomic.
BWSM93, 3 minutes
The Line That Picked Up 1000 Babes (And How It Can Work For You) by Eric Berlin

405
Joanne, 30s
When Joanne finds out that she has terminal bone cancer, she tells her best friend how she would like to die. Seriocomic.
BWSM93, 1.5 minutes
Lion in the Street by Judith Thompson

406
Margie, 30s
A sushi restaurant, Present
When Margie goes out on a blind date with Miles, an anal retentive perfectionist, she cracks under his intense scrutiny. Seriocomic.
BWSM93, 4 minutes
Loose Knit by Theresa Rebeck

407
Gina, 30s
An apartment in Manhattan, Present
When Gina is let go from her law firm, her usual reserve begins to crack a bit. Seriocomic.
BWSM93, 5.5 minutes
Loose Knit by Theresa Rebeck

408
Misty, 20-30
A wedding chapel in Las Vegas
Misty and Pete have decided to get married after only just meeting in a Las Vegas casino. Here, Misty tells the justice of the peace of the events that led to their hasty decision. Seriocomic.
BWSM93, 2 minutes
The Midnight Moonlight Wedding Chapel by Eric Berlin

409
Gi, 20s
The home of Mickey and Gi
Gi welcomes her baby son home with the following speech. Dramatic.
BWSM93, 3 minutes
Northeast Local by Tom Donaghy

410
An Old Actress, 70s
An old age home in Russia
Here, an old actress remembers her first kiss and her first love. Seriocomic.
BWSM93, 2 minutes
An Old Actress in the Role of Dostoevsky's Wife by Edvard Rodzinsky

411
Netty, 70-80
A bus stop, San Diego, Present
Netty's eyes are failing, and here she complains about eye doctors as she tries to catch a bus. Normally, she's a vigorous old lady, always in control of her life. But something has happened to her eyes. As she comes across the stage, traffic noise is heard, then angry horns. Seriocomic.
BWSM93, 10.5 minutes
The Old Lady's Guide to Survival by Mayo Simon

412
Cora, 20-30   A group therapy session
Here, Cora breaks down at her AIDS support group and finally explains how she became infected. Dramatic.
BWSM93, 4.5 minutes
Raft of the Medusa by Joe Pintauro

413
Geri, 17
Geneva's home in Arcata, California, Present
The daughter of a Vietnamese woman and an American GI, Geri is obsessed with finding her father. Here, she tells her Aunt Geneva why she can no longer handle the pressure of being a concert pianist.
BWSM93, 2.5 minutes
Redwood Curtain by Lanford Wilson

414
Francine, 20-30
A quilting bee for the Names Quilt Project, Present
Francine prowls the meat markets every night in search of sex with strangers. Here, she tells the tale of an encounter that didn't turn out quite the way she planned. Seriocomic.
BWSM93, 3.5 minutes
Screwed-Up Women And the Men Behind Them by Barbara Sellars

415
Joy, 17
A small town along the shore of an immense lake in Northern Saskatchewan, Present
Joy has hitched a ride to Saskatchewan with Duff, whom she now intends to marry. Following an argument, Joy tells Duff of the loneliness that she has experienced since leaving home. Dramatic.
BWSM93, 2 minutes
Serpent in the Night Sky by Dianne Warren

416
Jackie, 40s   A dating seminar, Present
Jackie's seminar is entitled: "Power Dating for the 90s: A Guide for Savvy Singles." Somewhere behind her psycho-babble rhetoric lurks an abhorrence for the opposite sex, as may be seen in the following speech. Seriocomic.
BWSM93, 2 minutes
Single and Proud by Frederick Stroppel

417
Jennifer, 30-40   A house in LA, Present
Here, Jennifer tells her best friend why she hates acting. Seriocomic.
BWSM93, 2 minutes
Snakebit by David Marshall Grant

418
Claire, 13
A country home in Connecticut, Present
Claire's younger brother, Christy, is dying. Here, she speaks to him for what she knows will be the last time. Dramatic.
BWSM93, 3 minutes
Spine by Bill C. Davis

419
Mary Louise, 60
A small service station in upstate Missouri, Present
While she makes egg salad, Mary Louise entertains a woman stranded at the service station with a tale of her first answering machine. Seriocomic.
BWSM93, 4 minutes
Stanton's Garage by Joan Ackerman

420
Mrs. Sims, 30-60   Here and Now
Mrs. Sims has allowed her dislike of a new neighbor to drive her to an act of violence. Seriocomic.
BWSM93, 3 minutes
Stories Women Tell by Janet Overmyer

421
Tina, 19   A city park, Present
Tina has confronted her boyfriend about her pregnancy and now realizes that she will have to go through it alone. Here, she reveals bitter insight about her future. Dramatic.
BWSM93, 2.5 minutes
Tough by George F. Walker

422
Brenna, 20-30   A farmhouse in Kansas
Brenna's husband has been driven to violence and madness and has locked her in her room to prevent her from escaping. Here, Brenna does her best to persuade him to release her. Dramatic.
BWSM93, 4 minutes
Trapped Daylight by Sharon Houck Ross

423
Fern, 30s
A home in suburban Kentucky, Present
Fern has been trapped in her house for many years. Here, she describes her first bout of agoraphobia. Seriocomic.
BWSM93, 3.5 minutes
The View from Here by Margaret Dulaney

424
Lottie, 14   Here and Now

Lottie is a romantic young girl anxiously awaiting her metamorphosis into womanhood. Here, she longingly contemplates the inevitable change that is to come. Dramatic.
BWSM93, 3 minutes
Watermelon Rinds by Regina Taylor

425
Joan, 35   **Here and Now**
Here, Joan shares a favorite daydream. Dramatic.
BWSM93, 3 minutes
What A Man Weighs by Sherry Kramer

426
Cheryl, 30s   **Here and Now**
When she was a little girl, Cheryl was abused by her father. After years of denial, she finally confronts him. Dramatic.
BWSM93, 2.5 minutes
What We Do With It by Bruce MacDonald

427
Belle, 20-30   **The Wild West**
The Wild West wasn't always kind to women as evidenced in the life story of Belle, a plucky gal who made a career for herself as a saloon singer. Seriocomic.
BWSM93, 5 minutes
Women of the Wild West by Le Wilhelm

428
Andrea, 30-40   **Here and Now**
After 13 years, Andrea has decided to leave her husband. Here, she speaks of the loneliness that drove her to make her decision. Dramatic.
BWSM93, 2.5 minutes
The Years by Cindy Lou Johnson

429
Peggy, 30s   **An apartment, Present**
Peggy and Mitch have just met and have chosen to withdraw to Mitch's apartment for a more intimate introduction. Here, Peggy demonstrates her oratory skills as Mitch pours wine. Seriocomic.
BWSM93, 2 minutes
Your Place Or Mine by Le Wilhelm

430
Billy, 16
In a tent in summer camp late at night, Present
Billy sits in his tent rereading a letter by flashlight that he has just penned to a friend.
YOUNG, 3.5 minutes
Album by David Rimmer

431
Chris, teenager
In a stranger's house, Present

Chris shares with Harold how an inspiring teacher influenced his life.
YOUNG, 5 minutes
Amulets Against the Dragon Forces by Paul Zindel

432
Randy, teenager
A Lutheran bible camp in Wisconsin, May 1947.
Randy addresses his fellow campers with a testimony: a declaration of faith.
YOUNG, 2 minutes
Ascension Day by Timothy Mason

433
Neal, married
Small North Carolina town, no time given.
Neal, his wife, Taw, and his best friend, Porter, travel a rocky and dramatic emotional journey of fifty-seven years, of friendship, love, confinement, and responsibility. Here Neal and Porter offer personal glimpses of themselves.
YOUNG, 2.5 minutes
August Snow by Reynolds Price

434
Porter
Small North Carolina town, no time given.
Neal, his wife, Taw, and his best friend, Porter, travel a rocky and dramatic emotional journey of fifty-seven years, of friendship, love, confinement, and responsibility. Here Neal and Porter offer personal glimpses of themselves.
YOUNG, 3 minutes
August Snow by Reynolds Price

435
Ma, young man
"ChinaMan railroad workers" on the transcontinental railroad in the hot summer of 1867.
Here Lone, disgusted with Ma's inability to learn from the past, challenges him to "be a locust till morning." If Ma cannot do this, Lone won't take him seriously and will refuse to continue to teach him.
YOUNG, 2.5 minutes
The Dance and the Railroad by David Henry Hwang

436
Dale
Back room of a small Chinese restaurant in southern California.
Here Dale, a second generation Chinese-American student, offers a hypothesis for the circumstances that bring Steve, the Chinese newcomer, to the United States.
YOUNG, 3 minutes
FOB (Fresh-Off-the-Boat) by David Henry Hwang

437
Carl
Cheap one-room apartment, Present
In this speech, a past boyfriend and pimp attempts to persuade Arlene to resume her former ways.
YOUNG, 5 minutes
Getting Out by Marsha Norman

438
Thorson
A farming community in Minnesota in the late 1920s
Here, Thorson attempts to make his intentions clear to Emma.
YOUNG, 3 minutes
In a Northern Landscape by Timothy Mason

439
Alan   **Evening, Present**
Alan's father left him and his mother to marry another woman. Throughout the evening, the audience is included in the reenactment of time spent during this rocky, emotional period in Alan's life.
YOUNG, 3.5 minutes
Lemon Sky by Lanford Wilson

440
Alan   **Evening, Present**
In this speech, Alan offers his early observations of California.
YOUNG, 2.5 minutes
Lemon Sky by Lanford Wilson

441
Hally, 17   **Port Elizabeth, South Africa, 1950**
For many years, Hally has come to rely on Willie and Sam, black waiters in the family-owned tea room, since his father is a dysfunctional, crippled drunk, and his mother is incapable of keeping the family on even ground. Hally, bitter about the news that his father is moving back home, harshly treats his trusted old friends. Here, Hally recalls fond memories of his youth with Sam.
YOUNG, 2.5 minutes
Master Harold...and the Boys by Athol Fugard

442
Hally, 17   **Port Elizabeth, South Africa, 1950**
In this speech, Hally has a telephone conversation with his mother in which he receives the news of his father's return home.
YOUNG, 3.5 minutes
Master Harold...and the Boys by Athol Fugard

443
Thami
A classroom of the Zolile High School in Camdebo, South Africa, August 1985
An argument concerning the need or not for violence to quell once and for all the injustice of apartheid (pronounced apart-hate). In this speech, Thami, a black student, sums up his concluding remarks in an inter-school debate about women. His opponent has been Isabel, a white female student.
YOUNG, 3.5 minutes
My Children! My Africa! by Athol Fugard

444
Thami
A classroom of the Zolile High School in Camdebo, South Africa, August 1985
In this second speech, Thami sets forth his passionate argument for action
YOUNG, 16 minutes
My Children! My Africa! by Athol Fugard

445
Dennis   **Sitting on bunks, Present**
Dennis has learned of the death of his friend, Scooter. Here, Dennis tells Scooter about Leslie Pinkus, a girl he thinks Scooter may like to meet.
YOUNG, 2.5 minutes
Scooter Thomas Makes It to the Top of the World by Peter Parnell

446
Scooter   **Present**
Here, Scooter finds himself in a bit of a predicament with Leslie.
YOUNG, 2.5 minutes
Scooter Thomas Makes It to the Top of the World by Peter Parnell

447
Lee
A Catholic school for boys in New York City's troubled Lower East Side.
Here Lee, a young Hispanic, who wants to be an artist, plays himself, his mother, and his older brother, Tyro, in Mr. Cain's "Stand-up Tragedy" style.
YOUNG, 5 minutes
Stand-Up Tragedy by Bill Cain

448
Timmy
Lebanon, Missouri, July Fourth, 1944
Here, Timmy, a young Marine killed in a Pacific battle of World War II, attempts an insightful communication with his father, which falls, like it might have in life, on deaf ears.
YOUNG, 2.5 minutes
Talley & Son by Lanford Wilson

449
Timmy
Lebanon, Missouri, July Fourth, 1944
Here, Timmy details his own death.
YOUNG, 3.5 minutes
Talley & Son by Lanford Wilson

450
Jud
Here, Jud tells his father about an incident
from his boyhood that particularly made him
angry.
YOUNG, 3 minutes
Tribute by Bernard Slade

451
Horace, 27
Christmas eve and Christmas day, 1917
Here, Horace is captured by a youthful re-
membrance, one that was painful, but one that
also set him on a determined course for the fu-
ture.
YOUNG, 2.5 minutes
Valentine's Day by Horton Foote

452
Ted, puberty
**Summer vacation on the Canadian shores of
Lake Erie near Buffalo, New York, 1945**
Here, Ted has just met Bonnie at the beach and
told her about his plans for their date that
night, but Bonnie has to ask her father.
YOUNG, 1.5 minutes
What I Did Last Summer by A.R. Gurney, Jr.

453
Rafe, teenager   **Present**
Here, Rafe, a Gulf War veteran, describes what
it is like to be a guard in a prison.
YOUNG, 2.5 minutes
Windshook by Mary Gallagher

454
Rafe, teenager
Rafe's camp at night, Present
Here, struggling with feelings about his family
and his resolve to do what he believes, Rafe re-
calls a time when the bond with his father was
strengthened, leaving a lasting impression that
still troubles him.
YOUNG, 3 minutes
Windshook by Mary Gallagher

455
Wallace, 16   **Present**
Wallace delivers a speech about his mother
(who committed suicide when Wallace was
six).
YOUNG, 3.5 minutes
Women and Wallace by Jonathan Marc Sherman

456
Wallace, 16
Psychiatrist's office, Present
Wallace confronts his psychiatrist with his
problems.
YOUNG, 4.5 minutes
Women and Wallace by Jonathan Marc Sherman

457
Elizabeth, a young girl
At a funeral service in Jackson, Indiana, Present
Elizabeth, confined to a wheelchair due to
being crippled at birth by cerebral palsy, is at
the funeral of her best friend, Zelda.
YOUNG, 4.5 minutes
*And They Dance Real Slow in Jackson by Jim
Leonard, Jr.*

458
Elizabeth, a young girl
In bed, Jackson, Indiana, Present
Here, in a dream sequence involving the cho-
rus of players, Elizabeth imagines that
dreamed-of-place where she may once and for
all feel free.
YOUNG, 6 minutes
*And They Dance Real Slow in Jackson by Jim
Leonard, Jr.*

459
Mary-Lois, teenager
**A Lutheran Bible camp in Wisconsin, May
1947.**
Mary-Lois speaks to her fellow campers dur-
ing a testimonial session.
YOUNG, 5 minutes
Ascension Day by Timothy Mason

460
Genevieve
Small North Carolina town, no time given.
Genevieve recounts a special episode she
shared with Neal years ago.
YOUNG, 6 minutes
August Snow by Reynolds Price

461
Laura   **Early 1920s**
Here, Laura struggles to understand some
basic truths in life by posing questions to her-
self and her sister that she simply couldn't ask
her father.
YOUNG, 4 minutes
Courtship by Horton Foote

462
Anne, 13
**A narrow attic in Amsterdam during World
War II**

Here, Anne speaks with her father about her desire to be a better person.
YOUNG, 4 minutes
The Diary of Anne Frank by Frances Goodrich and Albert Hackett

463
Anne, 13
A narrow attic in Amsterdam during World War II
Here, Anne talks with the Van Daan's son, Peter, about the need for each person to have faith in something.
YOUNG, 4.5 minutes
The Diary of Anne Frank by Frances Goodrich and Albert Hackett

464
Tillie   **Present**
Encouraged by a teacher, Tillie, a high school student, carries out a gamma ray experiment with marigold seeds that wins her a prize at the school Science Fair. Here, Tillie shows she has awakened to the wonders of science.
YOUNG, 1.5 minutes
The Effect of Gamma Rays on Man-in-the-Moon Marigolds by Paul Zindel

465
Tillie   **Present**
Here, Tillie again shows she has awakened to the wonders of science.
YOUNG, 2 minutes
The Effect of Gamma Rays on Man-in-the-Moon Marigolds by Paul Zindel

466
Joanne   **Present**
Here, Joanne, a Chinese-American raised in the Philippines, describes an early memory of her uncle Di-gou.
YOUNG, 5 minutes
Family Devotions by David Henry Hwang

467
Grace
Back room of a small Chinese restaurant in southern California, Present
Here Grace details a turning point in reconciling her feelings of not fitting in.
YOUNG, 2.5 minutes
FOB (Fresh-Off-the-Boat) by David Henry Hwang

468
Arlie
Locked maximum security cell, Present
In this flashback, Arlie tells an unseen officer her perceptions of her fellow inmates.
YOUNG, 3 minutes
Getting Out by Marsha Norman

469
Lucy, teenager   **England, Present**
Here, Lucy introduces us to Zara, her invisible friend.
YOUNG, 7 minutes
Invisible Friends by Alan Ayckbourn

470
Lucy, teenager   **England, Present**
Here, Lucy takes us through the series of events that lead to the fateful fall that caused Zara to materialize.
YOUNG, 8 minutes
Invisible Friends by Alan Ayckbourn

471
Lily Dale, teenager
Bedroom of her step-father's house, early 1908
Lily Dale's brother, Horace, has become sick while visiting them. Lily, spoiled and selfish, resents Horace's presence, particularly his persistent talks about the past.
YOUNG, 6 minutes
Lily Dale by Horton Foote

472
Frankie, 12
In the kitchen of her home, Present
Frankie, somewhat awkward and out-of-sorts searches for her place in this world. Here she speaks to the cook, Berenice, of her plans to leave her home with her brother, Jarvis, and his new bride.
YOUNG, 6 minutes
The Member of the Wedding by Carson McCullers

473
Helen
Boardinghouse in Harrison, Texas, 1952
Helen had an argument with her mother over Harvey Weems, whom she loved, but who could not overcome his drinking problems. Here, Helen attempts to explain her situation to Ralph, a new boarder at the house who is interested in her.
YOUNG, 6 minutes
The Midnight Caller by Horton Foote

474
Annie   **1800s**
Annie is one of the daughters of a pioneer family whose story is told through quilting. Here, Annie tells about her attempts to resist the quilting chores.
YOUNG, 3.5 minutes
Quilters by Barbara Damashek and Molly Newman

475
Beneatha
Small apartment in a black Chicago ghetto, 1950s
Beneatha has just learned that her brother, Walter, has lost the insurance money from her father's death, ending her dreams to become a doctor. Here, she speaks to Asagai, a young Nigerian student and friend of the family.
YOUNG, 3 minutes
A Raisin in the Sun by Lorraine Hansberry

476
Rebecca
Nebraska, late 1800s
In a flashback scene, Rebecca writes to her sisters.
YOUNG, 2.5 minutes
Scenes and Revelations by Elan Garonzik

477
Shivaree
Shivaree has moved into the home and life of Chandler, a hemophiliac young man who is innocent and lacking experience. Here, Shivaree answers Chandler's question about life as a professional (belly) dancer.
YOUNG, 3.5 minutes
Shivaree by William Mastrosimone

478
Bonnie, puberty
Summer vacation on the Canadian shores of Lake Erie near Buffalo, New York, 1945
Bonnie enjoys playing Charlie and Ted against each other. Here she anxiously waits to meet Charlie, at night, when he returns from his job gardening for a mysterious Indian woman.
YOUNG, 2.5 minutes
What I Did Last Summer by A.R. Gurney, Jr.

479
Mounette
A concentration camp for women of mixed nationalities during the Holocaust of World War II
Here Mounette speaks of the terrors of the night.
YOUNG, 6 minutes
Who Will Carry the Word? by Charlotte Delbo, tr. by Cynthia Haft

480
Rose, a young woman
Rose's apartment in Philadelphia, Present
Rose and Cliff, who are desperate for love, are in bed. Rose's vivid dream-life often fills her lonely world. Here, she describes a dream that involved Cliff.
YOUNG, 4 minutes
The Woolgatherer by William Mastrosimone

481
Wilma, a strong girl
Harrison, Texas, 1925
Wilma was left her childhood home by her mother on the mother's deathbed. Her father wants to sell the house and take his new bride to Houston. Wilma must live with her Aunt Gertrude. Here, she tells her good friend Arabella about the pull the house and property have on her.
YOUNG, 4 minutes
A Young Lady of Property by Horton Foote

482
Orestes   **Greece, 413 B.C.**
Apollo has urged Orestes to go to Electra (his sister) and avenge the murder of their father. Here, Orestes addresses the Chorus of Argive peasant women and his sister.
YOUNG, 3.5 minutes
Electra by Euripides, tr. by Emily Townsend Vermeule

483
Hotspur   **England, ca. 1597**
Warring factions are threatening King Henry IV's throne. A letter from one who refuses to join in the rebellion irritates the "fiery" Hotspur.
YOUNG, 3 minutes
Henry IV, Part 1 by William Shakespeare

484
Callimaco
Callimaco's house in Italy, 1513-1520
Callimaco anxiously awaits the return of Ligurio, the trickster he has employed to help him carry out his plan to win the favors of the beautiful Lucrezia, young wife of a rich and aged lawyer, Nicia.
YOUNG, 3.5 minutes
The Mandrake (La Mandragola) by Niccolò Machiavelli, English version by Frederick May and Eric Bentley

485
Callimaco
Callimaco's house in Italy, 1513-1520
Callimaco rhapsodizes to Ligurio about his night with Lucrezia
YOUNG, 3 minutes
The Mandrake (La Mandragola) by Niccolò Machiavelli, English version by Frederick May and Eric Bentley

486
Faulkland   **England, 1775**
Faulkland has reprimanded Julia (his love) for her lighthearted behavior in his absence, and she has run from the room crying.
YOUNG, 2 minutes
The Rivals by Richard Brinsley Sheridan

487
Benvolio   **Verona, ca. 1595**
In this scene Benvolio (Romeo's cousin) reports to the Prince the events of a fight in which Tybalt (Juliet's cousin) killed Mercutio (kinsman to the Prince and Romeo's friend), and Romeo in turn slew Tybalt.
YOUNG, 3.5 minutes
Romeo and Juliet by William Shakespeare

488
Horace   **France, 1662**
Horace, unaware that Arnolphe is Agnès' guardian, confides to him that he barely escaped discovery in the girl's chamber.
YOUNG, 4 minutes
The School for Wives (L'École des Femmes) by Jean Baptiste Poquelin De Molière

489
Giovanni, a teenage boy   **ca. 1633**
The young and brilliant Giovanni has developed a love for his sister, the beautiful Annabella. Likewise, Annabella, while courted by several suitors, is drawn to her brother's admirable qualities. Here, Giovanni expresses the torment building within him.
YOUNG, 2 minutes
'Tis Pity She's a Whore by John Ford, edited by N.W. Bawcutt

490
Electra   **Greece, 413 B.C.**
Electra speaks to the Chorus of Women of Mycenae of her lamentable life amidst the murderers of her father.
YOUNG, 6.5 minutes
Electra by Euripides, tr. by Emily Townsend Vermeule

491
Lady Percy
England, ca. 1597
Hotspur's wife, Lady Percy, senses something is weighing heavily on her husband's mind, and she attempts to gain his confidence.
YOUNG, 3 minutes
Henry IV, Part 1 by William Shakespeare

492
Iphigenia
Greece, ca. 414 B.C.
Eldest daughter of Agamemnon and Clytemnestra and sister to Orestes and Electra, Iphigenia speaks to her maidens of a dream she has had about the death of her brother.
YOUNG, 3 minutes
Iphigenia in Tauris by Euripides, tr. by Witter Bynner

493
Joan, 17   **Vaucouleurs, France, 1429**
Here, Joan begins her story.
YOUNG, 3 minutes
The Lark (L'Alouette)by Jean Anouilh, tr. by Lillian Hellman

494
Ondine   **1939**
Ondine, a beautiful water nymph is loved by Hans, the handsome knight who falls irretrievably in love with her. Unable to remain in a world vastly different from her own, Ondine says goodbye to her lover.
YOUNG, 3 minutes
Ondine by Jean Giraudoux, adapted by Maurice Valency

495
Julia   **England, 1775**
Julia scolds Faulkland (her lover) for his restless behavior.
YOUNG, 3.5 minutes
The Rivals by Richard Brinsley Sheridan

496
Agnès   **France, 1662**
Arnolphe asks Agnès to explain why she disobeyed his orders and received a young man in her chambers.
YOUNG, 7.5 minutes
The School for Wives (L'École des Femmes) by Jean Baptiste Poquelin De Molière

497
Annabella   **ca. 1633**
The young and brilliant Giovanni has developed a love for his sister, the beautiful Annabella. Likewise, Annabella, while courted by several suitors, is drawn to her brother's admirable qualities. Here, Annabella expresses the guilt which has been tormenting her.
YOUNG, 2.5 minutes
'Tis Pity She's a Whore by John Ford, edited by N.W. Bawcutt

498
Daughter   **Thebes, 1613**
In jail, Palamon encounters the jailer's daughter. She falls madly in love with him and helps him escape. Here, Daughter considers the possibilities of Palamon's returned love.
YOUNG, 3.5 minutes
The Two Noble Kinsman by William Shakespeare and John Fletcher

499
Sammy, 19   **An A&P Supermarket, Present**
Sammy, a checker, fantasizes over three girls

who enter the store one hot day, leading to an unexpected consequence.
YOUNG, 9.5 minutes
A&P by John Updike

500
Rafael Rosa, 19
A small hotel in New York City, Present
Rafael, a Puerto Rican, is a bellhop at the hotel. The second youngest of ten brothers, he is ready to serve and happy to talk about his hopes and dreams.
YOUNG, 4 minutes
American Dreams: Lost and Found by Studs Terkel

501
Will McLean, 20s
Carolina Military Institute, Present
Will is a defiant senior cadet whose personal code of honor is greater than his superiors. A young man of integrity, he risks his life and the love of his girlfriend to expose the injustice and corruption in the institution. Here, Will has just entered the Armory to play his last basketball game for the Institute.
YOUNG, 4 minutes
The Lords of Discipline by Pat Conroy

502
Will McLean, 20s
Carolina Military Institute, Present
Will confides in his friend Mark about his insecurities with women and his love for one particular girl.
YOUNG, 2.5 minutes
The Lords of Discipline by Pat Conroy

503
Owen, a young man
New Hampshire, Present
Owen believes he is an instrument of God. John, his lifelong friend is profoundly moved by Owen's beliefs, passions, and uniqueness. Here, the book's startling climax brings life to Owen's terrifying prophesy.
YOUNG, 7.5 minutes
A Prayer for Owen Meany by John Irving

504
Gene, 16
Devon, a boy's preparatory school in New England, 1942
Two sixteen-year-old friends, the academically brilliant and cautious Gene and the fearless and athletically gifted Phineas (Finny). Finny has just coaxed Gene into heading for the beach for a swim.
YOUNG, 8.5 minutes
A Separate Peace by John Knowles

505
Willie Metcalf
Town of Spoon River, near Petersburg, Illinois, Present
Spoon River Anthology is a series of poetic monologues spoken by real and fictional inhabitants of the imaginary town. All are now dead and "sleeping on the hill." Each character speaks their own epitaphs.
YOUNG, 3 minutes
Spoon River Anthology by Edgar Lee Masters

506
Harry Wilmans, 21
Town of Spoon River, near Petersburg, Illinois, Present
Spoon River Anthology is a series of poetic monologues spoken by real and fictional inhabitants of the imaginary town. All are now dead and "sleeping on the hill." Each character speaks their own epitaphs.
YOUNG, 3 minutes
Spoon River Anthology by Edgar Lee Masters

507
Pete, 16
In a bedroom Pete shares with his cousin, Sucker, Present
Here, Pete is attempting to make sense of recent events that have caused him and Sucker considerable emotional pain.
YOUNG, 4 minutes
Sucker by Carson McCullers

508
Linda Haas, 16
A large technical high school in Chicago, Present
Linda isn't certain whether she'll go on to college, but she does want to make her mark in the world.
YOUNG, 3.5 minutes
American Dreams: Lost and Found by Studs Terkel

509
Jennifer, a young mother   Present
In this scene, Jenny recalls a discovery she made in her favorite room in Grandmother's house.
YOUNG, 3 minutes
Artists by Lee Smith

510
Barbara Keller, 20
A college west of Chicago, 1988
Here, Barbara is beginning to find her direction in life.
YOUNG, 4 minutes
The Great Divide: Second Thoughts on the American Dream by Studs Terkel

511
Faith Matheny
Town of Spoon River, near Petersburg, Illinois, Present
Spoon River Anthology is a series of poetic monologues spoken by real and fictional inhabitants of the imaginary town. All are now dead and "sleeping on the hill." Each character speaks their own epitaphs.
YOUNG, 2 minutes
Spoon River Anthology by Edgar Lee Masters

512
Flossie Cabanis
Town of Spoon River, near Petersburg, Illinois, Present
Spoon River Anthology is a series of poetic monologues spoken by real and fictional inhabitants of the imaginary town. All are now dead and "sleeping on the hill." Each character speaks their own epitaphs.
YOUNG, 1.5 minutes
Spoon River Anthology by Edgar Lee Masters

513
Elsa Wertman
Town of Spoon River, near Petersburg, Illinois, Present
Spoon River Anthology is a series of poetic monologues spoken by real and fictional inhabitants of the imaginary town. All are now dead and "sleeping on the hill." Each character speaks their own epitaphs.
YOUNG, 3 minutes
Spoon River Anthology by Edgar Lee Masters

514
Leo, 20s   **NYC, Present**
Leo and Jeannie meet at a New Year's Eve party. Leo continuously complains about the loss of his umbrella a year ago. Jeannie suggests he look into his obsession and asks if he is in therapy. Leo snaps back.
EST, 3.5 minutes
Lost and Found by Peter Maloney

515
Calvin Jefferson, 18   **NYC, Present**
Calvin Jefferson has been admitted to City College on an open admissions policy. Underprivileged and desperate to succeed, he is "a bright, sensitive street person, trying to beat the odds." He realizes that his speech teacher is oblivious to him and other black students in her class, giving them "B's" whether they have earned them or not, and cheating him out of really learning something. Here, he defiantly confronts her, trying to make her see how she has been treating him.
EST, 4.5 minutes
Open Admissions by Shirley Lauro

516
Conrad Thacker, 30s
NYC, Present
Hearing a tape of his new play by Critic Bax Raving, Thacker argues with the critic and in an ensuing fight strangles him. He then exults.
EST, 1 minute
The Smash by Neil Cuthbert

517
Angelo, 45   **A movie theater, Present**
Angelo, a blue-collar guy, reveals his feelings about putting his father into a nursing home.
EST, 1 minute
Stuck in the Pictures on a Sunday Afternoon by Bill Bozzone

518
Richard, 35
A movie theater, Present
After making violent love to Beth Ann, Richard becomes enraged by her idiotic and inane responses to everything and bludgeons her to death with a bottle. Here, Richard describes the crime he has just committed to Angelo, who is also at the movie theater avoiding the fact that he has just committed his father to a state-run institution for the aged.
EST, 4.5 minutes
Stuck in the Pictures on a Sunday Afternoon by Bill Bozzone

519
Clark, middle-aged   **Suburbia, Present**
Clark has been fired from his job because of a disagreement with his boss, Mr. Spivak, who, according to Clark, is a "four-star horse's ass." When his son gets the flu, Clark takes over his paper route. He enjoys the freedom, the lack of stress and the fresh air, until he discovers that the contemptible Spivak is on his son's route. Clark decides that Spivak doesn't deserve the funnies and tears them out of Spivak's paper. Eventually, Clark, who refuses to look for a new job, loses everything. The play ends with Clark accepting an invitation for a drink with a woman who had befriended him on his morning route. Here, Clark describes the first morning he took over his son's paper route.
EST, 4.5 minutes
Routed by Jeffrey Sweet

520
Clark, middle-aged   **Suburbia, Present**
Here, Clark describes what happened to another friend who was fired from a job he hated.
EST, 2.5 minutes
Routed by Jeffrey Sweet

521
Frank, middle-aged
Midwest, Summer 1947
It was hard for women after the War. All the factory jobs reverted to the home-coming soldiers. Reba and April were forced into another line of work. April thinks she has found a way out of the "world's oldest profession" by marrying one of her customers—that is, until Frank, another regular customer, shows up after having shot his wife and her lover. Here, Frank describes how, after returning home with a birthday cake for his wife, he discovers her in bed with someone. Upset and confused, he shoots them both.
EST, 2.5 minutes
Bite the Hand by Ara Watson

522
Bobby, 20s   **NYC, Present**
Robert is a lonely attorney who stayed at the office very late in order not to worry about celebrating, or rather not celebrating, his thirtieth birthday. While walking home in the rain that night, he is solicited by a hustler named Bobby. On an impulse, Robert takes him home to his apartment. Robert is really seeking intimacy with a person, more than sex. Bobby, on the other hand, is cynical and all business. Ultimately, Robert realizes that Bobby doesn't understand warmth or compassion, but only reacts to coercion and humiliation. In this monologue, Bobby, realizing that Robert is sending him away, reacts by deliberately baiting Robert into retaliating physically.
EST, 4 minutes
Cash by Stuart Spencer

523
Jerry, 40s   **NYC, Present**
This is a surreal play about two ad executives, Jerry Tremendous and Paul Pill (Tremendous-Pill). Both are going through mid-life crises. Pill wants to sell out. Jerry, the intense partner, is becoming increasingly disinterested. In this monologue, Paul has just told Jerry of his plan to leave the business and move to Maine. Jerry, terrified that his sanity is slipping away from him, tries to persuade Paul to reconsider.
EST, 2.5 minutes
The Dolphin Position by Percy Granger

524
Rawley, 30s-40s
NYC, Present
Two friends, Rawley and Ron, have met for lunch at a new, trendy fast-food joint. A relatively happily married man, Ron has had a quarrel with his wife over her job, which would relocate them to San Francisco. During the course of the lunch, Ron has second thoughts and is now considering going along with his wife. Rawley is a divorced playboy and would dearly like to have Ron in the same condition to keep him company. Here, in order to convince Ron to leave his wife, Rawley paints a rosy picture of what it would be like if the two of them were to open a restaurant like the one they are sitting in.
EST, 4 minutes
Two Hotdogs with Everything by William Wise

525
Linc, 22   **Punk Rock Club, Present**
Linc and Mel are two friends who find an outlet for their confusion and directionless lives in punk rock slam dancing. Here, Linc, who is described as a "sometimes high school . . . brooding, pensive, but not without a sense of humor," tells Mel why he has decided to join the Marines.
EST, 4 minutes
Slam! by Jane Willis

526
Mel, 19   **Punk Rock Club, Present**
Mel, who is described as "not really inarticulate, just confused," responds that he, too, is fed up with his dreary life. Not as bright as Linc, he mistakes Linc's statement that he feels like a droid, a robot. Mel agrees that he feels like a droid, too.
EST, 4 minutes
Slam! by Jane Willis

527
Phil, 20s-30s   **New Jersey, Summer**
After holding up a convenience store, Phil and his girlfriend Rebecca are holed up in a hotel with the kidnapped manager Walt. Walt is being kept tied and blindfolded. He also happens to be a childhood friend of Phil. Rebecca's plan to make their way down to Florida, robbing convenience stores on the way, reaches a sticky point when she tries to convince Phil to shoot his old friend. Ultimately, Rebecca takes off with the money and leaves the two friends behind. Here, Phil tells Walt about his girlfriend, Rebecca.
EST, 4 minutes
Desperadoes by Keith Reddin

528
Bobbie, 26   **A bedroom, Present**
Coming from a dysfunctional welfare family with an alcoholic father and an abusive mother, Carol has made a success of her life over enormous odds. Carol's father is dying of cirrhosis of the liver. Carol has come to her younger brother's room to try to get him to

drop out of a self-destructive lethargy. She wants him to get clean of drugs and alcohol and face the reality of his life. Here, Bobbie finally reveals to Carol what has caused his alienation from life and triggered his downward spiral.
EST, 6.5 minutes
North of Providence by Edward Allan Baker

529
Willy, 30s-40s   **South Africa, Present**
In South Africa, black Africans like Willy, Samson, Henry and Pete live with the knowledge that dead-end jobs like painting walls is pretty much what they're stuck with – that indeed, they are lucky to have any job. Willy is the least resigned to his predicament. In this monologue, he explains to Samson why he was late for work.
EST, 6 minutes
Painting a Wall by David Lan

530
Willy, 30s-40s   **South Africa, Present**
Here, Willy vents his frustrations over the limits that lack of education places on him and his people.
EST, 5.5 minutes
Painting a Wall by David Lan

531
Samson, 30s-40s   **South Africa, Present**
Here, Willy's friend Samson tells an ironic story about his sister, who was once a clumsy maid for rich people, married well and now complains about her own clumsy maids.
EST, 5 minutes
Painting a Wall by David Lan

532
Bobby, 30s   **A gym, Present**
Bobby, an ex-con who runs a gym, is attracted to Laila, a woman who works out there obsessively. Laila, trapped in a troubled and abusive marriage, has Bobby arrested for rape in order to protect her husband. In this monologue, Bobby is angry at Laila for rejecting him. He accuses her of killing people with the cholesterol-rich food she serves in her catering business.
EST, 1.5 minutes
Mink on a Gold Hook by James Ryan

533
Lewis, 28   **An apartment, Present**
Lewis is a young doctor in residency at Lenox Hill hospital. Lewis is immature and confused about matters of the heart. He has recently broken up with Cecilia, a spoiled socialite, in order to date their mutual friend, Robin, a ju-

nior at Vassar. Even so, Lewis finds it hard not to sleep with Cecilia from time to time, for old time's sake. Here, after nearly losing Robin due to his philandering, Lewis confesses to her that he really loves her.
EST, 3.5 minutes
Moonlight Kisses by Stuart Spencer

534
Gordon, 60   **SoHo, 1982**
Gordon Tate, a sixtyish writer, who has been married several times, finds himself in love with Milly, a young student who makes him feel alive again. Gordon's various artist friends disapprove but tolerate this relationship. Grady, also a writer, and one of Gordon's ex-wives, regards his affair with Milly as a descent into a second childhood. Gordon tries to explain to Grady why he loves Milly.
EST, 1 minute
April Snow by Romulus Linney

535
Richard, 23   **West Texas, 1971**
Richard has just wandered into Sarah's house and made himself at home. He met Sarah a week ago and has not been heard from since. She asks him what he's been up to and why he has a bandage on his wrist.
EST, 3 minutes
Dinah Washington is Dead by Kermit Frazier

536
Billy, 20-30   **Lady of Fadima Hospital, 1987**
Terri, a young black woman who works for the hospital and needs her job desperately, is being sexually harassed by a superior. She turns to the older, more experienced Val for help. Here, Billy (the superior), trying to get Terri to be intimate with him, says it like it is.
EST, 1 minute
Lady of Fadima by Edward Allan Baker

537
Phil, 20s-30s
A beach house, Present
Batcho, a young gay man, has decided not to vacate his summer rental home at the end of the season to return to his business in the city. He prefers to stay with Gus, the ghost of his lover who died of AIDS. Batcho meets Phil, who has stayed to clean and close up the cottages. A mutual attraction develops, but Phil has lost friends to AIDS, too, and as a result is celibate. Here, Phil reveals to Batcho why he loves to watch the stars and remember remembering all the beautiful things he used to have before he lost so much.
EST, 1.5 minutes
The Last Outpost at the Edge of the World by Stuart Spencer

538
Hugh, 45   **A country home, Present**
Margie and Hugh are a brother and sister who
have had some major setbacks in their lives. In
the past, Margie had a child out of wedlock
who was frail and sickly and who she had difficulty supporting. Only her brother Hugh was
there to help her and be a father to little Billy.
Now, Margie is married and her life has im-
proved, but Hugh, an idealistic dreamer, has
lost his job and Margie is determined to help
him. Here, Hugh reveals both his touching optimism and his lack of realism when he clings
to the hope that if he is kind to all, someday he
will be left a lot of money in someone's will.
EST, 2 minutes
A Million Dollar Glass of Water by Anthony McKay

539
Terry, 30s
Maine, the week after Labor Day
Emma and her friend Heisey are old regulars
at a Maine resort. Emma, who writes a column
for a paper, needs the peace and quiet after the
season ends. Heisey is a retired English teacher
who enjoys the mental stimulation of Emma's
acerbic wit. Emma is a champion of causes and
rights for the disadvantaged, but she has a
great deal of trouble with personal relationships and is lonely and bitter. Terry, a stranger
to the hotel, arrives and connects with Emma.
Strange and desperately unhappy, he awakens
something in Emma. Here, Terry confides to
Emma some of the turmoil he has felt following the death of his wife.
EST, 4.5 minutes
Neptune's Hips by Richard Greenberg

540
Terry, 30s
Maine, the week after Labor Day
Here, Terry tells Emma about his tragic life.
EST, 1 minute
Neptune's Hips by Richard Greenberg

541
Tom, 36   **NYC, 1987**
Tom, a baker by profession, has been arrested
for the possible mercy killing of his AIDS-in-
fected gay lover. Here, Tom tells the police
about his relationship with Johnny and what
happened at the end.
EST, 10 minutes
A Poster of the Cosmos by Lanford Wilson

542
Man 1, middle-aged   **Break room, Present**
In this short play, two construction workers
are on a lunch break when, out of the blue, the
Blessed Virgin Mary appears to them, dressed
like a cafeteria worker. Here, Man #1 com-
plains about his job and his life in general.
EST, 7 minutes
Break by Michael John LaChiusa

543
Leroy, 48
A hospital waiting room, Present
Leroy Hamilton and Mr. Frick meet in the
waiting room of a state mental hospital. Both
of their wives are suffering from anxiety and
depression. This is Mr. Frick's first experience
at the hospital, whereas Mr. Hamilton has had
to admit his wife several times. Mr. Frick is a
successful businessman who could have easily
afforded a private hospital for his wife. He discovers that even though Leroy is descended
from Alexander Hamilton, he is "only" a car-
penter. Frick's condescension toward Leroy
and his line of work sparks this angry response
from Leroy.
EST, 3.5 minutes
The Last Yankee by Arthur Miller

544
Harvey, 20s   **A classroom, Present**
When Laura shows up for an adult Spanish
class, Harvey is already there. He has erased
the notice on the blackboard that the class has
been rescheduled. He wants a chance to talk to
her. Harvey is Laura's mailman and has loved
her from afar. He even went as far as opening
a "Dear Jane" letter from Laura's boyfriend.
Here, Harvey explains why he opened her
mail.
EST, 4.5 minutes
You Can't Trust the Male by Randy Noojin

545
Dotty, 50s   **NYC, Present**
Dotty, who lives in her own world, goes to the
rooftop on a cool summer's eve to dream and
remember.
EST, 2 minutes
Dotty the Dribbly Doodlin' Dame by Dimo Condos

546
She, 21   **A waiting room, Present**
A man and a woman are sitting in the waiting
room of an abortion clinic discussing their
pasts and their present situation. When she
tells him that she has faked orgasms with him,
he doesn't believe her. She responds angrily.
EST, 1 minute
Last Rite for Snow White by Robin Wagner

547
Rosemary, 26   **NYC, Present**
Rosemary and George are in a hotel room con-
templating sex as vengeance on their spouses,

who are having an affair. They are having problems getting it on. She becomes contemplative.
EST, 1.5 minutes
George and Rosemary by Robin Wagner

548
Diane, 20s　　　　　　　　**NYC, Present**
Diane visits her childhood Catholic schoolteacher, Sister Mary Ignatius. Sister criticizes Diane's lack of devotion to God and Catholicism. Diane explains her attitude.
EST, 2 minutes
Sister Mary Ignatius Explains It All for You by Christopher Durang

549
Lola, 50s　　　　　　　　**NYC, Present**
Upon hearing a preview of drama critic Bax Raving's scathing review of the show she has just directed, Lola approaches Raving.
EST, 1 minute
The Smash by Neil Cuthbert

550
Lola, 50s　　　　　　　　**NYC, Present**
Lola, having directed a play by Conrad Thacker, which is about to be panned, tries to encourage Thacker to go on.
EST, 2 minutes
The Smash by Neil Cuthbert

551
Florence, middle-aged　　　　**Suburbia, Present**
Florence Jones works as a housekeeper and baby-sitter to a white couple and their daughter Karen. Although she is not related to Karen, she has been the one constant, nurturing presence in Karen's life. When Karen learns that her self-centered parents are getting a divorce, her own guilt feelings lead her to accuse Florence of causing the breakup by usurping her love, which Karen feels might have kept her parents together. Here, Flo chides Karen, telling her that it is not Karen's fault that her parents are splitting up.
EST, 4 minutes
Blood Bond by Gina Barnett

552
Rebecca, 20s　　　　　　　**New Jersey, Summer**
After holding up a convenience store, Phil and his girlfriend Rebecca are holed up in a hotel with the kidnapped manager Walt. Walt is being kept tied and blindfolded. He also happens to be a childhood friend of Phil. Here, Rebecca describes their first robbery attempt to Walt.
EST, 3.5 minutes
Desperadoes by Keith Reddin

553
Vera Rose, 60　　　　**Midwest, December 1980**
Vera Rose's cosmopolitan daughter Rosa has come down to be with Vera while Ma Rose, Vera's mother, is dying. Vera Rose is very agitated and Rosa yells at her. Vera tells her daughter off.
EST, 1 minute
Ma Rose by Cassandra Medley

554
Cecilia, 27　　　　　　**An apartment, Present**
Lewis is a young doctor in residency at Lenox Hill hospital. Lewis is immature and confused about matters of the heart. He has recently broken up with Cecilia, a spoiled socialite, in order to date their mutual friend, Robin, a junior at Vassar. Even so, Lewis finds it hard not to sleep with Cecilia from time to time, for old time's sake. Although they have broken up, Cecilia is still attracted to Lewis and has spent the night with him. The next morning she speaks to Lewis.
EST, 1.5 minutes
Moonlight Kisses by Stuart Spencer

555
Milly, 20　　　　　　　　**SoHo, 1982**
Gordon Tate, a sixtyish writer, who has been married several times, finds himself in love with Milly, a young student who makes him feel alive again. In this monologue, Milly reminds Gordon of the nervous breakdown she had after the death of her parents.
EST, 2 minutes
April Snow by Romulus Linney

556
Milly, 20　　　　　　　　**SoHo, 1982**
Milly, hurt by Gordon's decision not to take her to Spain with him, goes out to a bar. Here, she describes to Gordon and his friends her disastrous experience.
EST, 1 minute
April Snow by Romulus Linney

557
Sarah, 43　　　　　　　**West Texas, 1971**
Sarah is having an affair with a man twenty years her junior. She is insecure and testy. They argue. He patronizes her. She defends herself.
EST, 2.5 minutes
Dinah Washington is Dead by Kermit Frazier

558
Val, middle-aged
Lady of Fadima Hospital, 1987
Terri, a young black woman who works for the hospital and needs her job desperately, is being sexually harassed by a superior. She

turns to the older, more experienced Val for help. Here, Val, who needs her job just as badly, angrily refuses to get involved.
EST, 2 minutes
Lady of Fadima by Edward Allan Baker

559
Jane, 37   **SoHo, Present**
Philip French is a young, successful director who is most effective directing women. He has been hired to direct a well-known actress, Jane Zane, in the lead in *Ibsen's Ghosts*. Jane has an unusual vision of how Mrs. Alving should be played. She tells Philip that rather than help her son to die, as the play implies, Mrs. Alving would do anything to save her son's life.
EST, 5.5 minutes
Juliet by Romulus Linney

560
Esther, 50   **SoHo, Present**
Philip's mother has overheard the exchange between Philip and Jane, including Philip's skepticism that a mother would go so far for a son. Esther makes an equally fantastic offer to her son. She reveals that, like Jane's Mrs. Alving, Esther and Philip have always shared repressed Oedipal feelings.
EST, 5.5 minutes
Juliet by Romulus Linney

561
Iris, 30s   **Rural New England, Present**
Wilbur Arnold, a black doctor, has married Iris and gone to live with her and his seven-year-old daughter in a small town. Iris has a history of deep insecurities which are returning after two years with Wilbur. She wants them to leave town. Wilbur assures her that this is a good place for them and that he has saved her. Iris blows.
EST, 1.5 minutes
Outside the Radio by Kermit Frazier

562
Venus, 20s
An eating disorder clinic, Present
Venus rejects the spa cure as the answer for her and explains why.
EST, 4.5 minutes
Pathological Venus by Brighde Mullins

563
Adel, middle-aged
A dining room, Present
Bethany is married to Alvin but in love with Carl. When Adel, Carl's wife, finds out about Bethany and Carl, she attempts suicide, then seeks revenge. Alvin is happy simply cooking. He equates life with a great kitchen. Carl is a writer whose characters are thinly disguised portraits of Bethany and Adel. Bethany hates Carl's portrayal of her in his novel and decides not to run away with him. Eventually, Carl persuades Adel to come back to him, leaving a confused Alvin and Bethany to sort it out. Here, Adel describes her feelings of paranoia to Bethany, since Carl cheated on her.
EST, 1.5 minutes
Self Torture and Strenuous Exercise by Harry Kondoleon

564
Adel, middle-aged
A dining room, Present
Here, Adel tells Bethany that marriage is a trap.
EST, 1 minute
Self Torture and Strenuous Exercise by Harry Kondoleon

565
Bethany, middle-aged
A dining room, Present
Bethany, who is unhappy in love, turns to poetry.
EST, 4 minutes
Self Torture and Strenuous Exercise by Harry Kondoleon

566
Agnes, any age   **A street corner, Present**
Agnes is about a woman who is trapped in a wheelchair, until she tricks a thief into setting her free. Here, Agnes laments about being stuck in her wheelchair, forever waiting to be let out.
EST, 4 minutes
Agnes by Michael John LaChiusa

567
Agnes, any age   **A street corner, Present**
Here, Agnes tells the man who is attempting to rob her that while watching a game show, she had a vision of a beautiful place where she was meant to go.
EST, 5 minutes
Agnes by Michael John LaChiusa

568
Jessica, 20s-30s   **An apartment, Present**
Jessica and Bill, who live together, are captive in a relationship that doesn't work anymore. When Arthur, a co-worker of Jessica's, makes a pass at her, she and Bill keep him captive in their apartment by tying him up. They hope the novelty of this bizarre situation will salvage their love. Jessica finally lets a confused and somewhat reluctant Arthur go. Bill admits that he no longer loves her and is leaving.

Here, Jessica predicts what will happen to her once she loses Bill.
EST, 3.5 minutes
Captive by Paul Weitz

569
Girl, late teens   **A hotel hallway**
In this short play, a motley group of residents of a single-room occupancy hotel wait to use a bathroom which, like everything else in the hotel and in their lives, needs to be fixed—hopefully by Mr. Hamm—who may or may not be dead. Here, a young girl rhapsodizes over San Francisco, where the boy who left her went, and where she hopes to go.
EST, 6 minutes
Eulogy for Mister Hamm by Michael John LaChiusa

570
Woman, 50s   **A hotel hallway**
Here, a female resident can't stand her room any more.
EST, 5 minutes
Eulogy for Mister Hamm by Michael John LaChiusa

571
Celeste, 40   **Perth Amboy, Present**
Celeste, a widow for 17 years, lives with her rebellious 18-year-old daughter and a large statue of The Sacred Heart, to which she constantly prays. When she makes a desperate plea to the statue to provide her daughter with a date to the prom, The Sacred Heart himself shows up, in a powder blue tux. Here, Celeste tells The Sacred Heart that even though his statue crushed her husband to death, she doesn't blame him or regret the lost years.
EST, 2 minutes
The Second Coming by Bill Bozzone

572
Wilma, 30s   **Northern Vermont, Present**
Wilma and Manny have a perfect marriage all year, until winter when Manny gets a case of cabin fever so bad he constantly deserts his wife. When he is there, he doesn't communicate with her. One snowy day, a man named Robbie Riddiker and his young daughter become snowbound with them. The vibrant widower and his precocious little girl become a catalyst for Wilma and Manny. Manny reacts to their presence with jealousy, Wilma with joy at the respite from boredom and frustration. Here, Wilma reveals to Robbie how she thrives on Manny's jealousy.
EST, 3 minutes
Stay Away a Little Closer by John Ford Noonan

573
Naomi, 50s   **A living room, Present**

In this absurdist comedy, John, a cross-dresser who wants to be just like his wife, brings her to visit his psychotic mother Naomi, who entertains them by screaming at them and making them move one piece of furniture to the other. Here, Naomi, insulted and furious because her son dresses like his wife but not like her, drives the couple out of the house.
EST, 3 minutes
Naomi in the Living Room by Christopher Durang

574
First Lady, 30s
Air Force 1, November 22, 1963
Over Texas is a poetical supposition of what it might have been like for the two personal secretaries of Kennedy and his wife on the day just before the assassination. Here, the First Lady recites what she saw, heard and felt as she rode through Dallas in the open car with her husband.
EST, 6.5 minutes
Over Texas by Michael John LaChiusa

575
Laura, 20s   **A classroom, Present**
When Laura shows up for an adult Spanish class, Harvey is already there. He has erased the notice on the blackboard that the class has been rescheduled. He wants a chance to talk to her. Harvey is Laura's mailman and has loved her from afar. He even went as far as opening a "Dear Jane" letter from Laura's boyfriend. Here, Laura reveals that she opened her boyfriend's mail to discover that he was cheating on her.
EST, 3 minutes
You Can't Trust the Male by Randy Noojin

576
Weller Martin, 70s
Retirement home, Present
Weller talks to his "girlfriend," Fonsia, about an experience of old age which recently befell him. Dramatic.
GMHUM, 1 minute
The Gin Game by D.L. Coburn

577
Weller Martin, 70s
Retirement home, Present
Weller loves to play gin rummy. He lives in a retirement home. He has taught the game to a recent arrival, Fonsia Dorsey, but has been unable to defeat her even one time. Rage and frustration is gradually overcoming him. He prepares to deal a new hand to Fonsia. Seriocomic.
GMHUM, 1.5 minutes
The Gin Game by D.L. Coburn

578
Arlie, 20s   **Southern prison, Present**
Arlie, who is in prison for murder, talks to a pillow in her cell as if it were the baby which was taken away from her and placed in a foster home. Dramatic.
GMHUM, 2 minutes
Getting Out by Marsha Norman

579
Roy, late 20s   **Texas, Present**
Roy is drunk on a Friday night outside Angel's bar. He tells about early experiences in his beloved pink convertible. Comic.
GMHUM, 2.5 minutes
Lone Star by James McLure

580
Annmarie, late 20s
Massachusetts, Present
Annmarie, who is a compulsive eater and who periodically spends time away from her husband, meets Delia, who has a similar story, at a motel. Annmarie tells Delia about her sex life. Dramatic.
GMHUM, 4.5 minutes
Chocolate Cake by Mary Gallagher

581
Chug, 20s   **Rural Indiana, Present**
Chug tells why he likes his girlfriend Freda (and let go of Moo-Moo). Seriocomic.
GMHUM, 5.5 minutes
Chug by Ken Jenkins

582
Edna Bloodwell, middle-aged
Iowa, Present
Due to a blizzard, Sandra Warsaw Stein, a Columbia University instructor has become stranded at the Lucky 6 Motel. Edna, a bitter and judgmental proprietor of the motel, decides to lecture politics to Sandra. Dramatic.
GMHUM, 2.5 minutes
Nothing Immediate by Shirley Lauro

583
Cemetery Man, 65   **Cemetery, Present**
Cemetery Man, the grave digger, is reminiscing about his career. Comic.
GMHUM, 5 minutes
Cemetery Man by Ken Jenkins

584
Raul, 30s   **Suburban house, Present**
Raul has forcibly entered Marjorie's house and is in the process of abusing and raping her. Dramatic.
GMHUM, 1.5 minutes
Extremities by William Mastrosimone

585
Raul, 30s   **Surburban house, Present**
Raul, in the process of abusing and raping Marjorie, has had the tables turned on him. He is now blindfolded and bound and is appealing to Marjorie, now his captor, for release. Dramatic.
GMHUM, 2 minutes
Extremities by William Mastrosimone

586
Marjorie, 20s-30s
Surburban house, Present
Marjorie has captured and bound Raul, who was in the process of abusing and raping her. She is now abusing him. Her roommate has returned home, and has accused Marjorie of becoming like Raul. Marjorie replies. Dramatic.
GMHUM, 1 minute
Extremities by William Mastrosimone

587
Lea, 14-16   **Lemas, France, 1933**
Lea and her sister, Christine, are hired out as domestics by their mother. Lea has just begun a new job and speaks to Christine, who is also her figure of mother-love. Dramatic.
GMHUM, 3.5 minutes
My Sister in This House by Wendy Kesselman

588
Sverre Lundgrensen, 40s
Montana, August 1915
Sverre Lundgrensen is a Norwegian immigrant who has found work fixing up Clara O'Keefe's farm. Having realized that Clara is not only crazy but also poor, he has just returned from town where he has gotten drunk and into trouble. Seriocomic.
GMHUM, 3 minutes
Clara's Play by John Olive

589
Sarah Johnson, 35   **Arkansas, 1959**
Sarah, an unsophisticated farm woman, surprises Jean, a sophisticated young (17) lady, with a cleverly presented ghost story. Seriocomic.
GMHUM, 4.5 minutes
A Different Moon by Ara Watson

590
Ric, late 20s   **Omaha, Present**
Ric finds his wife Beth hiding in her mother's mobile home. He tells her that he knows about her indiscretion. Dramatic.
GMHUM, 2.5 minutes
Full Hookup by Conrad Bishop and Elizabeth Fuller

591
Beth, 25   **Omaha, 1980-1981**
Beth is talking to her lover on the telephone. She is fearful of her husband finding out about the affair. Dramatic.
GMHUM, 3.5 minutes
Full Hookup by Conrad Bishop and Elizabeth Fuller

592
Joellen, late 20s   **Omaha, 1980-1981**
Office supervisor Joellen talks about Rosie, one of her office workers. Seriocomic.
GMHUM, 1.5 minutes
Full Hookup by Conrad Bishop and Elizabeth Fuller

593
Rosie, 50s   **Omaha, 1980-1981**
Rosie's daughter has been murdered by her son-in-law Ric but she believes he is innocent. Rosie practices her testimony for the defense for Ric's upcoming trial. Dramatic.
GMHUM, 5 minutes
Full Hookup by Conrad Bishop and Elizabeth Fuller

594
McCormack, 55   **City, Present**
Mrs. McCormack is interviewing a 35-year-old mainstream dropout, who wants to drop back in, for a night watchman's job. When she indicates "no," he complains about society's "vicious damn circle." She takes this personally and replies. Dramatic.
GMHUM, 4.5 minutes
Bartok As Dog by Patrick Tovatt

595
Emma Bredahl, 16   **Minnesota, 1926**
Emma has been persuaded by her mother to try on her wedding dress. Her brother, Samuel and his friend, Anders have been teasing her and have left for a college party. She is trying to remove the dress and is speaking angrily. Dramatic.
GMHUM, 2.5 minutes
In a Northern Landscape by Timothy Mason

596
Ambrose, 60ish
Metropolis, USA, Present
Ambrose is a derelict with style. He is invited into the apartment of a single young woman, Dafne, whose heart goes out to him. He is arrogant and argumentative in response to her kindness. In a burst of anger she throws a bowl of soup at him. She then apologies and hands him a towel. Ambrose responds. Dramatic.
GMHUM, 3.5 minutes
A Tantalizing by William Mastrosimone

597
Ambrose, 60ish
Metropolis, USA, Present
Ambrose, a derelict, has been welcomed by a young woman, Dafne, into her apartment. She has fed him and is attempting to clean him up when she discovers he is bleeding from a dog bite. She asks why the dog bit him. Dramatic.
GMHUM, 1.5 minutes
A Tantalizing by William Mastrosimone

598
Dafne, late 20s   **Metropolis, USA, Present**
Dafne has taken a derelict, Ambrose, into her apartment. He angrily bemoans his lot to her. His talk stirs memories of Dafne's father, who met with a tragic and untimely demise. Dafne speaks to Ambrose about her father. Dramatic.
GMHUM, 3 minutes
A Tantalizing by William Mastrosimone

599
Benny Silverman, 70
Hollywood Hills, Present
Benny's daughter, an aspiring actress, has just told him that she landed a part in a play which requires her to take her top off. Benny reacts negatively. She defends the play's seriousness. Benny replies. Seriocomic.
GMHUM, 1.5 minutes
The Value of Names by Jeffrey Sweet

600
Jim, 30s   **Wisconsin, 1979**
Jim reminisces to his sister-in-law, Doe, of a weekend with Nessa, his former girlfriend who has since chosen lesbianism as a result of her feminist philosophy. Dramatic.
GMHUM, 3 minutes
A Weekend Near Madison by Kathleen Tolan

601
Nessa, 30s   **Wisconsin, 1979**
Nessa, a lesbian who has recently "come out," defends her position to an old friend, David. Dramatic.
GMHUM, 2.5 minutes
A Weekend Near Madison by Kathleen Tolan

602
Laura, 17   **Harrison, Texas, 1917**
Laura and her older (20) sister Elizabeth have strict, overbearing parents. Laura reveals some of her fears to Elizabeth. Dramatic.
GMHUM, 2 minutes
Courtship by Horton Foote

603
Douglas Schmidt, 30s-40s

San Francisco, 1978
Douglas Schmidt, defense attorney for Dan
White who is on trial for the murder of San
Francisco Mayor Moscone and Supervisor
Harvey Milk, gives his closing statements to
the court. Dramatic.
GMHUM, 13.5 minutes
Execution of Justice by Emily Mann

604
Harry, 37   **Kentucky farm, Present**
Harry, who is visiting his parents at their farm
with his wife Bev, realizes that his parents can't
"make it" as farmers any longer because of the
"bureaucratic system." He discusses the un-
fairness of this situation with Bev. Dramatic.
GMHUM, 3.5 minutes
Husbandry by Patrick Tovatt

605
Harry, 37   **Kentucky farm, Present**
Harry, who has come to visit his folks at their
farm, realizes that they cannot "make it" as
farmers without his help. He tries to convince
his wife, Bev, that they should become farmers
in order to save the farm. Dramatic.
GMHUM, 2 minutes
Husbandry by Patrick Tovatt

606
Dee, 55   **Kentucky farm, Present**
Dee, realizing that she and her husband may
have to give up their farm, discusses with her
daughter-in-law, Bev, what will become of the
farm's contents. Dramatic.
GMHUM, 2 minutes
Husbandry by Patrick Tovatt

607
Desenelle, 55   **South, Present**
Desenelle is the super-secretary/office manager
who runs the show at Beuchel Goodee Motors
(car dealership). Here she returns from lunch.
Comic.
GMHUM, 2 minutes
Lemons by Kent Broadhurst

608
Connie, 56   **Rhode Island, 1944**
Connie, whose bad luck is giving her great
trouble, tells her sister about her confrontation
with a neighbor during their monthly bridge
game. Comic.
GMHUM, 2.5 minutes
The Octette Bridge Club by P.J. Barry

609
Martha, 64   **Rhode Island, 1944**
Martha, a widow in failing health, reveals

some of her frustrations to her sister during
their monthly bridge game. Dramatic.
GMHUM, 1.5 minutes
The Octette Bridge Club by P.J. Barry

610
Betsy, 47   **Rhode Island, 1944**
Betsy, who has recently returned from a
lengthy stay in an asylum, tells her sisters the
raw truth during their monthly bridge game.
Dramatic.
GMHUM, 3 minutes
The Octette Bridge Club by P.J. Barry

611
Joe Cernikowski, 40
Centralia, PA, Present
Centralia has fallen victim to a huge underground mine fire which is gradually destroying
the town above it and the people in it by fire or
noxious gases. Joe has just lost his wife Wilma,
daughter Doublemint, and son Skeeter. He
confronts his solitude and fears. Dramatic.
GMHUM, 4.5 minutes
The Roots of Chaos by Douglas Soderberg

612
Man, mid-20s   **Small Town, USA, 1945**
Tom is just home from the war. He has just
kissed his wife Margaret and tells her of his
optimism. Dramatic.
GMHUM, 2 minutes
The American Century by Murphy Guyer

613
Ora Belle Ivey, 50-60
Nursing home, Present
Ora Belle and Ruby are volunteers at a nursing
home. Ora Belle is a no-nonsense women who
unwittingly finds herself sharing an emotional
experience with Ruby and Ray, a nursing
home patient. Dramatic.
GMHUM, 4.5 minutes
Two Masters by Frank Manley

614
Ron Huber, middle-aged   **Bus, Present**
The driver of the 21A bus between
Minneapolis and St. Paul is doing a crossword
puzzle and telling about his route. Seriocomic.
GMHUM, 5 minutes
21A by Kevin Kling

615
Marty Staiger, 25-33   **Cleveland, Present**
Marty is unambitious but very focused on
Cover, his five-month-old son. He talks about
fatherhood. Dramatic.
GMHUM, 2 minutes
How to Say Goodbye by Mary Gallagher

616
Reverend Eddie, 30-50s
A church, Present
Reverend Eddie has nightmares that death has come for him. He wakes and then the lights go out. He speaks: Seriocomic.
GMHUM, 4.5 minutes
Some Things You Need to Know Before the World Ends (A Final Evening with the Illuminati) by Larry Larson and Levi Lee

617
Brother Lawrence, 30-50s
A church, Present
Brother Lawrence tells of a vision he has had. Dramatic.
GMHUM, 2.5 minutes
Some Things You Need to Know Before the World Ends (A Final Evening with the Illuminati) by Larry Larson and Levi Lee

618
Denny, 15   **Roberson City, Present**
Denny and his pal Casper are cruising a local mall. Denny notices a Camaro in an inside exhibit and has a fantasy. Dramatic.
GMHUM, 2 minutes
Fun by Howard Korder

619
Alex, mid-30s   **The Hamptons, Present**
Alex, perceived as dull and reclusive by a group of acquaintances with whom he has shared a beachhouse during the summer, opens up for the first time and tells Chris, a female roommate, how he came to discover computers. Dramatic.
GMHUM, 4 minutes
Alone at the Beach by Richard Dresser

620
Bob, 16-18   **Middle America, Present**
Bob is a boy raised by raccoons who has been adopted by human parents. He remembers his past. Seriocomic.
GMHUM, 2.5 minutes
Lloyd's Prayer by Kevin Kling

621
Paxton Spence, 40s   **San Bajo, Present**
Paxton discusses how he happened to be saved when the drinking supply of San Bajo was poisoned. Seriocomic.
GMHUM, 3 minutes
Incident at San Bajo by Brad Korbesmeyer

622
Erika Chadinoff, mid-20s
German Village, 1952
Erika Chadinoff, a Soviet spy, criticizes Blackford

Oakes, C.I.A. agent and would-be assassin of a West German political figure, for his government's hypocrisy and his own naiveté. Dramatic.
GMHUM, 1.5 minutes
Stained Glass by William F. Buckley, Jr.

623
Counsel, 56
Nuremberg, Germany, 1945-1946
Counsel, an attorney, is being interviewed by Herman Goering, who needs a defense for his war crimes trial. Goering asks Counsel what he thinks of him. Counsel answers. Dramatic.
GMHUM, 1.5 minutes
2 by Romulus Linney

624
Fraulein Mittel, 30s
Humboldt Desert, 1850
Here, a German pioneer woman who is dying of cholera speaks to a kind stranger. Dramatic.
GMHUM, 2 minutes
Infinity's House by Ellen McLaughlin

625
Mother, 50s   **Tennessee, Present**
Bigman, a wrestling promoter, has hired Mother's two daughters, called the Knockout Sisters, for his wrestling card. When Mother arrives and sees Bigman's "stable," she addresses them and Bigman. Comic.
GMHUM, 3 minutes
Cementville by Jane Martin

626
Henry Marlino, 40s   **Chicago, Present**
Marlino's sales manager has just died. Marlino calls the sales staff together for a meeting. He begins with an "inspiring" anecdote. Seriocomic.
GMHUM, 5 minutes
The Death of Zukasky by Richard Strand

627
S, 40s   **Boston, Present**
S is a woman who lives in a lonely world, alternating lives, mostly in her fantasies. Here, she enters into an escapist fantasy. Dramatic.
GMHUM, 4.5 minutes
Night-Side by Shem Bitterman

628
Jake, 20s   **NYC, Present**
Jake, a parapalegic, wakes up in the morning very hung over. Comic.
GMHUM, 5 minutes
Out the Window by Neal Bell

629
Andy, 20s   **NYC, Present**
Here, Andy tells her boyfriend, Jake, how she felt after his accident. Dramatic.
GMHUM, 1 minute
Out the Window by Neal Bell

630
Girl, 20s   **Hotel room**
Set in a hotel room, *Acrobatics* is about two women, called simply "Woman" and "Girl," who spend their time talking about love and their liaisons with men. Their relationship to each other remains unclear. Here, Girl, (20s), reads a letter she wrote to a Dutch boy she had a fling with.
GMWOMEN, 3.5 minutes
Acrobatics by Joyce Aaron and Luna Tarlo

631
Rachel, 40s   **In a hospital, America**
After the Revolution is a drama about one family and America, in a hospital. As Michael lies unconscious, hit by a car, muttering about distant planets, various members of his family confront each other and their own dreams, lies, betrayals. They urge him to wake up. Sitting next to her unconscious son, Rachel (40s), an ex-dancer, talks about her marriage to Fred whom she had met in a hospital after her suicide attempt which she calls "the flu."
GMWOMEN, 4 minutes
After the Revolution by Nadja Tesich

632
Rachel, 40s   **In a hospital, America**
After the Revolution is a drama about one family and America, in a hospital. As Michael lies unconscious, hit by a car, muttering about distant planets, various members of his family confront each other and their own dreams, lies, betrayals. They urge him to wake up. Still alone in a hospital room, Rachel (40s), talks about her marriage, her first love.
GMWOMEN, 2.5 minutes
After the Revolution by Nadja Tesich

633
Bonnie   **In a hospital, America**
After the Revolution is a drama about one family and America, in a hospital. As Michael lies unconscious, hit by a car, muttering about distant planets, various members of his family confront each other and their own dreams, lies, betrayals. They urge him to wake up. Bonnie, a former girlfriend of Robert, Rachel's radical brother, observes the two of them (Robert and Rachel) through the glass at the hospital, as she remembers her breakup with Robert.

GMWOMEN, 4 minutes
After the Revolution by Nadja Tesich

634
Pat   **Manhattan apartment**
Russell and Pat Baring have invited their friends Emily and Lewis to dinner in their Manhattan apartment. Throughout the evening, cracks in both the friendships and the marriages are revealed. Speaking to the audience, Pat reveals her obsession with Lewis.
GMWOMEN, 2.5 minutes
Amphibians by Molly Haskell

636
Debra
Debra O'Donnell, who is white, and her new lover Lew Claybrook, who is black, have invited her ex-husband, Jonathan Boyd, to dinner. Underneath a veneer of civility, the tensions between the three lead them into discussions of race, gender, and love. Here, Debra remembers Boyd's domineering nature.
GMWOMEN, 3.5 minutes
Black by Joyce Carol Oates

637
Esther, older black woman
Wagon train, heading West
This play deals with the hardships a mother and daughter face on a wagon train, heading West. Bluster, one of the officers on the wagon train, chatters incessantly to Helen as he digs a grave for her dying fourteen-year-old daughter. When Helen can endure no more of Bluster, Esther, an older black woman on the train, takes over the painful job of digging while dispensing both wisdom and comfort to the distraught mother.
GMWOMEN, 4.5 minutes
Breaking the Prairie Wolf Code by Lavonne Mueller

638
Rosa, 16   **Small apartment**
Rosa, a sixteen-year-old black girl addicted to crack, is chained by her desperate but misguided parents to the radiator of their small apartment. Rosa explains why Jesus started using crack.
GMWOMEN, 3 minutes
Chain by Pearl Cleage

639
Rosa, 16   **Small apartment**
Rosa, a sixteen-year-old black girl addicted to crack, is chained by her desperate but misguided parents to the radiator of their small apartment. After being chained for 5 days, Rosa begins to think about her addiction and to consider its consequences.

GMWOMEN, 3.5 minutes
Chain by Pearl Cleage

640
Rona   **Brooklyn, New York**
Set in Brooklyn, New York, *Holy Places* explores the prickly relationship between a mother, Helen, and her sensitive but less well-educated daughter, Rona. Rona, attracted to a handsome, younger man who is boarding with her mothers, has asked him if he ever visits his mother's grave. Rona admits she has never been in a cemetery.
GMWOMEN, 2.5 minutes
Holy Places by Gail Kriegel Mallin

641
Patricia Bosworth, as a young child
Her childhood summer
Choices is a collection of quotes and writings by various women of renown who have all had to make difficult choices in life. Playwright Patricia Bosworth describes the summer she pretended she was a boy.
GMWOMEN, 3 minutes
Choices, conceived by Patricia Bosworth, adapted by Cay Michael Patten and Lily Lodge

645
Colette
Colette in Love explores the famous French author's need to write and to love and the conflict between those two needs. Colette has just rejected her old lover and mentor, Willy. She is tired of 'ghost writing' his novels. This scene follows immediately after a quarrel in which Willy, as he is leaving, predicts her failure with him.
GMWOMEN, 2 minutes
Colette in Love by Lavonne Mueller

646
Betty, teens
Teenage Chinese-American Betty Sung's parents hadn't spoken in over five years when she walked in front of a car in a desperate attempt to bring them together. As they gather around her hospital bed, the family is finally forced to reveal their problems. Here, Betty rises from her coma to address the audience
GMWOMEN, 3.5 minutes
Eating Chicken Feet by Kitty Chen

647
Summer, 30s   **Southern USA**
A southern family comes together and remembers their shared past when Mamaw, the mother and grandmother who raised them, is dying. Summer, a recent divorcée in her thirties, describes a visit with her son, who lives with his father.

GMWOMEN, 2.5 minutes
Entry Points by Sharon Houck Ross

648
Mamaw, older woman   **Southern USA**
A southern family comes together and remembers their shared past when Mamaw, the mother and grandmother who raised them, is dying. From her hospital bed, Mamaw imagines telling her own mother about her new love.
GMWOMEN, 1.5 minutes
Entry Points by Sharon Houck Ross

649
Anna, middle-aged
Four Corners explores the life of a middle-aged women who is an acute agoraphobic, someone who is terrified to leave her house, and the resulting emotional distress on her teenage son and husband. Anna who hasn't left her house in ten years, describes why she refuses to go out.
GMWOMEN, 3 minutes
Four Corners by Gina Wendkos and Donna Bond

650
Anna, middle-aged
Four Corners explores the life of a middle-aged women who is an acute agoraphobic, someone who is terrified to leave her house, and the resulting emotional distress on her teenage son and husband. Fantasizing, Anna speaks on the phone as though someone were listening to her.
GMWOMEN, 3.5 minutes
Four Corners by Gina Wendkos and Donna Bond

651
Frida Kahlo
RCA building in NYC, 20th century
This musical play is based on the relationship of Frida Kahlo, one of the twentieth century's important surrealistic painters, with renowned painter/muralist Diego Rivera. While her husband paints a mural for the RCA building in New York, Frida is interviewed by a reporter.
GMWOMEN, 3.5 minutes
Frida: The Story of Frida Kahlo, book by Hilary Blecher, monologues and lyrics by Migdalia Cruz

652
Frida Kahlo   **NYC, 20th century**
This musical play is based on the relationship of Frida Kahlo, one of the twentieth century's important surrealistic painters, with renowned painter/muralist Diego Rivera. After selling a painting to the Louvre in Paris, Frida, back in New York, has a voluptuous conversation with her lover, Nickolas Muray, a famous photographer.

GMWOMEN, 3.5 minutes
Frida: The Story of Frida Kahlo, book by Hilary Blecher, monologues and lyrics by Migdalia Cruz

653
Eleonora, older woman from Boston
1950s-1960s
A series of short, fictional monologues dramatizing the experiences of real sportswomen. Eleonora Randolph Sears was a very versatile, high-spirited athlete from Boston who lived from the late 1800s to the 1960s. With great humor, she tells how she challenged a women's group who criticized her for wearing trousers.
GMWOMEN, 5.5 minutes
How She Played the Game by Cynthia L. Cooper

654
Althea, black woman
Wimbledon, England, 1957
A series of short, fictional monologues dramatizing the experiences of real sportswomen. Althea Gibson, the first black tennis player to win Wimbledon (male or female), talks about how she got her start in Harlem.
GMWOMEN, 12.5 minutes
How She Played the Game by Cynthia L. Cooper

655
Dorothy, 39   Kansas City, Summer 1919
In No Man's Land is set in a ward at the Sunset Ridge Maternity Hospital and Home for Unwed Mothers in Kansas City during the summer of 1919. Here, Dorothy, a puritanical thirty-nine-year-old legal secretary, describes how she became pregnant.
GMWOMEN, 3 minutes
In No Man's Land by Susan Kander

656
Monetty, middle-aged black woman   USA
Ladies is the poignant story of the difficult lives of various homeless women. Monetty, a middle-aged black woman, describes how she met her first husband.
GMWOMEN, 2.5 minutes
Ladies by Eve Ensler

657
Nickie   USA
Ladies is the poignant story of the difficult lives of various homeless women. Nickie, a tough, tattooed woman with a Brooklyn accent and a punk haircut, describes the heavy shopping bag she must carry as representative of all of life's burdens.
GMWOMEN, 1.5 minutes
Ladies by Eve Ensler

658
Dinah, middle-aged
Dinah LaFarge, a short plump, middle-aged woman, reveals her paranoia and her unique views on employment, society, eating, and the power of the mind in this one-woman show. Here, Dinah describes an encounter in a trendy restaurant.
GMWOMEN, 2.5 minutes
Lardo Weeping by Terry Galloway

659
Dinah, middle-aged
Dinah LaFarge, a short plump, middle-aged woman, reveals her paranoia and her unique views on employment, society, eating, and the power of the mind in this one-woman show. Here, Dinah expresses her dislike for power.
GMWOMEN, 2.5 minutes
Lardo Weeping by Terry Galloway

660
Ava, 20ish
Greyhound   Bus Terminal, Detroit, Michigan, 1970
Ava Johnson is a twentyish black woman who is headed to Atlanta to see the triumphant return to the ring of Muhammed Ali after three years of exile as a conscientious objector to the Vietnam War. Although a prostitute, Ava represents all black women and their "potential for...salvation." While waiting for a friend who is supposed to go to Atlanta with her, Ava paints her toenails and chatters to another black woman who looks abused but never speaks.
GMWOMEN, 4 minutes
Late Bus to Mecca by Pearl Cleage

661
Aurelia, speaking as 17-year-old
As seen through the eyes of Aurelia Plath, *Letters Home* reveals much about the life of her daughter, Sylvia Plath, the brilliant and often controversial poet. The play is structured as both a dialogue between mother and daughter, which takes place in Aurelia's mind, and letters that Sylvia wrote to her mother. Aurelia, speaking as the seventeen-year-old Sylvia, reveals her girlish dreams and trepidations for the future.
GMWOMEN, 4.5 minutes
Letters Home by Rose Leiman Goldemberg

662
Margaret Thatcher   Europe
Margaret Thatcher, ex-Prime Minister of Great Britain, has a momentous meeting with then-Soviet Premier Gorbachev. Gradually, as they cut through politics and policy, they con-

nect on a human level. Here, Maggie relates a humiliating experience that formed her determination to succeed.
GMWOMEN, 2 minutes
Maggie and Misha by Gail Sheehy

663
Missy, 14   **Southern USA, 1951**
Set in 1951, *Milk of Paradise* is a coming-of-age story of an aristocratic, southern family. Missy, a restless, dreamy fourteen-year-old, longs to escape from her stifling, provincial environment. While undressing a doll, Missy describes what it is like to be "felt up."
GMWOMEN, 3 minutes
Milk of Paradise by Sallie Bingham

664
Millie, older woman   **USA**
Millie tells the story of a funny, courageous, black woman who, for eleven years, has taken care of her severely brain-damaged husband. Millie, a grandmother who adores the singer, Teddy Pendergrass, describes how she rearranges her life to go to one of his concerts with her old friend, Sam.
GMWOMEN, 11 minutes
Millie by Susan J. Kander

665
Daisy Bates, older woman   **USA**
Parallax illuminates key moments in the life of Daisy Bates, the heroic teacher who fought for integration in Little Rock, Arkansas in the 1950s. Here, Daisy, addressing a large group of people, reveals why she feels no bitterness over the consequences of standing up for what she believes in.
GMWOMEN, 4 minutes
Parallax (In Honor of Daisy Bates) by Denise Hamilton

666
Ellen, young single woman   **NYC**
Personality is a one-woman play with many characters, primarily Ellen, a young, single woman in New York who is trying to find herself, and Lorette, Ellen's overbearing, Jewish mother who wants Ellen to have a good personality so she can get a man. Here, Ellen wistfully describes one type of woman she would like to be.
GMWOMEN, 3 minutes
Personality by Gina Wendkos and Ellen Ratner

667
Ellen, young single woman   **NYC**
Personality is a one-woman play with many characters, primarily Ellen, a young, single woman in New York who is trying to find her-

self, and Lorette, Ellen's overbearing, Jewish mother who wants Ellen to have a good personality so she can get a man. Ellen reveals her frustration over both her lack of money and the city's emphasis on the importance of having money.
GMWOMEN, 2.5 minutes
Personality by Gina Wendkos and Ellen Ratner

668
Ellen, young single woman   **NYC**
Personality is a one-woman play with many characters, primarily Ellen, a young, single woman in New York who is trying to find herself, and Lorette, Ellen's overbearing, Jewish mother who wants Ellen to have a good personality so she can get a man. Ellen points out some of the contradictions that society has placed on females.
GMWOMEN, 3 minutes
Personality by Gina Wendkos and Ellen Ratner

669
Ellen, young single woman   **NYC**
Personality is a one-woman play with many characters, primarily Ellen, a young, single woman in New York who is trying to find herself, and Lorette, Ellen's overbearing, Jewish mother who wants Ellen to have a good personality so she can get a man. This is a "tour de force" monologue with Ellen "becoming" each of many distinctive personalities, trying them on for size to see if any of them fits. All she really wants is to be accepted for herself.
GMWOMEN, 17 minutes
Personality by Gina Wendkos and Ellen Ratner

670
Carmen, 40s
Relativity describes the strange relationship which exists among three people, Carl, a scientist of some kind, Carmen, his wife, and Carmen's friend, Lucy. Carl lives in a scientific fantasy world, listening to tapes of himself speaking on relativity, and watching the Playboy channel. His wife dominates him in a peculiar, passive-aggressive alliance. Here, at the end of the play, Carmen, (40s), has completely dominated her husband and is enjoying humiliating him.
GMWOMEN, 4 minutes
Relativity by Marlene G. Meyer

671
Daphne, 30s   **Rural South Africa**
Daphne, thirties, and Ruth, late twenties, live with their parents, who exercise strict control over their daughters, in rural South Africa. Here, Daphne describes an argument with her abusive ex-husband to her sister.

GMWOMEN, 3.5 minutes
Scene of Shipwreck by Pamela Mills

672
Cheryl, 30s   **1978**
Set in 1978 and based upon actual interviews,
Still Life examines three people who have, in
one way or another, been deeply affected by
the Vietnam War. Cheryl, (30s), an abused
wife and a "survivor," describes why she stays
with Mark, her abusive husband.
GMWOMEN, 3 minutes
Still Life by Emily Mann

673
Nadine, 40s   **1978**
Set in 1978 and based upon actual interviews,
Still Life examines three people who have, in
one way or another, been deeply affected by
the Vietnam War. Nadine, (40s), a longtime
friend of Mark's and both a career woman and
mother, talks about the confusing role in society that men are asked to play.
GMWOMEN, 3 minutes
Still Life by Emily Mann

674
Joan of Arc, 1431   **Dungeon**
In this moving play, set in a dungeon in 1431,
Joan of Arc is being held prisoner when she is
visited by the Duchess of Bedford, cousin to
the King. The Duchess, in pity, has come to
offer her an escape from being burned at the
stake. Joan refuses, believing it is her destiny to
be a martyr. In this opening scene, Joan, having been subjected to a humiliating and painful
test for virginity the day before, is begging her
voices to speak to her once more.
GMWOMEN, 2.5 minutes
The Voices of Silence by Joan Vail Thorne

677
Fred, 45   **In a hospital in America**
After the Revolution is a drama about one
family and America, in a hospital. As Michael
lies unconscious, hit by a car, muttering about
distant planets, various members of his family
confront each other and their own dreams,
lies, betrayals. They urge him to wake up.
Fred, 45, sits alone in his son's room and talks
about his love and loneliness.
GMWOMEN, 10.5 minutes
After the Revolution by Nadja Tesich

678
Robert, 35   **In a hospital in America**
After the Revolution is a drama about one
family and America, in a hospital. As Michael
lies unconscious, hit by a car, muttering about
distant planets, various members of his family

confront each other and their own dreams,
lies, betrayals. They urge him to wake up.
Triggered by Michael's cries, "one, two three,
blast off, blast off" with Rachel nearby, Robert
remembers his youth, communal ecstasy on a
street in New York. The entire cast supports
him, the audience can join too.
GMWOMEN, 3 minutes
After the Revolution by Nadja Tesich

679
Bluster   **Wagon train heading West**
This play deals with the hardships a mother
and daughter face on a wagon train heading
West. Bluster, one of the officers on the wagon
train, chatters incessantly to Helen as he digs a
grave for her dying fourteen-year-old daughter.
GMWOMEN, 2.5 minutes
Breaking the Prairie Wolf Code by Lavonne Mueller

680
Jimmy, teens   **USA**
Four Corners explores the life of a woman
who is an acute agoraphobic, someone who is
terrified to leave her house, and the resulting
emotional distress on her teenage son, Jimmy,
and husband, Ralph. Jimmy expresses both rage
and pain in trying to cope with his mother's illness.
GMWOMEN, 4 minutes
Four Corners by Gina Wendkos and Donna Bond

681
Ralph   **USA**
Four Corners explores the life of a woman
who is an acute agoraphobic, someone who is
terrified to leave her house, and the resulting
emotional distress on her teenage son, Jimmy,
and husband, Ralph. Ralph enviously reveals
one of his co-worker's love-life.
GMWOMEN, 4 minutes
Four Corners by Gina Wendkos and Donna Bond

682
Jimmy, teens   **USA**
Four Corners explores the life of a woman
who is an acute agoraphobic, someone who is
terrified to leave her house, and the resulting
emotional distress on her teenage son, Jimmy,
and husband, Ralph. Jimmy, addressing the
audience, confides that he is afraid of becoming like his mother.
GMWOMEN, 1.5 minutes
Four Corners by Gina Wendkos and Donna Bond

685
Gorbachev   **Europe**
Margaret Thatcher, ex-Prime Minister of
Great Britain, has a momentous meeting with
then-Soviet Premier Gorbachev. Gradually, as

they cut through politics and policy, they connect on a human level. Misha reveals a painful memory about his birthmark that influenced who he became.

GMWOMEN, 2.5 minutes
Maggie and Misha by Gail Sheehy

686
Al
Niedecker presents the touching story of poet Lorine Niedecker, her friend, her husband, and the young man who loves and admires her. Al, "a rough outdoorsman" and the spiritual opposite of the quiet, gentle Lorine, describes the joys of fishing.

GMWOMEN, 3 minutes
Niedecker by Kristine Thatcher

687
Mark, 30s 1978
Set in 1978 and based upon actual interviews, *Still Life* examines three people who have, in one way or another, been deeply affected by the Vietnam War. Mark, an ex-Marine and Vietnam vet in his thirties, describes the process that made him into a killer.

GMWOMEN, 5 minutes
Still Life by Emily Mann

688
Mark, 30s 1978
Set in 1978 and based upon actual interviews, *Still Life* examines three people who have, in one way or another, been deeply affected by the Vietnam War. Here Mark, at last reveals some of the horror and pain he both suffered and inflicted, in Vietnam.

GMWOMEN, 10 minutes
Still Life by Emily Mann

689
Jerry, 30s Colorado suburb
Tales of the Lost Formicans concerns an assorted group of interrelated characters in a Colorado suburb being observed by what seems to be aliens from another planet. Jerry, an offbeat neighbor in his thirties, believes that the moon landing was faked by the government.

GMWOMEN, 2 minutes
Tales of the Lost Formicans by Constance Congdon

690
Alice, 11 A rabbit hole
As Alice falls down the rabbit hole, she delivers this commentary.

CHILD, 2.5 minutes
Alice's Adventures in Wonderland by Craig Slaight, from the novel by Lewis Carroll

691
Alice, 11 In Wonderland
A very confused Alice questions her identity after many baffling changes during her adventures in Wonderland.

CHILD, 3.5 minutes
Alice's Adventures in Wonderland by Craig Slaight, from the novel by Lewis Carroll

692
Cindy Sue, 10
Jackson, Indiana, a fifth grade schoolroom
Cindy Sue White delivers this oral report to her fifth grade classmates.

CHILD, 3.5 minutes
And They Dance Real Slow in Jackson by Jim Leonard, Jr.

693
Pony Blossom, 9 Taos, New Mexico
On this family trip across the country, everyone in the Blossom family experiences something important. In this speech, Pony confronts her fears about death with Aunt Olivia.

CHILD, 2 minutes
Approaching Zanzibar by Tina Howe

694
Daisy, 11 Jackson, Florida
In the private glimpse that Daisy's frank diary entries give us, we have a picture of an exciting childhood. Daisy's unique personality and adventurous spirit provide an intriguing character study, filled with laughs and thoughts for contemplation. Here, Daisy gives us her view of tap-dancing lessons.

CHILD, 2 minutes
Daisy Fay and the Miracle Man by Fannie Flagg

695
Daisy, 11 Jackson, Florida
In the private glimpse that Daisy's frank diary entries give us, we have a picture of an exciting childhood. Daisy's unique personality and adventurous spirit provide an intriguing character study, filled with laughs and thoughts for contemplation. Here, Daisy writes about her tonsillectomy.

CHILD, 3 minutes
Daisy Fay and the Miracle Man by Fannie Flagg

696
Daisy, 11 Jackson, Florida
In the private glimpse that Daisy's frank diary entries give us, we have a picture of an exciting childhood. Daisy's unique personality and adventurous spirit provide an intriguing character study, filled with laughs and thoughts for contemplation. Here, Daisy shares her experience with ringworm and vanity.

CHILD, 3.5 minutes
Daisy Fay and the Miracle Man by Fannie Flagg

697
Daisy, 11   **Jackson, Florida**
In the private glimpse that Daisy's frank diary entries give us, we have a picture of an exciting childhood. Daisy's unique personality and adventurous spirit provide an intriguing character study, filled with laughs and thoughts for contemplation. Here, Daisy explores her feelings about death.
CHILD, 3 minutes
Daisy Fay and the Miracle Man by Fannie Flagg

698
Jeanne Wakatsuki, 11-13
Manzanar, a Japanese internment camp during WWII
Taken from their home in Long Beach, CA, having no time to settle their belongings, Jeanne's family struggles to keep together and conserve their traditions in a hostile and disturbing environment. Here, Jeanne shares a memory of her mother.
CHILD, 2.5 minutes
Farewell to Manzanar by Jeanne Wakatsuki Houston and James D. Houston

699
Jeanne Wakatsuki, 11-13
Manzanar, a Japanese internment camp during WWII
Taken from their home in Long Beach, CA, having no time to settle their belongings, Jeanne's family struggles to keep together and conserve their traditions in a hostile and disturbing environment. Here, Jeanne tells us of two lovers in the camp.
CHILD, 4 minutes
Farewell to Manzanar by Jeanne Wakatsuki Houston and James D. Houston

700
Jeanne Wakatsuki, 11-13   **Manzanar, a Japanese internment camp during World War II**
Taken from their home in Long Beach, CA, having no time to settle their belongings, Jeanne's family struggles to keep together and conserve their traditions in a hostile and disturbing environment. Here, Jeanne speaks of her view of religion and the outside world.
CHILD, 3 minutes
Farewell to Manzanar by Jeanne Wakatsuki Houston and James D. Houston

701
Amy, 12   **Concord, Massachusetts, 1860s**
In this speech, the four sisters have been writing letters to their mother. Here, Amy reads her letter.
CHILD, 2 minutes
Little Women by Roger Wheeler, adapted from the novel by Louisa May Alcott

702
Amy, 12   **Concord, Massachusetts, 1860s**
Amy's sister Beth has been suffering from the fever, and because Amy feels that life is uncertain, she wants her wishes known. Here, Amy reads her Last Will and Testament.
CHILD, 2.5 minutes
Little Women by Roger Wheeler, adapted from the novel by Louisa May Alcott

703
Peter Pan, 12
Peter's hideout, Never Never Land
Peter talks to Tinker Bell, who first warns him that Hook has captured Wendy and the boys, and then drinks poison to save Peter's life.
CHILD, 2 minutes
Peter Pan by James Barrie

704
Peter Pan, 12
Wendy's parents' house, London
Peter and Tinker Bell plot to keep Wendy from returning home and run into Wendy's mother.
CHILD, 1.5 minutes
Peter Pan by James Barrie

705
Audrey, 8
Here, eight-year-old Audrey recounts a dream to Rosie, who has been with her since birth and is the dearest person to her heart. Rosie has just been told by Audrey's mother, Cele, that she is no longer needed in her position and must leave.
CHILD, 3 minutes
Picture Me by Margery Kreitman

706
Julie, 12   **Anywhere**
Julie delivers this impassioned defense of her vegetarianism when her father continues pressing her to eat the meat stew the family lives on.
CHILD, 2 minutes
Reindeer Soup by Joe Pintauro

707
Lucy   **A living room**
Lucy, a dynamic young lady with opinions that are bold and unchangeable, tells Linus of her dream of becoming a queen.
CHILD, 2.5 minutes
You're a Good Man, Charlie Brown by Clark Gesner, adapted from "Peanuts" by Charles M. Schultz

708
Huck, 13-14
Jackson's Island, the Mississippi River

Here, Huck tells of his escape from Pap and of his dream to be nothing but himself.
CHILD, 2 minutes
Big River: The Adventures of Huckleberry Finn by Roger Miller, adapted from the novel by Mark Twain

709
Buddy, 7   A warm kitchen, Christmastime
Buddy, a lonely little boy, recalls the careful preparations for the making of fruitcakes.
CHILD, 3 minutes
A Christmas Memory by Truman Capote

710
Horace, 13
A plantation in Houston worked by the convicts from the neighboring prison
Horace has been left to watch over a chained convict who has attempted to run away.
CHILD, 2.5 minutes
Convicts by Horton Foote

711
Rufus, 6-7   Anywhere
In this story of a family who lost their father in a tragic accident, Rufus shares his perception of the world. Here, he contemplates his life in the waking-darkness of the night.
CHILD, 3 minutes
A Death in the Family by James Agee

712
The Happy Prince, young man
A city square, nighttime
The Happy Prince, a statue come to life, tells a lonely, heartbroken swallow why he cries.
CHILD, 2.5 minutes
The Happy Prince by Oscar Wilde

713
Bibi, 12   Ottawa, Canada, a home
Bibi, a young man on the verge of adulthood, tells what happened to him at school when he was unfairly accused of drawing an inappropriate picture of a teacher.
CHILD, 3.5 minutes
The Happy Time by Samuel Taylor, based on stories by Robert Fontaine

714
Albert, 12-14   A ghetto
Walter, a young man in the ghetto, seems to have no other hope of bettering his life except through selling drugs. Here, Walter's little brother Albert stands up for himself while pretending to shoot hoops.
CHILD, 1 minute
Hey Little Walter by Carla Debbie Alleyne

715
Little Prince, young boy
The Sahara Desert
The Little Prince offers the pilot this argument for not trusting appearances.
CHILD, 2.5 minutes
The Little Prince by Antoine de Saint Exupéry

716
Little Prince, young boy
The Sahara Desert
The Little Prince tells the pilot about a special flower that at first fascinated him and caused him to love it deeply, then it seemed to become selfish and demanding.
CHILD, 1.5 minutes
The Little Prince by Antoine de Saint Exupéry

717
The Fox   The outdoors
Along the way in his Earthly journey, the Little Prince meets a wise fox who helps him understand how special his flower was and who shares a secret about life.
CHILD, 1.5 minutes
The Little Prince by Antoine de Saint Exupéry

718
Little Prince, young boy
The Sahara Desert
Here, the Little Prince, having arrived at the meaning of life, shares his feelings with the pilot.
CHILD, 2 minutes
The Little Prince by Antoine de Saint Exupéry

719
Wolfgang Mozart, 13   Bologna, Italy
Wolfgang Amadeus Mozart traveled around the world, fascinating audiences with his wonderful music. Here, he writes to his mother and sister from Bologna.
CHILD, 1.5 minutes
A Letter from Mozart by Wolfgang Amadeus Mozart

720
Toby, 10–11   Utah
Toby, living with his divorced mother, recalls a variation on archery practice that included some exciting risks.
CHILD, 4 minutes
This Boy's Life by Tobias Wolff

721
Toby, 10–11   Utah
Toby tells of a youthful success with two of his friends. Together, they succeed in getting away

with breaking windows and causing much trouble.
CHILD, 3.5 minutes
This Boy's Life by Tobias Wolff

722
Charlie Brown, boy   **The playground**
Charlie Brown alone on the playground, sits with his sack lunch.
CHILD, 4 minutes
You're a Good Man, Charlie Brown by Clark Gesner, adapted from "Peanuts" by Charles M. Schultz

723
Charlie Brown, boy   **Outdoors**
Charlie Brown tells of his newfound hope and "...confidence in the basic goodness of my fellow man."
CHILD, 1 minute
You're a Good Man, Charlie Brown by Clark Gesner, adapted from "Peanuts" by Charles M. Schultz

724
Schroeder, boy   **Shroeder's piano**
Schroeder's constant companion is the bold and brassy Lucy. Although she adores Schroeder and his brilliant piano playing, he doesn't respond. Here, Schroeder takes a moment to be extremely truthful with Lucy.
CHILD, 1.5 minutes
You're a Good Man, Charlie Brown by Clark Gesner, adapted from "Peanuts" by Charles M. Schultz

725
Speaker, male or female, any age
17th century
The prologue speaker reflects on poets and their craft. Dramatic.
RESTOR, .5 minute
The Way of the World by William Congreve

726
Speaker, male or female, any age
17th century
The prologue speaker comments on the audience's role as critic of the play. Dramatic.
RESTOR, 1 minute
The Double Dealer by William Congreve

727
Speaker, male or female, any age
17th century
The prologue speaker expresses the author's concern about unsympathetic critics. Dramatic.
RESTOR, .5 minute
The Wonder: A Woman Keeps a Secret by Susanna Centlivre

728
Speaker, male or female, any age
17th century
In this prologue, the speaker reflects on the nature of theater critics. Dramatic.
RESTOR, 1 minute
The Double Dealer by William Congreve

729
Speaker, male or female, any age
17th century
The prologue speaker comments on the critical nature of the audience and that the play's characters reflect the audience's foibles. Dramatic.
RESTOR, 1.5 minutes
The Man of Mode by George Etherege

730
Speaker, male or female, any age
17th century
The prologue speaker introduces the play and invites the audience's criticism. Dramatic.
RESTOR, 2.5 minutes
The Old Bachelor by William Congreve

731
Speaker, male or female, any age
17th century
In this prologue, the speaker comments on the audience and the purpose of theater-going. Dramatic.
RESTOR, .5 minute
The Rover; or The Banish'd Cavaliers by Aphra Behn

732
Tattle, 20s   **17th century**
Tattle plays his love game with Miss Prue, who is supposed to marry another. Since Tattle believes that every woman wants him, his modus operandi is sound and, in this instance, he succeeds. Dramatic.
RESTOR, 1.5 minutes
Love For Love by William Congreve

733
Angelica   **17th century**
Angelica decides to travel abroad. Her coach is broken, however, so she manipulates her uncle into lending her his. Dramatic.
RESTOR, 2 minutes
Love for Love by William Congreve

734
Ben   **17th century**
Ben is brought back from sea duties to marry Miss Prue. He wants nothing to do with her, however, and pleads his case to Mrs. Frail, a family friend. Dramatic.
RESTOR, 2 minutes
Love for Love by William Congreve

735
Lady Plyant   17th century
Lady Plyant attempts to break up the engagement between her step-daughter and Melefont by discussing her dissatisfaction with her own engagement. Dramatic.
RESTOR, 1.5 minutes
The Double Dealer by William Congreve

736
Loveless   17th century
Loveless finds that he is drawn to Berinthia. He is puzzled by his attraction since he still loves his wife. Here, he attempts to work out his dilemma. Dramatic.
RESTOR, 3.5 minutes
The Relapse by John VanBrugh

737
Child speaker   17th century
Rakes and lasses engage in love and badinage, but conventional morality is upheld and the tale ends beneficently. Dramatic.
RESTOR, 2.5 minutes
The Country Lasses by Charles Johnson

738
Lady Wishfort   17th century
Lady Wishfort's suitor, Sir Rowland, is servant to Mirabell, an enemy of Lady Wishfort. In another humiliating prank, Mirabell will have his man marry Foibile and then court Lady Wishfort. Dramatic.
RESTOR, 1.5 minutes
The Way of the World by William Congreve

739
Lopez   17th century
Lopez waxes bravely about what he would say to his master who has asked him to assist in some nocturnal wooing of Leonora. Dramatic.
RESTOR, 3 minutes
The Mistake by John VanBrugh

740
Maskwell   17th century
Maskwell has persuaded Melefont that the plot with Cynthia's aunt to break the match between Cynthia and Melefont is actually in the service of securing the marriage. Maskwell tells the audience his intrigues, which he believes are so well concealed he can share them with his victims. Dramatic.
RESTOR, 1.5 minutes
The Double Dealer by William Congreve

741
Angellica Bianca   17th century
Angellica falls in love for the first time with the philandering cavalier, Willmore. In this scene she expresses her anger and betrayal after discovering Willmore paying court to another woman. Dramatic.
RESTOR, 2.5 minutes
The Rover; or The Banish'd Cavaliers by Aphra Behn

742
Oroonoko, the captured leader of Angola
17th century
Oroonoko is more overwhelmed by grief than captivity. Blanford, one of the captors, has won Oroonoko's trust and here, listens to the warrior's story of his beloved. Dramatic.
RESTOR, 4.5 minutes
Oroonoko by Thomas Southerne

743
Lord Foppington   17th century
The fop, Lord Foppington, expounds indigently upon his daily habits before uninterested company. Dramatic.
RESTOR, 3 minutes
The Relapse by John VanBrugh

744
Lady Brute   17th century
After being abused again by her boorish husband, Lady Brute weighs faithfulness against happiness. Dramatic.
RESTOR, 2.5 minutes
The Provok'd Wife by John VanBrugh

745
Lady Truman   17th century
Lady Truman justifies her attention toward one of her many suitors. Dramatic.
RESTOR, 2 minutes
The Drummer by Joseph Addison

746
Millimant   17th century
Millimant is in love with Mirabell and sets forth her conditions for marriage when Mirabell proposes. Dramatic.
RESTOR, 3 minutes
The Way of the World by William Congreve

747
Mirabell   17th century
Mirabell responds to Millimant's conditions with his own compromises and provisos. Dramatic.
RESTOR, 3.5 minutes
The Way of the World by William Congreve

748
An enraged Frenchman   17th century
After sitting through an English play, this

Frenchman rails against the manners and customs of his enemy England and threatens to ruin the play. Dramatic.
RESTOR, 3 minutes
Sir Harry Wildair by George Farquhar

749
Speaker, male or female, any age
17th century
The epilogue speaker comments on the purpose of the epilogue. Dramatic.
RESTOR, .5 minute
She Would and She Would Not by Colley Cibber

750
Speaker(s), male or female, any age
17th century
In this epilogue, three speakers comment on different types of critics. Dramatic.
RESTOR, 1.5 minutes
The Double Dealer by William Congreve

751
Speaker(s), male or female, any age
17th century
Two epilogue speakers reflect on the play's critics. Dramatic.
RESTOR, 1 minute
The Way of the World by William Congreve

752
Mrs. Sullen   **17th century**
Mrs. Sullen is forced to share her marriage bed with Mrs. Bountiful. Here, she bemoans the misery of sharing her husband's bed. Dramatic.
RESTOR, 1.5 minutes
The Beaux' Stratagem by George Farquhar

753
Amanda   17th century
Posing as a seductive mistress, Amanda tries to woo her estranged husband. The next morning she confronts him with his cruelty. Dramatic.
RESTOR, 1.5 minutes
Love's Last Shift by Colley Cibber

754
Angellica   **17th century**
Dramatic.
RESTOR, 1.5 minutes
The Rover; or The Banish'd Cavaliers by Aphra Behn

755
Mrs. Pinchwife   **17th century**
Mrs. Pinchwife substitutes the "Dear John" letter her jealous husband has forced her to write and substitutes a passionate letter to her newfound love. Dramatic.

RESTOR, 2.5 minutes
The Country Wife by William Wycherly

756
Isabella   **17th century**
Isabella jumps from her window in a desperate attempt to free herself from an unwanted match. She is caught by Colonel Brighton and delivered to the home of Donna Violante where she relates her story. Dramatic.
RESTOR, 2 minutes
The Wonder: A Woman Keeps a Secret by Susanna Centlivre

757
Isabella   **17th century**
Isabella resolves to become a nun rather than bow to the customs of her country, which dictate she must obey her father and his choice of husbands for her. Dramatic.
RESTOR, 1.5 minutes
The Wonder: A Woman Keeps A Secret by Susanna Centlivre

758
Isabella   **17th century**
Here, Isabella proclaims her happiness when her suitor declares women his equal. Dramatic.
RESTOR, 2 minutes
The Wonder: A Woman Keeps a Secret by Susanna Centlivre

759
Aura   **17th century**
Epilogue to the play, spoken by Aura dressed in boy's clothes. Dramatic.
RESTOR, 3.5 minutes
The Country Lasses by Charles Johnson

760
Sophrenia   **17th century**
Sophrenia, a sister who is competing with her sibling for the same man, has offered to assist her mother in forcing an undesirable marriage onto her younger sister because the sisters are vying for the same gentleman. Here, Sophrenia's critical appraisal of her mother proves highly ironic. Dramatic.
RESTOR, 1.5 minutes
The Refusal by Colley Cibber

761
Amanda   **17th century**
Amanda, a woman posing as a seductive mistress, prepares to reveal her real identity to her husband and wonders if her scheme will be successful. Dramatic.
RESTOR, 1 minute
Love's Last Shift by Colley CIbber

762
Sir Harry Wildair   **17th century**
Lady Lurewell tests Sir Harry's good humor when she tells him the town Alderman has accused him of dishonorable dealings. Sir Harry beats the old man soundly with a cudgel and, here, relates his satisfaction with the deed. Dramatic.
RESTOR, 1.5 minutes
The Constant Couple by George Farquhar

763
Prince Volscius   **17th century**
To the dismay of his critics, Bayes, a playwright, has embodied the Prince's struggle in his footwear. The young royal debates his fate—boots on, or boots off? Dramatic.
RESTOR, 1.5 minutes
The Rehearsal by George Villars, 2nd Duke of Buckingham

764
Maskwell   **17th century**
Maskwell betrays his friend Mellefont Dramatic.
RESTOR, 2 minutes
The Double Dealer by William Congreve

765
Mr. Tattle   **17th century**
Mr. Tattle, a keeper of ladies, defends his reputation and accidentally lets details of his past liaisons slip. Dramatic.
RESTOR, 3 minutes
Love For Love by William Congreve

766
A tailor   **17th century**
An actor. Dramatic.
RESTOR, 1.5 minutes
The Rover; Or The Banish'd Cavaliers by Aphra Behn

767
Mr. Pinchwife   **17th century**
Mr. Pinchwife discovers his young wife writing a letter to her lover and threatens her life. Dramatic.
RESTOR, 2.5 minutes
The Country Wife by William Wycherly

768
Colonel Briton   **17th century**
Colonel Briton receives a love letter from a damsel-in-distress who requests a secret meeting. The Colonel sets off to the appointed place of rendezvous. Dramatic.
RESTOR, 2.5 minutes
The Wonder: A Woman Keeps A Secret by Susanna Centlivre

769
Sir Harry Wildair   **17th century**
Sir Harry tries to seduce Lord Bellamy's wife. The next morning Bellamy confronts the young gallant. Dramatic.
RESTOR, 3 minutes
Sir Harry Wildair by George Farquhar

770
Prometheus, 20s-30s
A mountain in Scythia
Chained to a mountain for stealing fire from Zeus, Prometheus here laments his fate.
CLASS, 4.5 minutes
Prometheus Bound by Æschylus, tr. by J. S. Blackie

771
Creon, 50s-60s
The royal palace in Thebes
When Creon assumes the throne of Thebes, he addresses his generals and commands that the body of Polyneises, son of Oedipus, be left to rot in the street in defiance of the rites of the dead.
CLASS, 3 minutes
Antigone by Sophocles, tr. by Sir George Young

772
Oedipus, 40s-60s   **The city of Thebes**
When Oedipus discovers that he has inadvertently killed his father and that his wife, Queen Jocasta, is his biological mother, he blinds himself with her brooch. Here, he explains his desire for sightlessness.
CLASS, 3.5 minutes
Oedipus Rex by Sophocles, tr. by Albert Cook

773
Strepsiades, 50s-60s   **Athens**
The querulous old farmer finds that he cannot sleep and frets about his numerous debts.
CLASS, 4 minutes
The Clouds by Aristophanes, tr. by T. Mitchell.

774
King Dushyanta, 20s-30s   **Ancient India**
While hunting, King Dushyanta encounters the beautiful young Sakoontalá and is instantly smitten.
CLASS, 4.5 minutes
Sakoontalá by Kálidása, tr. by Sir Monier Monier-Williams

775
Adam, 20s   **The Garden of Eden**
After surrendering to temptation, Adam here rages at Eve for having defied God.
CLASS, 4 minutes
Adam: The Mystery of Adam by Anonymous, tr. by Edward Noble Stone

776
God   **Heaven**
After lamenting the state of humankind, God summons Death and instructs this entity to bring his message to Everyman.
CLASS, 2 minutes
The Summoning of Everyman by Anonymous

777
Andronico, 30s-50s   **Medieval Venice**
Here, the bored Andronico ruminates on his latest acquisition: another man's wife.
CLASS, 4.5 minutes
Bilora by Angelo Beolco, tr. by Babette and Glenn Hughes

778
Bilora, 30s-40s   **Medieval Venice**
Bilora, a simple peasant, here plans to murder the man who has stolen his wife.
CLASS, 3.5 minutes
Bilora by Angelo Beolco, tr. by Babette and Glenn Hughes

779
Dr. Faustus, 30s-50s   **Dr. Faustus' study**
Here, we encounter the doctor in his study. As he pours over his collection of ancient texts, he reveals his desire for forbidden knowledge.
CLASS, 3.5 minutes
The Tragical History of Dr. Faustus by Christopher Marlowe

780
Dr. Faustus, 30s-50s   **Dr. Faustus' study**
Having sold his soul to the Devil in return for knowledge of black magic, Faustus now faces his damnation. Realizing his soul is lost, he despairs and repents before God.
CLASS, 3 minutes
The Tragical History of Dr. Faustus by Christopher Marlowe

781
Tamburlaine, 30s-40s   **Medieval Persia**
Following a successful military rout of Turkey, the bloodthirsty Tamburlaine takes a moment to gloat over his captives.
CLASS, 1.5 minutes
Tamburlaine the Great by Christopher Marlowe

782
Tamburlaine, 30s-40s   **Medieval Persia**
The conqueror of Turkey and Persia is smitten by the beautiful Zenocrate. Here, the shameless butcher is surprised by his feelings.
CLASS, 3 minutes
Tamburlaine the Great by Christopher Marlowe

783
Petruchio, 30s   **Medieval Padua**
Here, the stouthearted Petruchio divulges his plan to conquer his headstrong wife with kindness.
CLASS, 1 minute
The Taming of the Shrew by William Shakespeare, ed. by Robert Heilman

784
Puck, 15-20   **An enchanted forest**
Puck here reports to his master, Oberon, of Titania's love for an ass.
CLASS, 1.5 minutes
A Midsummer Night's Dream by William Shakespeare, ed. by Wolfgang Clemen

785
Mendoza, 20s-30s
The Duke's court in Genoa
Here, the minion of the Duchess waxes with eloquent enthusiasm on the benefits of being favored in the court.
CLASS, 3 minutes
The Malcontent by John Marston

786
Othello, 40s-50s   **Venice**
When the Duke and his men ask Othello how he was able to win the fair Desdemona, he offers the following explanation.
CLASS, 3 minutes
Othello by William Shakespeare, ed. by Norman A. Bert

787
Vindice, 20s-30s   **17th century Europe**
When the woman he loves is poisoned by the Duke for refusing his advances, Vindice allows himself to become filled with hatred.
CLASS, 2.5 minutes
The Revenger's Tragedy by Cyril Tourneur

788
Spurio, 20s-30s   **17th century Europe**
A man made bitter by the fact of his illegitimate birth here vows revenge upon his father.
CLASS, 1.5 minutes
The Revenger's Tragedy by Cyril Tourneur

789
Ralph, 20s-30s
London, Watham Forest and Moldavia
When his master writes a play, this simple grocer's assistant finds himself having to portray the May Lord.
CLASS, 3.5 minutes
The Knight of the Burning Pestle by Beaumont and Fletcher

790
Jasper, 20s-30s
London, Watham Forest, and Moldavia
When he is wronged by the merchant to whom
he had been apprenticed, Jasper feigns his own
death so that he can appear to his tormentor as
a "ghost" and punish him.
CLASS, 1 minute
*The Knight of the Burning Pestle by Beaumont and
Fletcher*

791
Morose, 30s-40s   17th century London
Morose, a man who craves silence, here lec-
tures his servant on the most effective way to
communicate without speaking.
CLASS, 4 minutes
Epicoene, or The Silent Woman by Benjamin Johnson

792
Charlemont, 20s-30s
A 16th century French baronial estate
Charlemont has gone to war against his fa-
ther's wishes. When he is visited in a dream by
his father's ghost, he awakens and questions
the meaning of the strange experience.
CLASS, 2 minutes
The Atheist's Tragedy by Cyril Tourneur

793
D'Amville, 40s-50s
A 16th century French baronial estate
A man haunted by his evil past is here tor-
mented by phantoms.
CLASS, 1.5 minutes
The Atheist's Tragedy by Cyril Tourneur

794
Sancho, 20s-30s   Leon, Spain
Here, Sancho speaks of his love for the beauti-
ful Elvira.
CLASS, 2.5 minutes
*The King, the Greatest Alcalde by Lope Felix de Vega
Carpio, tr. by John Garrett Underhill*

795
Dièque, 50s-60s   Seville
The noble father of Roderick—the Cid—here
defends his son to the king, who believes that
Roderick has killed the Count of Gormaz.
Dièque takes responsibility for the murder and
asks that he be punished in his son's place.
CLASS, 2 minutes
*The Cid by Pierre Corneille, tr. by Florence Kendrick
Cooper*

796
Deflores, 20s-40s
Allegant, a seaport on the east coast of

Spain
The ugly Deflores here speaks of his love and
lust for his mistress.
CLASS, 1.5 minutes
*The Changeling by Thomas Middleton and William
Rowley*

797
Leantino, 30s-40s   Florence
When his wife leaves him to become the
Duke's concubine, Leantino grieves her loss.
CLASS, 1.5 minutes
Women Beware Women by Thomas Middleton

798
Jeppe, 30s-50s
Rural 18th century Denmark
Following a rather blistering dressing-down
from his nagging wife, Jeppe bemoans his fate.
CLASS, 5 minutes
*Jeppe of the Hill by Ludvig Holberg, tr. by M.
Jagendorf*

799
Jeppe, 30s-50s
Rural 18th century Denmark
When the Baron and his men discover Jeppe
fast asleep in the middle of the road, they de-
cide to put him in the Baron's clothes and bed
for jest. Here, the confused Jeppe awakens in
the Baron's sumptuous bedchamber and ques-
tions his sanity.
CLASS, 6 minutes
*Jeppe of the Hill by Ludvig Holberg, tr. by M.
Jagendorf*

800
Mellefont, 30s   A room in an inn
A notorious womanizer, Mellefont has finally
fallen in love with the virtuous young Sara.
Even so, he cannot seem to make a commit-
ment to her.
CLASS, 2.5 minutes
*Miss Sara Sampson by Gotthold Ephraim Lessing, tr.
by Ernest Bell*

801
David, 30s-40s   Israelis' camp in Gilboa
On the eve of the battle between the Israelites
and the Philistines, David—a onetime favorite
of Saul—addresses his concerns for the future
to God.
CLASS, 1.5 minutes
Saul by Vittorio Alfieri, tr. by E. A. Bowring

802
Brackenburg, 20s   Brussels
While people threaten to revolt against
Spanish rule, passionate young Brackenburg
laments an unrequited love.

CLASS, 4 minutes
Egmont by Johann Wolfgang Goethe, tr. by Anna Swanwick

803
Egmont, 30s   **Brussels**
Count Egmont has led the rebellion against Spanish rule in the Netherlands. Captured and sentenced to death, Egmont bravely faces his executioners.
CLASS, 3 minutes
Egmont by Johann Wolfgang Goethe, tr. by Anna Swanwick

804
William Tell,
A woods in 14th century Switzerland
A Swiss patriot leading the rebellion against Austrian rule, Tell here lies in wait for his enemy, Gessler.
CLASS, 4.5 minutes
William Tell by Johann Christoph Friedrich von Schiller, tr. by Sir Theodore Martin

805
Don Ruy Gomez, 50s-60s
Castle of Silva in the mountains of Aragon
The don desires to marry his beautiful young niece. Here, he tells her of his desire to be young again.
CLASS, 3 minutes
Hernani by Victor Hugo, tr. by Mrs. Newton Crosland

806
Simon Legree, 40s-50s   **Louisiana, 1850s**
The notoriously cruel Legree here reveals the source of his evil nature to Cassie, his slave and concubine.
CLASS, 5 minutes
Uncle Tom's Cabin by George L. Aiken

807
Oliver, 30s-40s   **19th century Paris**
The rakish Oliver here offers an insightful interpretation of Parisian society.
CLASS, 8 minutes
The Demi-Monde by Alexandre Dumas Fils, tr. by Harold Harper

808
Jean, 20s-30s
Count's manor house, 19th century Sweden
Jean, a servant, has been in love with the Count's daughter since they were both children. Here, he confesses his feelings to her.
CLASS, 7 minutes
Miss Julie by August Strindberg, tr. by Evert Sprinchorn

809
Herod, 50s-60s   **The court of Herod**
Herod has promised Salomé whatever she desires in return for dancing at his birthday feast. When she demands the head of John the Baptist, Herod tries in vain to discourage her bloody request.
CLASS, 7 minutes
Salomé by Oscar Wilde

810
Jack, 20s-30s   **Late 19th century England**
The "gorgonesque" Lady Bracknell has declared that Jack may not court her niece. By way of retaliation, Jack here declares to his nemesis that he doesn't consider her beloved nephew a suitable suitor for his niece.
CLASS, 2 minutes
The Importance of Being Earnest: A Trivial Comedy for Serious People by Oscar Wilde

811
Cyrano, 30s-40s
The Hotel de Bourgogne, 1640
When a boorish fellow comments on the size of his famous proboscis, noble Cyrano illustrates that it is eloquence rather than cheap shots that wins the evening.
CLASS, 5.5 minutes
Cyrano de Bergerac by Edmond Rostand, tr. by Gertrude Hall

812
Astroff, 30s-40s
A country estate, 19th century Russia
Here, a passionate environmentalist chastises Voitski for destroying his forests for wood to burn.
CLASS, 2.5 minutes
Uncle Vanya by Anton Chekhov, tr. by Marian Fell

813
The Lawyer, 40s-60
The legendary Fingal's Cave
This bitter man reveals the sorrow of his life's worth to the daughter of Indra.
CLASS, 3.5 minutes
The Dream Play by August Strindberg, tr. by Edwin Björkman

814
Simone, 40s   **A palazzo in Florence, 1900s**
When Simone and his wife are paid a visit by the son of the Prince of Florence, he trips over himself to flatter his guest.
CLASS, 3.5 minutes
A Florentine Tragedy by Oscar Wilde

815
Bill, any age   **A lonely place**
Bill and Jim find themselves standing outside a large gate that they assume is the entrance to Heaven. As Bill tries to pry the gate open, he shares his vision of Paradise with Jim.
CLASS, 3 minutes
The Glittering Gate by Lord Dunsany

816
Esteban, 40s-50s
A farmhouse in Castille, 1920s
Esteban has fallen in love with his wife's daughter by her first husband and has murdered the young woman's fiancé in a jealous rage. When his wife confronts him with his evil deeds, he tries to explain.
CLASS, 3 minutes
The Passion Flower by Jacinto Benavente, tr. by John Garrett Underhill

817
Paddy, 50s-60s
An ocean liner, 1 hour after leaving NYC
As the hands gather to drink and gossip, the senior member of their ranks reminisces about days gone by.
CLASS, 4.5 minutes
The Hairy Ape by Eugene O'Neill

818
Mr. Zero, 45-50   **An unspecified city, 1920s**
When he is arrested and tried for murder, Mr. Zero addresses the jury with the sad state of his life.
CLASS, 13 minutes
The Adding Machine by Elmer Rice

819
Henry IV, 50
A solitary villa in Italy in our own time
A wealthy madman who has assumed the identity of Shakespeare's Henry IV here rants at his servants.
CLASS, 4 minutes
Henry IV by Luigi Pirandello, tr. by Edward Storer

820
Henry IV, 50
A solitary villa in Italy in our own time
Here, a wealthy madman who has assumed the identity of Shakespeare's Henry IV offers a fascinating treatise on madness.
CLASS, 2.5 minutes
Henry IV by Luigi Pirandello, tr. by Edward Storer

821
Ephraim Cabot, 70
The Cabot farmhouse in New England, 1850

Ephraim's young wife has been unable to conceive the son he desires to inherit his farm. Here, Ephraim tells her the story of his battle to carve out his own life and his need for an heir.
CLASS, 5.5 minutes
Desire Under the Elms by Eugene O'Neill

822
Mr. Scratch, 30s-60s
Cross Corners, NH 1841
Here, the clever Mr. Scratch summons the jury of the damned to sit in judgment on Mr. Stone.
CLASS, 2 minutes
The Devil and Daniel Webster by Stephen Vincent Benet

823
Willy Loman, 50s-60s
The Loman house, 1940s
Willy Loman has spent his life on the road. The realization that his children have grown up without him, combined with his growing disenchantment with the traveling life, leads Willy to make the following desperate plea to his boss.
CLASS, 3 minutes
Death of a Salesman by Arthur Miller

824
Lord Byron, 40s
A fantasy limbo called "Camino Real"
Here, Lord Byron describes the cremation of Percy Shelley.
CLASS, 2.5 minutes
Camino Real by Tennessee Williams

825
Johnny, 20s-30s
Lower East Side of Manhattan, 1950s
When his father comes to visit, Johnny is filled with memories of his childhood, which he here shares with his wife.
CLASS, 3 minutes
A Hat Full of Rain by Michael Vincent Gazzo

826
Don Juan, 30s-40s
The Great Wall of China
Don Juan here speaks to Christopher Columbus about the golden age of discovery and of mankind's desperate need for new horizons.
CLASS, 2.5 minutes
The Chinese Wall by Max Frisch, tr. by James L. Rosenberg

827
Hamm, 40s-50s   **A bare interior**

As Hamm's sense of reality disintegrates, he rambles endlessly about the weather, corn and porridge.
CLASS, 7.5 minutes
Endgame by Samuel Beckett

828
Aston, 20s-30s   A house in West London
Here, Aston describes receiving shock treatment in a mental institution.
CLASS, 9 minutes
The Caretaker by Harold Pinter

829
Davies, 50s-60s   A house in West London
Davies has been befriended by Aston, a younger man with brain damage. Sharing a house with Aston, however, becomes more than Davies can bear, as can be seen in the following attack.
CLASS, 4 minutes
The Caretaker by Harold Pinter

830
Io, 20s   A mountain in Scythia
Io, who has been transformed into a cow by Zeus in order to save her from the wrath of Hera, tells her unhappy story to Prometheus.
CLASS, 2.5 minutes
Prometheus Bound by Æschylus, tr. by J. S. Blackie

831
Antigone, 18-20
The royal palace at Thebes
When Antigone grants her brother a token burial in defiance of the decree of the king, she is sentenced to be buried alive. Here, she welcomes her fate.
CLASS, 2 minutes
Antigone by Sophocles, tr. by Sir George Young

832
Lysistrata, 20s-30s   Athens
Frustrated by Athens' involvement in the Peloponnesian War, Lysistrata convinces the women to withhold all services until peace is achieved. Here, she explains to a commander how governing the states of Greece is no more difficult than unraveling skeins of wool.
CLASS, 1.5 minutes
Lysistrata by Aristophanes, tr. by Donald Sutherland

833
Medea, 20s-30s
The royal palace at Corinth
Medea has sacrificed all for Jason, and when he rejects her and plans to marry another woman, she sinks into a dark despair and begins to plan revenge.
CLASS, 3 minutes
Medea by Seneca, tr. by Frank Justus Miller

834
Medea, 20s-30s
The royal palace at Corinth
Close to madness, Medea reviews the crimes she has committed for Jason, including the grisly death of her own brother.
CLASS, 2 minutes
Medea by Seneca, tr. by Frank Justus Miller

835
Zenocrate, 20s-30s   Medieval Persia
Following her ruthless husband's bloody conquest of Damascus, Zenocrate grieves for the dead.
CLASS, 2.5 minutes
Tamburlaine the Great by Christopher Marlowe

836
Kate, 20s-30s   Medieval Padua
The tamed shrew here counsels women on the proper way to manage a married relationship.
CLASS, 2 minutes
The Taming of the Shrew by William Shakespeare

837
Titania, 30s-40s   An enchanted forest
When Oberon feels that Titania has betrayed him, he confronts her with his jealous suspicions. The willful queen offers the following response.
CLASS, 3 minutes
A Midsummer Night's Dream by William Shakespeare

838
Aurelia, 20s-30s   The Duke's court in Genoa
Having fallen victim to the vicious intrigues of the court, the Duchess finds herself facing exile.
CLASS, 1.5 minutes
The Malcontent by John Marston

839
Aspatia, 20s   The city of Rhodes
When the king decrees that Aspatia may not marry Amintor, the young woman takes comfort in the company of her ladies-in-waiting and here counsels them on how best to fall in love.
CLASS, 2 minutes
The Maid's Tragedy by Francis Beaumont and John Fletcher

840
Castabella, 20s-30s
A 16th century baronial estate

When the evil D'Amville attempts to seduce the virtuous Castabella, she denounces his adulterous lust to God.
CLASS, 1.5 minutes
The Atheist's Tragedy by Cyril Tourneur

841
Phenix, 20s
The court of the King of Fez, Morocco
The young princess has discovered that her father intends to marry her to a man she does not love, and as a result she can no longer be moved by the earth's beauty.
CLASS, 1.5 minutes
The Constant Prince by Pedro Calderon de la Barca, tr. by Denis Florence MacCarthy

842
Elvira, 20s-30s   **Leon, Spain**
Elvira has been raped by the evil Don Tello. Here, she tells her story to the king and begs for justice.
CLASS, 3.5 minutes
The King, the Greatest Alcalde by Lope Felix de Vega Carpio, tr. by John Garrett Underhill

843
Chimène, 20s   **Seville**
The daughter of the Count of Gormaz here confronts her father's murderer, the Cid, who also happens to be the man she loves.
CLASS, 1 minute
The Cid by Pierre Corneille, tr. by Florence Kendrick Cooper

844
Beatrice, 20s-30s
A seaport on the east coast of Spain
Beatrice persuades her servant, Deflores, to murder her fiancé so that she can marry the man she loves. In return, however, Deflores demands that she sleep with him. On the eve of her wedding, Beatrice fears that her husband will detect her non-virginal status on their wedding night.
CLASS, 2.5 minutes
The Changeling by Thomas Middleton and William Rowley

845
Isabella, 20s-30s   **Florence**
When her aunt's marriage is announced, Isabella ruminates on the place of women and their responsibility to accept the husbands chosen for them.
CLASS, 1.5 minutes
Women Beware Women by Thomas Middleton

846
Bianca, 20s-30s   **Florence**
When Bianca's beauty captures the interest of the Duke, she allows him to seduce her. Here, she laments betraying her husband.
CLASS, 1.5 minutes
Women Beware Women by Thomas Middleton

847
Magdelon, 18-20
The house of Gorgibus, Paris, 17th century
Here Magdelon, a self-centered and rather silly young woman, explains the rules of courtship and chivalry to her father.
CLASS, 1.5 minutes
Two Precious Maidens Ridiculed by Moliére, tr. by Albert Bermel

848
Berenice, 20s-30s
The imperial palace in Rome
The Queen of Palestine has been brought to Rome to marry Titus, the Emperor. When a friend warns that marriage to foreigners isn't well regarded, Berenice points out the absolute authority of the Emperor.
CLASS, 1.5 minutes
Berenice by Jean Racine, tr. by R. B. Boswell

849
Phædra, 20s-30s   **Ancient Greece**
Here, Phædra confesses her forbidden passion for Hippolytus, her stepson, to her old nurse.
CLASS, 2.5 minutes
Phædra by Jean Racine, tr. by Robert Lowell

850
Mistress Bracegirdle, 30s-40s
17th century England
Here, an actress speaks to the audience in a prologue in which she condemns the playwright for having the audacity to have written three plays at once.
CLASS, 1.5 minutes
The Provok'd Wife by Sir John Vanbrugh

851
Lady Brute, 30s   **17th century England**
Having been rudely chastised for her questionable morality by her bitter husband, Lady Brute fumes as she considers the possibilities for her revenge.
CLASS, 3 minutes
The Provok'd Wife by Sir John Vanbrugh

852
Mrs. Sullen, 40s-50s
Litchfield, England, early 18th century
Here, Mrs. Sullen offers jaded counsel to young Dorinda, who fancies herself in love.
CLASS, 3.5 minutes
The Beaux-Stratagem by George Farquhar

853
Sara, 20s   **A room in an inn**
Sara, a young lady pure of heart, has run away
with the disreputable Mellefont. Here, she tells
Mellefont of a dream.
CLASS, 3 minutes
*Miss Sara Sampson by Gotthold Ephraim Lessing, tr.
by Ernest Bell*

854
Marwood, 30s
Marwood is a woman who was cast aside by
the rakish Mellefont and who has attempted to
take the life of Sara, his new lover. Here, she
rages about her base intentions and threatens
to take her own life as well.
CLASS, 2.5 minutes
*Miss Sara Sampson by Gotthold Ephraim Lessing, tr.
by Ernest Bell*

855
Miss Hardcastle, 20s   18th century London
This young lady posed as a barmaid in order
to win the man she loved. Here, she addresses
the audience on the different ages of women.
CLASS, 2 minutes
She Stoops to Conquer by Oliver Goldsmith

856
Rosine, 18-20
The house of Bartholo, a physician, in Seville
Here, the innocent young Rosine entertains a
lecherous count with a song of springtime.
CLASS, 3 minutes
*The Barber of Seville by Pierre Augustin Caron de
Beaumarchais, tr. by W.R. Taylor*

857
Clara, 20s   **Brussels**
Clara's lover is Count Egmont, the brave leader of
the rebellion against Spanish rule in the
Netherlands. Clara has heard rumors of his cap-
ture and here anxiously awaits their confirmation.
CLASS, 3 minutes
*Egmont by Johann Wolfgang Goethe, tr. by Anna
Swanwick*

858
The Locksmith's Wife, 30s-50s
A Russian village, 1830s
Believing a young bureaucrat to be the inspec-
tor general, the wife of the local locksmith
wastes no time in complaining to him about
the corrupt mayor, who has forced her hus-
band to join the army against her wishes.
CLASS, 2.5 minutes
*The Inspector General by Nikolai Gogol, tr. by
Robert Saffron*

859
Klara, 20s-30s
**A town of moderate size, the cabinet-
maker's house**
Klara reveals her love and concern for her
mother as she watches the older woman walk
to church.
CLASS, 3.5 minutes
*Maria Magdalena by Friedrich Hebbel, tr. by Carl
Richard Mueller*

860
Suzanne, 20s-30s   19th century Paris
Here, the manipulative Suzanne chastises her
ex-lover for treating her poorly.
CLASS, 2.5 minutes
*The Demi-Monde by Alexandre Dumas Fils, tr. by
Harold Harper*

861
Katerina, 20s-30s
The town of Kalinov, Russia, 19th century
Katerina here confides to her sister-in-law that
she is unhappy with the confinement of mar-
ried life and longs for the freedom she enjoyed
as a young girl.
CLASS, 4.5 minutes
*The Thunderstorm by Alexander Ostrovsky, tr. by
Florence Whyte and George Rapall Noyes*

862
Katerina, 20s-30s
The town of Kalinov, Russia, 19th century
Katerina has fallen in love with young Boris
and finally escapes the suffocating confines of
her husband's house. Rejected by all, she wan-
ders aimlessly, tortured by the knowledge of
her betrayal.
CLASS, 3 minutes
*The Thunderstorm by Alexander Ostrovsky, tr. by
Florence Whyte and George Rapall Noyes*

863
Julie, 20s
**The Count's manor house, 19th century
Sweden**
Julie has impulsively agreed to run away with
Jean, a servant in her father's employ. When
Jean kills her pet canary so as not to be bur-
dened with its cage on their flight, Julie erupts
with long-repressed rage.
CLASS, 3 minutes
*Miss Julie by August Strindberg, tr. by Evert
Sprinchorn*

864
Lady Windermere, 20s-30s
Late 19th century London
When she discovers her husband's infidelity,
Lady Windermere decides to run away with

the notorious Lord Darlington. Here, she anxiously awaits his arrival.
CLASS, 2.5 minutes
Lady Windermere's Fan by Oscar Wilde

865
Salomé, 15-20   The court of Herod
The fickle nature of youth is well-illustrated in Salomé's seduction of John the Baptist.
CLASS, 4 minutes
Salomé by Oscar Wilde

866
Salomé, 15-20   The court of Herod
When Herod reluctantly grants her demand for the head of John the Baptist, Salomé grieves for the loss of his life.
CLASS, 5.5 minutes
Salomé by Oscar Wilde

867
Magda, 30s-40s
A provincial 19th century European town
When her performance in a concert brings her back to her childhood home, Magda finds that reconciliation with her family is impossible. When her father threatens to kill her unless she marries the man who fathered her child, she explodes with years of stored anger.
CLASS, 3.5 minutes
Magda by Herman Sudermann, tr. by Charles Edward Amory Winslow

868
Helena, 20s
A country estate, 19th century Russia
Here, Helena takes a moment to muse over the unrequited love of her friend, Sonia, as well as her own forbidden feelings for the fiery Dr. Astroff.
CLASS, 2 minutes
Uncle Vanya by Anton Chekhov, tr. by Marian Fell

869
The daughter of Indra, 20s
The legendary Fingal's Cave
The daughter of the mighty god is approached by an earthly poet, who asks that she read a grievance in the form of a prayer to her father. Here, she reads it aloud.
CLASS, 4.5 minutes
The Dream Play by August Strindberg, tr. by Edwin Björkman

870
Nora, 40s
A cottage, County Wicklow, Ireland, 1900s
Believing her husband to be dead, Nora tells a young admirer of the reasons she chose to

marry and her fears for the future.
CLASS, 3 minutes
In the Shadow of the Glen by John M. Synge

871
Raimunda, 40s-50s
A farmhouse in Castille, 1920s
When she discovers that her husband is in love with her daughter, and has murdered the young woman's fiancé, Raimunda confronts him with his crimes.
CLASS, 2.5 minutes
The Passion Flower by Jacinto Benavente, tr. by John Garrett Underhill

872
Mrs. Zero, 45
An unspecified city in the 1920s
Mrs. Zero reveals her shallow and mean nature in the following verbal assault on her resting husband.
CLASS, 11 minutes
The Adding Machine by Elmer Rice

873
Joan, 20
The chamber of the assessors, 1431
Here, the maid of Orleans tells her captors that it is they who are ruled by the devil and not she.
CLASS, 2.5 minutes
Saint Joan by Bernard Shaw

874
Mrs. Tancred, 50s-70s
A tenement house, Dublin, 1922
When her son is killed by soldiers, Mrs. Tancred shares her grief with her friends.
CLASS, 2 minutes
Juno and the Paycock by Sean O'Casey

875
Mrs. Phelps, 50s-60s
Suburban America, 1920s
When her son brings home his new wife, Mrs. Phelps pleads with her new daughter-in-law to leave her some place in David's heart.
CLASS, 3 minutes
The Silver Cord by Sidney Howard

876
Christina, 20s-30s
Suburban America, 1920s
Christina fears that David's mother is ruining their marriage and tells him so.
CLASS, 4.5 minutes
The Silver Cord by Sidney Howard

877
Sabrina, 30s
A commuter's home in New Jersey, 1940s
Here, the family maid awaits the return of the master of the house while treating the audience to an entertaining introduction to his family.
CLASS, 6 minutes
The Skin of Our Teeth by Thornton Wilder

878
A Fortune Teller, 30s-60s
A commuter's home in New Jersey, 1940s
Here, an earthy Fortune Teller observes that it's much easier to tell a person's future than their past.
CLASS, 3 minutes
The Skin of Our Teeth by Thornton Wilder

879
Marguerite, indefinite age
A fantasy limbo called "Camino Real"
A woman trapped in limbo cautions her male companion not to fall in love with her.
CLASS, 3 minutes
Camino Real by Tennessee Williams

880
Margaret, 30s
"Big Daddy" Pollitt's home, Mississippi, 1950s
Maggie's husband, an alcoholic ex-football star, has lost interest in her sexually. Here, she tries to rekindle their relationship by making him jealous.
CLASS, 2 minutes
Cat on a Hot Tin Roof by Tennessee Williams

881
Margaret, 30s
"Big Daddy" Pollitt's home, Mississippi, 1950s
Brick holds Maggie responsible for the death of his best friend. Here, she passionately confronts his accusations.
CLASS, 4 minutes
Cat on a Hot Tin Roof by Tennessee Williams

882
Agnes, 20s-30s
International Bureau of Investigations, Paris, 1950s
When a timid woman is visited by the god of beauty, she speaks to him of her less-than-beautiful life.
CLASS, 3 minutes
The Apollo of Bellac; adapted by Maurice Valency, from the French of Jean Giraudoux

883
Jackie, 30s-40s
The Paradise Roadhouse, 1950s
When Bus returns to the small midwestern town of his childhood, he is confronted by Jackie, the woman he left behind.
CLASS, 2.5 minutes
Glory in the Flower by William Inge

884
Mrs. Curran, 60s   South Africa, Present
Mrs. Curran, a widow sick with cancer, tells a 12-year-old black activist who is just returning from a stay in the hospital about the realities of his situation and the fate of his compatriot.
CONLIT, 7.5 minutes
Age of Iron by J.M. Coetzee

885
Taylor, 20s   Arizona, Present
Taylor tries to console Esperanza, a Mexican who can barely understand English and who has lost her child.
CONLIT, 3 minutes
The Bean Trees by Barbara Kingsolver

886
Lou Ann, 20s   Arizona, Present
Here, Lou Ann describes a job interview she has just come from at a convenience store.
CONLIT, 1 minute
The Bean Trees by Barbara Kingsolver

887
Taylor, 20s   Arizona, Present
Taylor's daughter, Turtle, has just been molested. Here, Taylor is weeping as she explains the depth of her upset to her friend Lou Ann.
CONLIT, 3 minutes
The Bean Trees by Barbara Kingsolver

888
Persia, 31   Hammond, NY, Present
Persia has gone to the studio of her brother-in-law Leslie to be photographed with her daughter Iris. A thunderstorm and blackout traps them there. They drink and Persia gets drunk. She talks about life and her unsatisfactory relationship with her husband.
CONLIT, 3 minutes
Because It Is Better, and Because It Is My Heart by Joyce Carol Oates

889
Sugar Baby Fairchild, 20s   Hammond, NY, Present
Sugar Baby tries to convince his kid brother Jinx to shave points in an upcoming championship-round basketball game.
CONLIT, 4.5 minutes
Because It Is Better, and Because It Is My Heart by Joyce Carol Oates

890
Persia Courtney, 30s
Hammond, NY, Present
Persia, a deteriorating alcoholic, reacts to her daughter Iris' efforts to help her stop drinking.
CONLIT, 2 minutes
Because It Is Better, and Because It Is My Heart by Joyce Carol Oates

891
Grandfather, 60s   **Italy, 1960**
Grandpa responds to his daughter, who is pregnant but not by her husband, who is in America.
CONLIT, 1.5 minutes
The Book of Saints by Nino Ricci

892
Cristina, 30s   **Italy, 1960**
Cristina is leaving Italy for America. She has been given the "evil eye" by the villagers for being pregnant out of wedlock. She speaks to the people as she leaves.
CONLIT, 1 minute
The Book of Saints by Nino Ricci

893
Joseph Gallo, 60s   **NYC, Present**
Joe, consigliere to the Godfather, is depressed that one of their people is in the hands of the FBI and may talk. He speaks to the Godfather.
CONLIT, 1 minute
Boss of Bosses by Joseph F. O'Brien and Andris Kurins

894
Gloria Olarte, 20s   **NYC, Present**
Gloria is the Godfather's housekeeper and mistress. Here she expresses some concern to a "sympathetic" FBI agent.
CONLIT, 4.5 minutes
Boss of Bosses by Joseph F. O'Brien and Andris Kurins

895
Paul Castellano, 60s
NYC, Present
Paul, the Godfather, has been arrested and is in a car with two FBI agents on the way to being indicted. He becomes talkative.
CONLIT, 3 minutes
Boss of Bosses by Joseph F. O'Brien and Andris Kurins

896
Parker Jagoda, 35-40   **Chicago, Present**
Parker, although a family man, has developed an interest in sadomasochism. Here he tells a date (from a singles ad he has run) a story

which he has made up as a test for use at such occasions.
CONLIT, 3.5 minutes
Chicago Loop by Paul Theroux

897
Sofya, 50s   **Moscow, 1935**
Sofya's brother Mark, a communist party functionary, has attempted to justify and explain away the arrest and exile to Siberia of her twenty-year-old son Sasha. Sofya replies.
CONLIT, 3 minutes
Children of The Arbat by Anatoli Rybakov, translated by Harold Shukman

898
Grandpa Blakeslee, 59   **Georgia, 1906**
Grandma is on her deathbed. Grandpa recollects sweet moments to her through his pain.
CONLIT, 2 minutes
Cold Sassy Tree by Olive Ann Burns

899
Grandpa Blakeslee, 59   **Georgia, 1906**
Grandma is dying. Grandpa talks to God in his very personal style.
CONLIT, 2.5 minutes
Cold Sassy Tree by Olive Ann Burns

900
Grandpa Blakeslee, 59   **Georgia, 1906**
Grandpa has just eloped with his bookkeeper, Miss Love, three weeks after his wife of forty-odd years died. He comforts his children and grandchildren after dinner. All is tense until his good-bye.
CONLIT, 1.5 minutes
Cold Sassy Tree by Olive Ann Burns

901
Sam, 60s   **Atlantic Ocean, 1920-40**
Sam explains his distrust of women by recollecting a shipboard experience which occurred as he was fleeing from his unfaithful wife.
CONLIT, 4.5 minutes
The Death of Methuselah and Other Stories, A Peephole in the Gate by Isaac Beshevis Singer

902
G-Roc, 15   **An LA reform school, Present**
G-Roc, an incarcerated Crips gang member, eschews rape and tells why.
CONLIT, 3 minutes
Do or Die by Léon Bing

903
Faro, 17   **Los Angeles, Present**
Faro, a homeless gang member, explains the "rules of engagement."

CONLIT, 3 minutes
Do or Die by Léon Bing

904
Faro, 17   **Los Angeles, Present**
Faro, a homeless gang member, talks of life
and death.
CONLIT, 1.5 minutes
Do or Die by Léon Bing

905
Lefty, 30-40   **NYC, 1970s**
FBI agent Joseph F. Pistone has infiltrated the
mob using the alias Donnie Brasco. Here Lefty,
Donnie's mentor, lectures Donnie regarding
the proper attitude for a contract hit.
CONLIT, 1.5 minutes
*Donnie Brasco: My Undercover Life in The Mafia by
Joseph D. Pistone with Richard Woodley*

906
Man, any age   **Dictatorship, Present**
Traveling in a poor country, a man confronts
himself.
CONLIT, 2.5 minutes
The Fever by Wallace Shawn

907
Irina Asanova, 20s   **Moscow, Present**
Irina and her lover Arkady are caught between
two bad choices. She has spent many years in
Siberia and tells him this story.
CONLIT, 1.5 minutes
Gorky Park by Martin Cruz Smith

908
Arkady Renko, 30s   **Moscow, Present**
Police investigator Renko has discovered that
his lover is also the lover of the man he is
tracking. He confronts her with his knowl-
edge.
CONLIT, 1.5 minutes
Gorky Park by Martin Cruz Smith

909
Nivea, 50s   **South America, 1900**
Here, Nivea tells her daughter Clara a story
about a tree linked to both tradition and mis-
fortune in the del Valle family.
CONLIT, 3 minutes
The House of The Spirits by Isabel Allende

910
Nivea, 50s   **South America, 1900**
The mother of Clara and Rosa tells Clara a
cautionary tale about the girl's Uncle Juan,
who was the victim of an accident that had
tragic consequences.
CONLIT, 2.5 minutes
The House of the Spirits by Isabel Allende

911
Esteban Trueba, 30s   **South America, 1900**
Esteban is a tall, imperious man with a regal
demeanor, striking visage, powerful stride and
an explosive temper. Following the death of his
fiancée Rosa, Esteban comes to reclaim an
abandoned house occupied years ago by his
family. He decries the selfishness of the peas-
ants living in the town surrounding his ha-
cienda.
CONLIT, 3 minutes
The House of the Spirits by Isabel Allende

912
Mrs. Dupont, 50s   **NYC, Present**
Mrs. Dupont hitches a ride in a limousine in
New York's financial district. She says she is on
the way home from the hospital and then re-
veals some very personal matters to the male
passenger, Byron Coffin.
CONLIT, 2.5 minutes
The Imposter by Paula Sharp

913
Daisy, 38   **Wisconsin, Present**
Daisy has just been jilted for a younger, pret-
tier woman. She tells a friend how she feels
about it.
CONLIT, 3 minutes
The Imposter by Paula Sharp

914
Molly, 30-50   **Connecticut, Present**
Molly telephones Lily after midnight to tell her
that their friend Inez has just been found dead.
They talk for hours. Here, Molly dissects
Inez's live-in lover Kevin.
CONLIT, 2.5 minutes
*Interviewing Matisse or The Woman Who Died
Standing Up by Lily Tuck*

915
Molly, 30-50   **Connecticut, Present**
Molly telephones Lily after midnight to tell her
that their friend Inez has just been found dead.
They talk for hours. Here, Molly discusses
Inez's mother and her love for the telephone.
CONLIT, 1.5 minutes
*Interviewing Matisse or The Woman Who Died
Standing Up by Lily Tuck*

916
Molly, 30-50   **Connecticut, Present**
Molly telephones Lily after midnight to tell her
that their friend Inez has just been found dead.
They talk for hours. Here, Molly reminisces
about her hometown.
CONLIT, 4.5 minutes
*Interviewing Matisse or The Woman Who Died
Standing Up by Lily Tuck*

917
Fred, 26   **Queens, New York, Present**
The family is gathered at the Passover table.
Mom wants the whole ceremony. Dad wants
to paraphrase it for the assembled. Fred does it
instead.
CONLIT, 3 minutes
Kiss Out by Jill Eisenstadt

918
Mrs. Shtrum, 60   **Russia, 1939-1940**
Mrs. Shtrum, a Russian doctor who has been
trapped in her small village by the German invasion, writes to her son in Moscow about the
atrocities which have begun and the ominous
implications for the future. Here she concludes
with a farewell.
CONLIT, 4 minutes
*Life and Fate by Vasily Grossman, translated from
Russian by Robert Chandler*

919
Lila, 30s   **NYC, Present**
Phaedrus has picked up Lila during a drunken
evening and they have slept together. Now he
is trying to find out what she's all about. She
resists his interrogation.
CONLIT, 5.5 minutes
Lila by Robert M. Pirsig

920
Isadora Baily, 20s   **New Orleans, 1830**
Isadora answers her boyfriend Rutherford's
question as to why she has conspired with his
murderous creditors to blackmail him into
marriage with her.
CONLIT, 2 minutes
Middle Passage by Charles Johnson

921
Peter Cringle, 20s   **Atlantic Ocean, 1830**
Cringle, a finer type than the usual crewman,
explains how he came to be a seafarer.
CONLIT, 2.5 minutes
Middle Passage by Charles Johnson

922
Squibb, 50s   **Atlantic Ocean, 1830s**
Aboard a slaver, having suffered a successful
mutiny by the black prisoners, and where
everyone is starving and sick, Squibb explains
to a cabin boy from whence derived the meat
stew they have just eaten.
CONLIT, 4.5 minutes
Middle Passage by Charles Johnson

923
Del, 20s   **Greek Islands, Present**
Del, a camerawoman, lives with Frank, a film-
maker. She tells a friend why she respects
Frank.
CONLIT, 2 minutes
The Names by Don DeLillo

924
James, 30s   **Greece, Present**
James has become infatuated watching Janet, a
slim American, belly dance at a nightclub. He
talks to her at a table, trying to reach her in a
very direct and intense way.
CONLIT, 2.5 minutes
The Names by Don DeLillo

925
Peekay, 10   **South Africa, 1950**
Peekay, a farm boy, having just been sent to a
boys' boarding school, tells of his welcome.
CONLIT, 4.5 minutes
The Power of One by Bryce Courtenay

926
Magdalena, 40   **Albany, NY, 1850**
Magdalena, a traveling actress/"sensualist,"
includes in her entourage her precocious
twelve-year-old niece Maud, her dog, and her
maid and alter ego, Clara. A boating accident
claims Clara's life and injures Magdalena's
face. Maud is saved by a gallant fifteen-year-
old, Daniel Quinn. When Maud professes her
eternal love for young Quinn, Magdalena delivers a stern lecture to her.
CONLIT, 2.5 minutes
Quinn's Book by William Kennedy

927
Joey Ryan, 14   **Albany, NY, 1850**
Joey Ryan, his father, sister and mother are recent immigrants to America. His father has
just been killed by a drunken man who, having
been laid off at the foundry, looks for a newly
hired man to take vengeance on. When asked
where he came from in Ireland, Joey answers.
CONLIT, 2.5 minutes
Quinn's Book by William Kennedy

928
Daniel Quinn, 29   **Albany, NY, 1864**
Daniel Quinn, addressing an audience of local
people eager to know about the war firsthand,
relates a very personal war experience.
CONLIT, 2.5 minutes
Quinn's Book by William Kennedy

929
Daniel Quinn, 29   **Albany, NY, 1864**
Daniel Quinn, addressing an audience of his
hometown people, talks of a local boy who
didn't make good during the war.

CONLIT, 8.5 minutes
Quinn's Book by William Kennedy

930
Mr. Kohler, 19-20
A New England college town, Present
Kohler, a college physics major, attempts to convince Roger Lambert, a divinity professor, of the scientific basis of the existence of God. He is seeking support for a grant application for money to support research into his theory.
CONLIT, 1.5 minutes
Roger's Version by John Updike

931
Verna, early 20s
A New England college town, Present
Verna describes her situation and living conditions to her uncle, who has come to see her unexpectedly.
CONLIT, 1 minute
Roger's Version by John Updike

932
Verna, early 20s
A New England college town, Present
Verna suddenly believes that her uncle's unexpected interest in her welfare is based on his concern for her baby daughter, Paula.
CONLIT, 1 minute
Roger's Version by John Updike

933
Smiley, 60s   **London, 1960s**
Here, Smiley, a Secret Service agent, lectures a class of novice spies.
CONLIT, 2 minutes
The Secret Pilgrim by John le Carré

934
Hansen, 40s   **Cambodian jungle, 1960s**
Here, Hansen tells a fellow spy of his daughter Marie and how he discovered she had been captured by the Khmer Rouge.
CONLIT, 5 minutes
The Secret Pilgrim by John le Carré

935
Marie, late teens   **Cambodia, 1960s**
Here, Hansen's daughter Marie, having been captured and indoctrinated by the Khmer Rouge, identifies her father as a spy after he has been captured.
CONLIT, 2.5 minutes
The Secret Pilgrim by John le Carré

936
Reverend Buddy Winkler, 40s
NYC, Present
Buddy has run into his twenty-four-year-old niece Ellen Cherry on a street in New York. He has come on a fundamentalist "mission." She asks him why he objects to peace in the Middle East. Buddy answers.
CONLIT, 2.5 minutes
Skinny Legs and All by Tom Robbins

937
Boomer Petway, 20s
NYC, Present
Boomer has left his wife, Ellen Cherry. Although it is she who has studied art and come to New York to show, it is Boomer who has made it big in the New York art scene. Ellen Cherry didn't go to his opening. She calls to explain why. Boomer won't talk to her and here explains why.
CONLIT, 2 minutes
Skinny Legs and All by Tom Robbins

938
Buddy Winkler, 40s
NYC, Present
Buddy is a small-town fundamentalist preacher. Upon hearing that he and his zealots plan to blow up the Dome of the Rock in Jerusalem to hasten the advent of Armagedon, Ellen Cherry accuses Buddy of gambling with the lives of billions of people. He responds.
CONLIT, 1.5 minutes
Skinny Legs and All by Tom Robbins

939
Orfeo Quatta, 60s   **Rome, 1913**
Orfeo, a hunchback dwarf and madman, speaks to a sold-out auditorium in Bologna in the guise of the president of the University of Trondheim in Norway.
CONLIT, 2.5 minutes
A Soldier of the Great War by Mark Helprin

940
Guariglia, 30s   **Italy, 1916**
Guariglia is an imprisoned army deserter awaiting execution. He is a devoted father and here responds to his friend who refers to clouds as rafts for souls.
CONLIT, 3 minutes
A Soldier of the Great War by Mark Helprin

941
General, 30s   **Alpines, Italy, 1916**
Here, a general speaks to his troops before sending them into battle in the mountains between Italy and Austria.
CONLIT, 4 minutes
A Soldier of the Great War by Mark Helprin

942
Field Marshal Strassnitzky, 50s
Austria, 1917
Strassnitzky explains to his Italian prisoner Alessandro why he is a pacifist.
CONLIT, 1.5 minutes
A Soldier of The Great War by Mark Helprin

943
Alessandro, 70s
Italian countryside, 1960s
Alessandro tells his young friend Nicolo how he found his love after the great war.
CONLIT, 3.5 minutes
A Soldier of The Great War by Mark Helprin

944
Evelyn Matlock, 40   **London, Present**
During a murder investigation, Inspector Dalgliesh's subordinate Massingham accuses the maid of having an affair with the master of the house. Lady Ursula characterizes the accusation as ridiculous and grotesque. Evelyn responds.
CONLIT, 2 minutes
A Taste for Death by P.D. James

945
Canny, 7   **Fairground, Present**
Canny was stolen as an infant by Dotty and Wallace, whom she now knows as her parents. They live the life of hobos. Canny finds her Poppy (Wallace) in the parking lot of an amusement park and explains why she's late.
CONLIT, 2.5 minutes
Vanished by Mary McGarry Morris

946
Dotty, 20s   **Massachusetts, Present**
Dotty, Wallace and seven-year-old Canny have been "on the road" for five years. Here, Dotty tells her new friend Huller, an ex-con, how she kidnapped Canny.
CONLIT, 2.5 minutes
Vanished by Mary McGarry Morris

947
Dotty, 20s   **Massachusetts, Present**
Dotty finds Carl molesting her seven-year-old "daughter." She tries to kill him with a shovel. Then she tells a story about another young girl (herself).
CONLIT, 8.5 minutes
Vanished by Mary McGarry Morris

948
William, 30-40   **January 19, 1980**
Supreme Court Justice William O. Douglas authored the decision that assures a constitutional right to privacy among many others.

The great man is dying and is here transformed in his mind into his younger self. Seriocomic.
MEN80, 4 minutes
Mountain by Douglas Scott

949
Henri, 40-50   **France, early 20th century**
This play is a series of vignettes from the life of artist Henri Matisse. Each scene uses as its background a particular painting of Matisse. Here, Henri describes painting a prostitute. Seriocomic.
MEN80, 4 minutes
The Pink Studio by Jane Anderson

950
Streaky, 40-50   **London, Present**
The Rev. Donald "Streaky" Bacon has watched while his church is divided into two camps by the older vicar and an idealistic young priest. After several cocktails, Streaky shares some of his thoughts with God. Seriocomic.
MEN80, 2.5 minutes
Racing Demon by David Hare

951
Skolar, 40-50   **London, Present**
Skolar is the domineering and abusive patriarch of a West Indian family that has moved to England in search of a better life. When Skolar encounters Jacko, an old friend, he reveals his over-protective feelings for his youngest daughter. Dramatic.
MEN80, 2.5 minutes
Back Street Mammy by Trish Cooke

952
Jerome, 30s   **Brooklyn, Present**
Jerome is facing a mid-life crisis along with a touch of death anxiety brought on by the premature death of his friend in a motorcycle accident. Tortured by his fear of nothingness, Jerome is unable to sleep. He wakes his wife and confides his fears. Dramatic.
MEN80, 4.5 minutes
The End of I from Sex and Death by Diana Amsterdam

953
Jessep, 40-50
Washington, DC, Summer, 1986
This Marine Lt. Colonel is loyal to the Corps above all other things. When one of his men dies as a result of a "Code Red"—an unofficial act of internal discipline—Jessep finds himself giving testimony at the court-martial of the two men charged with the crime. When he is asked to tell the truth about "Code Red," he explodes with anger, revealing his fanatical de-

votion to the Corps. Dramatic.
MEN80, 2.5 minutes
A Few Good Man by Aaron Sorkin

954
Al Hoffman, 20s
Verona, New Jersey, 1930s
Al Hoffman has been set up on a blind date with Molly Farrell, a fiery young woman with a mind of her own. When their initial encounter goes poorly, an angered and bemused Al rails against women to his friend, Marty. Seriocomic.
MEN80, 1.5 minutes
Fighting Light by Greg Zittel

955
Weiskopf, 40-50
Vilna, Lithuania, 1939-1943
A Jew interred in the ghettos at Vilna, Weiskopf constantly strives to make the best of things. Here, the entrepreneurial Weiskopf admonishes the director of the ghetto's theater group for using the stage to complain about their situation. Dramatic.
MEN80, 3 minutes
Ghetto by Joshua Sobol in a version by David Lan

956
Ezra Pound, 50s   **Pisa, Italy, 1945**
The US Army has detained expatriate poet, Ezra Pound, in Italy at the close of the second World War. Pound stands charged with treason and here reveals his sardonic nature as he taunts the MP assigned to guard him. Seriocomic.
MEN80, 4.5 minutes
Incommunicado by Tom Dulack

957
King, 50   **Portugal, 14th century**
During a war with Spain, the King of Portugal orders the execution of his son's Spanish consort and her children. The old man knows that he has committed a great sin and despairs, for his own death is near. Dramatic.
MEN80, 2.5 minutes
Inés de Castro by John Clifford

958
Sanchez, 17   **Honduras, Present**
This young Nicaraguan has been turned into a brutal killer by his training at the Contra base in Honduras. After a devastating run-in with the Sandinistas, Sanchez flees over the mountains to Honduras, taking Emilio—a young boy whose father he has viciously tortured and murdered—with him. As they huddle next to a portable cooking-stove, Sanchez boasts to Emilio of his ability to kill and lectures on the state of the world, as he understands it. Seriocomic.
MEN80, 5 minutes
Kissing the Pope by Nick Darke

959
Max, 30s   **NYC, Present**
Max is a womanizing film producer who thinks he has finally fallen in love with a wholesome gal from Georgia. When she refuses to don some sexy lingerie that he has given her, he explodes comically, revealing his unrealistic expectations of their relationship. Seriocomic.
MEN80, 2.5 minutes
Lingerie from Sex and Death by Diana Amsterdam

960
Herbie, 40s   **Coney Island, 1965**
Herbie is Stewie's long-suffering father. Constantly struggling to make ends meet, Herbie is on the verge of a breakdown. On the evening following his son's Bar Mitzvah, Herbie explodes with years of pent-up anger and frustration, lashing out at his family and himself with a fury that none suspected he possessed. Dramatic.
MEN80, 4 minutes
The Loman Family Picnic by Donald Margulies

961
Spud, 40s-50s   **Glasgow, Present**
Spud is a former teacher forced into a life of petty crime by his drug addiction. He now lives a meager life in a Glasgow tenement where he barely survives in between jags. Here, he breaks down in front of Callum, a young man whom he has befriended. Dramatic.
MEN80, 3 minutes
Loose Ends by Stuart Hepburn

962
Oliver, 40s   **Greek Islands, 1990**
Oliver is the caretaker of Daniel, a best-selling author whom a stroke has left unable to communicate. Oliver and Daniel have spent many years together at Daniel's Greek Island home, and each depends on the other for daily sustenance. When Oliver discovers that he has AIDS, he feels that he must leave Daniel and here tenders his resignation. Seriocomic.
MEN80, 7 minutes
A Madhouse in Goa by Martin Sherman

963
General Burgoyne, 40s-50s
Saratoga, NY, 1777

At the close of the American Revolutionary War, General Burgoyne hides himself away while awaiting an opportunity to return to England. Defeated and bitter, the General surveys his hiding place and wonders what to say to his friends when he returns home. Seriocomic.
MEN80, 2.5 minutes
The Man Who Lost America by Michael Burrell

964
Brett, 30s   A mental hospital, Present
Brett visits his sister, Minna, in a mental hospital. Minna is pregnant and claims that benevolent space people have given her the child that will eventually save the world from nuclear war. Here, Brett pleads with Minna to have an abortion. Seriocomic.
MEN80, 3.5 minutes
Minna and The Space People from Family Life by Wendy Hammon

965
Caleb, 30-40
Tuskegee, Alabama, 1932-1972
Caleb and three of his friends have been diagnosed with syphilis and are participating in a government funded project to study the effects of the disease on the black male. Unknown to the patients, they are not being treated for the disease so that the government can study its unchecked effects. Here, Caleb is about to receive a spinal tap, and his fear of the procedure reminds him of a terrible day in his youth. Seriocomic.
MEN80, 2.5 minutes
Miss Evers' Boys by David Feldshuh

966
Dr. Brodus, 40-50
Tuskegee, Alabama, 1932-1972
Dr. Brodus is the black doctor working in conjunction with the government in the syphilis study. When confronted by the dedicated nurse who has been working with the infected men and demands that they be given treatment for the disease, Brodus responds by reminding her that they now have an opportunity to force the medical community to acknowledge physiological equality between the races. Dramatic.
MEN80, 2 minutes
Miss Evers' Boys by David Feldshuh

967
Mr. M, 40s   Camdeboo, South Africa, 1985
Anela Myalata teaches school in a black township in South Africa. Known as "Mr. M" to his students, Anela has long been an inspiration to the young minds which he helps to guide through the treacherous world of apartheid.

When he discovers that his finest students have organized an illegal political action committee, he reports those who have influenced them to the police. Here, he defends his actions to young Thami, his favorite student. Dramatic.
MEN80, 9.5 minutes
My Children! My Africa! by Athol Fugard

968
Prometheus, 20-30   Ancient Greece
Prometheus rages against Zeus for his imprisonment and begs for death so that he may at least become one of the people that he so dearly loves. Dramatic.
MEN80, 4.5 minutes
Seize The Fire by Tom Paulin

969
Archie, 30s   Massachusetts, Present
Archie is a British sort of fellow who works the baler in his uncle's factory. When Margy, the woman whom he has loved since the second grade, returns to town to visit her dying brother, Archie is surprised and pleased when she invites him out to dinner. She meets him at the factory, and he attempts to entertain her with a story of his childhood in the factory. Seriocomic.
MEN80, 6 minutes
The Widow's Blind Date by Israel Horovitz

970
George, 30s   Massachusetts, Present
George is an illiterate womanizer helping out his friend, Archie, in the baling press room at a wastepaper factory. When the two men are visited by Margy, a childhood friend, George becomes irritated by her refined mannerisms. He lashes out at her, his jealousy of her attention to Archie showing. Dramatic.
MEN80, 6 minutes
The Widow's Blind Date by Israel Horovitz

971
Monsoon, 18   Vietnam, December, 1968
When Bonney, an American GI in Vietnam, commits a war crime, the men in his unit are questioned about his state of mind. Here, Monsoon, a racist young Southerner, reveals his new insight into ethnic differences gained on the battlefield. Dramatic.
MEN80, 2 minutes
The Boys of Winter by John Pielmeier

972
Doc, 20   Vietnam, December, 1968
Here, the unusually insightful Doc points the finger of blame where it truly belongs. Dramatic.

MEN80, 2.5 minutes
The Boys of Winter by John Pielmeier

973
L.B., 18   **Vietnam, December, 1968**
The tragic horror of Vietnam is expressed in the following painful observations which eloquently link sex and death. Seriocomic.
MEN80, 3 minutes
The Boys of Winter by John Pielmeier

974
Bradley, 70s   **Upstate New York, 1970s**
As the family gathers for a cocktail hour before dinner, Bradley, the patriarch of the WASP's clan, laments the fact that no one drinks anymore. Comic.
MEN80, 2.5 minutes
The Cocktail Hour by A.R. Gurney

975
Gerald R. "Gunner" Smith, 30-40
A bar, 1973
Here, an experienced astronaut describes taking off in a Saturn V rocket to a couple of rookies. As he speaks, we can see his love for his work. Dramatic.
MEN80, 3 minutes
Darkside by Ken Jones

976
James, 50s   **London, Present**
The mysterious James has made a cash offer on a house being shown by Clair. James appears to be attracted to the young realtor and here reveals uncanny insight into her life. Seriocomic.
MEN80, 3 minutes
Dealing with Clair by Martin Crimp

977
Peter, 20s-30s   **Fire Island, Present**
A successful television executive, Peter has been diagnosed as being HIV positive. He instinctively retreats from reality by joining his sister and her lover, Stephen, at Stephen's summer house on Fire Island. Here, Peter offers Stephen a glimpse into the lifestyle that brought about his tragic end. Dramatic.
MEN80, 1.5 minutes
Eastern Standard by Richard Greenberg

978
Jake, 20-30   **NYC, Present**
Here, Jake speaks to the audience of his experience with relationships and offers insight into the sometimes befuddling realm of romance in the 1980s. Seriocomic.
MEN80, 3.5 minutes
A Girl's Guide to Chaos by Cynthia Heimel

979
Kerner, 40s
Indoor shooting range, Present
Kerner is a Russian physicist turned double agent in his new life in the West. The ever-cryptic Kerner here discusses Einstein and God with Mrs. Hapgood, a senior level British spy. Seriocomic.
MEN80, 2.5 minutes
Hapgood by Tom Stoppard

980
Lloyd, 30-50
Small town in mid-America, Present
When Lloyd is released from prison, he immediately embarks upon a career as an evangelist. Here, the wiley con-artist welcomes unsuspecting victims to "Lloyd's Holy World." Seriocomic.
MEN80, 2 minutes
Lloyd's Prayer by Kevin Kling

981
Gallimard, 65   **A Paris prison, Present**
Gallimard is a man facing the fact that his life has been based on a lie. Sent to China as a diplomat, Gallimard began a 20 year love affair with the beautiful Song Liling, a popular opera singer who, in reality, was a spy . . . and a man. Unbelievably, Song's gender remained unknown to Gallimard, who allowed himself to fall in love with his fantasy of Asian women as personified in the character Madame Butterfly. Gallimard spends his days and nights in prison reviewing his past, and has concluded that he must kill himself in order to restore honor. Here, Gallimard prepares to commit a ritual hara-kiri. Dramatic.
MEN80, 4 minutes
M. Butterfly by David Henry Hwang

982
Harry Hoveden, 40s   **Ireland, 16th century**
Harry is Hugh O'Neill's devoted secretary. When O'Neill, Earl of Tyrone, forms an alliance with Spain, war breaks out in Ireland. O'Neill and his men are forced into hiding. Harry has taken Mabel, O'Neill's pregnant wife, to a safe place. When Mabel dies in childbirth, Harry is faced with the painful task of telling O'Neill. As he tells his leader of his wife's death, he reveals that he, too has always loved Mabel. Dramatic.
MEN80, 5 minutes
Making History by Brian Friel

983
Blood, 20s
The Benjamins' home, Present
Blood is a young man struggling to come to

terms with the accidental shooting death of his ten-year-old brother. Vacillating between bouts of violence and despair, Blood here shares a memory of heartache with his father. Dramatic.
MEN80, 2 minutes
The Mojo and The Sayso by Aishah Rahman

984
Acts, 40-50
The Benjamins' home, Present
Acts is a man working hard to hold his family together after the tragic death of their youngest son. To him the task is rather like restoring a classic car: something to be done with care and love. When accused by his oldest son of never communicating his feelings, Acts delivers the following monologue. Dramatic.
MEN80, 2.5 minutes
The Mojo and The Sayso by Aishah Rahman

985
Tom, 36
NYC police station, 1987
When Tom is discovered in his lover's hospital room covered with blood, he is arrested for murder. Here, Tom begins his explanation to the police. When Johnny was diagnosed as HIV positive, Tom's own torment began as well. Even though Tom has remained AIDS-free, his desire to die with Johnny was strong enough to trigger his bloody act on Johnny's deathbed. Dramatic.
MEN80, 3.5 minutes
A Poster of the Cosmos by Lanford Wilson

986
Fourth Doctor, 30-50
Ohio and Alaska, Present
The chief suspect in a murder that she did not commit, Rachel lives her life on the run; constantly changing towns and her name. She always manages to find the time to see a psychiatrist, however, and here one of their number attempts to induce in Rachel a primal scream. Seriocomic.
MEN80, 2.5 minutes
Reckless by Craig Lucas

987
Gabby, 40s　　　　　**New Jersey, Present**
"Honest" Gabby Sandalson is at the end of his political rope. His campaign for president has all but stripped his soul. To win the popular vote, Gabby has grudgingly allowed his campaign manager to darken his eyebrows, mousse his hair, introduce him to TV evangelists, and dress him in pantyhose. When an investigative reporter exposes Gabby's ploys, the

good senator explodes the frustration in front of the TV camera and winds up with even more votes than he had before. Seriocomic.
MEN80, 2.5 minutes
The Senator Wore Pantyhose by Billy Van Zandt and Jane Milmore

988
Frankie, 16　　　　　**NYC, Present**
Sharon fills a void in her life through a volunteer program, where she becomes involved with Dawn, an underprivileged, defensive black woman, and Dawn's sensitive but troubled teenage son, Frankie. Here, Frankie tells the audience how he believes in the X-Men (comic book heroes) and identifies with them as mutants. Seriocomic.
MEN80, 4.5 minutes
Three Ways Home by Casey Kurtti

989
MacKenzie, 20s-30s
Scotland, During WWII
MacKenzie is a Chief Petty Officer in the Royal Navy stationed at home during WWII. One evening he is caught outside during a bombing raid. When the bombs begin to fall, MacKenzie hits the dirt and begins to bargain with God for his life. Seriocomic.
MEN80, 3.5 minutes
When We Were Women by Sharman Macdonald

990
Alec, 50s　　　　　**Scotland, During WWII**
Alec is an older man dancing with his daughter at her wedding. As they spin around the dance floor, he offers advice on married life and it is clear that his views reflect a more simple era when life was a little less complicated. Seriocomic.
MEN80, 3 minutes
When We Were Women by Sharman Macdonald

991
Patrick, 30s
Upper West Side apartment, 1987
Patrick is invited for lunch at his friend Himmer's apartment. During the course of their conversation, Patrick reveals his frustration with his career and the powerful and greedy people who control it. Dramatic.
MEN80, 1.5 minutes
Zero Positive by Harry Kondoleon

992
Will, 30s　　　　**Acapulco Plaza Hotel, Present**
Will is an actor working on location in Acapulco. Here, Will joins Steve, a fellow actor, at a hotel bar and tries to start up a con-

versation. Seriocomic.
MEN80, 5 minutes
Acapulco by Steven Berkoff

993
Steve, 30-40
Acapulco Plaza Hotel, Present
Steven, in turn, is a moody Brit who has just returned from an unsuccessful sexual encounter with a young woman. When Will asks him about his day, he launches into a philosophical and somewhat psychedelic accounting of his day's activities. Seriocomic.
MEN80, 6 minutes
Acapulco by Steven Berkoff

994
Tiny, 30s   **Here and Now**
Hapless Tiny is accustomed to playing the fool for his friends and is often the butt of the cruel jokes that they perpetrate. A disabled vet, Tiny here shows a rare flash of anger when he travels to Washington to collect his overdue pension. Rather than submit to the snail-paced bureaucracy of the Veteran's Administration, Tiny takes the entire building hostage. Seriocomic.
MEN80, 5.5 minutes
Archangels Don't Play Pinball by Dario Fo, translated by Ron Jenkins

995
Tiny, 30s   **Here and Now**
Tiny has been set up in a fake wedding by his friends, who only desire to play yet another joke on their personal jester. Tiny believes that his veiled bride is, in fact, Angela, a woman whom he loves. Unveiled, the "bride" is revealed as an ugly specimen. Enraged, Tiny finally turns on his friends and then on Heaven itself. Dramatic.
MEN80, 2 minutes
Archangels Don't Play Pinball by Dario Fo, translated by Ron Jenkins

996
Todd, 20-30   **Todd's apartment, Present**
Unknown to everyone, Todd's best-selling novel was really written by Gene, a pathetic gnome whom Todd has rescued from the street. Todd and Gene quarrel violently when Gene sneaks out of the apartment to go shopping. Here, Todd begs for Gene's forgiveness and reveals his feelings of isolation. Seriocomic.
MEN80, 6 minutes
The Author's Voice by Richard Greenberg

997
Colin, 30s   **Sydney, Australia, Present**

When Colin is offered the opportunity to produce a soap opera, he jumps at it. When his wife suggests that a soap opera isn't exactly a worthy showplace for his talents, he explains his motivation. Dramatic.
MEN80, 3 minutes
Emerald City by David Williamson

998
Johnny, 30-40   **NYC, Present**
On their first date, Frankie and Johnny return to Frankie's apartment for a round of passionate lovemaking. Johnny is clearly smitten with Frankie, who can't seem to overcome her fear of becoming emotionally connected. When he finally declares his love for her, she orders him to leave. Instead of leaving, Johnny phones the radio station that they've been listening to and makes the following request. Seriocomic.
MEN80, 4 minutes
Frankie and Johnny in the Clair De Lune by Terrence McNally

999
Samuel, 50s
Africa and West Indies, 1790s
Samuel Randall is a British merchant who has made his fortune in the slave trade. Samuel's morality is constantly attacked by his son, William. Here, he takes a moment to reflect upon the events that led to his decision to become a slaver. Dramatic.
MEN80, 2.5 minutes
Indigo by Heidi Thomas

1000
Ide, 20s   **Africa and West Indies, 1790s**
Ide is an African prince whose father has chosen to deal with the European slave traders. When Ide hears tales of Christianity, he is struck by the concept of a god who sends his only son out into the world. Ide decides to allow himself to be sold as a slave so that he can lead his people to freedom. Here, he performs one last tribal ceremony. Dramatic.
MEN80, 2 minutes
Indigo by Heidi Thomas

1001
Man, 30s   **Here and Now**
A man addresses the audience from a podium. He begins by telling of his experience in a personality workshop and of his daily battle with negativity. He then breaks from his prepared speech and recounts an unpleasant encounter he recently experienced in a grocery store. Seriocomic.
MEN80, 5 minutes
Laughing Wild by Christopher Durang

1002
Harold, 40s   **England, Present**
Arthur lives downstairs from Norma, his ex-wife, who is currently living with Harold, his best friend. When Norma tells Arthur that she no longer loves Harold, she pleads with him to break the bad news to his friend so she will be spared such a noisome chore. When the blow is dealt, Harold feels betrayed by both Arthur and Norma. Seriocomic.
MEN80, 2.5 minutes
Mixed Feelings by Donald Churchill

1003
Al, 50s   **Rural Wisconsin, 1963**
Al is an earthy man who has spent his life as a physical laborer. Al has come to Rock River, Wisconsin to do some fishing. There he meets Lorine, a poetess who he falls in love with and marries. Here, Al tells Lorine of the fine art of catching pike. Seriocomic.
MEN80, 3 minutes
Niedecker by Kristine Thatcher

1004
Gordon, 35   **Alcohol rehab center**
When Gordon is asked to welcome Sister Angelita to the rehab center, he greets her nervously, his fear of nuns—even one who is a fellow alcoholic—giving way to foolish banter about balding. Comic.
MEN80, 2.5 minutes
Penguin Blues by Ethan Phillips

1005
Gordon, 35   **Alcohol rehab center**
Here, Gordon is finally able to reveal the source of his fear of nuns to patient Angelita. Seriocomic.
MEN80, 3 minutes
Penguin Blues by Ethan Phillips

1006
Gallo, 40s   **Southwest, Present**
Gallo has spent the last several years in jail for manslaughter. Upon his release, he returns to his Chicano family in the southwest. His first visit, however, is to Zapata, the rooster that he bred and trained to fight in the ring. His love for the bird is nearly romantic, as can be seen in their first encounter. Seriocomic.
MEN80, 3.5 minutes
Roosters by Milcha Sanchez-Scott

1007
Hector, 20s   **Southwest, Present**
Hector is the son left behind when Gallo is sent to jail. This sardonic young man masks his feelings of abandonment and loneliness

with satiric wit. He works as a farm laborer and here reveals contempt for his life. Seriocomic.
MEN80, 2.5 minutes
Roosters by Milcha Sanchez-Scott

1008
Stone, 30   **San Antonio, TX, 1936-38**
Stone has traveled all the way to San Antonio is search of Johnson, a blues guitar player whom he hopes to sign in a recording contract. Here, Stone reveals his fatigue with life on the road. Seriocomic.
MEN80, 3.5 minutes
San Antonio Sunset by Willy Holtzman

1009
Johnson, 20s   **San Antonio, TX, 1936-38**
Here, the young bluesman reveals uncanny insight into the nature of the human soul as he explains his vision of God to Stone. Seriocomic.
MEN80, 2.5 minutes
San Antonio Sunset by Willy Holtzman

1010
Mordechai Weiss, 60-70   **Brooklyn, 1946**
Mordechai Weiss is the patriarch of a family of Polish Jews who was fortunate enough to have emigrated to New York before the war with his daughter, Rose. His wife and older daughter stayed behind, only to be swept into the whirlwind of war and swallowed up in the camps. Shortly after the war, Lusia, the older daughter who has survived the camps, makes her way to Brooklyn. Here, Mordechai encourages her to learn to adapt to her new life as quickly as possible. Dramatic.
MEN80, 4 minutes
A Shayna Maidel by Barbara Lebow

1011
T-Bone, 30s   **South Carolina, Present**
T-Bone is a small-time car thief traveling the backroads of South Carolina with his friend, Weasel. When Weasel is taken in by a scheming politician, T-Bone steals another car and winds up in a jail cell that he shares with a preacher, who he wastes no time in setting straight. Seriocomic.
MEN80, 2.5 minutes
T Bone N Weasel by Jon Klein

1012
Bert, 50s   **Up a creek**
Bert and his longtime friend, Charlie, are trout fishing on a mountain stream. As the two old buddies banter about everything from aesthet-

ics to Gandhi, trout come and go. Here, the pragmatic Bert lectures on the difference between hunting and fishing. Seriocomic.
MEN80, 2 minutes
Trout by William R. Lewis

1013
Charlie, 50s   **Up a creek**
In a moment of self-induced revelation, Charlie tells Bert of his mission in life. Seriocomic.
MEN80, 2 minutes
Trout by William R. Lewis

1014
Charlie, 50s   **Up a creek**
As the sun sets, Charlie tells Bert of a near-mystical experience he once had while fishing. Seriocomic.
MEN80, 4.5 minutes
Trout by William R. Lewis

1015
Kipps, 30-40   **A London Theatre**
Arthur Kipps is a man who is literally haunted by the past. In an effort to free himself from visitations from "the Woman in Black," a spectre who has attached herself to Kipps in order to avenge the death of her young child, Kipps hires out a theater and an actor and proceeds to reenact his first meeting with the phantom. His ghostly tale begins on Christmas eve. Seriocomic.
MEN80, 5 minutes
The Woman in Black adapted by Stephen Mallatratt from the book by Susan Hill

1016
Jim, 40s   **Australia, Christmas, 1967**
Jim's marriage to the shrewish Gwen has become more and more like a nightmare with each passing day. It was not always so, and here he tells his daughter of how different Gwen was when they were courting. Seriocomic.
MEN80, 2.5 minutes
Away by Michael Gow

1017
Harry, 40s   **Australia, Christmas, 1967**
Harry's son is dying of cancer. The family has recently moved from England to Australia and now they find themselves celebrating Christmas on the beach with new friends. Here, Harry tells Jim about his son's illness. Dramatic.
MEN80, 3 minutes
Away by Michael Gow

1018
Goose, 20-30
Underworld apartment, Recently
Goose and Tomtom are jewel thieves whose souls struggle for survival in a purgatory-like setting where they seem condemned to committing acts of violence. During his journey from life to this surrealistic place, Goose has been given insight into his true nature as he here reveals to Tomtom. Dramatic.
MEN80, 4 minutes
Goose and Tomtom by David Rabe

1019
Bingo, 30s
Underworld apartment, Recently
Tomtom and Goose have kidnapped Bingo's sister, Lulu, in an effort to recover diamonds which they believe were stolen from them by Bingo. Wandering through the underworld in search of his beloved Lulu, Bingo finally arrives at the home of Tomtom and Goose, where he tells his tale. Dramatic.
MEN80, 3.5 minutes
Goose and Tomtom by David Rabe

1020
Hal, 30-40   **Frank and Donna's house**
Hal is recently divorced and still somewhat reluctant to socialize. When Frank, a co-worker, invites him home for dinner, he accepts and finds that he actually enjoys being out after so many months of solitary existence in his lonely apartment. Here are Hal's ruminations as the evening progresses. Seriocomic.
MEN80, 4.5 minutes
Kvetch by Stephen Berkoff

1021
Frank, 30-40   **Frank and Donna's house**
Frank is the blustery host of the impromptu dinner party. As he tells a joke, he reflects with pride on his ability to amuse and then realizes with horror that he is boring everyone. Seriocomic.
MEN80, 3.5 minutes
Kvetch by Stephen Berkoff

1022
Leopold, 40s
Leopold's living room, Present
Professor Leopold Nettles has written a book which contains a paragraph considered offensive by the repressive government under which he lives. As menacing, shadowy figures begin appearing at his door to pressure him to sign a document which disavows his work, Nettles feels as though he has lost control of his life. Here, he confesses his despair to his lover. Dramatic.

MEN80, 3 minutes
Largo Desolato by Vaclav Havel, English version by Tom Stoppard

1023
Francis, 20-30   **Tasmania, 1935-1945**
When Francis and his friend, Peter, go camping in the wilds of Tasmania, they stumble upon the survivors of a shipwrecked group of convicts who have been living in a feral state since the Victorian age. Francis becomes attracted to Betsheb, a member of the strange tribe with a captivating lust for life. Although she doesn't understand English, Francis tells her about his world. Seriocomic.
MEN80, 3 minutes
The Golden Age by Louis Nowra

1024
Lord Gordon, 20-30   **London, 18th century**
Lord Gordon is a man suffering the effects of his ordinary appearance and demeanor. Here, he complains bitterly of his unnoticability. Seriocomic.
MEN80, 2 minutes
The Grace of Mary Traverse by Timberlake Wertenbaker

1025
Mr. Hardlong, 30-40   **London, 18th century**
Mary Traverse has run away from her wealthy father in order to experience life before resigning herself to marriage with a man she doesn't love. She had paid Mr. Hardlong to have sex with her. When she hesitates to join him in bed, he encourages her with the following words. Seriocomic.
MEN80, 4 minutes
The Grace of Mary Traverse by Timberlake Wertenbaker

1026
Franklin, 30s   **USA, 1950s**
Franklin has been wounded in Korea, losing his arm in the process. When he returns to his wife, Effie, they struggle to put their lives back together. One day, Effie and a friend plan to attend a matinee at the movies and here, Franklin tells the audience of the tragic event that occurred that fateful day. Seriocomic.
MEN80, 3.5 minutes
Life and Limb by Keith Reddin

1027
Shinji, 29
Hiroshima, 7 years after the bomb
As Japan struggles to rebuild following the devastation of the war, Shinji and Hisa struggle to rebuild their lives. Here, Shinji, who has been trying to convince Hisa to marry him, reminds her of the flowers that bloomed after the bomb. Dramatic.
MEN80, 3 minutes
The Mask of Hiroshima by Ernest Ferlita

1028
Bizet, 40s   **Paris, March 4, 1875**
On the opening night of his opera, "Carmen," Georges Bizet take a moment during the overture to comment on the mentality of the audience, and his love for his music and his disdain for those who listen to it are obvious. Seriocomic.
MEN80, 5 minutes
Opera Comique by Nagle Jackson

1029
Bizet, 40s   **Paris, March 4, 1875**
At the close of "Carmen," Bizet is confronted by a young woman in the corridor outside his box at the opera house. When she expresses her disappointment at the opera's ending, the composer explodes with anger. Seriocomic.
MEN80, 2 minutes
Opera Comique by Nagle Jackson

1030
Darrell, 20-30   **A house trailer, 1940s**
Darrell is a WWII vet traveling with his evangelical father and sister. They have just kidnapped his sister's baby from a medical lab and plan to escape in their house trailer to Canada. The child is badly deformed and here, Darrell addresses the baby in its crib. Seriocomic.
MEN80, 3.5 minutes
Tent Meeting by Larry Larson, Levi Lee and Rebecca Wackler

1031
Nobu Matsumoto, 68   **America, Present**
After 40 years of marriage, Nobu's wife, Masi, leaves him to start a new life for herself. Their marriage had been an unhappy one, and Nobu inflicted much emotional abuse upon Masi, leaving her with feelings of isolation and despair. When he discovered that Masi is seeing another man, he flies into a rage, buys a rifle and goes to her apartment. By the time he arrives his passion is spent. He and Masi confront one another, but the time for anger is over. Dramatic.
MEN80, 2 minutes
The Wash by Philip Kan Gotanda

1032
Robert Obosa, 40s   **An American Theater**
Based on an actual incident, this is the story of

two black South African actors who are prevented from performing in an American play festival by the South African National Council. If they perform, the Council has threatened reprisals on their loved ones, if they don't perform, the South African government will order them banned. Here, a defeated Robert tells a grim tale of the time he was imprisoned in his homeland. Dramatic.
MEN80, 3.5 minutes
Advice to The Players by Bruce Bonafede

1033
Jack, early 30s Chicago, Present
Jack's young lover is pregnant and has decided to give the child up for adoption. When the reality of this situation finally sinks in, Jack explodes with anger and frustration. Seriocomic.
MEN80, 3 minutes
Careless Love by John Olive

1034
Cop, 40-50 San Francisco, 1978-Present
When Harvey Milk and George Moscone are gunned down by Dan White, San Francisco is thrown into a period of violent chaos. A conservative voice is heard here in the guise of a policeman who wishes that things could be like they were in the old days. Dramatic.
MEN80, 5 minutes
Execution of Justice by Emily Mann

1035
Dr. Norman Bethune, 30-40
Michigan, 1930
Bethune was a Canadian physician whose passionate political beliefs brought him to field hospitals in the Spanish Civil War and the Chinese Resistance during the Japanese invasion of 1930. Here, the outspoken young doctor visits a friend in Michigan and lapses into a provocatively metaphysical monologue. Seriocomic.
MEN80, 10.5 minutes
Gone The Burning Sun by Ken Mitchell

1036
Eddie, 30s Hollywood, Present
Early morning finds Eddie, Phil and Mickey struggling to begin another day in LA Phil has just left his wife, Eddie is suffering from a terrible coke hangover and Mickey just wishes there was something to eat in the house. Eddie, a coke-addicted casting director thoroughly desensitized by life, needs to do a line of coke just to wake up and here comes to life after a snort. Seriocomic.
MEN80, 2 minutes
Hurlyburly by David Rabe

1037
Phil, 30s Hollywood, Present
Phil is a struggling LA actor who has recently left his wife. His contempt for women becomes evident when he verbally attacks Donna, a sixteen year-old waif who trades sex for a place to sleep, for distracting him from watching a football game on TV. Seriocomic.
MEN80, 2.5 minutes
Hurlyburly by David Rabe

1038
Willy, 30s Here and Now
Willy Rivers is a rock star who is struggling to make a comeback after an attempt has been made on his life. Willy was shot during the attack and is no longer able to play the guitar as he used to. Here, he tries to explain the magic of making music to a man in a three-piece suit. Seriocomic.
MEN80, 3 minutes
The Incredibly Famous Willy Rivers by Stephen Metcalfe

1039
Berk, 30-40 Poultry shop, Present
Berk is hired by Lorraine to kill chickens in her poultry shop. Lorraine is an alcoholic desperate for salvation and Berk becomes determined to help her to quit drinking. Lorraine's husband was killed by a drunk driver: Berk. In a highly emotional confrontation, Berk finally admits to being the driver of the car that killed her husband. Dramatic.
MEN80, 3 minutes
The Undoing by William Mastrosimone

1040
Daisy, 17 Here and Now
Daisy is a young man who has been raised as a girl by his parents. Here, he begins to tell his tale to an unseen voice which somewhat resembles that of psychoanalyst. As he speaks, Daisy begins to reveal details from his horrific childhood. Truly chilling, however, is his matter-of-fact descriptions of such a criminally distorted situation. Seriocomic.
MEN80, 3 minutes
Baby With The Bathwater by Christopher Durang

1041
Man, 20-50 Here and Now
Here, a regular kind of guy describes his relationship with his dog. Seriocomic.
MEN80, 3.5 minutes
The Dog by David Mamet

1042
Taylor, 30-40
A mountain ledge, September 4, 1977

Survival is the name of the game for two men stranded on a narrow ledge located on a 600 foot ice wall at 27,000 feet on K2, the world's second highest mountain. Harold's broken leg makes it impossible for him to assist Taylor in any plan to escape. When an argument regarding the best way for Taylor to got for help ensues, the volatile Taylor explodes at his friend, revealing years of pent-up frustration and resentment. Dramatic.
MEN80, 4 minutes
K2 by Patrick Meyers

1043
Don, 30s **Brine, Alabama**
As all of Brine, Alabama prepares for the annual Tara Parade and Ball, Don, the local hairdresser, helps Miz Zifty to make the transformation from dowdy old Southern Belle to Scarlett O'Hara look-alike. Miz Zifty has played the part of Scarlett in the parade for years, and only Don can help her to capture the essence of the role. Here, he chatters as he works. Seriocomic.
MEN80, 3 minutes
Coup/Clucks by Jane Martin

1044
Ryman 30-40 **Brine, Alabama**
Ryman is a Klan member in a small town in Brine, Alabama. Ryman has some very strange ideas about black people and time, as he here describes while assembling a bomb. Seriocomic.
MEN80, 2 minutes
Coup/Clucks by Jane Martin

1045
Gerry, 20-30 **London, 1980**
Gerry tells his lover, Edward, that he needs to go to the pub to clear his head after a minor spat. On his way, he describes a sexual encounter that he recently experienced on a train. Seriocomic.
MEN80, 3.5 minutes
Cloud Nine by Caryl Churchill

1046
Eamon, 30s **Ireland, Summer, 1970s**
The O'Donnell family has gathered at this ancestral home in Ballybeg for a wedding. Joining them is an American academic who is writing a thesis on the Catholic aristocracy in Ireland. Eamon, a local who married into the O'Donnell clan here reveals his resentment of the decaying class structure in Ireland. Seriocomic.
MEN80, 3 minutes
Aristocrats by Brian Friel

1047
Man, 50-60 **Columbus Avenue, Present**
An older merchant here gets a harsh dose of reality when he is evicted from his place of business. Dramatic.
MEN80, 4.5 minutes
Columbus Avenue by David Mamet

1048
Sir, 60s **English Theater**
This aging and ailing Shakespearean actor takes a moment during an intermission of "King Lear" to reflect upon his performance in the role that has eluded him for so long. He is at the end of his career and his life, much like the tragic king which he portrays. Dramatic.
MEN80, 2 minutes
The Dresser by Ronald Harwood

1049
Chris, 30 **Brighton Beach, England, Present**
Chris is deeply affected by the BBC news and has allowed herself to become obsessed with the stories. Her greatest desire is to be free from these worries as she here tells Hannah.
WOM80, 3 minutes
My Heart's a- Suitcase by Clare McIntyre

1050
Claudine, 40s **France, Early 1900s**
This play is a series of vignettes from the life of artist Henri Matisse. Each scene uses as its background a particular painting of Matisse. Henri's wife, Claudine, describes a portrait that Henri has painted of her.
WOM80, 5 minutes
The Pink Studio by Jane Anderson

1051
Maria, 40-50 **London, Present**
Maria works in a sweat shop hoping to make enough money to send her youngest daughter, Dynette, to college. She tells Dynette of her own dreams as a young girl in the Caribbean and urges her to succeed where she has failed.
WOM80, 2.5 minutes
Back Street Mammy by Trish Cooke

1052
Nell, 50s **A living room, Present**
Nell speaks to her retarded daughter.
WOM80, 2.5 minutes
Haiku by Katherine Snodgrass

1053
Nell, 50s **A living room, Present**
Nell tells Billie about the first time Louise really looked at her.
WOM80, 1 minute
Haiku by Katherine Snodgrass

1054
Actress, any age   An empty stage, Present
An actress recalls her father's death.
WOM80, 9.5 minutes
Impassioned Embraces by John Pielmeier

1055
Blanca, 30-40   Portugal, 14th century
Blanca is the legal wife of the prince and has spent many years hating Inés for having usurped her place in her husband's heart. Here, she confronts her adversary with feelings of grief and bitterness.
WOM80, 3 minutes
Inés De Castro by John Clifford

1056
Scheherezade, 20-30   London, Present
The famous storyteller here appears in an allegorical tale written during the furor that accompanied the publishing of The Satanic Verses. The ever-sagacious Scheherezade speaks to us of the necessity of resisting censorship and oppression.
WOM80, 4 minutes
Iranian Nights by Tariq Ali and Howard Brenton

1057
Doris, 38   Coney Island, 1965
Doris is floundering in her marriage to Herbie, with whom she hasn't communicated in many years. Bored, lonely and depressed, Doris uses her acerbic wit as a buffer as can be seen in the following monologue in which she introduces herself to the audience.
WOM80, 3 minutes
The Loman Family Picnic by Donald Margulies

1058
Sarah, 30s   Toronto, Present
Sarah is Eleanor's schizophrenic sister who likes to visit her in the law office in which she works. On one such visit, Sarah reveals her paranoid vision of reality to Eleanor and a client as she describes her worst fears.
WOM80, 3.5 minutes
Love and Anger by George F. Walker

1059
Mrs. Honey, 50-60   Greek Islands, 1966
David, a recent college graduate traveling around the world encounters the outspoken Mrs. Honey on the Greek Island of Corfu. It seems that the lonely widow has been globetrotting ever since the death of her husband. When David, whose heart has recently been broken, tells of his feelings of loss, she offers a brutally candid description of her own loss.
WOM80, 4.5 minutes
A Madhouse in Goa by Martin Sherman

1060
Heather, 40s   Greek Islands, 1966
Heather is a friend and legal guardian of Daniel, a best-selling author whom a stroke has left unable to communicate. Heather is dying of cancer, but is more terrified of the risk and danger offered by life to her son than of her own inevitable demise. Here, she expresses her fears to the nearly catatonic Daniel, whose help and guidance she needs now more than ever.
WOM80, 5 minutes
A Madhouse in Goa by Martin Sherman

1061
Mom, 40s   An American home, Present
Mom presides over a family in crisis in this absurdist glimpse into family communications. Persuaded by her oldest daughter that therapy is the only way to keep the other children from committing suicide, Mom begins to evaluate her own childhood.
WOM80, 5 minutes
Mom and the Razor Blades from Family Life by Wendy Hammond

1062
Isabel, 16-18   Camdeboo, South Africa
Isabel Dyson is a high school student with a passion for debate. When she is invited to participate in a debate a a school in a black township, she accepts and is pleased to meet Mr. M., a dynamic teacher who is an inspiration to his students. Here, Isabel describes the township and her feelings about it to the audience.
WOM80, 12 minutes
My Children! My Africa! by Athol Fugard

1063
Janet, 30s   A movie theater, Present
When the film gets sexy, Janet begins to ruminate on the breasts so gratuitously displayed by the actress on the screen. She observes that only a male director would devote so much footage to the female form.
WOM80, 4.5 minutes
One Naked Woman and a Fully Clothed Man from Sex and Death by Diana Amsterdam

1064
Molly, 40s   Small town in Ireland, Present
Molly has lived alone ever since Danger, the man she loved, left town with another woman. When he returns to persuade his lover's daughter, Eileen, to return to London with him, Molly's bitterness at having been rejected gets the better of her and she directs her animosity at Eileen.
WOM80, 2.3 minutes
Poor Beasts in the Rain by Billy Roche

1065
Io, 20s   **Ancient Greece**
Io is another who has fallen out of favor with
Zeus, who has transformed the unlucky young
woman into a cow. Here, she appears before
Prometheus and complains of her punishment.
WOM80, 3.5 minutes
Seize the Fire by Tom Paulin

1066
Molly, 30s   **London, Present**
Molly's art show has been a dismal failure.
Realizing that the time has come to reveal to
her lover, Adrian, the terrible truth that she
was molested as a child. Molly confronts him
in the gallery and tells her tale with a little help
from her sister, who was also a victim.
WOM80, 10 minutes
Sleeping Nightie by Victoria Hardie

1067
Louisa, 50s   **Brooklyn, Present**
During a wedding, three generations of the
DiVangilito family clash at an opulent
Brooklyn catering hall. During a lull in the ac-
tion, Louisa, the black sheep of the family,
shares a memory of her father with her daugh-
ter.
WOM80, 2.5 minutes
So When You Get Married . . . by Ellen Byron

1068
Valerie, 12   **Valerie's home, Present**
Valerie despairs and delights on getting her pe-
riod on her birthday.
WOM80, 16 minutes
The Valerie of Now by Peter Hedges

1069
Sherry, 30s   **London, Present**
Sherry is an impulsive young actress with a
definite flair for the dramatic as can be seen in
this colorful description of her commute home
on the train.
WOM80, 3.5 minutes
Valued Friends by Stephen Jeffreys

1070
Margy, 30s   **Massachusetts, Present**
Margy returns to the factory town in which
she grew up to visit her dying brother and to
confront some very painful memories. Margy
was gang-raped by her brother and several of
his friends when she was 17, and the need for
revenge still burns in her heart. When she finds
herself alone in a factory with two perpetra-
tors of the rape, Margy plays it cool, until
mention is made of her breasts.
WOM80, 3 minutes
The Widow's Blind Date by Israel Horovitz

1071
Margy, 30s   **Massachusetts, Present**
The evening in the factory finally breaks down
into an emotional confrontation in which
George - the first to rape Margy - describes the
horrific event as if it were a fond memory. In
his mind, Margy loved every moment of her
ordeal. Here, Margy finally explodes with 20
years of pent-up rage.
WOM80, 4 minutes
The Widow's Blind Date by Israel Horovitz

1072
Evelyn, 30s   **New Mexico, Present**
Zara Spook is an off-center comedy about sev-
eral women who are entering an important
bass fishing contest on a lake in New Mexico.
Evelyn, having won the trophy for catching the
largest bass, tells her audience her thrill at hav-
ing won.
WOM80, 4.5 minutes
*Zara Spook and Other Lures by Joan Ackermann-
Blount*

1073
Maureen, 39   **New York, Present**
Maureen "Spanky" Oberfeld is a New Yorker
visiting Minnesota. She hasn't "made it" in the
big city. Her life has constricted to exchanges
of audio tapes under the door with
"boyfriends," whom she never meets or sees,
and an obsessive interest in the New York
Yankees, past and present. She hasn't left her
apartment in 43 days. She is talking on the
phone with her "boyfriend," Jeffrey.
WOM80, 5.5 minutes
*All She Cares About Is the Yankees by John Ford
Noonan*

1074
Maureen, 39   **New York, Present**
Maureen "Spanky" Oberfeld is a New Yorker
visiting Minnesota. She hasn't "made it" in the
big city. Her life has constricted to exchanges
of audio tapes under the door with
"boyfriends," whom she never meets or sees,
and an obsessive interest in the New York
Yankees, past and present. She hasn't left her
apartment in 43 days. She is making a tape to
send to her father.
WOM80, 12.5 minutes
*All She Cares About Is the Yankees by John Ford
Noonan*

1075
Judith, 50s   **England, 1980**
A woman who has recently put her father in a
nursing home visits her family's home, now
empty, and remembers the past. She fears her
father's inevitable death, and pleads with him

not to leave her alone.
WOM80, 8 minutes
Borrowing Time by Michael Burrell

1076
Alice, 40-60   Central Park, Present
Alice is an aging and ailing woman whose loneliness propels her out into the night in search of human contact. Here, she confesses her need for love to an equestrian statue in the park.
WOM80, 3 minutes
Charity by Leonard Melfi

1077
Ann, 50-60   New York, Mid-1970s
A family reunion goes awry when John, a playwright, announces that his new play is about the family. Here, Ann, his well-meaning mother, encourages him to write a book instead.
WOM80, 2 minutes
The Cocktail Hour by A.R. Gurney

1078
Gigi, 30s   A party, 1973
When Gigi tells Bill that she no longer lovers her husband, Ed, he is slow to comprehend. His lack of understanding prompts the following tirade in which Gigi assures Bill that to her, Ed is already dead.
WOM80, 1 minute
Darkside by Ken Jones

1079
Phoebe, 20-30   NYC Restaurant, Present
When Phoebe and her brother, Peter, meet for lunch they usually trade gossip and dreams. Here, Phoebe describes a recent dream which vaguely details her disintegrating love life.
WOM80, 1.5 minutes
Eastern Standard by Richard Greenberg

1080
Emily, 30s   Manhattan, Present
Emily is a wonderful successful stockbroker who has everything she could possibly want except love. Drifting aimlessly from affair to affair, Emily has become numb to the possibility of falling in love until she encounters John, an aspiring actor who becomes the first man to break through her defenses. As Emily describes her history of sexual encounters to the audience, we can see John's welcome entrance into the bleak landscape of her dormant passion.
WOM80, 3.5 minutes
Emily by Stephen Metcalfe

1081
Agatha, 40s   Central Park, Present

When four friends hold a reunion in Central Park, all are amazed by their individual transformations. Here, Agatha, a wealthy divorcée, recalls the night Bobby Kennedy was shot.
WOM80, 2 minutes
Faith by Israel Horovitz

1082
Lipochka, 20s   Moscow, 1850
Lipochka is the spoiled and petulant daughter of a Russian merchant who dreams of marrying a nobleman who will take her far away from her parents. Here, the ungainly Lipochka fantasizes about attending a ball and the man she will marry.
WOM80, 3.5 minutes
A Family Affair by Alexander Ostrovsky

1083
Mitzi, 50s   Manhattan, Present
When Mitzi hears that a friend of her daughter Lucy has contracted the AIDS virus, she flies into a panic and rushes to New York City from Palm Beach to beg the promiscuous Lucy to settle down and get married in order to avoid a similar fate. When her initial hysteria has passed, Mitzi relents and admits to Lucy that it's better to be free.
WOM80, 2 minutes
Fast Girls by Diana Amsterdam

1084
Ophelia, 18-20   Elsinore Castle
Here, we are given a new look at tragic Ophelia as she entertains us with her own memory of Yorick.
WOM80, 6 minutes
The Girlhood of Shakespeare's Heroines from Cincinnati and Other Plays by Don Nigro

1085
Mariana, 20s   Vienna, 17th century
Mariana is a young woman spurned by her lover. Here, the pivotal character of *Measure for Measure* describes her plight.
WOM80, 9 minutes
The Girlhood of Shakespeare's Heroines from Cincinnati and Other Plays by Don Nigro

1086
Cynthia, 30s   NYC, Present
Here, the delightfully philosophical Cynthia reveals her admiration for Myrna Loy and details how acting like the actress has helped her to cope with her lover when he behaves badly.
WOM80, 7 minutes
A Girl's Guide to Chaos by Cynthia Heimel

1087
Mom, 30-50

Small mid-American town, Present
When childless Mom and Dad adopt Bob, a strange young boy raised by raccoons, the couple is suddenly forced to confront issues which neither seems capable of dealing with. Here, Mom reveals feelings on loneliness and disappointment when she urges Bob to seek a mate.
WOM80, 4 minutes
Lloyd's Prayer by Kevin Kling

1088
Philomele, 20s   **Ancient Thrace**
Tereus, King of Thrace, has fallen in love with Philomele, his sister-in-law. When she rejects his advances, he rapes her. Philomele confronts her attacker with his crime, and he responds by cutting her tongue out.
WOM80, 5 minutes
The Love of the Nightingale by Timberlake Wertenbaker

1089
Awilda, 40-50
The Benjamin home, Present
Awilda and her husband have finally received an insurance check for their son, who was mistakenly shot by a policeman. Awilda studies the check and wonders how they have managed to determine the cash value of the life of a ten-year-old boy.
WOM80, 3 minutes
The Mojo and the Sayso by Aishah Rahman

1090
Lolin, 30-40   **Long Island, Present**
Lolin is Lilia's outspoken and promiscuous next-door neighbor. Lolin is a single mother struggling to raise her rambunctious children in a suburban environment that grows more dangerous with every passing day. Here, Lolin describes the pitfalls of bringing home a date and exposing him to her wild brood.
WOM80, 2 minutes
The Promise by José Rivera

1091
Rachel, 30s   **Ohio and Alaska, Present**
It's a snowy Christmas eve and Rachel is so excited that she can't get to sleep. She speaks non-stop to her husband as she watches the snow fall; her love of Christmas nigh on becoming infectious.
WOM80, 2.5 minutes
Reckless by Craig Lucas

1092
Lynne, 30s   **Here and Now**
Lynne has nursed and comforted her best friend, Ellis, through a fatal round of cancer. The two women shared in the triumphs and horrors of Ellis' battle, bringing them to a place that few friends ever achieve. Lynne's final obligation to Ellis is to carry her ashes to an inlet in Maine and release them over the sea. Here, Lynne describes carrying Ellis' ashes to the sea and letting them go.
WOM80, 3 minutes
Starting Monday by Anne Commire

1093
Sharon, 32   **NYC, Present**
Sharon fills a void in her life through a volunteer program where she becomes involved with Dawn, an underprivileged and defensive black woman, and Frankie, Dawn's troubled teenaged son. Sharon, speaking to the audience, describes what first compelled her to try and help abused children.
WOM80, 9.5 minutes
Three Ways Home by Casey Kurtti

1094
Meg, 30s   **Manhattan, Present**
Meg has recently moved into an apartment occupied by three other women. Unknown to her at the time of her arrival, Wendi, the eldest of the four and the lessor or the apartment, is quite insane. Jusy and Denise have been humoring Wendi for a long time in order to keep the apartment. Meg has misinterpreted much of Wendi's behavior, and when she is finally told the truth of her condition, she finds it difficult to let go of the anger that she has harbored against the helpless madwoman.
WOM80, 2.5 minutes
The Wall of Water by Sherry Kramer

1095
Maggie, 50s   **Scotland during WWII**
As WWII rages in Europe, this Scottish matriarch takes a moment to share a memory of her pregnancy and of her courtship with her husband with her daughter, who is about to marry a naval officer.
WOM80, 3 minutes
When We Were Women by Sharman Macdonald

1096
Blondie, 30s   **Here and Now**
Blondie is a call girl who has been hired by a gang of pranksters to play the part of a bride in a fake wedding. Much to her surprise, Blondie finds herself attracted to the "groom," a melancholy man named Tiny who is constantly the butt of cruel jokes. Here, she reveals her feelings to a mannequin in her apartment.
WOM80, 4 minutes
Archangels Don't Play Pinball by Dario Fo translated by Ron Jenkins

1097

Mamila, 20s   **West Indies, 1790s**

Mamila is an African woman who has willingly followed her idealistic fiancé, Ide, across the Atlantic Ocean on a slave ship. Ide, a prince, desired to become a leader to his people in exile and lead them to freedom. When Ide dies on the journey, Mamila is left alone and pregnant. The owner of the ship frees her in Jamaica, and here she wonders about her past and her future.

WOM80, 2.5 minutes

Indigo by Heidi Thomas

1098

Catches Rain, 20s   **The desert, 1850**

Set against a desert backdrop, this play tells the story of three different eras in American history. Here, a young Indian woman entreats her gods to take her to them now that she has lost her family, her tribe, and has become a slave to a white man.

WOM80, 2 minutes

Infinity's House by Ellen McLaughlin

1099

Woman, 30s   **Here and Now**

Alienation and lack of communication are two themes explored by a woman in the following monologue. As she describes a mishap in a grocery store, we are presented with a character to whom the most simple of tasks has become a Herculean effort.

WOM80, 3 minutes

Laughing Wild by Christopher Durang

1100

Woman, 30s   **Here and Now**

As the woman keeps talking, it occurs to her that her non-stop gestalt may, in fact, be annoying the audience. She ponders this possibility ever so briefly and then renews her verbal attack with interesting commentary on Dr. Ruth Westheimer.

WOM80, 6.5 minutes

Laughing Wild by Christopher Durang

1101

Norma, 40s   **London, Present**

Norma is a promiscuous woman juggling two lovers at the same time. When she becomes more enamored of one than the other, she pleads with her ex-husband to break the bad news to the loser, who happens to be his best friend.

WOM80, 2.5 minutes

Mixed Feelings by Donald Churchill

1102

Katherine Mansfield   **England, 1923**

This is the story of the final years of literary great Katherine Mansfield, a New Zealand-born writer who died at the age of 35 of tuberculosis in England. Said to have inspired the character of Gundrun in the works of her friend, D.H. Lawrence, Katherine was a woman born ahead of her time and knew much passion in her short life. Here, the writer drifts ever closer to death and as she does so she becomes obsessed with trying to capture the essence of every experience she can remember.

WOM80, 2 minutes

The Rivers of China by Alma De Groen

1103

Chata, 40s   **The Southwest, Present**

Chata is an earthy woman trying to hold together a family that flounders after its patriarch is sent to prison for manslaughter. Here, the outspoken Chata describes the correct way to roll a tortilla.

WOM80, 2.5 minutes

Roosters by Milcha Sanchez-Scott

1104

Mrs. Chan, 60+   **America, Present**

Here, the elderly Mrs. Chan describes her life on the run. She is pragmatic about her nomadic existence and disavows the need for a home.

WOM80, 1.5 minutes

As the Crow Flies by David Henry Hwang

1105

Sandra, 40s   **America, Present**

Sandra is the alternate personality of Hannah, Mrs. Chan's cleaning woman. Here, Sandra confronts Mrs. Chan and describes Hannah, revealing the inner darkness of a multiple personality.

WOM80, 2 minutes

As the Crow Flies by David Henry Hwang

1106

Coral, 40s   **Australia, Christmas, 1967**

Since her son's death in Vietnam, Coral has drifted aimlessly through life. After attending a high school production of "A Midsummers' Night's Dream," she reflects on the unattainable magic of getting what you wish for.

WOM80, 1.5 minutes

Away by Michael Gow

1107

Dolores, 30s

Providence, Rhode Island, Winter, 1985

After a particularly violent encounter with Jerry, her husband, Dolores seeks refuge with her sister. Here, Dolores describes the night that she and Jerry first met.
WOM80, 2 minutes
Dolores by Edward Allan Baker

1108
Lulu, 20s
An underworld apartment, Recently
Lulu has been kidnapped by Tomtom and Goose in an effort to reclaim diamonds they believe her brother has stolen from them. Lulu reveals the cosmic nature of her existence to Tomtom in this surrealistic tale of souls floundering in purgatory.
WOM80, 2 minutes
Goose and Tomtom by David Rabe

1109
Lorraine, 30s   **Boston, Present**
At the meeting of a support group for adopted adults who are searching for their birth parents, Lorraine, the guest speaker, tells her own story, illustrating the frustration and heartache of her search.
WOM80, 3 minutes
Phantasie by Sybille Pearson

1110
Girl, 20s   **Here and Now**
Here, a young girl experiences a less-than-satisfactory sexual encounter with her boyfriend and finds that she got more than she bargained for.
WOM80, 6 minutes
Adult Orgasm Escapes from the Zoo by Franca Rame and Dario Fo, adapted by Estelle Parsons

1111
Moeller, 20-40   **A hospital, Present**
Moeller has been tortured and left for dead in a prison in an unknown country. She is saved just in time and here recounts the horrors inflicted upon her in the name of politics.
WOM80, 13 minutes
Adult Orgasm Escapes from the Zoo by Franca Rame and Dario Fo adapted by Estelle Parsons

1112
Strepponi, 50-60
Guiseppe Verdi's home, 1870
Following the success of "Aida," Verdi has retired to the countryside where he only wants to farm. All his friends and associates descend upon his home to beg him to write another opera based on Othello, but the composer is hard to convince. Strepponi, Verdi's wife of 20 years here offers some insight into her temperamental husband's psyche.

WOM80, 6.5 minutes
After Aida by Julian Mitchell

1113
Lena, 40-50   **NYC, Present**
Lena is a woman living in the past. She has spent her life trying to recreate the passion that she knew with her first love and has turned to alcohol to help in the quest. A kept woman, Lena fills the empty hours by commissioning a young artist to paint her portrait. Here, she tells him of her passion for sunsets.
WOM80, 3 minutes
Brown Silk and Magenta Sunsets by P.J. Gibson

1114
Fendi, 20s   **NYC, Present**
Fendi is Lena's daughter by her lost love. A constant reminder of that which could never be, Fendi was driven to suicide by Lena's inability to love her. Here, Fendi angrily confronts Lena on the subject of her birth.
WOM80, 1.5 minutes
Brown Silk and Magenta Sunsets by P.J. Gibson

1115
Olimpia, 40-50
A Latin American Country, Present
Olimpia is a middle-aged serving woman employed in the household of an army officer who specializes in torture. The simple-minded Olimpia clings to her daily schedule and the solace provided by routine as can be seen by her response when her mistress asks that she do something different.
WOM80, 4 minutes
The Conduct of Life by Maria Irene Fornes

1116
Nena, 13-18
A Latin American country, Present
Nena is a destitute young girl who had been kidnapped and kept as a prisoner by a sadistic army officer. Even though she has been subjected to unthinkable horrors at the hands of the fiendish torturer, the young girl still seeks for the goodness that she believes lives in all people.
WOM80, 9 minutes
The Conduct of Life by Maria Irene Fornes

1117
Mary, 20s   **London, late 18th century**
Mary Traverse is the daughter of a wealthy merchant. She is being prepared for her life as a wife by her father, who selects every last word that she may say to a potential suitor. It is Mary's greatest wish that she be able to walk on the carpeting without leaving an impression. Here, she practices her art.

WOM80, 2.5 minutes
The Grace of Mary Traverse by Timberlake Wertenbaker

1118
Merteuil, 30s   **Paris, 1780s**
Valmont and his cohort, play games of sexual intrigue and conquest, until Valmont is finally destroyed by love. Mme. de Merteuil tells Valmont how she succeeds in the arenas love and intrigue.
WOM80, 5 minutes
Les Liaisons Dangereuses by Christopher Hampton

1119
Effie, 30s   **USA, 1950s**
When her husband is sent to fight in Korea, Effie wishes him well and prepares for his absence. Here, she tells the audience about the year 1953 and the effect it had on her life.
WOM80, 4 minutes
Life and Limb by Keith Reddin

1120
Fanny, 30s   **Terra Incognita, 1888**
Three intrepid Victorian ladies have embarked upon a daring expedition of exploration to "Terra Incognita," a semi-mythological land which presents the ladies with an endless array of mysterious artifacts. Here, Fanny describes the menu of her last dinner at the Explorers Club.
WOM80, 2.5 minutes
On the Verge or The Geography of Yearning by Eric Overmyer

1121
Viviane, 17   **Paris, March 3, 1875**
Vigneron and Madam Corniche have been lovers for many years. They plan to arrange the marriage of their children, Hector and Viviane, and introduce them at the opera house during the performance of Carmen. Viviane is more attracted to Hector's father and tells him so.
WOM80, 3.5 minutes
Opera Comique by Nagle Jackson

1122
Rachel, 50+   **New York, Present**
Rachel is a former opera star whose long marriage to the famous conductor, Vito De Angelis, is at an end. Knowing that Vito has fallen in love with the attractive young ghostwriter of his autobiography and anticipating his request for a divorce, the resourceful Rachel has all the details taken care of ahead of time as she here delights in telling him.
WOM80, 4 minutes
Peccadillo by Garson Kanin

1123
Marguerite   **France, 1348**
When Marguerite's lover falls victim to the Black Death, this lusty young woman becomes a nun. When her convent is raided by a band of brigands, Marguerite is saved from being raped by Father Flote, a traveling cleric committed to bringing laughter to the despairing masses. Marguerite joins Flote's comedy troupe and here tells her story to the mute bellringer, Master Bells.
WOM80, 4.5 minutes
Red Noses by Peter Barnes

1124
Masi Matsumoto, 67   **America, Present**
After 40 years of marriage, Masi leaves her husband, Nobu, to seek a new life. When she is confronted by her daughters, Masi breaks down and tells them of the unhappiness and emotional abuse inflicted upon her by Nobu over the years.
WOM80, 2 minutes
The Wash by Philip Kan Gotanda

1125
Shelley, 30s   **The desert, Present**
Shelley and Candy's car has broken down in the middle of the Nevada desert leaving the two New Yorkers stranded. When Shelley confesses to having slept with Candy's exboyfriend, Candy gets angry and threatens not to speak to her ever again. Here, Shelley offers a feeble explanation for her actions.
WOM80, 5.5 minutes
Candy & Shelley Go to the Desert by Paula Cizmar

1126
Bonnie, 30s   **Hollywood, Present**
Bonnie is a hard core member of the LA scene whose sexual prowess is legendary amongst the human vultures that make up the film industry's minor hierarchies. She has been summoned to the home of Eddie and Mickey, who hope that her skills will cheer up their friend Phil, who has recently left his wife. Here, Bonnie speaks of her lust for drugs.
WOM80, 5 minutes
Hurlyburly by David Rabe

1127
Blonde, 20s   **Here and Now**
This young woman has wound up in bed with Willy Rivers, a famous rock star who is struggling to make a comeback after an attempt has been made on his life. Willy is unable to perform sexually, and the Blonde tells him that he is very different than she imagined he would be.
WOM80, 2.5 minutes
The Incredibly Famous Willy Rivers by Stephen Metcalfe

1128
Lorraine, 40s   A poultry shop, Present
Lorraine is an alcoholic desperately seeking
salvation which finally arrives in the form of
Berk, a man who understands her addiction
and becomes determined to help her quit. In a
particularly emotional confrontation between
the two, Lorraine breaks down and tells the
horrible story of the night that her husband
was killed by a drunk driver.
WOM80, 3.5 minutes
The Undoing by William Mastrosimone

1129
Lorr, 20s   A poultry shop, Present
Lorr is the daughter of an alcoholic and has
been enabling her mother's addiction. She resents her mother for many reasons and here reveals to Berk, a man strangely determined to
help her mother quit booze, that she never
thought that her mother deserved a man like
her father, who was killed by a drunk driver.
WOM80, 3 minutes
The Undoing by William Mastrosimone

1130
Vari, 30s   Scotland, Present
Morag wishes that her daughter was married
with children just like her friend, Vari. When the
three women meet on the beach, Vari reveals the
fact that her marriage and motherhood have
been quite detrimental to her happiness.
WOM80, 4 minutes
*When I Was a Girl I Used to Scream and Shout . . .
by Sharman Macdonald*

1131
Fiona, 20s   Scotland, Present
Fiona is the daughter of the outspoken Morag,
who is attempting to start a new life with a
new love. Fiona fears that she may be pregnant
and here pleads sensibly with God to spare her
from ruining the lives of those around her
whom she loves.
WOM80, 4 minutes
*When I Was a Girl I Used to Scream and Shout . . .
by Sharman Macdonald*

1132
May, 30s
A motel near the Mojave Desert, Present
May and Eddie have fallen in love despite the
fact that they share the same father. Their mer-
curial relationship has brought them to the
edge of the desert wilderness where they confront one another with their past, present and
future. This scenario is complicated by Martin,
a man who has been dating May. When Eddie
spitefully reveals the true nature of their relationship to Martin, May flies into a rage and

re-tells the tale from her own perspective.
WOM80, 6.5 minutes
Fool for Love by Sam Shepard

1133
Joan of Arc, 17-20   Medieval France, 1429
Joan is criticized by one of her officers as her
army makes its way to Orleans. When the
pompous officer refuses to relent in his nit-
picking, Joan lashes out at him, and her peasant upbringing proves more than a match for
his refined background.
WOM80, 2 minutes
Little Victories by Lavonne Mueller

1134
Danielle, 20-30
Danielle Edwards' home, 1948
Danielle is the young wife of Nelson, an
olympic medalist who has decided to never
again leave his bed because of the futility of life
as a black man in America. Here, the outspoken Danielle laments the loss of her jet-setting
lifestyle.
WOM80, 2 minutes
The Brothers by Kathleen Collins

1135
Elizabeth, 30s
New York State, 1962-1970
This is a memory play about the indelible ex-
perience of growing up in a Catholic school as
observed by several characters, particularly
Elizabeth. Here, Elizabeth berates God for tak-
ing away her Grandmother.
WOM80, 4.5 minutes
Catholic School Girls by Casey Kurtti

1136
Rachel, 28   Ukraine, 1665
Rachel is a homely young woman trying to
support herself and her mother in a small
Jewish village in the Ukraine. When her aunt,
the local matchmaker, suggests matrimony
with a fruit merchant many years her senior,
Rachel discusses her plight with God.
WOM80, 4.5 minutes
Messiah by Martin Sherman

1137
Rebecca, 50   Gallipoli, Turkey, 1655
When news of Sabbatai Sevi, a self-proclaimed
Messiah on his way to be crowned in
Constantinople, spreads throughout the
Ukraine, Asher convinces Rachel, his uncle's
widow, and Rebecca, her mother, to travel to
Turkey. When they arrive in Gallipoli, Rachel
and Asher are swept away by the fervor sur-
rounding the Messiah's every thought, word
and deed. Rebecca, however, has been mute

ever since the death of her husband and child at the hand of the Cossacks. A moonlight encounter with Sarah, the wife of the Messiah, helps break Rebecca's silence and at long last she addresses her old adversary: Death.
WOM80, 4 minutes
Messiah by Martin Sherman

1138
Paula, 18   **Girls' locker room, 1976**
For years, Paula has been forced to live in the shadow of her popular older sister who was once crowned "Queen of Hearts" in the annual beauty contest. Forced by her mother to enter the contest, Paula is disqualified during the evening for drunk and disorderly behavior. As she sobers up with her friends in the locker room, Paula tells them a story about her sister, revealing her deep-seated resentment.
WOM80, 7 minutes
The Real Queen of Hearts Ain't Even Pretty by Brad Bailey

1139
Marsha, 30s   **NYC, Present**
Marsha is a frustrated, neurotic New Yorker who nearly falls to pieces when confronted by her wholesome, church-going, country-bred neighbor as the following monologue illustrates.
WOM80, 3 minutes
Sally and Marsha by Sybille Pearson

1140
Betty, 40-50   **London, 1980**
Betty is a middle-aged woman who has recently walked out of a stifling marriage. In a frank discussion of sex, Betty reveals the forced repression that she has been subjected to since her childhood.
WOM80, 2.5 minutes
Cloud Nine by Caryl Churchill

1141
Madeleine, 30s   **Here and Now**
Madeleine is a prostitute struggling to break out of society's pre-established roles for her. Here, she offers a bleak manifesto of her life.
WOM80, 3 minutes
The Fairies Are Thirsty by Denise Boucher

1142
Melanie, 30-40   **England, 1960s**
Melanie has devoted her adult life to teaching English to foreigners and to caring for her mother, who has suffered a stroke. The pressures of her career and home life have finally accumulated to a point where Melanie feels hopeless and desperate as she here confides to her friend, Henry.

WOM80, 4.5 minutes
Quartermaine's Terms by Simon Gray

1143
Josie, 34   **England, Present**
Josie is involved in a very abusive relationship with a man upon whom she is totally dependent. Her only sanctuary is the steam room of the local public baths where she can confide her problems to her friends. Here, Josie describes one of the less violent encounters with her man.
WOM80, 3.5 minutes
Streaming by Nell Dunn

1144
Ludivinda, 20s   **NYC, Present**
This young émigré from the Philippines describes her marriage to a U.S. Marine, her new home in New York City and her love of American television.
WOM80, 6.5 minutes
Tenement Lover no palm trees/in new york city by Jessica Hagedorn

1145
Judith, 40s   **Ireland, Summer, 1970s**
Judith is the oldest of the O'Donnell clan of Ballybeg. She has devoted her life to caring for her invalid father at their ancestral estate in County Donegal. When pressured by Eamon, the man who once wanted to marry her, to explain why she never accepted his proposal, Judith responds by saying that she cannot bear to have her daily routine interrupted.
WOM80, 2 minutes
Aristocrats by Brian Friel

1146
Fernande, 40s
Outremont, Canada, Present
Fernande is a snobbish woman who likes to live in the past. She is constantly at odds with her sisters and is the cause of many arguments when they have occasion to get together. At a birthday party for her sister, Lucille, Fernande explains her contempt for contemporary theater.
WOM80, 4.5 minutes
The Impromptu of Outremont by Michel Tremblay

1147
Marie, 30s   **Here and Now**
In this contemporary treatise on the state of marriage, Marie has decided to leave her maddeningly affable husband, Bruce. After a morning of tantrums, and an afternoon of showers and the destruction of his favorite typewriter, Marie sets out to meet him at a friend's party where she plans to inform him of

her decision to leave. Here, Marie describes her particularly surrealistic experiences en route to the party.
WOM80, 7.5 minutes
Marie and Bruce by Wallace Shawn

1148
Rose, 20s   **South Philadelphia, Present**
Rose is a dreamer who never ceases to be amazed by what she learns about life. When she meets pragmatic Cliff, she is put off by his grim and practical view of things. Here, Rose tells Cliff the tragic story of the death of some rare cranes that she was unfortunate enough to have witnessed.
WOM80, 3.5 minutes
The Woolgatherer by William Mastrosimone

1149
Casey, 20s
A small prison cell, Present
Casey, a soldier, has been captured by the enemy and locked in a cramped prison cell. Time and loneliness have taken their toll on him. He tries to explain to his Captain what life in the prison cell has been like for him. Dramatic.
STREET, 5.5 minutes
Home by Glenn Alterman

1150
Herschel, middle-aged
Poolside at a resort, Present
Herschel, a loud, sleazy, two-bit talent agent has just met a new friend while having drinks around the pool. After they've gotten to know each other, he shares his views on fame, women, and the good life. Comic.
STREET, 8 minutes
The Big Pool by Glenn Alterman

1151
Ethan, 30s-50s   **A street, Present**
Rebelling against a society he felt was too constricting, Ethan became a loner. He describes what he does, what he thinks, and where he goes during a typical day in his life. Seriocomic.
STREET, 12 minutes
Ethan by Glenn Alterman

1152
Raphael, 20s
Broadway, near Times Square, Present
Raphael recounts to his buddy Nino the earth shattering drug experience he had the night before. Seriocomic.
STREET, 8 minutes
Raphael by Glenn Alterman

1153
Tommy, 30s-50s   **Anywhere, Present**
Every Friday night Tommy leaves his wife and family in New Jersey and sneaks into New York for some hot sex with street hookers. Seriocomic.
STREET, 4 minutes
Tommy by Glenn Alterman

1154
Robert, 40s-60s,
A waiting room, Present
Robert is one of the wealthiest, most successful men in the world. However, Robert yearns for anonymity—to be just one of the guys. Dramatic.
STREET, 8 minutes
The Best Dilemma by Glenn Alterman

1155
Sid, middle-aged
A crowded restaurant at lunch time, Present
Sid, a scheming, aggressive, New York talent agent, has recently experienced his partner's death in their office. While at lunch with is future son-in-law, he weaves the story of the death scene into a plan he has for his son-in-law's future. Seriocomic.
STREET, 9 minutes
Sid by Glenn Alterman

1156
Larry, 20s-40s   **Anywhere, Present**
Since their first meeting, Larry and his wife have always had very intense feelings for each other. The intensity of those feeling have, on occasion, gone out of control. One evening the passion of their love almost destroyed them. Dramatic.
STREET, 5 minutes
Larry by Glenn Alterman

1157
Edward, any age   **Edward's desk, Present**
For a writer, getting writer's block is always a painful, frustrating experience. For Edward it's a nightmare that is frighteningly real. Seriocomic.
STREET, 8 minutes
Edward by Glenn Alterman

1158
José, 20s-30s   **A street, Present**
José, a drug addict, had a beautiful vision of heaven last night. He tells another junkie what he saw. Seriocomic.
STREET, 2 minutes
José by Glenn Alterman

1159
Sal, 30s-50s
Sal's All Night West Side Diner, Present
Sal, the owner of a diner, thought he'd seen it all. But one night, a strange little man came into his diner and literally shook the place up. Comic.
STREET, 7 minutes
Sal by Glenn Alterman

1160
Melvin, 20s-40s
Fifty-Second Street, Present
Melvin lives a Jekyll-Hyde existence. During the day he's Mr. Stein, a proper and respectable teacher. On weekends he's a pill-popping drug addict who runs around Times Square like a madman. Seriocomic.
STREET, 9 minutes
Melvin by Glenn Alterman

1161
John, 20s-40s   A dark street, Present
On his way home from work, John is mugged. As his life and death struggle with the mugger unfolds, John learns a great deal about who he is and his power to survive. Dramatic.
STREET, 7.5 minutes
John by Glenn Alterman

1162
Joe, 20s-40s
A neighborhood bar, Present
All his life Joe wanted the American dream—home, wife, family. When his dream becomes a reality, it is more than he can handle. One night, while spending a quiet evening with the family, Joe has a major anxiety attack and leaves. Later, he tries to understand what has happened. Seriocomic.
STREET, 3 minutes
Joe by Glenn Alterman

1163
Vince, 40s-50s   A police car, Present
Vince, a New York City cop, has just been assigned a new partner—his brother Joey. As the two drive through a dangerous neighborhood together, Vince prepares Joey for the rough times ahead. Seriocomic.
STREET, 5.5 minutes
Vince by Glenn Alterman

1164
Michael, 30s-50s   A street, Present
Even though he had a successful career in business, Michael chose to chuck it all and move to New York to live the life of a bum. Now, free of worry and all pressure, he describes the many joys and adventures of the lifestyle he finds so satisfying. Seriocomic.
STREET, 6.5 minutes
Michael by Glenn Alterman

1165
Big A, 30s-60s   A bar, Present
After discovering his wife and another man in bed together, Big A drives into the city to get drunk. Seriocomic.
STREET, 7 minutes
Big A by Glenn Alterman

1166
Tony, 20s-30s   Anywhere, Present
Tony, a blue collar worker, thinks of himself as quite a romantic catch. However, he never seems to last in any relationship. He laments to a close friend how his last girlfriend did him wrong. Comic.
STREET, 6.5 minutes
Tony by Glenn Alterman

1167
Prince, 30s-40s   A street, Present
Prince thinks of himself as the smoothest pimp in town. He strolls down Eighth Avenue, beginning his nightly search for some new, young "talent." Seriocomic.
STREET, 7.5 minutes
Prince by Glenn Alterman

1168
Harris, 20s   A bar, Present
Harris just can't figure out why he never seems to score with the ladies. The way he sees it he's doing everything right but nothing seems to pay off. Awaiting the arrival of a blind date, he looks for some last minute reassurance from a close friend. Comic.
STREET, 3 minutes
Harris by Glenn Alterman

1169
Ralph, 20s-30s   A bar, Present
Once again Ralph met the perfect girl. In the middle of their two day sexual marathon the strangest thing happened; they accidentally had a moment of genuine intimacy. Comic.
STREET, 4 minutes
Ralph by Glenn Alterman

1170
Lefty, 30s-50s   Anywhere, Present
Lefty's been having sex with prostitutes for years. Here he describes the night he got more than bargained for in a life-and-death scene with a hooker in a cheap hotel room. Seriocomic.
STREET, 2.5 minutes
Lefty by Glenn Alterman

1171
Piano Man, 30s-50s   **Anywhere, Present**
Piano Man couldn't stand it anymore. Everywhere he looked he saw moral decay, filth, and perversion. One night in a church he expresses his feelings to Jesus. Seriocomic.
STREET, 4.5 minutes
Piano Man by Glenn Alterman

1172
Helen, middle-aged   **Anywhere, Present**
Her husband Morty is asleep, so it's another night of T.V. and boredom for Helen. Hearing a knock on the door, Helen answers and meets her tiny new neighbor, Hal, and her life changes forever. She recalls that first meeting. Comic.
STREET, 10.5 minutes
Helen by Glenn Alterman

1173
Lila, 40s-50s   **Anywhere, Present**
Lila, an earthy exotic dancer, has spent much of her life desperately looking for a man. Along the way her dancing career began to plummet as she accepted one sleazy job after another. She recalls how the events in her life lead her to an epiphany one night in a cheap club in New Jersey. Seriocomic.
STREET, 6.5 minutes
Lila by Glenn Alterman

1174
Myra, middle-aged
A tenement apartment, Present
Alone another night, Myra dreams up a romantic evening for herself. In tonight's fantasy, she is Lotte Lenya, adored and lusted after by a young soldier during the war. Seriocomic.
STREET, 8.5 minutes
Myra by Glenn Alterman

1175
Flora, 40s-50s
New York Port Authority Bus Station, Present
Flora, a waitress, has just escaped from a terribly dull life in the middle of New Hampshire. This morning she stole away on a bus to New York. Immediately upon arriving she shares her story with the first person she meets. Comic.
STREET, 4 minutes
Flora by Glenn Alterman

1176
Ruthie, middle-aged
Ruthie's kitchen, Present
Ruthie has been married to Sol, an alcoholic, for nearly thirty years. He's always been difficult to live with, but recently Sol's become im-

possible. Here, Ruthie tell her sister, Pearl, about a life-threatening scene that's just occurred between Sol and the family. Dramatic.
STREET, 9 minutes
Ruthie by Glenn Alterman

1177
Waitress, 20s-30s   **A bar, Present**
To help make ends meet, the waitress occasionally has sex with customers from the bar for cash. She describes an unpleasant scene she had with a crude fat man in the parking lot. Dramatic.
STREET, 6 minutes
Waitress by Glenn Alterman

1178
Mary, 20s-40s
A pickup bar, Present
Mary gets turned on by meeting men in bars. The man she met last night called himself Captain Midnight. Comic.
STREET, 3 minutes
Mary by Glenn Alterman

1179
Marie, middle-aged
Marie's kitchen, Present
Marie and Antony have been married for many years. One night while they're having dinner, Marie sees a ghost come in the window. Antony is unaware of the ghost. After it leaves, a terrified Marie tries to explain to Antony what has just happened. Seriocomic.
STREET, 3 minutes
Marie by Glenn Alterman

1180
Mary-Anne, 30s-40s
A street corner, Present
Mary-Anne's just had a few drinks in her neighborhood bar. On her way home she accidentally stumbles and falls. When she looks up from the curb, there stands a stranger; Mr. Right. Mary-Anne awkwardly tries to pick him up.
STREET, 5 minutes
Mary-Anne by Glenn Alterman

1181
Eva, 20s-30s   **Liberty Island, Present**
It is a few days after the great Apocalypse and most of the world has been destroyed. Eva's decided to take her kids over to Liberty Island for a day trip. While there, she meets another woman and they strike up a friendship. Dramatic.
STREET, 6 minutes
Eva by Glenn Alterman

1182
Beth, any age   **A street, Present**
Beth is a timid, tense, terrified lady. Everything and everyone in the city scares her. In this monologue she describes her nightly journey coming home from the subway. Seriocomic.
STREET, 9 minutes
Beth by Glenn Alterman

1183
Carousel, 20s-40s   **A bar, Present**
Carousel's got the whole bar scene all figured out. There isn't a scene or angle she hasn't played. Most importantly, Carousel must always be the star and be 'featured'. Comic.
STREET, 3 minutes
Carousel by Glenn Alterman

1184
Shirl, 30s-50s
Outside her bathroom door, Present
Shirl's drunk again. Tonight's Mr. Wonderful has, for some reason, locked himself in her bathroom. While anxiously waiting for him to come out, Shirl shares her feelings about love, loneliness, and the magic of movies. Seriocomic.
STREET, 3 minutes
Shirl by Glenn Alterman

1185
Anna, 30s-60s
A woman's shelter, Present
Anna, a homeless woman, has been broken by living out on the streets for too long. She tries to make contact with another woman in a shelter and warns her of the dangers of street life and shelter living. Dramatic.
STREET, 8.5 minutes
Anna by Glenn Alterman

1186
Brenda, 20s-30s
A laundry in Memphis
Brenda's felt trapped with Moe and their kids for a long time. Being their full-time maid and slave was not the kind of life she'd planned on. She dreams of some day being free of them. Seriocomic.
STREET, 11 minutes
The Wash by Glenn Alterman

1187
Angela, 20s-40s   **A bar, Present**
Angela is an adept game player in her bar scene. She has mastered the art of being a turn-on and a tease. Sometimes coy, always cunning, she usually gets her man exactly where she wants him. Seriocomic.

STREET, 4 minutes
Angela by Glenn Alterman

1188
Lisa, 20s-30s
Backstage at a theatre, Present
Lisa's dream was to be a great actress. After getting a leading role in a show and tremendous encouragement during rehearsals it looked like she was on her way to becoming a star. But on opening night, just a few minutes before she's to go on, a disaster occurs. She discovers that her "character" has   deserted her. Seriocomic.
STREET, 8 minutes
Lisa by Glenn Alterman

1189
Velvet, 30's-50s   **A bar, Present**
Usually, Velvet thinks of herself as a no-nonsense business woman. But one night she met a very exciting man who showed her a whole new side of herself. Seriocomic.
STREET, 7.5 minutes
Velvet by Glenn Alterman

1190
Vernice, 20s-40s
A dressing room in a strip joint, Present
Vernice, a stripper, loves being a woman who can arouse men. A customer from the club where she works has come back to her dressing room to ask for a date. Seriocomic.
STREET, 5 minutes
Vernice by Glenn Alterman

1191
Angel, 20's-40s   **A piano bar, Present**
Feeling stuck in a cold water flat in New Jersey with a junkie husband, Angel always dreamt of escaping to New York to become a famous singer. Here she recalls the night she took the risk and followed her dream. Dramatic.
STREET, 8.5 minutes
Angel by Glenn Alterman

1192
Kathy, any age   **Anywhere, Present**
Nighttime was special for Kathy because she knew she'd always see her father. He would tuck her into bed, give her a goodnight kiss, and promise to see her later in her dreams. Dramatic.
STREET, 3 minutes
Kathy by Glenn Alterman

1193
Stella, 30s-40s   **A pickup bar, Present**
When Stella makes love to a man her mind

drifts off to places far away. Her fantasies have little to do with the man she's actually with. This is the story of one of her sexual encounters. Seriocomic.
STREET, 4.5 minutes
Stella by Glenn Alterman

1194
Hannah, 20s-40s   **A bar, Present**
All her life Hannah has always been the polite, sweet little girl. With men she always feigns complete interest in their every word, and makes sure to always have a loving smile pasted on her face. Dramatic.
STREET, 3 minutes
Hannah by Glenn Alterman

1195
Rose, any age   **A bar, Present**
Rose has been dumped on by men all her life. But last night something changed and she finally defended herself. Comic.
STREET, 2 minutes
Rose by Glenn Alterman

1196
Lulu, 30s-40s
At her close friend's apartment, Present
Desperately looking for a man, Lulu thought she finally found one. But as so many times before, Mr. Right is another dud. And once again, Lulu is crushed. Seriocomic.
STREET, 5.5 minutes
Lulu by Glenn Alterman

1197
George, middle-aged
A first-class cabin aboard an ocean liner, 1930s
One partner of a successful playwriting team has reacted to the Depression by becoming a Communist who only wants to write serious plays with a message. Here, George, the other half of the team, tells his agent that he was once as idealistic as Max, until an incident opened his eyes to his true character.
TAPER, 3.5 minutes
An American Comedy by Richard Nelson

1198
Indian Elizabeth, any age
West Tennessee woods, 1830s
Indian Elizabeth, distraught at the prospect of being forced to leave her tribal land and move West, decides to impersonate a white woman in order to stay.
TAPER, 3.5 minutes
The Bear Facts by Jo Carson

1199
Davy Crockett
West Tennessee woods, 1930s
Davy Crockett describes his technique for hunting bear.
TAPER, 1.5 minutes
The Bear Facts by Jo Carson

1200
Anna, 20s-30s   **Anna's loft, Present**
Anna has returned from out of town where she attended her roommate Robbie's funeral and met his family. Here, she describes the experience to her friend, Larry.
TAPER, 4.5 minutes
Burn This by Lanford Wilson

1201
Pale, 20s-30s   **Anna's loft, Present**
Robbie's older brother, Pale, shows up at Anna's loft at midnight to collect Robbie's things. Talking non-stop he complains about a guy who talks too much and people who don't listen.
TAPER, 5 minutes
Burn This by Lanford Wilson

1202
Pale, 20s-30s   **Anna's loft, Present**
Pale, still talking incessantly, tells Anna what turns him on.
TAPER, 1.5 minutes
Burn This by Lanford Wilson

1203
Suna, 25-30   **LA, Present**
Suna tells her friend Satu about a girl she is jealous of and how she would like to deal with her.
TAPER, 1.5 minutes
The Distance Of You by Adelaide MacKenzie

1204
Lieutenant Halsey, over 40   **LA, Present**
Lieutenant Halsey, an Arizona police officer, unexpectedly arrives at Satu's house, much to the consternation of Suna, who seems to want to avoid him. Lt. Halsey claims to be friends with Joe Wambaugh, a former LAPD cop, now a successful novelist and screenwriter. It becomes clear that Suna has killed someone in Arizona and that Lt. Halsey was the arresting officer. He has become obsessed with Suna and has pursued her, not to arrest her, but to possess her. Here, he makes it clear that he wants to make her live with him and become totally dependent on him.
TAPER, 1.5 minutes
The Distance Of You by Adelaide MacKenzie

1205
Petra,   **LA, Present**
Alone, Petra angrily denounces Reed, condemning her own obsession with him.
TAPER, 1.5 minutes
The Distance Of You by Adelaide MacKenzie

1206
Lana, 40   **LA, Present**
Lana is married to Drew, a fringe criminal and "troubleshooter" for Wilson, owner of their apartment building. While smoking a joint, Lana confides to Marliss, an addict who turns tricks for drug money, how she always wanted to have a baby.
TAPER, 2 minutes
The Dream Coast by John Steppling

1207
Gros-Jean
West Indies, no specific time
Gros-Jean, the eldest, describes a bet he made with a white planter (the devil in disguise) as to who could lose his temper first.
TAPER, 4.5 minutes
Dream On Monkey Mountain: Ti-Jean And His Brothers by Derek Walcott

1208
Afa, over 40
West Indies, no specific time
Afa explains why he must live and die by the harshness and beauty of the sea.
TAPER, 2 minutes
Dream On Monkey Mountain: The Sea At Dauphin by Derek Walcott

1209
Afa, over 40
West Indies, no specific time
Afa describes the death of Bolo, an old fisherman.
TAPER, 2.5 minutes
Dream On Monkey Mountain: The Sea At Dauphin by Derek Walcott

1210
Camagitello, 30s-40s
NYC, Present
Camagitello is a cop working undercover for the DEA in hopes of getting off for shooting a young boy by mistake. Here he describes what happened that night to his fellow officers.
TAPER, 2.5 minutes
Hells Kitchen Ablaze by Thomas George Carter

1211
June, 20s   **A coffee shop, Present**
June's ex-boyfriend attempts to fix her up with

Frank, a well-meaning but bland teacher who is determined to go out with June. Here, June describes an incident to Frank that explains how her destructive pattern in relationships began.
TAPER, 3 minutes
The Interpreter of Horror by Kelly Stuart

1212
Horror
A coffee shop, Present
Horror relates a story to June meant to warn June against being lulled into becoming a victim.
TAPER, 2 minutes
The Interpreter of Horror by Kelly Stuart

1213
Star, 17   **Rural Kentucky, 1776**
Star, in labor with Michael's child, describes her feelings for the child and its father.
TAPER, 2 minutes
The Kentucky Cycle: The Courtship of Morning Star by Robert Schenkkan

1214
Mary Ann
Rural Kentucky, 1920
Mary Ann realizes that her marriage to Tommy, whom she never loved, has been a sham. Here, she defiantly takes back her name and renounces her marriage to the man she no longer trusts.
TAPER, 1.5 minutes
The Kentucky Cycle: A Fire in the Hole 1920 by Robert Schenkkan

1215
Mary Ann
Rural Kentucky, 1920
After their leader's murder, the men are disheartened and decide to give up fighting for the union. Mary Ann and the other women are left alone, feeling helpless and defeated. Here, Mary Ann showing enormous courage and resolve, rallies the women to stand up for what they believe.
TAPER, 1.5 minutes
The Kentucky Cycle: A Fire in the Hole 1920 by Robert Schenkkan

1216
Patrick, 40s   **Rural Kentucky, 1819**
Here, Patrick, who does not yet know Jeremiah's identity, begs not to be thrown off his land.
TAPER, 1.5 minutes
The Kentucky Cycle: Ties That Bind 1819 by Robert Schenkkan

1217
Jeremiah
Rural Kentucky, 1819
Jeremiah reveals who he is to Patrick and gloats over his revenge on the Rowens.
TAPER, 2 minutes
The Kentucky Cycle: Ties That Bind 1920 by Robert Schenkkan

1218
Joshua, 65   **Rural Kentucky, 1975**
Here, Joshua recounts a dream where he sees his son and his parents, who are trying to tell him something vitally important.
TAPER, 2 minutes
The Kentucky Cycle: The War On Poverty 1975 by Robert Schenkkan

1219
Joshua, 65   **Rural Kentucky, 1975**
Joshua's friends are pressuring him to sell off his share of the land for strip mining, which would mean the ultimate rape of the land. In a turmoil, Joshua vividly remembers his mother, the courageous Mary Ann, and the other miners who still believed in something and were not afraid to fight for it. He comes to believe that this is the message from the dream and that, at last, he too must take a good stand.
TAPER, 2.5 minutes
The Kentucky Cycle: The War On Poverty 1975 by Robert Schenkkan

1220
Paul   **Present**
Here, Paul describes his first sexual encounter after his wife's death.
TAPER, 1.5 minutes
Life after Time by Paul Linke

1221
Alma, middle-aged   **Buckram, Present**
Here Alma tries to explain to her son why she felt compelled to place the personal ad.
TAPER, 1.5 minutes
The Mind with the Dirty Man by Jules Tasca

1222
Wayne, middle-aged   **Buckram, Present**
Wayne, having imbibed too much wine, drunkenly confesses his past indiscretions to his wife.
TAPER, 1.5 minutes
The Mind with the Dirty Man by Jules Tasca

1223
Jack, 20s   **Vietnam, 1968s**
Here, Jack tells his wife that he deeply admires the ancient and mysterious peoples, the

Etruscans, more than anyone he can think of.
TAPER, 4 minutes
Muzeeka by John Guare

1224
Jack, 20s   **1968s**
Jack reveals a secret plan he has formulated for Muzeeka once he has accepted a job there.
TAPER, 7.5 minutes
Muzeeka by John Guare

1225
Paige, 20s   **LA, Present**
Paige has become involved with Junior, an angry man who works with Ike. Here, referring to her ex-husband, Deak, Paige talks about driving past the homes of the wealthy in Brentwood.
TAPER, 1 minute
My Crummy Job by John Steppling

1226
Father John
A church, during homily, Present
Father John, representing religious zealots, perpetuates the discrimination experienced by the disabled. Here, he warns all who will listen that the devil lives in the crippled and deformed.
TAPER, 3 minutes
PH*Reaks by Doris Baizley and Victoria Ann-Lewis

1227
Angie   **Doctor's office, Present**
Angie, a dwarf, angrily responds when a Doctor asks her why she displays herself in a sideshow. Why shouldn't they pay to look at her when she is stared and gawked at all the time anyway?
TAPER, 1.5 minutes
PH*Reaks by Doris Baizley and Victoria Ann-Lewis

1228
Joe, middle-aged
A hospice cottage, Present
Joe is visited by his wife, Maggie, who can't accept his illness, and his teenage son. Here he reveals the nightmare he has every night.
TAPER, 2 minutes
The Shadow Box by Michael Cristofer

1229
Brian, middle-aged
A hospice cottage, Present
Brian, a gay man, is being cared for by his lover, Mark. Brian angrily responds to the fuss his wife and lover are making over a champagne stain on Mark's jacket.
TAPER, 2 minutes
The Shadow Box by Michael Cristofer

1230
Beverly, middle-aged
A hospice cottage, Present
Brian, a gay man, is being cared for by his lover, Mark. Here, his ex-wife, Beverly, warns Mark that Brian is using him.
TAPER, 1.5 minutes
The Shadow Box by Michael Cristofer

1231
Maggie, middle-aged
A hospice cottage, Present
Maggie, defiantly and still in denial, tells Joe she wants him to come home with her.
TAPER, 1.5 minutes
The Shadow Box by Michael Cristofer

1232
Sharon Tate, 20s   **Her room, 1969**
After describing the evening leading up to the murders, Sharon describes the murders themselves.
TAPER, 3 minutes
Stalin's Daughter by August Baker

1233
Richard Nixon, 56
Psychiatrist's office 1969
Richard Nixon is being interviewed by Dr. Rita Gains, a psychiatrist. Here, Nixon describes a botched bombing attempt in Vietnam.
TAPER, 2.5 minutes
Stalin's Daughter by August Baker

1234
Megan, 20   **Her home, 1969**
Megan, a young woman who lives in Princeton, New Jersey, reveals to her parents an earlier incident between her brother, who is missing in action in Vietnam, and their celebrity neighbor, Stalin's daughter.
TAPER, 2 minutes
Stalin's Daughter by August Baker

1235
Father Ed Larkin, middle-aged
A Catholic school for Hispanic boys in lower East side Manhattan, Present
Father Ed Larkin, a Jesuit priest and principal of the school, reveals that he is disillusioned with a God who proves His love by allowing His Son to die.
TAPER, 2 minutes
Standup Tragedy by Bill Cain

1236
Tom Griffin, middle-aged
A Catholic school for Hispanic boys in lower East side Manhattan, Present
Tom Griffin, an increasingly cynical teacher, describes his frustration when trying to find a battered women's shelter for the mother of one of his students.
TAPER, 2.5 minutes
Standup Tragedy by Bill Cain

1237
Adnan, middle-aged
Venice California, Present
Adnan, a middle-aged aphasic, explains his daily routine since his stroke.
TAPER, 4.5 minutes
Struck Dumb by Jean-Claude van Itallie and Joseph Chaikin

1238
Adnan, middle-aged
Venice California, Present
Adnan talks about a little dog he likes and man's relationship with animals.
TAPER, 4.5 minutes
Struck Dumb by Jean-Claude van Itallie and Joseph Chaikin

1239
Prosecutor (Maggie Thatcher)
Courtroom, Present
Here, the prosecutor, whose name is Maggie Thatcher, makes her summation to the jury.
TAPER, 4.5 minutes
Tap Dancer by Conrad Bishop and Elizabeth Fuller

1240
Father Daniel Berrigan, 49
Catonsville, Maryland, 1970
Daniel Berrigan, a Jesuit Priest and chief defendant, recalls the day he was ordained and his feelings about the priesthood.
TAPER, 3.5 minutes
The Trial of the Catonsville Nine by Daniel Berrigan

1241
Mary Moylan, 20s
Catonsville, Maryland, 1970
Mary Moylan, while on the stand, describes the incident that awakened her social consciousness.
TAPER, 2.5 minutes
The Trial of the Catonsville Nine by Daniel Berrigan

1242
Victoria, middle-aged
Victorian England, late 1900s
Victoria confides to Wanda and Forgiveness that her husband, a physician, has convinced her that removal of her ovaries will get rid of her "hysteria" which manifests itself in biting,

and an arm spasm which causes her to hit her husband. In fact, her arm flings involuntarily whenever she utters the word, "husband".
TAPER, 3 minutes
The Waiting Room by Lisa Loomer

1243
Wanda, 40
NYC barroom, Present
Wanda has been told that she has a tumor in her breast which may be malignant. She will need a biopsy as soon as possible. When she leaves the office, she goes across the street to get drunk. Downing double Jack Daniels, she describes to the bartender, and anyone within earshot, the bet she made with her mother to beat the statistic and marry by age 40, which she is now.
TAPER, 6 minutes
The Waiting Room by Lisa Loomer

1244
Dr. Douglas McCaskill, middle-aged
Present
Douglas, the three women's doctor, makes a desperate, emotional phone call to a fellow healer.
TAPER, 2 minutes
The Waiting Room by Lisa Loomer

1245
Warren   **Present**
Warren, in a straightforward and practical manner, asks Luisa to live with him.
TAPER, 4.5 minutes
Whole Hearted by Quincy Long

1246
Jewel, older woman   **Present**
Jewel, Warren's childhood Nanny, tells a younger Warren a touching story about a prodigal son, hoping it will help his relationship with his father.
TAPER, 10 minutes
Whole Hearted by Quincy Long

1247
Jack Rover   **1880s**
Here, Jack Rover describes a chaotic night where he was shot by Indians and chased by a bear.
TAPER, 2 minutes
Wild Oats by James McLure, adapted from John O'Keefe

1248
Chiro   **A bar, Present**
Here, Chiro tells Rene about an incident with one of his clients, who turns out to be Rene's former employer.

TAPER, 2 minutes
The Woman Who Tried to Shout Underwater by Kelly Stuart

1249
Rene, 45   **A bar, Present**
Rene has spurned Chiro. Alone, she recalls when her baby was taken away from her.
TAPER, 3 minutes
The Woman Who Tried to Shout Underwater by Kelly Stuart

1250
Scott, 20s-40s
Outside the bedroom door, Present
After a dish-breaking fight, Scott tries to apologize to his wife, who's locked in the bedroom. Seriocomic.
TWOMIN, 3 minutes
Scott by Glenn Alterman

1251
Simon, any age
A subway station, Present
Simon tells a police officer about a horrible experience he just had in the subway car. Seriocomic.
TWOMIN, 4 minutes
Simon by Glenn Alterman

1252
Perry, Late teens to late twenties
Dreamland, Present
Here Perry, a "sprite," tells the "dreamer" about his dream. Seriocomic.
TWOMIN, 4.5 minutes
Perry by Glenn Alterman

1253
Beau, 30s-50s
A sandy area not far from the water, Present
After tirelessly filling bags with sand, Beau takes a break. Here he shares his feeling with a stranger. Dramatic.
TWOMIN, 2 minutes
Beau by Glenn Alterman

1254
Crying Johnny's Dad, 20s-40s
Anywhere, Present
While on an amusement park ride, Johnny's father has a very erotic encounter with a strange lady. Seriocomic.
TWOMIN, 3.5 minutes
Crying Johnny's Dad by Glenn Alterman

1255
Mr. Reynolds, 30s-50s
Anywhere, Present

Mr. Reynolds, a businessman, describes a life and death experience he had with another man in an elevator. Dramatic.
TWOMIN, 3 minutes
Mr. Reynolds by Glenn Alterman

1256
The Bee-Bop King, any age
Sitting in a room on a chair
Here the Bee-Bop King, a disturbed man, tells how he was violently forced out of Candyland. Seriocomic.
TWOMIN, 3 minutes
The Bee-Bop King by Glenn Alterman

1257
Carlie, 30s-40s
In a parked car in a rest area on a thruway, Present
Carlie is a lonely gay man who seeks out other men at rest areas to have sex. Here he tells a man he's just met how similar they are. Dramatic.
TWOMIN, 1.5 minutes
Carlie by Glenn Alterman

1258
Rodney, 30s-50s   A bar, Present
Rodney, a colorful, drunken womanizer, tells a friend about his previous night's sexual encounter. Comic.
TWOMIN, 2 minutes
Rodney by Glenn Alterman

1259
Zeke, any age   Anywhere, Present
Zeke recalls the terrifying dream he had as a little boy, the night his father died. Dramatic.
TWOMIN, 2.5 minutes
Zeke by Glenn Alterman

1260
Herbie, 20s-40s
A police station interrogation room, Present
Here Herbie nervously tries to explain why he had to kill a woman he never met before in her apartment. Seriocomic.
TWOMIN, 3.5 minutes
Herbie by Glenn Alterman

1261
Herbie, 20s-40s
The living room of a stranger he just met, Present
After coming up to a stranger's apartment, hopefully for sex, Herbie decides to tell her a little about himself. Seriocomic.
TWOMIN, 1.5 minutes
Herbie (II) by Glenn Alterman

1262
Mr. Al, 30s-60s   A vacant building, Present
Mr. Al trains young boys to pick people's pockets. Here he instructs and encourages a newfound student. Comic.
TWOMIN, 1.5 minutes
Mr. Al by Glenn Alterman

1263
Ronald, 30s-50s   Anywhere, Present
Ronald, a neurotic businessman, recalls a gruesome murder. Comic.
TWOMIN, 2 minutes
Ronald Silverman by Glenn Alterman

1264
Roy, 40s-50s   Anywhere, Present
Roy recalls the night he met and fell in love with his wife. Comic.
TWOMIN, 3.5 minutes
Roy by Glenn Alterman

1265
Sheridan, 30s-40s   A living room, Present
For the last two years, Sheridan has secretly been writing a full-length play every waking minute when he wasn't with his wife. Now that it's complete he finally tells her about his obsession. Comic.
TWOMIN, 1.5 minutes
Sheridan by Glenn Alterman

1266
Mort, 30s-40s
A furnished basement in Brooklyn, Present
While waiting for their connection in a drug deal, Mort and Harry, two old friends, high on coke, recall the day when Harry taught Mort to ride a bike. Seriocomic.
TWOMIN, 1.5 minutes
Mort by Glenn Alterman

1267
Mort, 30s-40s
A furnished basement in Brooklyn, Present
Here Mort lambastes his best friend Harry for trying to cheat him out of money in a phony drug deal. Seriocomic.
TWOMIN, 2 minutes
Mort (II) by Glenn Alterman

1268
Marcus, 30s-50s
A street corner near Times Square, Present
Here Marcus, an injured, mentally deranged, Vietnam vet, while panhandling, bounces back and forth in his mind between New York and memories of Vietnam. Seriocomic.
TWOMIN, 4 minutes
Marcus by Glenn Alterman

1269
Jethro, 20s-40s   **Anywhere, Present**
After they successfully rob a bank, Jethro and
Zeb are hiding out in a small hotel room wait-
ing for Miss Dolly to arrive with the loot. Here
Jethro talks about the difficulty of being stuck
with ugly old Zeb. Seriocomic.
TWOMIN, 3 minutes
Jethro by Glenn Alterman

1270
Dave, 50s-60s
The Rosenstein kitchen in the Brighton Beach
section of Brooklyn, Present
After her son died of AIDS, Vernice Rosen-
stein's personality radically changed. Here
Dave, her husband, tells their other son Barry
what she's been like. Seriocomic.
TWOMIN, 2.5 minutes
Dave Rosenstein by Glenn Alterman

1271
Dave, 50s-60s
The Rosenstein kitchen in the Brighton Beach
section of Brooklyn, Present
Here Dave describes the helplessness he felt
when his son, who had AIDS, had a seizure at
the dinner table. Seriocomic.
TWOMIN, 1 minute
Dave Rosenstein (II) by Glenn Alterman

1272
Dave, 50s-60s
The Rosenstein kitchen in the Brighton Beach
section of Brooklyn, Present
After his wife has refused to talk to him for
nearly a year, Dave unleashes his rage at her.
Seriocomic.
TWOMIN, 1 minute
Dave Rosenstein (III) by Glenn Alterman

1273
Leon, 20s-40s   **Anywhere, Present**
Leon finds love, himself, and his calling when
he meets a girl on the streets late one night.
Comic.
TWOMIN, 3 minutes
Leon by Glenn Alterman

1274
Mickey, 20s-40s   **The kitchen, Present**
After learning that he's been diagnosed with
AIDS, Mickey tells his brother. Dramatic.
TWOMIN, 1.5 minutes
Mickey by Glenn Alterman

1275
Fred, 30s-50s   **On his farm, Present**
Here Fred, a farmer, recalls the wonderful mo-

ment he realized he'd won ten million dollars
in a lottery. [Comedic]
TWOMIN, 4 minutes
Fred by Glenn Alterman

1276
Wally, 30s-60s   **Anywhere, Present**
After being fired from his job for racist behav-
ior, Wally tries to explain his side of the story.
Comic.
TWOMIN, 3 minutes
Wally by Glenn Alterman

1277
Harry, 30s-40s
A furnished basement in Brooklyn, Present
Harry and Mort have been close friends most
of their lives. These two small-time wheeler-
dealers are about to do their first big drug deal
which Harry has set up. While snorting some
coke and waiting for their connection, Mort
starts having doubts. Here Harry chastises him
for not trusting him. Seriocomic.
TWOMIN, 1 minute
Harry by Glenn Alterman

1278
Harry, 30s-40s
A furnished basement in Brooklyn, Present
Harry and Mort have been close friends most
of their lives. These two small-time wheeler-
dealers are now involved in a drug deal which
Harry has set up. When Mort expresses some
doubts about the deal, here Harry tries to re-
assure him everything will be okay.
Seriocomic.
TWOMIN, 1.5 minutes
Harry (II) by Glenn Alterman

1279
Rod, 20s-40s   **A bar, Present**
While putting the make on a young lady in a
bar, Rod has a "heated" encounter with the
devil. Comic.
TWOMIN, 2.5 minutes
Rod by Glenn Alterman

1280
Vincent, 30s-50s   **His apartment, Present**
After seducing a woman he met at his health
club, under false pretenses, Vincent decides to
come clean with her. Comic.
TWOMIN, 2.5 minutes
Vincent by Glenn Alterman

1281
Norm, 20s-40s
A bar, late afternoon, Present
Norm, a shy businessman, agonizes as he tries

to get the nerve to talk to an attractive woman across the bar. Seriocomic.
TWOMIN, 3.5 minutes
Norm by Glenn Alterman

1282
Nick, 30s-50s
A chair in a hospital room, Present
Here Nick, a small-time gangster, tells how a big drug deal fell through. He sits in a chair, wearing sunglasses, speaking slowly. Dramatic.
TWOMIN, 2 minutes
Nick by Glenn Alterman

1283
Brian, 50s-70s   A gay, hustler bar, Present
Brian, an older gay man, goes to hustler bars to meet young men for sex. Here he tells about how he feels about what he does. Dramatic.
TWOMIN, 4 minutes
Brian by Glenn Alterman

1284
Stanley, any age   Anywhere, Present
Here Stanley tenderly recalls some early memories of his mother. Seriocomic.
TWOMIN, 2 minutes
Stanley by Glenn Alterman

1285
Joyce, 30s-40s
A hotel suite, Present
Joyce, a successful executive, uses her business skills and directness to seduce an executive she just met at a business meeting. Comic.
TWOMIN, 2.5 minutes
Joyce by Glenn Alterman

1286
Maureen, 30s-50s   Her home, Present
Maureen, an agoraphobic, was once a successful executive at an advertising company. Here she tells the terrifying story of the day she tried to leave home to go to an important meeting but realized she couldn't. Dramatic.
TWOMIN, 3 minutes
Maureen by Glenn Alterman

1287
Alison, 30s-50s
Her son's bedroom, Present
After her son informs her he will not attend her wedding, Alison becomes enraged and lets him know who's boss. Comic.
TWOMIN, 2 minutes
Alison by Glenn Alterman

1288
Mary Ellen, 40s-50s   Anywhere, Present
After being in the company for twenty years, Mary Ellen recalls the moment her boss unexpectedly told her she was laid off. Dramatic.
TWOMIN, 2 minutes
Mary Ellen by Glenn Alterman

1289
Gwen, any age   In her home, Present
Gwen finally tells off her abusive, alcoholic husband. Dramatic.
TWOMIN, 2 minutes
Gwen by Glenn Alterman

1290
Kami, 20s-40s
The living room, Present
Kami, a mysteriously seductive woman, invites a man up to her apartment. Here she entices him with a strange story about the rear bedroom. Dramatic.
TWOMIN, 1.5 minutes
Kami by Glenn Alterman

1291
Rita, 30s-50s   A movie set, Present
After too many years of doing extra work on movies, Rita, a somewhat cynical yet hopeful actress, talks to another extra about her dream to be a star. Seriocomic.
TWOMIN, 2.5 minutes
Rita by Glenn Alterman

1292
Janine, 40s   Anywhere, Present
Janine remembers how a fun-filled afternoon with some boys on a rooftop turned into a nightmare. Dramatic.
TWOMIN, 3 minutes
Janine by Glenn Alterman

1293
Mary Elizabeth, 30s-60s
The jungle, Present
Here Mary Elizabeth, a missionary, tells a new arrival to the jungle about how she came to accept and love the people of the village. Seriocomic.
TWOMIN, 3 minutes
Mary Elizabeth by Glenn Alterman

1294
Evelyn, 20s-40s   Anywhere, Present
After her miscarriage, Evelyn had an emotional breakdown. Here she fantasizes about the son she never had. Dramatic.
TWOMIN, 3 minutes
Evelyn by Glenn Alterman

1295
Josephine, 30s-50s
Her lawyer's office, Present
After being tormented and harassed by her
creditors, Josephine, a successful business-
woman, has decided to file for bankruptcy.
When her lawyer suggests that she hold off on
such a drastic measure, she exploded.
Seriocomic.
TWOMIN, 2 minutes
Josephine by Glenn Alterman

1296
Janice, late teens-twenties
A jewelry store, Present
Here Janice talks about the day a strange boy
came into her father's jewelry store looking for
a job. Comic.
TWOMIN, 3.5 minutes
Janice by Glenn Alterman

1297
Esther, 30s-50s   Esther's house, Present
Here Esther tells about the day she discovered
her best friend in bed with her husband.
Comic.
TWOMIN, 2.5 minutes
Esther by Glenn Alterman

1298
Susannah, 20s-40s
In her apartment, Present
Susannah, an obsessive fan, plans on finally
seeing the man of her dreams tonight.
Seriocomic.
TWOMIN, 3 minutes
Susannah by Glenn Alterman

1299
Sylvia, 40s-60s
An expensive Park Avenue apartment,
Present
After being told by her "kept" young lover
that he wants to see his dying mother, Sylvia, a
wealthy Park Avenue lady, gives him an ulti-
matum. Seriocomic.
TWOMIN, 2.5 minutes
Sylvia by Glenn Alterman

300
Louise, 50s-60s   Her home, Present
After their children have left home, Louise be-
gins to notice that her husband is avoiding her.
Upset about this, she finally confronts him.
Dramatic.
TWOMIN, 1.5 minutes
Louise by Glenn Alterman

1301
Meredith, 40s-50s   At her home, Present
Meredith, talking to her daughter, recalls the
day she had to go to Puerto Rico to have an il-
legal abortion. Dramatic.
TWOMIN, 2 minutes
Meredith by Glenn Alterman

1302
Josie, any age   Anywhere, Present
Josie remembers the terrifying day she was al-
most kidnapped when her father took her to
Radio City Music Hall. Dramatic.
TWOMIN, 3.5 minutes
Josie by Glenn Alterman

1303
Jean, any age   Anywhere, Present
After getting an appointment for an important
audition, Jean finds out to her horror that she
only has two minutes to show her stuff.
Comic.
TWOMIN, 2 minutes
Jean by Glenn Alterman

1304
Ivy, 20s-40s   Anywhere, Present
Ivy has a serious problem with intimacy. The
mornings after always terrify her. Here, she de-
scribes a recent Sunday morning. Dramatic.
TWOMIN, 2 minutes
Ivy by Glenn Alterman

1305
Janet, any age
The unemployment office, Present
Here Janet recalls an uprising in the unem-
ployment office. Seriocomic.
TWOMIN, 4.5 minutes
Janet by Glenn Alterman

1306
Dotty, 50s-60s   Anywhere, Present
Here Dotty recalls a day a long time ago when
she and her sister picked up some sailors in a
movie theater and had a romantic afternoon.
Seriocomic.
TWOMIN, 2.5 minutes
Dotty by Glenn Alterman

1307
Michelle, 20s-30s   Anywhere, Present
Michelle imagines an exciting night-life for
herself as she escapes to Manhattan.
Seriocomic.
TWOMIN, 2.5 minutes
Michelle by Glenn Alterman

1308
Pamela, 20s-40s   A living room, Present
Pamela has just found out that her husband has been secretly sneaking off writing a play for the last two years. To boot, he now informs her that he's thinking of starting another one, a musical. Hearing this, she becomes enraged. Comic.
TWOMIN, 1.5 minutes
Pamela by Glenn Alterman

1309
Christina, 20s-40s   Anywhere, Present
Christina, a sensualist, describes her nightly ritual. Seriocomic.
TWOMIN, 3.5 minutes
Christina by Glenn Alterman

1310
Jessie, 30s-40s   The kitchen, Present
After Jessie's son has a near-fatal accident, a social worker is sent to her house to find out if it was indeed an accident and not child abuse. If it's child abuse, he warns, Jessie may lose both of her children. Here she pleads with the social worker on her own behalf as she tells him what happened. Dramatic.
TWOMIN, 2 minutes
Jessie by Glenn Alterman

1311
Yvette, any age   Anywhere, Present
Here Yvette tells of a harrowing experience she had during her first night as an usher in a Broadway theater. Comic.
TWOMIN, 3.5 minutes
Yvette by Glenn Alterman

1312
Charlene, any age   Anyplace, Present
After finding out her best friend has stolen her new boyfriend, Charlene confronts her. Comic.
TWOMIN, 1.5 minutes
Charlene by Glenn Alterman

1313
Dulcy, 40s-60s   Her kitchen, Present
Still upset by the murder that just occurred in her building, Dulcy serves her husband dinner. Comic.
TWOMIN, 3 minutes
Dulcy by Glenn Alterman

1314
Eleanor, 30s-40s   Her home, Present
Eleanor has just found out that her husband has been sexually abusing their daughter. Here she confronts him after he has just apologized.

Dramatic.
TWOMIN, 1.5 minutes
Eleanor by Glenn Alterman

1315
Evelyn, 30s-60s   Her office, Present
After being constantly bothered and harassed by her new young boss, Evelyn tells him off. Comic.
TWOMIN, 2.5 minutes
Evelyn Reid by Glenn Alterman

1316
Celeste, 30s-60s   A room, Present
Here Celeste, a medium, talks about how she channels spirits. Comic.
TWOMIN, 2 minutes
Celeste by Glenn Alterman

1317
Vernice, 50s-60s
The Rosenstein kitchen in the Brighton Beach section of Brooklyn, Present
It is a year since Vernice's son, Mickey, died of AIDS. The family is gathering to go to the cemetery. Vernice, still distraught, lashes out at her other son, Barry, when he asks her to get dressed so they can leave. Seriocomic.
TWOMIN, 1 minute
Vernice Rosenstein by Glenn Alterman

1318
Vernice, 50s-60s
The Rosenstein kitchen in the Brighton Beach section of Brooklyn, Present
It is a year since Vernice's son died of AIDS. The family has gathered to go to the cemetery. After an emotional blow up, Vernice talks to her other son, Barry, about her feelings of loss and grief. Seriocomic.
TWOMIN, 1.5 minute
Vernice Rosenstein by Glenn Alterman

1319
Lily, 20s-40s   A bar, Present
Here Lily, clinging to her groceries, nervously sits on a bar stool talking to a stranger she's just met. Seriocomic.
TWOMIN, 3 minutes
Lily Vernice, 50s-60s by Glenn Alterman

1320
Marvin, 30s-50s
An airline waiting area at the Miami Beach Airport, Present
Marvin is a high-strung, somewhat volatile man who has just missed his plane. Here he pours out his rage to an innocent fellow traveler who just happens to be seated in the wait-

ing area. Comic.
UPTOWN, 3 minutes
Marvin by Glenn Alterman

1321
Mr. Piano Player, 30s-50s
The Limbo Lounge, a piano bar, Present
The Limbo Lounge is a dream-filled, fantasy, piano bar. Here, Mr. Piano Player, your host, welcomes you to this magical place. Seriocomic.
UPTOWN, 9 minutes
Mr. Piano Player by Glenn Alterman

1322
T.S., 50s-70s
A very chic cocktail party in a gallery in Soho, Present
T.S., a very sophisticated older gentleman, has always been a prominent fixture in the art world. He's always invited to the most "in" parties, knows the most up and coming artists, and is always seen with the "right" people. Here, while walking with a new "protégé," showing him around, he admits his one secret yearning. Seriocomic.
UPTOWN, 8 minutes
T.S. by Glenn Alterman

1323
Barry, 30s-40s
Sitting at the kitchen table, Present
Mickey, Barry's brother, has committed suicide because he knew he was dying of AIDS. Here, Barry tells his parents about the last time he saw his brother. Dramatic.
UPTOWN, 2.5 minutes
Barry by Glenn Alterman

1324
Gregory, any age   A small town, Present
While going out for the morning paper, Gregory sees something horrible written across the front of his house. The shock, and how he deals with it, is what the monologue is about. Dramatic.
UPTOWN, 3 minutes
Gregory by Glenn Alterman

1325
Raheem A/K/A/ Leroy, 20s-40s
A black rally headquarters, Present
Here, Raheem, a black militant, attempts to convince another black man to join a looting group. Dramatic.
UPTOWN, 3 minutes
Raheem A/K/A Leroy by Glenn Alterman

1326
Merv, 30s-50s   Anywhere, Present
Merv decided to sneak away; escape from his responsibilities by going to a movie. Here he tells about the life and death experience he had while watching the movie, Termin-ator Two. Seriocomic.
UPTOWN, 5 minutes
Merv by Glenn Alterman

1327
Douglas, 30s-50s   Anywhere, Present
Douglas, a bald man, talks about his obsession with being bald, and how he finally resolved it. Seriocomic.
UPTOWN, 6.5 minutes
Douglas by Glenn Alterman

1328
Arnold, early 20s
Arnold's friend Harry's apartment, Present
Arnold, a young, aspiring, stand-up comic, has finally booked his first gig. Here he excitedly tells his teacher and mentor what has happened. Comic.
UPTOWN, 3 minutes
Arnold by Glenn Alterman

1329
Murray, 60s-70s   The bedroom, Present
Edna, Murray's wife, has revealed to Murray a secret she's held on to for over forty years. She's told him that her sister Martha accused Murray of trying to force himself on her one day when they were alone in a blueberry field. Murray becomes furious when he hears what Martha accused him of. Here, he tells Edna his side of the story. Dramatic.
UPTOWN, 3.5 minutes
Murray by Glenn Alterman

1330
Reggie, any age   Anywhere, Present
Reggie makes out very well in bars. Both he and "the jazz man" have a seductive technique that never fails. Seriocomic.
UPTOWN, 4 minutes
Reggie by Glenn Alterman

1331
Jim, 30s-40s   Anywhere, Present
Here, Jim, a street person, talks about how his life changed after the night he fought with his two angel friends. Seriocomic.
UPTOWN, 7 minutes
Jim by Glenn Alterman

1332
Morris, 60s-80s   Anywhere, Present

While sitting with his grandson, Morris remembers the good old days when he was a young man in Miami. Seriocomic.
UPTOWN, 2.5 minutes
Morris by Glenn Alterman

1333
Johnny Star, 20s-30s
Backstage at a huge sports arena, Present
Here, Johnny Star, a mega rock and roll star, tells what it's like everytime he goes out on the stage to perform. Seriocomic.
UPTOWN, 2.5 minutes
Johnny Star by Glenn Alterman

1334
Jeb, 30s-50s   A street corner, Present
After a torrential summer rain, Jeb, a homeless man, meets up with his friend Zack. The two get drunk together and Zack tells Jeb about a miracle that occurred during the storm. Here Jeb shares Zack's story. Seriocomic.
UPTOWN, 6 minutes
Jeb by Glenn Alterman

1335
Juan, 20s
A trench in Vietnam during the war
It's Christmas in Vietnam. Juan and a buddy are in the trenches, stoned. Here Juan tells his friend about a Christmas at home. Seriocomic.
UPTOWN, 2 minutes
Juan by Glenn Alterman

1336
Marty Cool, 20s-40s
A singles bar, Present
Marty Cool thinks of himself as Mr. "It," the make out man. He hasn't quite realized yet what a jerk he is, and how his come on is really a big turn-off. Seriocomic.
UPTOWN, 5 minutes
Marty Cool by Glenn Alterman

1337
Jeremy, 20s-40s
A small room at the State of Grace Motel, Present
Planning on going on a shooting spree, Jeremy, an unhappy, somewhat mentally disturbed man, starts drinking and planning his strategy. Seriocomic.
UPTOWN, 2.5 minutes
Jeremy by Glenn Alterman

1338
Dave, 50s-60s
At the kitchen table, Present
For a year, since their son died of AIDS,

Vernice has hardly said a word to Dave. He's tried everything to break down her wall but was only left frustrated. Here he finally releases his pent-up feelings by telling his wife how he felt their son really died. Dramatic.
UPTOWN, 2 minutes
Dave by Glenn Alterman

1339
Mark, 30s-50s   Anywhere, Present
Mark has a very unusual encounter with a beautiful woman in the elevator of his office building. Here he recalls that encounter in erotic detail. Comic.
UPTOWN, 7 minutes
Mark by Glenn Alterman

1340
Paulie, any age   Anywhere, Present
Paulie, a two-bit loser, tries to convince an old friend to invest in a show. Comic.
UPTOWN, 6 minutes
Paulie by Glenn Alterman

1341
Sam, 30s-50s   A mid-town bar, Present
Sam thought he'd seen it all. It's very difficult to shake up a mid-town bartender. But one night a mysterious stranger came into his bar and everything changed. Seriocomic.
UPTOWN, 4 minute
Sam by Glenn Alterman

1342
Bill, 30s-50s   Anywhere, Present
Bill, a story line writer for a soap opera tells of how he finally learned to deal with the pressure of a deadline. Seriocomic.
UPTOWN, 7 minute
Bill by Glenn Alterman

1343
Michael, 20s-30s
The Rosenstein kitchen in Brooklyn, Present
Here Michael tells his brother how he learned and accepted that he had AIDS. Dramatic.
UPTOWN, 1 minute
Michael by Glenn Alterman

1344
Claire, 30s-40s   Anywhere, Present
Last night Claire met a handsome stranger at the fruit and vegetable stand. Here she excitedly recalls their meeting. Comic.
UPTOWN, 6 minutes
Claire by Glenn Alterman

1345
Patrice, any age   Anywhere, Present

Patrice was an abused child. Here she describes her special fantasy place. The place she went when in danger. Dramatic.
UPTOWN, 7.5 minutes
Patrice by Glenn Alterman

1346
Margerie, 40s-60s
An executive office, Present
Margerie is a successful, always direct, in control, executive. She has just been given an ultimatum by the board of directors of her company. Here, she shares her feelings with a secretary. Seriocomic.
UPTOWN, 3 minutes
Margerie by Glenn Alterman

1347
Tonya, 30s-40s   Anywhere, Present
Each night, when everyone in her family is asleep, Tonya takes her nightly bubble bath. It is there that she allows her "wings" to come out. Here she talks about the journeys she takes, her night flights. Seriocomic.
UPTOWN, 4 minutes
Tonya by Glenn Alterman

1348
Laura, any age   Sitting at a table, Present
Laura has found something that's changed her life. Here she talks to another woman about it. As she talks she constantly smiles and seems genuinely happy. Seriocomic.
UPTOWN, 4.5 minutes
Laura by Glenn Alterman

1349
Rosa, 30s-60s   Rosa's kitchen, Present
Here Rosa, a hearty Italian housewife, tells an amazing story about a wooden Madonna that cried blood tears, and the effect it had on her family. Seriocomic.
UPTOWN, 7 minutes
Rosa by Glenn Alterman

1350
Shelly, 20s-50s
A hospital cafeteria, about two a.m., Present
Shelly, a nurse, rambles as she tries to express her feelings about the loss of a young patient. Dramatic.
UPTOWN, 2.5 minutes
Shelly by Glenn Alterman

1351
Edna, 60s
The kitchen, sitting at the kitchen table, Present
Edna's sister Martha is in the hospital dying of a terminal illness. Every day Edna goes to visit her hoping for a miracle. Here Edna tells her husband Murray about her visits. Dramatic.
UPTOWN, 1.5 minutes
Edna by Glenn Alterman

1352
Dora, 40s-60s
The security office of an expensive department store, Present
Dora, a very wealthy lady, loves to go "shopping." Having just been arrested for shoplifting, she explains her side of the story to the store detective. Comic.
UPTOWN, 4 minutes
Dora by Glenn Alterman

1353
Henny, 20s-40s   A bar, Present
Henny's just had a run-in with a mugger in her apartment. Here she describes what happened to a man she's just met. Seriocomic.
UPTOWN, 7 minutes
Henny by Glenn Alterman

1354
Terry, 30s-40s   A living room, Present
Terry, a strong, attractive, female cop tells her "friend" about an incident of sexual harassment she recently experienced on the job. Seriocomic.
UPTOWN, 5 minutes
Terry by Glenn Alterman

1355
Vernice, 50s   At the kitchen table, Present
It's been a year since Vernice's son died. His death has left her depressed, manic, and sometimes paranoid. Here she tells her other son, Barry, that her husband is secretly leaving the water overflow in the bathtub every night, flooding the house. Seriocomic.
UPTOWN, 1.5 minutes
Vernice by Glenn Alterman

1356
Sheila, any age   Anywhere, Present
On her way home, Sheila's car went out of control on a patch of ice. Here she recalls that terrifying experience. Seriocomic.
UPTOWN, 3.5 minutes
Sheila by Glenn Alterman

1357
Dixie, 20s-40s
A sleazy strip joint, Present
Just as they're ready to go on, Dixie, a perky, happy-go-lucky stripper, tells the new girl to

dos and don'ts of the job. Comic.
UPTOWN, 2 minutes
Dixie by Glenn Alterman

1358
Maxine, 30s-40s
The attic of Maxine and Hank's house, Present
Rough times have fallen on Maxine and her husband Hank. Hank has been out of work for a long time and is feeling the pressure. He has started closing himself off from the rest of the family. Here Maxine tries to convince Hank to come down from the attic and join the rest of the family for dinner. Dramatic.
UPTOWN, 2 minutes
Maxine by Glenn Alterman

1359
Jane, 30s-40s   **Anywhere, Present**
Jane has met and dated her share of men over the years, but never met the right one. After giving up for a while, she's decided to start dating again. Here she talks about a man she met the night before, and her renewed hope. Seriocomic.
UPTOWN, 1.5 minutes
Jane by Glenn Alterman

1360
Elizabeth, 20s-40s
An apartment on the West Side in Manhattan, Present
Elizabeth's sister was recently murdered. Elizabeth has come to New York to sort out her sister's belongings and close out the apartment. While packing some of her sister's things a man sneaks in and attempts to rape her. Here she tells what happened. Dramatic.
UPTOWN, 2.5 minutes
Elizabeth by Glenn Alterman

1361
Georgette, 30s-60s
On the bed in their bedroom, Present
Here Georgette tells her husband about a dream she just had where she was the royal chair to a king. Seriocomic.
UPTOWN, 4 minutes
Georgette by Glenn Alterman

1362
Edna, 60s   **The bedroom, Present**
For over forty years Edna has kept an important secret from her husband Murray. Her sister Martha once told her that Murray tried to seduce her when they all went up to the country one weekend. Here Edna blurts out the secret she's held on to all those years. Dramatic.

UPTOWN, 1.5 minutes
Edna (II) by Glenn Alterman

1363
Yvonne, 30s-40s
A small southern town, Present
Yvonne, a divorcée with a small son, has started dating again. She has finally met the man of her dreams, and they have a date Saturday night. Here she tells her best friend about her hopes for that date. Comic.
UPTOWN, 1.5 minutes
Yvonne by Glenn Alterman

1364
Sadie, 30s-50s
In her livingroom, Present
Here Sadie, a full-of-life divorcée, tells about an exciting encounter she had with a rabbi. Comic.
UPTOWN, 4.5 minutes
Sadie by Glenn Alterman

1365
Lou Anne, 30s-40s   **Her bedroom, Present**
As she's finishing getting dressed, Lou Anne tells about the dinner she was at the night before. At that dinner, the daughter of the man she wants to marry did everything she could to upset her. Comic.
UPTOWN, 5 minutes
Lou Anne by Glenn Alterman

1366
Sydelle, 40s-60s   **A waiting room, Present**
Seeing her son stoned on drugs was a harrowing experience for Sydelle. Here she recalls that night to a woman she's just met. Dramatic.
UPTOWN, 5 minutes
Sydelle by Glenn Alterman

1367
Celia, 20s-30s   **Anywhere, Present**
Celia's been a runaway, a drifter, since she was fifteen. Here, she tells about the day she tried to get her belongings from an apartment of two men she was staying with. One of the men refused to let her take her stuff. Here is how she handled it. Dramatic.
UPTOWN, 6 minutes
Celia by Glenn Alterman

1368
Lord Byron, 40s
A fantasy limbo called "Camino Real"
The preceding dissertation moves Byron to ruminate on the loss of his heart's innocence.
CLASS, 3.5 minutes
Camino Real by Tennessee Williams

1369
Cleopatra, Queen of Egypt, 30-40
Alexandria
Mark Antony has moved out of their palace quarters and taken up solitary residence in the Temple of Isis. His old friend and fellow Roman, Ventidius, has convinced him to leave Cleopatra and fight Octavius. Here, the Queen mourns her lover's departure. Dramatic.
NEO, 3 minutes
All for Love or The World Well Lost by John Dryden

1370
Hermione, 20s
Epirus, after the fall of Troy
Hermione has betrayed Pyrrhus, the man she loves, who has forsaken her to marry the captive Andromache. The vengeful Hermione has persuaded Orestes, the Greek Ambassador, to murder Pyrrhus. Here, she anticipates the news of his death. Dramatic.
NEO, 4 minutes
Andromache by Jean Racine

1371
Mrs. Sullen, 20-30   **Lichfield**
Squire Sullen is a terrible husband whose coarse and brutish ways have driven his wife to despair. Here, she confesses to his sister her desire to end her marriage. Dramatic.
NEO, 3 minutes
The Beaux Stratagem by George Farquhar

1372
Thalia, the muse, any age   **A theater**
Lack of funds forced Holberg to close the Lille Grønnegade Theatre in 1727. This play was written to commemorate that sad event. This speech, performed by Thalia, the muse of the theatre, is a bittersweet and eternally pertinent statement. Seriocomic.
NEO, 3 minutes
The Burial of Danish Comedy by Ludvig Holberg

1373
Lucia, 18-20   **Utica**
Lucia's father was the best friend of Cato, the fallen hero of Rome. She was in love with Cato's son, Marcus who was killed in battle. Here, the grieving Lucia offers insight into the frustrating role that women must play in a world swept along by male politics. Dramatic.
NEO, 4 minutes
Cato by Joseph Addison

1374
Lady Easy, 20-30   **Windsor**
When Lady Easy discovers her husband with her maid, she forces herself to remember her vow of obedience. Dramatic.
NEO, 3 minutes
The Careless Husband by Colley Cibber

1375
Lucile, an independent young lady, 18
A country house in France
It is decided that Lucile shall marry Damis, the son of her father's good friend. Unfortunately, the last thing headstrong young Lucile wants is to be married. She decides to write Damis a letter to this effect, and when her motives are questioned by her maid, she explains her desire to remain free of marital obligations. Seriocomic.
NEO, 3.5 minutes
Careless Vows by Marivaux

1376
Amelia, 20s   **Ancient Rome**
When her father is executed by Augustus, Amelia convinces her lover and trusted member of the court, Cinna, to stage a coup. Here, she sets the scene for vengeance. Dramatic.
NEO, 5.5 minutes
Cinna by Pierre Corneille

1377
Miss Sterling, 18-20   **London**
The scheming Miss Sterling is about to marry Lord Melvil, a man well above her in London's caste system. Here, she wastes no time to rubbing her poor sister's nose in her newfound wealth. Seriocomic.
NEO, 2 minutes
The Clandestine Marriage by George Coleman and David Garrick

1378
Maria, 18-20   **New York**
Maria has been engaged to a man she neither loves nor likes by her domineering father. Here, she laments her plight and indeed the plight of all members of the "weaker" sex. Dramatic.
NEO, 5.5 minutes
The Contrast by Royall Tyler

1379
Maria, 18-20   **New York**
Here, Maria contemplates her filial responsibility. Dramatic.
NEO, 2.5 minutes
The Contrast by Royall Tyler

1380
Parthenia, 18-20   **Arcadia**
Parthenia is the most beautiful nymph in Arcadia, but here she curses her appearance, for it has brought her nothing but trouble.

Dramatic.
NEO, 3 minutes
Dione by John Gay

1381
Silvia, 18-20   The Prince's palace
The Prince has brought the beautiful young Silvia to his palace against her will for the express purpose of wooing her and making her his wife. Unfortunately for the Prince, Silvia remains true to her first love, Harlequin. Here, she lashes out at the Prince's servant. Dramatic.
NEO, 2 minutes
The Double Inconstancy by Marivaux

1382
Lady Randolph, 30-40
Lord Randolph's castle in the west of Scotland, 12th century
Lady Randolph's first husband, Douglas, was slain in battle along with her brother. To make matters worse, their infant son was then lost in a flood. Years later, the unhappy woman has remarried and spends her days wandering her husband's estate mourning those she has lost. Dramatic.
NEO, 2.5 minutes
Douglas by John Home

1383
Calista, 20s   Genoa
Calista's passion for the notorious Lothario has ruined her life. Husband, father and friends have all turned from her. When the womanizing Lothario is killed in a duel, Calista keeps a lonely vigil by his body. Dramatic.
NEO, 4.5 minutes
The Fair Penitent by Nicholas Rowe

1384
Countess, 30s   A country estate in France
The Countess here breaks off her love affair with the unscrupulous Lelio, whose jealousy is too much for her to bear. Dramatic.
NEO, 2.5 minutes
The False Servant by Marivaux

1385
Charlot, 20-30   Penryn in Cornwall
Charlot, a young woman whose fiancé has been missing for seven years, has waited patiently for the missing Wilmot to return from India. When a friend suggests that she get on with her life, she replies that she intends to stand by the promise she made to Wilmot to love only him. Dramatic.
NEO, 2 minutes
Fatal Curiosity by George Lillo

1386
Agnes, 40-50   Penryn in Cornwall
Years of hard living have left their mark on Agnes. When a mysterious stranger, who is really her long-lost son in disguise, gives her a small casket to look after, curiosity compels her to open it. When she beholds the jewels inside, Agnes knows with sudden certainty that she'd rather kill than surrender them. Dramatic.
NEO, 4 minutes
Fatal Curiosity by George Lillo

1387
Lamira 20-30   England
Lamira, a wealthy widow, is in love with Gramont. Not knowing of his secret marriage to Felicia, she forces Gramont to marry her by holding her wealth as a carrot to his greedy father. When the unhappy Gramont refuses to touch her on their wedding night, she confronts him angrily. Dramatic.
NEO, 4 minutes
The Fatal Friendship by Catherine Trotter

1388
Nille, 30s   A village in Denmark
Here, shrewish Nille complains of Jeppe's slothful ways. Seriocomic.
NEO, 2.5 minutes
Jeppe of the Hill by Ludvig Holberg

1389
Lady Arabella, 20-30
When a younger friend suggests that married people must become so familiar to one another that they have to struggle to make conversation, Arabella hastens to assure her that married people find things to talk about that single folk could never imagine. Seriocomic.
NEO, 2 minutes
A Journey to London by Sir John Vanbrugh

1390
Mrs. Dickenson, any age   England
Here, a nasty Witch tells of a recent adventure. Seriocomic.
NEO, 1.5 minutes
The Lancashire Witches by Thomas Shadwell

1391
Armande, 18-20   Paris
Clitandre once courted Armande but soon tired of her esoteric prattle. He then transferred his affections to Armande's younger sister, whom he now plans to marry. Enraged, Armande insists that the union not be permitted. This eventually leads to a confrontation between Armande and Clitandre in which she

reviles her former beau for his physical lust. Seriocomic.
NEO, 2.5 minutes
The Learned Women by Molière

1392
Maria, 20-30   **Spain**
Maria has given up everything to follow Don Juan in a mad pursuit of vengeance. Here, she reveals her hatred for the infamous libertine as well as for the entire male race. Dramatic.
NEO, 3.5 minutes
The Libertine by Thomas Shadwell

1393
Millwood, 30s   **London**
Millwood is an unscrupulous woman who preys on younger men. Here she awaits the arrival of her latest victim. Seriocomic.
NEO, 4 minutes
The London Merchant or The History of George Barnwell by George Lillo

1394
Mrs. Woodcock, 40-50   **A village**
Mrs. Woodcock has discovered that her niece has planned to elope with her music teacher. Here, she sets the impulsive young woman straight. Seriocomic.
NEO, 1.5 minutes
Love in a Village by Isaac Bickerstaff

1395
Astrea, 20s   **London**
After a strange courtship consisting of many letters passed back and forth, Astrea here boldly confesses her love for Lycidas in yet another letter. Seriocomic.
NEO, 4.5 minutes
Love Letters to a Gentleman by Aphra Behn

1396
Arsinoé, 20s   **Paris**
Bitchy Arsinoé here pays a visit to her friend, Célimène, for the express purpose of "warning" her about the unsavory things being said about her recent behavior. Seriocomic.
NEO, 4 minutes
The Misanthrope by Molière

1397
Célimène, 20s   **Paris**
Here, Célimène repays Arsinoé's advice with a few choice words of her own. Seriocomic.
NEO, 5 minutes
The Misanthrope by Molière

1398
Zerbinette, 18-20   **Naples**

Zerbinette has fallen in love with the son of an infamous miser. Following many misadventures, she unwittingly tells the tale to Géronte, the miser in question. Seriocomic.
NEO, 6 minutes
The Mischievous Machinations of Scapin by Molière

1399
Aricie, a captive princess, 18-20
Trezene, a city in the Peloponnesus
Here, Aricie confesses her love for Hippolyte, the son of Theseus, her captor. Dramatic.
NEO, 5 minutes
Phèdre by Jean Racine

1400
Phèdre, 30s
Trezene, a city in the Peloponnesus
Believing Theseus to be dead, Phèdre finally feels free to confess her love for his son, Hippolyte. When she does so, the young man recoils in horror, for his heart belongs to Aricie. Enraged, Phèdre dares him to strike her down. Dramatic.
NEO, 4.5 minutes
Phèdre by Jean Racine

1401
Phèdre, 30s
Trezene, a city in the Peloponnesus
When Phèdre discovers that her husband is still alive, she realizes that her life is over and laments her unhappy fate. Dramatic.
NEO, 4.5 minutes
Phèdre by Jean Racine

1402
Cora, 20s   **Peru**
Cora's husband, Alonzo, has deserted Pizarro's ranks because he became disgusted by the brutality of the Spanish against the Incas. Following a bloody battle, Cora is told that Alonzo has been taken prisoner by Pizarro. Here, she vows to march into Pizarro's camp and find her husband. Dramatic.
NEO, 3 minutes
Pizarro by Richard Brinsley Sheridan

1403
Polly, 16-18   **London**
Here, Polly takes a great delight in reading a cheap romance novel out loud. Seriocomic.
NEO, 3 minutes
Polly Honeycombe by George Coleman

1404
Queen, 40s   **Ctesiphon**
When the Queen discovers that her husband has fallen in love with the beautiful young

Evanthe, she flies into a dark rage. The first
part of her revenge is to turn one of their sons
against the other as she here confesses to her
maid. Dramatic.
NEO, 3 minutes
The Prince of Parthia by Thomas Godfrey

1405
Evanthe, 18-20   **Ctesiphon**
Evanthe was rescued from the evil Vonomes by
his brother, the brave Arsaces. Here, she speaks
of her love for the noble prince. Dramatic.
NEO, 3.5 minutes
The Prince of Parthia by Thomas Godfrey

1406
Lady Brute, 20-30   **England**
Sir John has been treating her very poorly as of
late and here the provoked woman takes a mo-
ment to blow off a little steam. Seriocomic.
NEO, 3 minutes
The Provoked Wife by Sir John Vanbrugh

1407
Ambition, any age   Mytho-poetic England
Here, Ambition appears to a young country
girl and offers to teach her the ways of the
world. Seriocomic.
NEO, 3.5 minutes
Psyche Debauched by Thomas Duffett

1408
Redstreak, 30s   Mytho-poetic England
Here, this good-hearted provincial woman
fantasizes about what it would be like to be
Queen. Seriocomic.
NEO, 2.5 minutes
Psyche Debauched by Thomas Duffett

1409
Amanda, 20-30   **England**
Amanda has just discovered her wayward hus-
band in the arms of another woman. Here, she
fumes as she contemplates her response.
Dramatic.
NEO, 3 minutes
*The Relapse or Virtue in Danger by Sir John
Vanbrugh*

1410
Statira, 20-30   **Babylon**
Those who conspire against Alexander have
told Statira that her husband has broken his
vow to her by sleeping with Roxana, his sec-
ond wife. Here, the Queen reacts with jealous
grief. Dramatic.
NEO, 5 minutes
*The Rival Queens or The Death of Alexander the
Great by Nathaniel Lee*

1411
Statira, 20-30   **Babylon**
Following an emotional reconciliation with
Alexander the Great, Statira, his wife, awaits
him in her bedchamber. While she dozes, the
ghosts of her parents appear in a dream to
warn her of her impending death. When she
wakens, she contemplates his unhappy visita-
tion. Dramatic.
NEO, 2.5 minutes
*The Rival Queens or The Death of Alexander the
Great by Nathaniel Lee*

1412
Mrs. Malaprop, 50s   **Bath**
Mrs. Malaprop's niece, Lydia, has refused to
marry the well-appointed son of Sir Anthony
Adverse. Sir Anthony blames the young lady's
willfulness on her education, which he feels no
young lady should have. Here, Mrs. Malaprop
defends her decision to educate young women.
Seriocomic.
NEO, 2 minutes
The Rivals by Richard Brinsley Sheridan

1413
Bassima, 18-20   **The Middle East**
Bassima has been married to the Prince of
Colchis for political reasons. The unfortunate
young woman soon finds herself pursued by
Osman, the Prince's Grand Visier. Here, she
does her best to dissuade the relentless Osman.
Dramatic.
NEO, 4 minutes
The Royal Mischief by Mary Delarivier Manley

1414
Jane Shore, 30s   **London, June 1483**
Following the death of Edward IV, his brother,
the Duke of Glouster, hastens to seize power.
Jane Shore, a married woman of renowned
beauty, was once the favorite of Edward, but
now lives in poverty, her properties seized by
Glouster. When her friend, Alicia, suggests
that Jane learn to seek pity from the men who
control her life, Jane makes the following re-
play. Dramatic.
NEO, 2 minutes
The Tragedy of Jane Shore by Nicholas Rowe

1415
Jane Shore, 30s   **London, June 1483**
Alicia's treachery has caused Jane to be turned
out of her home. Here, poor Jane wanders the
streets, desperate and starving, and suddenly
finds herself at Alicia's door. Dramatic.
NEO, 2.5 minutes
The Tragedy of Jane Shore by Nicholas Rowe

1416
Zara, 18-20   **Jerusalem**
Zara was brought to Jerusalem as a child and
though a Christian, raised Saracen. She has
grown up to be the favorite of the Sultan, who
plans to marry her as soon as possible. When
Selima, another slave, asks Zara how it is pos-
sible for her to turn her back on her Christian
heritage, she makes the following reply.
Dramatic.
NEO, 2.5 minutes
The Tragedy of Zara by Aaron Hill, Esq.

1417
Belvidera, 18-20   **Venice**
Belvidera's husband, Jaffier, has just joined in a
conspiracy against the Venetian Senate, of
which her father is a member. When she forces
Jaffier to turn in his fellow conspirators, the
guilt he feels at his betrayal eventually drives
him to an attempt on Belvidera's life. Here, she
confronts her father and begs him to release
Jaffier's friends from prison. Dramatic.
NEO, 4 minutes
*Venice Preserved or A Plot Discovered by Thomas
Otway*

1418
Muslin, 20-30   **London**
When her mistress complains about not being
able to keep her husband interested in their
marriage, the knowing young maid offers both
chastisement and advice. Seriocomic.
NEO, 6 minutes
The Way to Keep Him by Arthur Murphy

1419
Alison, 20-30
**An inn lying on the road between London
and Canterbury**
When a fellow traveler claims to have been vis-
ited by an apparition, this earthy woman re-
veals her knowledge of the spirit world.
Seriocomic.
NEO, 3 minutes
The Wife of Bath by John Gay

1420
Mark Antony, 40s   **Alexandria**
On the last day of his life, Mark Antony enjoys
a dark and melancholy fantasy of his death.
Dramatic.
NEO, 3 minutes
All for Love or The World Well Lost by John Dryden

1421
Ventidius, 40-50   **Alexandria**
When Ventidius discovers his old friend in
Alexandria, he knows instinctively that Mark
Antony's life has come to an end. Dramatic.

NEO, 2 minutes
All for Love or The World Well Lost by John Dryden

1422
Orestes, 30-40
Epirus, after the fall of Troy
Orestes has traveled to Epirus to pursue his
love for Hermione, the daughter of Helen, and
to take Hector's son prisoner. Here, he speaks
of his unrequited love and his mission.
Dramatic.
NEO, 8 minutes
Andromache by Jean Racine

1423
Pyrrhus, 20-30   **Epirus, after the fall of Troy**
Pyrrhus has fallen in love with Andromache,
the captive widow of Hector. Here, he offers to
save her son from the Greeks if she will con-
sent to marry him. Dramatic.
NEO, 3 minutes
Andromache by Jean Racine

1424
Dick, 18-20   **An English Village**
Dick is a rascally youth who harbors a desire
to make a life for himself on the stage. When
he discovers it is his father's wish that he become an apprentice to an apothecary, he rejects the notion in the following melodramatic
explosion. Seriocomic.
NEO, 3 minutes
The Apprentice by Arthur Murphy, Esq.

1425
Macheath, 30s   **London**
Here, the infamous Macheath, a notorious
highwayman, greets the strumpets he has sum-
moned to his lair for an evening's entertain-
ment. Seriocomic.
NEO, 2.5 minutes
The Beggar's Opera by John Gay

1426
Cato, 40s   **Utica**
Conservative Cato backed Pompey in his
struggle against Caesar and then accompanied
the losing general into exile. When Cato is in-
formed of the defeat of the Roman nobility of
Caesar's legions in North Africa, he contem-
plates taking his own life. Dramatic.
NEO, 4 minutes
Cato by Joseph Addison

1427
Brass   **London**
Brass and Dick are a couple of nefarious ne'er-
do-wells who have scrambled from one

scheme to the next with Dick always coming out on top of things. Here, Brass finally objects to always playing second fiddle Seriocomic.
NEO, 1.5 minutes
The Confederacy by Sir John Vanbrugh

1428
Pinchwife, 20-30   **London**
When the philandering Pinchwife discovers that his wife has written a letter to a gentleman admirer, he flies into a rage and threatens to kill her. Seriocomic.
NEO, 2.5 minutes
The Country Wife by William Wycherley

1429
Mopus, 30-50   **London**
Here, a glorified fortune-teller muses over a book on astrology and wonders how to best bilk people out of their money. Seriocomic.
NEO, 3.5 minutes
The Cheats by John Wilson

1430
Lycidas, 20s   **Arcadia**
Lycidas has forsaken everything in order to pursue Parthenia, a lovely nymph who eludes his every advance. Here, the love struck young man has finally discovered Parthenia asleep in the woods, and marvels at her sleeping beauty. Dramatic.
NEO, 4 minutes
Dione by John Gay

1431
Glenalvon, 30s
Lord Randolph's castle in the west of Scotland, 12th century
A man driven by forbidden desire, Glenalvon here reveals his passion for Lady Randolph, the wife of his uncle and benefactor. Lady Randolph has recently taken in a young stranger, and Glenalvon believes that she loves the unknown young man. Here, Glenalvon vows to find the stranger and kill him. Dramatic.
NEO, 3.5 minutes
Douglas by John Home

1432
Douglas, 18-20
Lord Randolph's castle in the west of Scotland, 12th century
Douglas believed he was the son of a simple shepherd until Lady Randolph informs him that he is, in fact, her long-lost son. Following a poignant meeting with the good-hearted man who raised him, Douglas rejoices at being reunited with his true mother. Dramatic.
NEO, 2 minutes
Douglas by John Home

1433
Horatio, 20s   **Genoa**
Horatio is married to Lavinia, the sister of his best friend, Altamont. Here, he discovers a letter written by Altamont's fiancée, Calista to the notorious Lothario. It is obvious that although she has accepted Altamont, Calista still lusts after womanizing Lothario. When he has finished reading this most illicit love letter, poor Horatio wonders what he should do. Dramatic.
NEO, 5 minutes
The Fair Penitent by Nicholas Rowe

1434
Cecil, 40-50   **London**
After promising to help his nephew court a certain young lady, Cecil takes a moment to ponder the dramatic changes that love tends to make in our lives. Seriocomic.
NEO, 2 minutes
False Delicacy by Hugh Kelly

1435
Trivelin, 30-40   **A country estate in France**
After making his way in the world for 15 years, this crafty opportunist has returned home. Here, he delivers a philosophical description of his life to an old friend. Seriocomic.
NEO, 3 minutes
The False Servant by Marivaux

1436
Old Wilmot, 50-60   **Penryn in Cornwall**
Wilmot has lost both his fortune and his son, who has been missing at sea for seven years. Here, the beleaguered man muses on the nature of man's impermance. Dramatic.
NEO, 2 minutes
Fatal Curiosity by George Lillo

1437
Gramont, 20s   **England**
Gramont's secret marriage to Felicia has brought both of them nothing but misery. Gramont's father has also fallen in love with Felicia, and—not knowing that she is in reality his daughter-in-law—commanded that Gramont marry Lamira, a wealthy widow. Gramont and Felicia have a baby son who has just been kidnapped by pirates. Here, Gramont reacts to the news of his son's misfortune. Dramatic.
NEO, 3.5 minutes
The Fatal Friendship by Catherine Trotter

1438
Mortimer, 30-40   **An English manor**
Mortimer has murdered the uncle of Helen, the only woman he has ever loved. Here, the unhappy man confesses his deed to a faithful

servant. Dramatic.
NEO, 6 minutes
The Iron Chest by George Coleman

1439
Jeronimus, 40-50   A village in Denmark
His daughter's fiancé has traveled to Paris, and
Jeronimus objects to the lad's new pretentious
Parisian mannerisms as they manifest in the
letters that he sends home. Seriocomic.
NEO, 4 minutes
Jean de France or Hans Frandsen by Ludvig Holberg

1440
Jeppe, 30-40   A village in Denmark
Jeppe has spent the morning shirking his re-
sponsibilities and here debates whether or not
he should go home, or go back to the inn for
another drink. Seriocomic.
NEO, 3 minutes
Jeppe of the Hill by Ludvig Holberg

1441
The Devil   England
Here, the Devil tells his witches what they may
expect in return for their loyalty. Dramatic.
NEO, 2.5 minutes
The Lancashire Witches by Thomas Shadwell

1442
Chrysale, 40-50   Paris
Chauvinism was alive and well in 17th century
France as can be seen in the following speech
delivered by the much-harried Chrysale to his
wife in which he condemns the emphasis she
places on the education of their daughters.
Seriocomic.
NEO, 6 minutes
The Learned Women by Molière

1443
Barnwell, 18   London
Barnwell's love for the unscrupulous Millwood
has led him to embezzle money from his em-
ployer and flee the city. Now the treacherous
Millwood demands that Barnwell murder his
uncle. Here, the unhappy young man considers
his options. Dramatic.
NEO, 3.5 minutes
*The London Merchant or The History of George
Barnwell by George Lillo*

1444
Alceste, 30s   Paris
When a trivial disagreement sparks an argu-
ment between Alceste and his friend, Philinte,
the misanthrope reveals his utter contempt for
people he describes as being "men of style."
Seriocomic.
NEO, 2.5 minutes
The Misanthrope by Molière

1445
Acaste, 20s   Paris
Here, the boastful Marquis takes a moment to
sing his own praises. Seriocomic.
NEO, 2.5 minutes
The Misanthrope by Molière

1446
Maître Jacques, any age.   Paris
When Harpagon, the miser, asks Maître
Jacques to tell him what the people in town are
saying about him, he is less than pleased with
the servant's reply. Seriocomic.
NEO, 2.5 minutes
The Miser by Molière

1447
Harpagon, 40-50   Paris
Harpagon lives a Scrooge-like existence and
guards his possessions with paranoid zeal.
When he is robbed of his most precious trea-
sure chest, he falls into a great panic.
Seriocomic.
NEO, 3 minutes
The Miser by Molière

1448
Sancho, 20-30   Spain
When he and his master are both slighted by
the women they love, Sancho delivers the fol-
lowing misogynistic observation of the fairer
sex. Seriocomic.
NEO, 3.5 minutes
The Mistake by Sir John Vanbrugh

1449
Gonsalez, a sycophant, 40-50   Granada
Gonsalez wishes the Princess of Granada to
marry his son. Here, he greets the young lady
in the palace, and in as flowery a manner as
possible, tells her of her father's return from
doing battle with the Moors. Dramatic.
NEO, 3 minutes
The Mourning Bride by William Congreve

1450
Knight, 20s   Jerusalem
Despite himself, this young Knight Templar
has fallen in love with a Jewess. Here, he ago-
nizes over his impossible passion while await-
ing the young lady's father. Dramatic.
NEO, 5 minutes
Nathan the Wise by Gotthold Ephrain Lessing

1451
Las-Casas, 50s   Peru
When Pizarro and his bloodthirsty men call for
battle with the Incas, Las-Casas, General in the
Spanish Army occupying Peru, makes a plea

for peace. Dramatic.
NEO, 3.5 minutes
Pizarro by Richard Brinsley Sheridan

1452
Hippolyte, 20-30
Trezene, a city in the Peloponnesus
Hippolyte is a stern young man who has dis-avowed love. When he meets the captive princess, Aricie, however, his resolve begins to waver and confusion sets in. When his old friend and tutor asks him whether or not he's fallen in love with the young woman, he offers the following reply. Dramatic.
NEO, 5 minutes
Phèdre by Jean Racine

1453
Henrich, 40-50   **Hamburg**
When young Antonious arrives to ask for his mistress' hand in marriage, Henrich gives the lad advice then takes a moment to recall the time he proposed. Seriocomic.
NEO, 2.5 minutes
The Political Tinker by Ludvig Holberg

1454
Herman, 40-50   **Hamburg**
Herman wastes no opportunity to publicly criticize the city council and has consequently drawn their fire. In order to punish pompous Herman, the council conceives a plot in which they tell Herman he has been declared Burgomaster. It is their belief that a simpleton like Herman will soon crack under the strain of command. Here, an ecstatic Herman tells his wife and servant how their lives will change now that he is Burgomaster. Seriocomic.
NEO, 5 minutes
The Political Tinker by Ludvig Holberg

1455
Vardanes, 20s   **Ctesiphon**
Here, sullen Vardanes reveals his hatred of his brother, Arsaces, who is the King's favorite. Dramatic.
NEO, 2 minutes
The Prince of Parthia by Thomas Godfrey

1456
Leanchops, any age   **London**
Leanchops works for the most miserly gentle-men in London. Here, he complains bitterly of his employers' thrift. Seriocomic.
NEO, 3.5 minutes
The Projectors by John Wilson

1457
Sir John Brute, 20-30   **England**

Sir John can no longer tolerate his wife, as he here so eloquently states. Seriocomic.
NEO, 1.5 minutes
The Provoked Wife by Sir John Vanbrugh

1458
Faulkner, 20s   **Bath**
Faulkner and Julia are bound to marry by con-tract. When Faulkner questions her love for him, she leaves in tears. Here, the unhappy young man calls after her. Seriocomic.
NEO, 2 minutes
The Rivals by Richard Brinsley Sheridan

1459
Rogero, 30s   **A subterranean vault**
Rogero has been held prisoner for eleven years. Here, he wanders his underground gaol and thinks of Matilda, his one true love. Seriocomic.
NEO, 3.5 minutes
The Rovers by George Canning, John Hookman Frere, and George Ellis

1460
Sir Peter Teazle, 40s   **London**
Sir Peter married a country woman much younger than he in hopes of sharing his life with someone as yet untainted by material de-sires. When his wife quickly adapts to city ways, he finds himself at his wits' end. Seriocomic.
NEO, 2 minutes
The School for Scandal by Richard Brinsley Sheridan

1461
Mr. Rant, 50-60   **London**
Mr. Rant is distressed about his profligate son's drunken lifestyle. Here, he finally takes the youth to task. Dramatic.
NEO, 7 minutes
The Scowrers by Thomas Shadwell

1
462
Osmond, Lord High Constable of Sicily, 20-30
Palermo, Sicily
Osmond has been granted the Lord Chancellor's daughter's hand in marriage. When Sigismunda is informed that she will marry Osmond, she collapses in despair. Here, Osmond reacts to Sigismunda's rejection of his suit and subsequently becomes determined to have her for himself. Dramatic.
NEO, 3.5 minutes
Tancred and Sigismunda by James Thompson, Esq.

1463
Fossile, 30s   **London**

A mere three hours after the wedding ceremony, Fossile intercepts a suggestive note addressed to his new bride, and is here horrified that she may be in love with someone else. Seriocomic.

NEO, 2 minutes
Three Hours after Marriage by John Gay

1464
Osman, Sultan of Jerusalem, 30s   Jerusalem
Here, the powerful Sultan greets Zara and speaks of his love for her. Dramatic.
NEO, 2.5 minutes
The Tragedy of Zara by Aaron Hill, Esq.

1465
Osman, Sultan of Jerusalem, 30s   Jerusalem
Osman has unjustly suspected Zara of falling in love with a European emissary to his court. When she protests her innocence, Osman regrets having doubted her love for him. Dramatic.
NEO, 3 minutes
The Tragedy of Zara by Aaron Hill, Esq.

1466
Sir Formal Trifle, 40-50   London
When Sir Formal is challenged to display his self-proclaimed talent for oration, he asks that a young lady in the company select the topic upon which he is to speak. Her choice? A mousetrap. Seriocomic.
NEO, 2.5 minutes
The Virtuoso by Thomas Shadwell

1467
Chaucer, 30-40
An inn lying on the road between London and Canterbury
Here, the rascally Chaucer makes overtures to Myrtilla, a fellow traveler, while pretending to be a ghost. Seriocomic.
NEO, 2 minutes
The Wife of Bath by John Gay

1468
Chaucer, 30-40
An inn lying on the road between London and Canterbury
Chaucer here masquerades as a conjurer known as "Dr. Astrolabe" in order to further his suit with the unwitting Myrtilla. Seriocomic.
NEO, 2.5 minutes
The Wife of Bath by John Gay

1469
Dol Common, 30s   England
When her two partners argue over who the leader of their nasty little band should be, swords are drawn and mortal threats are made. Here, Dol admonishes the two hotheads for their petty bickering. Seriocomic.

REN, 3.5 minutes
The Alchemist by Ben Jonson

1470
Alice, 20s   England
Willful Alice has been having an affair with Mosbie, a man in her husband's employ. When Mosbie tries to end things, Alice erupts with great fire, revealing the depth of her obsession. Dramatic.
REN, 2 minutes
Arden of Feversham by Anonymous

1471
Alice, 20s   England
Following a botched attempt to murder her husband, Alice here does her best to convince him of her innocence. Dramatic.
REN, 3 minutes
Arden of Feversham by Anonymous

1472
Mother, 20-30   Persia
When the king's counsel, Praxaspes, criticizes the king's drinking, the enraged ruler demands that Praxaspes' young son stand at a distance so that he may shoot at him with a bow and arrow. He strikes the boy in the heart claiming that such a feat could not have been accomplished by a drunken man. Here, the boy's mother discovers his body. Dramatic.
REN, 3 minutes
Cambyses, King of Persia by Thomas Preston

1473
Bethsabe, 20-30   Israel
David's illicit passion for Bethsabe leads him to engineer her husband's death in battle. Here, tormented by feelings of guilt and grief, the widowed Bethsabe laments her loss. Dramatic.
REN, 3 minutes
David and Bethsabe by George Peele

1474
Lelia, 14-16   Modena
Lelia has run away from the convent to help the man she loves to woo another woman. Here, she steals through the city streets, disguised as a boy, fearing that she may be accosted by a group of young men. Seriocomic.
REN, 2 minutes
The Deceived by Gl'Intronati Di Siena

1475
Pasquella, 50-60   Modena

When Pasquella is sent on yet another errand by her love-sick mistress, she takes a moment to rue the ravages of young love. Seriocomic.
REN, 2.5 minutes
The Deceived by Gl'Intronati Di Siena

1476
Pasquella   **Modena**
Willful Lelia has been masquerading as a boy in order to win the love of Flamminio. When her long-lost brother, Fabrizio returns to Modena, he is mistaken to be Lelia by their father. Thinking that he has finally captured the wayward Lelia, their father locks up Fabrizio with the beautiful young Isabella. Here, Pasquella describes the shocking scene that greeted her when she unlocked Isabella's door to see how the two "girls" were doing. Seriocomic.
REN, 2.5 minutes
The Deceived by Gl'Intronati Di Siena

1477
Leonora, 40s   **Naples**
Here, passionate Leonora is driven mad with grief at the news that her son has murdered Contarino, a nobleman with whom she was very much in love. Dramatic.
REN, 5 minutes
The Devil's Law-Case by John Webster

1478
Lady Ager, 40-50
When her son is accused of being illegitimate, he challenges his accuser to a duel. Here, the distraught Lady Ager fears for the loss of her son. Dramatic.
REN, 3.5 minutes
A Fair Quarrel by Thomas Middleton and William Rowley

1479
Corisca, 20s   **Arcadia**
Corisca has fallen in love with Mirtillo, who is himself in love with the beautiful Amarillis. When her passion remains unrequited, the fiery nymph vows to win his heart and make all suffer. Dramatic.
REN, 14.5 minutes
The Faithful Shepherd by Giambattista Guarini

1480
Amarillis, 16-20   **Arcadia**
Here, Amarillis greets the day with great joy in her heart while reflecting upon the inner wealth that poverty may provide for the spirit. Dramatic.
REN, 5.5 minutes
The Faithful Shepherd by Giambattista Guarini

1481
Amarillis, 16-20   **Arcadia**
Although Amarillis is promised in marriage to Silvio, her heart belongs to Mirtillo. During an innocent game of blindman's bluff, Mirtillo tricks Amarillis into kissing him. When she realizes that she has been deceived, she chastises him as best she can. Dramatic.
REN, 6 minutes
The Faithful Shepherd by Giambattista Guarini

1482
Amarillis, 16-20   **Arcadia**
After she has sent Mirtillo away, Amarillis laments their impossible love for one another. Dramatic.
REN, 3.5 minutes
The Faithful Shepherd by Giambattista Guarini

1483
Corisca, 20s   **Arcadia**
When Amarillis confesses her forbidden love for Mirtillo to the scheming Corisca, the nymph does her best to incite the unhappy young woman to risk death by defying her contracted engagement to Silvio. Dramatic.
REN, 5 minutes
The Faithful Shepherd by Giambattista Guarini

1484
Telusa, 18-20   **Mythological Tudor England**
When the virgin nymph of chaste Diana feels the first stirrings of romantic passion, she agonizes over her maidenly state. Seriocomic.
REN, 2.5 minutes
Gallathea by John Lyly

1485
Diana, 20s   **Mythological Tudor England**
When Diana discovers that her virgin nymphs have all allowed themselves to fall in love, she lectures them on the importance of remaining chaste. Dramatic.
REN, 3.5 minutes
Gallathea by John Lyly

1486
Hebe, 16-20   **Mythological Tudor England**
Hebe has been selected to be sacrificed to the monster Agar to appease Neptune. As she is led to her doom, she bids farewell to life. Dramatic.
REN, 4.5 minutes
Gallathea by John Lyly

1487
Videna, Queen of Britain, 40-50
Legendary England
When her beloved son, Ferrex, is murdered by his brother, the grieving queen vows to avenge

his death. Dramatic.
REN, 8 minutes
Gorboduc by Thomas Sackville and Thomas Norton

1488
Anus, 40-50 **Mythic Britain**
Here, the aging Anus bemoans the fact that men seem to prefer younger women. Seriocomic.
REN, 2 minutes
Hey for Honesty by Thomas Randolph

1489
Celestina, 18-25 **The Strand**
Here, the crafty young widow reveals her secret for attracting men. Seriocomic.
REN, 3 minutes
The Lady of Pleasure by James Shirley

1490
Lena, 20-30 **Ferrara**
Married Lena has been having an affair with Fazio. When the lovers quarrel over money, Fazio sees an opportunity to end things. Here, Lena rages against being dumped by her lover. Seriocomic.
REN, 2 minutes
Lena by Ludovicio Ariosto

1491
Constance, 40s **France**
Constance is incensed that England should be ruled by the weak and foolish John and pushes her son, Arthur, to claim the British throne for France. Here, she demands that Arthur press his suit. Dramatic.
REN, 3.5 minutes
The Life and Death of King John by William Shakespeare

1492
Fortune, any age **Non-specific**
As Wrath, Discipline, and Idleness discuss their sovereignty over a simple foolish man, Fortune appears and reminds them that she is ruler over all. Dramatic.
REN, 3.5 minutes
The Longer Thou Livest by W. Wager

1493
Remilia, Princess of Assyria, 20s **Assyria**
Here, this foolishly self-centered young woman encourages her ladies-in-waiting to praise her beauty. Seriocomic.
REN, 6 minutes
A Looking Glass for London and England by Thomas Lodge and Robert Greene

1494
Mother, 40-50 **London**

Here, the mother of a well-used courtesan reveals her plan for the girl's future. Dramatic.
REN, 3 minutes
A Mad World, My Masters by Thomas Middleton

1495
Courtesan, 20-30 **London**
Here, the brassy courtesan tells another woman how to best make her husband jealous. Seriocomic.
REN, 2.5 minutes
A Mad World, My Masters by Thomas Middleton

1496
Evadne, a woman holding a terrible secret, 20s
The city of Rhodes
The King of Rhodes had forced young Amnitor to renounce his beloved Aspatia to marry Evadne, the king's secret mistress. On their wedding night, Evadne confesses her affair with the king to Amnitor and begs his forgiveness. Dramatic.
REN, 2 minutes
The Maid's Tragedy by Beaumont and Fletcher

1497
Evadne, 20s **The city of Rhodes**
When her hotheaded brother discovers the truth about her relationship with the king, he demands that Evadne murder her lover in the name of righteousness. Here, Evadne approaches the sleeping king and prepares to carry out her brother's wishes. Dramatic.
REN, 3 minutes
The Maid's Tragedy by Beaumont and Fletcher

1498
Hag, any age
The meeting of a witches coven
Here, a lowly witch reports on her nefarious activities to a superior. Seriocomic.
REN, 4.5 minutes
The Masque of Queens by Ben Jonson

1499
Mrs. Page, 30s **Windsor**
When Mrs. Page receives a love letter from the rascally John Falstaff, she vows to revenge herself of his impudence. Seriocomic.
REN, 2.5 minutes
The Merry Wives of Windsor by William Shakespeare

1500
Mistress Low-Water, 30-40 **London**
Mistress Low-Water would very much like to improve her material lot in life. Here, she agonizes over her lack of legitimate options. Dramatic.

REN, 3 minutes
No Wit, No Help Like a Woman's by Thomas Middleton

1501
Lady Katherine Gordon, 20-30   Ireland
Katherine is a woman of noble Scottish birth married to Perkin Warbeck, a scheming pretender to the throne of Henry VII. Warbeck's claim is backed by James IV of Scotland. Eventually, a treaty between James and Henry results in Warbeck and Katherine's exile to Ireland. Here, the homesick Scot shares a lonely moment with her maid. Dramatic.
REN, 4 minutes
Perkin Warbeck by John Ford

1502
Amie, 16-18   The Sherwood of Robin Hood
Amie has fallen in love, but is ignorant of the cause of this strange new malaise. Here, the unhappy young woman describes her "symptoms" to Maid Marian. Seriocomic.
REN, 3 minutes
The Sad Shepherd by Ben Jonson

1503
Bel-Imperia, 20s
Bel-Imperia's lover, Horatio, has been murdered by the Prince of Portugal and his accomplices. Here, the grief-stricken young woman goads Horatio's father, Hieronimo, into seeking justice for his son's death. Dramatic.
REN, 3 minutes
The Spanish Tragedy by Thomas Kyd

1504
Isabella, 40-50
When Isabella is told her beloved son, Horatio, has been murdered, she goes to the arbor where the killers hung his body and destroys it just before taking her own life. Dramatic.
REN, 4 minutes
The Spanish Tragedy by Thomas Kyd

1505
Winter, 30-60   The changing of the seasons
As Summer prepares to pass his crown to Autumn, the seasons squabble amongst themselves. Here, Winter delivers a damning speech in which she reveals her contempt for those who admire the other seasons. Seriocomic.
REN, 18 minutes
Summer's Last Will and Testament by Thomas Nashe

1506
Annabella, 20s   Italy
Annabella has allowed herself to be seduced by

her brother, Giovanni. Here, she bemoans her sin as she wanders unhappily through the castle. Dramatic.
REN, 4 minutes
'Tis Pity She's a Whore by John Ford

1507
Tamora, 40s   Rome
Tamora is a captive Queen of the Goths, now married to the Roman Emperor Titus Andronicus. When he sacrifices one of her sons to appease the spirits of the members of his family slain in the war with the Goths, Tamora vows revenge. During a royal hunt, Tamora slips away with Aaron, her beloved Moorish attendant to plot her redress. When the two are discovered by Latvinia and her husband, Bassanius, the former accuses Tamora of adultery against the emperor with Aaron. Calling for her two remaining sons, Tamora tells the following lie, that she hopes will clear her of any adulterous charge while inciting the boys to murder Bassinius. Dramatic.
REN, 2.5 minutes
Titus Andronicus by William Shakespeare

1508
Julia, 16-20   Milan
Julia has received a love letter from Proteus and, in a fit of pique, tears it up before having read it. Here, the impetuous young woman gathers all the scraps and tries to piece the letter back together again. Seriocomic.
REN, 2.5 minutes
The Two Gentlemen of Verona by William Shakespeare

1509
Daughter, 18-20   Athens
The jailer's daughter has fallen in love with Palamon, a captive Thebian knight, and here agonizes over whether or not to help him escape from her father's prison. Dramatic.
REN, 3.5 minutes
The Two Noble Kinsmen by John Fletcher and William Shakespeare

1510
Daughter, 18-20   Athens
After defying both her father and her king, the jailer's daughter here plans to rendezvous with the escaped Palamon in the woods. Dramatic.
REN, 4 minutes
The Two Noble Kinsmen by John Fletcher and William Shakespeare

1511
Emilia, 20s   Athens
Palamon and Arcite, two knights of Thebes, have both fallen in love with Emilia, who here

agonizes over which of the two she loves in return. Dramatic.
REN, 5.5 minutes
The Two Noble Kinsmen by John Fletcher and William Shakespeare

1512
Hermione, 20-30 Sicilia
Leonates has accused his wife of bearing the child of his onetime friend, Polixenes. When she is formally charged with high treason, Hermione makes the following speech in her own defense. Dramatic.
REN, 3.5 minutes
The Winter's Tale by William Shakespeare

1513
Hermione, 20-30 Sicilia
Here, the accused queen demands that she be judged by the Delphic Oracle. Dramatic.
REN, 2.5 minutes
The Winter's Tale by William Shakespeare

1514
Francisca, 20s Ravenna
Francisca is nearing the time when she will no longer be able to keep her pregnancy a secret from her family. Here, she ponders her unfortunate circumstances. Dramatic.
REN, 3 minutes
The Witch by Thomas Middleton

1515
Elizabeth Sawyer, 50-70 Edmonton
Believed by all to be a witch, Elizabeth here reveals her desire to live up to everyone's expectations so that she may wreak revenge on those who have abused her. Dramatic.
REN, 2.5 minutes
The Witch of Edmonton by William Rowley, Thomas Dekker, and John Ford

1516
Elizabeth Sawyer, a hag, 50-70 Edmonton
Elizabeth has been sent a dog-like familiar from the dark lord she has promised to serve. The familiar has committed much mischief at her bequest and has become very dear to the old witch. Here, she calls for her satanic familiar. Dramatic.
REN, 2.5 minutes
The Witch of Edmonton by William Rowley, Thomas Dekker, and John Ford

1517
Anne, 30s England
Anne has been lured into an unfortunate dalliance by the unscrupulous Wendoll, a supposed friend of her husband's. When the affair is found out, she tearfully abases herself in front of her husband. Dramatic.
REN, 2 minutes
A Woman Killed with Kindness by Thomas Heywood

1518
Livia, 30-40 Florence
When Livia discovers that her brother, Hippolito, has fallen in love with their niece, Isabella, she does her best to provide him with sympathetic advice. Dramatic.
REN, 4.5 minutes
Women Beware Women by Thomas Middleton

1519
Sophonisba, Princess of Carthage and wife of Massinissa, 20s
Libya
Sophonisba rejected the suit of Syphax of Libya in favor of Massinissa. When an enraged Syphax joins forces with the Roman army in a brutal attack on Carthage, Massinissa is forced to abandon their bridal bed to help defend the city. As the battle rages, Sophonisba reflects on their fate. Dramatic.
REN, 3 minutes
The Wonder of Women or The Tragedy of Sophonisba by John Marsten

1520
Erictho, any age Libya
Syphax's unrequited passion for Sophonisba brings him close to madness. In desperation, he summons the enchantress, Erictho, who promises him that the princess will soon share his bed. Dramatic.
REN, 5 minutes
The Wonder of Women or The Tragedy of Sophonisba by John Marsten

1521
Allwit, 20-30 England
Allwit's wife is carrying Sir Walter's child. The knight has arranged to keep the Allwits in fine style as they await the birth of the child. Here, broad-minded Allwit contentedly contemplates his good fortune. Seriocomic.
REN, 5 minutes
A Chaste Maid in Cheapside by Thomas Middleton

1522
Captain Ager, 20s England
When Captain Ager is accused of being illegitimate, he challenges his accuser to a duel. Here, he rages against this unwholesome slight to his mother. Dramatic.
REN, 3.5 minutes
A Fair Quarrel by Thomas Middleton and William Rowley

1523
Master Penitent Brothel, 20-30   London
A man of questionable morality, Penitent here contemplates the possibility of committing adultery. Seriocomic.
REN, 3 minutes
A Mad World, My Masters by Thomas Middleton

1524
Wendoll, 30s   England
The unscrupulous Wendoll has managed to lure the lovely Anne into an illicit affair. When Anne is subsequently banished by her husband, Wendoll realizes that he is responsible for her unhappy life. Dramatic.
REN, 3 minutes
A Woman Killed with Kindness by Thomas Heywood

1525
Gostanzo, 50-60   Florence
Here, this talkative braggart lectures his son on the finer points of entertaining ladies. Seriocomic.
REN, 4 minutes
All Fools by George Chapman

1526
Valerio, 20s   Florence
Here, Valerio offers a drunken salute to the age he lives in; where all are fools being fooled by other fools. Seriocomic.
REN, 8 minutes
All Fools by George Chapman

1527
Michael, 16-20   England
Master Arden's young wife and her lover have hatched a plot to murder Michael. When he discovers their plan, Michael agonizes whether or not he should take action. Seriocomic.
REN, 3 minutes
Arden of Feversham by Anonymous

1528
Mosbie, 20s   England
Mosbie's affair with the passionate young wife of Master Arden has led to a wicked scheme of murder. When Mosbie realizes how easy it was for Alice to plot to kill her husband, he begins to worry about his own future. Dramatic.
REN, 4.5minutes
Arden of Feversham by Anonymous

1529
Borachio, 30-40   A banquet
Borachio's master is brother to a wealthy baron, whose estate Borachio covets. He has convinced his master to do away with his nephew, Charlemont, so that he will inherit the baron's estate. Here, Borachio dons a disguise and falsely informs the baron that Charlemont has been drowned. Dramatic.
REN, 5.5 minutes
The Atheist's Tragedy by Cyril Tourneur

1530
Quarlous, 30-40   The Bartholomew Fair
Here, the rascally Quarlous chides a friend for his habit of romancing older women. Seriocomic.
REN, 4 minutes
Bartholomew Fair by Ben Jonson

1531
Ambidexter, 30-40   Persia
The crafty Ambidexter has wormed his way into the court of Cambyses by playing all sides against one another. Here, he takes a moment to speak out against marriage. Seriocomic.
REN, 3 minutes
Cambyses, King of Persia by Thomas Preston

1532
Sylla, ghost of a Roman dictator, 50-60
Rome
As the unhappy spirit of the murdered Sylla wanders the palace, he encounters the treacherous Catiline, who is in the process of planning a deadly coup. Dramatic.
REN, 7.5 minutes
Catiline by Ben Jonson

1533
Cicero, Roman statesman and orator, 40s
Rome
Having discovered the evil Catiline's plot to overthrow the empire, Cicero here muses over those who have attempted similar feats. Dramatic.
REN, 5 minutes
Catiline by Ben Jonson

1534
Posthumus, 30s   Britain
Posthumus has been tricked into believing that his wife has been unfaithful. In a rage, he orders his servant, Pisanio, to murder her. Fortunately, Pisanio is unable to carry out his master's orders and takes Imogen to Wales, instead. In the meantime, Posthumus has joined with the Roman army that now threatens Britain. Here, the unhappy man grieves for the wife he believes is dead. Dramatic.
REN, 3.5 minutes
Cymbeline by William Shakespeare

1535
David, King of Israel, 40s   Israel

David's son, Absalon, has murdered his brother, Amnon. Here, the grieving king leads his people in mourning the loss of his son. Dramatic.
REN, 3 minutes
David and Bethsabe by George Peele

1536
Faustus, 30-40   **Germany**
As he prepares to summon the evil spirits that will reveal to him the secrets of necromancy, Faustus fantasizes about the many feats that he will command the spirits to perform. Dramatic.
REN, 4.5 minutes
Doctor Faustus by Christopher Marlowe

1537
Freevill, 20-30   **London**
Here, Freevill defends the right of women to prostitute themselves when the need arises. Seriocomic.
REN, 3.5 minutes
The Dutch Courtesan by John Marston

1538
Cocledemoy, 30-40   **London**
During an evening of revelry, Cocledemoy takes a moment to raise his glass in salute to an old bawd. Seriocomic.
REN, 3 minutes
The Dutch Courtesan by John Marston

1539
King Edward, 30-40
Kenilworth Castle, England
Edward is a weak and foolish king whose flamboyant ways have earned him nothing but scorn from many earls attending the court. This animosity finally leads to rebellion and Edward is taken to Kenilworth Castle where he is held prisoner. Edward has long suspected that his wife, Queen Isabella, has been having an affair with young Lord Mortimer, the leader of the coup, and here laments his fate to the Earl of Leicester. Dramatic.
REN, 7.5 minutes
Edward II by Christopher Marlowe

1540
Sir Amorous La-Foole, a knight, 30-40
London
La-Foole—a talkative and foolish man—here invites some friends to dinner while offering at the same time a history of his family. Seriocomic.
REN, 3 minutes
Epiocene or The Silent Woman by Ben Jonson

1541
Truewit, a friend of Morose, a gentleman
who loves no noise, 40s   **London**
Morose has decided to marry to prevent his nephew from enjoying his inheritance. Here, his friend Truewit does his best to discourage him. Seriocomic.
REN, 5.5 minutes
Epiocene or The Silent Woman by Ben Jonson

1542
Knowell, 50-60   **London**
Knowell's son has received a mysterious letter from someone in the Jewery. Knowell managed to intercept and read the letter before it was delivered, and has therefore learned of his son's intention to visit the writer of the letter. Deciding to follow at a distance, the older man reflects on the differences between their generations and on the responsibility of fathers to their sons. Seriocomic.
REN, 7 minutes
Every Man in His Humor by Ben Jonson

1543
Frank, 20s   **London**
When he suspects that he is falling in love, Frank cannot help waxing rhapsodically about the young lady in question. Seriocomic.
REN, 7 minutes
The Fair Maid of the Exchange by Thomas Heywood

1544
Friar Bacon, 50-60   **Oxford**
The industrious Friar Bacon has constructed a strange brass head that he hopes will grant him dominion over the forces of evil. Here, the friar instructs his student to watch over the head while he sleeps. Seriocomic.
REN, 3.5 minutes
Friar Bacon and Friar Bungay by Robert Greene

1545
Diccon, 30-50   **Tudor, England**
When the wandering Diccon arrives at the home of Gammer Gurton, he finds all in an uproar due to the loss of the lady's sewing needle. Seriocomic.
REN, 2.5 minutes
Gammer Gurton's Needle by William Stevenson

1546
Ralph, 20s
At the presentation of a play
Ralph's employer has written a play and insists that his simple assistant portray the title role of the Knight of the Burning Pestle. Here, Ralph hams it up in an elaborate and long-winded death scene. Seriocomic.
REN, 5.5 minutes
The Knight of the Burning Pestle by Francis Beaumont

1547

Malevole, 30-40   **Genoa**

When his power is usurped, the duke disguises himself as the dire Malevole, which allows him to roam freely in the court. Here, he takes a moment to council a foolish vassal, who intends to leave his young wife at court while he travels abroad. Dramatic.

REN, 3 minutes

The Malcontent by John Marston

1548

Andrew Lethe, 20s   **London**

Here, a scheming young man plots to wed the daughter of a wealthy merchant while simultaneously seducing the girl's mother. Seriocomic.

REN, 3.5 minutes

Michaelmas Term by Thomas Middleton

1549

Hellgill, 20-30   **London**

Hellgill here does his best to convince a country wench to provide amorous services for his master. Seriocomic.

REN, 2 minutes

Michaelmas Term by Thomas Middleton

1550

Father, 40-50   **London**

When his daughter runs away from home to become the mistress of the roguish Andrew Lithe, her father resolves to find her. Dramatic.

REN, 4 minutes

Michaelmas Term by Thomas Middleton

1551

Benedick, 20s   **Messina**

When Benedick's friend Claudio falls in love, Benedick contemplates the strange changes that love can make in the heart of a man. Seriocomic.

REN, 2.5 minutes

Much Ado About Nothing by William Shakespeare

1552

Vindice, 20-30   **A ducal court**

When Vindice's mistress refused the Duke's advances, the enraged nobleman poisoned her. Here, the grieving Vindice roams the castle with her skull, speaking to it as if she were still alive. Dramatic.

REN, 6 minutes

The Revengers' Tragedy by Cyril Tourneur

1553

Ghost of Andrea, 20-30   **Spain**

Here, the ghost of a soldier slain in the recent war with Portugal wanders the corridors of the royal castle while lamenting his fate. Dramatic.

REN, 8.5 minutes

The Spanish Tragedy by Thomas Kyd

1554

Hieronimo, the Marshal of Spain, 40-50 Spain

Hieronimo's son, Horatio, has been murdered by the Prince of Portugal with his accomplices. Here, the Marshall discovers his son's body which has been hung by the murderers in an arbor. Dramatic.

REN, 3.5 minutes

The Spanish Tragedy by Thomas Kyd

1555

Segismund   **The Polish frontier**

Imprisoned in a desolate fortress and held by a large and heavy chain, Segismund, a captive prince, here vents his spleen to the night sky. Dramatic.

REN, 7.5 minutes

Such Stuff as Dreams Are Made of by Calderon de la Barca

1556

Tamburlaine, 30s   **Damascus**

Here, Tamburlaine persuades Techelles, a captain of the Persian army, to join with him in his war against the king. Dramatic.

REN, 4.5 minutes

Tamburlaine the Great by Christopher Marlowe

1557

Prospero, 50-60   **An enchanted island**

When his dukedom is restored to him, Prospero renounces his magic. Dramatic.

REN, 2.5 minutes

The Tempest by William Shakespeare

1558

Don Lope de Urrea, a man pleading for the life of his son, 50-60

The court of Arragon

Don Urrea's son has been condemned for killing another man in a duel. Here, Don Urrea pleads his son's innocence to the king in hopes of extracting a royal pardon. Dramatic.

REN, 6.5 minutes

Three Judgments at a Blow by Calderon de la Barca

1559

Timon, 30-50   **A cave near Athens**

When his friends desert him during a time of financial distress, Timon takes his leave of Athenian society and makes a new home in a desolate cave, where he intends to live out his days. Here, Timon curses the shallow nature of humankind as he digs in the earth of roots. Dramatic.

REN, 5 minutes
Timon of Athens by William Shakespeare

1560
Giovanni, 20s   **Italy**
Here, Giovanni confesses his forbidden passion for his sister, Annabella. Dramatic.
REN, 2 minutes
'Tis Pity She's a Whore by John Ford

1561
Richard II, King of England, 30s
A castle on the shore of Wales
When Richard returns to England from his war with Ireland, he discovers that the lords of the realm have risen in revolt. Here, Richard greets his native soil. Dramatic.
REN, 2.5 minutes
The Tragedy of King Richard II by William Shakespeare

1562
Richard II, King of England, 30s
A castle on the shore of Wales
When the severity of the revolt is revealed to the King, he reminds his followers that no one is ever very far from the grave and that kings are just as ruled by death as any man. Dramatic.
REN, 3.5 minutes
The Tragedy of King Richard II by William Shakespeare

1563
Arcite, a knight of Thebes, 20s   **Athens**
Arcite has recently escaped the royal prison in Athens. Here, he takes a moment to ponder his love for Emilia, a noblewoman of Athens. His thoughts then turn to Palamon, his cousin, who is still imprisoned in Athens. Dramatic.
REN, 3 minutes
The Two Noble Kinsmen by John Fletcher and William Shakespeare

1564
Wooer, 20s   **Athens**
When the Wooer discovers the daughter of the royal jailer wandering in the woods, he wastes no time in reporting this to her father. Dramatic.
REN, 5.5 minutes
The Two Noble Kinsmen by John Fletcher and William Shakespeare

1565
Arcite, a knight of Thebes, 20s   **Athens**
As Arcite prepares to meet Palamon in a deadly tournament that will decide which of the two knights will gain Emilia's hand in marriage, he pauses to pray to Mars, the god of war. Dramatic.
REN, 3.5 minutes
The Two Noble Kinsmen by John Fletcher and William Shakespeare

1566
Palamon, a knight of Thebes, 20s   **Athens**
On the eve of a tournament that will determine who shall wed the lovely Emilia, Palamon offers a prayer to the gods. Dramatic.
REN, 7 minutes
The Two Noble Kinsmen by John Fletcher and William Shakespeare

1567
Antigonus, a lord of Sicilia, 30s   **Sicilia**
The Queen of Sicilia has been charged with high treason and adultery for bearing a child the king refuses to believe is his own. Although the Delphic Oracle has proclaimed the queen's innocence, the king has demanded that the infant be abandoned on the desolate shore of Bohemia. Lord Antigonus has been charged with this unhappy task, and here wishes the baby well as he sets her ashore. Dramatic.
REN, 4.5 minutes
The Winter's Tale by William Shakespeare

1568
Almachildes, 30-40   **Ravenna**
Following an evening of drunken revelry, Almachildes foolishly purchased a love charm from a witch. In the sober light of day, he takes a moment to examine his strange new possession. Seriocomic.
REN, 3.5 minutes
The Witch by Thomas Middleton

1569
Leantio, 20s   **Florence**
As he returns home after a day's work, Leantio extols the virtues and joys of matrimony. Seriocomic.
REN, 3 minutes
Women Beware Women by Thomas Middleton

1570
Syphax, King of Libya, 30s   **Libya**
When Syphax is rejected by Sophonisba, a princess of Carthage, he flies into a rage and joins with the great Roman general, Scipio, who plans to invade Carthage. Dramatic.
REN, 5 minutes
The Wonder of Women or The Tragedy of Sophonisba by John Marston

1571
Alcmene, 20s
The Palace of Amphitryon in Thebes Alcmene has been tricked by Zeus into thinking that the

lusty god is, in fact, her husband. The lord of Olympus has prepared a series of misadventures for the real Amphitryon that will keep him away from the palace while he seduces Alcmene. When the real Amphitryon finally returns to his home, Alcmene no longer recognizes him, and here demands that he leave. Dramatic.

ROM, 3 minutes

Amphitryon by Heinrich von Kleist, tr. by Martin Greenberg

1572
Amy, 20-30   **London**
Amy's husband, Edward, has run afoul of a plot to ruin him financially. His enemy's final coup is to trick Edward into thinking that Amy has been unfaithful. When Edward angrily demands that Amy leave their house, she tearfully begs him to allow her to stay, if only to be a mother to their children. Dramatic.

ROM, 3 minutes

The Bankrupt by George Henry Boker

1573
Amy, 20-30   **London**
Believing her to have been unfaithful, Edward demands that Amy leave and take the children with her, for after all, he has no reason to suspect that they are his. This is the final insult to virtuous Amy, whose patience is finally at an end. Dramatic.

ROM, 2.5 minutes

The Bankrupt by George Henry Boker

1574
Imogene, 30s   **England**
Believing her beloved Bertram to be dead, Imogene marries a man she doesn't love to save her father from ruin. When Bertram returns and discovers her marriage, he kills her husband in a jealous rage. Imogene takes her young son and flees to a monastery. Here, she is haunted by the grisly spectre of her husband's corpse. Dramatic.

ROM, 3 minutes

Bertram or The Castle of Aldobrand by Charles Robert Maturin

1575
Bianca, 18-20   **14th century Milan**
Bianca's father, the Duke of Milan, has just decreed that she will marry Sforza, a young nobleman with whom she has always been in love. Here, she shares the happy news with her servants. Dramatic.

ROM, 3 minutes

Bianca Visconti or The Heart Overtasked by Nathaniel Parker Willis

1576
Bianca, 18-20   **14th century Milan**
Following her wedding to Sforza, Bianca discovers that her childish dreams of life together won't be enough to hold the interest of a man intent on glory. Here, she vows to win his love in earnest, even if it means the death of her heart's desire. Dramatic.

ROM, 5 minutes

Bianca Visconti or The Heart Overtasked by Nathaniel Parker Willis

1577
Frau Martha, 40-50   **A Flemish village**
In the midst of a domestic altercation, Frau Martha's prized jug was smashed. Determined to be compensated for her loss, she brings the matter before the local magistrate. Here, she describes the jug to the court. Seriocomic.

ROM, 7.5 minutes

The Broken Jug by Heinrich Von Kleist, tr. by Martin Greenberg

1578
Jane Warfield, 20   **Bath, England**
While visiting her sister in London, Jane is kidnapped by a gang of ruffians who intend to hold her for ransom. Fortunately, Jane manages to escape, and here seeks refuge in a churchyard. Dramatic.

ROM, 3 minutes

The Bucktails or Americans in England by James Kirke Paulding

1579
Eve   **The land without paradise**
Upon discovering the fact that Cain has murdered Abel, Eve curses her surviving son and banishes him from her sight. Dramatic.

ROM, 4.5 minutes

Cain by Lord Byron

1580
The Captive, 20s   **A dungeon**
Accused of madness, this desperate woman struggles with futile abandon against the chains that imprison her in Bedlam. Dra-matic.

ROM, 7 minutes

The Captive by Matthew G. Lewis

1581
The Marchioness, 50s   **London**
When she learns that her son, an army captain, is about to be posted to India, the Marchioness pays him a visit and offers the following advice. Dramatic.

ROM, 6 minutes

Caste by Thomas William Robertson

1582
Angela, 20s   **England**
Although Angela is being courted by the
wealthy Osmond, she finds no substance in his
lavish gifts and pines instead for the unencum-
bered days of her youth. Dramatic.
ROM, 2.5 minutes
The Castle Spectre by Matthew G. Lewis

1583
Beatrice, 20s   **16th century Rome**
Beatrice once loved Orsino, who has since
taken the vows of priesthood. When he con-
tinues to make romantic advances, she quickly
rebuffs him. Dramatic.
ROM, 5 minutes
The Cenci by Percy Bysshe Shelley

1584
Beatrice, 20s   **16th century Rome**
When her father causes the deaths of her
brothers, the evil man hosts a feast to celebrate. Here, desperate Beatrice begs the gathered lords of Rome to save her from her father's insane bloodlust. Dramatic.
ROM, 3 minutes
The Cenci by Percy Bysshe Shelley

1585
Ruth, 30-40   **A funeral**
Years of frustration with her brother's social-
climbing wife finally erupt in an angry con-
frontation with her at his funeral. Dramatic.
ROM, 3 minutes
The Climbers by Clyde Fitch

1586
Marion, 30s
Paris during the Reign of Terror
Here, as they tarry in bed, the earthy Marion
tells Danton of her first lover, his death and the
awakening of her endless longing. Dramatic.
ROM, 5 minutes
*Danton's Death by George Buchner, tr. by Henry J.
Schmidt*

1587
Anna   **Spain**
Anna's unrequited passion for Don Juan has
driven her nearly mad. Here, she confronts her
sister and the Don as they plan their future together. Their happiness is more than Anna can
bear, and here she tells them a dark tale ending
in threats. Dramatic.
ROM, 5 minutes
Don Juan by James Elroy Flecker

1588
Anna   **Spain**

Anna is the sister of Isabella, who is to marry
Don Juan. Here, she makes a startling confes-
sion to her sister's fiancé. Dramatic.
ROM, 2 minutes
Don Juan by James Elroy Flecker

1589
Elfie, 30s   **NYC**
When Elfie discovers that a young friend has
lost her heart to a man, she delivers the fol-
lowing sobering sermons. Dramatic.
ROM, 3 minutes
The Easiest Way by Eugene Walter

1590
Elfie, 30s   **NYC**
When Elfie discovers that a young friend has
lost her heart to a man, she delivers the fol-
lowing sobering sermons. Dramatic.
ROM, 4 minutes
The Easiest Way by Eugene Walter

1591
Margit, 22   Solhoug, Norway, 14th century
On the eve of her anniversary feast, Margit
finds herself in a melancholy mood. Here, she
takes stock of her marriage and reveals that
she feels trapped in a "gilded cage." Seriocomic.
ROM, 5.5 minutes
The Feast at Solhoug by Henrik Ibsen

1592
Signë, 18-20
Solhoug, Norway, 14th Century
Signë is an energetic young woman who here
bursts into her sister's chamber and tells her
that Gudmund, their childhood friend upon
whom they both had crushes, is coming to the
feast. Seriocomic.
ROM, 6 minutes
The Feast at Solhoug by Henrik Ibsen

1593
Margit, 22   Solhoug, Norway, 14th Century
Margit and Gudmund were once secret lovers.
Gudmund deserted Margit to pursue another
woman, and Margit has never forgiven him. In
fact, Margit blames Gudmund for her unhappy married life. At the feast, the guests demand that Margit entertain them all with a
tale. Driven to desperation by Gudmund's
presence, Margit impetuously tells her own
sad story, and then collapses. Dramatic.
ROM, 4.5 minutes
The Feast at Solhoug by Henrik Ibsen

1594
Margit, 22   Solhoug, Norway, 14th century

Following her collapse, Margit recovers in her bedchamber, her thoughts on Gudmund and suicide. Dramatic.
ROM, 5 minutes
The Feast at Solhoug by Henrik Ibsen

1595
Rhodope, 20-30   The kingdom of Lydia
The king has allowed Gyges to wear a ring that renders him invisible so that his visitor may behold his beautiful wife in her most natural of states. When Rhodope discovers that she has been so violated, she falls into a deep depression and no longer wishes to live. Here, she asks the gods why they have visited so much misery upon her. Dramatic.
ROM, 3.5 minutes
Gyges and His Ring by Friedrich Hebbel, tr. by Marion W. Sonnenfeld

1596
Judith, 20s   Bethulia
Judith has boldly volunteered to kill the dread Holofernes. When her goal is questioned by Ephraim, a man she despises, Judith explodes with feminist passion. Dramatic.
ROM, 3 minutes
Judith by Friedrich Hebbel, tr. by Marion W. Sonnenfeld

1597
Lady Inger, 40s   Norway, 1528
Lady Inger's allowed her first child, a son born out of wedlock to a Danish nobleman, to be taken from her in order to keep quiet a conspiracy concerning King Christian II. Years later, she is again approached to play a role in the maddeningly complex realm of Scandinavian power struggles. The price of her cooperation is the return of her son. Here, she tells the story to an old friend. Dramatic.
ROM, 8 minutes
Lady Inger of Östråt by Henrik Ibsen

1598
Lady Inger, 40s   Norway, 1528
Lady Inger has agreed to Nils Lykke's demands in order to be reunited with her son, but in doing so, renounced his right to the throne. Here, she agonizes over her decision. Dramatic.
ROM, 3.5 minutes
Lady Inger of Östråt by Henrik Ibsen

1599
High Betty Marlin (Betsey), 20s
The mountains outside of Sacramento
Betsey has received a letter from Jess, the man she loves, and makes up her mind to follow him into the California wilderness. She is soon lost in the mountains with her wagon and sick uncle. Here, she takes a moment to lament her

desperate state. Seriocomic.
ROM, 2 minutes
A Live Woman in the Mines by "Old Block" Alonzo Delano

1600
Svanhild, 20s   Norway
Falk, a would-be writer who rents a room from Svanhild's mother, has just proposed. Here, Svanhild turns the pompous young man down. Dramatic.
ROM, 5 minutes
Love's Comedy by Henrik Ibsen

1601
Lucrezia Borgia, 20-30   Ferrara
When Lucrezia comes to believe that her husband's people are mocking her, she angrily confronts him and demands that he do something about it. Dramatic.
ROM, 4.5 minutes
Lucrezia Borgia by Victor Hugo, tr. by George Burnham Ives

1602
Marion, 20s   France, 1638
Didier has been found guilty of participating in a duel and has been sentenced to death. Here, Marion desperately pleads with Louis XIII to spare his life. Dramatic.
ROM, 3 minutes
Marion de Lorme by Victor Hugo, tr. by George Burnham Ives

1603
Mrs. Warren, 40s   England
Mrs. Warren has supported her daughter, Vivie, by managing prostitutes. When Vivie discovers the truth about her mother's profession, she is sympathetic. Here, Mrs. Warren makes no apologies for her chosen career. Dramatic.
ROM, 2 minutes
Mrs. Warren's Profession by George Bernard Shaw

1604
Mrs. Warren, 40s   England
When Vivie discovers that her mother is still a working madam, she angrily announces her intention to sever all ties with her. Here, Mrs. Warren does her best to point out to idealistic Vivie that life is hard, and to survive, you need all the help you can get. Dramatic.
ROM, 2 minutes
Mrs. Warren's Profession by George Bernard Shaw

1605
Lady Auranthe, 20s   Germany
Scheming Auranthe has plotted to gain the crown by marrying Otho's son. When her plot-

ting is discovered, she fears, correctly, that the title "Empress" is now forever out of her grasp. Dramatic.
ROM, 3 minutes
Otho the Great by John Keats

1606
Penthesilea, 20-30   A battlefield near Troy
This brave warrior woman has fallen in love with Achilles. The fact that they are sworn enemies in battle has driven her near to madness. As the Trojan general approaches, Penthesilea calls her warriors to battle. Dramatic.
ROM, 3.5 minutes
Penthesilea by Heinrich von Kleist, tr. by Martin Greenberg

1607
The Earth
A ravine of icy rocks in the Indian Caucasus
Here, the spirit of the Earth visits Prometheus, a man who boldly stole fire from the gods and who is now chained to a mountain by Zeus. Dramatic.
ROM, 7 minutes
Prometheus Unbound by Percy Bysshe Shelley

1608
Panthea, 16-20   An oceanside
Here, the mystical young sprite tells her sister of a strange dream. Dramatic.
ROM, 7.5 minutes
Prometheus Unbound by Percy Bysshe Shelley

1609
Rita, 20s   A society party
Here, the passionate Rita tells the tale of her first love to Van Tuyl, an older man to whom she is very much attracted. Seriocomic.
ROM, 4.5 minutes
Romance by Edward Sheldon

1610
Rose Maybud, 18-20
The fishing village of Rederring in Cornwall
When asked by her aunt why she has yet to accept a suitor, Rose reveals that she lives by very strict rules of etiquette, and may therefore never reveal her true feelings to a man. Seriocomic.
ROM, 1.5 minutes
The Ruddigore or The Witch's Curse by William Schwenk Gilbert

1611
Salomé, 16-18   The court of Herod
Salomé has danced for Herod for which she receives the head of John the Baptist. Here, she addresses her grief to the prophet's severed head. Dramatic.
ROM, 4 minutes
Salomé by Oscar Wilde

1612
Paula, 30s   England
Paula longed to marry Aubrey Tanqueray in order to improve her place in society. She was unprepared, however, for the tedium of life on a country estate. The endless succession of days have made her quite stir-crazy as she here reveals to Aubrey. Dramatic.
ROM, 3 minutes
The Second Mrs. Tanqueray by Arthur Wing Pinero

1613
Paula, 30s   England
Here, Paula confronts Ellen, Aubrey's daughter from his first marriage, and begs the young woman to accept her as her new mother. Dramatic.
ROM, 1.5 minutes
The Second Mrs. Tanqueray by Arthur Wing Pinero

1614
Paula, 30s   England
Paula's constant anxiety over life minutiæ has finally caused her marriage to fail. Aubrey suggests that they travel abroad and try to begin again. It is too late, however, for Paula's descent into madness is complete. Here, she rejects Aubrey's notion of a better future and darkly alludes to her plan to commit suicide. Dramatic.
ROM, 3.5 minutes
The Second Mrs. Tanqueray by Arthur Wing Pinero

1615
May, 20s   London
May's husband has been sent to prison, leaving her with no money. Here, the destitute woman reads a recent letter from him aloud to her canary. Dramatic.
ROM, 2.5 minutes
The Ticket-of-Leave Man by Tom Taylor

1616
Mrs. Willoughby, 40-50   London
Here, May is paid a visit by her talkative landlady, whose favorite topic of conversation seems to be herself. Dramatic.
ROM, 3 minutes
The Ticket-of-Leave Man by Tom Taylor

1617
Sonya, 20-30
A country estate in Russia
Sonya realizes that there is no marriage in her future and that she will live out her days as a spinster on her father's country estate. Here, she commiserates with Uncle Vanya, who shares a similar fate. Dramatic.
ROM, 2 minutes
Uncle Vanya by Anton Chekhov, tr. by Stark Young

1618
Vera, 20s   **Moscow, 1800**
When the Czar declares martial law, Vera speaks passionately in favor of revolution. Dramatic.
ROM, 2 minutes
Vera or The Nihilists by Oscar Wilde

1619
Blanche, 18-20   **London**
Blanche has rashly broken off her engagement to Harry, with whom she is still very much in love. Several months later, Harry visits Blanche and she greets him with anger which soon melts into affection. Seriocomic.
ROM, 3.5 minutes
Widowers' Houses by George Bernard Shaw

1620
Melville, 40s
The village of Tappan, NY during the revolutionary war
Melville is standing the night watch at an encampment outside of Tappan. Here, he takes a moment to reflect on the dark nature of war. Dramatic.
ROM, 2 minutes
André by William Dunlop

1621
Major André, 20-30
The village of Tappan, NY during the revolutionary war
On the last night of his life, this convicted British spy contemplates his impending death. Dramatic.
ROM, 2.5 minutes
André by William Dunlop

1622
Nicola, 30-40   **Bulgaria, 1885**
Nicola takes his position in the Petkoff household very seriously. When Louka, a peasant-girl-turned-chambermaid, behaves in a manner he believes to be above her station, he lectures her on the importance of knowing one's place. Seriocomic.
ROM, 3 minutes
Arms and the Man by George Bernard Shaw

1623
Bertram, 30s   **England**
After wandering the land as a bandit for several years, Bertram has finally returned home to the woman he loves, only to discover that she has married his rival. Here, he roams the forest at night and considers his revenge. Dramatic.
ROM, 3.5 minutes
Bertram by Charles Robert Maturin

1624
William, 30s   **The harbor**
After many months at sea, William finally returns home, his thoughts on one person only: his lovely wife Susan. Dramatic.
ROM, 2 minutes
Black Ey'd Susan by Douglas Jerrold

1625
William, 30s   **The harbor**
Here, William spins a dark yarn about St. Domingo Billy, a man-eating shark he encountered in the Caribbean. Seriocomic.
ROM, 3.5 minutes
Black Ey'd Susan by Douglas Jerrold

1626
Reginald, 50s   **England**
Reginald has been kept in a dungeon by his scheming brother for many years. Here, he paces this lonely cell and longs for freedom. Dramatic.
ROM, 2 minutes
The Castle Spectre by Matthew G. Lewis

1627
Count Francesco Cenci, 50s
16th century Rome
Count Cenci has come to wield great power in Rome. Here, he reveals the delight he takes in the suffering of others. Dramatic.
ROM, 2.5 minutes
The Cenci by Percy Bysshe Shelley

1628
Robespierre, 30-40
Paris during the Reign of Terror
At a meeting of the National Committee, Robespierre speaks out in defense of the use of violence. Dramatic.
ROM, 8 minutes
Danton's Death by George Buchner, tr. by Henry J. Schmidt

1629
Camille, 40-50
Paris during the Reign of Terror
Here, the sardonic Camille bemoans the fact that art generally goes unappreciated by the masses. Dramatic.
ROM, 2 minutes
Danton's Death by George Buchner, tr. by Henry J. Schmidt

1630
Darnley, 30-40   **London**
When Darnley's foolish wife requests that they separate, he takes a moment to verbally vent his frustration with the fairer sex. Dramatic.

ROM, 1.5 minutes
Darnley by Edward Bulwer-Lytton

1631
De Montfort, 20-30   **A village in Germany**
De Montfort has spent the better part of his life hating his childhood rival, Rezenvelt. Indeed, this hatred has driven him away from his home and loved ones. Jane, his loving sister, has followed De Montfort, determined to bring him back, but when a stranger informs De Montfort that Rezenvelt intends to marry Jane, he falls into a murderous rage. Dramatic.
ROM, 4 minutes
De Montfort by Joanne Baillie

1632
Don Juan, any age   **Spain**
Here, the legendary womanizer introduces himself and describes his life. Dramatic.
ROM, 7 minutes
Don Juan by James Elroy Flecker

1633
Ghent, 30s   **A village in Massachusetts**
Ghent saved Ruth from a group of toughs in a frontier town by purchasing her from them. A simple man, Ghent assumed that she was therefore his to keep. Some nine months later, they have a child. Ruth is finally able to make her way back home to Massachusetts, where she lives in shame with her family. Ghent has followed, and here he eloquently pleads his love for her and their child. Dramatic.
ROM, 7.5 minutes
The Great Divide by William Vaughn Moody

1634
Ernest, 30s   **Madrid**
The agony of writer's block is here defined by Ernest as he struggles to find words to put down on paper. Seriocomic.
ROM, 2.5 minutes
The Great Galeoto by Jose Echegaray

1635
Ernest, 30s   **Madrid**
When a friend tries to persuade Ernest to give up his struggle, the playwright perseveres, and he finally finds the words he was searching for. Dramatic.
ROM, 3 minutes
The Great Galeoto by Jose Echegaray

1636
Satan   **Constantinople**
Here, the Lord of Darkness reviles Christ when both gather at Constantinople for the conversion of Mahmud. Dramatic.

ROM, 4 minutes
Hellas by Percy Bysshe Shelley

1637
Hernani, 20-30   **Spain, 1519**
Here, the passionate Hernani vows to revenge himself against the treacherous Don Carlos. Dramatic.
ROM, 3.5 minutes
Hernani by Victor Hugo, tr. by Mrs. Newton Crosland

1638
Don Ruy, 50-60   **Spain, 1519**
Even though he knows of her love for Hernani, Don Ruy is determined to marry the beautiful Dona Sol. Dramatic.
ROM, 5.5 minutes
Hernani by Victor Hugo, tr. by Mrs. Newton Crosland

1639
Hernani, 20-30   **Spain, 1519**
Here, the infamous outlaw pleads with Dona Sol to forsake the love that they share. Dramatic.
ROM, 5 minutes
Hernani by Victor Hugo, tr. by Mrs. Newton Crosland

1640
Joaquin, 18   **A monastery in Mexico**
Brooding Joaquin has lived his entire life behind the protective walls of the monastery. Here, he muses on his strange and empty existence. Dramatic.
ROM, 4.5 minutes
Joaquin Murieta de Castillo, The Celebrated California Bandit by Charles E.B. Howe

1641
Garcia, 30-50   **A monastery in Mexico**
When his life is spared by young Joaquin, Garcia impulsively vows to never harm his savior. When Joaquin subsequently rescues a band of pioneers that Garcia had threatened to rob and kill, the bandit rages privately. Dramatic.
ROM, 3 minutes
Joaquin Murieta de Castillo, The Celebrated California Bandit by Charles E.B. Howe

1642
Holofernes, 40s   **Bethulia**
Here, the dread general of Nebuchadnezzer muses on the importance of keeping himself a mystery to his underlings. Dramatic.
ROM, 3 minutes
Judith by Friedrich Hebbel

1643
Holofernes, 40s   **Bethulia**
The general finds himself attracted to Judith, a captured Jew who is secretly plotting to kill him. Here, the self-centered man contemplates his assured victory over Judith, while especially relishing the thought of driving the God she loves from her heart. Dramatic.
ROM, 3 minutes
Judith by Friedrich Hebbel

1644
Holofernes, 40s   **Bethulia**
As he prepares to seduce Judith, Holofernes cannot help taking a moment to preen in front of his captive. Dramatic.
ROM, 43 minutes
Judith by Friedrich Hebbel

1645
Melnotte, 20s   **Alsace**
Melnotte is a simple country boy who has fallen in love with the daughter of a wealthy merchant. When his mother chides him for courting a woman above his station, he assures her that he is more than capable of achieving his goal. Seriocomic.
ROM, 3 minutes
The Lady of Lyons by Edward Bulwer-Lytton

1646
Lord Darlington, 20-30   **London**
Here, Lord Darlington does his best to seduce the virtuous Lady Windermere. Dramatic.
ROM, 3.5 minutes
Lady Windermere's Fan by Oscar Wilde

1647
Stensgård, 20-30
A market town in Norway
Stensgård, an idealistic young attorney, here reveals his political ambition. Dramatic.
ROM, 2.5 minutes
The League of Youth by Henrik Ibsen

1648
Prince Leonce, 20s
The mythical kingdom of Popo
Privilege and sloth have turned Leonce into nothing short of a fop. Here, he lazily contemplates his feelings for Rosetta. Seriocomic.
ROM, 2.5 minutes
Leonce and Lena by George Buchner, tr. by Henry J. Schmidt

1649
Sir Christopher, 50s   **London**
When his friend, Ned, plans to run off with the very married Lady Jessica, Sir Christopher does his best to talk them both out of their foolish passion. Seriocomic.
ROM, 6.5 minutes
The Liars by Henry Arthur Jones

1650
Count Manfred, any age
The high Alps
On a dark night, Manfred climbs into the mountains in order to summon the spirits that he hopes will have the power to end his earthly suffering. Dramatic.
ROM, 5 minutes
Manfred by Lord Byron

1651
Count Manfred, any age
The high Alps
Manfred has caused the death of the woman he loved and now his soul is also dead. Here, he looks upon the beauty of the Earth but is unmoved by it. Dramatic.
ROM, 5 minutes
Manfred by Lord Byron

1652
Count Manfred, any age
The high Alps
The ghost of Manfred's beloved has appeared to tell him that his time on Earth is at an end. Here, he observes his final sunset. Dramatic.
ROM, 35 minutes
Manfred by Lord Byron

1653
Didier, 20s   **France, 1638**
Here, the impetuous Didier declares his passion for Marion. Dramatic.
ROM, 5 minutes
Marion de Lorme by Victor Hugo, tr. by George Burnham Ives

1654
Tom, 20-30   **London**
Tom is a member of an eccentric family, which he claims resembles molluscs. Here, he defines his odd zoological thesis. Seriocomic.
ROM, 3.5 minutes
The Mollusc by Hubert Henry Davies

1655
Graves, 30-40   **London**
Here, a man of caustic sensibilities expresses his dislike of newspapers. Seriocomic.
ROM, 1.5 minutes
Money by Edward Bulwer-Lytton

1656
McCluskey, 30s
Terrebonne Plantation, Louisiana
To possess the beautiful Zoe, McCluskey murders the mail carrier who was bringing evidence of her status as a freed slave. When his crime is discovered, he escapes into the bayou where he is pursued by justice and nightmares. [Dramatic]
ROM, 1.5 minutes
The Octoroon by Dion Boucicault

1657
Albert, 20s   **Germany**
Albert has discovered the Lady Auranthe's treachery against the Emperor. As he returns to court, he mourns the passing of his youth and regrets his unwitting involvement in the traitorous plot. Dramatic.
ROM, 3 minutes
Otho the Great by John Keats

1658
Peer Gynt, 20s   **Norway**
Here, the lazy Peer Gynt lies in a field watching the clouds go by and fantasizing that he is a great king. Seriocomic.
ROM, 3 minutes
Peer Gynt by Henrik Ibsen, tr. by Paul Green

1659
Peer Gynt, 20s   **Norway**
Marooned in Morocco, Peer wanders the hot desert with his tattered umbrella and tries to make the best of his situation. Seriocomic.
ROM, 3.5 minutes
Peer Gynt by Henrik Ibsen, tr. by Paul Green

1660
Peer Gynt, 20s   **Norway**
At the end of his life, Peer is confronted by visions of the countless things his vanity prohibited him from accomplishing. Here, Peer bemoans his wasted life just before he is transformed into a troll. Dramatic.
ROM, 2 minutes
Peer Gynt by Henrik Ibsen, tr. by Paul Green

1661
Prometheus, 20-30
A ravine of icy rocks in the Indian Caucasus
Prometheus has stolen from the gods and his punishment is to be nailed to a mountain where an eagle eats his liver by day, which then grows back by night. Here, the unhappy man curses the gods and his fate. Dramatic.
ROM, 7 minutes
Prometheus Unbound by Percy Bysshe Shelley

1662
The Chevalier de Mauprat, 20
The court of King Louis XIII
This dashing young chevalier has fallen in love with Julie, the ward of the powerful Cardinal Richelieu. Here, de Mauprat gives voice to his passion. Seriocomic.
ROM, 4.5 minutes
Richelieu by Edward Bulwer-Lytton

1663
Cardinal Richelieu, 40-50
The court of King Louis XIII
Richelieu takes a few moments in the dead of night to consider matters of life and death as well as his place in history. Dramatic.
ROM, 11.5 minutes
Richelieu by Edward Bulwer-Lytton

1664
Richelieu, 40-50
The court of King Louis XIII
During a disagreement, Louis XIII threatens to terminate Richelieu's power. The Cardinal here reacts with both fury and scorn. Dramatic.
ROM, 5.5 minutes
Richelieu by Edward Bulwer-Lytton

1665
Vyvyan
England, 1588—the year of the Spanish Armada
Vyvyan has just returned home from a long time at sea. During a joyful reunion with his wife, he takes a moment to correct her when she refers to the sea as being "cruel." Dramatic.
ROM, 3 minutes
The Rightful Heir by Edward Bulwer-Lytton

1666
Van Tuyl, 51   **A society party**
When Van Tuyl discovers that the beautiful young Rita is attracted to him, he does his best to discourage her. Seriocomic.
ROM, 3 minutes
Romance by Edward Sheldon

1667
Herod, 50s   **The court of Herod**
Here, lusty Herod begs his wife's daughter, Salomé, to dance for him. Dramatic.
ROM, 4.5 minutes
Salomé by Oscar Wilde

1668
Ravensbane, 20-30
A village in Massachusetts, late 1600s
The evil spirit of a scarecrow inhabits a mirror

belonging to Ravensbane, and he has fallen under its spell. Here, he addresses the figure in the mirror. Dramatic.

ROM, 4.5 minutes
The Scarecrow by Percy MacKaye

1669
Gerardo, 36
A city in Austria
When Gerardo is accosted in his hotel room by an obnoxious composer who believes that art is "...the highest thing in the world," the seasoned performer wastes no time in setting the young man straight. Dramatic.

ROM, 4 minutes
The Tenor by Frank Wedekind, tr. by André Tridon

1670
Voinitsky (Uncle Vanya), 47
A country estate in Russia
Uncle Vanya has sacrificed his own dreams in order to run the country estate of his brother-in-law, whom all believe to be a great scholar. Uncle Vanya even gave up any claim he may at one time have had on the professor's wife, with whom he is still very much in love. When at last he discovers that the professor is a fake, he realizes that he has wasted his life and his love for nothing. Dramatic.

ROM, 2.5 minutes
Uncle Vanya by Anton Chekhov, tr. by Stark Young

1671
Jamie, 20-30
An open, fluid space evocative of a burnt-out bayou, Present
Here, a restless young spirit tries to come to terms with his life and death while experiencing the wounds that killed him. Dra-matic.

BMSM94, 6 minutes
Alchemy of Desire/Dead-Man's Blues by Caridad Svich

1672
Irv, 20s   **Here and Now**
Here, Irv introduces himself to the audience with a slightly obsessive tale of one of his volleyball teammates. Seriocomic.

BMSM94, 5.5 minutes
Allen, Naked by Robert Coles

1673
Valentine Coverly, 25-30
A large country house in Derbyshire, Present
When a visiting scholar discovers an iterated algorithm in the schoolwork of a young girl who lived in his home some 180 years ago, Valentine does his best to explain the special significance of such a discovery. Here, he re-

veals his love of the mystery of creation, which he understands in purely mathematical terms. Seriocomic.

BMSM94, 3 minutes
Arcadia by Tom Stoppard

1674
Arthur, 64   **LA, Present**
Arthur is an alcoholic who has been selling pieces of junk to his sister and telling her that they are valuable family heirlooms. Arthur and Leila usually meet in the park for their exchanges, and here, the pigeons that patrol the ground nearby remind Arthur of the birds that they used to keep on the roof when they were children. Seriocomic.

BMSM94, 3.5 minutes
Arthur and Leila by Cherylene Lee

1675
Arthur, 64   **LA, Present**
Leila is desperate for her brother to seek help for his drinking and gambling. When she presents him with the business card of a highly-recommended therapist, Arthur demands that they engage in a role-playing game in which Leila is Arthur and Arthur is the doctor. The game turns serious when Arthur, as the doctor, reveals his despair over his condition. Dramatic.

BMSM94, 2.5 minutes
Arthur and Leila by Cherylene Lee

1676
Sugar Man, 30-50
A narrow street that clings to the end of the world on a barren strip of earth, World time 1948
Sugar Man is as street smart as they come. Here, he shares a tale with an important message. Seriocomic.

BMSM94, 2.5 minutes
Bailey's Cafe by Gloria Naylor

1677
Wendal, 30s   **Here and Now**
After a difficult bout in the hospital, Wendal returns home where he hopes to find the strength to fight his illness. When his mother discovers he has AIDS, she flies into a rage and demands that he pray to God for forgiveness. Here, Wendal reacts to his mother's condemnation with anger and frustration. Dramatic.

BMSM94, 3 minutes
Before It Hits Home by Cheryl L. West

1678
Patrick, 40s
A private school for boys, Present

Here, Patrick addresses the student body on the subject of kissing. Seriocomic.
BMSM94, 2.5 minutes
Body Politic by Steve Murray

1679
Scott, 30
A private school for boys, Present
Scott, a recovering alcoholic, has chosen to return to his prep school and confront Patrick, his former teacher and mentor upon whom he had a terrible crush. Here, he reveals his thoughts and feelings to Patrick. Dramatic.
BMSM94, 3 minutes
Body Politic by Steve Murray

1680
Jacky, 20s   **Here and Now**
Following several years of drifting, Jacky returns to his former lover's apartment and discovers her sleeping on the bed. Here, he greets the sleeping woman and proceeds to "catch up." Seriocomic.
BMSM94, 5.5 minutes
Careless Love by Len Jenkin

1681
Spin Milton, 40-50   **Here and Now**
Here, a road-weary lounge singer raps with the audience. Seriocomic.
BMSM94, 2.5 minutes
Careless Love by Len Jenkin

1682
Old Wilder, an old man   **Here and Now**
Here, Old Wilder shares a special memory of his mother. Dramatic.
BMSM94, 1.5 minutes
Cross-Dressing in the Depression by Erin Cressida Wilson

1683
Augustus, 20s
A plantation in antebellum South Carolina
Augustus has lived an unusual life. He first belonged to a sea captain who treated him as his own son. During those years Augus-tus was able to travel the Atlantic and Caribbean, learning what he could along the way. He has since been purchased by a plantation in South Carolina where he tells his fellow slaves the story of the violent uprisings that gave birth to the Republic of Haiti. Dramatic.
BMSM94, 7 minutes
The Darker Face of the Earth by Rita Dove

1684
Frank, 40s   **Here and Now**
Frank is a quiet man who writes a column on

gardening for a free newspaper. Follow-ing a minor exchange of words with someone who refuses a copy of the paper, Frank is reminded of his early interest in insects. Seriocomic.
BMSM94, 3.5 minutes
The Ends of the Earth by Morris Panych

1685
Walker, 40s   **Here and Now**
Walker has convinced himself that a stranger is following him with the worst of intentions. Here, this most paranoid individual describes his very unlucky life. Seriocomic.
BMSM94, 7 minutes
The Ends of the Earth by Morris Panych

1686
Jorge, 20s
The Amazon rain forest, Present
After spending a month or so in the jungle, Jorge is beginning to gain insight into his life. Here, he contemplates his life in the United States as he waits for night to fall. Dramatic.
BMSM94, 6.5 minutes
Entries by Bernardo Solano

1687
Barn, 30s   **Here and Now**
Barn's mother was killed by a wing that had fallen off a statue of an angel. Since that day, wings have become the central theme of his art. Here, Barn does his best to explain his obsession to the woman he loves. Dramatic.
BMSM94, 2 minutes
Floating Rhoda and the Glue Man by Eve Ensler

1688
Kiyoshi "Sam" Yamamoto, 60-70
A hospital room, Present
In 1945, Sam was a soldier in the 522nd Artillery of the 442, a division that helped to liberate Dachau. On that day in April, Sam saved the life of Leon Ehrlich, one of the many thousands of prisoners set free by the allies. Years later, the two men meet again in the United States and become best friends. It is now 50 years after the day that fate brought them together in Germany, and Leon is dying in the hospital. Here, Sam pays a final visit and gives his old friend a very special gift. Dramatic.
BMSM94, 2 minutes
The Gate of Heaven by Lane Nishikawa and Victor Talmadge

1689
Rev. Neal Hoffman, 50s   **England, Present**
Rev. Hoffman and his entourage have arrived in England with the intent of purchasing Hartstone, the home of a missionary family

and sight of a supposed miracle. Here, the Reverend entertains Hartstone's skeptical owner with the story of how his miserable life was saved by the Lord. Dramatic.
BMSM94, 3.5 minutes
Grace by Doug Lucie

1690
Harry, 30-40   **Here and Now**
Harry's marriage is on the rocks. Lack of communication is the primary source of their marital woes as can be seen when Harry erupts in a stream-of-consciousness tirade following a shopping expedition. Seriocomic.
BMSM94, 4 minutes
The Harry and Sam Dialogues by Karen Ellison

1691
Harry, 30-40   **Here and Now**
Driven by loneliness and despair, Harry's wife has turned to his best friend, Sam, for love. When Harry realizes that his neglect of Marge has pushed her away and cost him a friend in the bargain, he makes an honest effort to mend his ways. Here, he runs into Sam at their favorite watering hole and does his best to say that he doesn't want to throw away 20 years of friendship because of one mistake. Seriocomic.
BMSM94, 2 minutes
The Harry and Sam Dialogues by Karen Ellison

1692
Dorian, 30   **A hospital room, 1969**
Dorian's best friend has informed him that the mob wants him dead. Before he takes it on the lam, he pays a final visit to his comatose grandmother in the hospital. Dramatic.
BMSM94, 9 minute
The House on Lake Desolation by Brian Christopher Williams

1693
Leslie, 29   **Here and Now**
Years and sit-coms later, Leslie suddenly finds himself longing to return to the South. His experience as a television star has provided him with the insight that has finally made it possible for him to embrace his homeland along with all of its quirky characters and imperfections. Seriocomic.
BMSM94, 6.5 minute
Hysterical Blindness and Other Southern Tragedies That Have Plagued My Life Thus Far by Leslie Jordan

1694
John Dory, 20-30
The middle of the Pacific Ocean, Present
John has been lost at sea for nearly four years.

He finally manages to climb aboard a small boat inhabited by Mary, a young woman who has been drifting for nearly as long. Here, John tells Mary his story. Dramatic.
BMSM94, 6 minutes
John Dory by Craig Wright

1695
Mr. Miranda, 40s   **Hoboken, NJ, Present**
When a student approaches him for romantic advice, Mr. Miranda automatically (and incorrectly) assumes that the young lady has a crush on him. Seriocomic.
BMSM94, 2.5 minutes
Julie Johnson by Wendy Hammond

1696
Michael Rowen, 35
A crude cabin in southeastern Kentucky, 1776
Michael has carved a home for himself out of the Kentucky wilderness and has kidnapped a young Cherokee woman with the intention of making her his wife and mother of his heir. When she tries to escape, Michael severs the tendon of her heel, so that she can never run again. Here, he takes a moment to contemplate the violence with which he has forged his life. Dramatic.
BMSM94, 6 minutes
The Kentucky Cycle by Robert Schenkkan

1697
Hunter, 60s   **Here and Now**
During a conversation with an employee, Hunter reveals his prejudice and ignorance. Dramatic.
BMSM94, 3 minutes
The Last Time We Saw Her by Jane Anderson

1698
Austin, 50s   **Boston, Present**
Austin has been reunited with Ruth, a woman with whom he had a fling 30 years earlier. Here, he tells her of his divorce and the depression that followed. Seriocomic.
BMSM94, 2.5 minutes
Later Life by A.R. Gurney

1699
Burke, 40s   **Here and Now**
Here, Burke describes his first meeting with Mia, the woman he loves. Seriocomic.
BMSM94, 3 minutes
Life Sentences by Richard Nelson

1700
Tony, 40-50
Driven by feelings of guilt, Tony here confesses his feelings of love for another woman to his

wife. Seriocomic.
BMSM94, 13 minutes
Love Always by Renée Taylor and Joseph Bologna

1701
Man, 30s   **Here and Now**
Here a deformed Man reveals an interesting if
sad aspect of his relationship with his father.
Dramatic.
BMSM94, 3 minutes
Mambo Quasimodo by Steven Tannenbaum

1702
Man, 30s   **Here and Now**
Here, the hunchback discusses the death of his
mother. Seriocomic.
BMSM94, 4 minutes
Mambo Quasimodo by Steven Tannenbaum

1703
Jason, 30-40   **Corinth, ancient times**
Jason has foolishly forsaken his first wife,
Medea, in order to marry the daughter of
Creon. Driven mad with rage, Medea kills
their two young sons in a horrifying quest for
revenge. When Jason discovers her crime, he
curses her from the palace battlements.
Dramatic.
BMSM94, 3 minutes
Medea by Euripides, tr. by Alistair Elliot

1704
Ralph, 50s   **Here and Now**
Ralph's best friend Andy is on his deathbed.
Here, Ralph shares some insight into Andy
and soccer. Seriocomic.
BMSM94, 3 minutes
Moonlight by Harold Pinter

1705
Joseph, 20-30   **Here and Now**
Here, the suffering Joseph relates a strange
dream about Susan, the woman he loves, to his
psychiatrist. Seriocomic.
BMSM94, 5 minutes
My Funny Jarvik-7 by Richard Strand

1706
Joseph, 20-30   **Here and Now**
Joseph here describes the night he first met
Susan, the woman who broke his heart.
Seriocomic.
BMSM94, 3 minutes
My Funny Jarvik-7 by Richard Strand

1707
Howie, 40s   **Here and Now**
Here, Howie shares an unhappy memory of
his first day of high school. Seriocomic.

BMSM94, 2.5 minutes
1969 or Howie Takes a Trip by Tina Landau

1708
Walter, 20-30   **India, Present**
Walter's mother, Katherine, is traveling to
India on a quest to relieve her feelings of guilt
and grief over his death. Here, Walter watches
over Katherine from the wing of the airplane
and tells the story of his murder to Ganesha,
the Hindu elephant god. Dra-matic.
BMSM94, 4 minutes
A Perfect Ganesh by Terrence McNally

1709
James, 60-70   **Here and Now**
Here, James visits his wife's grave and tells her
that he thinks he is about to die. Dramatic.
BMSM94, 9 minutes
Perpetual Care by Jocelyn Beard

1710
Royal Boy, 14   **A police station, Present**
To prove himself to the Police Boys, a violent
gang, Royal Boy selects to rape and possibly
murder a woman he has grabbed in the park.
Following the rape, Royal Boy is filled with
feelings of remorse for the fact that everything
nice gets destroyed one way or another. Here,
he tells his victim the story of the birth of his
son. Dramatic.
BMSM94, 4 minutes
Police Boys by Marion Isaac McClinton

1711
Arthur, 50-60   **Here and Now**
When his wife informs him about Todd's dis-
ease, Arthur retreats into denial and memories
of happier times. Dramatic.
BMSM94, 1.5 minutes
Pterodactyls by Nicky Silver

1712
Vinetti, 40-50   **Here and Now**
Dr. Max Ziggerman specializes in the treatment of adult survivors of satanic ritualistic
abuse. Max's wife is dying of cancer, and when
the patient with whom he is currently working
suddenly declares that the cult now possesses
his wife's soul, he rushes to the hospital to find
that she has died. Max doubts that Detective
Vinetti will believe his claim of cult involvement in his wife's death, but here, Vinetti surprises him. Dramatic.
BMSM94, 3.5 minutes
Satan in Wonderland by Ron Mark

1713
Max, 40s   **Here and Now**

Max's patient, a terrified woman with multiple personalities, warns him that the cult that ritualistically tortured her is too strong for them to fight. Here, Max reminds her that humankind has survived a greater evil than a cult, and will always continue to do so. Dramatic.

BMSM94, 8 minutes
Satan in Wonderland by Ron Mark

1714
Aleksii Antedilluvianovich Prelapsarianov, 90s
Moscow, March 1985
Here, a man who's seen it all cautions against radical social and political change. Dramatic.
BMSM94, 4 minutes
Slavs! by Tony Kushner

1715
Yegor Tremens Rodent, 50s   Siberia, 1992
When Rodent is confronted by a woman whose daughter has been deformed by her exposure to toxic materials, he sidesteps the issue and tries to woo her political sympathy. Dramatic.
BMSM94, 3 minutes
Slavs! by Tony Kushner

1716
Oscar Wilde, 27   Toronto, 1882
Oscar Wilde has hired Stephen, a black manservant, to accompany him on his lecture tour of North America. Stephen was freed from slavery by the Union Army and may or may not be wanted for the murder of a former slave owner in Baltimore. Wilde has discovered a book on slavery as well as some radical political pamphlets among Stephen's things which have given him a new insight into the question of rights for blacks. Here, he shares his feelings with Stephen. Dramatic.
BMSM94, 4.5 minutes
Stephen and Mr. Wilde by Jim Bartley

1717
Harry, 50s
A house on the Ottawa River, 1972
Harry's secret life has finally caught up with him. A closet homosexual, Harry has served as Canada's Ambassador to Egypt, Mexico, Greece and the Soviet Union. His young Russian lover has been murdered, and Harry is the prime suspect. Here, Harry shares an important moment with his wife and best friend, Marian. Dramatic.
BMSM94, 2.5 minutes
The Stillborn Lover by Timothy Findley

1718
Pen Tip, 20-30
Pen Tip was once a radiologist but now serves Uncle Mao under the brutal reign of the Khmer Rouge. He obsesses on his fellow laborer, Dr. Haing Ngor, and in a fit of envy, reveals the doctor's identity to the Khmer Rouge. Here, Pen Tip describes Ngor's first round of torture. Dramatic.
BMSM94, 4 minutes
The Survivor: A Cambodian Odyssey by Jon Lipsky

1719
Brady, 40   Here and Now
When Dr. Brady appears before the members of the review board that will decide his fate, he explains that the incident in question—an alleged sexual attack on a male student—occurred when he had blacked out from too much alcohol. Since, as he claims, he was not aware of anything happening at that point in time, he feels that he isn't responsible for his actions. Dramatic.
BMSM94, 5 minutes
The Trap by Frank Manley

1720
David, 20
David has never gotten along with his strict father. His visits home from college become more and more strained until it becomes quite obvious that something has to give. During a particularly charged Easter visit, David finally confronts his father with the following observations about their relationship. Dramatic.
BMSM94, 3 minutes
Trophies by John J. Wooten

1721
Chief/Retiree, 60s
Here, the Chief closes his speech with some thoughts on murders. Dramatic.
BMSM94, 4.5 minutes
What Cops Know by Kenn L.D. Frandsen, based on the book by Connie Fletcher

1722
Simone, 20-30
An open, fluid space evocative of a burnt-out bayou, Present
Jamie has been killed in an unspecified war. Following his funeral, Simone contemplates the mess left behind those who had come to the house to pay their respects as well as her love for Jamie. Dramatic.
BWSM94, 9 minutes
Alchemy of Desire/Dead-Man's Blues by Caridad Svich

1723
Simone, 20-30
An open, fluid space evocative of a burnt-out bayou, Present
Simone has been driven to the edge by haunting visitations for Jamie. Here, she burns his clothes in an effort to break from the past. Dramatic.
BWSM94, 7 minutes
Alchemy of Desire/Dead-Man's Blues by Caridad Svich

1724
Jos Lubenowich, 17   **Here and Now**
While playing a game of Trivial Pursuit with her friend, Jos relates the story of her meeting with Tallulah Bankhead. Seriocomic.
BWSM94, 3 minutes
The Autobiography of Aiken Fiction by Kate Moira Ryan

1725
Jesse Bell, 40s
A narrow street, 1948
Here, Jessie reveals her life's tragedy as well as her love affair with heroin. Dramatic.
BWSM94, 3 minutes
Bailey's Cafe by Gloria Naylor

1726
Reba, 50s   **Here and Now**
When Wendal comes home to fight his illness, Reba cannot accept him. She can't even bring herself to touch the things that he has touched. Here, Reba blames Wendal for the death of everything she ever loved. Dramatic.
BWSM94, 2 minutes
Before It Hits Home by Cheryl L. West

1727
Kath, 30s   **A classroom, Present**
Here, Kath conducts an interesting class discussion on "The Tempest." Seriocomic.
BWSM94, 3 minutes
Body Politic by Steve Murray

1728
Marlene, 40-50   **Here and Now**
Here, a road-weary lounge singer raps with the audience. Seriocomic.
BWSM94, 2 minutes
Careless Love by Len Jenkin

1729
Nuala, 20s   **Ireland, Present**
Following a passionate lovemaking session, Nuala tells Terry, her lover, about a poem that she's working on. Dramatic.
BWSM94, 2 minutes
The Cavalcaders by Billy Roche

1730
Sabrina, 50s   **A funeral parlor, Present**
Sabrina's best friend, Connie, has died of a heart attack. Here, Sabrina shares a last moment together with the coffin. Serio-comic.
BWSM94, 3 minutes
Connie and Sabrina in Waiting by Sandra Marie Vargo

1731
Amalia, 20s
A plantation in antebellum South Carolina
When her husband sees that the baby is clearly half black, he threatens to find the slave who has "offended" Amalia and have him whipped to death. Here, Amalia corrects his assumption of rape. Dramatic.
BWSM94, 3 minutes
The Darker Face of Earth by Rita Dove

1732
Bianca, 20s   **The Palace of Cyprus, ages ago**
Bianca has ben recrafted as a lusty prostitute in this retelling of Othello. Here, she entertains Desdemona and Emilia with a tale of one of her quirkier johns. Seriocomic.
BWSM94, 3.5 minutes
Desdemona by Paula Vogel

1733
Emilia, 30s   **The Palace of Cyprus, ages ago**
When Desdemona discovers that Cassio has given her handkerchief to Bianca, she knows that she's in big trouble with Othello. She pleads her case to Emilia, not knowing that it was she who took the handkerchief in the first place. The two share several glasses of wine, and Emilia reveals the following insight into the relationship between married people. Dramatic. Seriocomic.
BWSM94, 4 minutes
Desdemona by Paula Vogel

1734
Willy, any age   **Here and Now**
Willy is an unusual woman who seems to be the proprietress of a ramshackle hotel on an island at the end of the world. Willy doesn't seem to experience the same reality as the other characters in the play, and here tells two of her guests how she happened to arrive at the hotel so many years ago. Seriocomic.
BWSM94, 3 minutes
The Ends of the Earth by Morris Panych

1735
Clara, 20-30   **LA, Present**
In her lowly capacity of production assistant, Clara has seen it all. Here, she offers her im-

pression of Los Angeles to one of the show's new writers. Seriocomic.
BWSM94, 3 minutes
The Family of Mann by Theresa Rebeck

1736
Clara, 20-30   **LA, Present**
Clara is slowly turning into an angel. As such, she here delivers her opinion on the USA. Seriocomic.
BWSM94, 2 minutes
The Family of Mann by Theresa Rebeck

1737
Georgeanne, 30s
A wedding reception in Knoxville, TN, Present
When Georgeanne sees the man with whom she had a flaming affair in college at a friend's wedding she is bombarded with memories—most of them unpleasant. Seriocomic.
BWSM94, 2.5 minutes
Five Women Wearing the Same Dress by Alan Ball

1738
Mindy, 30s
A wedding reception in Knoxville, TN, Present
Mindy is a lesbian whose lover has been specifically uninvited to her brother's wedding. This, when combined with the usual catastrophes and a good amount of booze, leads Mindy to the following melancholy observations. Seriocomic.
BWSM94, 1.5 minutes
Five Women Wearing the Same Dress by Alan Ball

1739
Rhoda, 30s   **Here and Now**
Rhoda is someone who has been hurt by life. Here, she tries to recall the time before the pain. Seriocomic.
BWSM94, 2 minutes
Floating Rhoda and the Glue Man by Eve Ensler

1740
Miss Leah, 73
Outside the all-black town of Nicodemus, Kansas, 1898
Miss Leah has lived more life than most women her age, and accumulated more heartache than many. Here, she describes her first meeting with James, the man she loved, when they were both being used as breeding stock on a southern plantation. Dramatic.
BWSM94, 2.5 minutes
Flyin' West by Pearl Cleage

1741
Miss Leah, 73
Outside the all-black town of Nicodemus, Kansas, 1898
Here, Miss Leah describes her horror of having her babies taken from her at birth and sold to neighboring plantations. She goes on to describe a bit of her life with James following the Civil War and of her need to go west. Dramatic.
BWSM94, 3 minutes
Flyin' West by Pearl Cleage

1742
Ruth, 50s   **England, Present**
Ruth's early years were spent in Africa with her missionary parents. Their mission a failure, the family returns to England, where Ruth's sister, Grace, falls victim to a mysterious fatal illness. Grace's death becomes the subject of a book written by their mother in which she details the event with divine visitations. Years later, an American evangelist who is a devotee of Grace's story makes an offer on Ruth's house with the intention of making it the vanguard of his European mission. Driven by her contempt for evangelism, Ruth is forced to finally reveal the truth about Grace's death. Dramatic.
BWSM94, 5 minutes
Grace by Doug Lucie

1743
Ella O'Casey, 18-20   **Dublin, Present**
Here, Ella prepares herself for her wedding. A young woman madly in love, she cannot stop thinking about the handsome young soldier—a drummer in the King's Liverpool Regiment—who she is about to marry. Seriocomic.
BWSM94, 2 minutes
Grandchild of Kings by Harold Prince

1744
Terry, 20-30   **Here and Now**
Terry hasn't gotten a role in a while, so when the opportunity to read for a lead in a film comes along, she embellishes certain aspects of her past in order to get the part. Seriocomic.
BWSM94, 5.5 minutes
Hand to Hand by Max Mayer

1745
Eloise, 60-70   **A hospital room, 1969**
Eloise was brought to the hospital when her spine collapsed and has been comatose ever since. Here, she begins to come to, but clearly thinks that she is dead. Dramatic.
BWSM94, 5 minutes
The House on Lake Desolation by Brian Christopher Williams

1746
Hazel, 40s   **Here and Now**
Here, Hazel angrily confronts her son, who has turned to a life of petty thievery, and does her best to impress upon him the transitory nature of our lives. Dramatic.
BWSM94, 3.5 minutes
Hunters of the Soul by Marion Isaac McClinton

1747
Hazel, 40s   **Here and Now**
Hazel's ex-husband, a man with whom she had a very complex relationship, has just died. When Sylvester refuses to wear a tie that she has selected for him to wear to the funeral parlor, Hazel unleashes the full fury of her grief and rage. Dramatic.
BWSM94, 3.5 minutes
Hunters of the Soul by Marion Isaac McClinton

1748
Mary, 20-30
The middle of the Pacific Ocean, Present
Mary has been lost at sea for three long years and has recently lost her only companion. When a strange young man climbs aboard her little boat, she tells him the sad tale of how she came to be all alone at sea. Dramatic.
BWSM94, 3.5 minutes
John Dory by Craig Wright

1749
Morning Star, 16
A crude cabin in southeastern Kentucky, 1776
Morning Star is a Cherokee woman who has been kidnapped from her tribe by the brutal Michael Rowen for the express purpose of providing him with an heir. As she suffers through the agony of childbirth, Morning Star calls in desperation to her lost people. Dramatic.
BWSM94, 7 minutes
The Kentucky Cycle by Robert Schenkkan

1750
Fran, 40s   **Here and Now**
Fran's boss hasn't a clue as to why Fran wants everyone in the office to know that she's gay. Here, she does her best to explain it to him. Dramatic.
BWSM94, 1.5 minutes
The Last Time We Saw Her by Jane Anderson

1751
Mia, 20s   **Here and Now**
Here, a thoughtful young woman speaks of her love of gardening. Dramatic.
BWSM94, 3 minutes
Life Sentences by Richard Nelson

1752
Mother, 30-40   **Here and Now**
Just before her daughter's Sweet 16 party, this woman takes a moment to offer the excited young girl some depressing advice. Dramatic.
BWSM94, 4 minutes
Love Allways by Renée Taylor and Joseph Bologna

1753
Barbara, 20-30   **Here and Now**
Here, an exhausted and ecstatic woman greets her child for the first time. Seriocomic.
BWSM94, 5 minutes
Love Allways by Renée Taylor and Joseph Bologna

1754
Medea, 30s   **Corinth, ancient times**
Medea has sacrificed everything for Jason, who has now announced his intention to marry another woman and banish Medea. Driven by jealous rage, Medea here contemplates taking the life of her two young sons to punish Jason for his betrayal. Dramatic.
BWSM94, 6 minutes
Medea by Euripides, tr. by Alistair Elliot

1755
Lydia, 25
The night of August 20, 1991. The Ukrain Hotel, Moscow. The Coup.
Lydia is engaged to Mikhail, who is hosting a 60th birthday celebration for himself at the Ukrain Hotel. When she finds herself to be surrounded by Mikhail's bitter ex-wives, she describes her love for him in the following account of their first night together. Dramatic.
BWSM94, 3 minutes
Misha's Party by Richard Nelson and Alexander Gelman

1756
Katia, 40-50
The night of August 20, 1991. The Ukrain Hotel, Moscow. The Coup.
Mikhail has invited all his ex-wives and their husbands to attend his 60th birthday celebration. Here, his first wife, Katia, shares the sad story of his cruel desertion of her. Dramatic.
BWSM94, 4.5 minutes
Misha's Party by Richard Nelson and Alexander Gelman

1757
Maria, 50s   **Here and Now**
Here, a woman about whom we know very little, shares happy memories from a more carefree time in her life. Dramatic.
BWSM94, 3 minutes
Moonlight by Harold Pinter

1758
Sandra, 20-30   **London, Present**
Here, a policewoman on her way up the career
ladder bemoans the endless amount of paper-
work required to perform her job. Seriocomic.
BWSM94, 2 minutes
Murmuring Judges by David Hare

1759
Susan Miller, 40s   **Here and Now**
When she drops her youngest son off at col-
lege, Susan is reminded of the panic that she
felt on the day that she dropped him off at day
camp for the first time. Dramatic.
BWSM94, 3 minutes
My Left Breast by Susan Miller

1760
Rebeka, 18   **Here and Now**
Rebeka has been in love with Ira ever since
they were kids sneaking Margaritas when their
parents weren't looking. Now, they both are
facing the uncertain future that all college
freshmen must face. On a last evening together
before leaving for their respective schools, Ira
complains that it won't be possible for him to
follow his dream of becoming a filmmaker. In
response, Rebeka shares a story her father
used to tell her when she was a little girl.
Seriocomic.
BWSM94, 3 minutes
One Man's Dance by Aaron Levy

1761
Annette, a young woman
Annette has just received a rejection letter
from an editor. When her lover teases her
about it, she unleashes the following torrent of
anger and frustration. Dramatic.
BWSM94, 3 minutes
Paddywack by Daniel Magee

1762
Margaret, 40-50   **India, Present**
Margaret and Katherine have traveled to
India, each on a separate quest of spiritual lib-
eration. Margaret hopes to escape from the
grim reality of the lump she has recently discovered in her breast. The Hindu god,
Ganesha, has been monitoring their journey
and has appeared to Margaret in the guise of a
sympathetic Japanese tourist. Margaret finds
herself telling Ganesha about the lump, and
before she realizes what she's saying, she reveals a secret from her past that is darker and
deeper than the lump. Dramatic.
BWSM94, 8 minutes
A Perfect Ganesh by Terrence McNally

1763
Katherine, 40-50   **India, Present**
Katherine shares Margaret's journey to India
where she hopes to be able to escape the
haunting visions of her son who was murdered
in a gay-bashing incident. Here, Katherine
confesses her humble origins to Margaret and
tells the story of her courtship. Dramatic.
BWSM94, 4.5 minutes
A Perfect Ganesh by Terrence McNally

1764
An angel, 20-30   **Here and Now**
This angel has been sent to earth to observe the
death of James Delacroix. In human guise, the
angel has rented a room from James and has
become quite friendly with him. When they
share a cup of tea, James confesses his disappointment that his late wife never had an opportunity to know their grandchildren. Here,
the angel does her best to provide him with
some soul comfort. Dramatic.
BWSM94, 3 minutes
Perpetual Care by Jocelyn Beard

1765
Christie, 20-30
The Eleventh Avenue Rep. Theatre, Present
Christie has been locked in the theatre with
Monica, a rival actress, who uses their forced
time together to accuse Christie of using the-
atre as a place to assuage her vanity. Here, the
spirited Christie sets her straight. Seriocomic.
BWSM94, 4 minutes
Phantom Rep by Ben Alexander

1766
Emma, 20-30   **Here and Now**
Emma's fiancé, Tommy, has fallen in love with
her brother, Todd, who has AIDS. When
Emma discovers that Tommy has contracted
the virus from Todd, she shoots herself. Here,
Emma's ghost speaks to us from the hereafter.
Seriocomic.
BWSM94, 4.5 minutes
Pterodactyls by Nicky Silver

1767
Katherina Serafima Gleb, 20s
Moscow, March 1985
Katherina is a night security guard at the Pan-
Soviet Archives For The Study of Cerebro-
Cephalognomical Historico-Biolog-ical Materialism.
(Hew!) Here, she fantasizes about making her
job a bit more (?) glamorous. Seriocomic.
BWSM94, 2 minutes
Slavs! by Tony Kushner

1768
Bonfila Bezhukhovona Bonch-Bruevich, 30s
Siberia, 1992
As one who treats children's cancers, Bonfila is an unhappy witness to the devastating effects of exposing large portions of Russia's population to toxic materials of one kind or another. Here, she angrily confronts a government official. Dramatic.
BWSM94, 2 minutes
Slavs! by Tony Kushner

1769
Mrs. Shastlivyi Domik, 40s
Moscow, Siberia, 1992
Mrs. Shastlivyi Domik's daughter has been deformed by her exposure to toxic materials. When she demands compensation for her plight from a government official, he sidesteps the issue by trying to convert her to a new political movement. Here, the furious woman wastes no time in telling him exactly what she thinks of him. Dramatic.
BWSM94, 1.5 minutes
Slavs! by Tony Kushner

1770
Brenda, 20s
Brenda and her friend Allan have traveled to Nick and Sara's upstate home for Christmas. Sara is shocked to discover Brenda's pregnancy is the result of a rape. When she asks Brenda if she's angry about her situation, she receives the following philosophical reply. Dramatic.
BWSM94, 2 minutes
Snowing at Delphi by Catherine Butterfield

1771
Diana, 20-30
A house on the Ottawa River, 1972
Diana's father, Harry, has just been recalled from his post as Canadian ambassador to Moscow following the mysterious death of a young Russian. When Diana finds out that the Russian was her father's male lover, she angrily confronts him with the lie of his life. Dramatic.
BWSM94, 3 minutes
The Stillborn Lover by Timothy Findley

1772
Marian, 50s
A house on the Ottawa River, 1972
Marian's daughter, Diana, has just discovered that her father, an ambassador in the Canadian diplomatic corps, is gay. Here, Marian confesses her strange role in Harry's covert life. Dramatic.
BWSM94, 5 minutes
The Stillborn Lover by Timothy Findley

1773
Stony, 20-30   **Here and Now**
Bone has confessed to sleeping around with white women. Here, Stony asks him if their relationship would change if she were white. Dramatic.
BWSM94, 2 minutes
Stones and Bones by Marion Isaac McClinton

1774
Jessica, 30   **Here and Now**
Jessica has been involved with commitment-shy Jeffrey for many years. Following a Sunday drive, Jessica returns home and tells one of her roommates that she thinks there's been a major breakthrough in Jeffrey's fear of matrimony. Dramatic.
BWSM94, 4 minutes
Sunday on the Rocks by Theresa Rebeck

1775
Elly, 30   **Here and Now**
Elly has just discovered that she is pregnant. Here, she passionately defends her decision to have an abortion to her pro-life roommate. Dramatic.
BWSM94, 1.5 minutes
Sunday on the Rocks by Theresa Rebeck

1776
Huoy My Chang, 20s
The rice fields of Cambodia, 1970s
Huoy is offered a bit of sugar by Pen Tip, a man who once turned her husband in to the Khmer Rouge. After an internal moral debate, Huoy gives in and eats the sugar. Here, she describes her delight in its sweet taste. Dramatic.
BWSM94, 2.5 minutes
The Survivor: A Cambodian Odyssey by Jon Lipsky

1777
Anne, 20s   **NYC, Present**
Anne's husband keeps her tied up in their apartment. When she finally manages to escape, she decides to sell her story to a television agent. The agent is very interested in Anne's story and has put her up in an expensive hotel. Here, she speaks of her empty new existence. Dramatic.
BWSM94, 3.5 minutes
The Treatment by Martin Crimp

1778
Sophia La Cruz, 25
An apartment in Vladivostok, Present
Sophia plays the title role in "Forever Angelina," a Mexican soap opera that is the number one show in Russia. During an arduous 10-city personal appearance tour that her

manager insisted she make, Sophia is kidnapped by a crazed fan in Vladivostok. When she realizes that her captor is relatively harmless, Sophia unleashes a passionate torrent of anti-Russian sentiment, none of which she actually means. Dramatic.
BWSM94, 5 minutes
Vladivostok Blues by Jocelyn Beard

1779
Amelia, 30-40   **A laboratory**
A famous lost aviator. Amelia describes her obsession with flight.
BWSM95, 3 minutes
Amnesia by Robert Anasi

1780
Celeste, 20s   **New York City**
A guardian angel. An angelic visitor begs forgiveness from one of her charges.
BWSM95, 2 minutes
Blink of an Eye by Jeremy Dobrish

1781
Jo-Lynne, 30s   **Here and Now**
A woman desperately seeking to avenge her husband's death. A dispute between neighbors ends in bloodshed, and the grieving Jo-Lynne becomes obsessed with finding someone to kill the man who killed her husband. She finally approaches Chick, a man that she knew years before, and offers him money to execute her neighbor. When Chick refuses, Jo-Lynne reminds him of something that he once said that left her with the impression that he could easily take a life.
BWSM95, 4 minutes
bliss by Benjamin Bettenbender

1782
Dana   **Dusk**
A jogger at beach. Dana attempts conversation with jogger, Willy—he jogs off—she responds.
BWSM95, 2 minutes
By the Sea by Terrence McNally

1783
Maddy, 42   **The suburban northeast**
A woman who has picked up a man at a bar, intelligent and perceptive. Following a night out on the town, Maddy has brought home John, a frightening volatile ex-Marine who turns violent when their sex play goes awry. When John threatens her physically, Maddy demonstrates a streak of nihilism that makes her fearless.
BWSM95, 2 minutes
A Candle in the Window by Tom Gilroy

1784
Alice, 30s   **America in the 50s and 60s**
An economically frustrated woman. The success of her friends drives Alice into a fit of pique while sharing perfume in the powder room.
BWSM95, 2.5 minutes
A Cheever Evening by A.R. Gurney

1785
Christina, 30-40   **America in the 50s and 60s**
A driven over-achiever. Christina's high level of energy helps to distance her from the empty nature of her life. She describes her technique for relaxation.
BWSM95, 2 minutes
A Cheever Evening by A.R. Gurney

1786
Han, 20-25   **A prison**
A North American Native. Han is being held in a mysterious prison with no true knowledge of her captors or the crime with which she has been charged. To help pass time, she and her fellow prisoners play a game in which each person tries to create a movie script based on three pre-assigned words. The following western fantasy is what Han is able to make from "poachers," "clinical" and "dig."
BWSM95, 3 minutes
Collateral Damage by Mansel Robinson

1787
Jeanne, 30-35   **A prison**
Franco-Ontarian. Jeanne and her husband, Henry, have been held without charge for several weeks in a mysterious prison. The claustrophobic confines of their physical and emotional space is beginning to affect their relationship in a negative way. When Jeanne realizes that Henry still carries adolescent prejudice against Franco-Canadians in his heart, she does her best to punish him.
BWSM95, 2 minutes
Collateral Damage by Mansel Robinson

1788
Anne Marie Garrett, 30s   **Corporate offices**
A corporate VP. Anne Marie's authority has been usurped by a male co-worker. She bemoans the system that has led her to the "glass ceiling."
BWSM95, 4 minutes
Company Policy by Michael Ajakwe Jr.

1789
A. LaShaun Lee, 20-30   **Corporate offices**
A woman starting a new job. A very driven young black woman prepares to begin a new

job in white corporate America.
BWSM95, 6 minutes
Company Policy by Michael Ajakwe Jr.

1790
Crow, 40s   **Darwin, Australia, 1942**
A black woman fighting to keep her land. When Crow's white husband dies, she can not by law inherit the tin mine that they worked together. The determined woman approaches a local judge and demands that he make an appeal on her behalf. When he speaks coarsely of her mixed marriage, Crow angrily denounces his provincial racism.
BWSM95, 3.5 minutes
Crow by Louis Nowra

1791
Eve, 30s   **New York City**
Very excitable. Hyper. She has a tough edge. Wild. The bombastic Eve has been stood up by a man she has dated only once before. She offers a scathing review of their disastrous date.
BWSM95, 4 minutes
Dates and Nuts by Gary Lennon

1792
Eve, 30s   **New York City**
Very excitable. Hyper. She has a tough edge. Wild. Eve has finally met a man she just might be able to love. On their two week anniversary, Eve takes a chance and tells him of her life in the lonely years before they met.
BWSM95, 3 minutes
Dates and Nuts by Gary Lennon

1793
Nickie, 38   **Providence, 1994**
Nickie arrives at the home of her lover, Lonnie, and practices telling her husband she wants out.
BWSM95, 2 minutes
A Dead Man's Apartment by Edwin Allan Baker

1794
Laura, 30-40   **Cambridge, MA**
An unhappy spirit. Laura has been summoned back to earth by her husband, who fancies himself a modern Faust; sacrificing all to be reunited with his one true love. Laura angrily confronts Peter with the fact that she died childless—at his insistence.
BWSM95, 3.5 minutes
Demons by Robert Brustein

1795
Madeline, 30s   **Here and Now**
A good blue-collar Catholic girl raised in Queens who made the long trip into Manhattan

to go to NYU so she could have an interesting life. Madeline takes a moment to confront a statue of the Virgin Mary with the fact that she hasn't been able to forgive her for abandoning her in a time of great need.
BWSM95, 3.5 minutes
Dog Opera by Constance Congdon

1796
Bernice, 60s   **Here and Now**
A tough old broad; irascible and matter-of-fact. Bernice has fallen in her bathroom. She contemplates her predicament before calling for help.
BWSM95, 2.5 minutes
Dog Opera by Constance Congdon

1797
Lil, 50-60
A summer cottage in Rhode Island, 1960s
A woman caring for her husband, a stroke victim. Lil and Peter have returned to their beach house the summer following Peter's stroke. Lil does her best to catch Peter up on family news.
BWSM95, 5 minutes
Down By The Ocean by P.J. Barry

1798
Celina, 20-30   **Here and Now**
A cigar-smoking Latina hedonist. Celina has struggled to stay "clean" ever since rehab. The passionate young woman describes the experience that led her back to heroin use.
BWSM95, 3 minutes
Drive Like Jackson Pollock by Steven Tanenbaum

1799
Dancer   **The North Pole**
A reindeer. When Santa is accused of sexual misconduct with Vixen, her sister reindeer, the tabloid press quickly descends upon the other reindeer for their comments. Dancer shares her favorite Santa story.
BWSM95, 4 minutes
The Eight Reindeer Monologues by Jeff Goode

1800
Emma Miller, 19   **Hospital, intensive care**
A birth mother. Emma describes seeing the father of her son in a bar.
BWSM95, 1.5 minutes
Emma's Child by Kristine Thatcher

1801
Jean Farrell, 40   **Hospital, intensive care**
Adoptive mother. Jean is talking to the newborn, describing a school trip she had taken in tenth grade where she saw a mongoloid baby for the first time.

BWSM95, 2.5 minutes
Emma's Child by Kristine Thatcher

1802
Jean Farrell, 40   Hospital, doctor's office
Adoptive mother. Jean is arguing with Henry, her husband, to keep the mongoloid baby they would have adopted had it been born healthy. She declares her devotion to the child.
BWSM95, .5 minute
Emma's Child by Kristine Thatcher

1803
Jen, 20s   The US Virgin Islands, Present
A young woman considering moonlight. While sharing a romantic moment with a friend, Jen reveals her occasional fear of moonlight.
BWSM95, 1.5 minutes
Emotions by Robert Coles

1804
Woman Cop, 30-40   Here and Now
A down-to-earth police officer entertains a writer with a few anecdotes and some hard-won wisdom.
BWSM95, 4 minutes
Gunplay by Frank Higgins

1805
Joan, 30s   Here and Now
A woman struggling to define her sexuality. Joan confesses feelings of asexuality to a man that she is briefly considering going to bed with.
BWSM95, 2.5 minutes
Half-Court by Brian Silberman

1806
Rachel, 60s   Guilford, CT
A well-educated woman. Rachel has driven to Connecticut to be with Jessica, her ex-daughter-in-law, whose lover of eight years has died. The acerbic Rachel muses over the oddity of offering comfort to the woman who left her son.
BWSM95, 2.5 minutes
If We Are Women by Joanna McClelland Glass

1807
Kristen, 16   An AIDS clinic
Kristen has developed AIDS. Following a hospitalization for pneumonia, Kristen again vents her spleen upon her therapist.
BWSM95, 3 minutes
Jaws of Life by Jocelyn Beard

1808
Kristen, 16   An AIDS clinic

HIV positive. A one night stand has destroyed young Kristen's life. Here, she angrily confronts her clinic therapist with the fact of her forced mortality.
BWSM95, 3.5 minutes
Jaws of Life by Jocelyn Beard

1809
Sarah Ponsonby, 23   Ireland and Wales, 1778
A young woman seeking to escape from an abusive home. Sarah, an orphan, has been forced to live an unhappy life in the home of her lecherous uncle. When she is finally presented with an opportunity to escape, she confronts her uncle with the intention of blackmailing him for his crimes.
BWSM95, 1.5 minutes
Lady-Like by Laura Shamas

1810
Lady Eleanor Butler, 30s
Ireland and Wales, 1778
A woman escaping the brutal confines of an unhappy home. While in the process of fleeing intolerable lives in Ireland, Eleanor and Sarah travel by boat across the sea to Wales. When Sarah becomes seasick during a gale, Eleanor shares a story from her childhood that she hopes will provide some comfort.
BWSM95, 1.5 minutes
Lady-Like by Laura Shamas

1811
Max, 20   A college dorm room
A college junior trying to emerge from an affluent love-starved adolescence. Max and her mother, a minor film star, have never enjoyed an ideal relationship as may be seen in the young woman's following attempt to communicate via answering machine.
BWSM95, 10 minutes
Living in Paradise by Jack Gilhooley

1812
Linney, 30-40   New Zealand, Present
The oldest of three sisters mourning the death of their mother. When their mother dies, the sisters gather at the family home to settle the estate. Linney remembers a summer that was a turning point for their family.
BWSM95, 2 minutes
Love Knots by Vivienne Plumb

1813
Blossom, 20-30   New Zealand, Present
A woman mourning the loss of her mother and her childhood. Blossom has returned home following a long absence to help her sisters to settle their mother's estate. Blossom and her

mother parted on bad terms, and now she finds herself struggling to cope with unresolved feelings of guilt. She makes a project out of digging in the garden for a doll that her mother once buried there and when she finally discovers it, she begins to make a little sense of her memories.

BWSM95, 2.5 minutes
Love Knots by Vivienne Plumb

1814
Mona, 40   **Present, a dump**
Mona has decided to leave her husband, Roy, and head west to begin a new life—she tells Roy her thoughts.

BWSM95, 1 minute
Middle-Aged White Guys by Jane Martin

1815
Sky, 21
New York City during the Bush administration
A college student. A somewhat confused and vaguely nihilistic young woman does her best to explain why she voted for George Bush.

BWSM95, 2.5 minutes
The Monogamist by Christopher Kyle

1816
Rennie, 17   A liposuction clinic waiting room
A young woman tortured by her body image. An unhappy young woman details the origins of her yo-yoing weight and the complex emotions that rule her life.

BWSM95, 6 minutes
The Most Massive Woman Wins by Madeline George

1817
Sebastian, 30s
The Nevada/Utah desert near an abandoned nuclear testing site
A new age mystic. Sebastian has been reunited with Verdree, an old friend, under the trying circumstances of traveling cross-country on bicycle. Old grievances soon pop up, and before long the two women find themselves arguing over what it means to be black in America. Sebastian points out the difference between their two viewpoints.

BWSM95, 1.5 minutes
My Darling Gremlin by Greg Tate

1818
Julie, 30s   **Here and Now**
A woman whose health is compromised by the fact that her mother took the drug DES while she was pregnant. When she is released from the hospital following her surgery, Julie withdraws into the world of soap operas until her husband makes an attempt to bring her back to life.

BWSM95, 2 minutes
My Virginia by Darci Picoult

1819
Alice, 54   Farmhouse in western Connecticut
A woman whose lover has just committed suicide. When Harry commits suicide, Alice finds herself surrounded by his family, including his twin brother, to whom she reveals Harry's philandering ways.

BWSM95, 2 minutes
New England by Richard Nelson

1820
Martha, 20s   **Here and Now**
A young woman struggling to cope with her husband's unexpected disability. When Martha's husband, Singer, receives a serious head injury, the quality of their lives rapidly deteriorates. She verbally attacks Singer, who slips in and out of consciousness, and vents all of her frustration and rage.

BWSM95, 3 minutes
Our Own Marguerite by Robert Vivian

1821
Anne Bittenhand, 40s   **Here and Now**
A poet. Following a doomed affair with the American Poet Laureate, Anne has decided to take the final plunge. She prepares to take her own life.

BWSM95, 2.5 minutes
The Psychic Life of Savages by Amy Freed

1822
Anne Bittenhand, 40s   **Here and Now**
A poet. Anne is a dangerously self-absorbed woman who uses her poetry as an outlet for her psychoses. She has recently signed herself into a mental institution following an unpleasant scene at her daughter's birthday party and here complains to her husband, Tito, on the phone.

BWSM95, 1.5 minutes
The Psychic Life of Savages by Amy Freed

1823
Marie-Antoinette   **Paris, October 1793**
Former Queen of France. On the evening before she is to appear before the Revolutionary Tribunal, Marie-Antoinette is visited in her prison cell by Chauveneau-Lagarde, the idealistic young attorney who has been commanded to defend her. When he asks that she beg the Tribunal for a postponement, she flatly refuses and offers an explanation.

BWSM95, 2 minutes
The Queen's Knight by Frank Cossa

1824
Marie-Antoinette   Paris, October 1793
Former Queen of France. When the former
Queen is questioned by her attorney on the
evening before she is to appear before the
Tribunal, their dialogue eventually devolves
into a philosophical discussion of human
rights. When her attorney insists that people
are born with such rights, Marie-Antoinette is
quick to correct such a notion.
BWSM95, 2 minutes
The Queen's Knight by Frank Cossa

1825
Kate, 35
Chiswick, England December 1, 1888
A music hall entertainer. Kate has been hired
by James Kenneth Stephen, scholar and one-
time tutor of Prince Albert Victor, heir to the
throne of England. On a December evening,
James pays Kate to reenact the brutal deaths
suffered by the prostitutes slaughtered by the
killer known as Jack the Ripper for the benefit
of the Prince, who is implicated in the crimes.
Kate confronts the Prince with the most gruesome death of Catherine Eddowes.
BWSM95, 3.5 minutes
Saucy Jack by Sharon Pollock

1826
Woman, 20-30   Here and Now
Recently discovered her birth mother. Woman
details her search for her biological parents
and goes on to explain how it has affected her
eating habits.
BWSM95, 7 minutes
Self-Defense by Michael P. Scasserra

1827
Robin, 20
A New England college campus, 1990
A young woman delivering the valedictory
speech at her commencement. Robin does her
best to make sense of her four years as an un-
dergraduate.
BWSM95, 2.5 minutes
Sophistry by Jonathan Marc Sherman

1828
Woman, 40-50   Here and Now
A woman shares her plans for a facelift with a
television audience.
BWSM95, 4.5 minutes
Talk/Show by Michael P. Scasserra

1829
Arden Shingles, 30s   Southern CA, Present
Arden teaches workshops and seminars on
self-defense. She "works" a crowd.

BWSM95, 1.5 minutes
*Tough Choices For the New Century by Jane
Anderson*

1830
Dorothy Trowbridge, 30s
A New England College town, 1936
Wealthy and disturbed, Dorothy seeks deliver-
ance from the demons of her past in the care of
Dr. Hatrick, a psychiatrist. After months of
fruitless sessions, Dorothy finally reveals the
source of her pain.
BWSM95, 3.5 minutes
Twelve Dreams by James Lapine

1831
Flo, 30s   Here and Now
A woman desperate to have a baby. Flo's husband has refused to have sex with her for over
a year. The worst part is that he seems incapable of offering an explanation for his unexpected aversion. Flo offers a glimpse of her
inner torment.
BWSM95, 2 minutes
Watbanaland by Doug Wright

1832
Nella Rae, 30s
Heavyset. Nella tells how she overcame her
poor self-concept as a black woman.
BWSM95, 2 minutes
Your Obituary Is A Dance by Bernard Cummings

1833
Setsuko, 20
Island of Shikoku, last days of WWII
The story of the Shimidas, a Japanese family.
Amidst exploding bombs and the screams of
people fleeing for their lives, Setsuko, the
younger daughter, pensively eats a handful of
locusts that she has taken from a handkerchief;
she attempts to share them with the audience.
MMYA, 1 minute
Asa Ga Kimashita by Velina Hasu Houston

1834
Hannah, 16-18
An intimate tapestry of rural America focusing
on five diverse families from 1911 to the pre-
sent. Moving back and forth through time, the
play depicts over a century of family evolution.
Hannah Carolina Vangger, a spirited young
Mennonite, applies as a volunteer to care for
refugees from the Russian Revolution.
MMYA, 2 minutes
Becoming Memories by Arthur Giron

1835
Rachel, 17

A search for happiness, Buba dramatizes the story of the title character, a middle-aged Israeli who is in conflict with his brother and himself. In the course of the play Buba meets and falls in love with Rachel, a young wanderer. Rachel, whom Buba has just discovered sleeping with his brother, asserts her independence.

MMYA, 3 minutes
Buba by Hillel Mitelpunkt; translated by Michael Taub

1836
Normal, mid-teens
George Wolfe shatters racial stereotyping in a series of eleven exhibits that expose the "myths and madness of black/Negro/colored Americans." In "Permutation," the exhibit that follows, Normal Jean Reynolds is about to give birth to a baby she hopes will transform the world.

MMYA, 6 minutes
The Colored Museum by George C. Wolfe

1837
Tafia Shebagabow, 11
Reserve near Thunder Bay, Ontario, Canada
A young Ojibway girl struggles to balance the demands of the modern world with the rich cultural values of her people. In the introductory speech to her story, Tafia sets her life in context.

MMYA, 3.5 minutes
Dancing Feathers by Christel Kleitsch and Paul Stephens

1838
Rose, early teens
Spirit Bay, northern Ontario, Canada
The story of two Ojibway youths, Rose and Rabbit, whose rivalry turns to friendship and trust. Rose recounts a dramatic episode during a challenging game of broom hockey.

MMYA, 3 minutes
Dream Quest: The Big Save by Amy Jo Cooper

1839
Rose, early teens
Spirit Bay, northern Ontario, Canada
The story of two Ojibway youths, Rose and Rabbit, whose rivalry turns to friendship and trust. Rose Tells her friend Mavis how she came to be raised by her grandmother.

MMYA, 5 minutes
Dream Quest: The Big Save by Amy Jo Cooper

1840
Leah, 18-20
Dybbuk recounts the tragic love of Channon and Leah. Having been denied Leah's hand in marriage by her father in favor of a wealthier suitor, Channon turns to the magic of Kabala in hopes of winning her love but dies in the mystical attempt. In death, Channon returns as a Dybbuk—or evil spirit, and possesses Leah's body on her wedding day. Leah, not yet possessed, shares with her grandmother her beliefs about the spirit world.

MMYA, 4.5 minutes
The Dybbuk by S. Ansky; translated by Henry G. Alsberg and Winifred Katzin

1841
Nicole, 16
Miguel Piñero focuses on a young couple, David and Rosemarie, who are in search of a better life than the street offers. Unfortunately their dreams are corrupted through their involvement with robbery, drugs and prostitution. Tonight, Rosemarie's sister Nicole (who is secretly having an affair with David) brings two school friends home for a proposed sexual encounter with two "clients" David has set up. Nicole tells her sister that she loves David and that she is determined to win him for herself.

MMYA, 2 minutes
Eulogy For A Small Time Thief by Miguel Piñero

1842
Elaine, 16
Miguel Piñero focuses on a young couple, David and Rosemarie, who are in search of a better life than the street offers. Unfortunately their dreams are corrupted through their involvement with robbery, drugs and prostitution. Tonight, Rosemarie's sister Nicole (who is secretly having an affair with David) brings two school friends home for a proposed sexual encounter with two "clients" David has set up. Elaine has just discovered one of her "clients" is her own father and attempts to justify her reasons for hustling.

MMYA, 2.5 minutes
Eulogy For A Small Time Thief by Miguel Piñero

1843
Julia, 18
Margareta Garpe, one of Scandinavia's leading contemporary dramatists, explores the relationship between mothers and daughters and the unique place young people hold in our modern world. Julia offers the Prologue to the play.

MMYA, 1 minute
For Julia by Margareta Garpe; translated by Harry G. Carlson

1844
Masha, 14   Six o'clock in the evening
The story of two Russian teenagers, Masha

and Valerka, who live next door to one another. First produced in Moscow in 1969, this play mixes fantasy with reality as it explores the struggles and emotions and beliefs and insecurities of its young protagonists. Young Masha has just climbed a hill and found her friend Valerka, a boy she has met during the summer.
MMYA, 3.5 minutes
Hey, There—Hello! by Gennadi Mamlin; translated by Miriam Morton

1845
Amelia, 18-20
Santiago de Cuba, during revolutionary turmoil
A Little Something to Easy the Pain explores the conflict between exile and freedom. Amelia, a child of the revolution, is speaking to Carlos Rabel (Paye), a visiting exile. Amelia reaffirms her passionate commitment to the principles that charged her people to unite and rebel.
MMYA, 1.5 minutes
A Little Something to Easy the Pain by René R. Alomá

1846
Flotilda, a young woman
A collection of wild and wacky characters who represent the truths of life, however bizarre they may be. Flotilda, a young actress, takes the audience through the role of Juliet, which she is currently playing at Shakespeare in the Slums.
MMYA, 8 minutes
Live And In Color! by Danitra Vance

1847
A Young Woman
My Life Story is a poem from Naomi Shihab Nye's anthology This Same Sky, a Collection of Poems from Around the World. Ms. Nguyen's poem depicts the struggle and pain of growing up in war-torn Vietnam.
MMYA, 1.5 minutes
My Life Story by Lan Nguyen

1848
Beneatha, 18-20   A Chicago ghetto, 1950s
The story of how three generations of the Younger family overcome their conflicts and bring their divergent hopes and dreams into common focus. Beneatha, who has just learned that her brother Walter has lost the family's money in a poor investment, speaks to her friend Asagai, a student from Nigeria.
MMYA, 2 minutes
A Raisin in the Sun by Lorraine Hansberry

1849
Girl, early to mid-twenties
Explores a young African-American woman's dream of dangerous and exciting entanglement with Shango, a fire god, and her eventual journey to face him in what becomes a mythic coming-of-age ritual. Jackson interlaces the style of a classic myth with language that is rich, almost bluesy, in its contemporary sound. The Girl approaches and addresses Shango.
MMYA, 3.5 minutes
Shango Diaspora by Angela Jackson

1850
Rose, 20s   1946
A Shayna Maidel focuses on the recently reunited Weiss family. Although Rose and her father escaped the horrors of Nazi Germany, her mother, who remained in Poland to care for Rose's ailing sister Lusia, perished in a concentration camp. Lusia survived and has now made her way to New York to be reunited with her family. On Luisa's first day in America, Rose welcomes her to her home.
MMYA, 3 minutes
A Shayna Maidel by Barbara Lebow

1851
Sugar, 15-18
The characters in Miguel Piñero's Sideshow are Black and Puerto Rican teenagers—a collection of prostitutes, hustlers, drug dealers, and pimps who present their lives in a series of improvised and real scenes. All have a unique story to share concerning their life on the streets and the danger and pain of existing on their own at such a young age. Sugar, who's just been beaten by her "man" Lucky, a pimp, tries to quell her need for a fix and the pain that accompanies her "jones coming down" by resting. She speaks to the memory of her mother, whom she misses.
MMYA, 3 minutes
Sideshow by Miguel Piñero

1852
Della, 18-20
Reynolds Price's The Surface of Earth is one of two novels tracing the lives of the Mayfield family. The complexities of relationships, both within the family and with others who affect their lives, becomes a dramatic patchwork of struggle and survival. The Surface of Earth spans the years 1903 to 1944. Della, the lifelong serving girl to Rachel Ravens, tells Robinson Mayfield (Rachel's fiancé) of a troubling dream that lead to Rachel's illness. Della is no stranger to Rob. She is described as Rob's "generous friend who had helped him in need." Although Della and Rob have been

physically intimate, Della has promised that she will leave after Rob and Rachel marry.
MMYA, 2.5 minutes
The Surface of Earth by Reynolds Price

1853
Eila, early 20s
Shay Youngblood's mysterious play deals with three generations of women: Ruth, in her early sixties; Baybay, Ruth's daughter, and Baybay's daughter, Eila. Ruth hears voices—voices that she feels are intended to advise her and her family. As Ruth approaches the final days of her life, she becomes more impassioned about the voices and their message. At odds with Ruth is her daughter, Baybay, who seeks escape from the confines of this family and responsibility. In the middle is Eila, who cares equally for Baybay and her grandmother, Ruth. Eila attempts to gain some understanding from her mother about the voices she has heard.
MMYA, 2 minutes
Talking Bones by Shay Youngblood

1854
Eila, early 20s
Shay Youngblood's mysterious play deals with three generations of women: Ruth, in her early sixties; Baybay, Ruth's daughter, and Baybay's daughter, Eila. Ruth hears voices—voices that she feels are intended to advise her and her family. As Ruth approaches the final days of her life, she becomes more impassioned about the voices and their message. At odds with Ruth is her daughter, Baybay, who seeks escape from the confines of this family and responsibility. In the middle is Eila, who cares equally for Baybay and her grandmother, Ruth. Eila addresses Oz, a homeless man who's come into the Ancestor's Books & Breakfast, the residence of Eila, her mother and grandmother
MMYA, 1 minute
Talking Bones by Shay Youngblood

1855
Eila, early 20s
Shay Youngblood's mysterious play deals with three generations of women: Ruth, in her early sixties; Baybay, Ruth's daughter, and Baybay's daughter, Eila. Ruth hears voices—voices that she feels are intended to advise her and her family. As Ruth approaches the final days of her life, she becomes more impassioned about the voices and their message. At odds with Ruth is her daughter, Baybay, who seeks escape from the confines of this family and responsibility. In the middle is Eila, who cares equally for Baybay and her grandmother,

Ruth. Eila in a trance, recounts to her mother, Baybay, a vision that came to her.
MMYA, 2 minutes
Talking Bones by Shay Youngblood

1856
Bet, 15   **Florida Everglades**
In Troubled Waters, Brian Kral uses as his jumping off point a series of newspaper articles he read that dealt with hunters converging in a "mercy kill" of deer. The play centers around two brothers, J.D. and Michael, their sister, Sandra, and their friend, Bet, an American-Indian girl. After recent droughts and later flooding weaken the deer population, government officials decide to kill the undernourished deer in order to save healthy deer. When there is a large public outcry against this, the children are forced to consider the moral and ecological issues raised by such a "mercy kill." Bet stands alone facing the audience.
MMYA, 2 minutes
Troubled Waters by Brian Kral

1857
Anima/Animus, ageless
Judith Alexa Jackson created WOMBmanWARs out of her reaction to the Anita Hill-Clarence Thomas hearings. Ms. Jackson puts forth the view that if "we all have some woman in us and we all have some man in us, then the Hill-Thomas event was a form of self-bashing rather than woman-bashing." In WOMBmanWARs she demonstrates that there are constant wars that go on within women as they try "to be whole in the world." Anima/Animus, fetus/spirit child who represents the male/female that exists in all of us, has just sprung forth from her mother's womb.
MMYA, 3.5 minutes
WOMBmanWARs by Judith Alexa Jackson

1858
Danisha, 12
Judith Alexa Jackson created WOMBmanWARs out of her reaction to the Anita Hill-Clarence Thomas hearings. Ms. Jackson puts forth the view that if "we all have some woman in us and we all have some man in us, then the Hill-Thomas event was a form of self-bashing rather than woman-bashing." In WOMBmanWARs she demonstrates that there are constant wars that go on within women as they try "to be whole in the world." Danisha, daughter/girl child, is coaxed into a playmate's makeshift tepee.
MMYA, 2 minutes
WOMBmanWARs by Judith Alexa Jackson

1859
Alirio, teenager
Mary Gallagher's compelling drama depicts the lives of Hispanics in the Rio Grande Valley of Texas and is concerned with the rights of refugees and their encounter with the INS (Immigration and Naturalization Service). The title refers to the shortened Spanish phrase for the question "Where are you from?" This is the first phrase heard by Hispanics suspected of being aliens. Alirio, a Salvadoran refugee and student activist, talks with Kathleen, an Anglo nun, about the conditions in the Processing Center.
MMYA, 3 minutes
¿De Dónde? by Mary Gallagher

1860
Rabbit, early teens
Spirit Bay, northern Ontario, Canada
The story of two Ojibway youths, Rose and Rabbit, whose rivalry turns to friendship and trust. Rabbit relives a dramatic episode during a challenging game of broom hockey; he has just warned his teammate Rose: "You better not goof up today because I don't want to lose."
MMYA, 4 minutes
Dream Quest: The Big Save by Amy Jo Cooper

1861
Rabbit, early teens
Spirit Bay, northern Ontario, Canada
The story of two Ojibway youths, Rose and Rabbit, whose rivalry turns to friendship and trust. Rabbit is tired of his teammates' "It doesn't matter, it's just a game" attitude every time they lose a game.
MMYA, 2.5 minutes
Dream Quest: The Big Save by Amy Jo Cooper

1862
Clay, a young man   On a New York subway
Dutchman is a fiery and ultimately violent racial debate between a young black man (Clay) and a bold, dangerous white woman (Lula). After first trying to seduce Clay and failing, Lula engages in a vicious verbal assault that provokes Clay to a heated response. A series of biting and coarse racial arguments ensue and the play ends with Lula murdering Clay. In the final few moments before his murder, Clay speaks of the violent passion that racial injustice breeds.
MMYA, 4.5 minutes
Dutchman by Amiri Baraka (LeRoi Jones)

1863
Eddie, 18   A college cafe
Lynne Alvarez's Eddie Mundo Edmundo concerns the journey of a young Hispanic American who travels to Nautla, Mexico, in search of his family's past and his own future after the death of his mother. Confronted with deep conflicts between the culture in which he was raised (as a Hispanic in New York City) and the culture he faces in Mexico, Eddie seeks his true identity and a place in the world. Along the way he is touched and moved by his Aunt Chelo and her fiancé of many years, Nyin, and stirred with love for a young local girl. The speech takes place in a college cafe in America two years after Eddie's experiences in Nautla.
MMYA, 1.5 minutes
Eddie Mundo Edmundo by Lynne Alvarez

1864
Eddie, 18   Nautla, Mexico
Lynne Alvarez's Eddie Mundo Edmundo concerns the journey of a young Hispanic American who travels to Nautla, Mexico, in search of his family's past and his own future after the death of his mother. Confronted with deep conflicts between the culture in which he was raised (as a Hispanic in New York City) and the culture he faces in Mexico, Eddie seeks his true identity and a place in the world. Along the way he is touched and moved by his Aunt Chelo and her fiancé of many years, Nyin, and stirred with love for a young local girl. Eddie, confused about his feelings for Alicia, the local girl he has fallen in love with, talks through his troubles with Mundo, a silent, lonely young man with mutant features whom Eddie has befriended.
MMYA, 3.5 minutes
Eddie Mundo Edmundo by Lynne Alvarez

1865
Eddie, 18   A college cafe
Lynne Alvarez's Eddie Mundo Edmundo concerns the journey of a young Hispanic American who travels to Nautla, Mexico, in search of his family's past and his own future after the death of his mother. Confronted with deep conflicts between the culture in which he was raised (as a Hispanic in New York City) and the culture he faces in Mexico, Eddie seeks his true identity and a place in the world. Along the way he is touched and moved by his Aunt Chelo and her fiancé of many years, Nyin, and stirred with love for a young local girl. The speech takes place in a college cafe in America two years after Eddie's experiences in Nautla. Eddie shares through poetry his Mexican experience.
MMYA, 1 minute
Eddie Mundo Edmundo by Lynne Alvarez

1866
A Young Man
A Headstrong Boy is a poem from Shihab Nye's anthology This Same Sky, a Collection of Poems from Around the World. Mr. Cheng, a young Chinese poet, lives in exile between New Zealand and Germany. His poem speaks not only of the pain of exile but of the passionate hope for beauty and truth in life.
MMYA, 2.5 minutes
A Headstrong Boy by Gu Cheng; translated by Donald Finkel

1867
Walter, teen   **A ghetto**
Walter, who like so many other young boys in similar circumstances, seems to have no other hope of bettering his life except through selling drugs. Hope is found in the inspiration of Walter's sister, Latoya, who paints a picture at school of her dreams—a family that is safe and together. The speech is the opening scene in the play.
MMYA, 1.5 minutes
Hey Little Walter by Carla Debbie Alleyne

1868
Valerka, 14
Hey, There—Hello! is the story of two Russian teenagers, Masha and Valerka, who live next door to one another. First produced in Moscow in 1969, this play mixes fantasy with reality as it explores the struggles and emotions and beliefs and insecurities of its young protagonists. Valerka recounts to his friend Masha what happened during the previous night's entertainment at the Seamen's Club.
MMYA, 2.5 minutes
Hey, There—Hello! by Gennadi Mamlin; translated by Miriam Morton

1869
Valerka, 14
Hey, There—Hello! is the story of two Russian teenagers, Masha and Valerka, who live next door to one another. First produced in Moscow in 1969, this play mixes fantasy with reality as it explores the struggles and emotions and beliefs and insecurities of its young protagonists. Valerka looks to the heavens and muses about the Stars.
MMYA, 1.5 minutes
Hey, There—Hello! by Gennadi Mamlin; translated by Miriam Morton

1870
Swahili, 20s Memphis, Tennessee, early 1968
I Am a Man depicts the events following a tragic incident in which two African-American garbage workers were crushed to death in the loader of their truck. The play unfolds through Bluesman, a blues singer and blues guitarist, who takes us back to the momentous strike of the Memphis Sanitation Works that followed the deaths of the two men. Swahili, an enraged young proponent of the "Black Nation," has come with a fellow brother to help protect Jones, one of the leaders of the strike.
MMYA, 2 minutes
I Am a Man, by OyamO

1871
Swahili, 20s Memphis, Tennessee, early 1968
I Am a Man depicts the events following a tragic incident in which two African-American garbage workers were crushed to death in the loader of their truck. The play unfolds through Bluesman, a blues singer and blues guitarist, who takes us back to the momentous strike of the Memphis Sanitation Works that followed the deaths of the two men. Swahili remains defiant when he senses that the leaders of the strike may be selling out.
MMYA, 2 minutes
I Am a Man, by OyamO

1872
Roger, early teens
In David E. Rodriguez's short play I'm Not Stupid, which was a winner in the Young Playwrights Festival and first performed at Playwrights Horizons in New York, Rodriguez looks at a dysfunctional mother and her abusive relationship with her learning disabled son, Roger. The mother, an alcoholic, resents the attention her husband gave to their son and, now that the father has died, her animosity has grown because he left the bulk of his money to Roger. Attempts by the boy's psychologist to intervene fail and the mother succeeds in carrying out her evil plan to kill the boy. In the speech which opens the play, Roger sits in a chair rocking back and forth.
MMYA, 1.5 minutes
I'm Not Stupid by David E. Rodriguez

1873
Angel Garcia, a young man
In the opening pages of John Leguizamo's collection of one-man scenes, the author offers that "This book is for all the Latin people who have had a hard time holding on to a dream and just made do." Mr. Leguizamo's characters are often irreverent but always startlingly truthful in portraying the diverse dynamics of Hispanic machismo. Behind the hilarity is a unique voice that is pointed and honest. Angel Garcia, who is handcuffed in jail, calls home.
MMYA, 3 minutes
Mambo Mouth by John Leguizamo

1874
Pepe, a young man
In the opening pages of John Leguizamo's collection of one-man scenes, the author offers that "This book is for all the Latin people who have had a hard time holding on to a dream and just made do." Mr. Leguizamo's characters are often irreverent but always startlingly truthful in portraying the diverse dynamics of Hispanic machismo. Behind the hilarity is a unique voice that is pointed and honest. Pepe encounters an Immigration official and lays bare the ignorance of racial prejudice.
MMYA, 6 minutes
Mambo Mouth by John Leguizamo

1875
Johnny, 19-22
No Place to Be Somebody, which was awarded a Pulitzer Prize in 1969 (the first to be awarded to an African-American playwright), is a dynamic and compelling study of an ambitious black man named Johnny who owns a bar in a black neighborhood controlled by white thugs. When Johnny begins to buy property and attempts to get into the rackets himself, the local Mafia rough him up. Soon Johnny's life—including the lives of his closest friend and girlfriend—is irretrievably enmeshed in the machinations of the underworld, which leads to a violent conclusion. Johnny threatens his old mentor, Sweets, who has recently been released from prison and seems to have had a change of heart.
MMYA, 2 minutes
No Place to Be Somebody by Charles Gordone

1876
Gabe, 19-22
No Place to Be Somebody, which was awarded a Pulitzer Prize in 1969 (the first to be awarded to an African-American playwright), is a dynamic and compelling study of an ambitious black man named Johnny who owns a bar in a black neighborhood controlled by white thugs. When Johnny begins to buy property and attempts to get into the rackets himself, the local Mafia rough him up. Soon Johnny's life—including the lives of his closest friend and girlfriend—is irretrievably enmeshed in the machinations of the underworld, which leads to a violent conclusion. Gabe, Johnny's friend and the play's storyteller, makes a confession
MMYA, 1.5 minutes
No Place to Be Somebody by Charles Gordone

1877
Gabe, 19-22
No Place to Be Somebody, which was awarded a Pulitzer Prize in 1969 (the first to be awarded

to an African-American playwright), is a dynamic and compelling study of an ambitious black man named Johnny who owns a bar in a black neighborhood controlled by white thugs. When Johnny begins to buy property and attempts to get into the rackets himself, the local Mafia rough him up. Soon Johnny's life—including the lives of his closest friend and girlfriend—is irretrievably enmeshed in the machinations of the underworld, which leads to a violent conclusion. Gabe recalls his boyhood girlfriend, Maxine.
MMYA, 2.5 minutes
No Place to Be Somebody by Charles Gordone

1878
Machito, 20   **New York City**
Once Upon a Dream explores the world of Hispanic exiles' and refugees' struggles to build a life in the urban world far removed from their Caribbean origins. We encounter a widowed mother, Dolores Jiménez, and her family, each of whom is tossed and torn between his or her native culture and the obstacles they confront in the city. Throughout, fantasy and nostalgia confront the cold realities of the present and force the characters to rediscover who they are. Machito, the blind son, lashes back at his mother, who has accused him of taking a check from her checkbook.
MMYA, 4 minutes
Once Upon a Dream by Miguel González-Pando

1879
Peer, 20
Henrik Ibsen's Peer Gynt spans the life of its title character, Peer, a kind of Norwegian folk hero whose mischievous and roguish ways lead him through a fanciful yet wasteful lie. In old age, however, he learns the virtue of living simply and honestly when he is reunited with his first true love, Solveig, who has remained faithful to him throughout the years. Young Peer has just returned from deer hunting in the mountains. His mother has been scolding him for leaving her at harvest time, and then returning empty handed having torn his coat and lost his gun. Peer spins a fantastical yarn about his encounter with a magnificent buck.
MMYA, 4 minutes
Peer Gynt by Henrik Ibsen; translated by Gerry Bamman and Irene Berman

1880
Christy, 20   **A small County May pub**
Christy Mahan, a shy Irish lad who is hired on to clean pots in a small County Mayo pub, soon becomes the hero of the village when it is revealed that he has killed his tyrant of a father. Christy has the affections of a local

widow—the publican's daughter, Pegeen Mike—and the other townspeople until old Mahan shows up wounded but very much alive. Despite these circumstances, Christy uses his newfound assurance to tame is father and then walks out on Pegeen Mike; he truly proves to be the "Playboy of the Western World." Christy, who now has "two fine women fighting for the likes of [him]," is cleaning a pair of Pegeen's boots and counting dinnerware in the pub.

MMYA, 2 minutes
The Playboy of the Western World by John Millington Synge

1881
A Young Man
The Prison Cell is a poem from Naomi Shihab Nye's anthology This Same Sky, a Collection of Poems from Around the World. Darwish's poem expresses the power of the human spirit—in this case a young Palestinian's—to escape the confinements that adversaries may impose.

MMYA, 2 minutes
The Prison Cell by Mahmud Darwish; translated from the Arabic by Ben Bennani

1882
Asagai, 18-20   A Chicago ghetto, 1950s
The story of how three generations of the Younger family overcome their conflicts and bring their divergent hopes and dreams into common focus. After Walter Younger loses the family's savings, his sister Beneatha, who has had aspirations of becoming a physician, loses faith in the goodness of people and gives up her dream. However, Asagai, a student from Nigeria who has become friends with Beneatha, admonishes her not to give up hope or to believe that the truth about all people is that they are "puny, small and selfish."

MMYA, 3.5 minutes
A Raisin in the Sun by Lorraine Hansberry

1883
Clearnose Henry, 13-15
The characters in Miguel Piñero's Sideshow are Black and Puerto Rican teenagers—a collection of prostitutes, hustlers, drug dealers, and pimps who present their lives in a series of improvised and real scenes. All have a unique story to share concerning their life on the streets and the danger and pain of existing on their own at such a young age. Clearnose Henry, a Puerto Rican glue-sniffer, introduces himself to the audience.

MMYA, 1.5 minutes
Sideshow by Miguel Piñero

1884
Clearnose Henry, 13-15
The characters in Miguel Piñero's Sideshow are Black and Puerto Rican teenagers—a collection of prostitutes, hustlers, drug dealers, and pimps who present their lives in a series of improvised and real scenes. All have a unique story to share concerning their life on the streets and the danger and pain of existing on their own at such a young age. In Clearnose's speech we see elements of the young man's source of pain and the reason for his drug addiction; he is alone on the roof.

MMYA, 2 minutes
Sideshow by Miguel Piñero

1885
Malo, 15-16
The characters in Miguel Piñero's Sideshow are Black and Puerto Rican teenagers—a collection of prostitutes, hustlers, drug dealers, and pimps who present their lives in a series of improvised and real scenes. All have a unique story to share concerning their life on the streets and the danger and pain of existing on their own at such a young age. Malo, the "Merchant," explains his trade to the audience.

MMYA, 5.5 minutes
Sideshow by Miguel Piñero

1886
Phil, 19
"The Slab Boys" of John Byrne's title are three young men who work mixing and matching paints for a carpet company in Scotland. Each of the boys dreams of a better life, perhaps a future that would evaluate their place in the world beyond that of their parents. Phil dreams of going to art school but is constantly worried that the mental illness that has tormented his mother for years is somehow in his future as well. Phil tells Spanky (a fellow slab boy) about a time his mother took him to visit a convalescent home. It was sometime after this visit that Phil's mother started being hospitalized from time to time as a result of her mental illness.

MMYA, 2.5 minutes
The Slab Boys by John Byrne

1887
Phil, 19
"The Slab Boys" of John Byrne's title are three young men who work mixing and matching paints for a carpet company in Scotland. Each of the boys dreams of a better life, perhaps a future that would evaluate their place in the world beyond that of their parents. Phil dreams of going to art school but is constantly worried that the mental illness that has tor-

mented his mother for years is somehow in his future as well. Phil has just been told that his mother has escaped the mental hospital. In his fright and anger he attacks Alan.

MMYA, 1 minute
The Slab Boys by John Byrne

1888
Johnny, 18-20
Luis Valdez wrote Solado Razo in 1971, in part, for the Chicano Moratorium on the War in Vietnam. The short play revolves around the story of Johnny, a young Chicano soldier killed in Vietnam. Johnny reflects on the life he is about to leave behind as he goes to war.

MMYA, 2 minutes
Solado Razo by Luis Valdez

1889
Johnny, 18-20
Luis Valdez wrote Solado Razo in 1971, in part, for the Chicano Moratorium on the War in Vietnam. The short play revolves around the story of Johnny, a young Chicano soldier killed in Vietnam. This speech is a letter home.

MMYA, 2 minutes
Solado Razo by Luis Valdez

1890
Shinji, 18-20 A small Japanese fishing village
Yukio Mishima was one of the leading Japanese writers of fiction and drama in the 20th Century. The Sound of Waves is a short novel recounting the first love of a boy and girl growing up in a small Japanese fishing village. Although this story is simply told, the struggle of Shinji to win the love of the beautiful Hatsue is a compelling, universal picture of young love the world over. In a village where work is everything, Shinji and Hatsue steal brief, important moments together that build their love for one another. Shinji, in a precious few hours alone with Hatsue, shares his dreams of a future that is both plentiful and peaceful.

MMYA, 2 minutes
The Sound of Waves by Yukio Mishima; translated by Meredith Watherby

1891
Spence, early teens
Take a Giant Step depicts the coming of age of Spence, a young African-American boy who experiences a sense of estrangement from his white friends as he emerges into adulthood. Confused by the prejudices of the adult world, his anger leads to his expulsion from school and a series of low-life encounters that leave him even more bewildered. It is not until he has a confrontation with his parents, confides his fears to the family maid, and experiences the death of his grandmother that he is able to make sense of what he may become. Spence tells his grandmother why he got kicked out of school.

MMYA, 3 minutes
Take a Giant Step by Louis Peterson

1892
Zippy, 17-21   A youth center
Mustapha Matura, perhaps the leading dramatist of West Indian origin, wrote Welcome Home Jacko after visiting a community youth center in Sheffield, England. The center was a place for young people to socialize apart from the pangs of social oppression and racism. The play, set in just such a center, concerns a group of young people struggling for a Black identity. As the four young West Indians interact in the club, exploring their place in the world, they assert their beliefs. Sandy, the white girl who manages the club, is preparing to welcome home Jacko, who has spent the last five years in prison for raping a girl. Zippy, in Rastafarian robe, explains to Jacko why he and his friends like gathering at the center.

MMYA, 1 minute
Welcome Home Jacko, Mustapha Matura

1893
Jacko, 20-25   A youth center
Mustapha Matura, perhaps the leading dramatist of West Indian origin, wrote Welcome Home Jacko after visiting a community youth center in Sheffield, England. The center was a place for young people to socialize apart from the pangs of social oppression and racism. The play, set in just such a center, concerns a group of young people struggling for a Black identity. As the four young West Indians interact in the club, exploring their place in the world, they assert their beliefs. Sandy, the white girl who manages the club, is preparing to welcome home Jacko, who has spent the last five years in prison for raping a girl. Jacko tells Sandy why the Rastafarian dreams and hopes expressed by the young men in the center are nothing to him but unrealistic nonsense.

MMYA, 1 minute
Welcome Home Jacko, Mustapha Matura

1894
Andrei, 17   Former Soviet Union
The Young Graduates defends the right of its young characters to assert their individuality and to make their own decisions concerning the course of their lives. Rozov defends young people's rights to criticize the shortcomings of

society, including adults and parents who behave in hypocritical ways. Likewise, the play reinforces the values that make the individual and society spiritually strong and dynamic. Andrei, a young man who recently graduated from a Moscow 10-year school (an accelerated program) has been attempting to prepare for his college entrance exams and to find his "calling" in life.

MMYA, 2 minutes

The Young Graduates by Victor Rozov; translated by Miriam Morton

1895

Ralph Burke, 60s   New York City, Present

A good-looking successful corporate executive. Ralph is with his advertising agency representative, enjoying a successful new product introduction macho-style, when he suddenly reveals the truth of his existence.

BMSM95, 1.5 minutes

Barking Sharks by Israel Horovitz

1896

Vincent, 16   Milwaukee, WI 1920s

An orphan. Vincent recounts a traumatizing incident at the orphanage to a sympathetic Seta.

BMSM95, 1 minute

Beast on the Moon by Richard Kalinoski

1897

Aram Tomasian, 30s-40s   Milwaukee, WI 1920s

Aram, orphaned as a child, finally explains to his barren wife his obsession to have children.

BMSM95, 3.5 minutes

Beast on the Moon by Richard Kalinoski

1898

Announcer, any age   New York City

Following an appearance by the one and only Julius Caesar, the Mephisthophelean Announcer does his best to peddle life's ultimate commodity: death.

BMSM95, 1.5 minutes

Blink Of An Eye by Jeremy Dobrish

1899

Matthew, 30-40   New York City

A homicidal manic. Matthew, a triplet, has escaped from a mental institution with the intention of tracking down and killing his two brothers in a misguided effort to integrate his hopelessly divided personality. He introduces himself.

BMSM95, 1.5 minutes

Blink Of An Eye by Jeremy Dobrish

1900

Chick, 30s   Here and Now

Chick has been hired by Jo-Lynne to kill Curtis, the man who killed her husband. Here, Chick rushes into Curtis's home and makes his intention clear.

BMSM95, 4 minutes

bliss by Benjamin Bettenbender

1901

Chick, 30s   Here and Now

A man poised to kill. Chick, who has killed once before, explains why it's important to give his intended victim an opportunity to beg for his life.

BMSM95, 5.5 minutes

bliss by Benjamin Bettenbender

1902

Willy   Dusk

A jogger at the beach. Willy tries to talk to swimmer, Marsha—she rejects him—he responds.

BMSM95, 2 minutes

By the Sea by Terrence McNally

1903

Willy   Dusk

A jogger at the beach. Willy having met Dana, a jogger, and Marsha, a swimmer on beach at dusk, tries to impress them with this obviously tall tale.

BMSM95, 1.5 minutes

By the Sea by Terrence McNally

1904

John, 27   The suburban northeast

An ex-marine, inarticulate and occasionally violent. A veteran of the Gulf War, macho John has been tortured by the possibility that he may have slept with Nathan, his best friend, while they served in the Marines. A few years and a broken marriage later, John allows himself to be picked up by Maddy, a pragmatic woman he meets at a bar. When their lovemaking goes awry, Maddy is able to coax the story of his night with Nathan from him, beginning with the description of the night he first met his wife.

BMSM95, 2 minutes

A Candle in the Window by Tom Gilroy

1905

Thingamajig, 20-30

Washington, DC, sooner than you think

A piece of the universe's primordial goo visiting earth in the form of a human being. Thingamajig has transformed himself into a human for the express purpose of delivering a

warning to the leaders of the planet. The pattern of ecological destruction must be halted, or the earth will be destroyed. Unfortunately, Thingamajig's mission is soon forgotten as he gets sucked deeper and deeper into the ennui of human life. The poor lost creature struggles to remember his purpose.
BMSM95, 2.5 minutes
Cannibal Cheerleaders on Crack by Billy Bermingham

1906
Ethan, 40s   America in the 50s and 60s
A man whose wife has just left him, again. Ethan describes a series of nocturnal visits by a prowler that culminate in an interesting discovery.
BMSM95, 3.5 minutes
A Cheever Evening by A.R. Gurney

1907
Lance Malone, a young man   Corporate offices
Starting a new job. When his boss, a white woman, makes a sexual advance upon him, Lance does his best to turn her down. When she insists that she understands the pain that he must feel as a black man trapped in the white corporate world, he becomes furious and tells her exactly what he thinks.
BMSM95, 1 minute
Company Policy by Michael Ajakwe Jr.

1908
Stu, 40s   The US Virgin Islands, Present
A transplanted New Yorker now living in the Caribbean. When Arthur, a harried New Yorker comes for a visit, Stu is reminded of the state he was in when he first arrived in the Virgin Islands. He tells Arthur the tale of that first visit, and cautions his impatient friend that it will take three days for the process of unwinding to be complete.
BMSM95, 2.5 minutes
Conversations With The Pool Boy by Robert Coles

1909
Vince, 20s   Darwin, Australia, 1942
The son of a racially mixed couple, Vince sadly belongs to neither's world. Instead, he travels the Outback as a tent boxer. He describes a typical night of boxing matches to his mother and brother.
BMSM95, 3.5 minutes
Crow by Louis Nowra

1910
Vince, 20s   Darwin, Australia, 1942
A tent boxer. Vince has returned to Darwin to claim Ruth, the woman he loves. When he discovers that she is pregnant with another man's

child, he flies into a rage. His passion nearly spent, Vince confesses the agony of his life on the road.
BMSM95, 3.5 minutes
Crow by Louis Nowra

1911
Lonnie, 38   Summertime, apartment, Present
Lonnie is having an affair with Nickie. Nickie's daughter, Valerie, is morose and claims to want out of life. Lonnie talks some of his style of common sense to her.
BMSM95, 1.5 minutes
A Dead Man's Apartment by Edward Allan Baker

1912
Kirt, 20s
Kirt relates a story of corporate privilege far removed from anything he had experienced before.
BMSM95, 3.5 minutes
Dog Eat Dog by Karen Smith Vastola

1913
Jackie, 17   Here and Now
An ingenious street hooker. Jackie has been working the streets for a year or so and in that time has managed to accumulate an amazing store of knowledge from watching educational TV in motel rooms.
BMSM95, 1.5 minutes
Dog Opera by Constance Congdon

1914
Henry Farrell, 46   Doctor's office
Jean, his wife, has asked Henry's blessing to care for and possibly adopt the severely retarded and sick infant who, if born healthy, would have been their adoptive son. Henry responds.
BMSM95, 1 minute
Emma's Child by Kristine Thatcher

1915
Sam Stornant, 40s
Sitting in the woods in the rain
Sam remembers when he began to date Franny, and what fatherhood came to mean to him.
BMSM95, 3 minutes
Emma's Child by Kristine Thatcher

1916
Dan, a teenager   Here and Now
Dan, along with his brothers and sister, has been abandoned by his parents and communicates with them by fax only. He reflects on his mother.
BMSM95, 2 minutes
Every 17 Minutes the Crowd Goes Wild! by Paul Zindel

1917
A Man, 30-40   **Here and Now**
A self-proclaimed ladies' man reveals his secret for scoring with dates.
BMSM95, 4 minutes
Gunplay by Frank Higgins

1918
David, 30s   **Here and Now**
A man looking for someone to share his life with (or so he thinks). David has decided to attend a "Men's Gathering" in order to gain a sense of "empowerment." He works up his courage and entertains the group with the tale of an early sexual encounter.
BMSM95, 5 minutes
Half-Court by Brian Silberman

1919
Mike, 30s   **Here and Now**
A man offering advice to a friend. Down-to-earth Mike tells his friend, David, the trick of acting as though one is well-endowed when one isn't.
BMSM95, 3 minutes
Half-Court by Brian Silberman

1920
Trucker, any age   **A hash house**
A king of the road. A hard-living trucker tells a strange tale of giving a man who may or may not have been Elvis Presley a ride to Graceland a few years after his death.
BMSM95, 5.5 minutes
Him by Christopher Walken

1921
Dave, 30s   **New York City, Present**
An unemployed advertising executive. Dave tells the story of the day he and his wife first met.
BMSM95, 1.5 minutes
Kept Men by Richard Lay

1922
Phil, 30-40   **New York City, Present**
An unemployed mob hitman. Phil describes the pleasure he finds in the act of killing someone he doesn't know.
BMSM95, 1 minute
Kept Men by Richard Lay

1923
Randye Mooglair, 20s   **Washington, DC**
African-American male who doubles as a Diana Ross impersonator. Randye is a world-weary drag queen whose indomitable spirit keeps him going from day to day. We join Randye as he prepares for a performance and celebrates his love of Diana Ross.
BMSM95, 5 minutes
Metamorphoses by Michael Winn

1924
Moon, 46   **A dump, Present**
A mercenary. Mona, Roy's abused wife, is firing at Ray when Moon appears and tells her to "cool it."
BMSM95, 1 minute
Middle-Aged White Guys by Jane Martin

1925
James Baldwin, 54
St. Paul de Vence, France, April 4, 1978
African-American novelist, essayist and dramatist. On the tenth anniversary of the death of Martin Luther King, Baldwin, now an expatriate living in France, describes a dream that he had about King.
BMSM95, 2.5 minutes
The Midnight Hour by James Campbell

1926
Dan, 30-40   **Here and Now**
A man whose wife is terminally ill. Julie's illness has been long and devastating but Dan has stood by her every step of the way. When someone finally asks him how he is feeling, he describes the horror of having to watch the one you love die a slow and agonizing death.
BMSM95, 2 minutes
My Virginia by Darci Picoult

1927
Tom, 40   **A farmhouse in western Connecticut**
A British acting coach living in New York City. While visiting his ex-sister-in-law's country home, Tom is caught up in a domestic tragedy. He does his best to entertain a room full of grieving fellow Brits with a tale of one of his American acting students.
BMSM95, 2.5 minutes
New England by Richard Nelson

1928
Man, 20-40   **Here and Now**
An imaginative romantic takes a moment to offer rhapsodic observations about his sleeping lover.
BMSM95, 5 minutes
The Only Thing Worse You Could Have Told Me by Dan Butler

1929
Hippolytus, 20s
A young man who has just discovered that his step-mother lusts after him. When Hippolytus is informed of Phaedra's secret passion for

him, he reacts with youthful indignation. He attempts to cast her out with a vengeance bordering on violence.
BMSM95, 3 minutes
Phaedra by Elizabeth Egloff

1930
Luke Laban, 50-60
A rundown publishing house in Eastern Europe
A retired policeman. Luke's professional life was spent conducting the surveillance of Teya Kry, a dissident intellectual considered a dangerous enemy of the state. In the years that he followed Teya, Luke became obsessed with his quarry and saved all of his speeches and stories. Luke's son, a college professor eager to seek intellectual freedom in the West, helped his father to bind all of Teya's writings into several volumes before his own escape. Now that communism has fallen, Luke finds himself out of a job and driving a taxi. Luke seeks out Teya, who is now the head of a publishing house, and presents him with the volumes of his forgotten stories. Luke reveals that in the beginning, he was tempted to kill Teya on several occasions.
BMSM95, 2 minutes
The Professional by Dusan Kovacevic, translated and adapted by Bob Djurdjevic

1931
Luke Laban, 50-60
A rundown publishing house in Eastern Europe
A retired policeman. Luke's professional life was spent conducting the surveillance of Teya Kry, a dissident intellectual considered a dangerous enemy of the state. In the years that he followed Teya, Luke became obsessed with his quarry and saved all of his speeches and stories. Luke's son, a college professor eager to seek intellectual freedom in the West, helped his father to bind all of Teya's writings into several volumes before his own escape. Now that communism has fallen, Luke finds himself out of a job and driving a taxi. Luke seeks out Teya, who is now the head of a publishing house, and presents him with the volumes of his forgotten stories. Luke recalls one of Teya's sardonic tales which has an uncomfortable parallel meaning to his own existence.
BMSM95, 1.5 minutes
The Professional by Dusan Kovacevic, translated and adapted by Bob Djurdjevic

1932
Dr. Robert Stoner, 60s   **Here and Now**
American Poet Laureate. After a long drunken weekend, the cantankerous Dr. Stoner turns on his young protégé and debunks his intellectual pretensions in a passionate outburst.

BMSM95, 1.5 minutes
The Psychic Life of Savages by Amy Freed

1933
Ted Magus, 30s   **Here and Now**
A young English poet. The pretentious poet/professor regales his students with his own special insight into the process of creating poetry.
BMSM95, 1.5 minutes
The Psychic Life of Savages by Amy Freed

1934
Staff, 40s   Dusk, farmhouse porch, Present
An ex-farmer. Staff tells about his recent fall from the roof, which left him confined to a wheelchair.
BMSM95, 4.5 minutes
Rain by Garry Williams

1935
Bob, 50s   **A cop's home**
A psychotic lawman. When his wife is visited by distant relations, Bob is delighted to be put in charge of a pot-smoking, teen-aged hellraiser. He delivers his first warning to the errant youth.
BMSM95, 1.5 minutes
Safe House by Douglas Michael

1936
Bob King, late 40s
A luxury housing estate in the north of Australia
An internationally renowned investigative journalist. John has pushed Bob to the limit of his physical and spiritual endurance, causing the tortured man to finally confess the horror that forced him into retirement.
BMSM95, 5.5 minutes
Sanctuary by David Williamson

1937
Aging Hippie, 40-60   **Here and Now**
A charter member of the Age of Aquarius takes a moment to lambaste life in the 80s and 90s.
BMSM95, 4 minutes
Self-Defense by Michael P. Scasserra

1938
Igor, 20   A New England college campus, 1990
An introspective college student. When he is accused of putting the moves on his friend's recent ex-girlfriend, Igor does his best to protect his relative innocence from the young woman in question.
BMSM95, 2 minutes
Sophistry by Jonathan Marc Sherman

1939
Street, 40s   **New York City, Present**
A coke addict dying of cancer. Street encounters Boogie, a young hustler who has just stolen a brick of coke in a subway station men's room. A hard-core addict, Street wastes no time in tapping the coke and shooting up. Now high, Street describes his love of storytelling.
BMSM95, 2.5 minutes
Sugar Down Billie Hoak by Brian Silberman

1940
Man   **Here and Now**
Channel surfing becomes a metaphor for life in the exaltation of the power of using the remote control.
BMSM95, 3.5 minutes
Talk/Show by Michael P. Scasserra

1941
Malice, 30-40   **A street corner**
A tough-talking man with twisted insight into the relationship between men and women. Malice makes love to a photo in a magazine.
BMSM95, 2 minutes
The Ties That Bind by Regina Taylor

1942
Malice, 30-40   **A street corner**
A tough-talking man with twisted insight into the relationship between men and women. Malice informs an acquaintance that he should have married a white woman.
BMSM95, 1.5 minutes
The Ties That Bind by Regina Taylor

1943
Bob Dooley, 30s-40s
Southern California, Present
Bob Dooley runs seminars about safety during natural disasters. He works the audience over pretty well.
BMSM95, 2.5 minutes
Tough Choices For the New Century by Jane Anderson

1944
Buonarroti of Michaelangelo
Winter 1506, a farm outside of Florence
Buonarroti has just come up from the cellar of a farmer, Giovanni, and his son, Enrico, an aspiring artist. Buonarroti responds to Enrico's comment about being an artist like the one who made the sculpture.
BMSM95, 2.5 minutes
Water and Wine by Stuart Spencer

1945
Park, 40   **Here and Now**
A man driven to despair by the birth of his disabled son. One night of drunken revelry with his secretary has resulted in the birth of a child with severe birth defects, leaving Park shattered by the realization that the baby's condition was a result of his genetic legacy. In the meantime, his wife, Flo, is desperate for a child of her own. Lashed by guilt, Park cannot bring himself to confess the truth. Instead, he writes everything down in letters that he eats rather than sends. Park struggles his way through one such letter.
BMSM95, 2 minutes
Watbanland by Doug Wright

1946
Sharon, 40   **Here and Now**
A political lobbyist, Jewish. Sharon has become attracted to her chiropractor, Dr. Matthew Cohen, who is a rather self-righteous Orthodox Jew. When she hears through the political grapevine that Matthew's rabbi cheated on his taxes, she takes great delight in telling him of his hero's misdeed. Matthew is unconvinced of the rabbi's guilt, however, and expresses his disapproval of Sharon's un-Orthodox lifestyle. Sharon reacts to his insulting suggestions with anger.
BWSM96, 3 minutes
The Adjustment by Michael T. Folie

1947
Jean, 60   **A park bench**
A woman confronting her first lover. Jean and Kate were separated by Kate's parents when they were 20, and the young lovers made a vow to meet on the last day of September in their 60th year. Forty years later, their long-anticipated reunion is made uncomfortable by the memory of their youthful affair. Jean tells Kate the difficult story of her life as a teacher in a small town.
BWSM96, 6.5 minutes
Alphabet Of Flowers by Elyse Nass

1948
Anne de Jumelle, 20-30   **16th century France**
Wife of the famous seer. Being the wife of a prophet can be quite difficult as Anne reveals.
BWSM96, 1 minute
Ask Nostradamus by R. J. Marx

1949
Julianna, 40   **A hotel room in Florida**
A woman vacationing with her sister. Julianna and Wilson have journeyed to St. Augustine, Florida at the request of Morgan, Wilson's twin sister who has been dead for two years.

Wilson has been uncommunicative with Julianna since Morgan's death, withdrawing into a state of functional catatonia. Julianna has tried to deal with her grief in a more proactive manner as she describes.
BWSM96, 4.5 minutes
The Batting Cage by Joan Ackerman

1950
Claudia, 40s A farmhouse in Provence, France
A woman on the verge of self-discovery. Claudia has been struggling to make her life make sense for quite some time. Now on holiday in the south of France with her best friend, Heddy, she seems ready to confront the demons she's thus far avoided so neatly. When a younger Frenchman, Alex, asks her out on a date, she accepts without considering the consequences. She expresses her feelings of loneliness and alienation to Heddy, who has passed out from a combination of Xanax, red wine and jet lag.
BWSM96, 3.5 minutes
Burning Down The House by Jocelyn Beard

1951
Claudia, 40s A farmhouse in Provence, France
A woman on the verge of self-discovery. While on holiday in the south of France, Claudia falls in love with Alex, a younger man whose wife was killed by a sniper in Sarajevo. When she accidentally causes a fire that burns down the house once inhabited by Alex and his wife, Claudia flees to a nearby lavender field where she hopes to be able to collect her thoughts. She is discovered by Alex's sister, Juliette, to whom she explains the reasons why she isn't ready for a relationship.
BWSM96, 1.5 minutes
Burning Down The House by Jocelyn Beard

1952
Erin, 30s   A wooden church
A woman tortured by memories of the past and fears of the future. The sole survivor of a vicious serial killer, Erin has spent the years battling to hold onto her daughter, who was conceived during her capture. Erin finally tells her terrifying and heartbreaking story to a caring friend.
BWSM96, 3.5 minutes
The Church Of The Holy Ghost by Ludmilla Bollow

1953
Sally, 30s   Here and Now
A woman fighting her addiction to love. Sally has finally given the boot to Jack and Talbot, two men who have taken turns using her. She describes her first moment without a man in her life

BWSM96, 3.5 minutes
Dance With Me by Stephen Temperley

1954
Vanessa, 63
San Miguel Allende, Guanajuanto, Mexico
Elegant and graceful, the wife of a great painter. Vanessa and Ed live in Mexico where they are paid a visit by a young photographer and his girlfriend, Chloe. Vanessa tells Chloe the unhappy story of her first husband's death.
BWSM96, 4 minutes
Detail Of A Larger Work by Lisa Dillman

1955
Chloe, 20s
San Miguel Allende, Guanajuanto, Mexico
A young woman with a terrible secret. Chloe and Zach have traveled to this part of Mexico to visit Vanessa and Ed, who were close friends of Duane, a man who allowed Zach to chronicle his slow death from AIDS in photographs. Unknown to Ed and Vanessa, Chloe could no longer bear Duane's suffering, and smothered him with a pillow. When this secret is revealed, Vanessa is horrified and demands that Chloe and Zach leave immediately. Chloe attempts to leave Vanessa with a happier memory of her dear friend.
BWSM96, 2.5 minutes
Detail Of A Larger Work by Lisa Dillman

1956
Young Woman, 20s   The deck of a cruise ship
When the ship's photographer offers to take her picture, the young woman ruminates on her appearance.
BWSM96, 2.5 minutes
Doppleganger by Jo J. Adamson

1957
Old Woman, 60-70   The deck of a cruise ship
Passenger on a cruise ship. Here, an older woman speaks of her newly discovered love of reading.
BWSM96, 2 minutes
Doppleganger by Jo J. Adamson

1958
Cathy, 30s   A hospital sitting room
A woman torn apart by her daughter's terminal illness and her failing marriage. When Cathy fears her husband, Daniel, is near to a complete breakdown, she leaves her terminally ill daughter to visit him in the Balkans where he has been working as a geologist on a dam project. Daniel informs Cathy that he hates her for their daughter's illness and then leaves her in the tiny village to go seek out a wise man who is rumored to have the power to cure the sick. Back in London, Cathy reveals to Daniel

what she did when left alone in the village.
BWSM96, 3 minutes
The Ends Of The Earth by David Lan

1959
Maureen, 20s
Events throughout the life & death of Jack Wilson
Jack's mother. The determined young Maureen frets over her sick baby.
BWSM96, 3 minutes
Fragments by John Jay Garrett

1960
Maureen, 40s
Events throughout the life & death of Jack Wilson
Jack's mother. Some 20 years later, Maureen recalls finding out that Jack was killed in Vietnam.
BWSM96, 3 minutes
Fragments by John Jay Garrett

1961
June, 40s   **Here and Now**
An alcoholic mom with a wry sense of humor. Because of her drinking, June's daughter, Claire, has been removed from her care several times. The philosophical booze hound addresses Claire's concerned teacher.
BWSM96, 2 minutes
A Girl's Tie To Her Father by Sari Bodi

1962
Orrine, 30s   **A cemetery**
A woman trying to make peace with her past. Orrine visits her mother's grave on her birthday and does her best to put to rest the demons that haunt her memory.
BWSM96, 10 minutes
Grace by Albert Verdesca

1963
June, 30s   **Here and Now**
A woman remembering her past. Restless June compares her current lover to her first lover.
BWSM96, 4 minutes
Hot Air by Richard Willett

1964
Cathy X, 20s
New York City and the infrared mirror world
A young woman with a shocking dual identity. A quirk of dimensional displacement has landed Cathy X in the mirror image world of Infrared where she determines to act as a missionary of the soul. She preaches to Infrared's inhabitants.
BWSM96, 1.5 minutes
Infrared by Mac Wellman in collaboration with Jane Geiser

1965
Linda, 40-60   **Here and Now**
A former Bond Girl. A one-time starlet recounts the chance meeting of a former comrade in arms at a Del-Mart.
BWSM96, 6 minutes
James Bond's Old Girlfriends by Toni Schlesinger

1966
Anna, 20s
A resort on Yalta, the turn of the century
A young woman who has been unfaithful to her husband. While on holiday in Yalta, Anna has become involved with the unscrupulous Dimitri. She indulges in a bit of self-loathing.
BWSM96, 1.5 minutes
The Lady With The Toy Dog by Sari Bodi
Adapted from "The Lady With the Toy Dog" by Anton Chekhov

1967
Anna, 20s
A resort on Yalta, the turn of the century
A young woman who has been unfaithful to her husband. Anna has tasted both passion and freedom during her holiday in Yalta. When her forgotten husband sends a telegram demanding that she return home, Anna wonders if she will able to go back to her old life.
BWSM96, 2.5 minutes
The Lady With The Toy Dog by Sari Bodi, adapted from "The Lady With the Toy Dog" by Anton Chekhov

1968
A Lesbian, 30-40   **Here and Now**
A woman dying of AIDS phones her mother to say good-bye before taking her own life via drug overdose.
BWSM96, 2.5 minutes
Lesbian's Last Pizza by Jeff Goode

1969
A Lesbian, 30-40   **Here and Now**
A woman preparing to commit suicide. The dying lesbian calls her father, to whom she hasn't spoken in years, to say good-bye.
BWSM96, 6 minutes
Lesbian's Last Pizza by Jeff Goode

1970
Elizabeth, 50s   **A summer house**
A woman on the verge of momentous change. Elizabeth has come to realize the emptiness in her life as a signal for change. She has therefore resolved to leave her husband for a new life as a volunteer worker in Africa. When her family pressures her to stay, she makes a declaration.
BWSM96, 2 minutes
Losers Of The Big Picture by Robert Vivian

1971
Jean, 50s   **A summer house**
An aging alcoholic. When her sister-in-law accuses her of having killed her husband, Fritz, by enabling his drinking, Jean readily agrees.
BWSM96, 1.5 minutes
Losers Of The Big Picture by Robert Vivian

1972
Oya, 20-30   **The kingdom of King Shango**
The king's first wife. When Shango finds true love with his second wife, Osun, Oya's jealousy drives her to commit desperate acts of betrayal. The jealous queen vents her rage.
BWSM96, 1.5 minutes
Many Colors Make The Thunder-King by Femi Osofisan

1973
Sarah, 8-11
Backyard, & homestead in the TX panhandle
A young girl with a vivid imagination. Young Sarah describes in detail her favorite pastime: pretending.
BWSM96, 6.5 minutes
Migrant Voices by Martha King De Silva

1974
A grieving mother, 30s
Backyard, & homestead in the TX panhandle
A care-worn farmer's wife remembers her daughter's death.
BWSM96, 6.5 minutes
Migrant Voices by Martha King DeSilva

1975
Myra, 17
America during Eisenhower Administration
The bad twin. The devilish Myra remembers a surrealistic air raid drill.
BWSM96, 4.5 minutes
The Mineola Twins by Paula Vogel

1976
Myra, 17
America during Eisenhower Administration
The bad twin. After sleeping with her twin sister's fiancé, Myra tries to convince the straight-laced young man to go out on the town with her.
BWSM96, 2 minutes
The Mineola Twins by Paula Vogel

1977
Kate, 30-40
A private school for autistic children
A teacher of autistic children. Kate claims to have made an amazing breakthrough in communication with one of her students, a young woman named Eve who has written a book while "speaking" to Kate via computer keyboard. Kate expresses a rather negative world view to Eve's concerned father.
BWSM96, 1.5 minutes
Miracles by Frank Higgins

1978
Kate, 30-40
A private school for autistic children
A teacher of autistic children. Kate claims to be able to communicate with seventeen-year-old Eve by "facilitating" the autistic girl's use of a keyboard. When Eve's father begins to suspect that Kate has fabricated everything that Eve has supposedly said via the keyboard, he storms out of the school with threats to remove Eve. Kate desperately pleads with an unresponsive Eve to communicate.
BWSM96, 3.5 minutes
Miracles by Frank Higgins

1979
Judy, 40s   **Here and Now**
A philosophical lesbian. Judy's relationship with the vivacious and younger Lois is coming to an end. Realizing that a break-up is inevitable, Judy takes a moment to reflect on her life and her sexuality.
BWSM96, 3.5 minutes
Missing Pieces by Barbara Quintero

1980
Lois, 20s   **Here and Now**
A young woman with a lust for life. Lois has been involved in a gay relationship but now wants to move on. She describes her parents' unhappy existence, revealing the fear that keeps her moving from place to place and person to person.
BWSM96, 5 minutes
Missing Pieces by Barbara Quintero

1981
Dolores, 20-30   **A desolate lighthouse**
A circus clown who has washed ashore at the lighthouse. Dolores has come to care for Ollie, the misanthropic lighthouse keeper. When she tries to return to her life in the circus, she discovers that she misses Ollie. She then returns to the lighthouse to confront Ollie with her feelings. She finally washes off her clown make-up.
BWSM96, 1.5 minutes
Mr. Melancholy by Matt Cameron

1982
Molly Sweeny, 30s   **Ireland**
A woman who has been blind since birth.

Molly describes her father's efforts to help her to "see" the world.
BWSM96, 5.5 minutes
Molly Sweeny by Brian Friel

1983
Barbara, 30-40   **The Bronx Zoo**
A woman visiting the zoo with her family. Barbara is inspired by one of the zoo's denizens to make a telling observation about sex and monogamy.
BWSM96, 2 minutes
Naked Mole Rats In The World Of Darkness by Michael T. Folie

1984
Jean, late 20s   **An inner city**
A woman confronting her HIV-positive lover. When her estranged lover, Arlington, demands to see their eleven-year-old son, Jean angrily refuses, citing her reasons, her anger and her fear.
BWSM96, 1.5 minutes
No Mean Street by Paul Boakye

1985
The Virgin Mary   **The home of Mary and Joseph**
Mary lectures her famous son about the power of the media.
BWSM96, 2 minutes
Portrait Of The Virgin Mary Feeding The Dinosaurs by Jeff Goode

1986
The Virgin Mary   **The home of Mary and Joseph**
As she does the ironing, Mary carps about her thankless role as messianic mom.
BWSM96, 2 minutes
Portrait Of The Virgin Mary Feeding The Dinosaurs by Jeff Goode

1987
Alma, 30-50   **A farm in rural Georgia**
A woman haunted by memories of the past. Alma shares a memory of her mother, Ruth, a killer executed by the state of Georgia.
BWSM96, 4 minutes
The Red Room by S. P. Miskowski

1988
Martha, 30-50   **A farm in rural Georgia**
A woman haunted by memories of the past. Martha's mother died in the electric chair. Now, she and her sisters, Alma and Louise share the family farm where all three struggle to cope with demons from the past. Martha shares a dream.
BWSM96, 2.5 minutes
The Red Room by S. P. Miskowski

1989
Juliette (Jules), 30s   **Here and Now**
A restless spirit. Jules has been haunted by her sister's ghost since she was five. In an effort to atone for her part in her sister's death, Jules and her best friend, Alexandra, have taken several road trips which have turned into spiritual quests, the most recent of which landed the women in New Orleans. Unfortunately for Jules, the Big Easy is to be her final destination in this life. Her spirit describes coming to New Orleans and her death.
BWSM96, 3 minutes
Romancing Oblivion by Steven Tanenbaum

1990
Janet, 40-50   **Here and Now**
A woman confronting her aging mother. Janet reveals her fears about her daughter, Cory, to her mother while challenging the older woman not to die.
BWSM96, 1.5 minutes
Second Sunday In May by A. Giovanni Affinito

1991
Roach, 30s   **Slaughter City, USA**
A black woman who works at the slaughter house. Roach remembers a time in her childhood when she felt special.
BWSM96, 4 minutes
Slaughter City by Naomi Wallace

1992
Simone, 20-30   **Here and Now**
A woman who has just discovered that she is HIV positive. Simone has always allowed herself to be ruled by passion, both emotional and physical; an indulgence for which she must now pay the ultimate price.
BWSM96, 3 minutes
Smoke & Mirrors by Eric C. Peterson

1993
Natalie, 30s   **Here and Now**
A woman who never tries too hard because she's happy right where she is. When Natalie's neighbor, Helen, kidnaps another woman's baby from the hospital, reporters waste no time in beating a path to her door. Pragmatic Natalie fields their questions.
BWSM96, 5 minutes
The Souvenir Of Pompeii by Sari Bodi

1994
Jennifer, 20s   **Here and Now**
A young woman whose baby has just been stolen from the hospital. Desperate Jennifer demands to be released from the hospital so she may search for her kidnapped child.

BWSM96, 2.5 minutes
The Souvenir Of Pompeii by Sari Bodi

1995
Marie Rossini Williamson, 40-60   **NYC**
A highly successful playwright. Marie and her
husband, Charlie are a winning writing team
who have recently separated. Marie describes
her lonely new single life to her agent.
BWSM96, 1.5 minutes
The Split by Jack Gilhooley and Jo Morello

1996
Babe, 40-50
Glen Daniel, West Virginia, a coal mining town
The outspoken widow of a coal miner. Babe is
obsessed with getting her daughter, Libby, out
of Glen Daniel. She is determined that Libby
won't know the same kind of life that she's
lived in their insular community. When she
convinces a childhood friend of Libby's to convince the girl to go to college, her motives are
questioned by her mother and best friend. She
does her best to explain her feelings.
BWSM96, 2 minutes
The Sweet By 'n' By by Frank Higgins

1997
Samantha, 20s   **NYC**
A young woman desperate to hang on to her
boyfriend. When Billy decides to go home to
Texas following college graduation, pregnant
Samantha begs him to stay without revealing
her secret.
BWSM96, 2.5 minutes
Texans Do Tap Dance by Richard Lay

1998
Ma, 50-60   **NYC**
A woman of the world, Texas-style. An earthy
ex-tart provides details of her life as a hooker
in suburban Texas.
BWSM96, 3 minutes
Texans Do Tap Dance by Richard Lay

1999
Myrna, 20s   **Here and Now**
Myrna came to New York City with one burn-
ing ambition: to become a hooker. She tells the
story of how she was sidetracked into acting.
BWSM96, 4 minutes
Twinges From The Fringe by Bob Jude Ferrante

2000
Edna, 30s   **A restaurant**
Edna announces her intention to leave her hus-
band and start a new life.
BWSM96, 1.5 minutes
Wait by Brian Christopher Williams

2001
Kate, 40-50   **A hospital**
A woman whose daughter has been brutally
raped. Lee has been in a state resembling catatonia since her rape and beating by a serial
killer. Strong-willed Kate does her best to get
her daughter to speak.
BWSM96, 5.5 minutes
When Language Fails by Gail Noppe-Brandon

2002
Jeni, 30s   **A hospital**
Jeni has been doing her best to encourage Lee,
a victim of a brutal rape, to describe her attacker, a serial killer who has raped and murdered
several other young women. Unfortunately, Lee
remains in a catatonic state and refuses to
speak. Jeni dispenses with the mask of concerned police officer and speaks to Lee on a
level she hopes will break through the terrified
girl's defenses.
BWSM96, 4.5 minutes
When Language Fails by Gail Noppe-Brandon

2003
Laura, 18   Augusta, Georgia, the early 1960s
A young woman trapped in an abusive marriage. Laura's husband, Marty, is about to be
shipped to Vietnam and has become increasingly violent as a result. Laura confesses her
dream to one day become an artist to her sympathetic neighbors.
BWSM96, 2 minutes
When Starbright Fades... by Sandra Marie Vago

2004
Laura, 18   Augusta, Georgia, the early 1960s
A young woman trapped in an abusive mar-
riage. Laura was sexually abused by her father
when she was a small child. She relates the
events of a sadly parallel dream.
BWSM96, 2 minutes
When Starbright Fades... by Sandra Marie Vago

2005
Lyn, 33   **The United Kingdom**
Following her second miscarriage, Lyn receives
a bothersome phone call from her mother, who
seems more interested in the pending nuptials
of Lyn's childhood nemesis than in her daughter's personal tragedy. Lyn complains of her
mother's lack of sensitivity to her lover, Kofi.
BWSM96, 4 minutes
Wicked Games by Paul Boakye

2006
Judith, 20s   **Here and Now**
A young woman handed an extraordinary op-
portunity. Judith describes how she came to at-

tend the University of Natal in South Africa.
BWSM96, 13 minutes
Yankee Kugel by Judith Silinsky Pasko

2007
Mr. Windenough, 20-40   A crypt, mid-1800s
A man entombed alive by mistake. When his
neighbor, Mr. Lacko'breath is also mistakenly
entombed alive, Windenough (who has been
having an affair with Lacko'breath's wife)
takes a moment or two to complain about his
situation.
BMSM96, 3.5 minutes
*Blackwood by Jocelyn Beard Based Upon "Loss of
Breath," a short story by Edgar Allen Poe*

2008
Alex, 30 A lavender field in Provence, France
Alex's Croatian wife, Soja, was killed in
Sarajevo nearly three years ago. Since her
death he has retired to his family's estate in
Provence where he eventually encounters
Claudia, an American woman who shares with
him a passion for art and the need to begin
again. He explains to Claudia why he is finally
ready to resume living.
BMSM96, 3 minutes
Burning Down The House by Jocelyn Beard

2009
Giddy Rourke, 70s
The Short Warf Cafe, on the Chesapeake Bay
A screenwriter in exile. During the communist
witch hunt of the 1950s, Giddy fled
Tinseltown for an obscure life fishing for crabs
on the Chesapeake. Nearly thirty years later,
he is discovered by an idealistic young director
who becomes determined to make Giddy's unfinished masterpiece into a motion picture.
Two very different generations of filmmakers
clash as Giddy reacts to the younger man's
sense of style.
BMSM96, 2.5 minutes
Cheap Sentiment by Bruce Graham

2010
Hunt, 50   The 124th Precinct
A morally bankrupt detective. Years on the
force weigh heavily on Hunt. When a murder
suspect whom he has illegally detained commits suicide in his jail cell, internal affairs
threatens to bring charges against him. The
soul-weary Hunt does his best to describe the
reality in which he is forever caught.
BMSM96, 2.5 minutes
The Coyote Bleeds by Tony DiMurro

2011
Hunt, 50   The 124th Precinct
A morally bankrupt detective. Hunt reveals a

glimpse of his tortured soul.
BMSM96, 2.5 minutes
The Coyote Bleeds by Tony DiMurro

2012
Talbot, 30s   Here and Now
A histrionic, self-centered crybaby. Talbot has
been cheating on Sally with Daisy, a younger
woman who is currently spending a romantic
weekend with Sally's lover, Jack. (Got that?)
The melodramatic Talbot tortures himself by
imagining Jack and Sally together.
BMSM96, 2 minutes
Dance With Me by Stephen Temperley

2013
Gil, whatever his age, he does not look it
A motel along the I-40, somewhere in Missouri
A documentary filmmaker from Orange
County California. Gil has encountered Matthew,
a young writer, in a motel in the middle of
nowhere. During a bout of drug-taking, ten-
sion flares when Gil makes a play for
Matthew's young lover, Fay. When Matthew
makes the mistake of asking Gil his age, he re-
ceives the following reply.
BMSM96, 2 minutes
Day Break by Nathan Parker

2014
Gil, whatever his age, he does not look it
A motel along the I-40, somewhere in Missouri
A documentary filmmaker from Orange
County California. Gil surreptitiously reads
Matthew's journal and discovers that the
younger man has described him in less than
flattering terms. Enraged, Gil tells Matthew
exactly what he thinks of his writing.
BMSM96, 2.5 minutes
Day Break by Nathan Parker

2015
Seth, 40   Here and Now
While trying to inspire passion in his fiancé,
Seth ponders the problematic nature of panty-
hose.
BMSM96, 3.5 minutes
Dead Or Alive by Karen Smith Vastola

2016
Frank, 80   Here and Now
A man who has just discovered he has a brain
tumor. Frank has lived his life with passion
and tenacity. The news of his tumor has made
him determined to use whatever time he may
have left in pursuing life's joys as he here discusses with a photo of his dead wife.
BMSM96, 2 minutes
Death Wears Dancing Shoes by Nannette Stone

2017
Frank, 28   **Here and Now**
A blue-collar brother from the 'hood with no kids. Frank recalls his first encounter with Sherry, the woman with whom he has fallen in love.
BMSM96, 2 minutes
Double Or Nothing by Michael Ajakwe, Jr.

2018
Daniel, 30   A hospital sitting room, London
A geologist whose young daughter is dying. Daniel has recently returned from the Balkans where he had been working on a dam project that was causing unrest in the local population. He has returned to London to be with his wife and daughter, who is terminally ill. In a quiet moment, Daniel reveals the dichotomy that has all but severed his soul.
BMSM96, 3.5 minutes
The Ends Of The Earth by David Lan

2019
Mitch, 40s   **New York City**
When Mitch is fired from a Wall Street firm, he phones his estranged son, Eric, and begs him to meet him in Central Park at Strawberry Fields. Mitch cautions Eric to abandon his youthful idealism.
BMSM96, 3.5 minutes
Event Horizon by Christopher Kyle

2020
Boyd, 20s and Walter, 60s   Here and Now
Boyd has just murdered his father and has become possessed by Walter's wrathful ghost.
BMSM96, 15 minutes
Family Of Horrors by William Gadea

2021
Biff, 30s   **Here and Now**
A well-meaning brother. Biff explains how his brother, Ray, came to lose his head.
BMSM96, 2.5 minutes
Family Of Horrors by William Gadea

2022
Henry, 20-30   **A field**
A man haunted by his experiences in war. Once a soldier, Henry now works as a surveyor. He reveals a bit of his empty soul to Joseph, his partner.
BMSM96, 1.5 minutes
Feasting by S. P. Miskowski

2023
Jack, 15
Events during the life and death of Jack Wilson
A young man on the verge of adulthood. Jack's best friend has tricked him into asking out Rachel. Jack makes an awkward attempt to convince her to go out on a date.
BMSM96, 3 minutes
Fragments by John Jay Garrett

2024
Ethan, 18
Events during the life and death of Jack Wilson
A young man struggling to know his dead father. Ethan's father, Jack, died in Vietnam before he was born. Ethan visits the Vietnam War Memorial in Washington, DC and reads a letter that Jack wrote when he found out that he was going to be a father.
BMSM96, 4 minutes
Fragments by John Jay Garrett

2025
Louis, 20-30   **Rikers Island**
A hitman contemplating entering the Witness Protection Program. Patrician Louis is determined to get out of serving time as he explains to Joey, his partner in crime.
BMSM96, 2 minutes
Gangster Apparel by Richard Vetere

2026
Louis, 20-30   **Arizona**
A hitman contemplating entering the Witness Protection Program. When Louis and Joey are relocated to Arizona by the Feds, Louis chafes at life in the desert. Joey, on the other hand, seems to finally come into his own. When he proudly shows Louis his garden, the former hitman is reminded of his father, a bricklayer.
BMSM96, 2 minutes
Gangster Apparel by Richard Vetere

2027
Man, 20-30   **New York City**
A petty thief-turned-killer weaves a gritty tale of betrayal and retribution.
BMSM96, 13 minutes
The Good Luck Charm by James M. O'Donoghue

2028
Roman Kozachenko, 78
The Sussex countryside, England
A Ukranian citizen of the UK accused of war crimes. Due to a change in British law, individuals suspected of having committed war crimes may now be formally charged. One such person is Roman, a seventy-eight year-old man accused of participating in the murder of 817 Jews in Ukraine. The nearly senile Roman explains why he could never have killed in cold blood.

BMSM96, 2.5 minutes
The Handyman by Ronald Harwood

2029
Al Bean-Fletcher, 45   **Here and Now**
On the first anniversary of his son's murder by
a street punk, who has been freed after serving
only nine months in a juvenile detention center, Al prepares to exact vengeance of a more
permanent nature.
BMSM96, 3.5 minutes
Happy Anniversary, Punk! by Michael Ajakwe, Jr.

2030
Chad, 30s   **Here and Now**
A gay man recalling a one-night stand. Chad
reminisces about the heyday of gay dance
clubs like the Saint, and one night in particu-
lar.
BMSM96, 4.5 minutes
Have It All by Robert Coles

2031
Joe, 40   **A southern college town**
A filmmaker. When a friend despairs of ever
being able to understand women, Joe offers
the following helpful information.
BMSM96, 1 minute
Hawk Dreaming by Frank Cossa

2032
Artie, 30s   **A bar in Queens**
Artie has mistakenly agreed to go out on a date
with Laura, a loquacious and shallow woman
with several ex-husbands to carp about.
Beleaguered Artie finally explains why he
wants to end the date and go home.
BMSM96, 4.5 minutes
*How To Go Out On A Date In Queens by Richard
Vetere*

2033
Narrator, 30-40
NYC and the infrared mirror world
An ungainly self in search of validation. The
narrator is a being whose sole purpose seems
to be that of proactive self-discovery.
Following a rather surreal visit to the world of
infrared, he muses on how much more he has
to learn about life.
BMSM96, 2 minutes
Infrared by Mac Wellman

2034
Jack, 30s   **Here and Now**
Jill's residency is proving more than their marriage can bear, and Jack can no longer provide
her with the kind of support she needs to endure the long hours and stress. During a rather

serious argument, Jill accuses Jack of being too
involved with trying to be nice to be truly effective. Jack fumes over being called "nice."
BMSM96, 2 minutes
Jack And Jill by Jane Martin

2035
Yomoma, 50s
The empty front room of Yomoma's Rest Home
An eccentric gay man. The enigmatic Yomoma
uses make-up and costumes to transform him-
self into "the kissing cousin of Aunt Jemima"
as he explains why he decided to open up a
rest home.
BMSM96, 3.5 minutes
The John Doe Variations by Silas Jones

2036
Tinatine, 20s
The fantastical kingdom of King Gordogan
The son of King Gordogan. Tinatine is in
search of his true love, who has been impris-
oned in a white tower. The luckless young man
complains about his fruitless search.
BMSM96, 4.5 minutes
*King Gordogan by Radovan Ivsic, translated by
Roger Cardinal, American Version by Allan
Graubard*

2037
The Fool, 20-50
The fantastical kingdom of King Gordogan
The King's fool. The talkative Fool indulges in
some rather philosophical stream of con-
sciousness.
BMSM96, 3 minutes
*King Gordogan by Radovan Ivsic, translated by
Roger Cardinal, American Version by Allan
Graubard*

2038
Dimitri, 30-40
A seaside resort in Yalta, the turn of the century
A sophisticated cad. A man addicted to the
joys of romantic pursuit makes a canny obser-
vation regarding his quarry.
BMSM96, 1 minute
*The Lady With The Toy Dog by Sari Bodi Based on
the short story, "The Lady With the Toy Dog" by
Anton Checkov*

2039
Rummy, 50s   **A summer home**
Prosperous but dismayed. Rummy stands on
the threshold of his golden years with a nice
pocketful of money but no understanding of
life; past, present or future.
BMSM96, 1.5 minutes
Losers Of The Big Picture by Robert Vivian

2040
Warren, 30s   **Troy, NC**
A man who has just realized his marriage is over. When his wife's artistic slump is cured by the arrival of her old flame, Warren realizes that he can't compete with her passion for art—nor does he wish to try. He tells his wife and her suspected lover about a liberating experience he enjoyed at a diner given in his honor by the Jaycees.
BMSM96, 7.5 minutes
Magnets by Phil Hines

2041
Father, 30s   **Here and Now**
A man recalling the traumatic birth of his first child. Childbirth isn't always a walk in the park, as women know all too well. A new father reveals his own struggle to cope with his wife's compromised labor.
BMSM96, 10 minutes
Master Of The Obvious by Kevin Fisher

2042
Frank, 40s   **Ireland**
A man trying to help his blind wife to see the world. Frank recalls the first time he asked Molly out on a date.
BMSM96, 4.5 minutes
Molly Sweeny by Brian Friel

2043
Jack, 40s   **The Bronx Zoo**
A man suffering from a mid-life crisis. Jack describes his unhappy state to his wife, Barbara.
BMSM96, 2 minutes
Naked Mole Rats In The World Of Darkness by Michael T. Folie

2044
Stephan Hoffman, 25   **Vienna, 1986**
An American music student. The former child prodigy has traveled to Vienna to study piano. Before he may study with Professor Schiller, however, he must first study singing with the eccentric professor Mashkan. Stephan, who is Jewish, assumes that Mashkan is an anti-Semite based upon the old man's caustic commentary. Stephan angrily tells Mashkan of his weekend visit to Dachau just prior to discovering the telltale tattoo on the professor's arm.
BMSM96, 6 minutes
Old Wicked Songs by Jon Marans

2045
Jake, 57   **A bar in Chicago**
A bar owner. Jake tells the story of his brief and unhappy marriage to a stranger.
BMSM96, 2 minutes
An Ordinary Woman Under Stress by Sandra Marie Vago

2046
Lou Barbota, 30s   **Queens**
Handsome Queens gangster; intelligent and dangerous. Lou is being sent to prison for fifteen years. Knowing that he won't survive without his wife, Diane, he summons artist Nick Dante to one of his illegal garbage dumps and demands that Nick paint a portrait of Diane.
BMSM96, 6 minutes
Painting X's On The Moon by Richard Vetere

2047
Charlie, 30s   **Queens**
A gangster's bodyguard; an abuser of women. When young Stephanie makes herself a gangster's whore by throwing herself at Charlie, he responds with acid misogynistic insight.
BMSM96, 1 minute
Painting X's On The Moon by Richard Vetere

2048
Mephistopheles   **A wilderness**
A devilish guy. A waggish Mephistopheles mocks the Ten Commandments.
BMSM96, 3.5 minutes
Portrait Of The Virgin Mary Feeding The Dinosaurs by Jeff Goode

2049
The Ghost of Moliere   **Here and Now**
The timeless playwright addresses his future audiences.
BMSM96, 1.5 minutes
Sad Laughter by Charles Deemer

2050
Jon Davies, 40s   **A stage**
An actor concerned with the preservation of all of Shakespeare's works, whether politically correct or not. When his performance as Shylock meets with public outrage, Jon (who is Jewish) examines the character both within and without its historical and cultural context. Jon recalls his first encounter with the Bard of Avon.
BMSM96, 6.5 minutes
Shylock by Mark Leiren-Young

2051
Abe, 70   **Here and Now**
Abe is in the beginning stages of Alzheimer's. He muses about a photograph he keeps in his wallet.
BMSM96, 1.5 minutes
Six At Twenty Six by Seth Kramer

2052
Abe, 70   **Here and Now**

A man suffering from Alzheimer's Disease. Abe seems to have found an odd and unsettling peace with his infirmity.
BMSM96, 1.5 minutes
Six At Twenty Six by Seth Kramer

2053
Brandon, 20s   **Slaughter City, USA**
A young worker in a slaughter house. As he shows a new worker how to pull loins, Brandon details his history at the slaughter house.
BMSM96, 1 minute
Slaughter City by Naomi Wallace

2054
Tuck, 40s   **Slaughter City, USA**
A supervisor in the slaughter house. Tuck, who is black, derides Cod, a new employee in the slaughter house for being Irish.
BMSM96, 2 minutes
Slaughter City by Naomi Wallace

2055
Tom, 30s   **Here and Now**
Apparently, there aren't enough women in town to satisfy Tom's needs. He describes what is, unfortunately, a typical night in his life.
BMSM96, 3 minutes
Smoke & Mirrors by Eric C. Peterson

2056
Sam, 30-40   **Here and Now**
A man whose wife has just kidnapped a baby from the hospital. When Helen disappears with another woman's child, Sam must do his best to answer questions about her motives and possible whereabouts.
BMSM96, 3.5 minutes
The Souvenir Of Pompeii by Sari Bodi

2057
Landon, 20s-30s   **Here and Now**
A poet. Landon reveals his sense of alienation as he describes his disassociative feelings about sex.
BMSM96, 2 minutes
Tell Me What You Want by Robert Coles

2058
Audie, 40s   **A psychiatric hospital**
Brought on by chronic alcohol abuse and exacerbated by head trauma, Audie's Korsakoff's Syndrome manifests itself in the patient as the inability to remember anything that happened the day before. Part of Audie's therapy has been to read from prepared scripts which retell certain events in his life. He forces himself to read a script in which he visits his dying father in the hospital.
BMSM96, 2 minutes
Tuesday by Paul Mullin

2059
Desmond, 20-40   **Here and Now**
The ever-inquisitive Desmond speculates about the reality of what it must be like when an entire continent disappears.
BMSM96, 3.5 minutes
Twinges From The Fringe by Bob Jude Ferrante

2060
Mr. Green, 86
The upper west side of Manhattan
A retired dry cleaner; a man hiding from life. When Mr. Green is nearly run over by Ross, an executive with American Express, the judge sentences Ross to helping Mr. Green one day a week. After many uneasy weeks, the cantankerous Mr. Green tells Ross the tale of how he met his beloved wife, Yetta.
BMSM96, 2.5 minutes
Visiting Mr. Green by Jeff Baron

2061
The Broker, 20-30   **Here and Now**
A man with a sardonic, yet practical view of life. A young stock broker reveals an incident from his past that changed his life.
BMSM96, 2.5 minutes
White Men by Michael P. Scasserra

2062
John Creek, 50-60
A white supremacist compound, Idaho
Charismatic and dangerous leader of the Brethren, a white supremacist militia. When a plane belonging to a popular Democratic senator—who happens to be black—crashes on his mountain in a blizzard, Creek is astonished when the senator makes an appearance at his home to beg for help in searching for survivors before the FAA and authorities arrive. Creek wisely concludes that the small plane was carrying a passenger whose identity could ruin the senator's career, and takes the upper hand in this most volatile situation.
BMSM96, 2 minutes
Whiteout by Jocelyn Beard

2063
Kofi, 31   **The UK and Ghana**
A British social worker, mixed race. Kofi stops by the beauty salon where his pregnant lover, Lyn works. As she washes his hair, Kofi entertains her with a story of a recent encounter with a new South African client.
BMSM96, 2 minutes
Wicked Games by Paul Boakye

2064
Leo, 34   **The UK and Ghana**
A sports instructor, black. Leo has recently discovered that his close male friend, Kofi, harbors romantic feelings for him. Leo muses on his tendency to give the wrong impression to other men with Kofi's female lover, Lyn.
BMSM96, 2 minutes
Wicked Games by Paul Boakye

2065
Rafe, 20   **The Catskills**
Rafe has returned home from the Gulf War only to discover that his father has sold the land that he intended to farm. Devastated, Rafe moves onto the site of an old hunting camp where he makes his home in a tent. He tells a visiting friend about the first time he went deer hunting with his father.
BMSM96, 2.5 minutes
Windshook by Mary Gallagher

2066
Rafe, 20   **The Catskills**
A disillusioned vet. Rafe is determined to buy back the land his father sold. To that end he takes a job as a prison guard. He describes his state of affairs.
BMSM96, 2 minutes
Windshook by Mary Gallagher

2067
A Man, 30s   **A funeral home**
Paying his respects at a friend's funeral. A friend describes his relationship with the deceased.
BMSM96, 7.5 minutes
Working Class by Richard Hoehler

2068
Meg, 20-30   **Here and Now**
A young woman momentarily dazzled by a glimpse of life's Big Picture. Impatient Meg reveals the brief yet profound epiphany she experienced while waiting for a friend in the rain.
BWSM97, 8.5 minutes
Bad Grrrls by Linda Eisenstein

2069
Mabel, 11   **Here and Now**
A young victim. An eleven year-old girl waits in the hall outside speech class and confides a troubling experience (in a roundabout way) to a friend.
BWSM97, 5 minutes
Big Bang by Ellen Reif

2070
Susie, 20s   **Here and Now**
A young woman who has just hit her boyfriend with his car. A remorseful Susie pleads for her boyfriend's life in the ER
BWSM97, 3.5 minutes
Big Bang by Ellen Reif

2071
Bill, 30s
A beach, the week of the Perseid Meteor Showers
A confused, chemically-dependent American aristocrat. When she visits her lover at the beach where he works, Bill (who has recently been released from rehab) reveals her fear and loathing of the ocean.
BWSM97, 2 minutes
By the Sea, By the Sea, By the Beautiful Sea: "Day" by Lanford Wilson

2072
Carol, 40s   **Here and Now**
A woman whose daughter has disappeared. Weeks after Anna has disappeared without a trace, Carol has slowly returned to her life where she is haunted by dark dreams of her daughter's most likely demise.
BWSM97, 3 minutes
The Dark Parent by Victor Bravo

2073
Anne, 30s   **A psychiatrist's office**
A woman coming to grips with her tragic childhood. Anne reveals a childhood filled with horror and abuse during a particularly intense therapy session.
BWSM97, 4.5 minutes
Dialogue of Self and Soul by Jo J. Adamson

2074
Teddie, 40s   An ad agency in Portland, Oregon
The president of an ad agency, recently widowed. Teddie has returned to the office following a lengthy bereavement. She describes a perfectly miserable Christmas.
BWSM97, 2 minutes
Drawing Down Clio by Doug Baldwin

2075
Wilma, 20-30   **The rural Mid-West**
A woman driven over the edge of reason by the death of her child. Wilma and her husband, Matthew, have been on the run since the death of their baby. Wilma has burned down a dozen or more churches in a tragic effort to express her feelings of guilt and rage. She muses about her growing disassociation from the world.
BWSM97, 3 minutes
Easter by William Scheffer

2076
Lief, 15
A mythical time in the NY tri-state area, specifically the underworld

A young woman in search of her father. Lief has left Penelope, her mother, to go in search of her missing father, Ulysses. When she falls into a river, she drowns and dies. Lief wakes up dead in Pluto's underworld.
BWSM97, 1 minute
Epic Poetry by James Bosley

2077
Woman, 30s   **New York City**
A denizen of the Big Apple ruminates on the city's more esoteric qualities.
BWSM97, 3 minutes
F.O.B. To U-Haul: New York Lessons by Steven Tanenbaum

2078
Rosie, 44   **An apartment in New York City**
An artist. After an evening of drinking, Rosie has returned to her apartment with three men in tow. She explains her motives.
BWSM97, 4 minutes
Forget-Me-Not by Richard Lay

2079
Deola, 30s   **A card game**
A hard-working African American business woman who can also predict the future. Deola is host to a weekly game of bid whist at which she and her friends meet to play cards and share their lives. On this particular evening, she is cooking chitlins, much to the olfactory consternation of her friends. She gamely defends chitlins' place in American culinary history.
BWSM97, 2.5 minutes
Four Queens—No Trump by Ted Lange

2080
Edna, 30-40   **A card game**
An African American woman trying to restart her life after an unhappy marriage. Edna has begun dating a white man whose family, she has just discovered, comes from the same small town in Texas as does her own. It was in this small town that her grandmother was raped and beaten by a white lynch mob in 1922. She remembers her grandmother's pain and her own efforts to bring the older woman some comfort.
BWSM97, 2.5 minutes
Four Queens—No Trump by Ted Lange

2081
Lorinda Wyndham, 30
The garden of the Wyndham Estate, 1920
A woman driven to dispair and madness by the death of her unborn child. Once full of life, Lorinda has deteriorated in the years that have

passed since she lost the baby she was carrying. She has decided to give the beautiful estate to an order of Catholic nuns and comes to the garden a final time to bid her lost child farewell.
BWSM97, 5 minutes
A Garden of Women by Ludmilla Bollow

2082
Jolene, 42   **Here and Now**
A college professor. Surrounded by blue books, Jolene explodes with frustration at her students' lack of interest and initiative.
BWSM97, 2 minutes
Golden Elliot by Linda Stockham

2083
Evie, 40   **A condo in the Pacific Northwest**
A woman trying to reconstruct her life following a divorce. Evie has divorced Duncan and left him behind in New England. She now fancies herself in love with Carter, a fellow divorcee. She describes the final days of her marriage with Duncan to Carter as they share a bottle of wine.
BWSM97, 1.5 minutes
Gunshy by Richard Dresser

2084
Sally, 20s   **Iowa**
An unhappy wife. Sally has manipulated her husband's life in practically every regard as she reveals in the heat of argument.
BWSM97, 4 minutes
Hazing the Monkey by Marcus A. Hennessy

2085
Altagracia, 30s   **A beach house**
A woman whose face is noticeably deformed and whose spirit is noticeably amazing. Altagracia has rescued her brother from the state hospital and is hiding with him in an empty beach house. Beau, a man claiming to know the owner of the house has arrived on the scene wearing a ski mask which he asserts hides a hideous face disfigured in a car crash. Altagracia tells him about her high school prom in an effort to help him come to terms with his newfound ugliness.
BWSM97, 2.5 minutes
Icarus by Edwin Sanchez

2086
The Gloria, 40-60   **A beach house**
An aging beauty. A woman who is desperate to hold on to her looks describes going to a power party and encountering a new blonde.
BWSM97, 3 minutes
Icarus by Edwin Sanchez

2087
Paulette, late 'teens–early 20s
Backyard of a trailer home in Deerfield, OH.
Aug., 1978
A woman who has just been raped by her husband. The death of their child has driven an irrevocable wedge between Paulette and her husband, Denny. On a hot night in August, Denny finally explodes with pent-up rage and sexual frustration, forever killing any chance the couple may have had to fix their marriage as she describes.
BWSM97, 2.5 minutes
In Search of the Red River Dog by Sandra Perlman

2088
Jackie, 30s JFK's funeral, 1963
Recently widowed in Texas. Jackie Kennedy takes a moment to reflect upon her loss.
BWSM97, 1.5 minutes
Jackie: An American Life by Gip Hoppe

2089
Ying-Ying St. Clair, 50-60 Here and Now
A woman divulging an old secret. Ying-Ying tells her daughter the passionate and tragic story of her first husband.
BWSM97, 4.5 minutes
The Joy Luck Club by Susan Kim. From the Novel by Amy Tan

2090
Tovah, 20s Here and Now
A Hasidic woman who has recently left her husband. Brave Tovah explains why she chose to leave her husband and her community.
BWSM97, 3 minutes
Lasso the Alamo by Olga Humphrey

2091
Christina, 20s Here and Now
A woman agonizing over whether or not she should marry her abusive fiancé. When her friends intervene in an effort to keep Christina from marrying the man who bit off her nose, the victim offers the reasons for going through with the nuptials.
BWSM97, 2.5 minutes
Lasso the Alamo by Olga Humphrey

2092
Marilyn, 20-30 Here and Now
An Asian-American prostitute. When a regular client, Dookie, proposes, Marilyn offers the violent thug a refusal.
BWSM97, 1.5 minutes
L'Eboueur Sleeps Tonight (For Worlds Are Destroyed by Day) by Jerome D. Hairston

2093
Sue, 39 Here and Now
A semi-worried mother. When she notices that her teen-aged daughter is missing from the house, Sue wonders how upset she should allow herself to become.
BWSM97, 1.5 minutes
L'Eboueur Sleeps Tonight (For Worlds Are Destroyed by Day) by Jerome D. Hairston

2094
Judy, 30s Here and Now
Judy bemoans the repression of sexuality rampant in our age and longs for the comfort of companionship. She describes an unsavory experience she recently had at a party.
BWSM97, 3.5 minutes
Lions, Tigers and Bears by Michael P. Scassera

2095
Libby, 20-30 New York City
A young woman whose life has bottomed-out. When Taylor, the man she loves, marries her sister, Libby thinks her life is pretty lousy until she loses her job and finds that it's worse than lousy. Just when things couldn't get worse for this recovering alcoholic, they do, as she describes.
BWSM97, 5.5 minutes
The Maiden's Prayer by Nicky Silver

2096
Caitlin, 30s The simplest possible car
Caitlin suffers from crippling panic attacks when she drives on the Mass Pike. She drives onto the dreaded highway to test the response time of her new beau.
BWSM97, 5 minutes
Marcus is Walking by Joan Ackerman

2097
Marla, 30s Here and Now
A woman seeking to change her life. Marla has recently begun to engage in systematic prostration—not unlike Buddhist pilgrims—in an effort to know her spiritual self. She offers some observations regarding the concept of devotion.
BWSM97, 1.5 minutes
Marla's Devotion by Linda Eisenstein

2098
Alison, 18
An apple orchard in Pine City, MN. Fall, 1965
A young woman on the verge of motherhood. The father of Alison's baby has shipped out for Vietnam, leaving her unwed and in the lurch. When her well-meaning aunt sets her up with Alec, a somber young mortician who has loved

her from afar, Alison does her best to be the earnest young man's friend.
BWSM97, 2.5 minutes
Molly's Delicious by Craig Wright

2099
Alicia, 30-40   **Here and Now**
A novelist and academic on the verge of a melt-down. Years of frustration have led Alicia to quit writing. She has invited her inner circle of sister scribes to participate in the ritualistic destruction of her work via fire. When someone suggests that Alicia needs to accept change in her life she makes a reply.
BWSM97, 1 minute
The Names of the Beast by Linda Eisenstein

2100
Nebekenezer, 30-40   **A bar**
A barkeep. On a dark and stormy night, Nebekenezer regales the denizens of her saloon with a colorful take on the Biblical Noah.
BWSM97, 5.5 minutes
Noah's Archives by Stephen Spoonamore

2101
Buns, 20-30   **A bar**
A.k.a. Judith, a temp/actress obsessed with her body. A woman who has extended lots of time and energy on making her body perfect reveals her hatred of men.
BWSM97, 6.5 minutes
Noah's Archives by Stephen Spoonamore

2102
Kelsey, 22
A beat-up old car heading north to Canada
Kelsey has been living with Zephyr in an isolated cabin in Canada. Following a visit home to California, Kelsey no longer wants to rough-it in the woods. She prepares to give Zephyr the bad news.
BWSM97, 2.5 minutes
The Northern Lights by Lauren McConnell

2103
Eurydice, 18-20
Pier at the edge of the city. Late 1990s, night
A young woman wandering through the underworld. As she crosses the River of Forgetfulness, Eurydice tells Orpheus and Persephone of her compelling need to forget.
BWSM97, 1.5 minutes
Polaroid Stories by Naomi Iizuka

2104
Persephone, 20s
Pier at the edge of the city. Late 1990s, night
A woman teetering on the edge. Rage and grief

over the loss of her son have driven Persephone to trash a public restroom.
BWSM97, 1.5 minutes
Polaroid Stories by Naomi Iizuka

2105
Lisa, 30s   **Here and Now**
Lisa has been sleeping with Adrian, a Brit who is directing her and her husband, Matthew, in a new play. Lisa reveals her overwhelming feelings of fear and guilt to a therapist.
BWSM97, 1.5 minutes
Private Eyes by Steven Dietz

2106
Barbara Kepler, 25
Benatek Castle, near Prague. 1600
A short-tempered, melancholy woman once married to a wealthy merchant and now married to a penniless—through brilliant—astronomer. Barbara's new husband, Johannes Kepler, has been invited to join Tycho Brahe at Benatek Castle. When Barbara and the children finally arrive she finds the environment of the scientists not at all to her liking.
BWSM97, 1.5 minutes
Reading the Mind of God by Pat Gabridge

2107
Woman, 30-40   **Here and Now**
A woman whose childhood was defined by her intense fear of demons (courtesy of the overactive imagination of her Sunday School teacher and a stolen glance at The Exorcist) describes a scene from her past that foreshadowed endless nights of terror.
BWSM97, 2 minutes
Scared of Demons by Michael Steffens-Moran

2108
Winnifred, 20-30   **A white room, Present**
A young woman claiming to have been aboard the Titanic. When Winnifred is discovered floating on an iceberg in the North Atlantic and dressed in late nineteenth century clothes, the only word she utters to her rescuers is: Titanic. A mysterious and seemingly wealthy man named John has Winnifred brought to Maine where he and a doctor endeavor to discover the truth about her origins. At first, John claims to be a great-grandson of John Jacob Astor, an American millionaire who went down with the overly famous ship. Winnifred eventually reveals that she knows his true identity and describes the first time she ever met John aboard a certain ship, many years ago...without Leonardo and Kate romping on the foredecks.
BWSM97, 4.5 minutes
Scotland Road by Jeffrey Hatcher

2109
Meg, 40s   **Here and Now**
A compassionate midwife who's seen it all.
Meg shares a story about her father, a preacher
man.
BWSM97, 4 minutes
Singing the Bones by Caitlin Hicks

2110
Nicole, 37   **Here and Now**
Determined Nicole tells her midwife why she
wants to deliver her twins at home, even if it
means risking her babies' lives.
BWSM97, 9 minutes
Singing the Bones by Caitlin Hicks

2111
Aunt Boat, 42   **A bedroom**
A large woman who resembles a peasant in
one of Jules Breton's nineteenth century pas-
toral paintings. Aunt Boat has just poisoned
her sister, House, who was too obese to leave
her bed. Boat addresses herself to her sister's
enormous body.
BWSM97, 2 minutes
The Sister Upstairs by Robert Vivian

2112
Sally, 20s
A small American town. Summer, 1969
When her fiancée shipped-off for Vietnam,
Sally eventually turned to booze to dull her
fear and boredom. She does her best to explain
why she drinks.
BWSM97, 3 minutes
Soda Fountain by Richard Lay

2113
Ma, 40-50
A small American town. Summer, 1969
A woman grieving over the death of her son.
When Francis is found drowned, Ma does her
best to cope with the loss. She describes how
she had come to love this child who was born
less-than-perfect.
BWSM97, 1.5 minutes
Soda Fountain by Richard Lay

2114
Bethany, 40
A low-heat steam room in a NYC health club
An attractive, neurotic woman who has had
extensive face and body work to maintain the
illusion. When Bethany encounters a long-lost
childhood friend in a steam room, she finds
that she must account for the unusual amount
of work that has gone into creating and main-
taining her "perfect" body.
BWSM97, 2.5 minutes
Some-Bodies by Gail Noppe-Brandon

2115
Michaela, 30s   **Here and Now**
A woman attending her younger sister's wed-
ding. Michaela remembers an incident from
her childhood that would become an enduring
bone of contention between her and little sister
Erin.
BWSM97, 2.5 minutes
Something Blue by Michaela Murphy

2116
She, 30s
**Manhattan; penthouse terrace on a summer
night**
A woman describes an act of marital infidelity
that she recently committed to a man she has
just met at a party.
BWSM97, 3 minutes
Stars by Romulus Linney

2117
Shary, 16-18   **New York City**
Shary committed suicide when she could no
longer bare being secretly pregnant, her par-
ents' violent arguments and being accepted at
Vassar all at the same time. Her restless spirit
recalls one of her parents' more unpleasant
confrontations.
BWSM97, 2 minutes
Sticky and Shary by Rob Handel

2118
Shary, 16-18   **New York City**
Shary describes her suicide, which unfortu-
nately claimed the life of her younger brother,
Sticky.
BWSM97, 5.5 minutes
Sticky and Shary by Rob Handel

2119
Svetlana, 20s   **Coney Island**
A recent Russian émigré. Svetlana is starting a
new life in Brighton Beach where she is beginning her American adventure by learning how
to be a fire-eater for a sideshow The spirited
young woman muses on the etiquette of fire-
eating.
BWSM97, 1.5 minutes
Svetlana's New Flame by Olga Humphrey

2120
Eve, 40s-50s
A homeless woman's makeshift campsite
A homeless woman; brash, spunky and possi-
bly crazy. Loquacious Eve entertains passen-
gers from a tour bus with a tale of alien visita-
tion.
BWSM97, 9 minutes
Tea Time by Dori Appel

2121
Linda, 34
Family garage in suburban Finland
A woman nearly trapped in a generational cycle of subservience. Married to a man she doesn't love, Linda describes her unfortunate legacy.
BWSM97, 1 minute
To Each His Own (Dead and Gone to Granny's) by Jussi Wahlgren

2122
Elsie Smith, 60s
The kitchen of a very ordinary house
Recently, things have happened to Elsie which have convinced her that it's time to shuffle off this mortal coil. The sassy granny describes the unfortunate incident which has inspired her to take her own life.
BWSM97, 9 minutes
Twockers, Knockers and Elsie Smith by Jean Stevens

2123
April, 30s **Queens, NY**
An alcoholic mourning the death of her father. Following her father's funeral, April and her sisters gather around the dining room table and catch up with one another. April is fascinated that her younger sister, Moira, is pregnant. She waxes rhapsodically on the subject of creation.
BWSM97, 3.5 minutes
Vegetable Love by Tammy Ryan

2124
Brigit, 50s **Queens, NY**
On the day of her husband's funeral, Brigit finds herself surrounded by her daughters. One is pregnant, one anorexic and one an alcoholic. She recalls a dream she once had.
BWSM97, 2 minutes
Vegetable Love by Tammy Ryan

2125
Jane, 20s **New York City**
An intense street person. Jane plays complicated rhythms on plastic tubs with drumsticks as she offers a passionate stream-of-consciousness diatribe on the nature of the city.
BWSM97, 5.5 minutes
Voices in the Dark by Heidi Decker

2126
Woman, 30s **New York City**
A homeless person whose time on the streets has been filled. A destitute woman offers some insight into the ghastly reality of her daily life.
BWSM97, 4.5 minutes
Voices in the Dark by Heidi Decker

2127
Louisa Mae Alcott, 45
The home of Bronson Alcott. Concord, MA
A writer; an unhappy woman. When her mother's health deteriorates, Louisa finds herself facing the inevitable conclusion that she will soon die. Plagued by nightmares, Louisa describes one to her father and sister.
BWSM97, 2 minutes
The Wax Cradle by Jo J. Adamson

2128
Bessie, 20s **Chicago**
An African American woman trying to keep it all together. When Bessie is admonished for not praying regularly to God by her wheelchair-bound mother, the pragmatic younger woman takes the advice offered and offers a prayer.
BWSM97, 4 minutes
Wedding Dance by Dominic A. Taylor

2129
Mantha, 20-30 **The southwest of England**
A young woman whose life has been forever changed by violent crime. Mantha's boyfriend, Davy, went on an unexpected and unexplained killing spree. Several years later, Mantha has started a new life with a new man. The past cannot be silenced, however, and she is soon tracked down by a journalist seeking the "truth." Mantha speaks about Davy to the persistent journalist.
BWSM97, 2.5 minutes
Went Down to the Crossroads by Philip Goulding

2130
Therese, 30s **Here and Now**
A manipulating player of games. When her partner hears word that a friend from his past has died, Therese reveals a bit of the spleen that has helped to make her the hard woman she has become.
BWSM97, 2 minutes
What Cats Know by Lisa Dillman

2131
Marty, 20-30 **Diva's, a cabaret in New Orleans**
A young woman seeking a career in show business. Marty has just been hired as the new act at Diva's, a club that usually headlines singers. Marty, whose act is more like performance art than anything else, does her best to describe her elation at being hired to the mega-divas who perform regularly at the club.
BWSM97, 3.5 minutes
When a Diva Dreams by Gary Garrison

2132
Miss Red, 50s
Diva's, a cabaret in New Orleans
The proprietor of Diva's, a woman with drive and moxie. When Miss Red is incapable of paying the mortgage, it looks as though Diva's will have to be closed. Enter Delle, Miss Red's estranged sister who has more than enough money to keep the cabaret afloat, if only Miss Red can forgive her for walking out on the family. Miss Red describes the effect that Delle's running away had on their father.
BWSM97, 4.5 minutes
When a Diva Dreams by Gary Garrison

2133
Rebecca Tattinger, 60
The home of John Creek; a white separatist and militia leader, Idaho
The wife of a powerful and well-liked African American US senator facing-off against the enemy during a blizzard. Dan Tattinger's private plane has crashed on land belonging to John Creek, the leader of the country's largest private militia. Onboard the plane was Tattinger's secret illegitimate daughter. Public knowledge of this woman's existence could prove lethal to his political career. Dan has gone to Creek to beg help in rescuing his daughter. Rebecca, a woman of enormous intelligence and power, arrives soon after. When Creek's daughter reveals that she already knows everything there is to know about Dan and Rebecca from their intelligence group, Rebecca angrily explains why the racists know nothing about her.
BWSM97, 13 minutes
Whiteout by Jocelyn Beard

2134
Peer, 20s   The Puget Sound Territory, 1851
An imaginative young scalawag. When the girl that he fancied for himself is about to be married to another, Peer spies on the wedding festivities from a hill above the town and daydreams about becoming a pirate.
BMSM97, 6 minutes
Alki by Eric Overmeyer

2135
Peer, 20s   The Puget Sound Territory, 1851
An imaginative young scalawag. Peer has stolen Ingrid from her wedding and is subsequently chased into the woods by an angry posse. In the forest, Ingrid is forgotten as Peer is seduced by a band of feral girls. The following morning Peer awakes on the cold earth feeling much the worse for wear.
BMSM97, 3 minutes
Alki by Eric Overmeyer

2136
David, 50s   The atelier of a Tudor-style house
in Croton, NY, Autumn 1972
A successful concert vocalist. David's longtime companion, Peter, has lost his passion for musical composition and has suffered a recent heart-attack. Walker, a younger man who has wandered into their lives, seems to have a beneficial effect on Peter and is encouraging him to write a book as he recuperates. David soon becomes jealous of Walker's influence on Peter and confronts the younger man with his concerns.
BMSM97, 4.5 minutes
Autumn Canticle by John W. Lowell

2137
Peter, 50s
The atelier of a Tudor-style house in Croton, NY, Autumn 1972
A former musical prodigy now ailing and played-out. Peter has had to cope with the loss of his passion for music as well as the disintegration of his body. When his longtime relationship with David, his heart and soul mate, is threatened, he reacts with fear and longing.
BMSM97, 3.5 minutes
Autumn Canticle by John W. Lowell

2138
Sayles, 30-40
The conference room of a small defense contractor in the declining Southern California defense/aerospace industry
An aggressive and optimistic player on the project team. Sayles and his co-workers are hard at work on what may be their final project. As they ponder the unknown threat to their continued employment, Sayles explodes with frustration and anger.
BMSM97, 2 minutes
Bafo Best and Final Offer by Tom Strelich

2139
P.K., 30-40
The conference room of a small defense contractor in the declining Southern California defense/aerospace industry
A disgruntled former employee toting a loaded AK-47. P.K. has burst into the offices of the company from which he was recently fired, and he is loaded for bear. After shooting at several people, he corners his former co-workers in a conference room. P.K. takes a moment to survey the project they have been working on and then advises them that they have failed to identify the threat to their work, a mandatory function for corporate survival. He offers them chilling insight into the necessity of being fearful.
BMSM97, 5 minutes
Bafo Best and Final Offer by Tom Strelich

2140
Clay, 50s
The conference room of a small defense contractor in the declining Southern California defense/aerospace industry
A retired Colonel now employed in the defense industry. When he and his co-workers are taken hostage by an ex-employee brandishing a loaded AK-47, the stress of the situation enables this otherwise cool and collected commander of men to make a confession.
BMSM97, 3.5 minutes
Bafo Best and Final Offer by Tom Strelich

2141
Robert, 30s   **Here and Now**
A man whose wife has committed suicide. Gayle's death has left Robert bitter and alienated. He shares a memory of his father.
BMSM97, 3 minutes
A Body Not Greatly Changed by Jo J. Adamson

2142
Quentin, 30s
A beach at dawn, the week of the Perseid meteor showers
A man coping with the loss of his mother. Their mother's last wish was that her ashes be scattered over the sea. To this end, Quentin and his sisters have gathered on the beach where their pre-dawn vigil has degenerated into petty sibling bickering. When his sisters condemn his wife for cheating on him, Quentin valiantly defends the woman he loves.
BMSM97, 2.5 minutes
By the Sea, By the Sea, By the Beautiful Sea "Dawn" by Joe Pintauro

2143
Willy, 30s
The beach during the week of the Perseid Meteor Shower
An attractive beachcomber. A glib ladies' man chats up a couple of women he's just met on the beach.
BMSM97, 1.5 minutes
By the Sea, By the Sea, By the Beautiful Sea "Dusk" by Terrence McNally

2144
Carl, 30s   **A passenger van**
An aggressive member of the carpool. When they witness an accident on the way to work, Carl lectures his fellow car-poolers on the importance of paying attention to their environment.
BMSM97, 1 minute
Carpool by Laura Hembree

2145
Willard, 40-50   **A passenger van**
A man whose wife has been diagnosed with cancer. Willard tells his fellow commuters about the recent changes in his home life.
BMSM97, 1.5 minutes
Carpool by Laura Hembree

2146
Carl, 30s   **A passenger van**
An aggressive member of the carpool. Bitter about his divorce, Carl cautions his romantically involved friend about the dangers of home redecorating.
BMSM97, 3 minutes
Carpool by Laura Hembree

2147
Reporter, 20s-30s   **British Columbia**
A city boy struggling to make sense of his new home in remote northern B.C. The reporter describes a murder case that he covered for the local paper.
BMSM97, 9 minutes
City Boy in a Cowboy Town by Mark Leiren-Young

2148
Pilot, 60s
The Smithsonian Air & Space Museum
The man who flew the Enola Gay. The man who helped Einstein and Oppenheimer create modern reality relives his famous flight before an audience at the Smithsonian.
BMSM97, 17 minutes
The Confession of Many Strangers by Lavonne Mueller

2149
Corporal William Garabents, 20s
Kobi Tan Tan Valley, Vietnam. July 1966
A tunnel rat. The sole survivor of his unit, Corporal Garabents finds himself alone in the jungle of Vietnam facing the dark and gaping maw of a tunnel which he has been ordered to secure. He encounters the ghost of his father, a G.I. who was killed in the Battle of the Bulge, and confronts the spirit with his childhood feelings of grief and abandonment.
BMSM97, 2.5 minutes
Daddy and the Tunnel Rat by Mark Blickley

2150
Matthew, 20-30   **A small town in the mid-west**
A man whose wife has been driven to madness by the death of their child. Matthew and Wilma have been on the run since the death of their baby. Wilma's suppressed grief and rage have caused her to act out by burning down churches. Matthew finally tells his story to a strange old man who is constantly tuned-in to television...with or without a TV set.

BMSM97, 5 minutes
Easter by Will Scheffer

2151
Ulysses, 40s-50s
The Amazon Saloon. A mythical time in the NY tri-state area
A lost hero. A modern incarnation of a familiar wanderer tells his son, Jason, about the importance of taking care of one's mother.
BMSM97, 3.5 minutes
Epic Poetry by James Bosley

2152
Bod, 30s **A train**
Bod rides trains in search of a woman with whom he has fallen in love. He tells his story.
BMSM97, 2 minutes
Feathers in the Dust by Richard Lay

2153
Judah ben Bezalel Loew, 50
The Jewish Quarter of Prague, Spring, 1592
Chief Rabbi of Prague. The Rabbi tells the tale of how he first met and fell in love with his beloved late wife, Perl.
BMSM97, 2 minutes
The Golem by Andrew C. Ordover

2154
Horatio, 30s **Here and Now**
A genetic engineer suffering from an attack of conscience. Although Horatio has devoted his professional career to improving the genetic structure of humanity, he has recently come to respect the importance of serendipity, as he describes.
BMSM97, 12.5 minutes
Good Guy's Wear Yellow by Daphne Hull

2155
Joseph, 20s **A provincial town**
A disgruntled valet to a minor government clerk. Joseph's employer is a traveling clerk whose extravagant habits have depleted their funds. Stranded in a small town in the country, Joseph grouses as he polishes his master's shoes.
BMSM97, 3 minutes
The Government Inspector by Nikolai Gogol. New Adaptation by Philip Goulding

2156
Petty, 20s **A provincial town**
A foolish young clerk. When Petty is mistaken for a Government Inspector, the people of the small town roll out the red carpet for the young impostor. Enjoying his unexpected status, Petty babbles inanely to an attractive young woman.

BMSM97, 4 minutes
The Government Inspector by Nikolai Gogol, New Adaptation by Philip Goulding

2157
Roger, 20s **Here and Now**
A disillusioned young man. Roger walked away from life as a musician in a bar band to marry Sally and settle down. His new job has taken him well inside the corporate milieu, where he is driven crazy by the new generation of business-speak mumbo jumbo. When his CEO, Mrs. Kaiser, has a heart attack at the office, Roger finally explodes as his co-workers debate the correct office protocol to handle the emergency.
BMSM97, 2 minutes
Hazing the Monkey by Marcus A. Hennessy

2158
Beau, 20-30 **A beach house**
A man hiding from the past and from himself. Beau wears a mask which he claims hides a face that has been horribly disfigured in a car crash. When he meets Altagracia, a remarkable woman who was born with a horribly ugly face, Beau is transformed by her strength and inner beauty, making it possible for him to finally reveal his own, perfect, face and confess his sad story.
BMSM97, 2 minutes
Icarus by Edwin Sanchez

2159
Denny, 20s
A trailer home in Deerfield, OH. Aug., 1978
A young man ruined by tragedy. Denny has lost his job, his child and his wife's love in a very short amount of time. Frustrated and ultimately enraged by his wife's refusal of physical closeness, he savagely rapes her. As she prepares to leave him, he begs her to stay.
BMSM97, 3 minutes
In Search of the Red River Dog by Sandra Perlman

2160
Jon, 70s **New York City**
While walking near the 59th Street Bridge, Jon and others watched in amazement as a homeless man flew. Lonely Jon describes the remarkable event to his dead wife.
BMSM97, 8 minutes
Jack Flew by David Ippolito

2161
Dookie, 30s **Here and Now**
A small-time hit man in love. Years of living a violent life have left an indelible mark on Dookie, who has fallen for Marilyn, a prosti-

tute. He makes an awkward proposal of marriage.
BMSM97, 3.5 minutes
L'Eboueur Sleeps Tonight (For worlds are destroyed every day.) by Jerome D. Hairston

2162
Nathan, 12
Small town on the plains of West Texas, 1962
Nathan must learn how to make his Bar Mitzvah by listening to an old LP recording made by his grandfather many years before. Frustrated by the poor quality of the recording, Nathan draws an impertinent analogy to his predicament.
BMSM97, 3.5 minutes
The Legacy by Mark Harelik

2163
Taylor, 20s   A grand house in the country
A man with a history of substance abuse and sexual experimentation. Taylor has cleaned-up his act and settled down with Cynthia, who is devoted to making their life together perfect. The happy couple has moved into Taylor's family home in the country where they are expecting the arrival of their first child. The formerly dissolute Taylor confesses that he's finally found peace in the country.
BMSM97, 1.5 minutes
The Maiden's Prayer by Nicky Silver

2164
Taylor, 20s   A grand house in the country
A man with a history of substance abuse and sexual experimentation. When Cynthia suffers a miscarriage, their marriage slowly deteriorates. Eventually, Cynthia leaves Taylor, who is tempted to revert to his previous lifestyle of substance abuse. He tells his best friend that he no longer wishes to live.
BMSM97, 2 minutes
The Maiden's Prayer by Nicky Silver

2165
Charles Manson, 60s
The prison cell of Charles Manson
Infamous Charlie shares a psychedelic memory of his time in the wilderness in which he received his first "vision" of Helter Skelter.
BMSM97, 13 minutes
Manson by Mark Roberts

2166
Henry, 30s   The simplest car possible
After making love with Lisa for the first time (in the back seat of his car, no less), Henry makes the following declaration of love.
BMSM97, 3 minutes
Marcus is Walking by Joan Ackerman

2167
Paul, 20s   A bar in New York City
A young man who has everything, except a future. This wealthy young executive has been diagnosed with a brain tumor. He sips a martini and wonders aloud if he should still propose to his girlfriend.
BMSM97, 4 minutes
Martini by Richard Lay

2168
Jerry, 18
Apple orchard in Pine City, MN. Fall, 1965
A young soldier on leave from the war in Vietnam. Jerry has returned to Pine City from Vietnam to discover that Alison, his girlfriend, is carrying his child. When he prepares to do the right thing and proposes, Alison balks, soliciting a confession.
BMSM97, 3.5 minutes
Molly's Delicious by Craig Wright

2169
Joaquim, 20s
Lobby of the Hotel Imperial, in Africa
A former soldier, now the bell boy of a crumbling old hotel. Made desperate by personal privation and the constant political upheaval in his country, Joaquim has taken a handful of guests hostage at the dilapidated Hotel Imperial. In a quiet moment, this frustrated young African reveals the pathology of his growing sense of emotional nihilism.
BMSM97, 1.5 minutes
Mud, River, Stone by Lynn Nottage

2170
Cupid, any age
Ancient Greece, or thereabouts
God of love. This cherubic cutie reveals some interesting facts regarding his modus operandi.
BMSM97, 3 minutes
Narcissus & Echo, Book and Lyrics by Jeff Goode, Music by Larrance Fingerhut

2171
Narcissus, 20s Ancient Greece, or thereabouts
A young nymph. Narcissus encounters his own reflection and is appropriately impressed.
BMSM97, 2 minutes
Narcissus & Echo, Book and Lyrics by Jeff Goode, Music by Larrance Fingerhut

2172
Louis, 40s
A booth store known as "The Blow Hole"
An edgily neurotic man in search of his lover. Louis has recently begun to suspect that Edwin's nightly jog is more than it seems. This night he has followed Edwin on his nightly run

with disastrous results. He describes his traumatic experience to a friend, whom he has called for help.
BMSM97, 4 minutes
A Night at the Blow Hole by Robert Coles

2173
Shem, 30-40   **A bar**
Earthy Shem reveals uncanny insight into the nature of love.
BMSM97, 6 minutes
Noah's Archives by Stephen Spoonamore

2174
Shem, 30-40   **A bar**
A man contemplating his life's love. Shem ruminates on the ultimately finite nature of human sexual relations.
BMSM97, 4.5 minutes
Noah's Archives by Stephen Spoonamore

2175
Giuseppe Verdi, 27
Milano, Italy. A winter evening in 1841
A young composer. Following the deaths of his beloved wife and children, Verdi has retreated into a world of grief and despair. When he is pressured by the Inspector General of the Royal and Imperial Austro-Hungarian Theatre to write a new opera, he is forced to reveal the depth of his sorrow.
BMSM97, 1.5 minutes
On Golden Wings by A. Giovanni Affinitio

2176
Lucky, 30-40   **A junk shop**
An ex-junkie. Lucky has created an emotionally comfortable niche for himself in the junk trade. Discarded coffee makers, radios and the like enjoy special attention at Lucky's place, where hopefully they can be rehabilitated and resold. The philosophical junkman describes meeting the love of his life at a methadone clinic.
BMSM97, 6.5 minutes
Patchwork "Lucky" by Vicki Mooney

2177
Detective Reid, 30s   **Brooklyn, NY**
A dwarf who has just committed suicide. The death of his normal-sized brother, Dwayne, has driven Detective Reid to the ultimate act of grief and despair. After shooting himself in the heart, he uses his last breaths to explain his love of Dwayne.
BMSM97, 2 minutes
The Pharmacist's Daughter by Monika Monika

2178
D(Dionysus), 18-25
A pier at edge of city. The late 1990s, night
A partying God. The god of celebration has turned way hip in this adaptation of Ovid's Metamorphoses. Here D describes his first meeting with Oklahoma Boy, a spray and video junkie.
BMSM97, 2 minutes
Polaroid Stories by Naomi Iizuka

2179
Narcissus, 20s
A pier at edge of city. The late 1990s, night
A self-infatuated young man. A smooth-talking Narcissus gives a contemporary spin to the myth of Proteus.
BMSM97, 2.5 minutes
Polaroid Stories by Naomi Iizuka

2180
Matthew, 30s   **Here and Now**
An actor whose wife is having an affair with their director. Matthew finally gives voice to his suspicions as he confronts his wife and director with a monologue he later claims is new script material.
BMSM97, 4.5 minutes
Private Eyes by Steven Dietz

2181
Matthew, 30s   **Here and Now**
An actor whose wife is having an affair with their director. Matthew reveals a dark fantasy about his wife's infidelity.
BMSM97, 1.5 minutes
Private Eyes by Steven Dietz

2182
Johannes Kepler, 29
Benatek Castle, near Prague. 1600
A brilliant astronomer. Kepler has recently arrived at Benatek Castle at the invitation of the great Tycho Brahe. Here he will join Brahe's team of astronomers who are in the process of charting the heavens as no one has done before. Kepler's first project is to chart Mars using data and instruments he has never had access to before. The passionate young man frantically makes new calculations on the Red Planet.
BMSM97, 3 minutes
Reading the Mind of God by Pat Gabridge

2183
Pops, 50s   **Here and Now**
A fallen priest. Pops has been sharing a house with his daughter, Joan, and his two sisters, Boat and House. Over the years, Pops and

Aunt Boat have overfed Aunt House to the point that she is no longer able to leave her bed. When Aunt Boat poisons her sister in an effort to end the poor woman's suffering, she and Pops must then confront their mutual culpability in House's condition. Boat encourages Pops to tell Joan about the sad demise of House and receives a response.
BMSM97, 1 minute
The Sister Upstairs by Robert Vivian

2184
Pops, 50s   **Here and Now**
A fallen priest. His idealistic Joan-of-Arc-obsessed daughter has reacted poorly to the news of her aunt's death and has managed to shoot herself in the foot with her bow and arrow in a fit of pique. Miserable Pops bemoans his unhappy and unsavory life.
BMSM97, 4.5 minutes
The Sister Upstairs by Robert Vivian

2185
Danny, 20s
A small American town. Summer, 1969
An alcoholic draft-dodger hopelessly in love with best friend's girl...who also happens to be his drinking partner. When Johnny shipped out for Vietnam he left his best friend and his fiancée behind to keep the home fires burning. Unfortunately, both Danny and Sally soon turned to booze in an effort to cope with their fears and sense of ennui. Philosophical Danny reveals his love for Sally.
BMSM97, 5.5 minutes
Soda Fountain by Richard Lay

2186
Danny, 20s
A small American town. Summer, 1969
An alcoholic draft-dodger hopelessly in love with best friend's girl...who also happens to be his drinking partner. When Johnny returns home from Vietnam a hero, he finds his fiancée and best friend have turned into drunks. Danny reflects on Johnny's homecoming.
BMSM97, 2.5 minutes
Soda Fountain by Richard Lay

2187
Guy, 30s   **Here and Now**
An African American Everyman with a good eye for detail. Guy's day begins with a visit from the Devil, whose offer of temptation the sharp-eyed mailman rejects. Later that same day, Guy meets the woman of his dreams and sees the route to true happiness. Perhaps the confluence of such cosmic forces have made to him a gift of insight or perhaps he had it all along. In any case, Guy shares a canny obser-

vation of the general personality of the young white power elite.
BMSM97, 2 minutes
Soul Survivor by Ted Lange

2188
He, 30s-40   Manhattan. A penthouse terrace on a summer night
While at a party featuring Manhattan's hoi polloi, our hero tells a woman whom he's just met the story of how he first got together with his wife.
BMSM97, 4 minutes
Stars by Romulus Linney

2189
Sticky   **New York City**
Sticky was accidentally killed when he slipped and fell on the bathroom floor when his sister, Shary, committed suicide. The wandering spirit shares a memory of an evening at home with his family before everything was lost.
BMSM97, 3 minutes
Sticky and Shary by Rob Handel

2190
Pip, 20-30   **New York City, 1995**
The son of a world-famous architect, an aspiring actor. Pip describes his parents' first meeting and his mother's current state.
BMSM97, 5 minutes
Three Days of Rain by Richard Greenberg

2191
Patrick, 36
Garage of family home, suburban Finland
A man who has lost everything that mattered to him in one day. Patrick plans on committing suicide. When his first effort is interrupted by the arrival of his younger brother, the two men find themselves sharing bittersweet memories of their childhood.
BMSM97, 1.5 minutes
To Each His Own (Dead and Gone To Granny's) by Jussi Wahlgren

2192
Dominic, 60s
The Twinkle Toes Dance Studio, Peoria, IL, 1984
A retired accountant. Dominic has recently moved-in with his divorced niece, Kendall, who runs her own dance studio. It becomes quite obvious that these two will have to go through a period of adjustment before settling in to a life together. Dominic helps things along when he tells Kendall the story of her birth.
BMSM97, 4.5 minutes
Unpacking Dominic's Trunk by Terryl Paiste

2193
A retired British soldier, 60s
Great Britain—there and now.
A soldier remembers his experiences in World War II.
BMSM97, 6.5 minutes
The War Monologue by Tom Greenwell

2194
Milton, 20-30
A wedding reception in Chicago
A man who is slightly retarded. Milton places centerpieces and place cards on the tables at a friend's wedding reception and reveals his keen sense of logic.
BMSM97, 3.5 minutes
Wedding Dance by Dominic A. Taylor

2195
Marty the Mover, 30s-40s
Bensonhurst, Brooklyn
A philosophical mover. Marty has been hired to empty out Benny's house by Angie, Benny's unhappy wife. When Benny furiously demands to know where Angie has gone, Marty does his best to offer a bit of calming insight.
BMSM97, 3 minutes
We Make a Wall by Gary Garrison

2196
Kent, 30s   **Chicago**
Kent has learned the hard way that it takes a lot of work to keep a marriage afloat. He describes the rather painful demise of his first marriage.
BMSM97, 3 minutes
What Cats Know by Lisa Dillman

2197
Gregory, 30s   **Chicago**
An artist. Gregory and Cass sleep together when Cass's partner, Kent, is away on business. When Cass subsequently announces that she and Kent are expecting a baby, Gregory makes an overly gushing response to the news.
BMSM97, 2 minutes
What Cats Know by Lisa Dillman

2198
Lipton, 60s   **Diva's, a cabaret in New Orleans**
Lipton has worked for many years for Miss Rose at Diva's. When lack of funds threatens to close the cabaret, all is dire until Miss Rose's sister, Delle, shows up out of the blue with enough money to keep Diva's afloat. Taking the money from the sister who walked out on her family and broke her father's heart presents an ethical dilemma for Miss Rose. Sage Lipton shares advice and wisdom with his old friend.
BMSM97, 2.5 minutes
When a Diva Dreams by Gary Garrison

2199
Senator Dan Tattinger, 60
The home of John Creek, a white separatist and militia leader. Idaho
An African American man trapped behind enemy lines and fighting to save the life of his illegitimate daughter. The Senator's private plane has crashed in a blizzard on mountain property belonging to John Creek, the racist leader of the country's largest private militia. The plane was carrying Dan's racially-mixed daughter, public knowledge of whose existence could ruin his political future. Dan's wife, Rebecca, is a proud African American woman who has made issues of race her only political concerns. A frustrated Dan finally explodes when she confronts him with the fact that she is furious because his illegitimate daughter is half-white.
BMSM97, 4 minutes
Whiteout by Jocelyn Beard

2200
Alice, 18-20   **Rural England**
A selfish and manipulating young wife. The plotting Alice reveals her desire to see her husband, Arden, dead.
UAB, 1 minute
Arden of Feversham by Anonymous

2201
Alice, 18-20   **Rural England**
When Arden chases off the thugs Alice has hired to murder him, the quick-thinking Alice, a selfish and manipulating young wife, does her best to cover her tracks.
UAB, 2 minutes
Arden of Feversham by Anonymous

2202
Margaret
England under the reign of Henry III
When a young man courts her at the Harleston Fair, Margaret, the keeper's daughter, wonders at his refined speech and manner.
UAB, 1 minute
Friar Bacon by Robert Greene

2203
Margaret
England under the reign of Henry III
Margaret, the keeper's daughter, prepares to enter a convent.
UAB, 2 minutes
Friar Bacon by Robert Greene

2204
Mary of Magdala, 20s **The empty tomb**
Mary, one of Christ's followers, laments the death of the man she loved.
UAB, 1 minute
The Resurrection by The York Pageant of the Carpenters

2205
Maudlin, 30-40 **England**
The ambitious Maudlin, a goldsmith's wife, nags her daughter, Moll, for not trying hard enough to find a husband.
UAB, 1.5 minutes
A Chaste Maid in Cheapside by Thomas Middleton

2206
Octavia, 30s **Alexandria, 30 BC**
Octavia, the wife of Marc Antony and sister of Caesar, has followed her husband to Alexandria with the intent of winning him back from Cleopatra. She offers to save Antony from her brother's wrath.
UAB, 1 minute
All for Love; or the World Well Lost by John Dryden

2207
Cleopatra, 30s **Alexandria, 30 BC**
Following the suicide of her lover, Marc Antony, the passionate Queen of Egypt prepares to join him in death. She presents her arm to the asp and suffers its fatal bite.
UAB, 2 minutes
All for Love; or the World Well Lost by John Dryden

2208
Mistress Otter, 30-40 **London**
Mistress Otter seems to relish the constant upbraiding of her subservient husband, as the harangue illustrates.
UAB, 2 minutes
Epicoene by Ben Jonson

2209
Bellinda, 20s **London**
Sad Bellinda, a woman who mistakenly believes the man she loves to be married to another, bemoans her loveless fate.
UAB, 1 minute
The Innocent Mistress by Mary Pix

2210
Celestina, 20-30 **London**
When her household steward tries to warn Celestina, an extravagant widow, that she is developing a questionable reputation for her excesses, she angrily scolds him.
UAB, 1.5 minutes
The Lady of Pleasure by James Shirley

2211
Armande, 20s **Paris**
Armande, a foolish young woman who fancies herself a philosopher, has put off Clitandre's proposal of marriage for two years in hopes that the young man's physical passion will evolve into something more spiritual. When the greatly frustrated Clitandre finally proposes to Armande's younger sister, Armande furiously demands that he account for his inability to express "perfect love."
UAB, 1 minute
The Learned Women by Moliere

2212
Fidella, 20s **London**
Fidella, a woman pining for the love of a man who loves another, loves Manly, and masquerading as a man, has followed him to sea. Now returned to London, Manly pursues Olivia. The heartbroken Fidella muses on the time she has wasted.
UAB, 1 minute
The Plain Dealer by William Wycherley

2213
Roxana, 20s **Babylon**
When Alexander takes the beautiful Statira as his second wife, passionate Roxana, the wife of Alexander the Great, flies into a rage. She threatens to ruin their honeymoon night.
UAB, 1 minute
The Rival Queens by Nathaniel Lee

2214
Bassima, 20s
The Castle of Phasia in Libardian
Bassima was married to Levan Dadiare for political reasons, but her heart belongs to Osman, the Chief Visier. The wretched Bassima reveals her illicit feelings to Osman.
UAB, 1 minute
The Royal Mischief by Mary Delarivier Manley

2215
Bassima, 20s
The Castle of Phasia in Libardian
Married to a man she doesn't love, Bassima pleads with Osman to never see her again.
UAB, 1 minute
The Royal Mischief by Mary Delarivier Manley

2216
Lady Knowell, 40-60 **London**
The well-read Lady Knowell, an affected learned woman, sings the praises of reading the classics in their original languages.
UAB, 1 minute
Sir Patient Fancy by Aphra Behn

2217
Mariane, 18-20   **17th century Paris**
Mariane's father, Orgon, has been conned by
the swindling Tartuffe into offering the
scoundrel his lovely young daughter in marriage. Poor Mariane begs her father to allow
her to enter a convent rather than marry a man
she doesn't love.
UAB, 1 minute
Tartuffe by Moliere

2218
Erictho, 30-40   Libya, the second Punic War
Erictho, a witch, has tricked the mighty
Syphax into believing that he has made love to
Sophonisba when in fact it was the old crone
herself in his bed. When the King discovers
that he has been with the witch, she laughs at
his outrage.
UAB, 1 minute
The Tragedy of Sophonisba by John Marston

2219
Sophonisba, 20s Libya, the second Punic War
Sophonisba has given herself to Syphax to save
her beloved Carthage from ruin by his armies.
When her rightful husband, Massinissa, de-
feats Syphax in battle and confronts her,
Sophonisba begs him to let her die a free
woman.
UAB, 1 minute
The Tragedy of Sophonisba by John Marston

2220
Belvidera, 20s   **Venice**
Belvidera has married Jaffeir, with whom she is
deeply in love. She greets her new husband
with great affection.
UAB, .5 minute
Venice Preserved; or, A Plot Discovered by Thomas Otway

2221
Celia, 20s   **Venice**
Celia's husband, Corvino, has offered her fa-
vors to the unscrupulous Volpone in a mis-
guided attempt to become the wealthy noble-
man's sole heir. The terrified Celia begs
Volpone to either let her go or kill her.
UAB, 1 minute
Volpone by Ben Jonson

2222
Elizabeth Sawyer, 40-60   **England**
A witch. A woman branded by all as a witch
indulges in a bit of self-pity.
UAB, 1 minute
The Witch of Edmonton by William Rowley, Thomas Dekker, John Ford

2223
Elizabeth Sawyer, 40-60   **England**
When Elizabeth, a witch, is accused of being a
witch, she angrily confronts her accusers with
the following insight.
UAB, 1.5 minutes
The Witch of Edmonton by William Rowley, Thomas Dekker, John Ford

2224
Mrs. Peachum, 40s   **London**
The Peachums are delighted when their daughter, Polly, catches the eye of the notorious
Macheath, who is prepared to pay handsomely
for her favors. When Polly announces that she
and the highwayman have been married, her
mother, a woman of questionable morality,
chides the girl for her foolishness.
UAB, 1 minute
The Beggar's Opera by John Gay

2225
Lady Easy, 20-30   **Windsor**
A long-suffering wife. Lady Easy's wayward
husband is making her crazy, as the following
diatribe illustrates.
UAB, 1 minute
The Careless Husband by Colley Cibber

2226
Lady Betty Modish, 20-30   **Windsor**
When Lady Betty, a vain and shallow woman,
is cautioned by a friend that the married man
she has been having an affair with will tell all
his friends about her intimate charms, the foolish homewrecker ignores the advice.
UAB, 1 minute
The Careless Husband by Colley Cibber

2227
Angela, 20s   **A castle**
The evil Osmond has taken Angela captive.
The anxious young woman waits to be rescued
by the man she loves.
UAB, 1.5 minutes
The Castle Spectre by Matthew G. Lewis

2228
Lady Randolph, 30-40
A castle in the west of Scotland, 12th century
When her new husband prepares to leave for
war against Danish invaders, Lady Randolph
is reminded of the bloody Scottish and English
wars that took the life of Douglas, her beloved
first husband.
UAB, 1 minute
Douglas by John Home

2229
Charlot, 20s   **Penryn in Cornwall**
When a stranger accuses Charlot of being un-
faithful to Wilmot while he was missing at sea,
she hotly protests her love.
UAB, 1.5 minutes
Fatal Curiosity by George Lillo

2230
Agnes, 50-60   **Penryn in Cornwall**
The family fortune gone and their son lost at
sea, Agnes and her husband are tempted to kill
a mysterious stranger for money. When her
husband balks at committing such a desperate
crime, Agnes angrily blames his excesses for
their shameful state.
UAB, 1 minute
Fatal Curiosity by George Lillo

2231
Lady Freelove, 30-40   **London**
Lady Freelove has used the innocent young
Harriet as a pawn in her idle affairs d'cour.
When Harriet's father accuses Lady Freelove
of having brought about Harriet's ruination,
the manipulating society matron protests her
innocence.
UAB, 1 minute
The Jealous Wife by George Colman

2232
Lady Bell, 20s   **London**
Lady Bell, a duplicitous young woman, de-
scribes the enjoyment she takes from torturing
the men who court her.
UAB, 1.5 minutes
Know Your Own Mind by Arthur Murphy

2233
Millwood, 30s   **London**
Millwood, an evil scheming woman, has deliberately seduced young George Barnwell in
order to ruin the innocent youth by forcing
him to perform criminal acts such as theft and
murder. When she is discovered and appre-
hended, she vehemently declares her hatred of
men.
UAB, 1.5 minutes
*The London Merchant; or The History of George
Barnwell by George Lillo*

2234
Maria, 20s   **London**
Maria's fiance, George, has been led astray by
the evil Millwood, for whom he has commit-
ted murder. Maria visits the man who betrayed
her love just before he is led off to the gallows.
UAB, 1.5 minutes
*The London Merchant; or The History of George
Barnwell by George Lillo*

2235
Kitty, 20s   **London**
When her mistress falls in love with the penni-
less Gayless, Kitty, an insightful ladies' maid,
laments the blinding property of love.
UAB, 1 minute
The Lying Valet by David Garrick

2236
Julia, 20s   **Bath**
Julia has been pushed to the limit by her fi-
ance's constant questioning of her loyalty and
love for him. She finally declares that their en-
gagement has ended.
UAB, 2 minutes
The Rivals by Richard Brinsley Sheridan

2237
Rebecca, 30s   **Algiers**
Rebecca and her son, Augustus, have been
taken captive in Algiers. Rebecca's unscrupu-
lous master has recently sold Augustus to an-
other household. Unhappy Rebecca worries
about her son.
UAB, 2 minutes
*Slaves in Algiers; or, Struggle for Freedom by Susanna
Haswell Rowson*

2238
Lady Racket, 20-30   **London**
Lady Racket entertains her husband by re-
counting her evening playing cards.
UAB, 2 minutes
Three Weeks After A Marriage by Arthur Murphy

2239
Alicia, 20s   **London, June 1483**
Alicia, a woman of dark passion, has sacrificed
her virtue and her birthright to Lord Hastings.
When he no longer desires her, Alicia angrily
accuses him of treason of the heart.
UAB, 1 minute
The Tragedy of Jane Shore by Nicholas Rowe

2240
Lady Wishfort, 30-40   **London**
Waitwell, a serving man and husband to
Foible, has masqueraded as "Sir Rowland" in
a scheme to distract Lady Wishfort from her
obsession with Edward Mirabell, Waitwell's
employer. When Lady Wishfort discovers that
she has been made the butt of this cruel joke,
she lashes out at Foible.
UAB, 1.5 minutes
The Way of the World by William Congreve

2241
Louisa, 18-20   **London**
Louisa has been advised by her brother to stop

thinking about Belcour, the man with whom she has fallen in love. The smitten Louisa questions the practicality of her brother's suggestion.
UAB, 1 minute
The West Indian by Richard Cumberland

2242
Rosina, 18-20   **Switzerland**
Rosina has just discovered that the man she loves is married. She bemoans her unhappy fate.
UAB, 2 minutes
Altorf by Frances Wright

2243
Louka, 18-20   **Bulgaria, 1885**
Louka, an ambitious and passionate servant, secretly loves Sergius, a young military hero recently returned from battle. When Sergius complains of the lack of bravery in the ranks he commands, Louka speaks with passion on what she would do with her life, if only she were allowed.
UAB, 1 minute
Arms and the Man by George Bernard Shaw

2244
Helen Popov, 20s-30s
The drawing room of Popova's country estate, somewhere in provincial Russia
A pretty young widow confronts her belligerent neighbor, who is demanding collection of a debt owed by her late husband, and who starts spouting philosophy about men and women in love.
UAB, 1.5 minutes
The Bear by Anton Chekhov, Trans. by Carol Rocamora

2245
Imogine, 20-30   **Sicily, 11th century**
Believing her beloved Bertram to be dead, Imogine marries St. Aldobrand to save her father from ruin. The lonely wife sits in her apartment and dwells with melancholy upon her fate.
UAB, 1 minute
Bertram; or, The Castle of St. Aldobrand by Charles Robert Maturin

2246
Mrs. Cregan, 40-50   **Ireland**
When her son announces that he plans to marry a woman of whom Mrs. Cregan, a nagging mother, does not approve, she offers the lad the following admonishment.
UAB, 1 minute
The Colleen Brawn by Dion Boucicault

2247
Sheelah, 40-50   **Ireland**
A young woman has been found drowned in a nearby stream. Sheelah, a superstitious woman, tells the tale to her feverish son.
UAB, 1 minute
The Colleen Brawn by Dion Boucicault

2248
Nora, 28-30   **Norway**
After eight years of marriage, Nora has finally realized that her life has never been her own. She confronts her husband just before leaving him.
UAB, 1 minute
A Doll's House by Ibsen, Trans. by Brian Johnston and Rick Davis

2249
Lady Florence, 18-20
A garden by Lake Como, Italy
Lady Florence confesses her love for Lumley Ferrers to the trees and flowers of her garden.
UAB, 1.5 minutes
Ernest Maltravers by Louisa Medina

2250
Helen, 20s   **The Isle of Mull**
To end war between the Campbells and the MacLeans, Helen has married a MacLean, and in so doing, loses De Gray, the man she has always loved. She tries to say farewell to De Gray, who has risked his life to visit her in the MacLean castle.
UAB, 1.5 minutes
The Family Legend by Joanna Baillie

2251
Charlotte Corday, 20-30
France during the Revolution
Though sympathetic to the Revolution, Charlotte, a French patriot, is horrified by the violence of the Reign of Terror and so murders the evil Marat. Charlotte awaits her execution in prison.
UAB, 1 minute
The Female Enthusiast by Sarah Pogson

2252
Pocahontas, 18-20
The banks of the Powhatan River in the land of Pawhatan named Virginia by Sir Walter Raleigh, 1609
When Pocahontas, the Forest Princess, daughter of Powhatan, is taken prisoner by Ratcliffe and his men, she angrily confronts those who conspire against her father.
UAB, 1 minute
The Forest Princess; or, Two Centuries Ago by Charlotte Mary Sanford Barnes

2253
Helene Alving, 40s
A country estate in West Norway
When she is accused by her pastor of being a bad mother for sending her son, Osvald, away to be raised by strangers, Helene reveals that her late husband was an abusive alcoholic whose profligate lifestyle led to his early demise. She sent her son away to save him from his father's evil influence.
UAB, 1 minute
Ghosts by Ibsen, Trans. by Brian Johnston and Rick Davis

2254
Helene Alving, 40s
A country estate in West Norway
Helen's inability to escape the memories of her unhappy past is evidenced in her speculation that ghosts—not only of people, but also of ideas—are everywhere, making progress to a better life impossible.
UAB, 1 minute
Ghosts by Ibsen, Trans. by Brian Johnston and Rick Davis

2255
Teodora, 20s   **Madrid**
When her sister-in-law informs her that her husband has been fatally wounded in a duel fought to preserve her honor, Teodora, a young woman wrongly accused of infidelity, passionately defends her love and loyalty.
UAB, 2 minutes
The Great Galeoto by Jose Echegaray, Trans. by Hannah Lynch

2256
Ella Rentheim, 30-40   **Norway**
Years ago, Borkman abandoned his love for Ella in order to advance his career. She angrily confronts him with his crime of the heart.
UAB, 1.5 minutes
John Gabriel Borkman by Ibsen, Trans. by Rolf Fjelde

2257
The Duchess of Berwick, 40-50   **London**
The pragmatic Duchess, a society matron, offers the following assessment of the character of men to Lady Windermere, whose husband has recently strayed.
UAB, 1.5 minutes
Lady Windermere's Fan by Oscar Wilde

2258
Mabel Vane, 22   **London**
Mabel has traveled to London to surprise her husband, Ernest. When she arrives, she discovers that Ernest has been having an affair with an ac-

tress. The distraught Mabel imagines what she would say to her rival should they ever meet.
UAB, 1 minute
Masks and Faces by Charles Reade

2259
Mrs. Warren, 40-50   **England**
When Mrs. Warren, a woman driven to prostitution by her need to survive, finally reveals the source of her income to her daughter, she explains why a young woman would turn to such a life.
UAB, 2 minutes
Mrs. Warren's Profession by George Bernard Shaw

2260
Julia, 20s   **London**
When the philandering Charteris announces that he wishes to end their relationship, Julia desperately begs him not to leave.
UAB, 1.5 minutes
The Philanderer by George Bernard Shaw

2261
Martha Bernick, 70-80
A small Norwegian seaport
All her life, Martha has loved Johan, who has just eloped with young Dina, a girl Martha has raised like her own daughter. Martha finally reveals her feelings to Lona, Johan's sister.
UAB, 1.5 minutes
Pillars of Society by Ibsen, Trans. by Rolf Fjelde

2262
Salome, 16-20   **The court of Herod**
Passionate young Salome, the tempestuous daughter of Herodias, escapes the stuffy confines of a royal banquet.
UAB, 1 minute
Salome by Oscar Wilde

2263
Salome, 16-20   **The court of Herod**
After hearing the captive John the Baptist cry out, Salome, the tempestuous daughter of Herodias, becomes determined to see him. She exerts her potent will on a guard.
UAB, 1.5 minutes
Salome by Oscar Wilde

2264
Cecil, 20s   **London**
Lacking the protection of husband or family, Cecil, with her baby, must beg in the streets of London in order to survive. The destitute woman has reached the end of her endurance.
UAB, 1.5 minutes
Smiles and Tears; or, The Widow's Stratagem by Marie-Therese DeCamp

2265
May, 20s London
When a surly restaurant owner demands she leave his establishment, May, a destitute young street singer, calls him cruel, but then regrets her hasty remark.
UAB, 1 minute
The Ticket-Of-Leave Man by Tom Taylor

2266
Mrs. Willoughby, 50-60 London
A gregarious landlady entertains a tenant with a typical soliloquy.
UAB, 1.5 minutes
The Ticket-Of-Leave Man by Tom Taylor

2267
Cassy, 20-30
Simon Legree's Plantation in Louisiana
When Tom refuses to whip a fellow slave, Legree becomes determined to break him. Cassy, Legree's slave and concubine, begs Tom to give in and save his life.
UAB, 2 minutes
Uncle Tom's Cabin by George L. Aiken

2268
Dona Sirena, 30s
A garden in an imaginary country
When informed that servants will not work or entertain at her party until she pays them, Sirena, an outspoken aristocrat, rages.
UAB, 1 minute
The Bonds of Interest by Jacinto Benavente, Trans. by John Garrett Underhill

2269
Emilia, 20-30 A cozy living room
When Egon refuses to speak to her, a dejected Emilia, an unfinished character, is forced to leave the stage, her passion unfulfilled.
UAB, 2 minutes
Egon and Emilia by Christian Morgenstern

2270
Tatyana, 28 A garden
As the world around her continues to change, Tatyana, an actress, finds that she can no longer find the proper voice with which to inspire passion in an audience.
UAB, 1.5 minutes
Enemies by Maxim Gorky, Trans. by Alexander Bakshy

2271
Maude, 20s Slovsky's Florist Shop
When Maude, a talkative and philosophical shop girl, receives an order for flowers for a baby's funeral, she is prompted to ruminate on the florist shop's place in the lives of the community.
UAB, 2 minutes
The Florist Shop by Winifred Hawkridge

2272
Mildred, 20s A transatlantic ocean liner
A member of the privileged class, Mildred, a passenger, has a desire to understand the life and needs of the common man as she explains to her aunt.
UAB, 1.5 minutes
The Hairy Ape by Eugene O'Neill

2273
Catherine, 20 Paris
Catherine's husband has taken great pains to see that she is cured of her inability to speak. Unfortunately, his efforts have backfired, for now the poor young woman can do nothing but speak, as she demonstrates.
UAB, 2 minutes
The Man Who Married a Dumb Wife by Anatole France

2274
Frank, 30s New York City
Frank, an unconventional woman, has raised Kiddie as if he were her own son. She tells the sad tale of how Kiddie arrived in her home.
UAB, 1 minute
a Man's World by Rachel Crothers

2275
Clara, 30s New York City
Clara, a struggling artist, has begun to despair of ever finding happiness in life. When a friend asks why she never married, she replies.
UAB, 1 minute
a Man's World by Rachel Crothers

2276
Lulu, 30s A middle class home
When Lulu discovers that her new husband is already married, she plans to finally break free from his brother's family for whom she has just worked as a servant for years. She finally tells the overbearing patriarch exactly what she thinks of the family and his lying brother.
UAB, 1.5 minutes
Miss Lulu Bett by Zona Gale

2277
Gram, 60s A primitive cabin in Tennessee
A blind mountain woman. All of Gram's family with the exception of her grandson, Clay, have been killed in a feud with a neighboring family. When a well-meaning neighbor suggests that Clay will soon have to take up arms himself, Gram reveals a family legacy of blood and sorrow.

UAB, 2.5 minutes
On Vengeance Height by Allan Davis

2278
Alice Roylston, 30-40
A home in Tarryville-on-Hudson, NY
Unhappy Alice confronts the woman she has convinced herself is having an affair with her husband.
UAB, 2 minutes
Servitude by Eugene O'Neill

2279
Gismonda, 18   **Italy, 15th century**
Gismonda, a flirtatious young wife, regrets having married an older man and leaving Rome as she indicates.
UAB, 1 minute
Torches by Kenneth Raisbeck

2280
Gismonda, 18   **Italy, 15th century**
When her husband discovers her affair with the young Pietro, he commands that she drink a cup of poison after first placing a ruby that she has long desired in the cup. After drinking the poison and gaining the ruby, Gismonda bids farewell to the world.
UAB, 1 minute
Torches by Kenneth Raisbeck

2281
Rose, 22
A squalid bedroom of a rooming house on the lower east side of Manhattan
With a baby, no money, an abusive man, and failing health, Rose's prospects don't look very good. When a kindly stranger asks why she doesn't give up a prostitute's life, she replies.
UAB, 1 minute
The Web by Eugene O'Neill

2282
Sylvia, 30s   **New York City**
When nosy Sylvia, a society busybody, pays a visit to a friend who happens to be taking a shower, her need to snoop far outweighs her sense of propriety.
UAB, 1.5 minutes
The Women by Clare Boothe

2283
Melissa, 30s   **The Russian Tea Room**
Hollywood and New York combine with predictable results as Melissa, a Hollywood development person, does her best to court a playwright for movie work.
UAB, 2.5 minutes
Business Lunch at the Russian Tea Room by Christopher Durang

2284
Eve, 20-30   **In the garden**
Eve begs Paul to leave even though she knows she can't let go.
UAB, 1 minute
The Danube by Maria Irene Fornes

2285
Cora, 30-50   A shabby New Orleans apartment
Cora, a good time gal, regales Stanley and Blanche with a tale about pipe dreams in a parody of the work of Tennessee Williams.
UAB, 1 minute
Desire, Desire, Desire by Christopher Durang

2286
Rosamund Brackett, 60s   **Los Angeles**
When Brackett, Director of an impoverished medical clinic, fires one of her doctors (an expatriate Brit with a bad attitude), she is shocked to discover that he has an original painting by Stubbs in his office. She explains her love for the artist.
UAB, 2 minutes
The End of the Day by Jon Robin Baitz

2287
Bunny, 40s
A neighborhood in Philadelphia, 1973
Bunny, a loud and vulgar woman, describes the terrible events that led to her being charged with assault.
UAB, 2 minutes
Gemini by Alberto Innaurato

2288
Verona, 30s   **Here and Now**
Verona, a fan of Mutual of Omaha's Wild Life Kingdom, shares a disturbing memory.
UAB, 2.5 minutes
Imperceptible Mutabilities by Suzan-Lori Parks

2289
Keely, 20-30   **A basement**
Keely has been kidnapped by a group of radical anti-abortion protesters who intend to keep her prisoner until she is forced to give birth to the baby she doesn't want. The furious Keely expresses her feelings to her jailer.
UAB, 1 minute
Keely and Du by Jane Martin

2290
Alison, 20s   A one-room flat in the Midlands
Alison left her emotionally abusive husband, Jimmy, when she discovered she was pregnant. Months later, she has lost the baby and returns to Jimmy, who still views her departure as a betrayal. Alison finally breaks down in front of

Jimmy and reveals her darkest self.
UAB, 1.5 minutes
Look Back In Anger by John Osborne

2291
Bette, 40-50   **Here and Now**
Matt fantasizes what his mother would say about her unrelenting quest to have children.
UAB, 1.5 minutes
The Marriage of Bette and Boo by Christopher Durang

2292
Bridget, 30s   **Here and Now**
Bridget, a restless spirit, wanders quietly through her parent's house on the night her father is dying.
UAB, 1 minute
Moonlight by Harold Pinter

2293
Kathleen, 40s East Gloucester, Massachusetts
Kathleen, an Irish Catholic Yankee, Gloucester native, now works for Jacob Brackish, a man she has secretly hated for having an affair with her mother. Now in his 80s and nearly deaf, Jacob is no longer the formidable schoolteacher he once was. Kathleen vents some spleen, knowing full well that Brackish can't hear her.
UAB, 2.5 minutes
Park Your Car in Harvard Yard by Israel Horovitz

2294
Lillian Barbow, 50s
The Woodvale Nursing Home, Madison, Tennessee, 1986
When Lillian, a southern matron, discovers that her mother is having a sexual relationship with a fellow patient at the nursing home, she and her brother rush in to put a stop to things. When the aged lovers inform their children that they intend to leave the nursing home and get married, Lillian does her best to dissuade her mother from what she feels is an unacceptable course of action.
UAB, 2.5 minutes
Songs of Love by Romulus Linney

2295
Marge Hackett, 50s   **New York City, Present**
Marge's late husband was involved in a city government scandal which left her a penniless widow. Now, Marge works for social services. She has been sent to evaluate Isaac Geldhart, a man whom she once met socially when they were both living happier lives. His children would like to have him committed to an old age home. She expected to find a senile, incompetent old man but discovers instead a bitter old man who is being victimized by his children.
UAB, 1.5 minutes
The Substance of Fire by Jon Robin Baitz

2296
Dilly, 18   **Montana, 1949**
A pistol, bright and cosseted. Dilly's father breeds roosters for cockfights. She describes the handler's experience.
UAB, 1.5 minutes
Summer by Jane Martin

2297
Janie, 20s   **California, the 60s**
Janie, a college student, and Monty have been friends for a while. When Monty, who is black, responds to Janie's interest sexually, she accuses him of raping her.
UAB, 2 minutes
The Taking of Miss Janie by Ed Bullins

2298
Janie, 20s   **California, the 60s**
Repressed Janie, a college student, does her best to justify her attraction to Monty.
UAB, 2 minutes
The Taking of Miss Janie by Ed Bullins

2299
Norma, 30s   **Malibu, the early 1980s**
The daughter of a well-known character actor describes how she, an actress, discovered that he had been black-listed in Hollywood.
UAB, 2 minutes
The Value of Names by Jeffrey Sweet

2300
Mrs. Dandywine, 50s   **An island**
Mrs. Dandywine, a self-aggrandizing matron, describes herself to a guest.
UAB, 1.5 minutes
Victory on Mrs. Dandywine's Island by Lanford Wilson

2301
Actress   **Here and Now**
The actress tells a sad tale about a pet iguana.
UAB, 1.5 minutes
Vital Signs by Jane Martin

2302
Black Will, 30-50   **Rural England**
A thug and murderer brags of his various misdeeds.
UAB, 2 minutes
Arden of Feversham by Anonymous

2303
Faustus, 30s   **The study of Dr. Faustus**
Faustus has summoned the powerful Mephistopheles from Hell, who has agreed to do his bidding. The foolish necromancer rejoices his dark accomplishment.
UAB, 1 minute
Dr. Faustus by Christopher Marlowe

2304
Lacy, 20s   **England under the reign of Henry III**
Lacy, the Earl of Lincoln, has fallen in love with Margaret, the keeper's daughter. He contemplates marrying her.
UAB, 1 minute
Friar Bacon and Friar Bungay by Robert Greene

2305
Prince Edward 20-30
England under the reign of Henry III
When his best friend, the Earl of Lincoln, reveals that he plans to wed Margaret, a woman the prince also desires, the royal heir vows to woo her for himself.
UAB, 1 minute
Friar Bacon and Friar Bungay by Robert Greene

2306
Herod, 50-60   **The court of Herod**
When the King of Judea's advisors warn him of Isaiah's prophecy that a child born to a virgin will become the Emmanuel, the despot flies into a rage.
UAB, 1 minute
Herod the Great by The Wakefield Pageant

2307
Hieronimo, 50s   **Spain**
Marshall of Spain. Hieronimo's son, Horatio, has been found murdered in the royal palace. The grieving father vows to avenge his death.
UAB, 1.5 minutes
The Spanish Tragedy by Thomas Kyd

2308
Tim, 20s   **England**
A bookwormish young man, Tim's marriage has been arranged by his overbearing parents. As he prepares to meet his bride-to-be, he laments his fate.
UAB, 1.5 minutes
A Chaste Maid in Cheapside by Thomas Middleton

2309
Sir Walter, 30-40   **England**
His desire for the chaste young Moll has driven Sir Walter to commit desperate crimes. He teeters on the edge of madness as he contemplates the base nature of his life.
UAB, 1 minute
A Chaste Maid in Cheapside by Thomas Middleton

2310
Subtle, 30-40   **London**
The clever Subtle, a quack and con-man, describes his plan to con Sir Epicure Mammon, by making the foolish man believe that he has a magical stone that will cure all disease.
UAB, 1 minute
The Alchemist by Ben Jonson

2311
Sir Epicure Mammon, 40-50   **London**
Sir Epicure Mammon, a foolish nobleman, has been conned by Subtle into believing that he possesses a stone that can cure all disease. The greedy Mammon describes the financial and social benefits of owning such a wondrous rock.
UAB, 1 minute
The Alchemist by Ben Jonson

2312
Serapion, 40-60   **Alexandria, 30 BC**
Cleopatra's priest of Isis recounts omens and portents which foreshadow the tragedy of Marc Antony's defeat and the final subjugation of Egypt.
UAB, .5 minute
All for Love; or the World Well Lost by John Dryden

2313
Marc Antony, 40s   **Alexandria, 30 BC**
As vengeful Caesar prepares to take Alexandria, history's two most famous lovers prepare to die together. Antony, General of Rome exiled in Alexandria, speaks his final words to Cleopatra.
UAB, 1 minute
All for Love; or the World Well Lost by John Dryden

2314
Sganarelle, 30-40   **Rural France**
Sganarelle, a woodcutter turned-physician, has been forced to masquerade as a doctor by his avaricious wife. He explains his predicament to a prospective client.
UAB, 2 minutes
The Doctor in Spite of Himself by Moliere

2315
Thibaut, 20s   **Rural France**
Thibaut, a simple country lad, tries to describe his mother's precarious health to a physician.
UAB, 1.5 minutes
The Doctor in Spite of Himself by Moliere

2316
Sir Francis Wildlove, 20-30   **London**
Sir Francis, a man about town, shares his thoughts on women.
UAB, 2 minutes
The Innocent Mistress by Mary Pix

2317
Clitandre, 20s   **Paris**
Clitandre first proposed to scholarly Armande, who scorned his passion and demanded that he turn his vulgar urges of the flesh into something spiritual. Two years later, the greatly frustrated Clitandre gives up on Armande and proposes instead to her younger sister. When Armande angrily confronts him with his inability to attain a state of "perfect love" for her, he offers a response.
UAB, 1 minute
The Learned Women by Moliere

2318
Gayman, 20-30   **London**
When Gayman, a spark of the town, receives a mysterious invitation to meet with an unknown woman promising love and fortune, the destitute charmer considers his options.
UAB, 1 minute
The Lucky Chance by Aphra Behn

2319
Manly, 20s   **London**
Manly, a sea captain in love, has returned from sea and is courting Olivia. When asked why he believes in her professed love for him, he offers an explanation.
UAB, 1.5 minutes
The Plain Dealer by William Wycherley

2320
Loveless, 30s   **Whitehall**
Loveless has vowed to turn over a new leaf by remaining faithful to his wife, Amanda. He tried desperately not to woo Amanda's cousin with whom he has become enamored.
UAB, 2 minutes
The Relapse; or, Virtue in Danger by Sir John Vanbrugh

2321
Cassander, 20s   **Babylon**
Alexander, an angry young man in the court of Alexander the great, has taken Statira to be his second wife, thus enraging Cassander. The furious Cassander contemplates revolt.
UAB, 1 minute
The Rival Queens by Nathaniel Lee

2322
Eglamour, 20-30   **Sherwood**
Eglamour's beloved, Earine, had been reported drowned. The grieving young man vows to somehow avenge her death.
UAB, 2 minutes
The Sad Shepherd by Ben Jonson

2323
Eglamour, 20-30   **Sherwood**
Eglamour tells his friend, Robin Hood, that he can no longer enjoy the springtime.
UAB, 2.5 minutes
The Sad Shepherd by Ben Jonson

2324
Cleante, 30-60   **17th century Paris**
Cleante is the exasperated brother of Orgon, a man who has allowed himself to be ruined by the scheming Tartuffe. When Orgon finally sees the errors of his ways, he flies into a belated rage. Cleante chides his foolish brother for his extreme ways.
UAB, 1.5 minutes
Tartuffe by Moliere

2325
Gelosso, 50-60   **Libya, the second Punic War**
Sophonisba has nobly offered herself to Syphax to save her beloved Carthage from being destroyed by his armies. Wise old Gelosso, a senator from Carthage, praises her bravery but fears the final outcome of her rash decision.
UAB, 1 minute
The Tragedy of Sophonisba by John Marston

2326
Volpone, 50-60   **Venice**
Volpone, a crafty nobleman, and his devious servant, Mosca, have plotted together to exploit his unscrupulous associates by making them believe that he is near death and that each has been named as the sole heir to his fortune. After being paid a visit by the aging Corbaccio—a man whose greed exceeds his concern over his ailing body—Volpone offers an observation on the effects of human disintegration.
UAB, 1 minute
Volpone by Ben Jonson

2327
Volpone, 50-60   **Venice**
The rascally Volpone, a crafty nobleman, attempts to seduce Celia, the lovely young wife of a man who has offered her favors to Volpone in hopes of becoming his sole heir.
UAB, 1.5 minutes
Volpone by Ben Jonson

2328
Macheath, 30s   **London**
When Macheath, a notorious jade and high-wayman, is arrested for having compromised Polly Peachum, he is taken to Newgate Prison to await his execution. The unrepentant cad muses over his fate.
UAB, 1 minute
The Beggar's Opera by John Gay

2329
Sir Charles, 30s   **Windsor**
The philandering Sir Charles has been discovered by his wife sleeping in the same room with a serving woman. When he realizes that he has been found in such an indelicate situation, he laments his careless ways.
UAB, 1.5 minutes
The Careless Husband by Colley Cibber

2330
Sir Charles, 30s   **Windsor**
Sir Charles doesn't appreciate his wife, as his declaration illustrates.
UAB, 1 minute
The Careless Husband by Colley Cibber

2331
Sir Charles, 30s   **Windsor**
When one of Sir Charles' many conquests threatens to leave him, he declares that he no longer has the strength or patience to keep women.
UAB, 1 minute
The Careless Husband by Colley Cibber

2332
Hassan, 20-40   **A castle**
When Hassan, a black slave, and Saib discuss the romantic foibles of their masters, Hassan is reminded of his own true love, lost to him forever in Africa.
UAB, 1 minute
The Castle Spectre by Matthew G. Lewis

2333
Hassan, 20-40   **A castle**
Hassan, a black slave, has long plotted to avenge his kidnapping and enslavement by destroying the man responsible for his miserable life. When his plan nears completion, Hassan takes comfort from the imminent devastation of his master's life.
UAB, 1.5 minutes
The Castle Spectre by Matthew G. Lewis

2334
Cato, 40s
The Governor's Palace of Utica, 46 BC

Cato, Roman statesman, has joined with Pompeii in his revolt against Caesar. When Pompeii is killed, Cato is faced with confronting Caesar's legions. After listening to his generals argue for both war and peace, conservative Cato calls for moderation.
UAB, 1.5 minutes
Cato by Joseph Addison

2335
Cato, 40s
The Governor's Palace of Utica, 46 BC
When Decius tries to persuade Cato, Roman statesman, to make peace with Caesar, the renegade statesman describes his contempt for the emperor.
UAB, 1 minute
Cato by Joseph Addison

2336
Monsieur, 30s
Mass. during the American Revolution
The monsieur, a man considering joining a group of Tories, is torn between his desire for a title and memories of his father's tales of escaping a life of oppression in France as he describes to a group of Tories.
UAB, 1.5 minutes
The Group by Mercy Otis Warren

2337
Hazelrod, 50-60
Mass. during the American Revolution
The passionate Hazelrod, a judge who presides over a group of Tories, reacts to a fellow conspirator's call for moderation.
UAB, 1 minute
The Group by Mercy Otis Warren

2338
Major Oakly, 30s   **London**
When his brother's marriage hits the rocks, this hind-sighted bachelor laments his sibling's inability to manage his life.
UAB, 1.5 minutes
The Jealous Wife by George Colman

2339
St. Pierre, 30s   **Louvain, France**
When the virtuous Julia announces that she'll join a convent rather than marry him, the evil St. Pierre vows to destroy her.
UAB, .5 minute
Julia of Louvain; or, Monkish Cruelty by J.C. Cross

2340
Mortimer, 40-50   **Castle Mortimer**
Lord Mortimer, an evil and powerful lord, ruminates on the tendency of men to deny their true natures.

UAB, 1 minute
The Kentish Barons by Francis North

2341
Osbert, 20s   **Castle Mortimer**
When Osbert, an unhappy young man, servant to the dread Mortimer, is ordered to assist his lord in the seduction of the virtuous Elina, he laments his inability to save Elina from Mortimer's clutches.
UAB, 1 minute
The Kentish Barons by Francis North

2342
George Barnwell, 20s   **London**
George has allowed himself to fall under the spell of the duplicitous Millwood, who has convinced him to steal from his employer. Barnwell contemplates his fall from grace.
UAB, 1 minute
The London Merchant; or, The History of George Barnwell by George Lillo

2343
Uncle, 50-60   **London**
A man about to be murdered here has a dark premonition immediately prior to his demise.
UAB, 2 minutes
The London Merchant; or, The History of George Barnwell by George Lillo

2344
George Barnwell, 20s   **London**
Millwood has convinced George to murder his uncle for money. Following the violent deed, Barnwell removes his mask and sobs over his uncle's body.
UAB, 2 minutes
The London Merchant; or, The History of George Barnwell by George Lillo

2345
Sir Anthony Adverse, 50s   **Bath**
When his son refuses to marry the young lady he has selected, Sir Anthony, an overbearing father, angrily confronts him with his willful disobedience. When the young man refuses to honor his father's demands, Sir Anthony flies into a rage and threatens to disown him.
UAB, 1.5 minutes
The Rivals by Richard Brinsley Sheridan

2346
Faulkland, 20s   **Bath**
Foolish Faulkland has allowed jealousy and poor judgment to drive away Julia, his fiancee. When she finally declares their engagement to be terminated, the young man laments his loss.
UAB, 1 minute
The Rivals by Richard Brinsley Sheridan

2347
Lord Hastings, 20-30   **London, June 1483**
Following a particularly harrowing encounter with Alicia, Hastings, a man torn between his love for Jane Shore and his dark passion for the tempestuous Alicia, reflects upon her stormy nature as he prepares to meet with calm and gentle Jane.
UAB, 1 minute
The Tragedy of Jane Shore by Nicholas Rowe

2348
Grizzle, 20-30
Court of King Arthur, and a Plain thereabouts
When Princess Huncamunca marries Tom Thumb, her erstwhile suitor, Grizzle, flies into a vengeful rage.
UAB, 1.5 minutes
The Tragedy of Tragedies; or, The Life and Death of Tom Thumb The Great by Henry Fielding

2349
Sir Wilfull Witwoud, 40   **London**
Before embarking on a journey for the purpose of improving himself, Sir Wilfull, a country gentleman, pays a visit to his aunt, Lady Wishfort, in whose home he encounters his estranged brother, Anthony, who has turned into a complete fop. The rusticated Sir Wilfull lambastes Anthony for his foolish city ways.
UAB, 1 minute
The Way of the World by William Congreve

2350
Censor, 30s   **London**
The jaded Censor, a man of Sardonic sensibility, chastises a friend for his inconsistent behavior with his mistress.
UAB, .5 minute
The Witlings by Francis Burney

2351
Dabbler, 30-40   **London**
When his work is interrupted, the pretentious Dabbler, a man who fancies himself a poet, has a hard time regaining his train of thought.
UAB, 1.5 minutes
The Witlings by Francis Burney

2352
Sergius, 20s   **Bulgaria, 1885**
Sergius, a young military officer, has recently returned from battle and is being hailed a brave hero. When asked by Louka, the servant girl he secretly loves, if he considers himself to be a brave man, he offers an insight.
UAB, 1 minute
Arms and the Man by George Bernard Shaw

2353
Grigory Stepanovich Smirnov, 40s
The drawing room of Popova's country estate, somewhere in provincial Russia
When Smirnov, a landowner in his prime, arrives at the home of the recently widowed Helen to collect one of her late husband's debts, he becomes outraged when she refuses to pay. He details his rather bleak opinion of the fairer sex.
UAB, 2.5 minutes
The Bear by Anton Chekhov, Trans. by Carol Rocamora

2354
Jacob Twig, 20s   A village by the sea
Jacob, village bailiff, a toady, had been in the employ of the evil Doggrass for whom he has done much dirty work. An encounter with mortality has inspired the young man to change his life, as he explains.
UAB, 1 minute
Black-Ey'd Susan by Douglas Jerrold

2355
William, 30s   A village by the sea
William, a sailor, has been away at sea for many months. When he returns, he discovers his wife, Susan, being seduced against her will by a senior officer, whom he attacks. Sentenced to death for his crime, William meets for the first time with his beloved Susan, and makes his final wish.
UAB, 1.5 minutes
Black-Ey'd Susan by Douglas Jerrold

2356
De Monfort, 20-30   A village in Germany
De Monfort, a man consumed with hatred and jealousy, has spent the better part of his life hating his childhood rival, Rezenvelt. When his enemy appears at his castle with the intent of marrying De Monfort's sister, he flies into a rage.
UAB, 1 minute
De Monfort by Joanna Baillie

2357
De Monfort, 20-30   A village in Germany
Driven insane by his hatred for Rezenvelt, De Monfort follows his enemy into the woods with murder on his mind.
UAB, 2 minutes
De Monfort by Joanna Baillie

2358
Dr. Thomas Stockmann, 30-40
A coastal town in Southern Norway
Dr. Stockmann is the staff physician at the

local mineral baths which provide the town with most of its income. When the baths are found to be contaminated, Stockmann orders them closed. He is out-voted by the people of the town, led by his brother, the mayor. The idealistic doctor confronts the entire community with their stupidity.
UAB, 2 minutes
An Enemy of the People by Ibsen, Trans. by Brian Johnston and Rick Davis

2359
John of Lorne, 20s   The Isle of Mull
John's sister and best friend have lost their chance for a life together because of clan warfare. John, a warrior, confesses his love of war.
UAB, 2 minutes
The Family Legend by Joanna Baillie

2360
Belcour, 20s   France during the Revolution
Virtuous Belcour has promised to help his best friend, Henry, win the heart of the woman he loves, only to discover that the woman in question is his own beloved Estelle.
UAB, 1 minute
The Female Enthusiast by Sarah Pogson

2361
Marat, 50s   France during the Revolution
Marat, French politician and co-conspirator of Danton and Robespierre, addresses a ragged Parisian mob.
UAB, 2.5 minutes
The Female Enthusiast by Sarah Pogson

2362
Gonzales, 40-60 The court of Francis the First
Gonzales, a Spanish monk, has become a part of the French Court in order to ruin Laval, a nobleman whose father destroyed his sister.
UAB, 1.5 minutes
Francis the First by Fanny Kemble

2363
Pastor Manders, 40—50
The country estate in West Norway
The unctuous Manders, a self-aggrandizing clergyman, confronts Helene Alving, the widow of his childhood friend who is soon to be honored with a memorial. The good pastor disapproves of Helene's parenting skills, and minces no words telling her so.
UAB, 1.5 minutes
Ghosts by Ibsen, Trans. by Brian Johnston and Rick Davis

2364
Ernest, 26   Madrid

Ernest, a passionate young man with poetic aspirations, has been working on a drama for the stage. When asked by his patron to describe it, he laments the impossibility of creating a character who represents everyone.
UAB, 2 minutes
The Great Galeoto by Jose Echegaray, Trans. by Hannah Lynch

2365
Jack, 20-30   **London**
The irascible Jack, a man with the wrong name, informs Lady Bracknell that he has no intention of allowing his ward, Cecily, to marry her nephew, Algernon.
UAB, 2 minutes
The Importance of Being Earnest: A Trivial Comedy for Serious People by Oscar Wilde

2366
John Gabriel Borkman, 50s   **Norway**
John Gabriel Borkman sacrificed everything, including Ella, the woman he loved, to advance his banking career. Years later, he has lost everything. When Ella returns to confront him, John Gabriel sinks into despair. On a cold night the two visit a place where they used to sit and dream of a future that never was to be. John Gabriel confesses that he never stopped loving Ella.
UAB, 1.5 minutes
John Gabriel Borkman by Ibsen, Trans. by Rolf Fjelde

2367
Manfred, 20-30   **A castle in the Alps**
Manfred, a necromancer, is determined to summon the ghost of the woman he loved to seek forgiveness for having caused her death.
UAB, 2 minutes
Manfred by Lord Byron

2368
Manfred, 20-30   **A castle in the Alps**
When he has successfully summoned the spirit of Astarte, he begs her forgiveness.
UAB, 2 minutes
Manfred by Lord Byron

2369
James Triplet, 30s   **London**
The hapless Triplet, a starving artist, pays a visit to Covet Garden only to find that his plays have been rejected and his children will have to go hungry.
UAB, 1.5 minutes
Masks and Faces by Charles Reade

2370
Aleksey Alekseich Zaytsev, 30s
Gloomy way station in provincial Russia
A young man, desperate, on the eve of his trial for bigamy, forgery, and attempted murder, contemplates suicide.
UAB, 2 minutes
The Night Before the Trial by Anton Chekhov, Trans. by Carol Rocamora

2371
Ivan Ivanovich Nyukhin, 30s-40s
Stage of an auditorium in provincial Russian
Tyrannized by his wife to give a public lecture on the harmful effects of smoking tobacco, a miserable, hen-pecked schoolteacher departs from his assigned topic to open his heart to the audience.
UAB, 2.5 minutes
On the Harmful Effects of Tobacco by Anton Chekhov, Trans. by Carol Rocamora

2372
Semeon Sergeevich Bortsov, 40-50
A tavern somewhere in southern Russia
His property lost, desperate and destitute, Bortsov implores a tavernkeeper for a drink.
UAB, 2 minutes
On the High Road by Anton Chekhov, Trans. by Carol Rocamora

2373
Yegor Merik, any age
A tavern somewhere in southern Russia
Merik, a tramp, describes demons and other apparitions to the superstitious patrons of a tavern in the remote parts of southern Russia.
UAB, 1.5 minutes
On the High Road by Anton Chekhov, Trans. by Carol Rocamora

2374
Peer Gynt, 30s   **An onion field**
Following many misadventures, the foolish Peer Gynt, a man in search of himself, finally achieves a moment of insight as he begins to peel an onion.
UAB, 2.5 minutes
Peer Gynt by Ibsen, Trans. by Rolf Fjelde

2375
Paramore, 40s   **London**
While reading through the British Medical Journal, Paramore, a self-styled medical researcher, discovers that the disease he believes himself to have discovered cannot exist. The ridiculous "scientist" vows to prove the disease really does exist.
UAB, 2 minutes
The Philanderer by George Bernard Shaw

2376

Bernick   **A small Norwegian seaport**

Years ago, when Bernick chose another woman for his bride, heartbroken Lona made her way to America where she made a home in the wilderness. Years later, Lona has returned only to find the man she once loved changed into a duplicitous businessman who cares for nothing save his place in society. Bernick complains bitterly of his position to Lona.

UAB, 1 minute

Pillars of Society by Ibsen, Trans. by Rolf Fjelde

2377

Frankenstein, 30s   **Geneva**

Since beginning his quest, Frankenstein, a man obsessed with discovering the secret of creation, has been able to think of nothing else. The scientist reflects on the nature of death before returning to his work.

UAB, 1.5 minutes

Presumption; or, The Fate of Frankenstein by Richard Brinksley Peake

2378

Frankenstein, 30s   **Geneva**

When he successfully reanimates his monster, Frankenstein, a man obsessed with discovering the secret of creation, finally realizes that he has forfeited his soul.

UAB, 2 minutes

Presumption; or, The Fate of Frankenstein by Richard Brinksley Peake

2379

Ivan Vasilevich Lomov, 40-50s

The drawing room of a country estate, somewhere in provincial Russia

Lomov, a portly, neurotic, hypochondriacal landowner, summons up his courage and calls on a neighbor to propose marriage to his daughter.

UAB, 1.5 minutes

The Proposal by Anton Chekhov, Trans. by Carol Rocamora

2380

Ulrik Brendel, 50-60

Rosmersholm, an old manor house in West Norway

When Brendel, a teacher, down on his luck, arrives unannounced at the home of his former student, John Rosmer, everyone is surprised by his shabby appearance. When a young woman of the household remarks that she has read many of his books, the professor claims that his best thoughts have never been put on paper.

UAB, 1 minute

Rosmersholm by Ibsen, Trans. by Rolf Fjelde

2381

Jokanaan, 30s   **The court of Herod**

When Jokanaan, John the Baptist, is released from Cistern so that Salome may see him, he calls out for Herod and Herodias.

UAB, 1.5 minutes

Salome by Oscar Wilde

2382

Colonel O'Donolan, 20-30   **London**

O'Donolan, a jealous hot-head, is in love with the capricious Lady Emily, who does her best to keep the poor man guessing. When she claims ignorance of his suffering, O'Donolan turns to an older woman for support.

UAB, 2 minutes

Smiles and Tears; or, The Widow's Stratagem by Marie-Therese DeCamp

2383

Vasily Vasilich Svetlovidov, 68

The empty stage of a provincial theatre, late at night, following a performance

Stumbling out drunk onto an empty stage in a dark, deserted theatre, an old character has-been actor faces the empty dreams of his career.

UAB, 2.5 minutes

Swan Song by Anton Chekhov, Trans. by Carol Rocamora

2384

Wyatt, 20s   **London**

Wyatt, a pragmatic country lad, offers astute commentary on his fashionable London counterparts.

UAB, 1 minute

Two Roses by James Albery

2385

St. Clare, 30-40   **New Orleans**

When St. Clare's northern cousin objects to his young daughter's lavishing much affection on his new slave, Uncle Tom, he gives his relative a lecture on northern hypocrisy.

UAB, 1.5 minutes

Uncle Tom's Cabin by George L. Aiken

2386

Professor Arnold Rubek, 40s

A health resort by the sea

As Rubek and his wife, Maja, enjoy a quiet moment at a spa, their conversation turns to his work. The world-weary artist reveals the dark secrets to be found in the simple portrait busts he sculpts for wealthy patrons.

UAB, 1.5 minutes

When We Dead Awaken by Ibsen, Trans. by Rolf Fjelde

2387
Satorius, 50s **England**
When his daughter's idealistic young suitor questions the living conditions in the slums he owns, the pragmatic Satorius, a wealthy landlord, offers insight into his tenants' sociological tendencies.
UAB, 1.5 minutes
Widowers Houses by George Bernard Shaw

2388
Leander, 20-30 **A garden in an imaginary country**
Leander has plotted with the unscrupulous Crispin to pretend to fall in love with the wealthy young Sylvia to gain her fortune. When Leander finds that he has truly fallen in love, he agonizes over his feelings.
UAB, 1.5 minutes
The Bonds of Interest by Jacinto Benavente, Trans. by John Garrett Underhill

2389
The Gambler, 40-50 **Europe, 1920s**
A man who has lost everything and is addicted to the thrill of the wager describes his experiences with Lady Luck.
UAB, 2.5 minutes
The Gambler by Klabund

2390
Boris, 20s **A landowner's house in Russia**
Boris, a young revolutionary, has entered the house of Alexis Alexandrovitch with the intention of assassinating him. When the cruel landowner reveals his knowledge of Boris's plot, the young man explains his intentions.
UAB, 1 minute
The Game of Chess by Kenneth Sawyer Goodman

2391
Alexis Alexandrovitch, 40s
A landowner's house in Russia
When he is confronted in his home by a would-be assassin, Alexandrovitch, a despotic landowner, dismisses the young revolutionary's attempt with scorn.
UAB, 1 minute
The Game of Chess by Kenneth Sawyer Goodman

2392
Yank, 20-30 **A transatlantic ocean liner**
Crude Yank, a stoker, rallies his fellow shipmates.
UAB, 1.5 minutes
The Hairy Ape by Eugene O'Neill

2393
Yank, 20-30 **A transatlantic ocean liner**
When Yank, a stoker, frightens a young female passenger who was exploring the ships nether regions, he becomes furious at the invective she hurled his way at the height of her scare.
UAB, 2 minutes
The Hairy Ape by Eugene O'Neill

2394
Satin, 40-50 **A crude flophouse in Russia**
One of several miserable denizens of the flophouse, Satin, a thief, shares a piece of alcohol-induced philosophy.
UAB, 2 minutes
The Lower Depths by Maxim Gorky, Trans. by Alexander Bakshy

2395
Leonard, 30s **Paris**
Leonard, a young judge, has recently married a woman who cannot speak. He laments his choice.
UAB, 2 minutes
The Man Who Married a Dumb Wife by Anatole France

2396
Gentleman, 30-40
A steamer's life raft, rising and falling slowly on the long ground swell of a glassy tropic sea
The gentleman, a former first class passenger, has survived the steamer's sinking along with two other shipmates. He describes his experience to a woman who was a dancer and to a man who was one of the deck hands.
UAB, 2 minutes
Thirst by Eugene O'Neill

2397
Ulysses, 40s **Ithaca**
When finally deposited on the shores of his beloved Ithaca, Ulysses, the wandering hero, thinks himself to be dreaming.
UAB, 2 minutes
Ulysses by Stephen Phillips

2398
Antipa Zykov, 50s **Russia**
When he is chastised by his idealistic young wife for not loving his own son, Zykov, a ruthless businessman, reveals the heartless philosophy with which he has governed his life.
UAB, 1 minute
The Zykovs by Maxim Gorky, Trans. by Alexander Bakshy

2399
Teach, 40-50 **A junk shop**
Teach, an ordinary guy, complains about the behavior of Ruthie, a woman who recently

beat him at cards.
UAB, 2.5 minutes
American Buffalo by David Mamet

2400
Goldberg, 50s
A house in a seaside resort town
Goldberg, a sinister man, and McCann have mysteriously appeared at a boarding house, their intent unclear. Goldberg boasts of his good health before suffering a brief break-down.
UAB, 2.5 minutes
The Birthday Party by Harold Pinter

2401
James, 18-20
The waiting room at a doctor's office
James, a young man in need of medical attention, is convinced that he has swallowed the moon. He describes the result.
UAB, 1.5 minutes
The Boy Who Ate the Moon by Jane Martin

2402
Dr. Shedman, 40s
A studio in a NYC hotel, August 1962
Shedman, an alcoholic in exile, has married his father's mistress, Pixie. In order to avoid a scandal, they move to a remote corner of Kansas where Pixie turns to poetry and Shedman to booze. The drunken doctor reads one of Pixie's poems and confesses that he's having an affair.
UAB, 2.5 minutes
The Captivity of Pixie Shedman by Romulus Linney

2403
JP, 50-60   **The Midlands**
JP, a man whose life has passed him by, is the older version of "Jimmy," who first appeared in Osborne's Look Back in Anger. Thirty years older, JP appears no wiser, as he reveals.
UAB, 1.5 minutes
Dejavu by John Osborne

2404
Edmond, 30-40   **A prison cell**
Edmond has been jailed for killing a girl. He is visited by his wife who asks him whether or not he committed the crime. His response reveals more than a simple confession.
UAB, 1.5 minutes
Edmond by David Mamet

2405
Edmond, 30-40   **A prison cell**
Edmond, a man suspected of murder, lashes out angrily at the prison chaplain.

UAB, 1 minute
Edmond by David Mamet

2406
Graydon Massey, 40-50   **Los Angeles**
Massey, a frustrated doctor and ex-patriot Brit, has given up his lucrative Beverly Hills psychiatric practice to run the oncology department of an impoverished clinic. The dire conditions in the clinic prove to be more than he can cope with, however, leading him to clash with the clinic's director.
UAB, 1 minute
The End of the Day by Jon Robin Baitz

2407
George Dillon, 30s
The home of the Elliot family, outside London
When the woman he loves prepares to leave him, George, a failed playwright, bitterly offers her his "epitaph."
UAB, 1.5 minutes
Epitaph for George Dillon by John Osborne and Anthony Creighton

2408
Tom, 20-30   **A southern home**
Tom, a sensitive southerner, could no longer bear to live with his nagging mother and alcoholic brother, so he finally left home as he relates.
UAB, 2 minutes
For Whom the Southern Belle Tolls by Christopher Durang

2409
Fran Geminiani, 45
A neighborhood in Philadelphia, 1973
Fran, a boisterous, friendly working-class dad, offers his Harvard-bound son some advice about women.
UAB, 1 minute
Gemini by Albert Innaurato

2410
Smith, 40-50   **Here and Now**
Smith, a military man reunited with his family, describes his desire to have done something noble.
UAB, 1.5 minutes
Imperceptible Mutibilities in the Third Kingdom by Suzi Lori Parks

2411
Jack, 20s-30s   **Here and Now**
Jack reacts to being described as "nice."
UAB, 2 minutes
Jack and Jill by Jane Martin

2412
Jimmy, 25   A one-room flat in the Midlands
A miserable and sometimes abusive young
man, Jimmy's enjoyment of a radio concert is
diminished by the sounds made by his wife,
who is ironing. He cruelly describes the clum-
siness of women.
UAB, 2.5 minutes
Look Back in Anger by John Osborne

2413
Jimmy, 25   A one-room flat in the Midlands
Jimmy, a miserable and sometimes abusive
young man, lashes out at Alison, his long-suf-
fering wife, whose upper-class upbringing has
always been a thorn in his side.
UAB, 1.5 minutes
Look Back in Anger by John Osborne

2414
Elvis, 40s   A dump
The King, a cosmic messenger, returns to Earth
to inspire White Anglo-Saxon men to wake up
and achieve their true potential.
UAB, 2.5 minutes
Middle-Aged White Guys by Jane Martin

2415
Marius Byleveld, 60s
New Bethesda, South Africa, 1974
Marius, a well-meaning Dominee, pays a visit
to an eccentric parishioner, Miss Helen, whom
he tries to entertain with a tale of his inspira-
tion for an upcoming sermon.
UAB, 2.5 minutes
The Road to Mecca by Athol Fugard

2416
Isaac, 60-70   New York City, Present
When Isaac, a floundering publisher trying to
reconcile his past through the works he publishes, refuses to publish what will certainly be
a popular book, he is confronted by his three
children who all own stock in the company.
They proceed to express concern for his recent
interest in publishing Holocaust-related material and threaten to take over the company
with their collective shares. His back against
the wall, Isaac reveals something about his obsession with the Holocaust just before firing
his oldest son.
UAB, 2 minutes
The Substance of Fire by Jon Robin Baitz

2417
Isaac, 60-70   New York City, Present
Three years later the company has gone bankrupt and Isaac's children are trying to have him
committed. Isaac, a floundering publisher trying to reconcile his past through the works he
publishes, reveals his feelings about his children to the social worker sent to evaluate his
case.
UAB, 2 minutes
The Substance of Fire by Jon Robin Baitz

2418
Monty, 20s   California, the 60s
Monty, a black college student with a street
background, analyzes Janie's interest in him.
UAB, 2 minutes
The Taking of Miss Janie by Ed Bullins

2419
Stromil, 50s   An apartment in Poland
When his son complains of the repressive life
they're forced to live under the regime created
by revolution, Stromil, a patriarch dedicated
to the principles of revolution, angrily reminds
him that life before the change was intolerable.
UAB, 1 minutes
*Tango by Slawomir Mrozek, Trans. by Ralph
Manheim and Teresa Dzieduscycka*

2420
Arthur, 25   An apartment in Poland
Arthur, a passionate young man, is committed
to changing his repressive world, and the first
step in his agenda is to reintroduce church
weddings. He proposes to the woman he
thinks he loves.
UAB, 2.5 minutes
*Tango by Slawomir Mrozek, Trans. by Ralph
Manheim and Teresa Dzieduscycka*

2421
Vladimir, any age   A country road, a tree
Vladimir, a man waiting, assures his compan-
ions that they are doing the right thing.
UAB, 1 minutes
Waiting for Godot by Samuel Beckett

2422
George, 30
**The baling-press room at a wastepaper
company, Wakefield, Massachusetts**
In high school, George and his friends gang-
raped Margy in a savage encounter that left
her scarred for life. Years later, Margy returns
to Wakefield to visit her dying brother, and discovers that George has allowed time to warp
his memory of the brutal event. George viciously taunts Margy with the "fact" that she
"loved" what he and his friends did to her that
night.
UAB, 2.5 minutes
The Widow's Blind Date by Israel Horovitz

2423
Winnie, about 50
A woman is buried in a pile of sand up to her neck. She reaches out to her silent husband Willie in a desperate attempt to receive reassurance and affection.
BVT, 2 minutes
Happy Days by Samuel Beckett

2424
Bawd II
Irish prostitutes are in a cemetery in Dublin where beggars and prostitutes gather to conduct their business. They are entertaining themselves as they wait for prospective clients to come along.
BVT, 1.5 minutes
Richard's Cork Leg by Brendan Behan

2425
Monica, late 50s A suburb of Dublin, Present
A woman's unhappy, childless marriage ends with her poisoning her husband Myles, a man who grew increasingly cruel and distant over the years. She has just returned from his funeral and is sorting through is possessions.
BVT, 3.5 minutes
The Holy Ground by Dermot Bolger

2426
Monica, late 50s
A living room in Drumcondra, an old suburb of North Dublin, Present
A woman has finished packing up her husband's papers and photographs. She's exhausted as much from the activities of this funeral day as she is by her revelation.
BVT, 3.5 minutes
The Holy Ground by Dermot Bolger

2427
Curtains, young woman   Ireland, Present
This play deals with the difficulties of male/female relations. Curtains, a young woman hidden behind a set of curtains, finally tells the story at the end of the play that she has been struggling to tell all along.
BVT, 2 minutes
Low in the Dark by Marina Carr

2428
Mrs. Galgoogley
In a library, Easter Monday, 1916
A worn little woman is the custodian of statues of historic insurgents and dead political rebels. The statues speak to her and tell her that her son, Oweneen, will be on the front lines of an impending revolution. She hears gunfire outside the library.

BVT, 1.5 minutes
Coggerers by Paul Vincent Carroll

2429
Greta, late 30s   England, Present
An Irish woman explains her dream to her newborn baby. Through this she relates her search for identity, culminating in a discovery of her mystical Irish roots.
BVT, 1.5 minutes
After Easter by Anne Devlin

2430
Queen
The Queen banquets with those who would be her enemies. She has tasted the feast and wine to show that it's not poisoned and now offers the return of land. Soon, however, she will unleash the floodwaters of the Nile and drown all the enemy leaders who have gathered in her trap.
BVT, 2 minutes
The Queen's Enemies by Lord Dunsany

2431
Janet Fraser, late 40s
An attractive woman speaks with her ex-husband James. He has proposed that she remarry him, in order to save his reputation. It seems his second wife, Elsie, for whom he divorced Janet, has decided to divorce him.
BVT, 2.5 minutes
The First Mrs. Fraser by St. John Ervine

2432
Madelene, 29   Canary Islands
Madelene is in love with Fergus, and both are staying at the same modern resort hotel on the Canary Islands. Fergus, a priest who is hiding his profession while on holiday, cannot return Madelene's advances. To appear nonchalant in the face of his spurning her, Madelene engages in promiscuous activity and begins drinking heavily. She lectures the people with whom she has been vacationing about their hypocrisy.
BVT, 3 minutes
Canaries by Bernard Farrell

2433
Mag, 17   Western Ireland, 1960s
Mag is described as "bubbling with life and inclined to be extreme in her enthusiasms." She has recently discovered that she is pregnant and must marry Joe, the seventeen-year-old father of her child.
BVT, 3 minutes
Lovers by Brian Friel

2434
Mag, 17   **Western Ireland, 1960s**
Recently engaged, both Mag and Joe are nearly seventeen. They have rented a poorly ventilated house at the edge of a slaughter-house field. Nearly hallucinatory with the heat, Mag stares out the window and talks to Joe, who isn't listening.
BVT, 2.5 minutes
Lovers by Brian Friel

2435
Ma
Cahill, nicknamed "the Quartermaster," has ostensibly murdered a British policeman in the name of the Irish Republican Army. He gives the gun to Donny, a mentally handicapped boy in his late teens, to throw into the river so that Cahill can pass through the police patrols. Ma discovers that Donny has not disposed of the weapon and finds it a badge of her son's bravery.
BVT, 3 minutes
Donny Boy by Robin Glendinning

2436
Mrs. Fallon, middle-aged
Mrs. Fallon has just returned to a town's fair where nobody has any business but "to be minding one another's business." Her husband, Bartley Fallon, has left to return a hay-fork to Jack Smith. This information, spread amongst the townspeople, has been transformed into an account of Bartley murdering Jack with a hayfork.
BVT, 2.5 minutes
Spreading the News by Lady Gregory

2437
Bella   **In a pub in Belfast**
A group of friends drink, dance and brag—they are the very image of "Oirishness." Bella, a brash young woman, is the first to call the men on their boasting.
BVT, 1.5 minutes
Says I, Says He by Ron Hutchinson

2438
Molly Nolan
The attractive young housemaid to the Justice of a small town, speaks to the highly principled Sean O'Fenetic. She has just rejected three separate proposals of marriage before Sean's entrance. He is a government inspector who was sent to investigate the local authorities.
BVT, 1.5 minutes
Step-In-The-Hollow by Donagh MacDonagh

2439
Maeve, 23   Turn of the century, County Clare
Set on the grounds of a ruined abbey, the play weaves together themes of loss, love, and the healing powers of mysticism. Maeve, a hand-some young girl calls on Queen Maeve, a fig-ure from Irish mythology, when her husband dies unexpectedly.
BVT, 3 minutes
Maeve by Edward Martyn

2440
Grace   **Ireland, Present**
Grace lives with her mother, a housekeeper at the "Guernica Hotel," a dilapidated seaside boarding house. Grace is getting ready to leave for college when her father Joe, whom she's never met, comes to pay a visit.
BVT, 3 minutes
The Guernica Hotel by Jim Nolan

2441
Nora, 22   **Dublin, 1916**
During the Easter Rebellion, Nora has just re-turned to her tenement. She has been searching Dublin unsuccessfully for her husband, a com-mandant in the Irish Citizen Army.
BVT, 2.5 minutes
The Plough and the Stars by Sean O'Casey

2442
Mrs. Grigson, around 40   Dublin, May 1920
Mrs. Grigson, an Irish Protestant has just left her tenement apartment which is being raided by British Auxiliary soldiers.
BVT, 3 minutes
The Shadow of a Gunman by Sean O'Casey

2443
Angela   **Ireland, 1990s**
A young married woman, is having an affair with Artie, a sacristan in a local church. In that church's belfry, they kiss and cuddle and fall deeply in love.
BVT, 4 minutes
Belfry by Billy Roche

2444
Angela   **Ireland**
A young married woman living in small town Ireland, is having an affair with Artie O'Leary, a timid church mouse who leads an otherwise lonely existence as sacristan of the local Catholic chapel.
BVT, 2.5 minutes
Belfry by Billy Roche

2445
Nora Burke, middle-aged
A married but excruciatingly lonely woman, speaks to Michael, a young shepherd, while her husband lies next to them pretending to be dead. A tramp wandering through the dark and isolated area has stopped to spend the night away from the pounding rain outside.
BVT, 2.5 minutes
In the Shadow of the Glen by John Millington Synge

2446
Mary Byrne, an old woman
Mary has just returned to her son Michael, a poor tinker with whom she travels, after a night of drinking. She is speaking to Sarah, a destitute young woman who, desperately wanting to be married, has convinced a priest to wed her and Michael.
BVT, 3 minutes
The Tinker's Wedding by John Millington Synge

2447
Nagg, 60
A sixty-year old man whose health is failing, lives inside a garbage can. He struggles to perform his favorite comic story for his companion, Nell.
BVT, 2 minutes
Endgame by Samuel Beckett

2448
Cronin   **Dublin**
In a church cemetery in Dublin, Cronin, an Irish nationalist posing as a blind man, tries his hand at seducing young Deidre.
BVT, 2.5 minutes
Richard's Cork Leg by Brendan Behan

2449
Cronin   **Dublin**
A group of bawds have gathered in a Dublin cemetery to mourn the death of one of their colleagues. Cronin, an Irish nationalist and lover of wine and women, has disguised himself as a blind man to gain sympathy and favors from the prostitutes.
BVT, 6 minutes
Richard's Cork Leg by Brendan Behan

2450
Conor, middle-aged man   **Ireland**
An inmate in an Irish prison has been sentenced to criminal confinement instead of the "political treatment" to which he is entitled. His cellmates rally to his cause with threats of a hunger strike.
BVT, 2 minutes
Design for a Headstone by Seamus Byrne

2451
Bill   **Outside the pearly gates of heaven**
Jim and Bill, two thieves, stand outside the pearly gates of heaven. Jim, an older man who has been shot in the head, has been there for some time and has given up all hope of entering paradise. Bill, recently dead and with a spiral lockpick in hand, is determined to open the gates.
BVT, 2 minutes
The Glittering Gate by Lord Dunsany

2452
James Caesar, mid-30s   **late 1800s**
A prosperous grocer has just found out that Hannah Ferguson has decided that she cannot marry him. She had agreed to it as a way of saving her family's farm from foreclosure. James speaks with Hannah's family.
BVT, 3 minutes
John Ferguson by St. John Ervine

2453
Joe, late teens
Joe and Mag, a married couple in their late teens, have just leased their first apartment, which is located at the edge of a slaughterhouse.
BVT, 1.5 minutes
Lovers by Brian Friel

2454
Private   **Ireland**
Private and Public are two sides of the same man, Gar O'Donnell, twenty-five. He is planning to go to Philadelphia to work in a hotel to escape the mundane routine of his life in Ireland. He addresses his father, S.B. O'Donnell, whom he refers to as Screwballs.
BVT, 2 minutes
Philadelphia, Here I Come! by Brian Friel

2455
Owen   **Ireland, 1833**
Owen and Yolland, two young soldiers, have been charged with Anglicizing the Gaelic names of towns across Ireland for a map company. This begins to weigh strangely on Owen's conscience.
BVT, 2 minutes
Translations by Brian Friel

2456
Finn   **Ireland in a far-off time**
Finn is a respected General who has been promised the hand of the beautiful Princess Grania. But on the eve of their wedding day, Grania falls in love with Finn's heretofore reliable friend and confidant, Diarmuid. The two

betray Finn by eloping, setting off a seven year battle which sends the lovers into exile.
BVT, 3 minutes
Grania by Lady Gregory

2457
Hanrahan, young man   Ireland
Hanrahan, living before the Irish potato famine, has erroneously informed upon a friend. The friend is now in jail due to Hanrahan's action. Now repentant, Hanrahan has sworn an oath of silence so that he may avoid all possibility of future sin. An old man, Coey, has just failed at making small talk with Hanrahan, who has chased him away with a rock.
BVT, 2.5 minutes
Hanrahan's Oath by Lady Gregory

2458
Daly, middle-aged
A blind man speaks of his aggressive friends. They are his ex-band musicians who have gone on without him. He has become a sort of hanger-on who follows them around to hear their music and drink.
BVT, 1.5 minutes
Eejits by Ron Hutchinson

2459
Parnell   In an empty nightclub
An aging drummer for a second-rate band, dramatically informs Mathewson why he sometimes performs while drunk.
BVT, 5 minutes
Eejits by Ron Hutchinson

2460
George   Late September 1927
A "well-seasoned and weather-beaten old salt," has just completed a tiny model of a ship in a bottle. A girl of thirteen, Blanaid, has been observing him with keen interest.
BVT, 2.5 minutes
The Moon in the Yellow River by Denis Johnston

2461
Younger man
Older man and younger man are playing cards. They are having a heated disagreement about Ireland's political future.
BVT, 2 minutes
The Old Lady Says "No!" by Denis Johnston

2462
Tetley, 30s   Ireland, 1916
Tetley is quiet, and a Commandant in the Irish Volunteers. It is the afternoon of Easter Monday, and the rebellion is now showing se-

rious signs of collapse.
BVT, 2 minutes
The Scythe and the Sunset by Denis Johnston

2463
Bishop   Ireland
The voice of the Bishop interrupts the action of this play concerning a land dispute in a small Irish village. Visiting from England, William Dee was attacked and accidentally killed by Bull and Tadhg McCabe, two local farmers, after bidding against them for a piece of land at a public auction. Convinced of their own right to the property and resentful of the outsider's bid, they were attempting to intimidate him to forget about buying the land for his sick wife.
BVT, 5 minutes
The Field by John B. Keane

2464
Kelly, mid-30s
Kelly and Seamus, both middle-class men in their mid-thirties, have played a bit too rough with a drinking buddy, and he has been pushed into the cellar where he has died. Kelly phones his lawyer.
BVT, 4.5 minutes
The Death and Resurrection of Mr. Roche by Thomas Kilroy

2465
Jasper Dean   Ireland, Turn of the century
Jasper is a dynamic, young alderman in a village in western Ireland. He finds himself embroiled in a conflict between Irish nationalism and loyalty to the British Empire when he comes under the influence of Ralph Kirwan, a mystic who dreams of a culturally independent society for Ireland.
BVT, 3.5 minutes
The Bending of the Bough by George Moore

2466
Joseph Shannon, middle-aged
A seaside hotel, 1990s
Joseph returns home to his family's seaside hotel after eighteen years' absence. His father, Francis, a faded revolutionary who now feels useless, has sold the hotel and wishes to retire. Joseph warns his father that he "must not despair."
BVT, 3 minutes
The Guernica Hotel by Jim Nolan

2467
Francis Shannon   A seaside hotel, 1990s
A group of faded revolutionaries gathers every year in remembrance of a fallen comrade-in-

arms. All are dead now, except for Francis Shannon, who holds his own lonely celebration.
BVT, 2.5 minutes
The Guernica Hotel by Jim Nolan

2468
McKeever, middle-aged
A mortician, was once in love with the town preacher's daughter, Elizabeth. Now Elizabeth's mother has passed away and McKeever is called upon to prepare the body for burial.
BVT, 3 minutes
Moonshine by Jim Nolan

2469
Artie O'Leary, 20s   **Ireland**
A sexton in a small Irish town has had an affair with Angela, his best friend's wife. Now the affair has ended in scandal and shame and Angela has returned to her husband.
BVT, 3 minutes
Belfry by Billy Roche

2470
Artie O'Leary, 20s   **Ireland**
A small-town sexton has taken under his wing a mentally handicapped boy, Dominic. He employed him as a custodian for the church until Dominic was sent to an institution. Concurrently, Artie's mother has passed away after a long, wasting disease.
BVT, 3 minutes
Belfry by Billy Roche

2471
Speaker
This selection is from Preface for Politicians (1907), which Shaw added to his earlier work, John Bull's Other Island, a commercial success in England. These essays were intended to give Broadbent, the play's English character, as well as the English audience, a "piece of (Shaw's) mind, as an Irishman."
BVT, 2.5 minutes
What is an Irishman? by George Bernard Shaw

2472
Forgael
The captain of a ship in isolated waters has just awakened. His crew, however, afraid that he had lost his mind, was plotting mutiny while he slept. Fortunately, they have spotted their first ship in over a month, a spice vessel which they can plunder.
BVT, 2.5 minutes
The Shadowy Waters by William Butler Yeats

2473
Martin   **Dublin, early 19th century**
A young laborer, whose religious fervor concerns his family, explains his beliefs to his parish priest.
BVT, 1.5 minutes
The Unicorn from the Stars by William Butler Yeats

2474
Female
Diner waitress' story of taking in stray pup evolves into meditation on marriage. "I mean, after all, hon — you can pick up a good enough husband anytime. But a good dog, well, now. . . they just don't come along that often, you know."
IBO, 2 minutes
Strays by L. E. McCullough

2475
Male
Lovestruck street corner romeo recounts courtship of his latest ex-wife. "All I know is, after leaving her that last night I got in my jeep and drove forty-two miles through a silver-thaw gullywasher with traces of hail and neon past Seven Sisters, past Wolf Springs, past Edgar and Diablo and the all-nite baile grande at The Rockin' M with Ruben De Luna y Su Conjunto Muy Caliente, halfway almost to Dime Box and the Pandora cutoff before my arms shook loose from the steering wheel's shuddering embrace and my mouth finally stopped kissing the moon-flecked fog wisps teasing my cheeks like moist dancing fingers and lingering tequila sighs."
IBO, 3 minutes
The Rest Was History by L. E. McCullough

2476
Female
Woman of the world who's been around the block shares her philosophy on higher education. "Well, let me tell you somethin's gonna hit you like a brick in the beeswax, Mister High-and-Mighty: real music don't come outa books. It come outa tarpaper shacks with mud floors and the stink of hog piss on your clothes, and a flock of hungry children eatin' red clay dirt in their salt mush, 'cause the last time they had a taste of meat or fresh vegetables was the last time their daddy whupped their mama and caught the midnight train for Memphis one step ahead of the lynchin' tree."
IBO, 1.5 minutes
Real Music Don't Come Outa Books by L. E. McCullough

2477
Female
Mother calling son's school from Domestic Relations Court, warning of ex-husband's imminent appearance. "Look, I just want to let somebody know that if Mr. Hollingsworth shows up and — he's very unstable and has a history, you have to stop him, please — listen, please, listen. Somebody, please. Please. Stop him. Please. . ."
IBO, 3 minutes
Somebody, Please by L. E. McCullough

2478
Female/Male
A loquacious bus passenger reveals secrets of the Universe. "Ask if they like porcupines. Expound your thoughts on telepathy. Inquire about their favorite food and whether or not they were aware that the letters in Seattle also spell 'Let's Eat'."
IBO, 2.5 minutes
Hey You Sitting There Looking at This by L. E. McCullough

2479
Female/Male
Old black-and-white photograph inspires a trip back in time. "Mostly I want to ask just how they can sit there and smile. And be so sure they'll still be smiling at each other this way half a century later. When they don't even know Madonna's last name. Or the price of cherry sodas in the Year of the Fax."
IBO, 2 minutes
Club Lido, Kansas City, 1944 by L. E. McCullough

2480
Male
Vietnam vet uses a fractured fairy tale to explain today's latest war to a child. "Hey mister, he says. Was you born in that wheelchair? Son, I says. Set down on that box of empties right there, and I'll tell you a story. About three bears lived in a jungle. Mama-san, Papa-san and Baby-san . . ."
IBO, 2 minutes
Three Bears Lived in a Jungle by L. E. McCullough

2481
Female
Feminist writer takes a stand with a tongue-in-cheek manifesto. "Biographically speaking I can't say much, other than I am of pure Dutch-Irish-Creole ancestry born in Mobile, Alabama and nearly murdered on a fetus-removal table in Denver nineteen years later."
IBO, 2 minutes
Have a Nice Day by L. E. McCullough

2482
Female/Male
Heartfelt tribute to a departed jazz minstrel. "They called you blind, Mr. Piano Man. But you could see into our hearts. Deep. Past skin tone and fashion fad. Deep. Past barroom cant and stoned soul supervibes. Deep."
IBO, 1.5 minutes
Sweet Blackberry Wine by L. E. McCullough

2483
Female
Abortion clinic worker relates a haunting, recurring dream. "I stood at the top of the Yellow Brick Road with Dorothy, who was in her second trimester and somewhat pale and visibly nervous. We were going to walk up that road, me and Dorothy together, holding hands all the way up the road to visit the big jolly green Doctor of Oz."
IBO, 3.5 minutes
Ice Babies in Oz by L. E. McCullough

2484
Female/Male
Comic political stump speech from a candidate wayyyyyyyy out in the deep grass-roots. "I would teach our children what they must learn in order to survive in this modern fiber-optic world. I would teach them that minute rice cooks best in an hour. And to beware the man whose mouth is so big he can eat a banana sideways. And never turn your back on the man who will do anything for the workers except become one. Or the woman who's had a seven-year itch every night the last two months."
IBO, 2.5 minutes
A Genuine Education President by L. E. McCullough

2485
Male
Otherworldly auto mechanic dispenses advice on repair of the Inner Vehicle. "Don't like to brag, sonny, but one glance under the hood and I know exactly what ails a person's soul. A broke-down axle or a busted fan belt ain't just a piece of metal or rubber gone bad. . . corresponds to some strained part of your psyche, a part of your spirit that's sick or twisted or about ready to go haywire and do you permanent damage."
IBO, 3.5 minutes
Jump Start by L. E. McCullough

2486
Female/Male
Foster-parent relates impact of racist incident on young boy. "The bus come about a minute later, and all the way downtown I could tell

the boy was upset and not likely just by his mother. I mean, there's plenty of time before he gets older till he's expected to hate people for no damn reason at all."

IBO, 2 minutes
Plenty of Time by L. E. McCullough

2487
Male
A love poem for the romantically-challenged outdoorsman. "Me — I like campfires. I like the way the slender nimble orange flamefingers reach into the air and sketch deft pictures of nymphs and goddesses dancing across eons and galaxies, twisting and weaving to the fluting sorcery of laughing Pan whistling his songs of seduction in the cool night breeze."

IBO, 3 minutes
Campfire Girl by L. E. McCullough

2488
Male
Spurned musician places curse on ex-partner. "Think you gonna throw ol' Staker away like a used-up toothpick! Well, merde on you! Go merde all over the whole damn world, you want! But, you remember this. . . we partners. . . now and forever!"

IBO, 1 minute
Partners Forever by L. E. McCullough

2489
Female
Chilling monologue of a woman's obsession with rain and death. ". . . the water stinging and smacking and pounding and punching and pushing and poking and gushing over your head up your nose in your eyes the sewer opened up like a big ugly scar gushing and screaming screaming screaming, pounding and punching, pounding and punching, screaming and screaming. . . what?"

IBO, 3.5 minutes
It's This Rain by L. E. McCullough

2490
Female
Aunt Lydia instructs her niece on the digital nuances of True Love. "Course, a man like Sonny Boy Dupree. . . he's got busy hands. They want to jump on top of every piano they bump up against, whether she's a shiny slick uptown baby grand, or a fallen-apart, stumpy-legged pile of rusty knobs and strings."

IBO, 2 minutes
Patient Hands by L. E. McCullough

2491
Male
Unhinged '60s folksinger on comeback trail. "You don't know my fans, little brother. They are a New Generation. They are dedicated, they are committed, they are warriors in the fight against fascism. They are dancing their butts off to bad bad disco."

IBO, 2 minutes
A New Generation by L. E. McCullough

2492
Female/Male
To the loan officer of the Future, your collateral is your life — literally! "Do you recall your Bible, Mr. Nelson? Third Gospel of St. Trump, may he earn in peace, amen, The Book of The Deal, I'll paraphrase here: 'Life is a precious social resource that can no longer be left to the mere individual to piss away.'"

IBO, 2.5 minutes
Credit Check by L. E. McCullough

2493
Female/Male
An eerie tale from Cajun country of a late-night encounter in the bayou. "Then bazzam! — the Cadillac and the talent agent man with the bright red walking stick were gone, just in the instant you blink your eye, cher — not a trace of the man or his car but a thin puff of black, black smoke twisting slowly through the live oak trees and cypress."

IBO, 2.5 minutes
The Flames of Hell by L. E. McCullough

2494
Female/Male
A childhood memory of a parent's final voyage. "It was night with a big orange full moon peeking through a curtain of dark clouds being swept along by a stiff northeasterly breeze that had just enough push to send a shiver through you when you weren't expecting it, which made it an even stranger kind of shiver than a just plain cold breeze shiver."

IBO, 4 minutes
Shiver by L. E. McCullough

2495
Male
Ever had the feeling somebody's watching you? Maybe they are. "I look up and there is a big brown shape of somethin' gettin' bigger and bigger and comin' straight at me. I step aside, gracefully, and bazoomba! — this giant jumbo raisin bagel size of a German Shepherd smashes into the pavement and busts the sidewalk to pieces after missin' my noggin by like this much. Eight, nine floors above, there's a

face stickin' out the window, and it's her! The old babe with the hair and the earrings and the damn scarf, and then zipporama! — she's gone. I'm quiverin'."
IBO, 4 minutes
Guardian Angel by L. E. McCullough

2496
Male
Smalltown mayor discourses upon moral corruption. "Nosir, I am crucially well-informed upon the subject of religion. As the Bible says, 'What does it profit a man to save his soul and lose his mistress in a poker game?'"
IBO, 1.5 minutes
The Twelve Commandments by L. E. McCullough

2497
Female/Male
A deathbed reunion dredges up decades of disdain. "But everything you did turned to failure; everything he did turned to success. Yes, yes, your brother is an incredibly lucky man. Pity. When will you ever admit the truth? Your brother's ambition was fueled by his complete and utter hatred for you."
IBO, 2 minutes
An Incredibly Lucky Man by L. E. McCullough

2498
Male
That panhandler on the subway — didn't he used to be Somebody? "Yeh, I was a CEO of a major medical research corporation. Uh-huh. Okay, okay. I made that up. I was a boxer took a bad punch. I was a stockbroker took a bad tip. I was a bricklayer got hit by a ton of bricks. I was a missionary got eaten by cannibals. I was a rock star, a rocket scientist, a rockette at Radio City Music Hall — hey, whatsit matter? I'm a human be-ing!"
IBO, 3 minutes
I Wasn't Always Like This by L. E. McCullough

2499
Male
Territoriality reigns supreme in the urban jungle. "I mind my own bidness, babe. You mind your bidness, I mind my bidness. Don't you try mind my bidness. . . I mind my bidness, hear? Now this corner my bidness."
IBO, 1.5 minutes
This Corner My Bidness by L. E. McCullough

2500
Male
Meet the promoter who never met an act he didn't like — or one you will. "I'm sorry, madam, but Mister Dinky the Clown from

Outer Gonzo Land is our most requested attraction — yes, I believe Mister Dinky has had his rabies and distemper shots — excuse me? He did what at your son's birthday party?"
IBO, 3 minutes
Our Most Requested Attraction by L. E. McCullough

2501
Male
A shade-tree handyman offers commentary on a variety of body parts. "Hey, how's your mamacita, cholo? She been workin' at the Denny's on 31 two, three weeks, now, huh? Man, I like that place. They got good eats, huh? Hey, you wanna see somethin' really boss? Check this out, my man."
IBO, 1.5 minutes
Your Mama She Lookin' Real Fine by L. E. McCullough

2502
Male
Psycho teen talk at a public pay phone. Ooops, wrong number! "This planet is headed toward total destruction in a matter of minutes. Cataclysmic, absolute, utter and complete obliteration! And you're worried about how the Federal Reserve interest rate and the price of bananacide in Zimbabwe is gonna affect your revolving charge account at Montgomery Ward? Get...a...grip!"
IBO, 3 minutes
Get a Grip by L. E. McCullough

2503
Female
A fragile, driven songwriter on the verge of winning — or losing — it all. "Okay, sure of course I'm tense maybe at times but that's where the inspiration comes from. . .you've got to have tension to create...tension is it!"
IBO, 2.5 minutes
That Odor Again by L. E. McCullough

2504
Male
A talent agent offers a benediction to his charges. "He will taketh my talent and maketh it yield a humongous annual net income I could never have conceivably pulled down without his expert assistance. Yea, though I walk through the Valley of Slimeball Hustlers, I will fear not the Sharpies nor the Weasels nor the Scumbuckets competing for my contract."
IBO, 2 minutes
So Help Me by L. E. McCullough

2505
Female/Male
Pep talk from Attila the Hun's chief legal coun-

sel. "As your attorney, Mr. Tubbernitz, I'd like to remind you that the key word in this situation is 'fear'. Fear is a key word, Mr. Tubbernitz. Fear is your friend. Always think fear."
IBO, 2 minutes
Key Word by L. E. McCullough

2506
Male
A modern Odysseus-in-exile hears the call to home. "Then one day in '89 I was laying drunk outside a flop house in Mexicali, thinking which one of the cantinas I'd visit that night, when I heard that old Son House song 'Death Letter Blues' on some loco homeboy's boombox."
IBO, 2 minutes
Home Again by L. E. McCullough

2507
Female
A fed-up wife finally solves an embarrassing household odor problem — Flamethowers 'R' Us! "You know, Delbert, I wish that for just one hour God would grant us a genu-wine miracle — giving you enough sense of smell to realize how much a room fulla cat pee really really really stinks."
IBO, 3 minutes
Only 159.95 by L. E. McCullough

2508
Female/Male
A transient discovers an unexpected find in a back alley dumpster. "I know a lot about garbage. Garbage stinks. Garbage rots. Garbage ebbs and garbage flows. But garbage don't cry. And after I rescued that corned beef and was closing the lid on the dumpster, I heard a sound down inside it, deep down. Something weak...and faint...and...and pissed off."
IBO, 3 minutes
Garbage Don't Cry by L. E. McCullough

2509
Female
Danger — road rage on Checkout Aisle 9! "Now what? She's gonna show the bag boy her family photo album? Go on, marry the kid, honey; take him home and marry him; get him bar mitzvahed first, then marry him, just get outa the line, get outa the line, get outa the line!"
IBO, 3 minutes
Express Lane by L. E. McCullough

2510
Male
A hit man explains his code of honor. "You got

kids? Sure you do. Now that's responsibility. Teaching a kid right from wrong. It's tough, I know, I know. I didn't get a good start in that department. My father didn't. . . take responsibility for that. So I had to find a way to get that responsibility into my life, you understand?"
IBO, 2.5 minutes
Family Man by L. E. McCullough

2511
Female
Calling home to Mom after a college girls' night out. "Are you really sitting down? Okay, we met this friend of his, and his name was Blade — I don't know, I guess it's his first name. Anyway, Blade drove me back to the dorm, just part-way cause his Harley ran out of gas right outside this bar on the edge of town, no, I don't know what town it was, but the bar was called The Doll House or something about toys."
IBO, 4 minutes
Girl Talk by L. E. McCullough

2512
Male
A lunch-counter Casanova spins his web of desire. "I'm lookin' at you, at that face, at that smile, at that beauty, at that essence, at that at that that uunnhh you got right there inside you, and I'm sayin', 'Hey. . . I could make her happen in a very, very big way. I could make her every dream come true. I could give her what she's always wanted. Cause I know what that is. I know exactly what this girl has always wanted, and I am here, right here at this counter in front of these mashed potatoes for the sole purpose of giving her what she wants — and needs.'"
IBO, 3 minutes
An Artist Like Me by L. E. McCullough

2513
Male
Hate those annoying phone solicitations? Don't get mad. . . get crazy! "Good evening, Robinson residence. Yes, this is Danny Robinson, who is this? Murray? Murray who? Sorry, I don't — what? Murray? Oh! That Murray K. Stephanopoulos, Junior! Well, why didn't you say so? Gosh, it's been, what, gosh, well, way too long! No, I was just kidding around, of course I knew who you were — only the best darn college roommate I ever had. Truly!"
IBO, 3 minutes
Thanks for Calling by L. E. McCullough

2514
Female
Some door-to-door salespeople just won't take No for an answer. "What a lovely home! Oh, I cannot tell you how utterly tasteful and healing this is. May I sit? Thank you. Now, if you wouldn't mind removing your shoe and sock — left or right, either one. There. My, what an interesting foot!"
IBO, 4 minutes
Door to Door by L. E. McCullough

2515
Male
The mind of a killer, the mind of a child. "It just went off. . . in the guy's face. . . as he was looking at me. . . his face just. . . like, blew up. . . and blood gushed everywhere and skin and and and and . . . and everybody just stood there and watched the guy lay on the ground, and I thought, 'This is, like, a movie; this is awesome!'"
IBO, 4 minutes
Something To Do by L. E. McCullough

2516
Male
Praise the Lord and pass the Valvoline — a preacher guides his flock in the NASCAR Belt. "His oil is the finest, made from His precious blood; his parts will last forever, they saved Noah from the flood. Don't let backsliders tempt you with a cheaper brand; just follow His directions, and you'll reach the Promised Land."
IBO, 4 minutes
Let Jesus Be Your Pit Stop in the Final Race to Heaven by L. E. McCullough

2517
Female
Speakeasy owner lays it out for her bandleader. "See this? Yeh, all these empty tables and chairs. Well, they mine. I own 'em. Every last one of 'em. And my business is to fill 'em up — every night — with hard-workin' men and women wanna drink lotsa liquor, drink it hard and drink it fast, so they can forget what a stink-ass world it is where they just come from. Now, your music supposed to help 'em forget. Your music ain't supposed to educate 'em, or give 'em Jesus or stir 'em up and get 'em marchin' outa here to go vote for no damn politicians gonna give us no damn new deal same as the old deal!"
IBO, 1.5 minutes
Help 'em Forget by L. E. McCullough

2518
Male
A wartime memory that refuses to fade. "At the Boogie Rock Club in Hue City, all the girls had American Top Forty names. There was White Rabbit. Mustang Sally. Inna Gadda Da Vida. Lucy in the Sky with Diamonds. Jennifer Juniper. Da Doo Ron Ron. Sugar Pie Honeybunch. The madam figured it made the boys feel more at home. And she was right."
IBO, 2.5 minutes
Love Me Two Times by L. E. McCullough

2519
Male
A man accidentally discovers the long-ago source of his wife's sudden change-of-heart. "Lowell George croons 'I will be your Dixie chicken, if you'll be my Tennessee lamb' on the all-nite oldies station, as I fluff a pillow next to my wife and watch tears suddenly spurt from her crumpling face. . ."
IBO, 1.5 minutes
Flashbacks Burn by L. E. McCullough

2520
Female/Male
A child beats the boogie man with his mother's magic. "Cause I know now that for the rest of my life, even when I get real old, like maybe nineteen or twenty, all I have to do to make bad people go away and not hurt me is take a kleenex and flush them down the potty."
IBO, 4 minutes
I Once Was Scared of the Dark by L. E. McCullough

2521
Female
Lessons for the lovelorn from one who's Been There, Done That. "If you ask me, you're too choosy, and in this world you're never going to find Mr. Right. Mr. Okay, Mr. Not-So-Bad, Mr. Could-Be-Worse — maybe. That is if some low-life like Glenda Ruble doesn't sink her hooks into him first and make shredded wheat out of him."
IBO, 2.5 minutes
Advice Lady by L. E. McCullough

2522
Female
Java junkie jams jolly on jittery joie de vivre. "But, you must understand, I am a connoisseur. A savant of the noble bean. A dedicated disciple of the demitasse. Coffee isn't a filthy habit like cigarettes or polo players; it's an art form. Are you feeling well, darling? You haven't said a word since we sat down."
IBO, 4 minutes
Disciple of the Demitasse by L. E. McCullough

2523
Male
Some lives are measured in deeds, others in songs. "Not a minute didn't go by without some song telling my whole world like it was and like it oughta be. Blame it on the Bossa Nova, it's the dance of love. Yeh, he's the Leader of the Pack. Earth Angel, Earth Angel, whoa-oh-oh-oh, please be mine. Return to Sender' address unknown. She's my little Four-Oh-Nine, Four-Oh-Nine, Four-Oh-Nine. Everybody's gone surfin', Surfin' U.S.A. He's So Fine, oo-lang, oo-lang. Hit the Road, Jack and don't you come back no more no more. Duke, Duke, Duke, Duke of Earl, Earl, Earl. Come on, baby, do-ooo The Locomotion with me with a ba-ba-ba, ba-ba-ba-ba and a ba-ba dit-dit dingaling dit-dit-dowwwwww. Damn, that was music!"
IBO, 4 minutes
Music of Your Life by L. E. McCullough

2524
Harper Pitt
From Washington, D.C., the South Bronx, Salt Lake City, Antarctica, and the Kremlin, to Hell, Heaven, Purgatory, and beyond. 1985-1990
An agoraphobic young Mormon woman with a Valium addiction, sits alone talking to herself. She is the wife of Joe Pitt, a young chief clerk for the Justice Department, who is struggling with his sexual identity.
GMYA2, 1.5 minutes
Angels in America by Tony Kushner

2525
Harper Pitt
From Washington, D.C., the South Bronx, Salt Lake City, Antarctica, and the Kremlin, to Hell, Heaven, Purgatory, and beyond. 1985-1990
An agoraphobic young Mormon woman with a Valium addiction. She is the wife of Joe Pitt, a young chief clerk for the Justice Department, who is struggling with his sexual identity. Harper is in a window seat on board an airborne jumbo jet headed for San Francisco.
GMYA2, 1.5 minutes
Angels in America by Tony Kushner

2526
Thomasina
A room on the garden front of a large country estate in Derbyshire, England. April, 1809
The young Thomasina is taking a lesson on Cleopatra and the classics from her handsome tutor, Septimus.
GMYA2, 1 minute
Arcadia by Tom Stoppard

2527
Lemon **A London flat, Present**
Through a series of flashbacks, Aunt Dan and Lemon tell the chilling story of Lenora (Lemon), an intelligent somewhat fragile young English woman who falls under the spell of an older family friend, Danielle (Aunt Dan). Gradually Aunt Dan becomes the central force in Lemon's life, shaping and corrupting her moral view of what it means to be a human being. In the end, which is where the play begins, Lemon has come to believe that only brute force, such as the Nazis exhibited, is the true order for mankind. Lenora (Lemon) speaks of her philosophy of life and how she acquired it.
GMYA2, 15 minutes
Aunt Dan and Lemon by Wallace Shawn

2528
Yachiyo **Kauai, Hawaiian Islands, 1919**
A poor peasant girl, with not much hope of raising herself beyond working in the sugar fields of Hawaii, is sent by her father to live with a pottery artist, Hiro Takamura, and his wife, Okusan. Okusan hopes to teach Yachiyo proper Japanese language and customs, and before long Hiro finds new inspiration for his work through the girl. Eventually the young Yachiyo and Hiro develop a deep relationship that leads to a tragic outcome. Yachiyo paints a picture of Takamura practicing his art.
GMYA2, 3 minutes
The Ballad of Yachiyo by Philip Kan Gotanda

2529
Yachiyo **Kauai, Hawaiian Islands, 1919**
A poor peasant girl with not much hope of raising herself beyond working in the sugar fields of Hawaii, is sent by her father to live with a pottery artist, Hiro Takamura, and his wife, Okusan. Okusan hopes to teach Yachiyo proper Japanese language and customs, and before long Hiro finds new inspiration for his work through the girl. Eventually the young Yachiyo and Hiro develop a deep relationship that leads to a tragic outcome. Yachiyo enters the waters of Polihale Beach.
GMYA2, 2.5 minutes
The Ballad of Yachiyo by Philip Kan Gotanda

2530
Darlene
An all-night coffee shop on New York's upper Broadway, late 60s
Balm in Gilead is a kaleidoscopic slice of life that centers on two characters Joe and Darlene, who have some hope of escaping the ugly world they have fallen into among the drug addicts, pimps, and petty criminals of New York's upper Broadway. Darlene is talk-

ing to Ann about "boyfriend" stuff and life in general.
GMYA2, 8 minutes
Balm In Gilead by Lanford Wilson

2531
Donna   An Unnamed City, The 1990s
A local boy, Corvette, has been missing for a few days. No one knows where he is or what happened, although speculation amongst his contemporaries is wild, especially from Donna, who is a close friend of Corvette and who feels she knows more than the others. Donna shares with the audience her inner-most fears.
GMYA2, 3 minutes
A Bird of Prey by Jim Grimsley

2532
Marie, 13   An Unnamed City, The 1990s
Marie struggles with the torment of a fractured and abusive family life. In a moment alone, on her way home from school, Marie confesses her need for the protection and fullness of school life.
GMYA2, 2.5 minutes
A Bird of Prey by Jim Grimsley

2533
Emma, teen   High school, 1990s
Emma recounts a life-altering encounter at a famous rock concert.
GMYA2, 3 minutes
Class Action by Brad Slaight

2534
Danielle, teen   High school, 1990s
Danielle reveals a secret that will soon be very public.
GMYA2, 1.5 minutes
Class Action by Brad Slaight

2535
Joan, 17
Cleveland during prom season and in the dreamtime of Joan, Present
The prom. In the Men's Room, the Mayor of Cleveland, who has been serving as a chaperone, has his head stuck in a towel dispenser. As others look for just the right tool to unwedge the Mayor, Joan holds vigil.
GMYA2, 4.5 minutes
Cleveland by Mac Wellman

2536
Nena, 12   A Latin American Country, Present
The Conduct of Life depicts the emotional torture and psychological and physical brutality exacted on several women by the men in their lives. There is much wisdom and insight into the human condition and the suffering some women have endured throughout history. Nena, recalls her destitute life in a home for girls.
GMYA2, 3.5 minutes
The Conduct of Life by Maria Irene Fornes

2537
Olimpia   A Latin American Country, Present
The Conduct of Life depicts the emotional torture and psychological and physical brutality exacted on several women by the men in their lives. There is much wisdom and insight into the human condition and the suffering some women have endured throughout history. When Leticia, the mistress of the household, asks the servant girl, Olimpia, to help her with a task the inflexible Olimpia details her daily routine.
GMYA2, 3.5 minutes
The Conduct of Life by Maria Irene Fornes

2538
Margot
The Pomme's decaying mansion, Present
A bizarre, biting, darkly humorous look at the Pommes, a family on the periphery of life. Margot conjures up a painful memory with Grandma, who has just suffered a bad episode herself.
GMYA2, 1.5 minutes
Death Comes To Us All, Mary Agnes by Christopher Durang

2539
Margot
The Pomme's decaying mansion, Present
A bizarre, biting, darkly humorous look at the Pommes, a family on the periphery of life. Margot tells her father about one of her disturbing dreams.
GMYA2, 2.5 minutes
Death Comes To Us All, Mary Agnes by Christopher Durang

2540
Rosacoke Mustian
Warren County, North Carolina and Mason's Lake, Virginia, summer, fall and winter 1957
Rosacoke and members of her family struggle with life in northeastern North Carolina, attempting to seek love and purpose amidst complex internal and external turmoil. Rosacoke declares the depth of her love for Wesley, gone these two years, and expected at any moment to appear on the road just beyond the open window in which Rosacoke sits.
GMYA2, 2.5 minutes
Early Dark by Reynolds Price

2541
Luisa, 16 **Present**
A romantic, theatrical tale of two crafty fathers who conspire to bring their children, Matt and Luisa, together—which they do. Luisa speaks of the awakening wonder of life.
GMYA2, 1 minute
The Fantasticks by Tom Jones and Harvey Schmidt

2542
Kerney Bascomb, 19
Eastern North Carolina, Late summer, 1938
Kerney attempts to find direction to her life and reconcile her relationship with a young man (Kipple Patrick), complicated by his long-standing involvement with Ora Lee, the daughter of his family's housekeeper. Issues of race and gender inform and deepen Kerney's choices while the adults around her offer advice and reflections from the past. Kerney has returned home from her date with Kipple, very late and a bit intoxicated. Finding her father still awake, their talk leads to Kerney's passionate plea for her independent womanhood, and her reluctance to marry.
GMYA2, 1.5 minutes
Full Moon by Reynolds Price

2543
Kerney Bascomb, 19
Eastern North Carolina, Late summer, 1938
Kerney attempts to find direction to her life and reconcile her relationship with a young man (Kipple Patrick), complicated by his long-standing involvement with Ora Lee, the daughter of his family's housekeeper. Issues of race and gender inform and deepen Kerney's choices while the adults around her offer advice and reflections from the past. Kerney, facing pressure from all sides to make a decision to marry Kipple or not, attempts to sort out her feelings in front of the insisting Kipple, and both of their fathers.
GMYA2, 3 minutes
Full Moon by Reynolds Price

2544
Polyxena **The shores of Thrace, 1184 B.C.**
Euripides fifth-century B.C. telling of the grief-ravaged Queen of Troy, Hecuba (Gk. Hekabe), and her revenge for the murder of her son, Polydorus. The plot draws on the classical tales of the Trojan War, and the characters of Odysseus, Agamemnon, and others. Odysseus has arrived to take Hecuba's daughter, Polyxena, away in order to sacrifice her to the ghost of Achilles, who has becalmed the ships of the Greeks returning from the Trojan War. Hecuba beseeches her daughter to fall upon her knees and beg for mercy but Polyxena refuses.
GMYA2, 3 minutes
Hekabe by Euripides, translated by Timberlake Wertenbaker

2545
Laura Dennis, 17
The fictitious small town of Harrison, Texas, on the Gulf Coast, 1938
Laura has lived with Lena Abernathy since the passing of her father. Laura has never been acquainted with her mother, as the mother abandoned the family when Laura was an infant and has since remarried and lives in South Dakota. As Laura faces the prospects of her adult life, she longs to understand the details that make up the history of her family, a history that ultimately unfolds with tragic consequences. Laura sits with Lena on the front porch. While Laura waits daily for a letter from her mother (which will never come), rumors abound that a local boy has impregnated one of Laura's school mates.
GMYA2, 2.5 minutes
Laura Dennis by Horton Foote

2546
Laura Dennis, 17
The fictitious small town of Harrison, Texas, on the Gulf Coast, 1938
Laura has lived with Lena Abernathy since the passing of her father. Laura has never been acquainted with her mother, as the mother abandoned the family when Laura was an infant and has since remarried and lives in South Dakota. As Laura faces the prospects of her adult life, she longs to understand the details that make up the history of her family, a history that ultimately unfolds with tragic consequences. Harvey, the young man Laura cared for very much, has been killed. Laura has subsequently learned that Harvey was, in fact, her stepbrother. She has also learned that her long lost mother has asked that Laura no longer attempt to make contact. Sitting with Lena (her one true support), Laura desperately struggles to hold on by remembering the riches of her past.
GMYA2, 2.5 minutes
Laura Dennis by Horton Foote

2547
Actress The stage of a drama school, Present
A sketch written for the Juilliard School's Drama Division's twentieth-fifth anniversary, April, 1994. The subject draws on Euripides' tragedy, The Trojan Women. The actress playing Medea comes to introduce the evening.
GMYA2, 2 minutes
Medea by Christopher Durang and Wendy Wasserstein

2548
Portia   **Venice, Italy, Circa 1596**
Antonio, a Venetian merchant, assists his friend Bassanio in wooing the beautiful young heiress, Portia. Antonio's good intentions land him in debt to the moneylender Shylock, however. When Shylock attempts to collect his interest payment of a pound of flesh, Portia successfully defends Antonio disguised as a judge, and all ends happily except for Shylock. Portia considers the strengths and weaknesses of her various suitors.
GMYA2, 5 minutes
The Merchant of Venice by William Shakespeare

2549
Portia   **Venice, Italy, Circa 1596**
Antonio, a Venetian merchant, assists his friend Bassanio in wooing the beautiful young heiress, Portia. Antonio's good intentions land him in debt to the moneylender Shylock, however. When Shylock attempts to collect his interest payment of a pound of flesh Portia, successfully defends Antonio disguised as a judge, and all ends happily except for Shylock. Portia longs for Bassanio to select the right casket and so win her hand in marriage.
GMYA2, 1 minute
The Merchant of Venice by William Shakespeare

2550
Birda, young lady
A circus arena in an unnamed location, The early 1900s
Megan Terry's adventurous and magical circus telling of a fictional meeting and the life stories of two celebrated women at the turn of the century is played out by a happy company of theatricals. Mollie Baily sets the stage in the first scene of the play as she describes the Mollie Bailey-Mother Jones, "...[the] history of two mothers, mothering the miners and the countryside, working every night and every day for motherhood, and sisterhood and brotherhood and The Union of the Workers, and the Union of Heaven with this beautiful Earth..." Part history, part magic, part fable, part fact but all passion, the play brings a band of players and musicians together to present an extraordinary theater event. Birda, one of Mollie's children is alone on stage with her horse (played by one of the ensemble actors), trying to teach the horse to dance.
GMYA2, 2.5 minutes
Molly Bailey's Travelling Family Circus With Scenes from The Life of Mother Jones, Book and Lyrics by Megan Terry, Music by JoAnn Metcalf

2551
Mae, mid-20s
A house on a rural promontory, Present
The story of three rural characters in the mud of life attempting to find human connections: Mae, a "spirited, single-minded" young woman; Lloyd, a "simple and good-hearted young man" (mid-twenties); and Henry, a big man (mid-fifties) with a "sense of dignity who can barely read." Their relationships are visceral, earthy, and fundamental. Mae tells Henry about the nature of her relationship with Lloyd.
GMYA2, 2 minutes
Mud by Maria Irene Fornes

2552
Elaine
Kitchen of the Mann house, an ordinary Tuesday morning
This absurdly comic play revolves around the life of the Mann's. The family is headed by Steve, a religious fanatic, and held together by the beleaguered mother, Eleanor. Colorfully rounding out the family are three sons: Donald, a pimp and dope peddler; Andy, a flamboyant homosexual; and Gary, the victim of a threshing accident that has left his penis little more than a stub. Into all this, comes, among others, Elaine, masquerading as Sister Annie De Maupassant, the radical nun of Bernardsville. The assassination of the new Pope is the result of these characters' interactions. Elaine challenges Mrs. Mann's perceptions of her sons.
GMYA2, 3 minutes
The Nature and Purpose of the Universe by Christopher Durang

2553
Elaine
Kitchen of the Mann house, an ordinary Tuesday morning
This absurdly comic play revolves around the life of the Mann's. The family is headed by Steve, a religious fanatic, and held together by the beleaguered mother, Eleanor. Colorfully rounding out the family are three sons: Donald, a pimp and dope peddler; Andy, a flamboyant homosexual; and Gary, the victim of a threshing accident that has left his penis little more than a stub. Into all this, comes, among others, Elaine, masquerading as Sister Annie De Maupassant, the radical nun of Bernardsville. The assassination of the new Pope is the result of these characters' interactions. The speech comes immediately after the Pope has shot and killed Andy Mann. Elaine offers some words of consolation.
GMYA2, 1.5 minutes
The Nature and Purpose of the Universe by Christopher Durang

2554
Morse, 12
A comfortable house in Axe yard, off King Street, Westminster, in London, 1665
A wealthy couple, quarantined in their home during London's historic plague, harboring a girl and a sailor. As death rages beyond their door the four lives entwine and disintegrate within. Morse is locked in an empty room. Alone. She wears a dirty, tattered, but once fine dress. The dress is pulled up to hide her face. She wears a torn pair of boy's britches under the dress. She repeats the words that her interrogator might have used earlier.
GMYA2, 2.5 minutes
One Flea Spare by Naomi Wallace

2555
Morse, 12
A comfortable house in Axe yard, off King Street, Westminster, in London, 1665
A wealthy couple, quarantined in their home during London's historic plague, harboring a girl and a sailor. As death rages beyond their door, the four lives entwine and disintegrate within. Morse sits alone on the floor.
GMYA2, 3 minutes
One Flea Spare by Naomi Wallace

2556
Morse, 12
A comfortable house in Axe yard, off King Street, Westminster, in London, 1665
A wealthy couple, quarantined in their home during London's historic plague, harboring a girl and a sailor. As death rages beyond their door, the four lives entwine and disintegrate within. It is early morning. Snelgrave is tied to a chair, slumped over. When Morse enters, she is wearing Snelgrave's shirt as a nightgown. She approaches him closer and closer until their faces are almost touching.
GMYA2, 2.5 minutes
One Flea Spare by Naomi Wallace

2557
Ana, 18
A tiny sewing factory in East Los Angeles, The first week of September, 1987
Ana, a Latina living in East Los Angeles, dreams of getting out of the barrio to get a good education and become a successful writer. In the meantime, stuck working in a small sewing factory, Ana chronicles her observations of the live's, loves and dreams of her co-workers, five heavy-set Mexican-American women. The very last moment in the play, Ana reflects on what she has learned since leaving home.
GMYA2, 1.5 minutes
Real Women Have Curves by Josefina Lopez

2558
Jaime, 19
New York City and the Hamptons, Present
The separate quests of a young New York street poet seeking fame and fortune, and a wealthy entrepreneur who will stop at nothing to find his son who committed suicide nineteen years before, collide with astrological proportions, helped by a mystical and androgynous couple. This is the first scene in the play, in which we find Jaime selling her poetry in New York City's Port Authority Bus Terminal.
GMYA2, 4 minutes
The Reincarnation of Jaimie Brown by Lynne Alvarez

2559
Sally Decker, 17
A large kitchen in a suburban home, Summer, present
The story of Sally Decker and her parents, Henry and Cynthia, and Christopher, her brother. Mom and Dad are not what they used to be, nor is the family; life is changing—nothing seems connected anymore. Sally speaks of her restlessness to her mother.
GMYA2, 2 minutes
Sally's Gone, She Left Her Name by Russell Davis

2560
Sally Decker, 17
A large kitchen in a suburban home, Summer, present
The story of Sally Decker and her parents, Henry and Cynthia, and Christopher, her brother. Mom and Dad are not what they used to be, nor is the family; life is changing—nothing seems connected anymore. Sally tells Christopher how difficult it is to say what we mean.
GMYA2, 2 minutes
Sally's Gone, She Left Her Name by Russell Davis

2561
Girl A girl's camp in West Virginia, July, 1963
Jayne Anne Phillips' novel recounts the experiences of a group of girls at a West Virginia camp in July of 1963. Two sisters, Lenny and Alma, confront life transforming events, tucked away in a forest dense wilderness, away from the normal influences of an urban world. The startling and moving coming-of-age story is seen through youthful eyes. Phillips' strikingly vivid and rich prose speaks to all of the senses, sharpened by adolescent perception. This is the first page of the novel. Although the speaker is not identified, this could be the view of any of the girls who spend this hot July away at camp.
GMYA2, 1.5 minutes
Shelter by Jayne Anne Phillips

2562
Annie Gayle Long, early 20s
Austin, Texas, Spring, 1928
The attendants of this spring dance are not members of the local community, but rather the patients of a sanitarium, a collection of souls crushed by their inability to exist in the real world. Although the normalcy of an evening dance is a pleasure for most people, here it brings about struggle among these patients, as they attempt to reach for a sane lifeline. At the center of the play is Annie Gayle Long, a young woman who over a period of years has lost her grip on life. Finally her family could no longer handle her situation and has sent her to this sanitarium, where she is surrounded by other lost souls. A section of enclosed garden adjoining a ballroom-auditorium where a dance is being held. Annie sits on a bench listening to the music. After a few moments, Annie notices that Dave (early twenties) has fallen asleep.
GMYA2, 2.5 minutes
Spring Dance by Horton Foote

2563
Annie Gayle Long, early 20s
Austin, Texas, Spring, 1928
The attendants of this spring dance are not members of the local community, but rather the patients of a sanitarium, a collection of souls crushed by their inability to exist in the real world. Although the normalcy of an evening dance is a pleasure for most people, here it brings about struggle among these patients, as they attempt to reach for a sane lifeline. At the center of the play is Annie Gayle Long, a young woman who over a period of years has lost her grip on life. Finally her family could no longer handle her situation and has sent her to this sanitarium, where she is surrounded by other lost souls. A section of enclosed garden adjoining a ballroom-auditorium where a dance is being held. Annie sits on a bench listening to the music. Annie has taken Dave's letter from his mother. Annie likes to read Dave's letters from home to hear the news of the people she misses.
GMYA2, 4 minutes
Spring Dance by Horton Foote

2564
Cecilia Monroe
Harrison, Texas, Late summer, 1923
Originally written for live television, Foote's short play is seen through the eyes of Cecilia, a young lady living with her mother and older sister in a boardinghouse. For the live television production, Cecilia was only a voice and the camera served as Cecilia's eyes, moving among the actors as the character would. The story concerns Cecilia's sister, Bessie, who is promised to an older man with means, but loves another. Cecilia tells the audience her inner thoughts as the drama plays out. Cecilia is seated on the front porch of the boardinghouse. Bessie, Cecilia's older sister, has just come onto the porch. Cecilia speaks to us.
GMYA2, 2 minutes
The Tears of My Sister by Horton Foote

2565
Cecilia   Harrison, Texas, Late summer, 1923
Originally written for live television, Foote's short play is seen through the eyes of Cecilia Monroe, a young lady living with her mother and older sister in a boardinghouse. For the live television production, Cecilia was only a voice and the camera served as Cecilia's eyes, moving among the actors as the character would. The story concerns Cecilia's sister, Bessie, who is promised to an older man with means, but loves another. Cecilia tells the audience her inner thoughts as the drama plays out. Near the end of the play, Bessie has been asked to put a stop to her affections for the young Syd Carr and to marry Stacey Davis (an older man who could take care of the family and find a home). Crushed with the fate life has handed her, Bessie weeps in her room as her mother consoles her. In her room, which she shares with Bessie, Cecilia listens.
GMYA2, 1 minute
The Tears of My Sister by Horton Foote

2566
Cassandra
Outside the walls of the fallen city of Troy, 1184 B.C.
Euripides' fifth-century B.C. tragedy set immediately after the fall of Troy, recounts the fate of Queen Hecuba, her daughters Cassandra and Polyxena, and Andromache, widow of the Trojan hero Hector at the hands of their Greek captors. Half-mad, Cassandra, who is to be taken as Agamemnon's concubine, prophesies that the indignity laid upon her will result in the fall of Agamemnon's house and great suffering for Odysseus.
GMYA2, 4 minutes
The Trojan Women by Euripides

2567
Jane
A rooming house in the French Quarter of New Orleans, the period between winter 1938 and spring 1939
"The Writer," a character in Vieux Carre fashioned after Mr. Williams, brings us into the world of a dilapidated rooming house in New

Orleans' French Quarter. Part player and part narrator, The Writer reflects on the past by reliving that past. The collection of troubled souls that occupy the rooming house form a bizarre tapestry: a brash and desperate landlady; a well-bred young lady having a steamy relationship with a hot strip joint worker; two older women clinging to the last remains of their dwindling income; a painter who is slowly dying; and our writer, struggling for purpose amidst conflicting feelings. A rich mix of humor, cruelty and poetry fuse together in the telling of this haunting story. In the first few moments of the play, Jane (a young woman of good breeding) has returned to the rooming house late, only to be startled by Mrs. Wire (the older landlady).
GMYA2, 2 minutes
Vieux Carre by Tennessee Williams

2568
Charlotte Bronte (1816-1855)
An unnamed place, Present
Charlotte explains the restlessness that consumed her life.
GMYA2, 2 minutes
A Voice of My Own by Elinor Jones

2569
Jane Austen (1775-1817)
An unnamed place, Present
Jane sits at the breakfast table discussing the latest events in her life with her sister, Cassandra.
GMYA2, 2.5 minutes
A Voice of My Own by Elinor Jones

2570
Albert   A big girded railway bridge, Present
This one-act stage play/radio play centers on Albert, a philosophy graduate, and bridge painter who succeeds in replacing all of the other painters and making the bridge his. Eventually a would-be suicide and fourteen other painters interfere with his life. Albert paints, observes, and comments on his world.
GMYA2, 6 minutes
Albert's Bridge by Tom Stoppard

2571
Chris, 16   Staten Island, 1995
A sensitive yet biting play that uncovers a complex story of a shy teenage boy forced to follow his mother, a practical nurse, from household to household as she nurses dying patients. Circumstances lead Chris and his mother to look after the dying mother of Floyd, a dockworker who drinks heavily and is a match for Chris's blunt and efficient overprotective mother. Chris attempts to convince Harold (late teens) to run off with him to see his father in Florida. As Harold resists the idea, Chris appeals to him.

GMYA2, 1 minute
Amulets Against the Dragon Forces by Paul Zindel

2572
Septimus
A room on the garden front of a large country estate in Derbyshire, England, April, 1809
The tutor, Septimus, reassures his pupil that learning and discovery is a lifelong process, and that although mankind has lost many ancient manuscripts, we must glean from those we have.
GMYA2, 2.5 minutes
Arcadia by Tom Stoppard

2573
Dopey
An all-night coffee shop on New York's upper Broadway, late 60s
Balm in Gilead is a kaleidoscopic slice of life that centers on Joe and Darlene, who have some hope of escaping the ugly world they have fallen into among the drug addicts, pimps, and petty criminals of New York's upper Broadway. Dopey, a drug pusher, speaks of the human need, on whatever level, to be cared for.
GMYA2, 4 minutes
Balm in Gilead by Lanford Wilson

2574
Dopey
An all-night coffee shop on New York's upper Broadway, the late 60s
Balm in Gilead is a kaleidoscopic slice of life that centers on Joe and Darlene, who have some hope of escaping the ugly world they have fallen into among the drug addicts, pimps, and petty criminals of New York's upper Broadway. Dopey, a drug pusher, lashes out at the ubiquitous cockroach.
GMYA2, 2 minutes
Balm in Gilead by Lanford Wilson

2575
Corvette, teen   An Unnamed City, the 1990s
We see Corvette who has recently been killed at the hands of a sexual predator and left in a shallow grave. As the lights rise, Corvette faces the audience. There are many wounds on his body, cuts and burns. Also on stage are the Street Angels, three young angels who had also died in their youth.
GMYA2, 6 minutes
A Bird of Prey by Jim Grimsley

2576
Evan, 14   An Unnamed City, the 1990s
Evan faces the audience and rages about his

brutal family.
GMYA2, 2 minutes
A Bird of Prey by Jim Grimsley

2577
Dennis, teen
Various parts of an unnamed high school, 1990s
Dennis confesses the dilemma of life as a genius.
GMYA2, 2 minutes
Class Action by Brad Slaight

2578
Waiter
Budapest, beginning in 1938, the play quickly shifts back and forth in time
A waiter in a small, working-class restaurant, addresses the audience in a rapid, declamatory style on the difference between the European and the American way of life.
GMYA2, 3 minutes
The Danube by Maria Irene Fornes

2579
Dan, teen   Staten Island, Present
The lives of the children in a large family turn complex when the parents abandon them in favor of traveling the country to the trotting races and Native American casinos. The absent parents (gone now for two months) have left no provisions and show no signs of returning, communicating only by fax machine. As the children are divided about the pluses and minuses of being parentless, the tensions mount. Dan, one of the older brothers in the family, faces the audience and recalls a time he observed his mother (a psychotherapist) acting overly neurotic, obsessed with a current patient she was seeing.
GMYA2, 2.5 minutes
Every Seventeen Minutes the Crowd Goes Crazy by Paul Zindel

2580
Dave, late teens   Staten Island, Present
The lives of the children in a large family turn complex when the parents abandon them in favor of traveling the country to the trotting races and Native American casinos. The absent parents (gone now for two months) have left no provisions and show no signs of returning, communicating only by fax machine. As the children are divided about the pluses and minuses of being parentless, the tensions mount. Dave has returned home to see his family. He tells Dan about the family he has been staying with.
GMYA2, 3 minutes
Every Seventeen Minutes the Crowd Goes Crazy by Paul Zindel

2581
Gil, early 20s
An archeological excavation site in Southern Mexico, 1977-1987
The Burgess family is living in Durban, South Africa, while the father (Harry) serves as a cultural attaché—bringing artists to South Africa to improve America's image. In an attempt to get the family out of Africa and secure a better position, Harry betrays his oldest son's (Alec) radical friends to the government. As events play through the next ten years, bitterness consumes the family, compounded by an emotionally overwrought mother, Patrice. The consequences are devastating. Patrice encounters Gil at an archeological excavation site in Southern Mexico. Many unresolved issues exist between mother and son, particularly surrounding the horrible death of Gil's brother, Alec.
GMYA2, 1 minute
A Fair Country by Jon Robin Baitz

2582
Matt, 20   Present
A romantic, theatrical tale of two crafty fathers who conspire to bring their children, Matt and Luisa, together—which they do. Matt speaks of his love for Luisa.
GMYA2, 1 minute
The Fantasticks by Tom Jones and Harvey Schmidt

2583
Irving Katz, 14
A NYC playground basketball court, Present
Irving Katz encounters Irving Allen, a former professional basketball star, on a New York City playground basketball court, and learns that Allen's son is the one who killed Katz's father during a robbery. As the short play unfolds, Allen attempts to atone for his son's actions. The game they play is almost a metaphor for the contest of life both man and boy has faced. Near the end of the play, Katz (small, slightly chubby) has been pushed by Allen to the breaking point.
GMYA2, 3 minutes
The Former One-On-One Basketball Champion by Israel Horovitz

2584
Hotspur   England and Wales, early 1500s
The fiery Hotspur, who has recently come from battling the Scots, attempts to explain to King Henry that he has not refused to turn over the prisoners he has captured, but that the King's emissary did anger him.
GMYA2, 2 minutes
Henry IV, Part I by William Shakespeare

2585
Prince Hal   England and Wales, early 1500s
Before the deathbed of King Henry, Prince Hal honors his father and prepares himself to be king.
GMYA2, 2 minutes
Henry IV, Part II by William Shakespeare

2586
Rudy, 25
Catchpole's Funeral Parlor. A very posh establishment on Ocean Boulevard in Swampscott, Mass., November 12, 1918
It's the night of the day after the signing of the Armistice ending World War One and the Schmidt—"Smith"—family is trying to have the funeral for their wife and mother, recently deceased. Their attempts are thwarted when the funeral director discovers their "Germanity" and throws all the grieving mourners out. Rudy (the Schmidt's son) has returned for his mother's funeral, only to find chaos. As he bonds with his father and sister, he recounts the events of his past few years.
GMYA2, 5 minutes
Home Fires by John Guare

2587
Boy, teen   Present
A divorced mother, caring for a teenage girl and boy, makes her living writing screenplays for adult films. When the kids find out mom's true profession, it's cool. But when the father barges back into their lives (breaking a restraining order), the family disorder builds to overwhelming proportions with dark consequences. Woman (the mother) takes a private moment with Boy (Calvin, the son) to inquire about Girl's (the daughter, Lesley Ann) weekend outings with her friend, Lisa.
GMYA2, 2 minutes
Hot 'N' Throbbing by Paula Vogel

2588
Jed Rowen, 20s
Eastern KY, the Rowen homestead, 1861
Jed flees his father Ezekiel's fire and brimstone preaching and tells of his own visions and the specter of William Clarke Quantrill, a fearless guerrilla fighter for the Southern cause.
GMYA2, 1 minute
The Kentucky Cycle by Robert Schenkkan

2589
Davis   Minneapolis, Minnesota, fall of 1967
A troubled young man recreates a turbulent year in his life (1968) with the hopes of finding answers to paths that have led to today. The journey back replays the complexities of relationships, the crisis of sexual identity, the

bonds of truthful friendship, and the search for purpose. Davis (the central character) begins the second act of the play with the historical context of 1967 on an international level and on a personal level.
GMYA2, 2 minutes
The Less Than Human Club by Timothy Mason

2590
Bob   A small town in mid-America, Present
We find Bob, a boy raised by raccoons, high in a tree talking to his shadow. A thunderstorm is moving in.
GMYA2, 2 minutes
Lloyd's Prayer by Kevin Kling

2591
Bob   A small town in mid-America, Present
Bob, a boy raised by raccoons, finds the answer to his existence.
GMYA2, 1 minute
Lloyd's Prayer by Kevin Kling

2592
Stony McBride
A galaxy of stars and an island off the coast of Norway, 1999
This comedy presents a bizarre picture of the future through the lives of Stony McBride, a movie director and adopted son of a former Hollywood legend, who is developing a screenplay about Marco Polo for his father to star in. Complications develop through a wild cast of characters, such as his wife and her lover, Tom, a politician who has a cure for cancer; Stony's mother, a transsexual; and Larry, who has a set of mechanical legs—among others. Stony sings the praises of man's "plant nature" to Tom.
GMYA2, 4 minutes
Marco Polo Sings A Solo by John Guare

2593
Stony McBride
A galaxy of stars and an island off the coast of Norway, 1999
This comedy presents a bizarre picture of the future through the lives of Stony McBride, a movie director and adopted son of a former Hollywood legend, who is developing a screenplay about Marco Polo for his father to star in. Complications develop through a wild cast of characters, such as his wife and her lover, Tom, a politician who has a cure for cancer; Stony's mother, a transsexual; and Larry, who has a set of mechanical legs—among others. Stony floats in space connecting with all that he is or ever has been.
GMYA2, 4.5 minutes
Marco Polo Sings A Solo by John Guare

2594
Hank, 17
Various locations in Florida and a mental hospital in Ohio, Present
Bessie has committed her life to caring for others, among them her invalid father and aunt. When she discovers that she has leukemia, she is forced to contact her long-estranged sister, Lee, about the possibility of a bone-marrow transplant. Lee arrives with her two sons, Hank and Charlie, who have problems of their own, and a difficult reunion ensues. Hank speaks to aunt Bessie of his dreams to be free of the psychiatric hospital where he has been placed because he burned down the house.
GMYA2, 1 minute
Marvin's Room by Scott McPherson

2595
Mark Dolson, early 20s
Autumn, The office of Father Tim Farley and St. Francis Church, Present
Mark Dolson, a young seminarian, comes to study and work with Father Tim Farley, an older priest who has burned-out internally (his faith and his passion), but has years of experience in the showmanship of the priesthood. When young Dolson begins to call Father Farley on his sloppy, passionless, theology and on his contradictions in his life, the fire roars. Mark gives his first sermon at St. Francis. He has just been introduced to the parishioners by Father Farley with: "There's a certain James Dean quality about him which I think you'll find very exciting. Will you welcome please— Deacon Dolson."
GMYA2, 3 minutes
Mass Appeal by Bill C. Davis

2596
Mark Dolson, early 20s
Autumn, The office of Father Tim Farley and St. Francis Church, Present
Mark Dolson, a young seminarian, comes to study and work with Father Tim Farley, an older priest who has burned-out internally (his faith and his passion), but has years of experience in the showmanship of the priesthood. When young Dolson begins to call Father Farley on his sloppy, passionless, theology and on his contradictions in his life, the fire roars. After Father Farley admonishes Mark for his recent sermon, Mark defends himself.
GMYA2, 2 minutes
Mass Appeal by Bill C. Davis

2597
Lorenzo   **Venice, Italy, Circa 1596**
Antonio, a Venetian merchant, assists his friend Bassanio in wooing the beautiful young heiress, Portia. Lorenzo, Bassanio's sensitive, music-loving friend, has fallen in love with Jessica, Shylock's daughter.
GMYA2, 2 minutes
The Merchant of Venice by William Shakespeare

2598
Otis   **An iceberg, Miami, Present**
Otis—is he an Eskimo?—directly addresses the audience.
GMYA2, 3.5 minutes
Moon Under Miami by John Guare

2599
Bo, 20s   **A large metropolitan city, Present**
Bo is having coffee with Miriam (also twenties) in a local coffee shop, divulging his self-esteem issues.
GMYA2, 2 minutes
Only You by Timothy Mason

2600
Leo, 20s   **A large metropolitan city, Present**
Leo enters his dark apartment, turns on the light, and is shocked to see Heather there. Heather has been sent by her friend Miriam (who has just broken up with Leo) to return Leo's keys. This is the final blow for Leo, the end of a miserable day. He confesses the depth of his desperation to Heather.
GMYA2, 10 minutes
Only You by Timothy Mason

2601
Rudy Pazinski, 12
The Pazinski apartment above "Chet's Bar & Grill" and other locales in a city somewhere in the Northeastern U.S., autumn, 1959
Rudy, angry with his father, has just run into the sanctuary of the church; he genuflects, kneels, and challenges Jesus to give him a sign that his prayers aren't landing on deaf ears.
GMYA2, 1.5 minutes
Over The Tavern by Tom Dudzick

2602
Rudy Pazinski, 12
The Pazinski apartment above "Chet's Bar & Grill" and other locales in a city somewhere in the Northeastern U.S., autumn, 1959
Rudy back in church, this time because his prayer to make Sister Clarissa ease up on him seems to have resulted in more than he intended.
GMYA2, 1.5 minutes
Over The Tavern by Tom Dudzick

2603
Jimmy

A squad room of a downtown precinct, Present

After the murder of an old woman, two suspects are hauled into the police station for questioning—Sean, a middle-aged homosexual, and Jimmy, his street-urchin friend who's on drugs. In the course of the action, Jimmy has gotten hold of one of the officer's guns. Now he forces them to listen, closely, to his story.

GMYA2, 5 minutes
A Prayer For My Daughter by Thomas Babe

2604
Christopher Decker
A large kitchen in a suburban home, Summer, Present

Christopher confronts his father and his sister, Sally, who seems to have driven Mother out of the family.

GMYA2, 2 minutes
Sally's Gone, She Left Her Name by Russell Davis

2605
Trinculo   An enchanted island, Circa 1611
The clown Trinculo seeks shelter from an approaching storm after being shipwrecked on an island.

GMYA2, 2 minutes
The Tempest by William Shakespeare

2606
Ariel   An enchanted island, Circa 1611
Prospero, who was banished from power in Milan by his brother, the King of Naples, holds dominion over an enchanted island, where he eventually heals old wounds through his powers and brings about the marriage of his daughter, Miranda, to Ferdinand, the son of his enemy. Prosper's chief spirit, Ariel, casts a charm on his master's enemies.

GMYA2, 2 minutes
The Tempest by William Shakespeare

2607
Writer, 20s
A rooming house in the French Quarter of New Orleans, the period between winter 1938 and spring 1939

"The Writer," a character in Vieux Carre fashioned after Mr. Williams, brings us into the world of a dilapidated rooming house in New Orleans' French Quarter. Part player and part narrator, The Writer reflects on the past by reliving that past. The collection of troubled souls that occupy the rooming house form a bizarre tapestry: a brash and desperate landlady; a well-bred young lady having a steamy relationship with a hot strip joint worker; two older women clinging to the last remains of their dwindling income; a painter who is slowly dying; and our writer, struggling for purpose amidst conflicting feelings. A rich mix of humor, cruelty and poetry fuse together in the telling of this haunting story. The Writer has confessed his sexual experience with a paratrooper to Nightingale, the ill painter who stays in the attic cubicle next to him. In the course of the scene, Nightingale has sympathized and then made his own sexual advance on The Writer. An hour later, in the reflection of the encounter, The Writer as narrator sits smoking on the foot of his cot, the sheet drawn about him like a toga. He speaks out front.

GMYA2, 2 minutes
Vieux Carre by Tennessee Williams

2608
Scott, adolescent
The family condo, Scott's room, and Willow Lake of an unnamed city, Present

The two characters in Mary Lathrop's powerful play are Meg, a single mother, and Scott, her adolescent son. The father of this family has been dead a year, and Scott is having difficulty accepting his death. It is Thursday afternoon. Scott with his bicycle. He takes a comb out of his pocket and combs his hair. He addresses the audience.

GMYA2, 1.5 minutes
The Visible Horse by Mary Lathrop

2609
Scott, adolescent
The family condo, Scott's room, and Willow Lake of an unnamed city, Present

The two characters in Mary Lathrop's powerful play are Meg, a single mother, and Scott, her adolescent son. The father of this family has been dead a year, and Scott is having difficulty accepting his death. It is Friday afternoon. Scott is wearing roller blades.

GMYA2, 1 minute
The Visible Horse by Mary Lathrop

2610
Scott, adolescent
The family condo, Scott's room, and Willow Lake of an unnamed city, Present

The two characters in Mary Lathrop's powerful play are Meg, a single mother, and Scott, her adolescent son. The father of this family has been dead a year, and Scott is having difficulty accepting his death. It is Monday afternoon. Scott stands on a skateboard.

GMYA2, 2 minutes
The Visible Horse by Mary Lathrop